Embracing Democracy in the Western Balkans

T0385531

Embracing Democracy in the Western Balkans

From Postconflict Struggles toward European Integration

Lenard J. Cohen and John R. Lampe

Woodrow Wilson Center Press
Washington, D.C.

The Johns Hopkins University Press
Baltimore

EDITORIAL OFFICES

Woodrow Wilson Center Press
One Woodrow Wilson Plaza
1300 Pennsylvania Avenue, N.W.
Washington, D.C. 20004-3027
Telephone: 202-691-4029
www.wilsoncenter.org

ORDER FROM

The Johns Hopkins University Press
Hampden Station
P.O. Box 50370
Baltimore, Maryland 21211
Telephone: 1-800-537-5487
www.press.jhu.edu/books/

Library of Congress Cataloging-in-Publication Data

Cohen, Lenard J.
    Embracing democracy in the western Balkans : from postconflict struggles
toward European integration / Lenard J. Cohen and John R. Lampe.
        p.   cm.
    Includes bibliographical references and index.
    ISBN-13: 978-1-4214-0382-3
    ISBN-10: 1-4214-0382-X
    ISBN-13: 978-1-4214-0433-2 (pbk. : alk. paper)   1. Balkan Peninsula—
Politics and government—1989–   2. Democratization—Balkan Peninsula.
3. Democracy—Balkan Peninsula.   I. Lampe, John R.   II. Title.
JN97.A91C64 2011
320.9496—dc22

                                                                    2011015223

**Woodrow Wilson
International
Center
for Scholars**

The Woodrow Wilson International Center for Scholars is the national, living US memorial honoring President Woodrow Wilson. In providing an essential link between the worlds of ideas and public policy, the Center addresses current and emerging challenges confronting the United States and the world.

The Center promotes policy-relevant research and dialogue to increase understanding and enhance the capabilities and knowledge of leaders, citizens, and institutions worldwide. Created by an act of Congress in 1968, the Center is a nonpartisan institution headquartered in Washington, D.C., and supported by both public and private funds.

Conclusions or opinions expressed in Center publications and programs are those of the authors and speakers and do not necessarily reflect the views of the Center staff, fellows, trustees, advisory groups, or any individuals or organizations that provide financial support to the Center.

The Center is the publisher of *The Wilson Quarterly* and home of Woodrow Wilson Center Press and dialogue television and radio. For more information about the Center's activities and publications, including the monthly newsletter *Centerpoint,* please visit us on the Web at www.wilsoncenter.org.

To our grandsons, Benjamin, Mark, and Joshua

Contents

Tables and Figures

Tables

Figures

Preface

Visiting Serbia in early 2010, the European Union's new representative for foreign affairs and security, Catherine Ashton, confidently reminded a Belgrade audience that was undoubtedly skeptical, given the current international financial crisis, that "compared to the 1990s, we have achieved real progress. The Balkans today is a different place." Ashton could point to the region's recent postconflict decade of pluralist politics and economic growth, and also to the persisting hopes of its citizens and elites to join the "EU family" in the not-too-distant future. It was an impression of such progress just under way in 2006, coupled with subsequent concern about its depth and sustainability, that prompted the two authors of this book to undertake a detailed inquiry during the past several years. Our intention was to take a close and unvarnished look at what indeed has happened in this Western Balkans region now consisting of seven states (only five states and one independence-seeking protectorate as we began), how the attendant changes have affected their diverse populations, and how their elites, rather than the international community alone, have affected these changes.

This book therefore focuses on the progress made and problems encountered in the challenging process of democratic consolidation in the Western Balkans, primarily in the period since 1999. Rather than subdividing our volume on the familiar country-by-country basis, we have pursued a comparative approach in order to examine the linkages and disjunctures within the region's common political, social, and economic dimensions. The introduction and nine chapters proceed through the specific challenges that constitute the crux of what we have termed "embracing democracy." Where have these respective polities succeeded and where have they fallen short, we ask, in their own domestic con-solidation of competitive multiparty politics; engaged civil societies; modern public administrations under the rule of law; open, upwardly mobile societies; and market economies? Having been free of armed conflict and civil disruption for barely a decade, the Western Balkans has now been confronted with a global financial crisis and the prospect of economic recession replacing its rapid growth of recent years. Also in the background for the Yugoslav successor states—minus Slovenia plus Albania—that became "the Western Balkans" in 1999 are the long pre-1989 decades under Communist regimes that equated democracy with their ruling parties and practice. We draw on our own long de-cades of tracking the region, traveling frequently, and publishing our research repeatedly, to keep its checkered legacies in mind. But we do not regard these surely relevant Communist legacies as predetermining the region's future. And still less relevant for our purposes is the less recent past, with its temptations to weigh down the present period with a simplifying moral narrative of victimization or illegitimacy applied to one polity or another.

We are grateful to the various officials, scholars, and friends both within and outside the region with whom we have met and who have assisted us in our research. They are of course in no way responsible for our account and its conclusions. Deborah Chang, Hyun Kim, John Kim, Jill Pokorney, and Dragan Pucar provided valuable assistance in the collection of materials and in the preparation of the manuscript. Finally, and not for the first time, our wives Terri Cohen and Anita Baker offered the support and forbearance that allowed us to visit the region regularly and to work jointly on the book in far closer coordi-nation than our locations at opposite ends of North America might otherwise have permitted.

Lenard J. Cohen and John R. Lampe

Embracing Democracy in the Western Balkans

Introduction: The Challenges of Postconflict Democracy Building

In recent years, most observers in the international community have chosen to follow the lead of the European Union since 1999, and so they have viewed Southeastern Europe as being composed of two parts. One part is unambiguously identified as "European." In that small, fortunate subgroup are the four present members of the EU—Greece and Slovenia, joined in 2007 by Bulgaria and Romania. In the other part, dubbed "the Western Balkans" by the international community during the past decade, we find a group of seven states—four of the initial successor states to the former Yugoslavia, plus recently independent Montenegro and Kosovo,[1] together with long-isolated Albania (figure I.1). These states are referred to as "Western" only because of their geographic location to the west of Bulgaria and Romania. Their designation as "Balkan" recalls a common geographical expression identifying the area, but one that too often became a pejorative synonym for ethnic division and violence. For many observers, this problematic "Balkans" region was not intrinsically part of Europe.

Yet for the already-independent states of Southeastern Europe and the Hapsburg borderlands, the effort to establish pluralist democratic polities had already begun by the start of twentieth century, or, for the Ottoman borderlands, immediately after World War I. Barely a decade later, there admittedly followed a prolonged dismissal of any multi-

1. "Kosova" is the Albanian spelling and is the preferred usage by the authorities in the new state, although less frequently used in English-language and non-Albanian sources. This book uses "Kosovo" unless citing the usage of the Albanian variant.

1

Figure I.1. The Western Balkans in 2010–2011

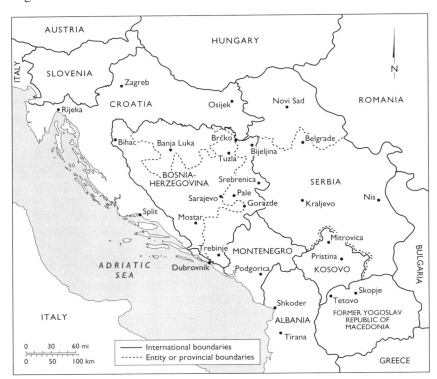

party model, from the authoritarian regimes of the 1930s through the upheavals of World War II and directly into more than four decades of Communist rule everywhere but Greece. Since the Communist collapse during the years 1989–90, a second democratic transition has proceeded in the region, under international conditions more auspicious than during the first effort. This time, of course, the violent dissolution of the second Yugoslavia has been accompanied by, and indeed has prompted, active engagement in democracy building. A large complement of international organizations has pushed democratic elites and publics to support pluralist democracy. Yet the magnitude and repercussions of the violence during the 1990s challenged this support, setting the Western Balkans apart from the rest of Southeastern Europe. Indeed, the consequences of armed struggle raised obstacles to democracy building that strengthened antipluralist resistance at both the elite and mass levels across much of the region.

At a time when the Western projection of postconflict democratization and pluralist state building is sorely troubled in many regions of the world,[2] compounded by the prolonged global economic downturn that began with the financial crisis in 2008, this book poses these basic questions: How and to what extent has this particular postconflict region of the Western Balkans actually embraced the democracy that its leaders now formally endorse? More specifically, have the region's institutions and populations evolved to support and accept pluralist values and political behavior to the extent necessary to make democracy self-sustaining? And finally, how have the region's economies reconstructed themselves since the Communist era? What progress have private sectors and public regulators made in creating the "functioning market economies" stipulated by the EU's Copenhagen Criteria as a qualification for membership?

For some, it has been tempting to dismiss the Western Balkans as still overwhelmed by the violent dissolution of the former Yugoslavia and Albania's upheavals during the late 1990s, not to mention the region's unhappy historical reputation, fair or unfair. Though granting the reality of the region's serious difficulties in the twentieth century and beyond, this book seeks to closely examine the prospects for democracy in the Western Balkans. Wider lessons for Western policy regarding the realities of democratic transition should also emerge from an inquiry into the experience of a region whose immediate postcommunist years were both conflicted and violent.

It is still useful to recall that during the 1920s, the independent states of the region we now call the Western Balkans struggled to establish parliamentary democracy and open economies, based on Western-style institutions that affirmed individual rights.[3] The illiberal regimes that followed, authoritarian in the 1930s and Communist after World War II, could play off of serious shortcomings in these pluralist frameworks.

---

2. See Christian W. Haerpfer, "Post-Communist Europe and Post-Soviet Russia," in *Democratization,* edited by Christian W. Haerpfer, Patrick Bernhagen, Ronald F. Inglehart, and Christian Wehel (London: Oxford University Press, 2009), 309–19. The 14th edition of Freedom House's comprehensive overview of democratic development reports considerable areas of democratic regression in fourteen of twenty-nine postcommunist countries during 2009: Freedom House, *Nations in Transit 2010* (Washington, D.C.: Freedom House, 2010).

3. John R. Lampe, *Balkans into Southeastern Europe, A Century of War and Transition* (London: Palgrave, 2006), 63–104; Lenard Cohen and Paul Warwick, *Political Cohesion in a Fragile Mosaic: The Yugoslav Experience* (Boulder, Colo.: Westview Press, 1983), 27–50.

Indeed, from the 1930s onward, these regimes pursued the creation of strong central governments, privileging a single party and using referenda on new constitutions and sometimes (as in the former Yugoslavia) multicandidate one-party elections as a substitute for genuine pluralist competition. The breakdown of parliamentary democracy at the end of the 1920s, and then the destructive course of World War II, also had much to do with the failure to accommodate pluralism after 1945. Moreover, even with Communist efforts to suppress them, the memories of civil war, genocide, and forced migration (really "ethnic cleansing") during World War II were left to resonate across the Western Balkans. These memories combined with the legacy of the former Yugoslavia and the postcommunist problems facing all of Eastern Europe to promote the warfare, forced migration, and other abuses that set the region apart from the rest of Southeastern Europe during the mid-1990s (table I.1).

Happily, by the start of the twenty-first century, democratic promise and postconflict challenges replaced ongoing or impending large-scale violence in the region. Some positive historical traditions have also facilitated recent democracy building. For example, the population of the Western Balkans is divided into the Orthodox, Catholic, and Muslim religions, along with other small faith communities. But the region can also draw on a long premodern cultural history of religious coexistence. There has also been a modern secular connection to the European mainstream. The cultural connections and intellectual life of Belgrade and Zagreb before World War I, and also that of Sarajevo, illustrate this connection.[4]

Conceptualizing and Evaluating Democratic Consolidation

The primary focus throughout this book is to evaluate the region's progress in consolidating democratic regimes, a process that has been proceeding with a largely successful if still-mixed record across the former "Eastern Europe" since the collapse of its post-1945 Communist regimes in the years 1989–90. At the center of such consolidation are not simply multiparty elections and the privatization of state enterprise.

4. See Lampe, *Balkans into Southeastern Europe*, 97–104; Robert J. Donia, *Sarajevo, A Biography* (London: Hurst, 2006); and Celia Hawkesworth, *Zagreb: A Cultural History* (Oxford: Oxford University Press, 2008).

Table I.1. Selected Features of the Western Balkan States, 2008 or 2009

State	Population	Size (km²)	Ethnic Composition: Major Groups (%)
Serbia, 2009	7,381,000	88,361	Serbs, 82.9; Hungarians, 3.9; Bosniaks, 1.8
Montenegro, 2009	628,000	13,812	Montenegrins, 43.2; Serbs, 32.0; Bosniaks, 7.8; Albanians, 5.0
Croatia, 2008	4,436,000	56,594	Croats, 89.6; Serbs, 4.5
Bosnia, 2008[a]	3,773,100	51,197	Bosniaks, 48.0; Serbs, 34.0; Croats, 15.4
Macedonia, 2008[b]	2,045,000	25,713	Macedonians, 64.2; Albanians, 25.2
Kosovo, 2009[c]	2,180,000	10,887	Albanians, 92; Serbs, 5.3
Albania, 2008	3,200,000	28,748	Albanians, 98.8; Greeks, 1.2

[a]No census has been taken in Bosnia since 1991, but one is planned for 2012. Ethnic data are based on a 2003 estimate. A survey sponsored by the Catholic Church estimated the number of Croats at between 14 and 15 percent in 2010 (or roughly 62.6 percent of those Croats living in the country in 1991); *Vjesnik*, February 19, 2010.

[b]Ethnic data are from the 2002 census.

[c]It is estimated that more than half of Kosovo's Serb population lives in north Kosovo, where they constitute approximately 96 percent of the population. North Kosovo consists of the country's three northernmost municipalities—Leposavić, Zvečan, and Zubin Potok—plus a relatively small portion of Kosovska Mitrovica municipality.

Electoral democracy, after all, sustained both Slobodan Milošević's regime in Serbia and Franjo Tudjman's in Croatia through the 1990s.[5] And during the same decade, across the region, hasty programs for voucher privatization left large enterprises in the hands of politically selected managements, new or old. To evaluate whether, and to what extent, the polities in the Western Balkans have made progress toward becoming institutionalized democracies, the following chapters examine the initial limits of institution building in the region during the late 1990s, and then proceed to explore more extensively the less turbulent political and economic environment of the post-2000 period.

Following many students of democracy, this book distinguishes between "regime transition" and "regime consolidation." As Andreas Schedler has put it, "The consolidation of democracy concludes when democratic actors manage to establish reasonable certainty about the continuity of the new democratic regime, abating expectations of authoritarian regression. . . . The emergence of uncertainty marks the beginning of regime change, and the fading away of uncertainty marks the successful culmination of consolidation."[6] Terry Karl has also drawn attention to this same conceptual distinction: "During transition from authoritarian rule there is an extraordinary state of uncertainty characterized by a high degree of unpredictability, lack of adequate information, sheer confusion among activists; . . . actions during transitions are undetermined choices and unspecified, and outcomes are uncertain. The consolidation of democracy is defined by the substantial reduction in the uncertainty that is so certain to transition. Indeed, it is about institutionalizing some relatively high degree of certainty through a common set of rules (both formal and informal), generally understood political rules and relatively well-defined policy arenas."[7]

5. Lenard J. Cohen, *Broken Bonds: Yugoslavia's Transition and Balkan Politics in Transition,* 2nd ed. (Boulder, Colo.: Westview Press, 1995); Lenard J. Cohen, *Serpent in the Bosom: The Rise and Fall of Slobodan Milošević,* 2nd ed. (Boulder, Co.: Westview Press, 2002); and John Lampe, *Yugoslavia as History: Twice There Was a Country,* 2nd ed. (Cambridge: Cambridge University Press, 2000), 365–415.

6. Andreas Schedler, "Taking Uncertainty Seriously: The Blurred Boundaries of Democratic Transition and Consolidation," *Democratization* 8, no. 4 (Winter 2001): 2.

7. Terry Karl, "From Democracy to Democratization before and after Transitions from Authoritarian Rule," in *The Diversity of Democracy: Corporatism, Social Order and Political Conflict,* edited by Colin Crouch and Wolfgang Streeck (Cheltenham, UK: Edward Elgar, 2006), 101, 106.

An analysis of democratic consolidation will raise a number of questions. For example, how successful have the Western Balkan political elites been at organizing and fine-tuning effective and legitimate institutions of state power, and the separation of powers between the executive, legislative, and judicial branches? How far have the political and administrative institutions of the region come to be considered structures of democratic governance? And can such institutions ward off pressures to prolong or renew vestigial authoritarian patterns, while also avoiding the chronic inefficiencies and endemic corruption that have contributed to state weakness in the region? Democratic theorists have emphasized that it is the "fading away of uncertainty" about the institutional continuity of a democratic regime that is the hallmark of its consolidation, or, as Juan Linz and Alfred Stepan have put it, that democratic regimes can only be regarded as consolidated when democracy is the "only game in town."[8]

The certainty and continuity that are intrinsic to democratic consolidation depend upon certain behavioral, attitudinal, and constitutional features of a society—behaviorally, when no significant political groups are trying to seriously terminate democracy or break up the state; attitudinally, "when even in the face of severe political and economic crises, the overwhelming majority" of the population embraces democratic procedures; and constitutionally, when all major governmental and nongovernmental actors channel their conflicting demands and grievances through the established laws and procedures of the democratic

8. Juan J. Linz and Alfred Stepan, "Towards Consolidated Democracies," *Journal of Democracy* 7, no. 2 (1996): 14–33; Juan J. Linz and Alfred Stepan, *Problems of Democratic Transition and Consolidation: Southern Europe, South America and Post-Communist Europe* (Baltimore: Johns Hopkins University Press, 1996); Guillermo O'Donnell, "Illusions about Consolidation," in *Consolidating Third Wave Democracies,* edited by Marc F. Platner et al. (Baltimore: Johns Hopkins University Press, 1997), 40–57. Larry Diamond observed in 2002 that "democracy is consolidated when all major parties and organizations and the overwhelming majority of the mass public believe that democracy is the best form of government for their society—better than any alternative they can imagine—and when they abide by the rules and constraints of the legal and constitutional system. . . . It is generally believed that Poland, Hungary, the Czech Republic, Slovenia and the Baltic states all have consolidated their democracies, but not the states of the Balkan region." Larry Diamond, "Assessing Global Democratization a Decade after the Communist Collapse," *Romanian Journal of Political Sciences,* issue 2 (2002): 7.

framework. As Linz and Stepan caution, however, even the "varieties of consolidated democracies" are vulnerable to the emergence of some "new dynamic," and also to problems that can reverse gains and even potentially destroy a democratic regime. Moreover, as Wolfgang Merkl has observed, in countries where the "state of the state" is precarious (revealing a "weakness of the state," or special problems with "stateness"), owing to internal territorial issues or high levels of ethnic conflict, the possibility for the "deconsolidation" of democracy is more probable. The question of when a democracy is "sufficiently robust" to be regarded qualitatively as "above the consolidation threshold" is not easily answered, even when based upon a careful analysis of the evidence.[9] Still, while granting that democratization is never a linear process, and the outcome of that process is indeterminate (periods of "democratic recession" and cases of "authoritarian regression" abound), it is fair to say that once a society becomes involved in democracy building for a protracted period, it becomes increasingly difficult to return to the authoritarian order.[10] As a democracy moves from an unconsolidated to a more consolidated stage, the number of "contingent democrats," "superficial democrats," and "nondemocrats" decreases, while those who can be regarded as "consistent democrats" form a critical mass in society.[11]

Some two decades after the collapse of the region's one-party systems, how do the various Western Balkans polities compare with regard to their record of institutional transformation and strengthening? Can the operation of formal and informal institutions in the region be deemed not only democratic in form but also deeply valued by those

9. Wolfgang Merkl, "Plausible Theory, Unexpected Results: The Rapid Democratic Consolidation of Central and Eastern Europe," IPG 2/2008.

10. For regimes that fall beneath the democratic "threshold," see Leonardo Morlino, "Hybrid Regimes or Regimes in Transition?" Fride Working Paper 7 (September 2008). See also Philippe C. Schmitter, "Twenty-Five Years, Fifteen Findings," *Journal of Democracy* 21, no. 1 (January 2010): 17–28; and Guillermo O'Donnell, "Schmitter's Retrospective: A Few Dissenting Notes," *Journal of Democracy* 21, no. 1 (January 2010): 29–32.

11. On the depth of democratic commitment to the consolidation process, see E. Bellin, "Contingent Democrats: Industrialists, Labor, and Democracy in Late Developing Countries," *World Politics* 52, no. 2 (January 2000): 175–205; Larry Diamond, "Democratically Correct Nation," *The Australian,* October 21, 2009; and Yun-han Chu, Larry Diamond, Andrew Nathan, and Doh Chull Shin, *How East Asians View Democracy* (New York: Columbia University Press, 2008).

taking part in the political process? As Jean Monnet aptly remarked in his memoirs, "Nothing is possible without men, nothing is lasting without institutions."[12] The initial phase of postcommunist transition and state reconfiguration was a wrenching experience in the Western Balkans and was "made possible" by leaders whose democratic credentials were spotty, or in some cases sorely lacking. In any event, in the longer term, it is the processes of consolidation and institutionalization that determine whether or not democracy acquires a more "lasting" quality. Because these processes are generally indeterminate and fluid, with a lack of clarity as to their starting and end points, it is important to closely examine the complex empirical record of the consolidation that has been achieved in the individual Western Balkan states.

The consolidation of democracy demands a great deal. First of all, it demands a rejection of clientelist commitments in favor of the contractual obligations that underlie the rule of law and a market economy. Behavior and governmental institutions shift substantially from interactions based on personal relationships to those based upon codified rules. The much cited but rarely defined concept of the "rule of law" further demands the separation of executive and legislative powers and an independent judiciary, supported by an independent media and a substantially depoliticized and transparent public administration responsive to civil society. Only a political elite committed to the values underlying genuine pluralism in governance, to individual rights and equality before the law, can create such a democratic institutional framework that will function in practice. And for the Western Balkan region—much disrupted by the turbulence of the 1990s—the prospect and attraction of such a pluralist framework must be a realistic, domestically based one for both the younger postcommunist elite and the bulk of the citizenry if they are to resist disillusionment or emigration.

By 2010, the Western Balkans had experienced roughly a decade without the armed conflict that initially set the region apart from the rest of postcommunist Eastern Europe. Prolonged warfare attended by criminal violence and ethnic cleansing ended with the Dayton Agreement on Bosnia-Herzegovina in 1995 and Serbia's forced withdrawal from Kosovo in 1999. More warfare erupted briefly in Macedonia two years later, but this time local representatives were able to cut short the dispute under international mediation. In August 2001, the leaders of

12. Jean Monnet, *Memoirs* (Paris: Fayard, 1976), 360.

the ethnic Macedonian majority and the Albanian Macedonian minority signed the Ohrid Agreement. Thus, under terms that avoided Dayton's division of Bosnia into separate entities, Macedonia has attempted to legitimize the republic's political, judicial, and economic institutions. But ethnic contention has continued to trouble the efforts in both Bosnia and Macedonia. Meanwhile, in Kosovo, since mid-1999, a military force (the Kosovo Force, known as KFOR) drawn largely from NATO members has remained in place with the mission of deterring renewed conflict. A reduced force, along with an EU civilian mission, has remained even since Kosovo declared its independence in early 2008. In both protectorates, Bosnia and Kosovo, moreover, international oversight has both pushed and held back domestic officials in catching up with the rest of the region's progress in establishing the kind of representative political process, independent legal system, and market economy associated with membership in the European Union. But in Bosnia and Kosovo, along with the five other less internationally dependent states of the Western Balkans, the critical steps to establish consolidated democratic regimes remain contingent upon domestic political forces.

This common set of postconflict struggles for democratic consolidation is framed both by the attraction to and the conditionalities of EU membership. Indeed, the region's prospects to advance as "the Western Balkans" date only from the European Union Summit of November 2000 in Zagreb. Its Final Declaration extended the prospect of EU membership beyond Slovenia, already a likely candidate, to all the other post-Yugoslav states, even to Bosnia-Herzegovina, to a then–united Serbia/Montenegro, and to a potentially independent Kosova (rather than a Kosovo still formally controlled by Serbia). The declaration substituted Albania for Slovenia to complete this collection of previously unlikely polities, calling them "the Western Balkans." The EU's Balkan Summit of 2003, convened in Thessaloniki under Greek presidency, established specific stages leading to the Stability and Association Agreements with the EU, and thereby to eventual EU membership for all countries in the region. The terms were admittedly less generous and the stages were to last longer than those for previous candidates, and they were laced with "conditionality" regarding standards that needed to be achieved. But these standards and stages had at least been set in place, and they have guided the course of the subsequent EU enlargement process. The terms set for association constitute just the sort of "gradual incentives and mechanisms" that have been called optimal for linking conditional support to Western leverage to avoid further ethnic conflict.[13]

Realistic chances to qualify for EU membership, more likely chances than the one offered to Turkey at a 1999 EU meeting in Helsinki, surfaced for Croatia and Serbia/Montenegro with the end of the Tudjman and Milošević regimes in 2000. Albania was already making progress following the conclusion of international intervention to stem the 1997 chaos in that country. Macedonia's opportunity to make progress in democratization followed from the Ohrid Agreement in 2001.[14] Since then, all the region's governments, their publics, and especially their emergent middle classes and younger professionals have been drawn to the prospect of EU membership. Croatia and Macedonia became regional leaders and were officially designated by the EU as "candidate countries." And the same magnetic attraction was clearly at work in Serbia, Bosnia, Kosovo, and Albania, which were designated by 2008 as "potential candidate countries" that still lagged behind on the path to EU association.

All the Western Balkan countries were scarred, most prominently the two international protectorates, by the conflicts of the 1990s. All the regimes in the region have struggled with establishing the political provisions of the EU's Copenhagen Criteria for candidate countries, namely, legitimate public institutions and the transparent separation of their powers under the rule of law, with respect for human and minority rights. First set down at Copenhagen in 1993, these provisions have been legal requirements for EU membership since 1997.[15] The region's economies have faced comparable challenges in meeting the provision stipulating a "functioning market economy." Sharp Communist-era distinctions, making Albania a separate, indeed exceptional case, have meanwhile receded. The former Yugoslav republic of Slovenia, which was fortunate to avoid the prolonged conflict of the 1990s and successful in making itself a member of the European Union by 2004,

13. Judith Kelly, *Ethnic Politics in Europe: The Power of Norms and Incentives* (Princeton, N.J.: Princeton University Press, 2004), 30–53.

14. Gerald Knaus and Marcus Cox, "The 'Helsinki Moment' in Southeastern Europe," *Journal of Democracy* 1, no. 16 (2005): 39–53.

15. On the origins and evolution of the EU's Copenhagen Criteria, see Milada Anna Vachudova, *Europe Undivided: Democracy, Leverage, and Integration after Communism* (London: Oxford University Press, 2005), 121–23.

has instead become the exception (and is no longer officially labeled "Balkan"). Hence, Slovenia has been excluded from the EU's initial definition of the region and from subsequent international surveys and indexes now tracking "the Western Balkans," and also from this volume.

This newly configured region has continued across the past postconflict decade to struggle with building democracy, facing internal challenges as well as addressing EU standards. The efforts of the various states in the region deserve systematic comparative analysis. They have enough in common so that the differences stand out, a classic standard for comparison. Existing scholarship has tended to deny these similarities and to neglect a careful comparison of the differences. The majority of scholarly studies have concentrated on single cases and distinctions in cultural history—on Yugoslavia's individual successor states, on the protectorates in Bosnia or Kosovo, or on Albania as the still-isolated exception. And yet all these polities have faced common challenges in consolidating pluralistic political institutions and democratic political cultures; in creating independent judiciaries and media; in reforming their educational and health systems; and in confronting the economic problems of high unemployment, initially flawed privatization, huge trade and budget deficits, and the challenge of attracting direct foreign investment. Their levels of domestic stability and international standings have of course varied, proceeding in the post-1999/2000 period downward in rough order from Croatia to Macedonia, Albania, and Montenegro, and then to Serbia, Albania, Bosnia, and Kosovo.

Despite a flood of official studies and studies by nongovernmental organizations of the post-1999 Western Balkans, much of the scholarly and popular literature has remained focused on the former Yugoslavia, on the warfare and war crimes of the 1990s, or on the diplomatic and military role of the international community. The complex internal political and socioeconomic dynamics of the postconflict period since then has been either ignored or assumed to be a continuation of wartime patterns. Unfortunately, much of the literature on the Western Balkans presents a brief snapshot of current events, often ignoring careful trend analysis and utilizing the latest "democratization index" or poll on the evolving situation without reference to what has really changed over time, or why. As Thomas Carothers has observed, such indexes and surveys, or what he calls "photographs of reality," can be valuable, "but they're less useful for telling you why reality is the way it is. If I say 'show me a photograph of this country,' these indices will say: 'The media is in this condition, the level of civil liberties is in that condition.' These photographs don't answer questions like 'How might it change?' 'How did it become this way?' 'Where are the fault lines?'"[16]

Another prominent analytical problem is the use of "moral narratives" in the study of the region. Their major purpose is to condemn or to excuse one party or the other, local or international. They tempt us to read the history of the twentieth century and early twenty-first century backward from the 1990s, thus freezing recent victims and the victimizers into enduring stereotypes. The relatively greater responsibility of certain actors (e.g., the Milošević regime for the post-1989 warfare and violence notwithstanding), such moral narratives have discouraged and distorted the comparative and policy-relevant analysis that the post-1999 period now merits. Broad-brush moral overgeneralizations are a poor substitute for careful analysis. Our own primary concern with the dynamics of the past decade resists any long-term historical projection of internal path dependency, that is, the normative temptation to simplify the multisided and complex character of political consolidation so that it fits a single preordained and externally determined path. At one extreme for this region, there is the assumption that the Western democratic model is not only a proven success but that it is also easily exportable to the Western Balkans if accepted at face value. Early affirmations by Western officials, centering on the promise of multiparty elections and multiethnic relations, are too numerous to mention. At the other extreme is the equally ad hoc dismissal of any such positive transfer of the Western model, typically from regional officials or Western academics. One of the latter simply asserts that only Slovenia and the Czech Republic across all the former Central and Eastern Europe have avoided a sham democratization, one that is in fact "a plutocratic-colonial structure" erected by "the plutocrats of

---

16. Thomas Carothers, "Democracy Assistance without a Plan," *Development and Transition,* no. 12 (April 2009): 11. Nenad Zakosek observes that despite their ostensible diachronic character most indices of democracy have a "static quality" that does not explain the "real dynamics of political regimes. Those indexing regimes rarely explain deviation from earlier ratings, why there are deviations from some ideal model of democratic consolidation, and how measuring tools may fail to cover the unique features of societies." Nenad Zakosek, "The Dynamics of Changes: How Different Are the Transformation Results in Post-Yugoslav Countries?" in *1989–2009 Years of Upheaval: Beginning of Inclusion or Exclusion?* edited by Heinrich Boll-Stiftung (Sarajevo: Heinrich Boll Stiftung, 2009), 159–66.

the West."[17] Both these extremes ignore the domestic political dynamics of the Western Balkans on which this volume concentrates.

Economic analysis has generally reached more evenhandedly across the region. But for some time, such analysis saw the post-1999 record as still held hostage to the unpromising decade that preceded it. This pessimism was indeed understandable when studies of the first few years after 1999 found the major economic indicators still discouraging. Following the economic upturn after 2003, however, the pendulum swung the other way. Many critics of Western engagement in the region now focused upon the close connection assumed between the neoliberal Washington Consensus of the early 1990s and the EU's initial reluctance even to consider membership for the Western Balkan states. This dismissive view saw the EU as concerned only with setting harsh, hegemonic terms for capitalist subordination rather than economic integration.[18] More recently, the economic downturn starting in the fall of 2008 has further encouraged an already-popular "Post–Washington Consensus" that touts the value of increased state intervention.

The analysis in the chapters that follow considers the decade of development in the Western Balkans after 1999–2000 as a departure from the experience of the 1990s. A "structural narrative" of the decade compares the region's struggles for institutional change, increasingly within a framework of EU candidacy offered by Brussels, and the impact of such postconflict struggles on elite transition and popular support.[19] This approach does not, however, privilege the central government's executive powers and national identity as dictated by the ethnic majority. Instead, the emphasis of the analysis is on the region's post-1999 strug-

---

17. Sabrina Ramet, *The Liberal Project and the Transition to Democracy: The Case of East Central Europe* (College Station: Texas A&M University Press, 2007), 29–32. See also, e.g., James Sadkovich's failed effort to prove that Croatia was "well on its way" to being a consolidated democracy by 1998 and was fully consolidated by 2003: James Sadkovich, "An Historical Test Case: Was Franjo Tudjman an Authoritarian Nationalist?" *Review of Croatian History*, no. 1 (2007): 219–49.

18. See the detailed case made by Mustafa Tuerkes and Goeksu Goegoez, "The European Union's Strategy towards the Western Balkans: Exclusion or Integration," *East European Politics and Society* 20, no. 4 (Fall 2006): 659–90.

19. As early as 1998, Jon Elster and his coauthors pointed to the importance of institutions in their volume on institutional design in postcommunist societies: Jon Elster, Claus Offe, and Ulrich K. Preuss, *Institutional Design in Post-Communist Societies: Rebuilding the Ship at Sea* (Cambridge: Cambridge University Press, 2005).

gles to retreat from exclusivist identities within constitutions, and to establish a separation of powers, while at the same time strengthening essentially weak state structures. A successful turn to checks and balances is crucial to both postcommunist democratization and broader European integration. Specifically, the analysis here focuses upon the deconcentration and sharing of institutional authority among separate branches of government and independent agencies, of devolution to local or regional levels of government, and potentially to the European Union. It must be acknowledged, however, that a good deal of structural struggle occurs in the ranks of political and other elites, both current and pending. These domestic elites face the promise of the European Union with their publics already feeling pressured by the conditionality demanded by international organizations from the 1990s forward.

The idea of "embracing democracy," as phrased in the title of this book, suggests a dual process—not only one of establishing appropriate pluralist institutional frameworks and procedures but also one of growing public acceptance and trust in their legitimacy. Democracy must be both embraced and practiced, as the current struggles to transform illiberal regimes have made clear, if the members of a society are to sustain the principles and practices of pluralist politics and market economics. The same dual process characteristic of a viable democratic state will be required for successful accession to the European Union. Yet the very process of accession among the new EU members from Central and Eastern Europe since 2004 has often neglected democratic practice, and thus has reinforced concern about the EU's own long-discussed "democratic deficit."[20] In the Western Balkans, accepting the *acquis communautaire* and the prospect of its supranational enforcement has already prompted public concern over the sacrifice of national sovereignty. And yet the undeniable attraction of EU membership still looms large across the region. This attraction is what has enabled the EU's "positive leverage" in mobilizing public support for membership and domestic reform.[21] At the least, EU leverage has pushed the region's legal and legislative frameworks to move

20. The Czech Republic, Hungary, Poland, Slovakia, Slovenia, Lithuania, Latvia, and Estonia joined the EU in May 2004; Bulgaria and Romania became members in January 2007.

21. Vachudova, *Europe Undivided,* 105–222.

toward advancing transparent public administration and reducing private corruption. Moreover, a stable and democratic future for the Western Balkans is also important to the European Union. Simply for its own security, the EU's original core members worry about leaving an unintegrated "black hole" or "ghetto" in a region now surrounded (with the accession of Bulgaria and Romania) by EU members.

Probing postcommunist patterns of political and societal change in the Western Balkans, as investigations of other Central and Eastern European countries, requires consideration of the closely related and overlapping issues of "transformation"—democratic transition and consolidation in our approach—and "Europeanization." As Alina Mungiu-Pippidi has pointed out, the two processes can, nonetheless, be distinguished: "Transformation is about *building* states," including the rule of law. "Europeanization is about *integrating* already functioning systems of this kind and rendering them compatible with the European model."[22] In postcommunist Central and Eastern Europe and the Western Balkans, the two processes sometimes come together and sometimes conflict. The concept of democratic consolidation in particular involves both the primarily domestic process of transformation and the process of Europeanization. Moreover, European integration, as Mungiu-Pippidi usefully reminds observers, should be seen not only as a process whereby countries "report" and negotiate with the EU on the requirements of the *acquis communautaire* but also in relation to the critical issues of how states "return to Europe" and "relate to Europe" in their internal political and societal transformations. Although most studies of the Western Balkans' integration with Europe have focused primarily on the formal EU accession process and its conditionalities, this book concentrates on the domestic impact of transformation and the Europeanization process.

By itself, however, the emphasis in the EU accession process on a full framework for the rule of law under reformed public administration

22. Alina Mungiu-Pippidi, "When Europeanization Meets Transformation: Lessons from the Unfinished Eastern European Revolutions," in *Democracy and Authoritarianism in a Post-Communist World,* edited by Valerie Bunce, Michael McFaul and Kathryn Stoner-Weiss (Cambridge: Cambridge University Press, 2010), 59–81. Branko Caraton takes the view of many observers that the Europeanization and transition processes have "essentially been one and the same process—the former, with its requirements has significantly helped and facilitated the latter." Branko Caraton, "The European Union, Southeastern Europe, and the Europeanization of Croatia," *Politička Misao* 46, no. 5 (2009): 171.

and regulated private enterprise has helped to push postcommunist state building forward, beyond the political transition from one-party rule and the economic maxims of the neoliberal Washington Consensus of the early 1990s. That initial low-cost, fast-track approach advocated new constitutions, immediate multiparty elections, and rapid privatization. Offered in return was Western financial support only to stabilize newly established currencies and discourage inflationary state budgets, along the very lines promoted but not supported by British and French central banks during the 1920s. Initially, at least, the longer list of international actors after 1989 still neglected the more daunting institutional enterprise of state building. Meanwhile, in the 1990s, the perils of "nation building" for ethnic minorities in regimes ruled by newly empowered ethnic majorities and their returning diasporas soon became all too clear.

After the conflicts of the 1990s, and their illiberal excesses, a new stage of what we may call a "liberal democratic consensus" emerged regarding the Western Balkans, not to mention many other areas of the world. It emphasized public and private institution building rather than simply financial stability and military security. It relied on a broader definition of liberal democracy and a market economy, one whose legitimacy rested on public institutions—that is, a more responsible state administration, a more representative government, and a framework for the regulation of legal business. Such legitimacy underpinned the national confidence that allowed the EU's initial six members to form the Common Market in 1957.[23]

However, a new mood regarding the future prospects of the Western Balkans emerged even before the global recession began in 2008. The defeat of a single Constitution for the European Union in 2005, and the rising sentiment in some member states against adding new members after the accession of Bulgaria and Romania, fueled the argument that the Western Balkans might not even have a long-term chance for membership. Questions arose about what the European Commission meant when it spoke about EU enlargement, and whether the Stability and Association Agreements could serve as real avenues to eventual membership for the Western Balkan polities. Indeed, the conditions imposed by the EU as a template for democratic state building are quite

23. See "Conclusions," in *The Frontier of National Sovereignty, History and Theory,* by Alan Milward, Francis M. B. Linch, Frederic Romero, Ruggero Ranieri, and Vibeke Sorenson (London: Routledge, 1994), 182–201.

daunting. Thus the question naturally arises about whether such conditionality will dampen the determination spreading through younger political and economic elites in the Western Balkans about proceeding with an EU accession process that seems invaluable in its own right. Such concerns come into sharper focus in the face of the problems posed by the international financial crisis at the end of the twenty-first century's first decade.

This Book's Lines of Inquiry

Chapter 1 of this book provides initial background, moving only from the legacy of the last years and dissolution of Communist regimes in Yugoslavia and Albania to the warfare of the 1990s that culminated with first diplomatic and then military international intervention in Bosnia and in Kosovo. In the process, the World Bank, the International Monetary Fund, and a variety of other organizations broadened the international presence in the region and helped open the way for the EU itself. After reviewing this familiar international activity, the chapter turns to the domestic struggle over the postcommunist transition in the face of real or threatened conflict. Common problems from the last Communist years spilled over into the initial efforts at economic privatization, leaving politically favored, often former Communist management in charge of enterprises. Hasty multiparty elections were left to lead the way in political democratization. The attendant abuses were at least being challenged across the region by the end of the 1990s.

Chapters 2 and 3 track the evolving frameworks for constitutional governance that the Western Balkan polities established, including their struggles to consolidate the positions of accountable executives and legislatures that could function democratically and implement their decisions through reformed and substantially depoliticized public bureaucracies. Generally, fair and democratic elections to the respective legislatures have now become routine in the Western Balkans. But have the winners overcome the legacy of dysfunctional interexecutive rivalry, a dismissive attitude toward legislative authority, and a manipulation of public administrations that have challenged the capacity for democratic governance? Indeed, it is progress in such areas of state building by which candidates for EU membership are now being judged. For Bosnia and Kosovo, the combination of direct international oversight and enduring ethnic divisions has made progress on reformed governance especially difficult. But across the region—even in Croatia, which is furthest away from the wartime conditions of the 1990s—reforming existing police forces, confronting corruption, and establishing independent judiciaries have remained critical challenges for political authorities unaccustomed to nonpartisan state administration and the separation of powers. What have domestic reforms to achieve democratic governance nonetheless accomplished, what accounts for their deficiencies, and where do they now stand?

The next two chapters appraise patterns of political participation. Chapter 4 addresses the civic engagement of populations in the Western Balkans as a bridge between the society and the state's organizational structure. The development of nongovernmental organizations (NGOs) is closely examined, as well as the role of both gender politics and the media in reflecting and reinforcing civil society and democratic change. How important has the role played by NGOs and the media been in sustaining the progress already made in the Western Balkans and addressing persistent problems? Have a more independent media and the free rein enjoyed by a range of NGOs empowered civil society to join in creating networks to monitor official activity?

Chapter 5 examines the changing role of the region's political parties, from the embryonic and rather "wild" pluralism of the 1990s to the evolution of more "European" models. How has public opinion evolved regarding the operation and value of political parties? Has the proliferation of parties that fragmented and to some extent destabilized early pluralist development been replaced by a more stable and defragmented party landscape? Have interest-based political party appeals replaced the symbolic emotional appeals that generated radical nationalism and ethnic polarization during the 1990s? To what extent are political parties still dominated by charismatic leaders, or has the personalization of party control given way to more internal party democracy? Have elections attracted the participation of citizens at a level conducive to democratic consolidation?

Chapters 6 and 7 turn to the social and attitudinal underpinnings of democratic consolidation. At issue is the classic, albeit disputed, claim that stable democracy is only possible if pluralist state institutions are supported and monitored by a robust middle class that is the product of economic development and social modernization. Chapter 6 explores whether classes and elites that are supportive of democracy have emerged in the Western Balkan states. What remains of the class structure and elite formations that were socialized and seasoned during the 1980s and 1990s and also of the Communist leaderships and corrupt elements that rose to prominence as Balkan one-party regimes crumbled? Have the preconditions for a strong, democratically oriented new middle class been put in place, and what impact have factors such as the emergence of new entrepreneurial forces, educational expansion and reform, and brain drain had on this process of class development? Chapter 7 examines the values espoused by elites and new middle classes, and by the general citizenry, as the region endeavors to demonstrate its "Europeanization" and fulfill EU conditions for democratic development and accession. Has the younger generation of postcommunist politicians that entered pluralist politics during and after 1989, and also in the post-2000 period, been able to free itself from the strong residual influence of former Communist beliefs and practices? Clearly, substantial value transformation has occurred throughout the Western Balkans. But has a critical mass of elite and popular support for democracy been consolidated? Have the appeals of radical nationalism and noncivic perspectives diminished to levels that are conducive to a stable democracy, and does a potential for tolerant cooperation among different ethnic groups—if not congenial coexistence—appear to be on the horizon?

Chapter 8 focuses on the nexus of democratic consolidation and social transformation with the belated economic transition that has been under way since the late 1990s. Leading the way have been efforts to reform tax systems, reduce enterprise costs for legal employment, and provide more accessible credit, following from the competitive stimulus of privatization and foreign banks. Streamlined procedures for starting new enterprises have eased market access, especially for smaller firms. Encouraged by growing foreign direct investment, rates of economic and export growth turned upward from 2003 to 2008 everywhere except Kosovo. Yet this boom created too few new jobs, even though levels of unemployment started to come down. Large enterprises would now confront the post-2008 problem of domestic and foreign markets contracting in the face of the international financial crisis. Huge trade deficits were already distinguishing the Western Balkans from the rest of Southeastern Europe. Low levels of per capita income persisted; less so in a Croatia free from domestic turmoil and large numbers of refugees or internally displaced persons. Within these constraints, what progress was made in conforming to the economic standards that constitute the majority of chapters in the EU's *acquis communautaire* during the boom years of 2004–8? And could the reform of higher education under way across the region, as well as the EU, generate the higher productivity of a limited labor force that would be needed to survive the post-2008 downturn and generate intensive growth?

Chapter 9 concludes the book by inviting attention to the experience of the Western Balkans as a cautionary tale for accelerating the complex process of democratic state building. Extracting simple lessons from the terminal, presumably triumphant, phases of the 1990s conflicts has proven to be of limited value. Without the difficult post-1999 decade of experience with pluralist democracy and a market economy, any movement in the Western Balkans toward regional reconciliation and European integration would have remained stillborn. But what effect has the region's challenging and continuing process of preparation for EU membership had on its actual domestic embrace of democracy? (For the reader's convenience, a comprehensive list of the abbreviations used is given at the end of the book.) A brief epilogue pursues this question into 2011, and considers the region's wider postauthoritarian lessons newly relevant for North Africa and the Middle East.

Beginning in 2008, the global financial crisis placed a new burden on the process of postcommunist consolidation in the Western Balkans. The crisis and the slow recovery that is apparently under way have threatened to derail the region's embrace of the European Union, making its prospects for membership more daunting and raising the risk of domestic frustration regarding the accession process, or even its rejection. Summarizing the findings from the preceding chapters, chapter 9 goes on to explore how the primarily domestic dimensions of democratic consolidation have been influenced by the global crisis, and it surveys the European Union's prospective relationship with the Western Balkans after a decade of promising engagement. Will the Western Balkans be able to attain both its "European" and democracy-building goals during this period of weak and uneven economic recovery? And can, as explored in the Epilogue, the participants in the "Arab Spring" of early 2011 learn any lessons from the experience of the Western Balkans?

Chapter 1

Legacies of Communism, Conflict, and International Intervention

The failings of the last decade of Communist rule and tragedies of ethnic warfare, civil disorder, and forced migration that unfolded across the Western Balkans for much of the 1990s are well known. Yet the linkage between the two decades has been neglected. Studies of the international role after 1989 have concentrated on the initially hesitant diplomacy and the final military intervention. Economic intervention has received less attention, and the domestic legacy of belated Communist efforts at economic reform in the 1990s even less. The domestic political legacy has also been neglected, with the exception of Serbia and the rise to power of Slobodan Milošević. The primary international interests throughout this initial postcommunist decade consisted of a strategic desire for stability combined with narrowly focused, low-cost support for a democratic transition.

Such strategic concerns surely predominated in 1999 when, in the wake of NATO's military intervention in Kosovo, barely four years after intervening in Bosnia, the European Union reconsidered its previous rejection of potential membership for these troubled states. Otherwise, the region newly dubbed the Western Balkans ran the risk of becoming a permanent "black hole" in the center of Southeastern Europe and on the borders of Central Europe. Enter the prospect of candidacy for the European Union in 1999. The region has since then seen the West's promotion of the market mechanism, as detailed in chapter 8; a turn to a broader program for building public institutions; and efforts to regulate as well as encourage private enterprise. Across the earlier period considered here, the neoliberal Washington Consensus, led by the United States and the International Monetary Fund, had pressed the successor regimes of the Western Balkans only to establish stable currencies and balanced budgets in order to suppress inflation. The regimes themselves were left to privatize their economies on the muddled terms of the last Communist reforms.

Accompanying this limited Western economic agenda had been the assumption that free, multiparty elections would bring in regimes with the capacity to consolidate democratic practice and their own legitimacy. As it turned out, however, the electoral winners drew on the supposedly defunct Communist framework to subvert the separation of powers and the privatization process to political advantage. These unpromising connections across the watershed of Communist collapse in 1989 also encouraged the violence of the 1990s. And this violence would in turn trigger international intervention and mark out the Western Balkans as a separate, deeply troubled region by the end of this initial post-1989 decade. This chapter reviews the region's discouragingly comparable experience up to that point.

The Failed Communist Reforms of the 1980s in Yugoslavia and Albania

Yugoslavia and Albania stood separated in 1980 by a famously wide political and economic gulf. Although the last years of Communist rule that lay ahead would hardly dent their disparities in political organization or levels of economic development, the decade did pose some common challenges. From having been poles apart, the responses of the two regimes were being drawn closer together. Most noticeably, as market-minded reformers in the Yugoslav Communist Party were stymied, the Albanian party was relaxing its rigid hold on what had become an autarkic economy.

New political diversity, if hardly new frameworks, emerged in the two parties to face their greatest common challenge: the death of their original leaders in the postwar consolidation of Communist power— Josip Broz Tito died in 1980, and Enver Hoxha in 1985. Their successors struggled with political resistance from within their respective Communist parties to confront slowing growth and mounting economic problems.[1] By 1986, Branko Mikulić in Yugoslavia and Ramiz Alia in

1. For an overview of both countries and the regional problems of the 1980s

Albania appeared to have consolidated their political positions. Their party memberships and some Western observers expected them to use their somewhat different positions to advantage—Mikulić as chair of the Federal Executive Council, and Alia as head of the Communist Party. As a Bosnian Croat, Mikulić seemed the best hope to strike a balance between the republic-based organizations in the six republics (Serbia, Croatia, Slovenia, Bosnia-Herzegovina, Macedonia, and Montenegro) plus Serbia's two autonomous provinces of Kosovo and Vojvodina that the 1974 Constitution had given near-republic status. Republic party interrelations—particularly between Serbia, Croatia, and Slovenia—had come to control the League of Communists of Yugoslavia. Mikulić was fresh from his apparent success in coordinating the Winter Olympics of 1984 in Sarajevo. He also brought experience in the multimember, rotating Federal Presidency created by the 1974 Constitution. And in the period 1983–84, the last major infusion of American support had mobilized a Western financial consortium to relieve the immediate burden of Yugoslavia's swollen external debt that would otherwise have confronted Mikulić.[2]

Alia had meanwhile survived the efforts of Hoxha's widow, Nexhmije, and her hard-line colleagues to use the 1986 congress of the Party of Labor of Albania (Partia e Punës e Shqipërisë) to block any relaxation in the central controls that the Great Leader's last years had tightened. Most affected were the collective or state farms in which all of Albania's peasant majority, still two-thirds of the population, were already assembled. Nexhmije and her associates were now set aside, although not as abruptly as Mao Zedong's widow and her Gang of Four, and some loosening now began in the strictest rural regime left in the Communist world.

Deteriorating economies still faced both the Mikulić and Alia regimes, with fateful consequences for their political positions. Their personal standings and their party's both suffered, but the economic crisis strengthened the public perception that authoritarian political leadership might still be needed. For Mikulić, rising inflation and a

---

for Southeastern Europe, see John R. Lampe, *Balkans into Southeastern Europe: A Century of War and Transition* (New York: Palgrave, 2006), 237–55.

2. The full package, called the Friends of Yugoslavia, mobilized $6.5 billion of new credit and longer-term repayment, as detailed by John R. Lampe, Russell O. Prickett, and Ljubiša Adamović, *Yugoslav-American Economic Relations since World War II* (Durham, N.C.: Duke University Press, 1990), 156–86.

scandal in his Bosnian base would force him to resign his position as chair of the Federal Executive Council, the equivalent of being prime minister, by the end of 1988. What had gone wrong? Problems for him and especially for the younger economic reformers that had accompanied him began with the party's political commission convened in 1986. Its task was to assess the appropriate response for the League of Yugoslav Communists to the still-limited reforms suggested by the party's economic commission, chaired by the Slovene economist Sergei Kraigher, in 1982–83. Its recommendations spoke of market-based reforms but left in place the social ownership of enterprises and the 1976 subdivision of workers' councils. A freer price regime served only to grant the growing number of loss-making firms the chance to raise their prices. The new political commission, headed by the Croat Josip Vrhovec, bridled at even even talk of a market economy. It rejected any limits on subsidizing the loss makers. Sacrificing political leverage to the market mechanism was "incompatible with the truly socialist system of self-management." This decision left the republics and their local governments free to continue collecting high "contributions" (*doprinosi*) from the profitable enterprises in order to keep the loss-making majority afloat.[3]

At the weak federal level, the Mikulić regime first rejected the International Monetary Fund's "enhanced monitoring" that its predecessor had accepted early in 1986 in hopes of renewing the so-called standby credits. Then, also under party pressure, it abandoned the IMF requirement that interest rates be set at least 1 percent above the rate of inflation. That rate promptly doubled, and rose to reach 150 percent by 1987. Only the National Bank of Yugoslavia might have reined in this new explosion of domestic credit. But it did not. Its location in the federal capital of Belgrade meant that the western republics of Slovenia and Croatia were likely to resist potentially restrictive powers, granted under a hasty new bank law open to potential Serbian leverage. In the meantime, domestic banks across Yugoslavia, but particularly in Serbia, continued to feed the desperate need for new credit to cover enterprise losses from the social sector. The sector's aggregate loss had

3. On the absence of a genuine liberal option for economic reform in Yugoslavia of the 1980s, see Vladimir Gligorov, "Yugoslav Economics Facing Reform and Dissolution," in *Economic Thought in Communist and Post-Communist Europe,* edited by Hans-Jurgen Wagener (London: Routledge, 1998), 329–61. The prescient critique is by Harold Lydall, *Yugoslavia in Crisis* (Oxford: Clarendon Press, 1989).

mounted since 1982, when a crisis in debt repayment had ended the ready access to Western banks' loans on which large new investments, most of them ill considered and unprofitable, had come to rely in the 1970s. Inventory values unadjusted for the accelerating rate of inflation allowed official statistics to hide the aggregate losses of the social sector from public scrutiny.[4]

The problem of these aggregate losses nonetheless surfaced in 1987 thanks to a major case of outright corruption. Several Bosnian Muslim party leaders were implicated in providing huge unsecured credits to the Agrokomerc conglomerate, many from the leading Slovenian bank, the Ljubljanska Banka. The fall of these key Bosnian Muslims altered a decades-long political balance between Bosnian Serbs, Croats, and Muslims in the republic's Communist leadership. It had served to insulate Bosnia from the liberal stirrings that were challenging Tito's regime in the late 1960s. Then it had allowed the Bosnian Muslims, recognized as a national group in 1971, to take economic advantage of growing Yugoslav trade with Islamic countries and finally of the 1984 Winter Olympics in Sarajevo. Meanwhile, the Bosnian Serb reliance on employment in arms manufacturing suffered from the downsizing of the Yugoslav National Army in the 1980s. For the Croat Mikulić, these Bosnian Serb tensions and the Muslim scandal in his home base also began to weaken wider political support. By the time he resigned in December 1988, the rate of inflation for that year had reached 250 percent.[5]

By that time, moreover, the newly consolidated, more popular, and increasingly nationalist regime of Slobodan Milošević in Serbia made

---

4. The recent recalculation of these aggregate losses, starting in 1983 and rising steadily to nearly 10 percent of social product (gross domestic product minus services but also depreciation) by 1989, is given by Michael Palairet, "The Inter-Regional Struggle for Resources and the Fall of Yugoslavia," in *State Collapse in South-Eastern Europe: New Perspectives on Yugoslavia's Disintegration,* edited by Lenard J. Cohen and Jasna Dragović-Soso (West Lafayette, Ind.: Purdue University Press, 2007), 225–33. The first, generally ignored recognition of Yugoslavia's negative growth rates as disguised by inflated inventory values is Lydall, *Yugoslavia in Crisis,* 128–34.

5. On the political disjuncture between Bosnian Muslims, Serbs, and Croats in the wake of the Bosnian financial scandals of the mid-1980s and the wider economic problems facing the Mikulić regime in Belgrade, see John R. Lampe, *Yugoslavia as History, Twice There Was a Country,* 2nd ed. (Cambridge: Cambridge University Press, 2000), 325–45.

the potential of his large republic's leverage a realistic threat to the others. He started with Serbia's two autonomous provinces, Kosovo and Vojvodina, forcing out their local party leaderships and ending the status as virtual republics that the 1974 Constitution had, as noted above, given them. In Serbia itself, he authorized large new credits that were funneled from the major Belgrade banks to large economic enterprises. Operating in 1989 at an aggregate net loss equal to 15 percent of social product, the largest for any republic, they received enough new credits to give Serbia alone a gain in net investment for the year.[6] More broadly, Milošević demanded that the other republics agree to recentralization in Belgrade as the only way out of the economic crisis. Open resistance had emerged only in Slovenia, where the interest of the Yugoslav National Army in both regional and economic recentralization exposed it to increasing criticism from the youth weekly *Mladina.* The arrest and clumsy trial of several *Mladina* journalists by the army's intelligence agency (KOR) for revealing "state secrets" in June 1988 only spread this critical attitude to the wider Slovenian public and higher Communist officials.[7] Then came the last straw, in June 1989: the critical coverage by Slovenian television of Milošević's remarks threatening Serb violence at the ceremony commemorating the anniversary of the Serbs' Kosovo battle with the Ottoman Turks in 1389.

In Albania, Alia was able to persuade his party congress in 1986 to accept some wage incentives for industrial and agricultural workers. Livestock were returned to the control of family or local units, from which they had been taken in 1981. Some peasant food sales were permitted in newly opened markets. The Five-Year Plan for 1981–85 had failed on its promise to increase industrial production. The harder agricultural regime only decreased the urban food supply, instead of increasing it as promised. Both failures suggested that far greater changes were needed. But the rigidly hierarchical party elite was reluctant to relax comparable control of the economy. In addition, the 1976 Constitution remained in place as a major barrier. It banned foreign investment or credit, and it forbade private ownership of even the smallest property or enterprise.

6. Palairet, "Inter-Regional Struggle," table 1, 230.
7. For the details, see Mark Thompson, *A Paper House: The Ending of Yugoslavia* (New York: Pantheon Books, 1992), 3–59.

Alia has himself been called "a reluctant reformer" at best.[8] He had risen through the Communist Party ranks to the Politburo by 1961 and advanced from there as a close associate of both Hoxha and his wife. Alia become the next in line for succession only after the eminent wartime Partisan and presumed heir apparent, Mehmet Shehu, had died in 1981, probably killed in a still-murky confrontation with Hoxha. In addition, Alia was one of the few northern Gegs in a party leadership otherwise dominated by southern Tosks. He placed his hopes in better results from the new Five-Year Plan for 1986–90. Its rigid central direction had been at least partly decentralized, and enterprise and farm managers had been given some limited autonomy. But the official statistical abstract of 1988, newly forthcoming, indicated that net material product per capita for the period 1986–88 had continued a decline that had already begun in 1981–85.[9]

By the start of 1989, in other words, the pressures for significant change had reached the boiling point in both countries. At the same time, the claims to legitimacy from the two Communist regimes stood their ruling parties in better stead than their counterparts across Central and Eastern Europe. This legitimacy rested on wartime Partisan origins, independence from Soviet control, and the advance of industrial development from a low prewar base. In none of the Soviet Bloc neighbors could their Communist parties draw on all three of these bases of support. Among Yugoslavia's republics, however, we might well note Slovenia's higher level of economic development and closer involvement with the Italian and Austrian economies. These ties had preceded the Communist era and then grown significantly starting in the 1960s. This distinction helps us to understand Slovenia's early exit from the region that has since become the Western Balkans. Elsewhere in the region, the period from 1989 to 1991 did not see the sort of transition that set the stage for peaceful if uneven progress and elec-

8. Nicholas Pano, "The Process of Democratization in Albania," in *Politics, Power and the Struggle for Democracy in South-East Europe,* edited by Karen Dawisha and Bruce Parrott (Cambridge: Cambridge University Press, 1997), 298–314.

9. Orjan Sjöberg and Per Sandstrom, *The Albanian Statistical Abstract of 1988: Heralding a New Era?* Working Paper 2 (Uppsala:, Uppsala University, 1989). Also see Orjan Sjöberg, *Rural Change and Development in Albania* (Boulder, Colo.: Westview Press, 1991).

tions won by opposition parties across Eastern Europe during the rest of the decade. For the Western Balkans, these initial years therefore deserve special attention.

The Two Interregnums, 1989–91

For both Yugoslavia and Albania, their postcommunist transitions struggled to take shape with Communist parties or at least their institutional frameworks still in place well past the collapse of comparable one-party regimes in the Soviet Bloc during the last months of 1989. Both those institutional frameworks were storing up trouble for the years ahead. So was the precedent of unchallengeable political leadership from the head of the ruling party, even if he was now the victor in a multiparty election.[10] Starting in 1991, a wider war followed from the confrontation between two of them, Croatia's Franjo Tudjman and Serbia's Slobodan Milošević. Tudjman's Croatian Democratic Union (Hrvatska demokratska zajednica, HDZ) received more votes than any other party in the 1990 elections on an anticommunist platform. It promised to challenge Croatia's obligation to remain in Yugoslavia and to marginalize the influence of the republic's large Serb minority. At the same time, Milošević's Communists, hastily renamed the Socialist Party of Serbia (Socijalistička Partija Srbije, SPS), had won the republic's own multiparty elections with claims of representing a Yugoslavia that would still include all Serbs.

In Albania, the Communists' Albanian Party of Labor used its rural leverage and organizational advantage to win two-thirds of the seats

10. On the patterns of political leadership connecting the last years of the former Yugoslavia and its breakup, see Dejan Jović, *Yugoslavia, A State That Withered Away* (West Lafayette, Ind.: Purdue University Press, 2009), 226–360; and Lampe, *Yugoslavia as History,* 332–64. On the rise of Milošević's influence in the JNA leadership, culminating in his becoming commander-in-chief in 1991, see Florian Bieber, "The Role of the Yugoslav People's Army in the Dissolution," in *State Collapse,* ed. Cohen and Dragović-Soso, 315–25. The course of events are described from the inside in interviews with former officials Vladimir Lončar, Raif Dizdarović, Željko Kovačević, and others for segments 9 and 10 of the film series *Pogled u prošlosti: Srbija, 1965–1991* (Looking into the Past: Serbia, 1965–1991), produced by the Helsinki Committee for Human Rights in Serbia in 2003, in Film Library, Open Society Archives, Budapest.

in the initial parliamentary election of March 1991. Alia was able to remain president until the following year. Before then, at least, a large crowd in Tirana had pulled down Hoxha's statue, and the feared secret police, the Sigurimi, had been disbanded. Reformers in the new Democratic Party could now openly clamor for change. As with disintegrating Yugoslavia, however, new parties including the reformed Communists were still contending for a monopoly of political power. The contest produced more turmoil than transition, in the economy as well.

Yugoslavia's dissolution moved ahead during this interregnum on the basis of relatively democratic, multiparty elections in all the republics. Like Czechoslovakia's peaceful dissolution in 1993, there were no elections for the country as a whole. Republic elections began with Slovenia and Croatia in April, and the four other republics held theirs in November and December. Only one party claimed to represent all of Yugoslavia and took part in all the elections remaining after its belated formation in July. This was the Alliance of Reform Forces (Savez Reformskih Snaga), led by the last chair of the Federal Executive Council in Belgrade, Ante Marković. His past experience as an enterprise director had made him a convinced market-based reformer. As a Croat, he might have appealed to voters in the western republics, had the party been formed in time for their elections. As it was, public opinion polling suggested that about 60 percent of voters in Slovenia's elections wished to preserve at least a confederal Yugoslavia. The several parties in Croatia's balloting who supported some sort of Yugoslavia, led by a Communist–Social Democrat coalition, won over more than half the votes between them. But in the absence of proportional distribution, the leading nationalist party, the HDZ, took 58 percent of the seats with only 41 percent of the vote.[11] But we may doubt, if Marković's Alliance had been formed in time, whether its presence would have changed the Croatian result. Witness its limited success even in Bosnia-Herzegovina, the most multiethnic republic and the one arguably most committed to preserving some sort of Yugoslavia. Preelection polling predicted that the Alliance would

11. On the way in which the HDZ plurality in these initial Croatian elections favored bipolar division and worked against the political center as well as the smaller and Serb minority parties, see Ivan Grdešić, Mirjana Kasapović, Ivan Šiber, and Nenad Zakošek, *Hrvatska u izborima '90* (Croatia in the 1990 Elections) (Zagreb: Naprijed, 2000).

attract less than 15 percent of the votes cast in Bosnia, and barely 5 percent elsewhere.[12]

As it turned out, even those modest percentages were optimistic forecasts, except in Macedonia and Montenegro. Although a September referendum in Macedonia had produced a clear majority of 71 percent for independence, Marković's Alliance and an associated party still combined to win 14 percent of the votes in the subsequent parliamentary elections, receiving 17 of 120 seats. Their presence at least helped to prevent the aggressively nationalist party that won the most votes, the Internal Macedonian Revolutionary Organization–Democratic Party for Macedonian National Unity (Vnatrešna makedonska revolucionerna organizacija—Demokratska partija za makedonsko nacionalno edinstvo), from forming a government. This result, as we shall see, led to a coalition government that included a party representing the minority Albanians. Such joint governments have sustained Macedonia ever since. Already in January 1991, the Albanian representatives joined the parliamentary majority in voting to elect as president the old Yugoslav economic reformer Kiro Gligorov. He promised that the newly independent Macedonia would at least "participate in the Yugoslav community."[13]

In Montenegro, the prospects of Marković's Alliance were less promising, given the overwhelming victory, with 56 percent of the votes and two-thirds of the parliamentary seats, of the one Communist party among Yugoslavia's republics that had not bothered to change its name. Led by Momir Bulatović, a protégé of Slobodan Milošević and some younger colleagues, they had ignored the representatives of Marković's Alliance and maintained the union with Serbia in Milošević's "Third Yugoslavia." Still, the Alliance finished second in the balloting, with 13.6 percent of the vote and 17 of 125 seats.[14]

Elsewhere, the electoral impact of this last effort to reach across the republics was even less successful. It had been formed too late, as noted above, for the parliamentary elections held earlier in 1990 in Slovenia

12. Lenard J. Cohen, *Broken Bonds: Yugoslavia's Disintegration and Balkan Politics in Transition,* 2nd ed. (Boulder, Colo.: Westview Press, 1995), table 3.2, 105.

13. Duncan Perry, "The Republic of Macedonia: Finding Its Way," in *Politics, Power and the Struggle,* ed. Dawisha and Parrott, 233–35.

14. Florian Bieber, "Montenegrin Politics since the Disintegration of Yugoslavia," in *Montenegro in Transition, Problems of Identity and Statehood,* edited by Florian Bieber (Baden-Baden: Nomos, 2003), 11–17.

and Croatia. In Serbia's December elections, Marković's Alliance received only 2.4 percent of the votes, and 4 seats out of 250, despite the fact that Milošević's SPS had fallen short of the 50 percent of the vote that its media and patronage monopoly had been promising to exceed. And in Bosnia-Herzegovina, where its founding had been announced in hopes of actually winning there, the Alliance won only 9.2 percent of the votes in the November elections of 1990 and 13 seats. Although a declaration of independence and open warfare were still more than a year away, the three ethnic parties representing the Bosnian Muslims, Serbs, and Croats had already carried 202 of the 240 seats in the two chambers—86 for the Party of Democratic Action (Stranka Demokratske Akcije), 71 for the Serbian Democratic Party (Srpska Demokratska Stranka), and 45 for the HDZ. Each promptly broke its campaign promises to serve the whole republic's best interests within some sort of Yugoslavia.[15] The Serb and Croat parties turned instead to exclusivist ethnic programs that would lead to violence and ethnic cleansing.

Marković was temporarily successful only in his monetary measures. The rest of his economic reforms did no more to prevent dissolution and left a large and unfortunate legacy to the successor states. His initial steps as chair of the Federal Council, taken in consultation with the American economist Jeffrey Sachs, did halt the hyperinflation that had reached 3,000 percent for 1989. A newly stabilized exchange rate for the dinar reopened the chance for international debt relief. The Milošević regime closed that opening, first by railing at the resulting end to domestic bank credit available at negative, inflation-fed rates of interest to Serbia's struggling enterprises. By the end of 1990, it slammed the door shut by using the republic's separate National Bank to ignore the authority of the National Bank of Yugoslavia and put "gray emissions" worth 10 percent of Serbia's social product into the hands of several Belgrade banks. Their "secret credits" allowed Serbian enterprises to cover some of their arrears but also put an end to any incentive for the other republics to stay within a single Yugoslav financial system.[16]

15. On the emergence of "mobilized nationalists" by 1990 and the subsequent electoral campaign, see Nevin Anđelić, *Bosnia-Herzegovina: The End of a Legacy* (London: Frank Cass, 2003), 140–92; and Paul Shoup, "The Bosnian Crisis of 1992," in *Beyond Yugoslavia,* edited by Sabrina Ramet and Ljubiša Adamović (Boulder, Colo.: Westview Press, 1995), 155–88.
16. Palairet, "Inter-Regional Struggle," 233–44.

The wider Marković program did dissolve the Basic Organizations of Associated Labor, which had been created in 1976 as Edvard Kardelj's capstone reform of the self-management system he had initiated in 1950. In practice, a number of now-subdivided Workers' Councils confronted each enterprise management, taking more time for meetings and discouraging efficient coordination. A bankruptcy law to see out at least some of the loss-making enterprises finally came into force, much to the political disadvantage of Marković's Alliance for Reform. But Marković's subsequent program for privatizing the surviving enterprises traded economic for political advantage. It recognized the legitimacy of the existing Communist framework for "social ownership" and allocated the majority of shares to managers and employees.[17] Its progress by 1991, as we shall see, helped to push ahead "insider privatization" by the existing, politically appointed management.

The interregnum of 1989–91 also did considerable economic damage in Albania. Both political change and the accompanying socioeconomic disorder gathered pace after the violent deposition of Nicolae Ceauşescu and the end of Romania's supposedly comparable "National Communist" regime in December of 1989. The hasty plenum called by the Albanian Communist Party in January 1990 faced more problems than the example of Ceauşescu's immediate trial and execution. Riots broke out in Shkoder, the main northern town, partly to protest the lack of food in the stores but also to demand some sort of democratic reform. At the plenum, Alia seemed to still be siding with the party hard-liners. They were fiercely resisting any substantive changes beyond allowing peasants to take back their livestock and to sell their own produce to the desperate urban markets. His rhetoric still glorified the party's all-important role and continued the castigation of Mikhail Gorbachev's Soviet concessions familiar from the late 1980s.

By the spring of 1990, however, Alia was sounding like Gorbachev himself as a variety of political pressures swelled up to the Central Committee from below.[18] The first pressure came in February, when an Albanian family desperate to leave the country took refuge in the

17. Saul Estrin and Lina Talka, "Reform in Yugoslavia: The Retreat from Self-Management," in *Industrial Reform in Socialist Countries,* edited by Ian Jeffries (Cheltenham, UK: Edward Elgar, 1992), 267–77.

18. A useful summary of this fateful year is given by Miranda Vickers and James Pettifer, *Albania: From Anarchy to a Balkan Identity* (London: Hurst, 1997), 20–54.

Italian Embassy compound. The regime was still refusing to issue passports to its own citizens, as caustically reported by the Western journalists just now allowed entry visas. More pressing were the domestic demands for editorial independence from the newspaper of the Democratic Front, which was soon followed by a variety of published reform proposals from within the previously subservient Front itself. Students from Tirana University began organizing their own protests and publishing their own pamphlets.

Alia's new emphasis on "openness" did nothing to address the growing urban unrest and rural absenteeism from the still-predominant collective farms. The decline in industrial and agricultural production now accelerated. The regime's May promise to issue passports went unfulfilled. Finally, the large number of students and unemployed young men gathering in Tirana began breaking into and occupying all the Western embassy compounds, demanding visas to leave. The Sigurimi, supported by the hard-liners around Hoxha's widow, tried but failed to hold down the embassy numbers from reaching 4,500. From there, or in open boats across the Adriatic, about 6,000 managed to flee the country. The security service was left only to threaten and harass their family members.

By July, Alia was moving away from the hard-liners. He dismissed the interior minister and several close associates and also the head of the Sigurimi. Within weeks, his regime had rescinded the law making flight from the country a treasonable act. It began issuing a limited number of passports, and by October a new election law was promising a secret ballot and the chance for unions or other authorized organizations to nominate candidates. But Alia's own readiness to accept initiatives from outside the PPSh, let alone from another political party, remained in doubt. Indeed, the party's November plenum made it clear that in this respect he and Nexhimije, "the first widow," were still in agreement.

The first of two hard winters followed. Urban food supplies and now public order were both in short supply. These desperate circumstances started another, larger exodus in December, mainly to Italy. By January 1991, about 10,000 people had left, and another 20,000 departed in February. The deepening crisis had already pushed some younger, more independent party members to step outside the Democratic Front, of which Nexhimije was still the titular head. They formed their own Democratic Party on December 12. Leading the way was the party

hospital's chief of staff and Hoxha's former physician, the heart sur-
geon Sali Berisha. It was he whom the Tirana Central Committee had
initially dispatched to meet with striking students at Tirana University
that fall. When Alia agreed to the establishment of at least one other
political party in December, Berisha proclaimed such a party on behalf
of the students. The economist Gramoz Pashko and several prominent
intellectuals quickly joined him in the leadership. The students' role in
prompting the party dissidents to go ahead now brought civil society
onto the Albanian stage as a political actor. The dissidents' own pressure against the party's regime continued. They demanded that Hoxha's
name be removed from the university, and then in February they mobilized a huge crowd to pull down his gold-plated statue in the center of
Tirana.

Now came two hard elections, in March 1991 and March 1992. Only
after the second one could it be said that Albania's Communist interregnum was over.[19] The PPSh had already promised parliamentary
elections for January 1991, but with candidates only from the party, its
Democratic Front, or the trade unions. After the concession to accept
one other party in December, Alia refused to accept the Democrats'
request to postpone the balloting until May. He finally agreed to a
date in March. By then, three other parties had taken advantage of
the opening. They all stepped forward with their own newspapers, led
by the Democrats' *Rilindja Demokratike*. But the PPSh countered this
challenge by concessions to the rural majority, enlarging the allowed
size of private plots and removing all controls on livestock. It also
established diplomatic relations with the United States a week before
the election on March 22. In the event, the PPSh's continuing leverage
in the countryside was largely responsible for its winning 56 percent of
the vote and, thanks again to the absence of proportional representation, 169 of 250 seats, versus the Democrats 75 seats, despite receiving
39 percent.

The new government made little progress in confronting the collapse of industrial production, which fell by another half in 1991. The
disintegration of the collective and state farms accelerated after their
equipment was looted or destroyed by former members that summer. A

19. The background and course of the two elections, starting with the formation of the Democratic Party in later 1990, is detailed by Pano, "Process of
Democratization," 303–19.

proposed new Constitution in April removed some powers of the presidential veto and left judicial oversight to the Parliament. Alia's choice of Fatos Nano as prime minister at least put forward a newer, younger, and reform-minded face. But simply reforming the existing Communist framework seemed too little to address the collapse of state institutions and public confidence. By September, the Democrats had split over the issue of continuing to work in any way with the Communist-led government. Berisha led the larger group, which favored refusing to do so. With another winter coming, Pashko and others argued for holding on to a working arrangement.

By December, Berisha had carried the day, and the Democrats withdrew from the government. Their withdrawal forced Alia to agree to new elections for March 22. This time, the Democrats won 67 percent of the vote. They took 90 of the 100 seats left to direct elections. It was the PPSh, now renamed the Socialist Party of Albania (Partia Socialiste e Shqipërisë), which took advantage of the smaller share of 40 seats provided by proportional representation to retain 32 of them. On April 4, 1992, Alia resigned as president, and the new Parliament elected Sali Berisha in his place. Now Albania's first transition—albeit deeply flawed, as we shall see—could begin. Its failure by 1997 was, however, so complete that it left the way open for a second one. This renewed transition has struggled but proceeded into consolidation without comparable conflict for the past decade.

The Western Balkans: From Warfare to International Intervention, 1991–99

The public's and policymakers' attention to the postcommunist period has focused largely, and understandably, on the wars of Yugoslavia's dissolution and the international response. Scholarly and popular publications have responded to this focus by concentrating on the wider role of Slobodan Milošević in Serbia and on the warfare and forced migration, first in Croatia, then in Bosnia-Herzegovina, and finally in Kosovo.[20] The peacekeeping interventions of the European Community

---

20. On Bosnia, see Steven L. Burg and Paul S. Shoup, *The War in Bosnia-Herzegovina, Ethnic Conflict and International Intervention* (Armonk, N.Y.: M. E. Sharpe, 1999); and on Kosovo, see Tim Judah, *Kosovo: War and Revenge* (New

(and its successor, the European Union, starting in 1992) and the United Nations in Croatia and Bosnia, and then the diplomacy surrounding the NATO-led military interventions in Bosnia and Kosovo, have received special scrutiny.[21] This conflict-ridden decade burdened the electoral politics and civil society needed to create a new middle class and support a market economy. Confronting these democratic prospects were the warfare and civilian abuse that prompted international intervention, first diplomatic and then military. Their combination helped to confine our region's initial postcommunist transition within an unpromising domestic framework.

The warfare in Croatia began immediately following its declaration of independence and lasted from July 1991 until January 1992. It bore little resemblance to the brief weeks of skirmishing in Slovenia. The Yugoslav National Army (Jugoslovenska Narodna Armija, JNA) had begun preparing to abandon the westernmost republic within five days after its declaration of independence on June 25, 1991. In Croatia, however, the Milošević regime in Serbia and the JNA's leadership were determined to remain because of the Serb-populated areas entirely absent in Slovenia. Earlier in the year, the army had already begun transferring arms to local Serbs in the newly proclaimed Serb Autonomous Regions, which included land around the Krajina on Bosnia's eastern

---

Haven, Conn.: Yale University Press, 2000). For the start of the debate on the origins of the Croatian and Bosnian conflicts, see the contrasting views of Susan L. Woodward, *Balkan Tragedy, Chaos and Dissolution after the Cold War* (Washington, D.C.: Brookings Institution Press, 1995); and James Gow, *The Triumph of the Lack of Will, International Diplomacy and the Yugoslav Wars of Dissolution* (New York: Columbia University Press, 1996).

21. The closest account of international diplomacy regarding Croatia and Bosnia, from a European participant first in the EC Monitoring Mission in 1991 and then in the International Conference on the Former Yugoslavia through 1996, is given by Geert-Hinrich Ahrens, *Diplomacy on the Edge: Containment of Ethnic Conflict and the Minorities Working Group of the Conferences on Yugoslavia* (Washington, D.C., and Baltimore: Woodrow Wilson Center Press and Johns Hopkins University Press, 2007), 116–210. On the leading American role in the two military interventions, see Ivo Daalder, *Getting to Dayton: The Making of America's Bosnia Policy* (Washington, D.C.: Brookings Institution Press, 2000); and Ivo H. Daalder and Michael E. O'Hanlon, *Winning Ugly: NATO's War to Save Kosovo* (Washington, D.C: Brookings Institution Press, 2000). Military analysis of the various local forces, with an emphasis on the JNA and its wartime Serbian base, is given by James Gow, *The Serbian Project and Its Adversaries: A Strategy of War Crimes* (London: Hurst, 2003).

border, an enclave in Western Slavonia, and land bordering Serbia's Vojvodina in Eastern Slavonia. Within these enclaves, local Serbs had begun forcing out all minority Croats, going beyond the dismissals of individual Serbs from their official and enterprise positions already under way on the Croatian side.

This forced migration, which was soon called "ethnic cleansing," became common practice—if not as centrally coordinated as each side assumed of the other—by the fall of 1991. In September, the JNA had shifted from any effort at peacekeeping between the two sides to defending Serb areas. On the Croatian side, Franjo Tudjman overcame his initial reluctance to challenge the Yugoslav army. Enough of his already-expanded police force had now been transformed into National Guard units (the Zengas) to surround those army garrisons not in Serb areas and to demand the surrender of their badly needed arms. The JNA responded not only by securing their garrisons in the Serb areas but also by trying to move out beyond them. Broader aims from Belgrade to take control of all of Croatia were apparently emerging. Milošević's army leaders, who were largely Serb but not yet purged to include only his allies, still thought in terms of holding all of Yugoslavia save Slovenia together, fearing the Soviet-fed fantasy of a NATO attack from the West if they failed to do so. Yugoslavia's former foreign minister, Budimir Lončar, aptly described the JNA mindset as "preserving the state for the army, rather than the reverse."[22] Early efforts by the European Community (EC) to bring the two sides together failed. When the EC put a small military contingent on the ground as peacekeepers, both sides ignored the white-clad detachments.

Then, however, two black marks against the Serbian side cut into the international impression that only peacekeepers were needed. First, the JNA sent Montenegrin units to surround storied Dubrovnik in October. They shelled it sporadically to no military advantage and savaged the surrounding area. In eastern Slavonia, the JNA's own heavy artillery leveled much of multiethnic Vukovar. Paramilitary infantry then entered to terrorize any Croat survivors and execute at least a

---

22. Interview with Lončar in segment 10, *Pogled u prošlosti.* Tracing the growing isolation of the JNA in the 1980s and its turn to Milošević's Serbian base after the collapse of the League of Yugoslav Communists in January 1990 are Bieber, "Role of the Yugoslav National Army," 301–32; and Miroslav Hadžić, *The Yugoslav People's Agony: The Role of the Yugoslav People's Army* (Burlington, Vt.: Ashgate, 2002), 38–131.

hundred wounded defenders. The Milošević regime had started down the road that would by 1992 make it the primary offender in the wars of Yugoslavia's dissolution. In the eyes of some Western observers and American officials, it became the only offender.

This last perception surely informed the German government's decision to recognize Croatia's independence in December 1991, which was made against the judgment of the EC's Badinter Commission that the Croatian Constitution offered insufficient protection to minority Serbs. German recognition then helped to bring along the rest of the international community.[23] But the still-debated timing of recognition had less to do with the Serbian decision to sign a cease-fire and peace-keeping agreement on January 2, 1992, than the military stalemate that had emerged between the two sides. In came 15,000 UN peacekeeping troops, called the United Nations Protection Force (UNPROFOR), with a mandate to confine the JNA within the several Serb enclaves. Yet taken together, the enclaves covered nearly one-third of the territory within the republic's 1989 borders. Within these borders, more than 10,000 people had been killed on each side, many of them civilians, and about 100,000 refugees, both Croats and Serbs, were forced to flee their homes.

The warfare and cleansing in Croatia was not over, however.[24] In two offensives in the summer of 1995, the expanded and fully equipped Croatian army, now trained with some still-controversial American assistance, swept aside the local Serb forces, first in western Slavonia and then in the Krajina. Resistance from the Bosnian Serb forces close by or the new Serbian-controlled Yugoslav Army was conspicuous by its absence. Some 160,000 Serbs in all fled to Bosnia or Serbia or initially to eastern Slavonia. About 1,000 of the few remaining Serbs were killed, and more of their houses burned. The Serbian side was also obliged to

---

23. On the much-debated issue of Germany's and then Western recognition of Croatia, see the judicious survey of its diplomatic background and strategic consequences given by Richard Caplan, *Europe and the Recognition of New States in Yugoslavia* (Cambridge: Cambridge University Press, 2005), 16–48, 106–20.

24. On the first as well as the final phase of the warfare in Croatia, with attention to the attendant controversies on the Croatian and Krajina Serb sides along with the military history, see Mile Bjelajac and Ozren Žunec, "The War in Croatia (1991–1995)," in *Confronting the Yugoslav Controversies: A Scholars' Initiative,* edited by Charles Ingrao and Thomas Emmert (West Lafayette, Ind.: Purdue University Press, 2009), 230–70.

accept that the UNPROFOR force would remain in eastern Slavonia until handing over the territory to Croatian sovereignty by the end of 1996. In the process, many of the 90,000 Croats displaced from the territory returned. Most of the 70,000 Serbs who had fled there from western Slavonia were pushed into Serbia.[25]

However, the conclusion of conflict in Croatia cannot be understood without turning to the warfare, ethnic cleansing, and intervention in Bosnia-Herzegovina that began in April 1992. Before it would end in December 1995, more than 100,000 people would die, nearly half of them noncombatants. And about 2.2 million would be forced to flee their homes. By the time Radovan Karadžić's Serbian Democratic Party (Srpska Demokratska Stranka) led Bosnian Serbs to boycott the republic's referendum on independence in February 1992, its followers had already established Serb Autonomous Regions in Eastern Bosnia. As in Croatia, they were receiving weapons taken by the JNA from the republic's stocks for territorial defense. Paramilitaries from Serbia launched the killing and cleansing of Bosnian Muslims on April 1, before the NATO allies recognized the independence of Bosnia-Herzegovina a week later. Thereafter, the Milošević regime quickly limited the JNA units in the republic to Bosnian Serbs only, and it continued to supply and pay officers salaries for what became in UN parlance the Bosnian Serb Army (BSA) under General Ratko Mladić. Its advantage in arms and numbers allowed it to take control of 60 percent of Bosnia-Herzegovina and lay siege to Sarajevo within a few months.

But several years of stalemate now followed. The Bosnian Muslim, or Bošniak, plurality of the population hastily assembled its own military forces under the leadership of Alia Izetbegović's Party of Democratic Action (Stranka Demokratske Akcije). The concentration of Croats in western Herzegovina set up their own Defense Council and drew heavily for support from neighboring Croatia's military buildup. The Bosnian Muslims had no such external support. They were thus most disadvantaged by the initial Western response to the conflict: an arms embargo imposed on all sides.

The second response in January 1993, a proposed UN-sponsored peace settlement called the Vance-Owen Plan (after its protagonists, David Owen and Cyrus Vance), which proposed majority rule and mi-

25. Richard Caplan, *A New Trusteeship: The International Administration of War-Torn Territories* (Oxford: Oxford University Press, 2002), 69.

nority rights in nine cantons and subdividing the republic, also had unintended consequences. The Croatian Council forces responded to Bosnian Muslim pressures to push out some of the Croat population in central Bosnia with more straightforward and brutal ethnic cleansing in their southern stronghold in western Herzegovina, from which they had already expelled the Serb population. The resulting warfare between Croat and Bosnian Muslim units helped to scuttle the Vance-Owen Plan. So did US reluctance to endorse it. Finally, an American lead did bring Tudjman's Croatia into a settlement of the Bosnian Croat and Muslim conflict. But an extension of the same UNPROFOR force keeping the peace in Croatia was left with the impossible task of making peace across Bosnia-Herzegovina with small scattered units capable only of delivering humanitarian aid. Ethnic cleansing proceeded behind the lines of all three sides, including harsh treatment for captured combatants in concentration camps. The Serb side received almost all the international condemnation, and in fact deserved the larger share.

The trigger for the third international intervention was the Bosnian Serb Army's brutal cleansing of the UN-designated "safe haven" at Srebrenica in July 1995. It culminated in the genocidal execution of nearly 8,000 captured Bosnian Muslim men with a small Dutch UN unit standing by. The NATO members responsible for most of the UNPROFOR contingents now concentrated their previously dispersed units and reinforced them. Under US leadership, NATO itself launched air strikes in September that destroyed the BSA's command and control. More decisive in the outcome, according to the US Central Intelligence Agency's published history of the war, was the advance of Croatian army units from the newly liberated Krajina to link up with Bosnian Muslim forces and push the BSA out of most of western Bosnia, threatening the major city of Banja Luka.[26]

This desperate military position on the ground persuaded the Bosnian Serb side to leave its representation at the December peace talks in Dayton to Slobodan Milošević. Despite his concession of Sarajevo and environs to the Bosnian Muslims, the Serb entity in the

---

26. *Balkan Battlegrounds: A Military History of Yugoslav Conflict, 1990–1995* (Washington, D.C.: CIA Office of Russian and European Analysis, 2002), 295. A searing Dutch account of Bosnian Serb execution of all male Bosnian Muslim prisoners at Srebrenica, sufficient to meet the UN definition of genocide, is given by Jan Willem Honig and Norbert Both, *Srebrenica: Record of a War Crime* (New York: Penguin Books, 1996).

confederal division of Bosnia-Herzegovina still retained almost half its territory. The rest of the complex Dayton Accords did provide for disarmament, which was initially enforced by 58,000 NATO troops and kept in place during their subsequent reduction over the decade that followed. But untangling Dayton's tangled provisions for reconnecting the two—really three—separate ethnic entities under the authority of an internationally appointed high commissioner has proved illusive. Subsequent chapters will consider Bosnia's postconflict political and economic transition within the international framework that was set by this peace agreement late in 1995 and is still in place at this writing.

Two more international agreements have set formal frameworks for postconflict transition in the Western Balkans, in Kosovo since 1999 and in Macedonia since 2001. But only Kosovo saw the creation of another international protectorate secured by the long-term deployment of NATO peacekeeping forces. The limited international presence in Macedonia following the Ohrid Agreement of 2001 seems comparable instead to the short-term, Italian-led force that prevented civil war in Albania in 1997 and left soon after facilitating new elections. Triggering NATO's 1999 military intervention in Kosovo was the sort of violence and ethnic cleansing seen in Croatia and Bosnia. Directly initiated this time by Serbia's Milošević regime, its army and police had carried out enough indiscriminate killings and massive expulsions by 1998 to generate Western demands for intervention, peaceful or not.[27] Whether because of the subsequent United States–led air campaign beginning in March 1999, a threatened NATO ground offensive, or the absence of Russian support, the Serbian side agreed to the withdrawal of its forces in June, albeit under a UN resolution that left the province technically part of Serbia. Resolution 1244 of the Security Council, which was set to run until the determination of the final status just now emerging, established the United Nations Mission in Kosovo (UNMIK) with interim administrative authority comparable to the High Commission in Bosnia. Again, 50,000 NATO troops began arriving to assure Serbian withdrawal and to secure the peace.

The United States–led case for intervention rested on the Kosovar Albanians' previous decade of suppression under the Milošević re-

---

27. On US and European diplomacy and NATO's military decisions before and during the intervention of March–June 1999 in Serbia as well as Kosovo, see Daalder and O'Hanlon, *Winning Ugly.*

gime and also on the final months of ethnic cleansing. Expulsion from the province's public and professional life made full independence the only acceptable alternative for the Kosovar Albanian majority of 90 percent. Beginning in 1991, the Serbian authorities simply dismissed two-thirds of the Albanians employed in schools, hospitals, courts, and public administration. The Kosovars responded with passive political resistance under the leadership of Ibrahim Rugova and his League for Democratic Kosovo (Lidhja Demokratike e Kosovës). They struggled to set up makeshift schools and medical facilities. Their more successful shadow economy of small operations served the majority population and left the established enterprises to languish with only Serb customers. But after an agreement on a common educational system failed in 1995, the huge security apparatus maintained by Milošević's Interior Ministry in Belgrade sought to tighten the screws on the province. At the same time, young Kosovar émigrés had organized the small Kosovo Liberation Army (Ushtria Çlirimtare e Kosovës, UÇK) in order to begin the terrorist attacks that did indeed produce the desired Serbian reprisals and win new recruits to their small guerrilla units.

Growing numbers of guerrilla attacks fed the increasing disposition of the Milošević regime to distract public attention from its domestic problems. Hence its decision for a major military offensive against all areas of resistance, real or potential, in 1998. After pushing 200,000 Kosovars from their homes by the summer, the regime agreed to the presence of a small mission from the Organization for Security and Cooperation in Europe (OSCE) that would monitor a military withdrawal from both sides. For Western opinion, the UÇK's violations were soon topped by the discovery that about forty Kosovars had apparently been executed by the Serb side. When Belgrade's representatives refused to accept the United States–brokered agreement to withdraw most of their forces in March 1999, the Milošević regime launched a massive campaign to expel all Kosovars from the capital of Priština and the major areas of resistance. The NATO bombing campaign also encouraged the exodus, but mass flight from Interior Ministry roundups seems to have been primarily responsible for driving 850,000 Kosovars into neighboring Macedonia or Albania. Their temporary presence in those two countries created problems for their subsequent transitions, as will be seen.

More important in Kosovo itself was the traumatic experience of expulsion, and the killing of at least 5,000 Kosovars in the process. All this made their rapid return after the Serbian capitulation in June 1999 hardly a promising one for the multiethnic terms of administration under which UNMIK was mandated to proceed. Indeed, unchecked Kosovar bands killed nearly 800 Serbs, burned several thousand houses, and destroyed nearly half the Serbian churches and religious sites in Kosovo during the first year of the new mandate. About 100,000 of the 220,000 Serbs living in Kosovo simply fled.[28]

Failed Economic Transitions and Crony Capitalism in the 1990s

Beyond the interethnic violence that led to military intervention and international mandates in Bosnia and Kosovo, the first decade of post-communist transitions elsewhere in the region had been sufficiently troubled to justify a new approach. Its international impetus came from the joint initiative of the World Bank and the European Commission, launched in June 1999 to address the internal disorder in Albania along with the wartime exigencies and excesses in all of Yugoslavia's successor states except Slovenia. It was a plan for coordinating democratic consolidation and domestic reform across what the initiative called the Western Balkans. Multiparty elections seemed a promising start. Yet the winning parties proved reluctant to abandon Communist-era pre-eminence for their leaders or to break up the Communist-era concentration of state (or republic) powers. The legitimacy and efficiency of public administration remained to be established, leaving the political framework too weak to resist authoritarian abuse.

There was also the problem of an economic framework ill suited to any coordinated transition to a market economy or to the institutions needed to regulate it. The obvious failings of this framework ironically helped to discourage further disengagement from the previous Communist practice of political control and to open the privatization process to political manipulation. The resulting corruption of private enterprise hampered the emergence of a politically independent middle class, which, as we noted in our introduction, was crucial to a

28. On the Kosovo conflict and attendant abuses before and after the NATO intervention, see Judah, *Kosovo;* and Iain King and Whit Mason, *Peace at Any Price: How the World Failed Kosovo* (Ithaca, N.Y.: Cornell University Press, 2006), 43–53.

democratic consolidation. In the longer run, however, corrupt privatization weakened the foundations on which the new monopolies of
political power actually stood.

The fractured economies in all Yugoslavia's successor states save
Slovenia saw their declared per capita incomes slide down during the
1990s toward the previously distant level for Albania. Indeed, the 1998
average of $1,500 for Serbia/Montenegro, Macedonia, and Bosnia-
Herzegovina was virtually the same as Albania's. Part of their precipitous
decline, and Croatia's fall from 1990 by one half to $4,400, may of course
be traced to the broken economic ties between the former Yugoslavia's
republics. These ties went beyond internal trade that exceeded foreign
trade to common enterprises and sources of bank credit. Just the loss
of deposits as well as further credit from Slovenia's Ljubljanska Banka
was a significant handicap. Still in place within the successor states,
however, were the republic's payment bureaus, through which currency
used in all commercial transactions had to pass. In addition to the fees
they charged, the payment bureaus delayed payments and left their final
approval open to political pressure. Their presence made sure that no
foreign bank, and few foreign investors, would open for business while
they remained. Meanwhile, domestic enterprises continued to pay the
variety of *doprinosi,* that is, contributions for social benefits and local
taxes that nearly doubled the cost of paying a legal wage. One combined
effect of these disruptions and restrictions was to limit exports and to
open up the same huge, two-to-one import surplus that Albania's postcommunist economy needed to survive. And as in Albania, remittances
from the swelling numbers of nationals working abroad soon became
the largest inflow shoring up current account balances.

Also feeding the import surpluses and attendant inflation were the
extralegal enterprises and associations that sprang up to take advantage
of wartime smuggling across the former republic's borders.[29] They paid
no added contributions for wages to employees and no fees to the payment bureaus. They led the way in creating the so-called gray economies
that provided for 40 to 50 percent of income generated, if not accounted
for, during the 1990s. Montenegro took an early lead, thanks to officially
sanctioned cigarette smuggling from Italy into Serbia in particular.

29. A special issue of *Problems of Communism* on "Transnational Crime and
Conflict in the Balkans," May–June 2004 (Peter Andreas, guest editor), contains
eight articles on the subject.

Albania soon caught up on the strength of its oil imports, which were ten times its still-limited domestic consumption, and then were sent on to Yugoslavia's successor states. Greece's trade embargo on Macedonia in the period 1994–95 added oil and other goods smuggled in from Bulgaria to the traffic to Serbia working around the international trade and financial sanctions of the period 1992–95. Smuggling services for transportation and money laundering also grew up in both Croatia and Serbia for traffic into Bosnia-Herzegovina, sometimes in cooperation with each other. Serbian and Kosovar Albanian groups also cooperated across ethnic battle lines, particularly for traffic in drugs and women. Jokes around the region identified such criminal networks as the only multinational enterprises that had found their way to the Balkans.[30]

Meanwhile, rates of unemployment in the legal economies ranged from 20 to 40 percent. The initial postcommunist push for privatization had done little to mobilize the capital that would have been needed to create new jobs. We may track a common pattern of manager and employee buyouts of vouchers or low-priced shares followed by the "re-nationalization" of major enterprises under indirect state control. This applied in the former Yugoslav republics, where the aforementioned Marković reforms of 1989 had started such sales in order to preserve firms as "socially owned enterprises," but also in Albania.

The rise of politically favored management was most striking in Croatia and Serbia/Montenegro. In Croatia, the transfer to restructured social ownership during the course of 1990 had affected few firms and little of the labor force (less than 2 percent). What became the new Croatian Privatization Fund in 1992 set a series of deadlines whereby all manufacturing enterprises had to be privatized, with employees soon limited to half the vouchered shares, or the firm would pass to the state as the buyer of last resort. Two-thirds of all enterprises had indeed been privatized by late 1995, but most were small firms and thus together accounted for only 9 percent of industrial capital. When the fund moved the next year to transfer ownership of what had become state-owned firms through a new set of vouchers in a new fund, the existing management and political favorites of the ruling HDZ party

---

30. For an overview of these interconnections, see David Binder, "Organized Crime in the Balkans," and Robert Hislope, "Crime and Corruption in Post-Ohrid Macedonia," *EES News,* Woodrow Wilson Center, May–June 2003; and *Atlas kriminalnih organizacija na Balkanu* (Belgrade: Vreme, 2005).

took up those that were offered for sale. These sales served to reduce public debt but not to attract significant new direct investment, particularly from abroad.[31]

Promising annual increases in Croatia's gross domestic product had indeed begun in 1993 with the stabilization of the currency. They accelerated to 5 or 6 percent with the clearing of the Serb enclaves in 1995. The reconstruction boom of 1995–96 to repair an estimated $4 billion in war damage attracted $1 billion in bilateral Western assistance, primarily from Germany. But the rebuilding created few new jobs while boosting wages. Manufacturing firms typically worked at a loss and relied on high-interest loans, often from politically favored banks with connections to the few genuinely profitable enterprises. These were the so-called cash cows in retail outlets or the press. Their owners in turn relied on low-interest loans from state-owned and new private banks. Then several of the favored owners and banks, like the poorly secured Dubrovačka Banka, went under. Their bankruptcies drew public attention to the wider pattern of political favoritism and corruption that two Croatian economists aptly dubbed "crony capitalism."[32] Two IMF loans to support the imposition of financial discipline on banks and state enterprises, $103 million in 1994 and 1995, obviously failed to make a difference. By 1998, Croatia's economic indicators had fallen to the problematically low levels of its neighbors in the Western Balkans, leaving its transition to job-creating growth and a transparent market economy to the decade that followed.

Serbia had no war damage to repair before 1999, but its economy bore two burdens that Croatia did not face: its half million remaining refugees and the international sanctions placed on its trade and finance in 1992, which were stiffened in 1993. Both these burdens encouraged the aforementioned smuggling and extralegal activities that extended further into the Serbian and also Montenegrin economies than Croatia's. Otherwise, their initial experiences with privatization were

31. Domogoj Račić and Vladimir Cvijanović, "Privatization, Institution Building and Market Development: The Case of Croatia," in *Path-Dependent Development in the Western Balkans, The Impact of Privatization,* edited by Siniša Kušić (Frankfurt: Peter Lang, 2005), 43–77.

32. Vojmir Franičević and Ivo Bićanić, "Dismantling Crony Capitalism: The Croatian Case," CERGE-EI Research Seminar Series, Prague, available at www .cerge-ei.cz. Also see William Bartlett, *Croatia between Europe and the Balkans* (London: Routledge, 2003), 87–116.

quite similar. By 1992, the Milošević regime had pushed through its own privatization law, facilitating an easier transfer of ownership to political favorites than the Marković law it replaced. In Kosovo, the new legislation served nicely to transfer the ownership of more than 80 percent of enterprise assets to firms based in Serbia.[33] That August, the allied regime of Momir Bulatović in Montenegro adopted a comparable Law on Transformation. As in Croatia, key enterprises were declared "strategic industries" and were nationalized under regime-appointed management. For the rest, new terms for manager or employee vouchers offered discounts that did not appear attractive until the regime turned hyperinflation loose late in 1992. It served to soak up the public's large reserves of Western hard currency. As in Weimar Germany in 1923, only stock values could keep up with the high rate of inflation. Existing or regime-appointed managers led the way in buying up nearly half the existing capital in Serbian firms by 1994. Once again, however, the Milošević regime intervened, first to restore a stable currency but also to "revalue social capital." The past two phases of privatization were now, as in Croatia, largely set aside, and the value of individually held shares fell drastically to under 5 percent of the total value. In Montenegro, a similar process dubbed "managerial transformation" did leave 25 percent in employees' hands but transferred the rest to several state funds. Acting for the ruling Democratic Party of Socialists (Demokratska Partija Socijalista), the funds appointed boards of directors who put all large enterprises in politically loyal hands.[34] Both regimes lacked any coordinating program that might be called an industrial policy. Instead, they simply turned their appointees loose to take what they could from firms under no pressure from independent shareholders or international competition. Their targets included the major enterprises in Kosovo, whose ownership and operation were simply folded into existing firms in Serbia.

33. The Milošević regime had already seen to the replacement of three quarters of the 160,000 Albanian employees in Kosovo's socially owned enterprises with Serbs or Montenegrins. On the absence of any further advancement in privatization there during the 1990s, see Isa Mulaj, "Delayed Privatization in Kosovo: Causes, Consequences and Implications in the Ongoing Process," in *Path-Dependent Development,* ed. Kušić, 123–46.

34. On Montenegro, see Dragan Djurić, "The Economic Development of Montenegro" in *Montenegro in Transition,* ed. Bieber, 147–49. On Serbia, see Milorad Filipović and Miroljub Hadžić, "Serbian Privatization: From Social toward Private Ownership and from Self-Management toward Proper Governing," in *Path-Dependent Development,* ed. Kušić, 101–21.

Nor was the introduction of private enterprise a more successful or for that matter a much different experience for Albania and Macedonia, the two states in the Western Balkans least affected by the wars of Yugoslavia's dissolution. Any process of privatization obviously had much further to go in Albania than anywhere else in Eastern Europe. In agriculture, popular resentment had already torn apart the widespread network of collective and state farms. Looting had destroyed most of their equipment by 1991. Pushing the privatization of all arable and pasture land ahead in 1992 were the demands of every rural family for its own holding—hence, the distribution of 95 percent of what now became private property into some 400,000 parcels; they averaged only 1.5 hectares apiece.[35] In addition to the handicap of such tiny holdings, the new owners found little bank or other credit available to support profitable activity. Younger family members in particular began to leave from these holdings for Tirana and other towns. By 1995, the population of Tirana had doubled to half a million, and the urban share of Albania's population had jumped from 34 to 44 percent.

Only the rapid restructuring of industrial enterprises supported by foreign direct investment could have provided the expanded activity needed to provide employment for the large urban influx. A new Agency for Enterprise Restructuring was created in 1992, but it closed in 1996 without having had any recorded impact on the same process of insider privatization under way in Yugoslavia's successor states. After simply declaring state-owned firms to be "socially managed enterprises" in 1991, the Berisha regime moved ahead in May 1993 to establish a series of local "privatization boards" empowered to auction off voucher shares in enterprises with fewer than 300 employees. Low prices allowed widespread employee purchases, also accompanied by sales of controlling shares, not only to precommunist owners but also to "special judicial and physical persons."[36] These were of course the political favorites of the Berisha regime, chosen to replace the Communist management of the former state enterprises. The ensuing

35. Harold Lemmel, "Tenure Security," and Rachel Wheeler and Harold Lemmel, "Credit Access and Collateral," both in *Rural Property and Economy in Post-Communist Albania,* edited by Harold Lemmel (New York: Berghan Books, 2003), 25–34, 93–102.

36. Fatmir Mema and Ines Dika, "Privatization and Post-Privatization in Albania: A Long Difficult Path," in *Path-Dependent Development,* ed. Kušić, 195–209.

sale of vouchers to a new set of private investment plans, deceptively called banks, fed the widespread speculative frenzy that followed from the high interest rates promised by these pyramid schemes. They acted as a substitute for the banking system that the Communist regime had never allowed to take shape. Their rise and spectacular collapse in 1997, as detailed below, brought down the Berisha government itself and is therefore left to the political accounting that follows in the next section.

Only in October 1993, months after Albania had launched its privatization boards and a year after Yugoslavia's other successor states has abandoned the 1990 Law on Social Capital, did Macedonia finally open a Transformation Agency to move its enterprises beyond the Marković reforms. They had not only lasted longer but gone further in Macedonia than elsewhere. By 1991, these semiprivatized firms accounted for 18 percent of estimated equity capital in Macedonia versus a Yugoslav average of 6 percent. Proceeds from the strictly internal sales of shares to managers and employees at discounted prices were collected in the prescribed Development Fund, whose political abuse left viable enterprises seeking other ways to attract the funds they desperately needed for new investment. The new 1993 law on transformation substituted paid sales for vouchers and left only 30 percent of enterprise equity to employees at discounted prices, with another 15 percent for pensions. Yet the sales effort mobilized minimal capital for buyouts, even by existing management. Most shares remained unsold and reverted to the state's Transformation Agency. Potential foreign investors were limited to only 30 percent of shares, well short of the majority interest needed to attract them to direct investment. And as elsewhere, a number of major enterprises were simply exempted from the process, including banks, agricultural cooperatives, and public utilities.[37]

The 1993 process has acquired a bad reputation, leaving new capital unmobilized and Macedonia's major enterprises in the hands of existing management for the rest of the decade and beyond. But as its director has fairly pointed out, the process began with no procedures or personnel in place to value enterprise equity. Once evaluations had been completed in 1995, they revealed that 50 to 70 percent of the major firms' equity, much more than had been presumed, had al-

37. Sašo Arsov, "Post-Privatization Retrospective of Macedonia: What Could We have Done Better?" in *Path-Dependent Development,* ed. Kušić, 167–73.

ready been transferred to insider hands under the voucher distributions of the Marković reforms.[38] It was these distributions that left existing management still in charge of these same, largely unprofitable "social enterprises," which were unrestructured and inaccessible to foreign investment. They also left the illegal import trade as the major source of profitable business largely in the hands of the aforementioned gray economy, which both corrupted public administration and further discouraged legal manufacturing.

Across the Western Balkans, therefore, the persisting, Communist-era pattern of politically managed enterprises had generated a process of privatization that only deepened the precipitous post-1989 decline in legal income and legal foreign or interrepublic trade. The major Western benchmarks for this initial transition—the creation of stable currencies, and the avoidance of large deficits in state budgets—were met in Milošević's Serbia, Tudjman's Croatia, and elsewhere. But meeting them proved irrelevant to the need to address the problems of a shrinking, increasingly illegal economy. The temptation for still-monopolistic political power to address such an economy by taking increasing control of it proved irresistible.

Electoral Democracies and Wartime Abuses

Simply freeing up the founding of political parties and holding multiparty elections, neither of which was permitted in the Communist period, failed to redistribute enough political power to overcome this temptation. We may doubt that any more benign outcome would have been able to pry enterprise managers and employees, and much of the general public, loose from the presumptive rights of social ownership. But the unchecked and uncoordinated monopolies on political power that emerged from these elections undoubtedly corrupted any institutional transition to a market economy and facilitated the recourse to warfare by which the 1990s are most often remembered. In the process, as will be seen in chapter 2, their political institutions lacked the legitimacy to strengthen weak state structures and insulate them from partisan abuse.

---

38. Interview with Verica Hadži Vasileva-Markovska, Skopje, October 5, 2005.

The abuse of presidential powers nonetheless worked across the region to muzzle the media and to leave the interior ministries or their agencies with some of the authority of their Communist predecessors and even less accountability. Economic sanctions from the international community, or just the threat of them, spilled over from the Bosnian warfare to encourage the extralegal economy, which reinforced both the justification and the abuse of these presidential powers. So did the corrupted process of initial privatization, as just described. In this fashion, the abuse of political authority—which had led to violence and international intervention in Croatia, Bosnia, and Kosovo—was working to undermine the embryonic democratic transitions all across the Western Balkans.

First came elections for legislative assemblies or constitutional referendums, which every regime in the region claimed had established its legitimacy and authority. Western policymakers and some analysts had hoped that these elections would see the start of a successful transition to liberal democracy and a market economy, as in large measure proved to be the case in the rest of postcommunist Central and Eastern Europe. The results were disappointing in various ways. And they were different enough for each state to justify the separate sections that follow—a separation that the region's more comparable efforts since 1999 do not justify and that our subsequent chapters seek to avoid.

Serbia and Montenegro

It seems appropriate to start with Serbia, where the confounding of any constructive transition is clearest—indeed, notorious. And yet more elections with more parties registered were held in Serbia than anywhere else, not just in the Western Balkans but in all Eastern Europe. They began during the post-1989 interregnum discussed above and continued with more of the old Communist institutions and personnel in place than elsewhere. Already in November 1989, the day after the Berlin Wall had fallen, Slobodan Milošević strengthened his position as leader of Serbia's League of Communists by winning a virtually uncontested election to the new position of president of Serbia. By July 1990, the regime did allow the single-party republic Assembly elected in 1989 to authorize the formation of other political parties. Without consultation, Milošević pushed through the aforementioned renaming of his own ruling party as the Socialist Party of Serbia (Socijalistička Partija Srbije, SPS).

One month before, his regime had already used the popularity gained by consolidating control of Kosovo to win almost unanimous approval of a proposed new Constitution for Serbia in a hastily staged referendum. Then in September, the republic's same preelection Parliament passed the new Constitution into law without amendment or debate. Its provisions concentrated a set of formidable powers in the hands of the president, who was now to be elected by direct vote. They eliminated the previous rights for provincial autonomy given to Vojvodina and Kosovo under Yugoslavia's 1974 Constitution. The new single Assembly, divorced from the two chambers of Yugoslavia's Federal Assembly, was given formal control over the judicial system, but its informal control was left to Milošević's ministerial authority. His presidential authority allowed him simply to suspend, in case of emergency or threat of war, any law previously passed by the Assembly. These provisions for a "semipresidential system" were unsurprisingly not changed, as detailed in chapter 2, by the new 1992 Constitution for the "Federal Republic of Yugoslavia" connecting only Serbia and Montenegro. In December 1992, Milošević himself had solidified his position by winning direct election, against an émigré candidate, to a five-year term as president of Serbia. The weaker position of "federal president" had already been given to the aging novelist Dobrica Ćosić. Montenegro remained under the subservient leadership put in place by Milošević around Momir Bulatović in 1989.

The flood of new parties founded in Serbia since 1990 worked in favor of Milošević's increasingly personal rule. He co-opted enough of them to rule by what has been called "dominating pluralism."[39] To start with, Serbia's initial multiparty election in December 1990 had left the regime with an overwhelming SPS majority in the Parliament. Although they had won only 46.1 percent of the votes cast, Milošević's SPS received 77.6 percent of the seats thanks to the two rounds of absolute-majority contests. (Also known as "first past the post" or "winner take all," this system serves two-party races as in the United States well but risks domination by a minority party in a multiparty field.) The two major opposition parties, the Serbian Renewal Movement (Srpski pokret obnove) led by Vuk Drašković and the Democratic

39. Lenard J. Cohen, *Serpent in the Bosom: The Rise and Fall of Slobodan Milošević* (Boulder, Colo.: Westview Press, 2001), 118; and on the consolidation of Milošević's hegemonic party system and parastate, ibid., 188–36.

Party (Demokratska stranka, DS) led by Zoran Djindjić, won 23.3 percent of the vote together but only 10.4 percent of the seats.

Nor did a turn to the more generally used European system of proportional voting in the parliamentary elections of 1992, 1993, and 1997 much reduce the weight of presidential leverage. Compensating for the decline in SPS votes and seats in 1992 (to 28.8 percent and 40.4 percent) was the rise of the blindly nationalist Serbian Radical Party (Srpska radikalna stranka, SRS), led by the same Vojislav Šešelj who was subsequently put on trial in The Hague for war crimes in Croatia and Bosnia before the International Criminal Tribunal for the Former Yugoslavia. The SRS's support for the regime allowed the Assembly to continue its record of approving more than 95 percent of the legislation put before it through the 1990s.[40]

How can we understand both the SRS's position as the second-largest single party in the 1992 and 1997 elections and the rise in SPS support to 36.7 percent in 1993 and, with its left-wing coalition, to 34.4 percent in 1997? Three interrelated elements worked in favor of the Milošević regime. First, although its control of the print media could not prevent the emergence of several opposition newspapers and weekly magazines, they were available mainly in Belgrade. The state television station blanketed the entire country with its news broadcasts, which favored the regime without fail, while also limiting exposure for rival party candidates during elections. Second, the democratic opposition remained divided among its members, initially between the SPS and the DS but then within this Democratic Party and also extending to other smaller parties which emerged.

The third handicap to challenging the Milošević regime, and his personal leadership in particular, was arguably the most formidable and surely the most ironic. It was the political and economic damage done to Serbia as a result of the regime's own conduct in the wars of Yugoslavia's dissolution. Its promotion of armed opposition to the declarations of independence by Slovenia and Croatia in 1991 and then Bosnia-Herzegovina in 1992 brought down international sanctions on Serbia and resulted only in final defeat for Serb forces in the former

---

40. For details on parties and elections, see Vladimir Goati, "The Party Systems in Serbia and Montenegro," and "The Electoral System in Serbia," both in *Between Authoritarianism and Democracy, Serbia, Montenegro and Croatia,* vol. 1, edited by Dragica Vujadinović, Lino Veljak, Vladimir Goati, and Veselin Pavićević (Belgrade: CEDET, 2003), 169–96, 259–78.

republics, as noted above. Still, these reverses and the tendency of the international community to identify reputedly intransigent Serbian nationalism as Milošević's major motive fed genuine public intransigence and helped to sustain his regime. So did the international sanctions placed on Serbia's trade and finance in 1992 and strengthened in 1993. Their imposition left the regime's corrupt connections and smuggling arrangements to dominate the Serbian economy. The regime's media was, however, free to blame the sanctions for the vast majority of the population's widespread hardship and increasing impoverishment. Then in 1995 came the defeat and expulsion of the Croatian Serbs and the retreat from around Sarajevo and elsewhere in Bosnia following the Dayton Peace Accords. The flow of Serb refugees into Serbia, with scant international assistance to accommodate them, reached 600,000. Their tales of ill treatment and trauma, both true and exaggerated, obscured the lack of justification for what the Serbian side itself had done, particularly in Bosnia.[41] The refugees themselves created a new constituency to which the regime or the SRS could easily appeal.

Both the wider Serbian society's own sense of being wounded from the outside and Milošević's internal advantages saved his regime from the serious challenge it faced late in 1996. The previously divided democratic opposition put forward candidates in that fall's parliamentary and local elections under the new banner of Zajedno (Together). Their coalition now included the largest opposition party, the DS led by Zoran Djindjić. Its absence had hurt the previous attempt at a coalition in 1992. Though they were badly defeated in the parliamentary elections, Zajedno's candidates nonetheless won a majority of the municipal elections, Belgrade included. When the regime's election authorities refused to recognize these results, demonstrators in Belgrade and the smaller cities poured into the streets, pulling the coalition's leadership along with them. Noisemaking to drown out the regime's evening television news program echoed across Belgrade, and university students led the way in a competition for the most damning slogan. Soon the Zajedno leaders were addressing mass meetings of 100,000 or more in the center of Belgrade. By January 1997, Milošević was forced to recognize the municipal results.[42]

41. A full set of critical appraisals from Serbian scholars and journalists of what was done and said is given by Nebojša Popov, ed., *The Road to War in Serbia: Trauma and Catharsis* (Budapest: Central European University Press, 1996).
42. For a sociological study of Zajedno and the student role in particular, see

Within a few months, however, Milošević had largely restored his commanding position. He artfully withdrew ministerial appointments for several of his wife's ill-qualified candidates from her own Yugoslav United Left (Jugoslovenska udružena levica) party. Divisions within Zajedno weakened the opposing coalition. Still supporting the regime along with state television were some 100,000 police and Interior Ministry forces. Western diplomacy had also accepted Milošević as a guarantor of the Dayton Accords. Trade if not financial sanctions had been duly lifted. It remained only for him to strengthen the powers of the Federal Presidency before receiving that appointment from its Parliament later in 1997. His second term as president of Serbia was coming to its mandatory end. The otherwise powerless Federal Parliament then duly voted him president. As for the direct election now needed for the Serbian Presidency, the Zajedno candidate, Vuk Drašković, finished third behind Milošević's handpicked successor and the SRS candidate, Vojislav Šešelj. In the second round's runoff between the two, Šešelj's violent rhetoric and erratic reputation made the SPS candidate, Milan Milutinović, seem the safer choice. This plus the fraudulent addition of more SPS votes from Kosovo than Serbs resident there assured an easy victory.[43]

With the opposition in growing disarray, the Milošević regime could now remain in power for the rest of the decade. The final military defeat in Kosovo in 1999, led this time by NATO air strikes against infrastructure in Serbia proper, was not enough. It took his refusal to recognize his own defeat in the elections for the Federal Presidency in 2000 by an opposition candidate, Vojislav Koštunica, to bring back enough demonstrators to force him out.

Croatia

The politically comparable regime of Croatia's president, Franjo Tudjman, and his ruling HDZ ended only with his death in December 1999 and the party's defeat in the elections that immediately followed.

Mladen Lazić, ed., *Protest in Belgrade* (Budapest: Central European University Press, 1997).

43. The progression of events in Serbian elections from 1990 through 1996 is well traced by Nicholas Miller, "A Failed Transition: The Case of Serbia," in *Politics, Power and the Struggle,* ed. Dawisha and Parrott, 155–88.

We do not refer here to his regime's military conduct and forced migration, actions equated by some with the worst excesses of Milošević's Serbia and excused by others as lesser abuses committed only in defense of Croatia's independence. Setting aside the controversial question of comparing Croatia's warfare with Serbia's, significant parallels may be seen in their practice of domestic politics and economic transition. Tudjman's increasingly personal and authoritarian regime as president extended to an unmonitored set of security services, corrupt advantages for economic insiders, a usually subservient judiciary, and a media under direct control or indirect pressure. The parallels with Serbia also include a series of multiparty elections and some significant opposition, not just by other party leaders but also openly stated in an embattled corner of the press or implied on state television.

Setting Croatian politics apart during the wartime years, however, were elections that gave the ruling HDZ the absolute parliamentary majority never enjoyed by Milošević's SPS. These elections came on the heels of military victories, first in winning independence and then in the two 1995 offensives to take control of the Serb-held areas of western Slavonia and the Krajina. In mid-1992, the HDZ abandoned the coalition "unity government" it had formed during the war of independence. It called for new parliamentary elections and a direct election for the presidency, previously determined by the more powerful lower chamber. In the August balloting, the HDZ trumpeted its championship of "homeland war" and won fully 59 percent of the increased number of seats for that chamber, from 80 to 137. Although receiving slightly more votes than it got in the 1990 election while still a republic of Yugoslavia, the opposition was now more divided. The previous opposition leader, the Social Democratic Party (Socijaldemokratska partija, SDP) of reformed Communists, fell from 28 to barely 5 percent of the votes cast. Franjo Tudjman won a clear majority, 57 percent versus former student leader Dražan Budiša of the Croatian Social Liberal Party (Hrvatska socijalno liberalna stranka) with 22 percent and still smaller shares for several candidates.

From this high-water mark, the HDZ's legislative majority would decline, albeit slightly, during the next elections.[44] This decline occurred

44. On the Croatian elections of 1992–96, see Lenard J. Cohen, "Embattled Democracy: Post-Communist Transition in Croatia," in *Politics, Power and the Struggle,* ed. Dawisha and Parrott, 69–121.

despite the sharp reduction of the Serbian minority and the allocation for the 1995 elections of 12 of the now 127 seats to the Croatian Diaspora, votes largely cast from the Croat concentration in Herzegovina. Fewer opposition parties allowed the survivors to begin taking some advantage of increased proportional representation, now determining 60 of the 138 seats in an enlarged lower chamber. Already in the 1993 elections, while winning a 54 percent majority in the upper chamber, HDZ candidates struggled to hold on in local government. They failed to win absolute majorities in two-thirds of the 68 towns and half the municipalities. In Zagreb and 7 of the 21 counties, they were defeated. On the Istrian Peninsula, the opposition Istrian Democratic Assembly (IDS) won all the seats.[45] Even the immediate postwar elections of October 1995, where the share of ethnic minority (mostly Serb) seats was reduced from 13 to 3 and the Diaspora Croats voted almost unanimously for the HDZ, its share of seats in the lower chamber remained at 59 percent. Its share of the total vote was only 1 percent higher than in 1992. The Croatian Peasant Party and the revived SDP now joined the Istrian Democratic Assembly and the Social Liberal Party (Hrvatska socijalno liberalna stranka) as the major opposition parties. In a number of local elections, HDZ candidates were simply defeated— decisively in the Zagreb City Council.

The remaining years of Tudjman's presidency may be instructively framed on one side by his refusal to accept this opposing municipal government in Zagreb, dissolving the council and appointing his own commissioner. On the other, he kept enough personal popularity to win reelection as president in June 1997 with 61 percent of the vote. In that campaign against a still-divided set of opposition candidates, Tudjman could still bask in the glow of an earlier military background and his leadership in two successful wars. With no more warfare in prospect, however, his party did not fare so well. Its internal unity was fraying noticeably. Already in 1994, the center-left group of eighteen former Communist reformers led by Stjepan Mesić, the last prime minister of Yugoslavia, had left the members of the HDZ's bench in the lower chamber to form their own small party. From 1996, the hard-right group known as "the Herzegovina lobby," for their family ties to that

45. Details on IDS origins may be found in Andreas Heilborn, "Istrien . . . Kroatiens gröste Ferienregion und sein Regionalpartei IDS," *Österreichische Osthefte* 37, no. 2 (1995): 637–56.

area and its claim to becoming part of Croatia, was left to contest with the party's larger but more disparate group of managers, technocrats, retirees, and villagers. Hard-right pressures forced the resignation of moderate foreign and defense ministers in 1998.

Holding the regime together as long as Tudjman remained alive, despite his deteriorating health, were the authoritarian powers that wartime had allowed his regime to accumulate. Pressing against these powers, however, were a variety of democratic stirrings. They did not spill over into the streets, as with Serbia's Zajedno demonstrations. Yet they also promised a change of direction that has proved to be more sweeping than that in Serbia since 2000. Although the censored state television station was forced to drop a late-night news program including coverage from Western Europe and elsewhere in the former Yugoslavia, talk shows increasingly discussed current political issues without mentioning either Tudjman's name or the HDZ. Some speakers went further. They lamented the "unlawful" state of Croatian affairs, called for greater transparency, and hoped that the public's civic passivity, reminiscent of "silent Croatia" in Yugoslavia's 1980s, would not continue.[46]

The regime's control of the judicial system through ministerial appointments needing only parliamentary approval began to slip. The previously compliant Constitutional Court refused to approve Tudjman's aforementioned decision to replace Zagreb's elected City Council with his own appointed commissioner. A lower court upheld the regime's libel suit against the wickedly satirical weekly *Feral Tribune* for detailing a 1991 war crime against Croatian Serbs. Yet its judgment imposed only an affordable fine and did not close down the paper, as the regime had hoped to do. The regime used control of an enterprise monopolizing the supply of newsprint to limit the circulation of the new weekly magazines *Globus* and *Nacional* but could not haul them into court. Both magazines published articles detailing the corruption and wealth accumulating among Tudjman's associates and within his own family, his daughter in particular. Such scrutiny would not have been dared in Serbia against Milošević's son Mirko and the corruption surrounding his activities.

Tudjman's own standing suffered when he forced the panel selecting Miss Croatia for 1997 to replace the selection of a Bosnian Muslim with

46. Drawn from the tapes of RTH news and talk shows reviewed in "Monitoring Croatian Television, 1996–1998," HU OSA 310, Open Society Archives, Budapest.

a "proper Croatian" woman. His support from an Interior Ministry and an intelligence service often assumed to be as oppressive as Milošević's suffered from a multiplication of agencies, which were sometimes at odds with each other. In addition, the most prominent of the several intelligence services was headed by his son Miroslav, who was hardly unintelligent but placed the agency's authority in a position that would not outlive his father. It was, however, the aforementioned faltering of the initial economic transition, seemingly more successful in Croatia than elsewhere in the Western Balkans, that cut most deeply into the personal authority that Tudjman had established. In the absence of renewed warfare after 1996, his regime's standing came to depend on prosperity rising as promised at independence.

Albania

Such was more starkly the case for Albania, which in Sali Berisha had an assertive president still in office and in good health. Only the 1996 collapse of the pyramid schemes that had spread since the early 1990s triggered the political crisis that forced Berisha from power. Immediately after his election by the Parliament as president in April 1992, he pushed through a law allowing the president to remain an active party leader. His Democratic Party (Partia Demokratike) had won a substantial victory over the former Communists, now the Socialist Party (Partia Socialiste e Shqipërisë), with 62 percent of the popular vote and 90 of the 100 seats directly elected. The Socialists received all but six of their 38 seats from the 40 allocated by proportional representation, which also added two seats for the Democrats and eight from their Social Democratic and Republican allies.

Even this predominance was not enough for Berisha, who was strongly supported by those who had suffered most under the Communist regime and now wished to exclude their successors from the political process. In this effort, he enjoyed a unique advantage over his counterparts elsewhere in the Western Balkans. Usefully at hand for him to attack were the leaders of the last Communist regime, including Hoxha's widow and the other members of his Politburo. Well-publicized trials, charging them all with financial corruption, soon sent most of them to prison for substantial terms. The need to hold these trials helped to justify the president's cleansing of the judicial system. All past judges and states attorneys were now replaced by appointees required only to complete a six-month training program. The convictions also helped to tie the Socialists to their Communist past and thus tar their present credentials.

Despite the high reputation that Berisha himself enjoyed among EU and US representatives until 1996, internal strains within his own regime were appearing by the summer of 1992.[47] They began with expulsion from the party of the economist Gramoz Pashko. He had already been excluded from the leadership for favoring a coalition with the Alia government in the chaotic events of 1991, as noted above. Troubles continued with the resignation of the majority of the party newspaper's editors after some eight party leaders had themselves resigned or been expelled. By September, they had formed a splinter party. Berisha then dismissed his newly appointed attorney general for objecting to a presidential procedure for selecting states' attorneys over his head. And so it went, on into 1993–94, with the formation of another splinter party, this time on the hard anticommunist right, and the departure of first the Social Democrats and then the Republicans from the coalition government. The Socialists, conversely, struggled with a still Marxist-Leninist party platform and the imprisonment of their leader, Fatos Nano, who was jailed in July 1993 on charges of diverting funds from the Italian-supplied food relief of 1991.

Berisha's emerging personal regime nonetheless held on to its wider public approval and suffered only one political defeat before 1996. His efforts in 1994 to replace the interim Constitution of 1991 with a permanent one were rejected. Draft provisions to strengthen the president's considerable powers over the judiciary and even his own Cabinet prompted a parliamentary boycott, led by the Socialists and the Social Democrats. Their absence denied Berisha the two-thirds majority that was needed for ratification. A lesser concern, and in part a source of wider Albanian support for the draft, was its requirement that bishops of the Orthodox minority in the south, mainly Albanian but including some Greeks, be resident in the country for at least twenty years. This provision would have excluded the Greek clergy who had fled to Greece before the end of the Communist era. Turning to a referendum where the small Greek vote would be overwhelmed and parliamentary opposition would be irrelevant, Berisha expected approval. Instead, Albanian voters turned it down decisively, by 57 percent to 43 percent.

47. The following account draws primarily on Pano, "Process of Democratization," 318–52; and Vickers and Pettifer, *Albania,* 74–117.

Trouble was therefore brewing for Berisha's regime as the 1996 elections approached. He was still able to use the centralized powers of what has been called his "executive presidency" against all possible adversaries.[48] These included censorship and pressure on the opposition press, growing in circulation by this time past the initially predominant Democratic Party paper. A reconstituted security service to replace the feared Sigurimi, now called SHIK, also pressed domestic opponents, although not arresting them in Communist fashion. These dangers were used to justify a strong presidency. The regime's restoration of religious rights was also counting in its favor, with Catholics in the north and with the Orthodox in the south, where the regime's redistribution of land favored them over Muslim claimants.

But when the election arrived in June 1996, the Berisha regime could simply not stand back and allow the campaigning and the balloting to proceed fairly. Other parties were rarely allowed to display their posters in public, their distribution of newspapers was restricted, and their meetings were disrupted. The accumulation of abuses prompted the Socialists and several other parties to withdraw from their support for the electoral process and their local representatives from polling stations, but only toward the end of election day. This unfortunate timing left the Democrats with the claim to a fair process for most of the day and then allowed their own representatives a free hand for the last two hours. The Berisha regime naturally stood by the results, which gave the Democrats 55.5 percent of the vote and 122 of the 140 seats in Parliament. The Socialists got just 20 percent and 10 seats. Objections from the large numbers of international observers, led by the OSCE, finally pushed Berisha to allow re-voting in 17 constituencies, hardly enough to change the overall result. Local elections in October produced the same result, buoyed by the reluctance of the rural majority to vote for a Socialist Party that they still identified with the Communist regime that had seized their livestock in the early 1980s. The Socialists decided in August to remove all Marxist rhetoric from their program, but it was too late for this election to make the difference it would subsequently register. Meanwhile, their leader, Nano, still languished in prison. Nor was the growing disenchantment of US representa-

48. Mirela Bogdani and John Loughlin, *Albania and the European Union: The Tumultuous Journey towards Integration and Accession* (London: I. B. Tauris, 2007), 122–27.

tives with the Berisha regime shared by key members of the European Union, Italy included.

Only the economic crisis and social unrest that erupted in December 1996 cut short the Berisha presidency and its abuses of personal power. The crisis followed directly from the collapse of the aforementioned pyramid schemes that had mushroomed since 1993. These 150 "investment houses" were able to pay the promised 20 to 30 percent rates of return on funds flowing in primarily from remittances only as long as the inflow increased, in the absence of any profitable new investments in the country. The larger houses nonetheless advertised chains for profitable domestic enterprises, and as Albanian economists now acknowledge, a speculative mania spread widely through the population. Not all the houses were linked to Berisha's Democrats, but when smaller ones began to fail in December, he took a fatal step. He stood behind the large VEFA enterprise, which was linked to several party members. Angry crowds began to confront the offices of the smaller failures in January. Berisha thereupon accorded VEFA and the other large house linked to his party the formal status of commercial banks. Their subsequent failure brought Vlora, the center for the largest pyramid, and several other southern coastal towns into open revolt by February.

The revolt's wider spread coincided not surprisingly with Berisha's March 3 decision to declare a state of emergency. This gave his regime unrestricted authority. At the same time, he dismissed his prime minister and pushed his reelection as president for another five-year term through the Democrat-dominated parliament in Tirana. The revolt's "Salvation Committees," whose primarily Socialist leadership was Berisha's justification for imposing martial law, now spread across the south and up the coast. The rest of the month saw this southern half of Albania come under the control of these committees and their local militias. Previously dismissed Socialist army officers took the lead, collecting weapons looted from the arsenals of a disintegrating national army that were not sold or taken to Kosovo and Macedonia. The militia's rank and file were familiar with these small arms from Communist training or family tradition. The fighting in the south and its start in the north took more than a thousand lives and surely threatened more if a full-scale battle for Tirana erupted.[49]

49. The most detailed treatment of the 1997 crisis and its troubled resolution is given by James Pettifer and Miranda Vickers, *The Albanian Question: Reshaping*

Instead, international intervention prevented civil war and allowed new elections. The balloting authorized a Socialist government that took office in July. Italian concern over another refugee influx had mobilized Operation Alba in April. Italy contributed nearly half its 6,300 troops. UN authorization and OSCE oversight were hastily added. The force kept the south's rebel units from clashing with the government's hastily assembled northern militias and the remaining members of the officially disbanded security service still in place in Tirana and elsewhere. It was under these internationally imposed conditions that the Democratic Party agreed both to new parliamentary elections and to a referendum on the return of the monarchy. The pretender, King Zog's son Leka, attempted to mobilize political and also armed support but failed. The Socialists were still the most popular alternative to the Berisha regime. The Socialist Party of Albania won 52 percent of the vote and 118 of 155 seats in the OSCE-supervised election of June 29, versus 20 percent and 24 seats for the Democrats. Leka's royalists won less than 4 percent of the vote, and the referendum to return the monarchy was defeated by a two-to-one margin. Berisha resigned as president on July 3. The Socialist leader Nano, long imprisoned and freed only in the March chaos, became the new prime minister. As the powers of the presidency were now made secondary to those of the Parliament, Albania's democratic transition received a new lease on life.

Macedonia

This late start for a genuinely democratic transition across the Western Balkans also extended to Macedonia, but under different political conditions and with less violence. Only there was the personal authority of the president used by the winning party's leader to restrain the abuse of executive power. Still, the abstention of major groups marred the electoral process until 1998, and even then did not resolve the ensuing ethnic conflict. Only international intervention in 2001 stopped it short of civil war. In 1991, the representatives of the Albanian minority population of 20 to 25 percent, recalling how their separate language

---

the *Balkans* (London: I.. B. Tauris, 2007), 3–92. Also see Paulin Kola, *The Search for Greater Albania* (London: Hurst, 2003), 321–29; and the various *Reports* on Albania by the International Crisis Group.

and educational rights had been squeezed down in the last years of Communist rule, abstained from voting in the referendum for independence. But with Serbia's pressure on their ethnic fellows in Kosovo rising and JNA troops still in the country, these representatives joined the ethnic Macedonian majority in the government formed in 1992. And there one Albanian party or another would stay, despite the stormy parliamentary politics that dominated the rest of the 1990s.

Helping to keep Macedonian Albanians' representation in cabinets formed by a prime minister from the ethnic Macedonian majority was the initial Parliament's choice for president, Kiro Gligorov. He would remain in office for two full terms and use his reconciling reputation to good advantage until retiring in 1999. As a leading reform economist in the 1960s and Central Committee member in the former Yugoslavia into the 1970s, he had helped to found the Social Democratic Party directly from the membership of the old League of Communists. He then worked to mediate its relations with other parties. He also took the initiative in 1992 in persuading the UN to detach a small part of its UNPROFOR force in Croatia, formally to secure Macedonia's border with Serbia. Informally, just the presence of these thousand Western troops, independently constituted as the United Nations Preventive Deployment Force (UNPREDEP) in 1995, helped to keep the domestic peace through the rest of Gligorov's term.

Gligorov's young prime minister, Branko Crvenkovski, had put together a coalition of four parties, the Albanian Party for Democratic Prosperity included, after the 1992 elections. Their seats combined to outweigh those won by the largest single party, the anticommunist and émigré-backed Democratic Party for Macedonian National Unity. Under the urging of their leader, the equally young Ljubčo Georgievski, they added the prefix "Internal Macedonian Revolutionary Organization" in honor of the illegal interwar organization famed for terrorist acts to promote a larger and independent Macedonia. Their presumed claims on Greek Macedonia posed problems for the republic in its relations with Greece that led the Athens government to institute an economic blockade in 1994–95. The contention has persisted since then, despite the party's retreat from such claims. Inside Macedonia, the Internal Macedonian Revolutionary Organization–Democratic Party for Macedonian National Unity abstained from the second round of parliamentary elections in 1994, charging ballot tampering after having won almost no seats in the first round.

President Gligorov won reelection, but by a narrow margin. He narrowly escaped assassination the next year, probably at the hands of the corrupt interests living off illegal trade with sanctioned Serbia. Quickly recovering, he worked to prevent the huge Social Democratic majority in Parliament from abusing its authority, without the major opposition party, which was boycotting its sessions. Prime Minister Crvenkovski's efforts to advance Albanian representation did not extend to the police force or higher education. Nor did his party's involvement in economic corruption help to preserve its position in the local elections of 1995, in which the VMRO–DPMNE won the majority of municipalities. This set the stage for their sweeping victory in the parliamentary elections of 1998. They formed a strong majority government by including what had now become the largest and most defiant Albanian party, the new Albanian Democratic Party (Demokratska Partija na Albancite) led by Arben Xhaferi.[50]

The victory for an opposition party, a commonly accepted indicator of democratic governance, suggests that a political transition was indeed proceeding in Macedonia by the late 1990s. Yet its framework was one that the Albanian minority had initially rejected and was tempted to reject again in 2001. NATO's final defeat of Serbia in Kosovo in 1999 allowed the rapid return of the 850,000 Kosovars who had fled to refugee camps in Macedonia and also to Albania. The example of Albanian rights affirmed in Kosovo encouraged small numbers in the largely Albanian northwest of Macedonia to form their own paramilitary National Liberation Army by 2000. Taking the Kosovars' UÇK as their example and drawing on some cross-border support, they had begun confronting Macedonia's small and ill-equipped police force and army by March 2001. Police abuses, particularly from the two paramilitary units hastily assembled by an Interior Ministry little changed from the Communist era, helped to escalate the conflict. In the months that followed, the fighting killed almost 1,000 people and displaced as many as 100,000.

However, public support for continuing the conflict was largely absent, particularly among the Albanian minority. Gligorov's successor as president, Boris Trajkovski, was free to moderate the confronta-

---

50. A flavor-rich survey of Macedonia's politics through the 1990s is given by John Phillips, *Macedonia: Warlord and Rebels in the Balkans* (New Haven, Conn. Yale University Press, 2004), 48–88.

tional approach of Prime Minister Georgievski and his harder-line interior minister, Ljube Boškovski. Trajkovski negotiated the sort of rapid international intervention absent in the earlier wars of Yugoslavia's dissolution. US, British, and EU representatives were determined to avoid another such conflict. They rushed to convene the parties at Lake Ohrid in August. Neither they nor President Trajkovski were deterred by ethnic Macedonian demonstrations in Skopje protesting the Western side's alleged bias toward the Albanian side, a view that would continue after the Ohrid Agreement. The ethnic Macedonian side accepted a Framework Agreement for revisions in the 1991 Constitution, detailed in chapter 2, to expand Albanian rights. The Macedonian Albanians agreed to the arrival of a small NATO contingent of 3,500 to disarm the rebel force of less than 2,000.[51] Amnesty for all but those Albanians charged with specific war crimes was the hardest provision for the ethnic Macedonian side to swallow. But the provision shortly allowed representatives of the former rebel group to form a political party under their erstwhile leader, Ali Ahmeti. As we shall see in chapters 2 and 3, their participation has been critical to a process of democratic transition that has subsequently gone forward to win the start of a Stability and Association Agreement for eventual membership in the European Union.

Legacies and Lessons

If warfare, forced migration, and international intervention framed the first postcommunist decade for the Western Balkans, what political legacy did the domestic regimes behind the lines leave to the consolidation of democracy and the transition to a market economy? The exercise of power did not operate under democratic ground rules once elections, even if relatively free and fair, had been held. The rule of law often seemed not to apply, frustrating the creation of strong public in-

51. On the diplomatic background to the small UN force (UNPREDEP) from 1992 to 1999 and then a summary of the Ohrid Agreement with its arms-collecting provision for NATO's "Operation Essential Harvest," see Ahrens, *Diplomacy on the Edge,* 377–462; and Alice Ackermann, "International Intervention in Macedonia, From Preventative Engagement to Peace Implementation," in *International Intervention in the Balkans since 1995,* edited by Peter Siani-Davies (London: Routledge, 2003), 107–19.

stitutions and a democratic political culture. The state structures of the postcommunist regimes remained weak. Nor were the 3 million refugees or internally displaced persons, with only the near million forced out of Kosovo returning intact, likely candidates for multiethnic reconciliation or skilled employment.

International initiatives before 1999 had consisted mainly of European or UN diplomacy and peacekeeping missions, followed by US-led military intervention. Aid for reconstruction was tied to maintaining stable currencies and some promise of debt repayment. Although EU members were furnishing 80 percent of this sizable assistance, there was until then no promise of any possible inclusion as EU members in return for the broader institutional reform, beyond privatization, that would be needed for this membership. The prospect of EU membership appeared only in 1999. It came, as we shall see, as part of the Stability Pact for broader structural assistance, which was proclaimed immediately after NATO's prolonged intervention in Kosovo and intended to preclude any more. Just proclaiming this joint initiative from the EU's European Commission and the World Bank suggests that an international lesson had been learned during the course of the 1990s.

If the region's own lessons learned are restricted to the 1990s, they probably came foremost from the specter of open warfare and forced migration. Its growing shock effect registered across the region as a cautionary tale. In Macedonia, violence was more limited, in significant measure because of the images of death and desperate flight in the wars of Yugoslavia's dissolution. The 1,000 people killed in 2001 paled in comparison to the roughly 20,000 dead in Croatia and the 100,000 in Bosnia between 1992 and 1995. As the decade drew to a close, more than a million Bosnian Muslims and half a million Serbs were still living as refugees and internally displaced persons. For Macedonia, forced migration was confined to the Kosovar Albanians driven there temporarily in 1999. The international military presence, in the form of UNPREDEP, was far smaller and yet continuous and more locally valued than elsewhere. Intervention from émigré groups or funds in internal politics was also less important than in Croatia, Albania, and Kosovo. There was none of the political-military interference projected by Serbia into Croatian and Bosnian territory or by Croatia into Bosnia. And even in Bosnia-Herzegovina itself, widespread weariness of war on all sides helped to keep the post-Dayton peace and maintain an internationally supervised demobilization.

Joining the wartime displacements and memories as burdens for the Western Balkans has, however, been the legacy of Communist political culture and economic control. Croatia and Albania, along with Serbia, paid a high price for political leaders whose attraction to personal power and clientalism, intolerance of criticism, and refusal to leave office willingly continued the pattern set by their predecessors in one-party Communist regimes. All were themselves former party functionaries, although none of them had advanced to the Central Committee, as had the one leader who did not abuse his post-1989 power or tenure, Kiro Gligorov.

A damaging economic legacy of the pre-1989 period was the Yugoslav model of the socially owned enterprise, which was belatedly adopted in Albania as a first step toward privatization. In both countries, the notion of ownership as the prerogative of exiting employees led straight to the ill-fated plans for voucher privatization that left industrial enterprises in the hands of existing management, well insulated from foreign direct investment. In the former Yugoslav republics, the process was already under way before the dissolution of the country, tying the hands of those making post-1989 plans for privatization, especially in Macedonia. Banks were neglected in these initial plans, while all financial transactions in Yugoslavia's successor states were left to struggle with the delays and overcharges of the official payment bureaus through which they had to pass. Only agricultural holdings were thoroughly privatized, but as family small holdings with little access to affordable credit for modern equipment. In Albania, a widespread sacking of collective and state farms in 1991 destroyed what little mechanized equipment there was.

The democratic promise let loose in 1989 did pose some challenges to the arbitrary regimes of the 1990s that their Communist predecessors never had to face. The otherwise dominating political leaders in Serbia, Croatia, and Albania still made their best efforts to keep the media largely state controlled or blindly partisan. But they could not suppress the independent journalism that persevered against restrictions in Belgrade, Zagreb, and Tirana. Popular support, at least in these capital cities, came into the open with large public meetings as it never could have in Communist times. If only on isolated occasions, new Constitutional Courts in Croatia and Albania displayed the potential benefit for the rule of law if the judiciary acted independently against the wishes of the regime's ministerial authority. Educational reform and independent new scholarship continued to lag, but university faculties and students in Belgrade and Zagreb resisted regime pressures for control and clientism, even when their administrators did not. And everywhere—except, ironically, in Macedonia—academic support spilled into the media for the market-based reforms needed to move toward the standards of the European Union.

Thus, the principal lesson to be drawn from this more farsighted perspective is that a longer transition to democracy should have been expected for the Western Balkans. The largely failed first efforts of the 1990s were doubly difficult, weighted down not only by the violence and disruption attending Yugoslavia's dissolution but also by the larger legacy from the late Communist era, which was also less discredited in local opinion than elsewhere in Eastern Europe.

And yet, although the troubled region still lacked the set of independent institutions and the democratic political culture needed to move beyond this legacy the moment that peace returned, at least some hopeful stirrings survived the conflicts of the 1990s. They helped to persuade the European Union to open its doors to membership for the region's states starting in 1999. How the states and societies of the Western Balkans have since struggled to consolidate the more promising "second transitions" that began with the new century, at least pointing toward European integration, also concerns the rest of this volume. Thus, the subsequent chapters systematically explore the complex dynamics of post-2000 state building, and the changes in the region's political culture and social structure, before turning finally to the economic challenges that are a crucial credential for EU membership. Surely complicating these challenges has been the international financial crisis that had reached across the region by 2009, and the slow recovery under way by 2010 for the European economy as a whole.

Chapter 2

New Regimes, Old Routines: Institutional Innovations and Governance Challenges

The conclusion of the war in Bosnia near the end of 1995 brought a modicum of stability to the Western Balkans, and it appeared that a promising new phase of postcommunist development had begun. But the legacy of problems spawned by Yugoslavia's dissolution and the recent violence had only partially abated. Moreover, most of the major political actors responsible for the region's difficulties in the early 1990s still remained dominant figures on the political landscape. Most notable in this respect was the continued rule of both Slobodan Milošević and Franjo Tudjman, the two leaders who had been most responsible for Yugoslavia's violent collapse, and whose regimes obstructed pluralist evolution in Croatia and Serbia/Montenegro respectively.

Democratic Institution Building in the Precarious 1990s

Although the Western Balkans had ostensibly begun a "postconflict" stage by 1996, democratic state building during the second half of the 1990s would prove very uneven and limited. Granted, a plethora of state institutions had already been established in Yugoslavia's successor states, and also in Albania. Indeed, most political actors in the region evinced a public commitment to the notion of democratic rule. But the region exhibited a hodgepodge of different institutional models and practices that had been rapidly cobbled together during its turbulent initial transition from Communist rule. It is fair to say that democratic structures were not yet deeply entrenched in the region, let alone fully understood by the general citizenry. As we saw in chapter 1, reconfig-ured or new constitutional frameworks had been adopted by most of the Western Balkan states, and multiparty elections were regularly held. Yet in Croatia and Serbia, as elsewhere, the region's political institu-tions did not yet exhibit the features of stability, relative sustainability, and legitimacy that are generally associated with "institutionalized" or "consolidated" forms of democratic rule.

Fledgling Constitutions on a Semipluralistic Platform

As the regimes in the Western Balkans began their postcommunist phase of political development in the early 1990s, the region's politi-cal elites hastily improvised a patchwork of different constitutional frameworks. The primary goal of most constitution making by political leaders in the region was to assert their countries' sovereignty and state-hood, both to distinguish their states from the previous Communist experience and also, in most cases, as successor states to the former Yugoslavia. Additionally, specific constitutional features, such as those stipulating the illegality of property ownership by foreigners, served to signal each state's post-Yugoslav independence and its noncolonial status in relation to the Hapsburg successor states or Italy.[1] In brief, the new or reconfigured constitutional frameworks in the Western Balkans were seen as legitimacy-building devices on at least two im-portant levels: (1) *polity legitimation,* that is, the process of defining the boundaries and membership of the state community, and also mobi-lizing consciousness or support for such state identity; and (2) *regime legitimation,* the process of generating acceptance for a particular set of institutions that are tasked with governance responsibilities and the provision of justice.[2]

---

1. Stefano Bianchini, "The Idea of the State in Post-Communist Balkan Societies," in *State-Building in the Balkans and Dilemmas on the Eve of the 21st Century,* edited by Stefano Bianchini and George Schopflin (Ravenna: Longo, 1998), 53–80.

2. See, e.g., Richard Belamy and Dario Castiglione, "Legitimizing the Euro-'Polity' and Its 'Regime': The Normative Turn in EU Studies," *European Journal of Political Theory* 2, no. 1 (2000): 7–34; and Neil Walker, "Central Europe's Second Constitutional Transition: The EU Accession Stage," in *Rethinking the Rule of Law after Communism,* edited by Adam Czarnota, Martin Krygier, and Wojciech Sadurski (Budapest: Central European University Press, 2005), 341–70.

For example, for the "new" polities that are successors to the former Yugoslavia, it was necessary for constitutional frameworks to provide, at least symbolically, the imprimatur of statehood. This proved to be the case even if there was already some historical record of state experience or aspiration before Yugoslavia's dissolution. In many of Yugoslavia's successor states, there was already a background of popular feeling of virtual state identification, owing to various cultural or emotional markers of distinctiveness or experiences that could be tapped by the new state units and their elites. The legitimation of the polity, or the development of state identity, was therefore generally not that difficult for most Croats in Croatia, ethnic Macedonians in Macedonia, and among "Yugoslavs" (mostly Serbs and Montenegrins), who felt a commitment within the new rump, two-unit Federal Republic of Yugoslavia. Even in Bosnia-Herzegovina, where relations among Croats, Serbs, and Muslims had been very severely strained by the warfare of the early 1990s, there was at least, on a general level, a sense of pan-ethnic identification with the external borders of the newly established polity. And in the case of Albania, where the postcommunist polity is continuous with the earlier state boundaries established in the first quarter of the twentieth century, ascendant elites still endeavored to legitimate the state community in constitutional terms. Meanwhile, all the states in the region desired to advance the further process of regime legitimation, that is, the mobilization of support for newly elaborated or reconfigured institutions of governance.

However, despite their early recognition of the importance of both polity and regime legitimation for overall state development, the Western Balkan states made only limited progress during the 1990s with the kind of constitutional development that could significantly enhance democratic consolidation. Politically driven flaws of both commission and omission were in large part responsible for this lack of progress. Thus, for the most part into the later 1990s, the region's political elites failed to mobilize broad public support for the constitution-making efforts that were undertaken. Flawed constitution making often frustrated both polity and regime legitimation in ethnically divided countries. Moreover, there was also a significant discrepancy between the institutional arrangements specified in constitutional frameworks and the reality of political practice.

For example, in Albania, the 1990 interim Constitution—the "Law on Major Constitutional Principles"—was not superseded until 1998.

And although throughout this period Albania was technically a parliamentary system with the president elected by the Assembly, the regime exhibited strong elements of presidentialism owing to the dominating role of President Sali Berisha, who initially served from April 1992 to July 1997. Berisha's position did not, however, prove strong enough, as we saw in chapter 1, to force through ratification of a new Constitution that would formally increase the powers of the presidency. Even the final draft, drawn up with the assistance of American lawyers, could not overcome the resistance of the opposition political parties in Parliament or persuade voters in a hastily called referendum. A long and acrimonious constitutional debate followed the collapse of Berisha's political authority in early 1997, and not surprisingly led to the adoption of a Constitution in 1998 that formally established a parliamentary regime.

In Croatia, the postcommunist political elite elected in May 1990 had first utilized an interim constitutional framework based on amendments to the existing socialist Constitution, but it moved to adopt a new Constitution near the end of the year. However, the new "Christmas Constitution" was adopted after only four weeks of political debate. Serb deputies in the Croatian Assembly boycotted the process because language in the proposed Constitution formally relegated the Serb community of Croatia to a minority status (rather than its earlier position as a constituent nation), and also because of a proposed article that permitted Croatia to secede from Socialist Yugoslavia based on a two-thirds vote in the Assembly. Although a constitutional law was added in 1991 in order to try to settle the Serb objection, the early constitutional dispute had already served to spark an armed uprising by Croatia's Serbs in August 1991. It continued into 1995. Indeed, the warfare surrounding the dissolution of Yugoslavia, combined with strong features of executive dominance deriving from the semipresidential features of Croatia's 1990 Constitution, severely retarded democratic state-building efforts in the country until President Tudjman left office in December 1999.[3]

In Macedonia, early difficulties with constitution making resulted in serious problems for future state building and democratization. The

3. See Mirjana Kasapović, "Semi-Presidentialism in Croatia," in *Semi-Presidentialism in Central and Eastern Europe,* edited by Robert Elgie and Sophia Mostrup (Manchester: Manchester University Press, 2008).

1991 Constitution remained in force until 2001 (with some modifications in 1993 and 1995). Because of a constitutional preamble that identified Macedonia "as a national state of the Macedonian people," it was adopted without the support of deputies from the Albanian minority. Equality for Albanians and other minorities was otherwise provided for in the Constitution, but they were not described as constituent nations at the same level as "the Macedonian people." The 1991 Constitution organized Macedonia in a manner that could be described as a mixed system, containing elements of a parliamentary and a presidential regime, but favoring the former. It was, as we discussed in chapter 1, the result of Kiro Gligorov's lengthy term as directly elected president that seemingly transformed the political system into a presidential regime. As one 1996 study concluded: "So far, . . . stability has been dependent less on institutions and procedures than on the personality and ability of one man, President Kiro Gligorov. Through his overpowering prestige, he effectively transformed what was purportedly a parliamentary system of government into a presidential one."[4] The fact that Gligorov was a strong but nonauthoritarian political executive assisted the process of democratic state building in Macedonia. But ethnic divisions and the post-Gligorov return of constitutional problems and weakened political authority discouraged the regime legitimation that might have prevented the near civil war of 2001.

In creating the Federal Republic of Yugoslavia (FRY, composed of Serbia and Montenegro), Milošević's hastily engineered Constitution of April 1992 failed both to foster cohesion between its two territorial units and to advance democratic state building. Indeed, he had used the delegates directly elected from the two republics in 1986 to the Chamber of Republics and Provinces in the now-defunct Federal Assembly to adopt the Constitution with no voice for the newly elected parliaments. Yet Milošević's "caesarist" control over the FRY derived from his extensive constitutional powers as president of Serbia from 1992 to mid-1997,[5] as noted in chapter 1, rather than from his constitutional authority in the new federation. In 1997, Milošević shifted his political-constitutional power base and had himself elected (at that

4. As cited in Svetomir Škarić, "Institutional Support to the Countries of South Eastern Europe, *National Reports–FYR Macedonia,* March 2001.

5. Slobodan Antonić, *Zarobljena zemlja: Srbija za vlade Slobodana Miloševića* (Belgrade: Otrovenje, 2002), 411–24.

time a prerogative of the legislature) president of the FRY. He then began transferring power to the presidency. Milošević's political acumen would permit him to survive in power following the 1999 war between Yugoslavia and NATO, and the de facto loss of control over Kosovo. But he would not survive the results and aftermath of the popular election he mistakenly called in September 2000, for which he had set the stage by adopting constitutional amendments in July that allowed him to run for a second term as federal president in a direct countrywide election. This vote was a fatal mistake that would lead to his fall from power in October 2000, and his eventual arrest and extradition to stand trial at The Hague Tribunal (where he died in March 2006, while in prison, during the course of the trial).

Milošević's 1992 constitutional initiatives would also reinforce provisions limiting the autonomy of the province of Kosovo within Serbia, a situation that would not be altered until the conclusion of Yugoslavia's 1999 war with NATO and the establishment of a UN protectorate for the province. Meanwhile, in Montenegro the October 1992 Constitution served to formally legitimate the regime, which was headed by Milošević's allies in the republic. It was not until the Montenegrin ruling elite, headed by Milo Djukanović, broke with the Serbian leader in the second half of the 1990s that the smaller republic began its own preliminary and preindependence efforts at democratic state building. But although Djukanović steered his own course away from Serbia throughout the decade after 1997, he utilized the same constitutional framework that had been set in place at the onset of the Milošević era.[6]

Bosnia's post-Yugoslavia odyssey in state building and democratization, struggling since 1996 with the separate entities left in place by the Dayton Peace Accords, could not call upon an auspicious constitutional legacy for interethnic reconciliation. For example, in an attempt to avoid violence in mid-1990, the last Communist-era legislature of the republic had adopted constitutional amendments strengthening the notion of consensus decisionmaking among the three ethnic groups— Serbs, Croats, and Bosnian Muslims—which all were designated as constituent peoples (alongside the country's minority "others"). But

6. European Stability Initiative, *Rhetoric and Reform: A Case Study of Institution Building in Montenegro 1918–2001* (Podgorica: European Stability Initiative, 2001).

provisions for fixed proportional representation of the constituent nations in the recruitment of officials at different levels of government, and also for consensus decisionmaking, soon turned into a mechanism leading to constitutional deadlock and state collapse.[7] Once each of the three major groups expressed its relative ethnic cohesion by voting respectively for three major nationalist political parties in the election of 1990, the country became deeply segmented along ethnic lines. The so-called unity government agreed to by the three ruling parties as a result of secret negotiations before the elections resulted in fragmented governance by separate party machines that divided up the few spoils available and failed to cooperate in a unified manner.

Constitutional deadlock ensued in October 1991 when Bosnia's secession from the dissolving Yugoslavia became a likely prospect. Serb representatives in the legislature used their constitutional right to block a resolution calling for the republic's secession. But after the Serb deputies left the legislature following its technical adjournment, Croat and Muslim representatives took advantage of the situation only an hour later to resume business and pass a Muslim-supported declaration of sovereignty. In response, the Serbs ceased their participation in the legislature altogether and initiated the formation of their own parallel institutions. Now the procedural road was open to their boycott of the March 1992 referendum on Bosnia's independence, their formation of their own parallel institutions, and the Belgrade-backed warfare that began the next month. Meanwhile, Muslims and most Croats voted in favor of statehood. For many Serbs, it seemed that war was the only alternative to inclusion in a state they opposed. Constitutional discourse regarding Bosnia was essentially suspended until the last stages of the violent struggle that ensued in the period 1992–95.

Bosnia's postwar Constitution is contained in Annex 4 of the General Framework Agreement for Peace adopted at the Dayton Peace Conference in November 1995. The Constitution, admittedly part of a formidable negotiation that ended a savage war, is a framework designed and imposed by the international community, and not a product of a democratic process of constitution making by Bosnia's political class and public. The Dayton Constitution provided Bosnia with a central

---

7. Robert M. Hayden, "'Democracy' without a Demos? The Bosnian Constitutional Experiment and the International Construction of Non-Functioning States," *East European Politics and Societies* 19, no. 2 (2005): 226–59.

government having only limited powers, and two ethnoterritorial enti-ties—the Republika Srpska, constituted as a "state of the Serb people"; and the Federation of Bosnia and Herzegovina (originally designed in the United States during 1994 to end fighting between the Muslims and Croats). A three-person collective Federal Presidency consisting of one representative from each of the three constituent nations was es-tablished to make decisions by consensus. Elected representatives from each of the constituent ethnic groups can also veto parliamentary and Cabinet decisionmaking.[8]

Early on in its operation, it became apparent that Bosnia's limited central authority was hostage to stalemate by any one of the three ma-jor ethnic groups. Thus, at the end of 1997, as the central government's weakness became more obvious and serious, the Peace Implementation Council (PIC), representing the international community in Bosnia, gave added decisionmaking authority—the so-called Bonn Powers—to the Office of the High Representative (OHR), which represented the PIC. This increased authority included the right to remove elected officials from office if they were obstructing "the will of the people." Unfortunately, working within the confines of the Dayton Accords framework, the routine intervention of the OHR to remove offending officials and to break logjams among domestic political actors—895 times from 1997 through early 2010[9]—did not constitute the kind of state-building progress that could advance the country's internal pro-cess of democratic consolidation (see below).

Thus, at the end of the 1990s it was clear that democratic state build-ing in the Western Balkans did not rest on solid constitutional foun-dations or effectively functioning institutions. All the countries in the region, as we saw in chapter 1, had undergone considerable transforma-tion, opening up to new political parties and meaningful elections while separating the state from direct control of the economy. But political institution building in the service of democratic consolidation had not advanced very far as the decade drew to a close. The constricted and

8. Ibid. Bosnia's Constitution has stipulated that only Bosniaks (Bosnian Muslims), Serbs, and Croats can get elected to top state bodies. In December 2009, the European Court of Human Rights reprimanded Bosnia for discriminating against Jews and Roma and asked the country to review its laws.
9. See Bart M. J. Szewczyk, *The EU and Bosnia and Herzegovina: Power, Decision and Legitimacy,* Occasional Paper 83 (Brussels: European Union, 2010), 35–42.

sluggish evolution of constitutional frameworks in the region both reflected and contributed to the difficulties at institutionalizing democracy. For example, on the cusp of the twenty-first century, Albania
was just beginning to function under its new 1998 Constitution, and
because the country was just recovering from complete state collapse,
internal political struggles and elite conflict remained at a high pitch.
Croatia was still operating under the constitutional interpretations of
state founder Franjo Tudjman's "imperial presidency." Macedonia's
political institutions were regarded as illegitimate by its large Albanian
community. And its executive and institutional framework had relied
on a "dictatorship of respect" for Kiro Gligorov (as President Tomáš
Masaryk's role in interwar Czechoslovakia has been described) more
than on a vital multiethnic democracy. Milošević still employed a "soft
dictatorship" to maintain control of Serbia. Although he was challenged politically by his former allies in Montenegro, the elite in that
small unit of the Yugoslav federation could hardy be described as fully
accountable democratic decisionmakers.

Meanwhile, Kosovo had been placed in mid-1999 under international
administration, and it still did not possess functioning domestic institutions. And Bosnia, although a more constitutionally and institutionally
elaborated ward of the international community, was still striving to
overcome the legacy of war. The deep mistrust among its major ethnic
groups, as much as the fragmented framework of the Dayton Accords,
impeded stable power sharing and democratic institution building. Not
only were the capacity and the ambit of Bosnia's central political institutions very limited, but in addition the internationally appointed high
representative had began to function in a manner that was soon to be
described as a "European Raj."[10]

In summary, at the onset of the twenty-first century, the region was
composed of weak states or international protectorates operating under fledgling constitutions. Despite some signs of promise in the second
half of the 1990s, the states of the Western Balkans had not established
their own accountable or fully legitimate executive authorities and the
separation of powers needed to consolidate democracy as the basis for
domestic institutions.

10. Gerald Knaus and Felix Martin, "Travails of the European Raj," *Journal of
Democracy* 14, no. 3 (July 2003): 66–74.

The Acceleration of State Building: A Second Transition in a New Constitutional Environment, 1999–2009

The climate for constitutional developments and democratic consolidation acquired new momentum at the end of the 1990s. Two factors were primarily responsible for this development: (1) the enhanced involvement of the international community in Southeastern Europe following the 1999 NATO war over Kosovo; and (2) the weakened influence and subsequent departure of the two leaders who had obstructed pluralist development and regional stability, Croatia's Franjo Tudjman and Serbia's Slobodan Milošević. Additionally, one can discern that a gradual, albeit still limited, maturation of democratic skills had begun to take hold in the region, particularly within the emerging postcommunist generation of political elites and civil society activists (see chapters 4 and 5).

Stabilizing the Balkans after the Kosovo war was viewed by most European states not only as a critical regional imperative but also as an opportunity for the EU both to assume a larger role in regional conflict management and to diminish US leadership in dealing with European crises. The United States had played the central role in forging the Dayton Peace Agreement for Bosnia in 1995, and also leading the subsequent NATO military interventions in Bosnia (the Implementation Force, known as IFOR; and the Stabilization Force, known as SFOR), and initially in Kosovo. But those American initiatives also were viewed with a certain chagrin by European elites, and thus helped motivate them to upgrade the EU's efforts to develop a capability in defense and foreign policy. EU and other European efforts to assist the Western Balkans had not been insignificant in the 1990s, particularly in funding. But after the war in Kosovo, European leaders improvised a more expanded role in the region.[11]

For example, the Stability Pact for Southeastern Europe (SPSEE) inaugurated in June 1999 was organized to enhance cooperation between

11. Lenard J. Cohen, "Managing Multilateralism? EU-US Relations and the Challenges of Regime Building in South Eastern Europe," in *The Transatlantic Divide: Foreign and Security Policies in the Atlantic Alliances from Kosovo to Iraq,* edited by Osvaldo Croci and Amy Verdun (Manchester: Manchester University Press, 2006), 77–91; John Lampe, *Balkans into Southeastern Europe: A Century of War and Transition* (London: Palgrave, 2006), 290–95.

and among the Southeastern European states on the one hand, and between those states in Europe and the United States and Russia on the other. The SPSEE utilized the regional approach in the effort to build a stronger and more prosperous region, and it was aimed at promoting stability and cooperation within the postcommunist Balkans region as a prelude to its integration into the European Union. Through the SPSEE, the EU—as the SPSEE's joint coordinating and facilitating agency with the World Bank—became more directly and deeply involved across the region. The SPSEE included both the successor states of the former Yugoslavia as well as Albania, and also Bulgaria and Romania, which were already in the forefront of the EU accession process. As such, the SPSEE became an "antechamber" of the European Union (and finally, in early 2008, a new Regional Cooperation Council superseded the SPSEE).

In May 1999, the EU elaborated a new concept—the Stabilization and Association Process (SAP) aimed at coordinating preaccession assistance for five countries: Bosnia-Herzegovina, Albania, Croatia, Serbia/Montenegro, and Macedonia. The SAP process offered the countries of what was now termed the "Western Balkans" region a European perspective. This regional approach to assistance for the Western Balkans had already been applied as early as 1996–97, but the SAP was a "new strengthened approach," which treated the countries in the area as a group but also on an individualized basis. The SAP not only emphasized stabilization and cooperation for the region's states but also provided the political, economic, and administrative criteria to guide them in achieving eligibility to become full candidates for EU membership.

At the Feria European Council meeting in June 2000, the heads of the EU's member states indicated that they regarded all the countries that were part of the newly established SAP as potential candidates for EU membership. The development and signing of Stabilization and Association Agreements under the SAP now became the designated "road to Europe." During the next five years, the EU would assume a major role in Western Balkan state building and economic development, although still not at the level of the kind of "member state building" that was already utilized for the Central European states and the Eastern Balkans (Romania and Bulgaria), or the style of so-called authoritarian state building that was emphasized in Bosnia and Kosovo.

Instead, the EU utilized the kind of "traditional state building" that focused on improving domestic institutional capacity and assisting with economic development.[12]

Thus, in November 2000 the EU adopted the Community Assistance for Reconciliation, Development, and Stabilization (CARDS) program to coordinate assistance to the Balkans and earmarked €4.6 billion for this initiative for the period 2000–2006. In brief, the EU was now aggressively involved in the Balkan state-building enterprise, although surveys showed that European elites and citizens were still quite ambivalent about whether the countries of Southeastern Europe, and particularly those in the Western Balkans, would or should quickly advance to EU membership (see chapter 9).[13]

The close coincidence between the adoption of the EU's new strategy toward the Western Balkans and the important trends in leadership succession in Croatia and rump Yugoslavia would also stimulate constitutional changes throughout the region. For example, in the spring of 2000, not long after the death of President Tudjman, presidential and legislative elections were held in Croatia. Tudjman's ruling party, the Croatian Democratic Union (Hrvatska demokratska zajednica, HDZ), lost power and in October 2000, the newly elected leaders adopted constitutional amendments changing the makeup of the regime from a semipresidential model to a parliamentary form. The willingness of two new political executives, President Stipe Mesić and Prime Minister Ivica Račan, to reach an agreement on such rules of the democratic game marked a new stage in Croatia's political development. Their agreement allowed the country to begin "a second transition." During 2000, the EU quickly responded to these changes and embarked on negotiations with Croatia for a Stabilization and Association Agreement. Discussions about major constitutional revisions in Croatia would only resume in the years 2009–10, as Croatia drew nearer to its EU accession goal.

For Macedonia, the Ohrid Framework Agreement of 2001 began a new stage in its constitutional development. The EU- and

12. European Stability Initiative, *The Helsinki Moment: European Member State-Building in the Balkans* (Berlin: European Stability Initiative, 2005).
13. Lenard J. Cohen, "The Europeanization of 'Defective Democracies' in the Western Balkans: Pre-Accession Challenges to Democratic Consolidation," in *The Boundaries of EU Enlargement: Finding a Place for Neighbours,* edited by Joan de Bardeleben (London: Palgrave, 2007), 205–21.

American-led negotiations cut short the incipient interethnic war, as described in chapter 1, in part by addressing the persistent complaints by Macedonia's Albanians concerning the 1991 Constitution. The Framework Agreement brokered with the four major political parties in the country—two ethnic Macedonian parties and two ethnic Albanian parties—was designed to accommodate Albanian demands for greater standing and equality in the state by changing the preamble to the Constitution (symbolically eliminating the ethnic nature of citizenship), altering the system of parliamentary voting, promising a larger representation of Albanians in the police, broadening the use of the Albanian language in official proceedings, and providing for more religious freedom and decentralization. But there was substantial ethnic Macedonian opposition to the agreement at both the popular and elite levels. Indeed, it took several months, and a good deal of political tension, before Macedonia's Parliament finally adopted fifteen amendments ratifying a modified version of the Ohrid provisions. For example, the new preamble to the constitutional changes agreed to at Ohrid was reworked under ethnic Macedonian pressure, acknowledging non-Macedonians as "peoples" instead of minorities but still recognizing the primacy of "the Macedonian people." These and other amendments and features of the Ohrid Agreement gave it a decidedly ethnic rather than civic character.[14] Minority rights were certainly enhanced under the Ohrid model, but interethnic relations remained tense. And considerable political controversy would lie ahead regarding the implementation of reforms in public administration, decentralization (see chapter 3), and the use of nonmajority languages.[15]

During 2001, Kosovo also began functioning within a new "provisional constitutional framework" that was instituted by the protectorate's "special representative of the UN secretary-general." This framework, which initiated a rather checkered phase of "state building without

14. Zhidas Daskalovski, "Language and Identity: The Ohrid Agreement and Liberal Notions of Citizenship and Nationality in Macedonia," *Journal on Ethno-Politics and Minority Issues in Europe* 1 (2002). See also Armand Reka, "The Ohrid Agreement: The Travails of Inter-Ethnic Relations in Macedonia," *Human Rights Review,* 2008, 9, 58–59.

15. Biljana Vankovska, "The Role of the Ohrid Agreement and the Peace Process in Macedonia," in *Walking on the Edge: Consolidating Multi-Ethnic Macedonia, 1989-2004,* edited by Z. Daskalovski (Chapel Hill, N.C.: Globic, 2006).

statehood" in Kosovo,[16] would continue right through the 2005–7 dis-cussion of Kosovo's future status. Kosovo's unresolved "final status" and the deep interethnic chasm between Serbs and Albanians would have a detrimental impact on democratic institution building within the protectorate. Moreover, after eight years of UN administration in Kosovo, a 2007 report concluded that the mission suffered from an acute "accountability gap" and had failed to establish itself as "a model of good governance practices."[17] Concerns over Kosovo's future and its government weaknesses would also negatively influence constitutional and political development in Serbia and Montenegro following the fall of the Milošević regime (see below). A plan to proceed to eventual state-hood for Kosovo through another and final interim period of "super-vised independence" was finally drawn up by a special UN envoy, Martti Ahtisaari, in 2007. The Ahtisaari plan envisioned a strong EU civilian and military presence, and it also aimed to establish "a multiethnic so-ciety exercising self-government" through its own legislative executive and judicial institutions.[18] But during the summer of 2007, regional and international disagreements obstructed the final decision on postprotec-torate status for Kosovo.

The Ahtisaari plan, however, became the working document for a group of twenty-one constitutional experts—established by Albanian leaders in Kosovo with foreign assistance—the "Constitutional Working Group." Following the Unilateral Declaration of Independence by the Kosovo Assembly, this group became the Constitutional Commission of Kosovo. With heavy influence from the US government and the US Agency for International Development in particular, and with support from many societal groups and experts, the Constitutional Commission

16. Lenard J. Cohen, "State Building before Statehood: Kosovo's Evolution from an Interim Polity to 'Conditional Independence,'" in *Interim Governments: Institutional Bridges to Peace and Democracy?* edited by Karen Guttieri and Jessica Piombo (Washington, D.C.: US Institute of Peace Press, 2007), 239–62.

17. Human Rights Watch, *Better Late Than Never: Enhancing the Accountability of International Institutions in Kosovo* (New York: Human Rights Watch, 2007). See also Iain King and Whit Mason, *Peace at a Price: How the World Failed Kosovo* (Ithaca, N.Y.: Cornell University Press, 2006); and Andrew J. Taylor, "'We Are Not Asking You to Hug Each Other, but We Ask You to Co-exist': The Kosovo Assembly and the Politics of Co-existence," *Journal of Legislative Studies* 11, no. 1 (Spring 2005): 105–37.

18. United Nations Security Council, "Comprehensive Proposal for the Kosovo Status Settlement," S/2007/168/Add.1, March 26, 2007.

developed a draft document that was publicly discussed before the Constitution's formal adoption in April 2008.

Although the Kosovo Constitution formally provides a modern and civic-oriented basis for democratic governance, the document has a number of flaws that potentially can impede or complicate democratic consolidation. For example, the fact that the international community played an enormous role in guiding and drafting the Constitution raises the issue of how much ownership domestic Kosovo political elites have in the document and its long-term legitimacy. More specific problems have also been identified. Thus, the language used in the Constitution has a civic tone and is devoid of "ethnonational ideology." But using a phrase inserted in the final stage of drafting, it also differentiates between the Albanians and "other" communities, which are not designated. Consequently, at least on a symbolic level, the Constitution establishes the "identity fiction" of a linkage between a majority population and the state.[19] There is, however, considerable provision in the Constitution for the representation of ethnic minorities in legislative and executive bodies, balancing quite effectively between individual and group rights, although in the face of the ethnic divisions in Kosovo, and the close ties between Serbia and the Kosovo Serbs, the constitutional provisions (and other far-reaching legislation to protect minorities) remain largely theoretical.

Moreover, because Kosovo is only "conditionally independent," and has a powerful international civilian representative, representing the international community, a continued role for the UN Mission in Kosovo (directed by a representative of the UN secretary-general), the "supremacy" of the Constitution, and also the state authorities of Kosovo, remained in doubt. Technically, the Constitution defined Kosovo as an independent state that is to be initially supervised by the international community (specifically, by the International Civilian Office and the European Union Rule-of-Law Mission, EULEX). This uncertainty made it difficult to identify who had paramount authority in Kosovo. For example, Vetan Surroi observed that Kosovo in 2009 was very much like the situation in 1999, at least de facto, with three coexisting state-like authorities: a so-called independent state, an international protectorate, and "a de facto partitioned country" (i.e., northern Kosovo

19. Joseph Marko, "The New Kosovo Constitution in a Regional Comparative Perspective," *Review of Central and East European Law* 33, no. 4 (2008).

under substantial Serbian control). The biggest challenges, as he saw it in 2009, were "how to make the country more independent, how to get rid of the protectorate, and how to unify the country territorially."[20]

Kosovo's "stateness" problem came into sharp focus in September 2009, when EULEX, headed by the international civilian representative (who was also the EU special representative), signed a protocol on police cooperation with Serbia—but without the consent of the Kosovo state authorities. The matter was further complicated because EULEX, although an EU mission, also operates ostensibly under the UN umbrella, and the UN is technically neutral regarding the issue of Kosovo's "status." Additionally, the fact that five EU countries did not recognize Kosovo's independence clouds the position of EULEX in dealing with sovereignty issues. At the end of 2009, one year after its deployment, EULEX still faced an uphill battle in fighting corruption and organized crime, and also in establishing its mandate throughout Kosovo.

A new phase of constitutional and political debate ensued with the July 2010 decision by the International Court of Justice (ICJ), ruling that the February 2008 declaration of Kosovo's independence did not contravene international law. In the wake of the ICJ ruling, Kosovo prime minister Hashim Thaçi requested, to no avail, that the International Civilian Office and EULEX renounce their executive powers in the country. Some of Kosovo's Albanian opposition leaders argued that the new state actually needed more externally "supervised independence" to establish law and order in the predominantly Serb-populated north, and also to fight government corruption and election fraud. For its part, Serbia completely rejected the ICJ's ruling and responded by submitting a draft resolution to the United Nations General Assembly calling for a dialogue between Belgrade and Priština. Belgrade's initial resolution was strongly opposed by the United States and most EU member countries. Under pressure, Serbia agreed to a new compromise draft in which Belgrade took "note" of the ICJ resolution but sidestepped specific recognition of Kosovo independence and emphasized the readiness for the EU to begin a "process of dialogue between the parties."

20. Vetan Surroi, writing in *Koha Ditore,* March 3, 2009. See also Kosova Democratic Institute, *Power in Post-Independence Kosovo* (Priština: Kosova Democratic Institute, 2009).

This compromise resolution was unanimously adopted at the UN in early September 2010. Serbian nationalists were offended by an outcome that put "the fate of Kosovo and Serbia . . . into the hands of Washington, Brussels and their bureaucracy," but more pragmatic observers viewed the compromise in a more positive light because it only vaguely dealt with the status of Kosovo and opened discussion that might assist the autonomy-seeking Serb minority in Kosovo.[21] The resolution was correctly described as an example of "constructive ambiguity" that for the moment at least would buy time for everyone to search for a more lasting solution.[22]

Serbia's own constitutional evolution was somewhat more convoluted than those of its neighbors. Milošević's 1992 Constitution continued in force under the regime of his successor as president of the Federal Republic of Yugoslavia, Vojislav Koštunica. At the beginning of his tenure, Koštunica, a conservative if democratic nationalist dedicated to legal continuity, hoped to keep restless Montenegro within the Yugoslav Federation, and also to regain de facto control over Kosovo. Thus, in 2002 the Koštunica presidency cooperated with the determined efforts of EU officials to elaborate their plan for a new state union of Serbia and Montenegro. However, the new state proved unworkable and short-lived. The Montenegrin political leadership moved actively toward its announced goal of full independence, having been emboldened by momentum from the Kosovo Albanians' drive for full independence vis-à-vis Serbia. The drive for Montenegrin sovereignty was finally achieved in May 2006 after a majority voted for independence, just exceeding the special EU requirement of 55 percent.[23] By early 2007, debate on a new constitution for Montenegro had begun, but it proved as internally acrimonious as the discussion that surrounded the issue of independence. The pro-Serb parties, for example, branded the draft Constitution as "anti-Serb," and they also asked that the Serbian Orthodox Church be given special recognition. In the end, however, Montenegro adopted a civic and secular Constitution in October 2007 that was given a positive evaluation by the Council of Europe.

21. Slobodan Samardžić of the DSS in *Radio B92,* September 9, 2010; and Dusan Janjic, Radio KiM, September 9, 2010.

22. *Guardian,* September 9, 2010.

23. Statehood was supported by 56.6 percent of those voting, a margin of approximately 45,000 votes. See Srdjan Darmanović, "Montenegro: A Miracle in the Balkans?" *Journal of Democracy* 18, no. 2 (April 2007): 152–59.

Meanwhile Serbia, now decoupled from Montenegro (and de facto without control of Kosovo) adopted the requisite legislation and symbols of independent statehood. In October 2006—five years after the fall of Milošević—the government of Prime Minister Koštunica held a referendum, and it managed by only a slim margin to push through the adoption of a new Constitution for Serbia. Although constitutional change in Serbia had been a source of debate and interparty controversy for years,[24] the constitutional draft was finally adopted by the Serbian Assembly in September, after only a brief public debate. Prime Minister Koštunica was able to secure approval for constitutional change by the major segments of Serbia's fractured "democratic bloc," largely because the constitution-making exercise in 2006 served primarily as an act of political symbolism to forestall territorial secessionism by Kosovo. This was ostensibly achieved through the inclusion in the preamble of a provision stipulating that Kosovo remains "an integral part of the territory of Serbia."[25] Indeed, during the constitutional referendum campaign, Serbian TV broadcast patriotic films suggesting that Kosovo would be lost to Serbia unless the Constitution received majority support.

For its part, the international community and the EU gave their grudging approval to Serbia's new Constitution—although with reservations regarding the level of judicial independence and provisions for local government—because they vainly hoped that a political consensus on the new framework might provide Serbia with sufficient political stability to calmly or at least peacefully accept the parallel Ahtisaari international plan that was being developed for Kosovo's "supervised independence." When the democratic parties proved victorious in the early 2007 parliamentary elections, it initially appeared that such foreign hopes may have been warranted. But extensive interparty wrangling during the spring of 2007—including the selection, albeit short-lived, of Tomislav Nikolić, the leader of the ultranationalist Serbian Radical Party (Srpska radikalna stranka, SRS), as speaker of Serbia's legis-

24. See, e.g., Nenad Dimitrijević, "Serbia as an Unfinished State" in *Between Authoritarianism and Democracy: Serbia, Montenegro, Croatia,* edited by Dragica Vujadinović, Lino Venjak, et al. (Belgrade: Dosije, 2005), vol. 2, 59–74; and Slobodan Samardžić, "Basic Issues of the State," in *Four Years of Transition in Serbia,* edited by Boris Begović, Milica Bisić, Milica Djilas, et al. (Belgrade: Center for Liberal-Democratic Studies, 2005), 403–28.

25. See www.legislationonline.org.

lature—delayed the formation of a new coalition of prodemocracy parties. Indeed, internal fractures in the government that was finally formed, as well as continued uncertainty regarding the Kosovo problem (as Russia advocated Serbian interests at the UN Security Council), raised continuing doubts about Serbia's longer-term stability. In May 2008, a new coalition of democratic parties achieved victory at the ballot box and promised to advance Serbia's democratic orientation. But the hastily drafted Constitution of 2006, designed by less liberal and more nationally oriented democratic elements, remained in force (and throughout 2009 and 2010, it was used to legitimate Serbia's intransigence on the question of recognizing Kosovo's statehood). Any further constitutional changes in Serbia awaited what President Boris Tadić has called "a wider political consensus."[26]

Debate concerning Bosnia's constitutional framework picked up as the political mood began to improve in the Western Balkans after 1999 and as the EU adopted a hands-on role in the region. Post–Dayton Accords constitutional changes had been suggested throughout the late 1990s, but they only began in earnest in July 2000 when the Constitutional Court of Bosnia and Herzegovina ruled that constitutional bylaws within the two entities differentiating the status of the three constituent peoples were discriminatory. The court elevated to the status of a constitutional principle the equality of all three constituent peoples throughout Bosnia. This outcome was the result of a five-to-four decision by the court, with the three foreign judges joining with the two Bosnian Muslim judges to outvote four others, two Serbs and two Croats who chose to dissent. Bosnian politicians subsequently moved to institutionalize this court ruling through provisions guaranteeing the interests of all three ethnic communities and their representation in decisionmaking bodies.[27]

By 2004, initiatives for a more comprehensive constitutional overhaul of the Dayton Accords gathered momentum. Various reform proposals were advanced by domestic actors as well as foreign think tanks. Many suggestions focused on reducing the power of the country's two entities, strengthening the role of the central government, and scaling back the plethora of governmental structures and responsibilities (e.g., Bosnia's government structure consisted of 3 rotating presidents at the

26. *Politika,* December 5, 2009.
27. Hayden, "'Democracy' without a Demos?"

state level, 2 presidents at the entity level, 13 prime ministers presiding over cabinets at various levels, as well as more than 180 ministers, 760 members of various legislative bodies, and 148 municipalities). Positions differed about whether the powers of the Office of the High Representative should be increased to leverage change at a faster rate, or should be reduced or even eliminated, as part of an effort to move quickly to local control.

There was little question that the dominant ethnically oriented political parties in Bosnia proved adept at utilizing the mechanics of the Dayton institutional structure in a manner that prevented effective political decisionmaking in the country's legislative and executive institutions. To eliminate such political paralysis, the OHR was compelled to step in and fill the decisionmaking vacuum. For example, data on legislative activity (see table 2.1) revealed the persistent difficulty of passing legislation, the necessity for the OHR to impose legislation (the extent of such intervention being contingent on the personality of the occupant of the OHR and the degree of concern shown by the international community), and the obstructionist role played by the entities, particularly the Republika Srpska. Thus, 156 of 260 draft laws and proposals (60 percent) did not pass from 1997 to 2007 because they failed to receive the support of the legislators in the two entities. And more than half of the failed laws (52.3 percent) resulted from the action of the Republika Srpska's Assembly (another 35 percent failed because of obstruction in the central legislature itself).[28]

Beginning in 2005, secret informal discussions among Bosnian leaders, but encouraged by the OHR and other external actors, took place concerning the issue of constitutional change. Although it could be convincingly argued that by the tenth anniversary of the Dayton Agreement in 2005, Bosnia's institutional framework had already been greatly transformed without formal constitutional alteration—and also that the powers of the two entities had already diminished considerably[29]—most observers felt that formal constitutional change could help resolve the internal constitutional contradictions and complexities that clearly were still in evidence. In March 2006, an agreement on

28. Konrad Adenauer Stiftung, *Proces Odlučivanja u Parlamentarnoj Skupštini Bosne i Herczegovine* (Sarajevo: Konrad Adenauer Stiftung, 2009).
29. Florian Bieber, "External De- and Re-Construction of Multi-Ethnic States: The Case of Bosnia," unpublished paper, 2005.

Table 2.1. Legislative Activity in Bosnia, 1997–2007

Year	Laws Adopted by Bosnia's Legislature	Laws Not Adopted	Laws Blocked by Entities		Laws Imposed by High Representative[a]	Other Decisions Imposed by High Representative
			Federation	Republika Srpksa		
1997	11	—	—	—	1	—
1998	4	9	—	1	4	—
1999	7	13	1	9	5	4
2000	8	2	—	—	20	15
2001	23	40	—	26	4	13
2002	12	43	—	26	24	15
2003	40	16	2	11	14	26
2004	73	32	2	16	13	26
2005	39	31	8	10	6	45
2006	37	36	6	13	6	23
2007	25	38	1	24	15	7
Total	279	260	20	136	112	174

[a]These are the occupants of the Office of the High Representative under the Peace Implementation Council, representing the international community in Bosnia: Carl Bildt, December 14, 1995–January 18, 1997; Carlos Westendorp, June 18, 1997–August 18, 1999; Wolfgang Petritsch, August 18, 1999–May 27, 2002; Paddy Ashdown, May 27, 2002–January 31, 2006; Christian Schwartz-Schilling, January 31, 2006–July 2, 2007; Miroslav Lajčák, July 2, 2007–March 26, 2009; and Valentin Inzko, March 26, 2009–present.

Source: Authors' reconfiguration of data in Konrad Adenauer Stiftung, *Proces Odlučivanja u Parlamentarnoj Skupštini Bosne i Hercegovine* (Sarajevo: Konrad Adenauer Stiftung, 2009).

constitutional reform was reached by six political parties, assisted by the external mediation of American consultants and the EU's Venice Commission.[30] However, in late April 2006 the constitutional reform package, which among other things would have strengthened the role of the central government, failed by just two votes to obtain the necessary two-thirds majority in Bosnia's House of Representatives (the principal spoiler was the Bosniak leader and Federal Presidency member Haris Silajdžić, who objected to the continued role of the entities).

Sofia Sebastian has accurately described the principal reasons for the failure of the "April package" and its important consequences for the future: "While the failure of this process was largely the result of ethnic power games, the United States–led initiative suffered a lack of democratic legitimacy and was constrained by tight deadlines. The lack of participation of key stakeholders led ultimately to an embittered political climate that resulted in a highly radicalized election campaign in 2006."[31] Partially as a result of the rising political attentions spawned by constitutional immobilism, the election of October 2006 was characterized by an increase in nationalism, interethnic antagonism, and distrust. The president of the Republika Srpska, Milorad Dodik, Bosnia's leading Serb politician, questioned the very cohesion of the country by suggesting that his entity—just as the citizens of Montenegro—should have the right to hold a referendum on secession. Meanwhile, Silajdžić remained adamant that the two entities needed to be abolished, and at the least, entity voting in Bosnia's Parliament should be ended. International organizations continued to emphasize the urgency of constitutional reform from 2006 through 2009, but the impasse among domestic actors continued to block progress on the issue, and also on other questions of institutional change such as police reform, which the EU deemed necessary for Bosnia to enter the Stabilization and Association Process. A new effort at constitution making would begin

---

30. Don Hays and Jason Crosby, *From Dayton to Brussels: Constitutional Preparations for Bosnia's EU Accession,* Special Report 175 (Washington, D.C.: US Institute of Peace Press, 2006). For an argument that recent constitutional initiatives in Bosnia have been elitist and nontransparent, and have also exaggerated the role of ethnoterritorial considerations, see Esref Kenan Rašidagić, "Ustavna promjene: Ambivalentan process, ambivalentiji resultati," *Puls demokratije,* November–December 2006.

31. Sofia Sebastian, "No Time to Wind Down in Bosnia," *Fride Policy Brief,* August 2009, 4.

in 2009, but it made little headway owing to the continuing deadlock among the principal ethnopolitical elites (see below).

Overall, the major political changes in the Western Balkans after the 1999 Kosovo war and during the first decade of the twenty-first century—or what amounted to a second postcommunist transition in the area—improved the environment for democratic consolidation and state building. The international community and the EU in particular were more directly involved in the region, and the attention of Western Balkan elites was now more concentrated on getting their states or entities on the "road to Europe." But if their regimes had a "tangible European perspective," they still remained in the early phase of the type of institutional transformation that has the potential for sustainable and stable democratic development. For example, the comprehensive report of the International Commission on the Balkans, completed in 2004–5, reported that the constitutional frameworks designed by international officials and local political leaders in Bosnia, Macedonia, Kosovo, and the union of Serbia and Montenegro shared certain common problems. First, they were power-sharing deals shaped by elite bargaining and therefore lacked popular legitimacy or a focus on implementing democratic rights. Second, they allocated power and resources to different ethnic or territorial groupings, thus focusing on collective rights, not individual rights. Third, they generally reinforced state weakness and the influence of nonstate and private actors (some of a criminal nature) by decentralizing power to various entities and localities (in Bosnia and Macedonia), to different federal units (in Serbia and Montenegro, before 2006), to unacceptable parallel structures (e.g., to the Serbs in Kosovo), or to powerful internationally appointed officials (in Kosovo and Bosnia).[32]

To address these problems quickly and assuage fears across the Western Balkans that the region might be left out of the EU integration process for the moment—particularly in view of the difficulties that EU members were having with their own constitutional framework—the International Commission on the Balkans argued that a combination of "classical state-building" policies (already under way in the area) and a "members' state-building" strategy (which would go beyond the sagging momentum of the EU accession process under the

32. International Commission on the Balkans, *The Balkans in Europe's Future* (Sofia: Center for Liberal Strategies, 2005), 15–17.

SAP mechanism) should be applied to jump-start democratic change and state development. Upon the completion of its very useful report, the commission still faced a dilemma that would continue though the next several years. The critical issue was how to overcome the considerable impediments to democratic state building in the Western Balkans and to advance the region toward EU accession, at a time when the EU member states themselves were faced with considerable difficulty finding an overarching constitutional model, and when considerable anxiety existed within the EU regarding the prospects of further enlargement. In 2008, the onset of the global economic crisis would further complicate the climate for smooth constitutional change in each country. The following section examines how governmental institution building in the Western Balkans had a direct bearing on the region's democratic consolidation and prospects for EU integration.

Interexecutive Rivalry and Reactive Parliaments: Balancing Power in Unfinished States

By the start of the twenty-first century, the Western Balkan states had traversed the first turbulent stage of postcommunist statehood and regime transition. A variety of constitutional frameworks and institutional mechanisms had already been established to express the democratic aspirations of the region's elites and citizens. The second transitional phase would therefore focus not on the tasks of democratic breakthrough and state formation but rather on the more routine issues of fine-tuning the structure and dynamics of democratic governance. And although the heightened involvement of the EU as an agent and monitor of change would be of critical importance, the challenge of improving the quality of governance necessary for building sustainable and stable democracies would depend largely on the region's own actors.

Nearly all the countries in the Western Balkans, just as most of the other postcommunist states, had adopted mixed or hybrid models of political governance, that is to say established polities in which executive power was divided between popularly elected and influential presidents on the one side, and prime ministers who were to be selected from, or responsible to, ruling party majorities and coalitions in the legislature on the other. Most of the region's political systems could therefore initially be defined as semipresidential or mixed presidential-parliamentary regimes. In terms of *formal* powers, there had been a trend toward vesting more authority in parliaments and heads of government, therefore tilting most systems in the region toward a "parliamentary-presidential" form of semipresidentialism. However, owing to the relative immaturity and fluidity of institutions in the region, as well as different formal and informal practices, and the rapidly changing balance of power between cohabiting executives—heads of state and heads of government—these regimes are quite difficult to categorize as anything but hybrid or eclectic forms of governance. And in the case of Bosnia-Herzegovina, with its rotating and directly elected tripartite Federal Presidency, as well as a rotating post of chairman of the Council of Ministers (only after 2002 did this prime-ministerial post get extended to a four year term), and its potentially powerful internationally appointed high representative, the constitutional system was designed principally as a mechanism to satisfy demands for balanced ethnic representation rather than to establish a coherent, efficient, and broadly legitimated model for governance.

The so-called syndrome of dual legitimacy in the Western Balkans and most other postcommunist states, whereby both heads of state *and* heads of government have substantial real or potential political powers, generally has created an inherent pattern of interexecutive rivalry in these polities.[33] At the minimum, such rivalry often weakens policy coherence and blurs lines of accountability, and at worst it creates polarization and deadlock in the system. The initial organizational and political turbulence in the postcommunist states of the Western Balkans, together with their highly fragmented party systems (see chapter 5) and typically zero-sum style of elite-level politics, have resulted

33. Juan Linz, "Presidential or Parliamentary Democracy: Does It Make a Difference?" in *The Failures of Presidential Democracy,* edited by Juan Linz and Arturo Valenzuela (Baltimore: Johns Hopkins University Press, 1994), 83–87; and Thomas A. Baylis, "Presidents versus Prime Ministers: Shaping Executive Authority in Eastern Europe" *World Politics* 38, no. 3 (April 1996): 297–323. See also Petr Kopecky, "Power to the Executive! The Changing Executive-Legislative Relation in Eastern Europe" *Journal of Legislative Studies* 10, nos. 2–3 (Autumn 2004): 142–53; Oleh Protsyk, "Politics of Intra-Executive Conflict in Semi-Presidential Regimes in Eastern Europe," *East European Politics and Societies* 19 (2005): 135–56; Mikhail Belaev, "Presidential Powers and Consolidation of New Post-Communist Democracies," *Comparative Political Studies* 39, no. 3 (2006): 375–98; and Elgie and Mostrup, *Semi-Presidentialism.*

in a complicated pattern of institutional development. Unfortunately, this pattern offers few insights pertinent to the vigorous debate among social scientists regarding the innate virtues or weaknesses of parliamentary systems vis-à-vis presidential systems.

In practice, throughout the Western Balkans, the reality of nascent institutional power struggles, both between and within different branches of government, reinforced by political and personal rivalries within the leadership structure of particular regimes, contributed to a pattern of persistent and sometimes intense interexecutive rivalry. In most cases, this pattern impeded the overall institutionalization of the regime and also undermined policy coordination. Granted, the political conflicts within the executive authority itself can be said to have pluralized the political system in comparison with the more monolithic power structure during the previous single party regime. But, except in Croatia (and then only tentatively), the character of institutional pluralism—or the separation and sharing of power, in practice—generally proved of relatively little assistance to the overall process of democratic consolidation. The transition from an authoritarian power structure to a pluralized power pattern had taken place, but, at least until 2010, the emergence of solidly legitimated polities with accountable and effective governance remained in the early stages.

Each state in the region has its own unique pattern of institutional evolution. For example, in Montenegro, where between 1991 and 2010 the dominant political leader, Milo Djukanović, has been prime minister four times, president once, and semiretired from late 2006 until February 2008 (but remaining president of the party in power), the locus of paramount executive power resided in one individual who kept changing posts. Conversely, Croatia and Serbia during the last decade provide illustrative examples of a rather complex, evolving, and frequently confused pattern of interexecutive power sharing and power struggles.

For example, as mentioned above, not long after the death of President Tudjman in 1999, Croatia moved to eliminate the semipresidential model. But the presidency remained a directly elected post, and its incumbent—the popular politician Stipe Mesić (who had broken with Tudjman in 1994 on the issue of excessive executive authority)—continued to exercise considerable informal influence. Mesić had cooperated with the new prime minister, Ivica Račan, the Social Democratic Party (Socijaldemokratska partija, SDP) leader who had won the 2000 legislative elections, to push through new constitutional amendments that also strengthened the legislature and the post of prime minister. But Mesić was determined that the presidency would not become a ceremonial one, simply reduced to performing protocol duties. Thus, during the constitutional debate, he intervened to make sure that the president would retain substantial power over the intelligence services and foreign affairs, as well as remain the commander in chief of the armed forces. He did scale back the trappings of presidential power, including a reduction in the size of the president's office staff. But in exercising the powers that he managed to retain, he shrewdly utilized the popular legitimacy deriving from the presidency's direct election. Mesic's independence and activism elicited considerable support. As one of Croatia's most astute analysts remarked at the end of 2004 in an interview with a Belgrade newspaper: "If Zagreb had a president who was elected in Parliament, Croatia today would not [have troops] in Iraq, our state would have signed a treaty that Americans would be exempted from trial for war crimes, generals who mix in politics would still be in the army, the affairs of the secret services would be kept totally secret."[34]

Beginning in 2000, the post of prime minister in Croatia, which drew its legitimacy from elections and the legislature, acquired new powers. But the fact that the incumbent was leading a coalition government considerably limited his personal power. Still, the opposition leader at the time, Ivo Sanader—the head of Tudjman's previously ruling party, the HDZ—suggested in 2001 that after two years of post-Tudjman government, Croatia had really not changed from a semipresidential into a parliamentary system, and that power now resided in a kind of quasi-presidential government in which the prime minister used the parliament as simply "voting machinery."[35]

Sanader would be elected prime minister in 2002 (Račan became opposition leader and served until his death in 2007), and he would subsequently coexist quite successfully with President Mesić, who was reelected as president in 2005 (to serve until early 2010). And although the two Croatian political executives had minor differences with respect to foreign policy—Mesić was more oriented toward Europeanization, while Sanader was an adherent of balancing between the EU and the

34. Interview with Ivan Šiber, *Politika,* December 24, 2004.
35. *HINA,* December 18, 2001.

United Nations—their differences were nothing like the contentious elite-level problems in some other Western Balkan states. Thus, Croatia had progressed successfully out of its "imperial" presidential model (which really made the Tudjman system more superpresidential than semipresidential), and had begun operating as a mixed system from the perspective of executive power.

Meanwhile, the oversight functions of the Croatian legislature (Sabor) were strengthened in 2000, although the fact that the legislature "did not yet possess a stable core of seasoned and competent representatives" put it at a clear disadvantage in relation to the executive branch.[36] Still, the "conflicting cooperation" between the two political executives in the country, and the fact that the multiparty legislature had slowly begun to function in a more vital manner than it had earlier, significantly improved the functioning of democratic pluralism in Croatia.[37]

When Sanader abruptly resigned the prime ministership in mid-2009, it appeared that the country would face the global economic crisis, and the final stages of the EU preaccession process, with the same interexecutive dualism that had persisted throughout the previous decade. Throughout 2009, a new and untested prime minister, Jadranka Kosor, seemed to be working effectively with President Mesić. Although Mesić critically described the ruling HDZ's hasty choice of Kosor to be head of the party as a "reduction of democracy" in the country, the criticism may have derived from the fact that Mesić had split away from the HDZ many years before and planned to form another party after leaving the office of president.

The effectiveness of Croatia's leadership succession process and pattern of executive cohabitation took a positive turn at the beginning of 2010, when the moderate and democratically oriented Ivo Josipović, from the SDP, won the country's presidential election. Initially, there was some tension between the prime minister and the new president regarding their respective political roles and powers. However, Josipović did

36. Vlasta Ilišin, "Hrvatski Sabor 2000: Struktura značajke i promjene," *Politička misao* 38, no. 2 (2001): 42–67.

37. Nenad Zakošek, *Politički sustav Hrvatske* (Zagreb: Fakultet političkih znanosti, 2002), 98–124. See also Siniša Rodin, "The Croatian Parliament in Transition: From Authoritarian Past to European Future," in *National and Regional Parliaments in the European Constitutional Order,* edited by Philipp Kiiver (Groningen: Europa Law Publishing, 2006), 98–113.

not hesitate to come out strongly against a proposed law to restrict his powers, and he left little doubt that he intended to continue the activist presidential role of his predecessor. He also substantially increased the size of the presidential staff, and took a number of controversial foreign policy initiatives aimed at achieving interstate reconciliation in the region. And he downplayed reports that his criticism of the HDZ, the prime minister's party, had been excessive. "I will continue to criticize them as well as to praise them when they deserve praise," Josipović remarked."[38] But gradually, interexecutive problems in Zagreb appeared to be smoothed out. Moreover, when former prime minister Sanader awkwardly and unsuccessfully tried to return to political life following the presidential race, he was quickly forced out of the HDZ, and Kosor emerged as a stronger figure in her own right as prime minister (she also purged Sanader supporters in Croatia's elite structure). Overall, the pattern of executive succession to both Sanader and Mesić reflected Croatia's substantial institutional stability and relative success at consolidating democracy.[39]

The structure of governance within the Federal Republic of Yugoslavia following the end of Milošević's superpresidential rule left the organization of executive authority very unclear. Indeed, extensive interexecutive rivalry would emerge as a dominant feature of Serbian political life, along with the difficulty of overcoming the legacy of the recent past. Vojislav Koštunica had defeated Milošević in the presidential election of September 2000, which precipitated the fall of the authoritarian regime, and would serve as the FRY's president until March 2004. However, Koštunica would soon be challenged by a rival power base, namely the Office of the Prime Minister of Serbia, which was headed—after the democratic coalition's sweep in the early 2000 election—by Zoran Djindjić, who was Koštunica's longtime rival in Serbian democratic opposition politics. When Djindjić extradited Milošević to The Hague in mid-2001 in defiance of federal authorities, Koštunica's influence was seriously weakened. The growing division between the FRY's two federal units, Serbia and the much smaller Montenegro (headed

38. *Vjesnik,* May 24, 2010.
39. Josipović dismissed reports that his initial steps in office were aimed at "overthrowing the government." As he put it: "I have good relations with Prime Minister Jadranka Kosor, but I would say that we are still seeking the right modus vivendi." *Vjesnik,* March 14, 2010.

by the popular president, Milo Djukanović, who would serve in that post from 1998 to June 2003), also undercut Koštunica's authority and weakened the role of the Federation. Meanwhile Djindjić, although not personally very popular with the Serbian public, was politically strengthened. He enjoyed good relations with the Montenegrin regime, maintained influence in the Serbian police and media, and found support among many of the democratically oriented parties within the Serbian Parliament.

The intense executive-level rivalry in Serbia and the FRY at the time was based on both personality and philosophy. On one hand, the internationally oriented and fast-moving Djindjić was more of a reform pragmatist, who embraced an essentially liberal democratic notion of patriotism (although he could play the nationalist card on occasion). On the other hand, Koštunica was essentially a conservative nationalist devoted to continuity with legitimate authority, anticommunism, and Serbian national-religious traditions. He was also very skeptical regarding the intentions of foreign countries (especially those in NATO).

Moreover, interexecutive rivalry in the FRY and in Serbia was primarily a question of the relationship between offices at two different levels of the federal system—the FRY's president, Koštunica, and Serbia's prime minister, Djindjić (the FRY's own prime ministerial office was quite weak and rather irrelevant, and the incumbent occupying the Serbian presidency initially was in disgrace owing to his earlier association with Milošević). This unique pattern of hierarchical interexecutive polarization was further complicated when the FRY was dissolved and replaced by the EU-negotiated state union of Serbia and Montenegro in early 2003. Koštunica left his position as federal president, and he was replaced by a weak union-level president (the loose union would subsequently dissolve in 2006, when Montenegro declared its independence).

For the moment, Zoran Djindjić seemed to hold the advantage. But the prime minister was tragically assassinated shortly afterward, creating an entirely new power equilibrium in Serbia. Djindjić's successor as prime minister, Zoran Živković, proved to be politically weak, as was Koštunica's successor as head of the nearly powerless state union, Svetozar Marović. Matters were only partially normalized in late 2003 and the first part of 2004 when Koštunica, in a turnaround of political fortunes, was elected prime minister of Serbia. Meanwhile, Boris Tadić assumed the post of president of Serbia, and a new phase of interexecutive rivalry began in Serbia during the period 2004–8. Tadić viewed himself as heir to the policy priorities of Djindjić. Thus, although inheriting a relatively weak post as Serbian president, Tadić became the natural political and institutional rival of Koštunica.

The post-2000 pattern of political instability, blocked reform, and leadership polarization in both the FRY and Serbia also took its toll on the development of Serbia's legislature. Thus the legislature's institutional strengthening was undermined during the 2001–4 period, and even atrophied in some respects compared to the Milošević period when the opposition was quite active.[40] For example, not only was the government dominant in initiating legislation, but the extent and quality of legislative activity diminished as the parties in Djindjić's ruling coalition, fearing for their survival and power, instructed their deputies not to put pressure on the government. The increasing use of accelerated procedures for the passage of legislation also was an indication of legislative weakness. Moreover, Djindjić's quasi-presidential style of exercising prime ministerial power in Serbia, and also his feud with Koštunica, would lead him to use high-handed methods in dealing with the Serbian Assembly. For example, in June 2002, Djindjić arranged the expulsion of twenty-one deputies representing the Democratic Party of Serbia (Demokratska stranka Srbije, DSS) for failing to attend parliamentary sessions. Djindjić employed a law whereby political party organizations in Serbia controlled their elected deputies, and technically Koštunica's DSS was part of the Djindjić-headed coalition, the Democratic Opposition of Serbia (Demokratska opozicija Srbije), which had triumphed in the 2001 elections. In response to Djindjić's move, all forty-five deputies from the DSS walked out of the Serbian Assembly (the party had already pulled out of the government in August 2001). Djindjić had essentially changed the composition of the Serbian legislature in a "parliamentary coup" that disqualified the participation of deputies from Koštunica's DSS.

Such problems in the Serbian Assembly—along with the egregious acts of incivility by members of the ultranationalist SRS, various corruption scandals, and rampant party factionalism—diminished the institutional capacity of the legislature and also undermined popular trust in the legislative process. In May 2003, a Constitutional Court

40. Slobodan Antonić, "Skupština Srbije danas," *Nova Srpska Politička Misao, Analiza* 1, no. 1 (2005): 13–22.

decision voided the law that allowed parties to control deputies, and this somewhat improved the functioning of the legislature. But the temporary boycott of the legislature by deputies of Tadić's Democratic Party (Demokratska stranka, DS) in the fall of 2005 further indicated the deep political fragmentation of the country, impaired legislative development, and also weakened the consolidation of institutional balance essential to a democratic polity.

However, as the question of Kosovo's future status grew in significance during 2006 and 2007, Prime Minister Koštunica and President Tadić grudgingly cooperated in order to present a superficial united front. This shallow alliance of convenience proved very effective in the adoption of a new Serbian Constitution in late 2006, which described Kosovo as being an integral part of Serbia. But when Tadić's DS received the largest share of the vote in the January 2007 Serbian election, the executive-level conflict reopened, along with a several-month interparty power struggle over the formation of a new government. And although Tadić had fewer powers compared with the prime minister and government, he embodied the continuity of governance. As one observer noted during the prolonged effort to organize a new government, "Until the new Assembly and government are constituted, the lines of all our institutions converge in the office that President Tadić discharges."[41]

The presidential / prime ministerial standoff in independent Serbia continued through early 2007. This was hardly an anomalous situation, considering the chronic difficulties of government formation that have followed elections in Serbia's fragmented multiparty environment, and the subsequently long periods of executive and legislative drift. The aforementioned election in May 2007 of the leader of the ultra-nationalist SRS, Tomislav Nikolić, as speaker of the Serbian Assembly convulsed Serbia's already deeply fragmented political process and shocked the international community. It also did not auger well for the country's legislative process. Nikolić was notorious for his chronic verbal harassment of other members of Parliament in the past, and also of individuals who held different views or were of non-Serbian ethnic backgrounds. But when it quickly appeared that Nikolić might use the interlude of a caretaker government, and also the new constitutional powers of the Parliament, in an authoritarian manner—by declaring a

41. Predrag Simić, *Večernje novosti,* February 9, 2007.

state of emergency to deal with the matter of Kosovo's potential independence—the democratic parties, at the eleventh hour, formed a new
government.

But even after the democratically oriented political parties formed
a marriage of convenience coalition government in May 2007, centered on Tadić's DS and Koštunica's DSS, it appeared that members
of the two-party constellation within the Cabinet often functioned as
parallel governments. In the usual Serbian executive-level deal making
between rivals, President Tadić retained control over defense and intelligence matters, while Vojislav Koštunica continued as prime minister.
Serbia's uneasy pattern of interexecutive cohabitation continued, but
now the political-institutional balance of power had shifted. Prime
Minister Koštunica was in second place in Serbia's political hierarchy,
with President Tadić in an informally much stronger position owing to
his party's greater representation in the National Assembly, and also
his substantial foreign support. Unfortunately, the rebalancing of executive power within the "democratic bloc" was not accompanied by
a close working partnership between Serbia's top two leaders and between their respective parties. And although the issue of government
formation had been resolved, Serbia again lost valuable time that could
have been used for reform. For example, the legislature was not able to
pass a single law from January to May 2007.

President Tadić's political clout in Serbia improved considerably after
the clear electoral victory in May 2008 of the party coalition headed by
his DS (in which he retained the position of party president). The wider
democratic forces were still not very cohesive, but Tadić had been able
to assume control of the country without the support of Koštunica,
and during 2009 and 2010 he enhanced his informal influence over the
legislature and governmental structure. Mirko Cvetković, the new prime
minister, was from Tadić's DS and was regarded as a nonambitious
technocrat carrying out presidential directions. "Unofficially," wrote
one Serbian analyst, "Tadić is practically a head of state, a premier, a
police minister and a foreign minister. He distributes money from the
budget, puts forth economic measures to curb the crisis, he commands
the army and as someone put it, edits major media."[42] Tadić's highly
presidentialized form of parliamentary system has been less charitably

42. Ivan Torov, "Strong President, Weak-State," *Helsinki Charter,* nos. 125–26
(December 2008).

described by members of the opposition in Serbia as a "democratically enlightened dictatorship" or as a "dictatorship with a typical presidential system."[43]

The extent to which executive-level institutional struggles impeded or facilitated state building and the gradual emergence of pluralist politics varied from polity to polity. In Serbia throughout most of the post-2000 period, a pattern of persistent and deep intra-elite and interparty polarization, and also the considerable confusion that accompanied the frequent reorganization and multiplication of state ministries and institutions, resulted in episodic political paralysis, popular disenchantment with the political class, and considerable discontinuity in policymaking. The situation improved after 2008, as President Boris Tadić acquired a more hegemonic role in the political executive sector, but this was tied to his personal role so that the further institutionalization of executive roles and their accountability to the public remained an outstanding challenge.[44]

In Croatia and most of the other Western Balkan states, the course of democratic consolidation was also influenced and disrupted by the political dynamics and tensions characterizing interexecutive relations, and the often complicated admixture of institutional powers within the state structure, but less severely than in the case of Serbia. Throughout the region, the intensity of conflict stemming from executive dualism and the unclear locus of power in the state usually depended less on constitutional rules and more on the personalities filling the top political posts, the prevailing political situation, and the evolving alignment of power among political parties. And overall, the shifting character of executive powers did very little to lessen the overall dominance of executive institutions in relation to relatively weak and only slowly developing legislatures. Western Balkan assemblies have become more

43. *Tanjug,* October 6, 2009.
44. For the evolving and highly personalized nature of Serbia's presidency, see Nenad Rava, "The Role of Presidency in Ensuring Accountability, Professionalism, Transparency, and Legitimacy of the Policy Process—The Case of Serbia," paper presented at Annual Conference of Network of Institutes and Schools of Public Administration in Central and Eastern Europe, Ljubljana, April 2006; and Christina Dallara and Irena Marčeta, "Serbia in Stability and Accountability," in *Democratization and the European Union: Comparing Central and East European Post-Communist Countries,* edited by Leonardo Morlino and Wojciech Sadurski (London: Routledge, 2010), 123–46.

stable in recent years owing to a pronounced decrease in party fragmentation and volatility (see chapter 5). But the character of party competition has not generally improved the overall oversight of executives (presidents or prime ministers) by legislators, or the "quality" of democracy.[45]

Therefore, from a positive perspective, the interexecutive and institutional contestation within these Western Balkan regimes described above at least has helped to forestall the reemergence of unchallenged or absolute power by any single political personality or institution. Indeed, within the context of the fragmented legislative assemblies and new party systems during much of the postcommunist transition period, it could also be argued that the assertion of political executive power, whether emanating from the office of presidents or from prime ministers and their cabinets, was helpful for overall economic development and state cohesion in these countries.

For example, in ethnically divided Macedonia, the hybrid or dual political executive model that evolved may have served the country better than the constitutionally provided allocation of dominant power to the institutions of Parliament and the prime minister. Thus, as mentioned above, the first directly elected president, Kiro Gligorov, although constitutionally quite weak, enjoyed considerable influence as a respected and strong political figure from the Titoist era. Gligorov would play an influential role until 1999, although gradually his involvement in decisionmaking diminished and his position became more "symbolic."[46]

The next president, the less experienced and less charismatic Boris Trajkovski of the Internal Macedonian Revolutionary Organization–Democratic Party for Macedonian National Unity (Vnatrešna makedonska revolucionerna organizacija–Demokratska partija za makedonsko nacionalno edinstvo, VMRO-DPMNE), was initially overshadowed by an incumbent prime minister. But Trajkovski emerged to play an important role in helping to contain the interethnic crisis of 2001, where recent research has also indicated that the Macedonian Parliament

45. Martin Brusis, "The Quality of Democracy in Market Economy in Southeast Europe," *Sudosteuropa: Zeitschrift fur Politik und Gesellschaft,* nos. 2–3 (2009): 146–67.

46. François Frison-Roche, "Semi-Presidentialism in the Republic of Macedonia (former Yugoslavian Republic of Macedonia)," in *Semi-Presidentialism,* ed. Elgie and Mostrup.

exercised a mainly reactive rather than a proactive influence in conflict management.[47]

After Trajkovski's untimely death in a plane crash, former prime minister Branko Crvenkovski of the Social Democratic Union (Socijaldemokratski sojuz na Makedonija, SDSM) was elected president. His experience as a former prime minister, his leadership of a major governing party for twelve years, and the fact that the new prime minister had no political base all strengthened the semipresidential features of Macedonia's technically parliamentary system. But when another stronger figure in the SDSM, Vlado Bučkovski, assumed the post of prime minister in 2004, interexecutive rivalry again asserted itself. In 2007, Bučkovski's successor as prime minister, Nikola Gruevski of VMRO-DPMNE, maintained that he would observe the constitutional pattern of "executive cohabitation," but that President Crvenkovski had only "insignificant powers." He went on to say that any interexecutive sparring was only normal interparty competition in the long run-up to the 2009 presidential election.[48]

The parliamentary component of executive cohabitation was strengthened in 2009 when Gjorge Ivanov, a relatively politically weak member of Prime Minister Crvenkovski's own party, was elected to the formally weak presidential post. After a hundred days as president, Ivanov's office produced a pamphlet to inventory his activities. But Macedonian analysts concluded that he was a "marginal figurehead," who was weaker than all previous presidents.[49] In September 2010, the president also lost some of his previous authority over the country's intelligence services. Macedonia had clearly become more parliamentary in operation, although it had a directly elected president. But overall, the "plasticity" of executive cohabitation between prime ministers and presidents in Macedonia since 1990 has not proven to be an impediment to the country's fragile democracy.[50]

47. Sašo Ordanoski, "UNDP's Global Conference on Strengthening Parliaments in Conflict-Post-Conflict Situations: Case Study—Macedonian Parliament," April 2005, Draft Report. A report in early 2009 found that only 25 members of Parliament out of 120 were regularly present in the Parliament from July to December. MAXFAX, January 19, 2010.

48. *MIA,* May 26, 2007.

49. *Dnevnik,* August 22, 2009, in *BBC Monitoring Service,* August 26, 2009; *Nova Makedonija,* September 24, 2010.

50. Frison-Roche, "Semi-Presidentialism."

A similar form of executive contestation was also apparent in Kosovo and Albania, both technically parliamentary regimes, but with presidents elected in the legislature. Thus, during 2006 and 2007, Kosovo, though still a protectorate with provisional institutions, experienced a "silent" tug of war between President Fatmir Sejdu on the one side and Prime Minister Agim Çeku on the other. Sejdu, who belongs to the Democratic League of Kosovo (Lidhja Demokratike e Kosovës, LDK) and is a constitutional lawyer, had been the ally and successor of the highly respected President Ibrahim Rugova, who died in 2006. Çeku was a member of the Alliance for the Future of Kosovo (Aleanca për Ardhmërinë e Kosovës), a former military officer in the Kosovo Liberation Army, and had strong ties to his former comrades in arms. But Çeku emphasized that his main preoccupation was governing and that he had little time "to engage in party issues."[51] And he also pointed out the critical factor that kept interexecutive conflict to a minimum in Kosovo until 2008: "I sometimes meet the president, the Assembly speaker three or four times a day. Every Monday at 9 we have a meeting with the president, and we examine the weekly agenda, the weekly positions, if we have any visitors, what position we should maintain if we go outside Kosova. I have good cooperation with the opposition leaders, too. . . . Politics is politics, . . . and the most important thing is that we have one hundred percent consensus and consent on the great issue of [Kosova's] status."[52]

After Kosovo's independence was declared in early 2008, a new phase opened in executive evolution, but rivalry between executives was initially muted by the formation of a grand coalition between the Party of Democratic Progress (Partija demokratskog progresa, PDP) of Prime Minister Hashim Thaçi and the Liberal Democratic Party (Liberalno-demokratska partija, LDP) of President Sejdu. During 2009, as political relations between the PDP and LDP deteriorated, a less unified pattern of coexistence developed between Sejdu and Thaçi. But "institutional relations" between the two executives remained civil in public, and the two executives continued to meet regularly once a week without media for a discussion over coffee. The chilly pattern of executive relations in the governing coalition and the divided nature of international

---

51. *Koha Ditore,* January 5, 2007, via World News Connection.
52. Ibid.

and domestic authority, however, created considerable ambiguity about where the locus of political power actually resided in the new state.[53] Near the end of September 2010, Kosovo's new institutions passed a key test—smooth legal succession—when President Sejdu quickly resigned in response to a Constitutional Court decision that he had breached the Constitution by simultaneously holding both the post of state president and that of LDK party president. The speaker of the Parliament temporarily assumed the role of acting president.

Meanwhile, the Albanian political system, although parliamentary in form, has been characterized by overt semipresidential features. Thus, early in postcommunist development, Sali Berisha of the Democratic Party (Partia Demokratike, PD), who served as president from 1992 to 1997 (and who was elected prime minister in September 2005), was able to exercise quasi-dictatorial powers despite the fact that his office was formally quite weak. Their exercise, even after the 1994 defeat of his constitutional referendum to expand his formal powers, exacerbated the drift toward the financial collapse in 1997 that forced Berisha to resign. More recently, President Alfred Moisu, a respected figure from the former Communist regime who was elected president in 2002, crossed political swords with Prime Minister Fatos Nano of the Socialist Party (Partia Socialiste e Shqipërisë), with regard to the latter's alleged abuse of excessive powers. Moisu also became involved in a struggle with the next prime minister, again Sali Berisha, over the president's refusal to remove the attorney general, who had been accused of crimes by the Berisha government and the Parliament. In March 2007, Berisha refused to attend a ceremony for the swearing in of his own ministers in the president's office, using the pretext that Moisu had violated the Constitution. But Berisha publicly asserted that Albania was a "functioning democracy," and in May 2007 he even congratulated the opposition for "exercising its constitutional rights" and demanding a vote of confidence on his performance as prime minister.[54]

The continued importance of the two top executive posts in Albania surfaced once again when interparty wrangling broke out in the sum-

---

53. In early 2010, Prime Minister Thaçi resigned as a member of Parliament in order to pursue his duties in a more "efficient" manner. *KosovaLive,* February 12, 2010. Should the new pattern continue, Kosovo will have two not popularly elected political-state executives.

54. *Albania,* May 12, 2007, via World News Connection.

mer of 2007 concerning who would succeed President Moisu. Bamir Topi, a member of Berisha's PD, was elected in July. In mid-2008, however, Berisha and Topi became embroiled in a conflict over the latter's use of decree powers to nominate judges to the High Court of Justice. When President Topi made nominations to the Court without consulting Berisha, a tug of war ensued that was ultimately won by the prime minister. Topi called the move a "political execution" after the prime minister broadened the consultation process through the formation of a group of experts, and he was able to get his judicial nominees approved in the legislature.

To some extent, the interexecutive institutional and personality clashes in Albania resemble similar tensions found elsewhere in the Western Balkans and other states, and are part of normal political dynamics and power struggles that characterize democratic political life. Whether or not such struggles contribute to democratic consolidation depends on the length and character of such conflicts. When overbearing and over-reacting executives such as Berisha are present, such conflicts are far more likely to occur and to detract from democratic development. In any event, in June 2009, Berisha was reelected to office in a controversial and close election (see chapter 5). The sharp polarization in the wake of the election, which continued throughout the first part of 2010, allowed President Topi to assume a higher-profile political role. Thus, at the urging of the EU, he was asked to mediate between the ruling government coalition and the opposition parties who were boycotting the legislature.

In Bosnia, the role of a strong externally mandated and guided political executive—the Office of the High Representative—has, together with other factors, made the framework of governance a unique and cumbersome structure. At the minimum, however, the unusual political system in Bosnia has helped to dampen violent conflict within a deeply divided society. But considerable potential for political competition, along with obstruction and deadlock both within and between Bosnia's political executive bodies, is built into the structure of the Dayton Accords. Total paralysis in Bosnia has been avoided due to the fact that the most powerful executive post, that of the high representative, is filled by a foreign appointee. This gives the political system a superpresidential character in practice. For example, between December 1997 and December 2008, the high representative fired or suspended 174 officials in the country for various offences (about half for noncompliance with The Hague Tribunal's search for war crime fugitives). Moreover, because the political deadlock among representatives of the three constituent peoples typically has led to inertia in the legislative organs of the country, the OHR, as mentioned above, has imposed much of the legislation necessary for the functioning of the state (see table 2.1). Moreover, a great many of the laws were only adopted as a result of "arm-twisting policies exerted by representatives of the international community . . . secretly and publicly exerted pressure, even blackmail, on behalf of the OHR, the [Organization for Security and Cooperation in Europe], the embassies of PIC member states, etc."[55]

As a result of such tactics, the OHR's special powers have been widely criticized for obstructing the emergence of a responsible and cooperative form of interethnic politics within the country, as the basis for homegrown democratic development. Paddy Ashdown, perhaps the most proactive occupant of the OHR (who served from May 2002 to January 2006), conceded that the extent of his authority "ought to make a liberal blush." And he also claimed that the near-dictatorial power he enjoyed constituted a "nuclear option" to break internal deadlocks and prevent the resumption of violence in the country.[56]

The ultimately failed constitutional reform package that was debated in 2005 and 2006 had been designed to move Bosnia toward a more parliamentary form of government by creating a single president, who along with two vice presidents would be indirectly elected by the legislature and who would govern for a longer term. Presidential powers would also have been reduced under the proposed reform. Under this proposal, the prime minister would have presided over a strengthened government and had the power to dismiss the Council of Ministers. The power of Bosnia's two entities and their top executives would also have been significantly reduced. But, as mentioned above, the proposal for constitutional revision was scuttled in April 2006 by the very obstructionist nationalist politics the reform was designed to eliminate. In early 2006, in a move that also bears on the evolution of executive authority,

55. Esref Kenan Rašidagić, "Government Effectiveness and Accountability," in *Democratic Assessment in Bosnia and Herzegovina* (Sarajevo: Open Society Fund Bosnia and Herzegovina, 2006), 204.

56. "Occupational Hazard in Post-War Bosnia: Overruling Voters to Save Democracy," *Wall Street Journal Online,* October 1, 2004.

the Peace Implementation Council that guides Bosnia's evolution on behalf of the international community replaced the extremely activist OHR occupant, Ashdown, who had served for forty-four months, with a new incumbent, Christian Schwarcz-Schilling, who adopted a less assertive interpretation of his responsibilities. At this point in time, there was speculation that the entire OHR would soon be phased out. In his final address to the Bosnian legislature, Ashdown remarked that the "'backstop' of a high representative in position has often been adopted by all sides as a default position. Bosnia and Herzegovina's politicians feel free to argue the case from one side, without any effort to build consensus, secure in the knowledge that in the end the high representative would ride to the rescue."[57]

The impasse over Bosnian constitutional reform, along with the country's continued ethnic-political fragmentation, and also widespread dissatisfaction with the initially laid-back and subsequently inconsistent style of Schwarcz-Schilling, Ashdown's successor as high representative, led to the decision in 2007 to extend the OHR for a limited period, but with a new incumbent (Miroslav Lajčák of Slovakia did in fact assume the post on June 30, 2007). High Representative Schwarcz-Schilling, chafing under criticism of his style, and particularly the fact that he had not been aggressive enough, defended his approach: "Since I took up my duties in February 2006, I deliberately chose not to follow the interventionist approach of my predecessors, opting instead for a policy of local ownership. . . . I have stuck to that principle. . . . Some critics are now demanding a return to the policy of international intervention, thereby throwing out the baby with the bathwater. It is, however, a dangerous illusion to think that it is possible to build a functional state, revive the economy, and foster reconciliation by imposition. Institutions and democratic processes will only function if the country's citizens buy into them."[58]

The severity of Bosnia's institutional and political cleavages was illustrated again in June 2007, when the Muslim and Croat members of the tripartite state Federal Presidency took it upon themselves to write directly to the UN secretary-general—ignoring the Presidency's Bosnian Serb member, who was serving as chairman—and asked for

---

57. Quoted by *BBC Worldwide Monitoring,* January 21, 2006.
58. Office of the High Representative and EU Special Representative, "Bosnia's Road to Ownership," February 24, 2007.

help in nullifying the result of the "genocide verdict" of not guilty against Bosnian Serbs. This move was directed against the Serb entity, and it was connected with the recent International Court of Justice decision regarding the role of that entity and Serbia in the Srebrenica massacre. Schwarcz-Schilling, less than ten days before the end of his OHR term, condemned the letter for contributing to the "deterioration of political relations in the country." The isolated Serb member of the Presidency described the letter as an attempt to "destroy the country's constitutional system."[59] Faced with persistent executive deadlock in Bosnia, the PIC decided to grant Schwarcz-Schilling's successor a broad mandate to address the situation during his term.

Unfortunately, the next high representative, Miroslav Lajčák, made little headway in addressing the basic deficiencies of Bosnia's political system. Not only had the climate for interentity and interethnic cooperation deteriorated, but the United States and the international community were also very distracted by the wars in Iraq and Afghanistan, along with other regional problems. Lajčák tried to nurture change in the country, but he was continuously frustrated by local politicians. "The state functions," he explained, "but it's like a car with square tires."[60] Despite Lajčák's difficulties, his tenure did coincide with some renewed discussion of constitutional reforms by the country's divided political class.

In November 2008, several months after Bosnia had made sufficient progress to be allowed access to the EU's Stabilization and Association Process, a new discussion of constitutional matters gained momentum. This time, however, the constitution-making discussion was dominated by the leaders of the three main ethnically oriented political parties. Thus, the so-called Prud trio (named after the location of their first meeting), reached agreement on a number of points (e.g., on state property, conducting a census, reconstructing the Council of Ministers, and forming a decentralized system of governance with four territorial units). But their very shallow consensus soon evaporated into reciprocal bickering about details, and the momentum of the Prud Process

59. Deutsche Presse-Agentur, June 19, 2007; *BBC Worldwide Monitoring,* June 19, 2007.

60. Quoted by Tina Wolfe, "Bosnia Struggles to Contain Sectarianism," *World Politics Review,* March 10, 2008.

quickly petered out. In July 2009, a new OHR occupant, Valentin Inzko, declared the Prud Process to be "dead, in a way."[61]

Both domestic and international observers continued, however, to seek a way forward with regard to constitutional reform. Some in the international community—probably overestimating what foreign experts can achieve—suggested that a new Dayton-type international conference be held to redesign Bosnia's constitutional architecture. Others believed that Bosnia's speedier advancement in the EU accession process, and its entry into NATO, would provide the momentum for changes. Many domestic political actors in the country felt that all externally guided strategies to establish a model for governance were doomed to fail, lacked a solid rooting in the country, and indeed smacked of imperialism. Views also differed about when the OHR should be phased out, recognizing that such a development must occur before the country could enter the European Union (although not necessarily during the preaccession phase). Perhaps the only matter on which broad agreement has existed is that Bosnia badly needed more functional institutions of governance, and also a new generation of leaders who would be willing to cooperate. In early October 2009, anxious for Bosnia to finally break out of its persistent syndrome of dysfunctionality, representatives of the United States and the EU convened a meeting of domestic party leaders to discuss constitutional reform. Four issues closely resembling the failed April 2006 package were at the forefront of the "new" effort (the so-called Butmir Proposals):

- Changes to eliminate overlap between the Federal Presidency and the Council of Ministers by dissolving the current three-person rotating Presidency and replacing it with a largely ceremonial institution headed by a single president and two vice presidents.
- Broadening the powers of the Council of Ministers to give it paramount authority with regard to EU integration.
- Increasing the size of the House of Representatives in the central legislature from forty-two seats to eighty-seven, with three of the seats guaranteed for ethnic minorities. It was hoped that a larger

61. Bosnian Serb Television, Banja Luka, July 19, 2009, in *BBC Worldwide Monitoring,* July 20, 2009.

number of deputies would assist in creating a more rapid legislative process (the House of Peoples would grow from fifteen to
twenty-one members).

• Undertaking a controversial initiative to reduce the significance
of the "entity vote" or "entity veto" by stripping the House of
Peoples of its legislative role, and the possibility of the entities
blocking legislation by invoking the notion of a threat to the vital
national interest.

Once again, it appeared that the crucial factor influencing the success
or failure of reform in Bosnia would be the attitudes and behavior of
Bosnia's principal political actors. High Representative Inzko put the
challenge succinctly: "Dayton was certainly the best constitution that
could have been written at an airport within a space of three weeks.
Above all, it put an end to the war and to people's suffering. But that
was fourteen years ago. Now the time is ripe for further steps. I hope
this is clear to the Bosnian politicians, too."[62] Unfortunately, such clarity was absent, and after the usual round of interentity and interethnic
sparring, the Butmir Process ran out of steam. In December, Željko
Komšić, the Croat chairing the country's Federal Presidency, claimed
that the latest constitutional reform package "had turned into a farce,"
and was "absolutely dead."[63] Although international officials involved
in the constitutional initiative did not share Komšić's view, temporarily most politicians in Bosnia and foreign officials hoped that the 2010
elections would create a new momentum for reform. Meanwhile, the
term of the high representative was extended until August 2011, although it was widely felt in the international community that the continued use of the Bonn Powers and Bosnia's heavy dependence on the
OHR were basically inconsistent with the country's eventual accession
to the EU.[64]

62. Die Presse.com, October 15, 2009.

63. Bosnia-Herzegovina Federation Public TV, December 5, 2009, in *BBC
Monitoring Europe,* December 7, 2009.

64. A 2010 poll indicated that 78 percent of Bosniaks in Bosnia support the ab-
olition of the entity level of government, as opposed to 9 percent of the Serbs in the
country (46 percent of whom desire the status quo). A majority of Croats (53 percent) prefer the formation of a third Croat entity. National Democratic Institute,
Public Opinion Poll: Bosnia and Herzegovina (BiH), August 2010 (Sarajevo:
National Democratic Institute, 2010), 42.

During 2009 and 2010, Bosnia's institutional structures remained deeply fractured and weakly legitimated. If a solution could not be found for Bosnia's problems, the country would be in danger of falling behind its Western Balkan neighbors on the road to EU membership, if not worse. Florian Bieber correctly observed that the county faced a serious crisis, but that it was wrong to attempt "quick crisis-style constitutional changes to overcome the current impasse, the emphasis should be on what the EU does best: process. How can there be confidence in Bosnian institutions if decisions are taken by party leaders under international supervision, far from parliament." Bieber aptly suggested a more incremental approach that would focus on matters less controversial than eliminating entity voting in order to "open the door" to constitutional change.[65] But even if Bosnia somehow succeeded in a constitutional makeover in either 2010 or 2011, the testing of new institutions to advance the country's functionality still lay ahead, whether outside or inside the European Union. One thing was clear: In view of what had happened in Bosnia during the 1990s, progress at building a more coherent and functional state had become a critical matter if the state was to survive.

Impressive Edifice, Troubled Dynamics

At the end of 2010, each state in the Western Balkans region had its specific pressing constitutional and institutional difficulties. Considerable institutional innovation, experimentation, and progress had occurred in the region during the post-2000 period, but the short-run and long-term challenges in the future remained formidable. The problems of fine-tuning constitutions, elaborating effective organizational frameworks, passing legislation, and balancing executive powers continued to be an important part of the overall state-building struggle. For example, the ongoing confusion over the locus of authority in Kosovo, and also the tentative legitimacy of the Ohrid framework in Macedonia, reflected the fragile constitutional settlements in those countries, although arguably they did not pose as much of a threat to state cohesion

---

65. Florian Bieber, "Dayton Bosnia May Be Over—but What Next?" *Balkan Insight,* December 10, 2009.

as the chronic decisionmaking paralysis in Bosnia. Meanwhile, Croatia, Albania, Montenegro, and Serbia were all far better off with respect to having achieved at least a fundamental consensus on workable, albeit still contentious, constitutional frameworks. But as will be explored in the next chapter, all the states in the region still faced pressing challenges regarding the intricacies of governance. This was particularly critical with respect to improving the effectiveness and depoliticization of their state administrative structures, and also in combating the scourge of corruption. Complex problems in these areas seriously weakened their overall capability for governance and their quest to legitimate the state institutions that are the sinews of democratic consolidation.

Chapter 3

Administrative Development, the Rule of Law, and the Struggle against Corruption

Democratic state building depends on the establishment of administrative institutions that have the capacity to efficiently and legally implement government policy and are also accountable to elected officials and the public. More broadly, the ability of civil servants to carry out their duties both effectively and honestly has an important influence on the overall performance and legitimation of the state. Forging an administrative culture that is professionally oriented, intolerant of corrupt practices, and unresponsive to illegal overtures by political party officials and financial interests is a critical facet of establishing a democratic political culture. And together with other factors, such as the manner in which administrative officials relate to other state institutions, and how such officials respond to the demands of individuals and groups within society, administrative change has a critical impact on the process of democratic consolidation. In view of the significance that administrative culture and capacity have on democratic state building, the EU has accorded public administration reform a high priority, both in the pre-accession process and also in the period after states are allowed to enter the EU.[1] Indeed, the experience of former EU candidate members who

1. On the general problems of administrative development in the area, see Svein Eriksen, "Institution Building in Central and Eastern Europe: Foreign Influences and Domestic Regimes," *Review of Central and East European Law* 32 (2007): 333–69; Organization for Economic Cooperation and Development, *Sustainability of Civil Service Reforms in Central and East Europe Five Years after EU Accession* (Paris: Sigma, 2009); and Tony Verheijen, *Administrative Capacity in the New EU Member States: The Limits of Innovation* (Washington, D.C.: World Bank, 2007).

have gone on to become successful applicants suggests that the quality of public administration in a country is critical to the ease with which it navigates the accession process.[2]

The question of how to reform public administration has acquired even more urgency as a result of the global economic crisis that began in 2008. Thus, political elites in the Western Balkans region, along with leaders of other postcommunist regimes, found themselves shifting their focus from the previous imperative of reducing the role of the state to redefining the quality of state institutions and making them more supportive of the market economy.[3] Indeed, it has become even clearer that public administration as the "state in action" was critically important for the ability of governments to deal with the socioeconomic impact of the crisis (see chapter 8).

The Evolution of Public Administration: Toward Depoliticization, Professionalization, and Accountability

Historical continuities and discontinuities in administrative development, particularly in transitional and postconflict settings such as the Western Balkans, have an important impact on the capacity of a particular bureaucratic apparatus. And although the impact of historical legacies and traditions on bureaucracy building can often be exaggerated, it is a formidable task to transform "administrative cultures," even after revolutionary episodes and the purge of personnel from the old regime. Thus, as one seminal study aptly reminds us, "The historical character of a bureaucratic apparatus must be taken into account in any attempt to explain its capacity, or lack of capacity to intervene."[4]

Despite disparate nineteenth-century origins in an autonomous Serbia and two imperial bureaucracies, followed by the discontinuities of the two world wars and Communist restaffing after 1945, those

2. *Convergence to the European Union: Challenges and Opportunities* (Skopje: Ministry of Finance, 2009), 26.

3. European Bank for Reconstruction and Development, *Transition Report 2009: Transition in Crisis* (London: European Bank for Reconstruction and Development, 2009).

4. Dietrich Rueshemeyer and Peter B. Evans, "The State and Economic Transformation: Towards an Analysis of the Conditions Underlying Effective Intervention," in *Bringing the State Back In,* edited by Peter B. Evans, Dietrich Rueshemeyer, and Theda Skocpol (Cambridge: Cambridge University Press, 1985), 59.

chiefly responsible for public administration in the Western Balkan regimes entered the postcommunist period with one historical legacy in common. They all lacked the experience of sustained democratic consolidation, that is, a transparency and separation of powers sufficient to make their bureaucracies responsible to legal norms and standards of efficiency, as well as external oversight. They were burdened instead with a heritage of clientelism and corruption not open to public view. By the 1930s, the democratic promise of full independence, new constitutions, and parliamentary government following World War I had clearly failed all across Southeastern Europe. Authoritarian regimes, now facing the Great Depression, struggled in vain to reduce the bloated bureaucracies that had already grown up in the 1920s. They also gave their interior ministries new extralegal powers that would set precedents for the Communist regimes after 1945.[5]

In both Yugoslavia and Albania, the occupations and divisions of World War II substantially destroyed the existing institutions of administration. The Communist personnel purges that followed World War II reconstituted administrative institutions, which were now staffed with new and much less experienced cadres. Neither of the new one-party regimes—which would quite quickly diverge in their structures and character—opened its respective public administrations to the representative or judicial oversight demanded by democratic norms. Yugoslavia's growing devolution of party and executive authority to its republics never provided this oversight. What continued instead, based on a pattern already established by the 1930s, was a state (or republic) apparatus whose reach was extensive, but whose basis for public support and legitimation was weak. As discussed in chapter 1, the growing tension of the 1980s between the federal and republic administrations contributed to the failure of Yugoslavia to survive the general crisis of Communist regimes in 1989. But unlike the post-1945 period, neither Yugoslavia's successor states nor Albania entered the new post-1989 period with significant turnover in public administration below the highest level. Thus, what continued in place were inefficient, nontransparent, and essentially nonaccountable "administrative cultures" throughout the region, from which the ethnic and political homogenization linked to the conflicts of the 1990s hardly freed it.

5. See John R. Lampe, *Balkans into Southeastern Europe: A Century of War and Transition* (London: Palgrave, 2006), 63-140.

Proceeding against the background of regional disruption and violence, the initial period of post-Yugoslavia and postcommunist institution building during the 1990s only reinforced the historical pattern of state weakness and fragility in the Western Balkans.[6] Thus, the turbulence and uncertainty that accompanied the initial stage of regime transition in each new polity often demoralized and traumatized personnel in the long-established state apparatuses of the former Yugoslav republics and provinces, and also Albania, reinforcing earlier Communist and precommunist problems in the administrative sectors. In many cases, administrative coherence, the rule of law, and efficiency were also undermined when segments of the former Communist elite took advantage of the transitional situation to stay in power and corrupt the new institutional structures and its officials through various modes of "state capture."[7]

At the same time, the new states of the Western Balkans were faced with an enormous burden: reorganizing their administrative structures as postcommunist states (and in most cases of Yugoslavia's successor states), removing those officials associated closely with the former single-party regimes, recruiting new personnel, creating a new administrative culture with respect to norms and behavior, and endeavoring to legitimate the new "democratic" system through effective governance. This heavy load on these states is reflected in comparative trend data with respect to the level of government spending as a percentage of gross domestic product (GDP) (see table 3.1).

Indeed, regional difficulties with regard to the scope and size of the state have continued throughout the postconflict period since 1999. The costs of having to establish new institutions for an independent state, and to perform new functions previously carried out by the pre-1991 Yugoslav Communist federation, were largely responsible for the

6. For the character of state weakness in the Balkans, see Albert Rakipi, "Weak States: A View from Within," *Building Stability in Weak States: The Western Balkans* (Vienna, 2002), 9–29; and Ivan Krastev, "Bringing the State Up," paper presented at the conference "Interethnic Relations in the Western Balkans: Problems, Instruments, and Prospects for the Future," Berlin, September 12–13, 2003.

7. See Venelin I. Ganev, "Dysfunctional Sinews of Power: Problems of Democracy Building in the Post-Communist Balkans," paper presented at the conference "Civil Society, Political Society, and the State: A Fresh Look at the Problems of Governance in the Balkan Region," Split, Croatia, November 23–24, 2001.

Table 3.1. Government Expenditures as a Percentage of Gross Domestic Product in the Western Balkans, Selected Years

Country or Group	1997	2001	2003	2005	2008
Albania	29.2	31.6	29.0	28.3	32.7
Bosnia-Herzegovina	55.4	46.9	52.4	50.2	49.7
Croatia	50.7	52.0	51.3	49.0	46.3
Kosovo	N.A.	N.A.	33.1[a]	31.3	27.3[b]
Macedonia	35.1	34.3	38.5	35.3	36.4
Montenegro	N.A.	42.8	39.9	40.4	42.9
Serbia	N.A.	36.2	46.7	44.4	45.2
European Union	N.A.	N.A.	47.4	46.9	46.6

Note: N.A. = not available.
[a]2004.
[b]2006.
Sources: IMF country reports; World Bank, "European Commission Spring 2009 Forecast," May 2009.

high public spending levels apparent in Bosnia-Herzegovina, Croatia, and Serbia and Montenegro, although in the first two cases the trend has gradually improved. Serbia's budget for administration costs increased sharply following the breakup of the state union of Serbia and Montenegro in 2006 (the number employed in various state services actually quadrupled between 2000 and 2008). In Bosnia, the complex institutional environment, with multiple units and levels of government, accounts for the large share of government spending—at almost 50 percent of GDP in 2008—and a high public-sector wage bill. High wage bills are particularly striking in the two entities. In the Federation of Bosnia and Herzegovina, there have been excessive salary outlays on war veterans, invalids, and the families of those killed during the war (40 percent of the Federation's budget in 2008 was spent on social welfare). Meanwhile, salaries in the Republika Srpksa were ten times higher than the country average. Requests by the International Monetary Fund during 2009 and 2010 for Bosnia's governments to cut public administration expenses met with resistance from both politicians and organized groups.[8] In April 2010, six thousand war veterans protested budget cuts in front of the Federation's government buildings, and sixty people were injured in clashes. However, the IMF resident representative in Bosnia remarked that the situation in Bosnia was

8. Anes Alić, "Bosnia: The IMF Money Crunch," *International Relations and Security Network*, Zurich, May 25, 2009.

different from Greece: "We started the reforms early here to avoid the cataclysms faced by Greece."[9]

Government spending in Albania and Kosovo has been lower (in the latter case, without the UN Mission in Kosovo's spending, about 33 percent in 2003 and 27.3 percent in 2006, but good trend data regarding this new state are not available). The implosion of the Albanian state in 1997 accounts in part for its lower level of public expenditures, but this level is also subsequently explained by the country's avoidance of inefficient resource allocation and limitations on social transfers and corporate subsidies. In most of the Western Balkan states, a number of factors have all played a role in high government spending levels, to one extent or another: postconflict reconstruction imperatives; ambitious new show projects; high welfare, health, and defense expenditures; and delayed reforms of the old socialist system. The economic impact of such high levels of governmental spending (see chapter 8) is to crowd private-sector activity, increase spending on consumption, and slow economic investment and growth. When the impact of the global financial crisis hit the Western Balkans in late 2008, the states in the region came under new pressure from international financial institutions to downsize their administrative sectors and wage bills.

Montenegro has stood out in the relative size of its state administration as a percentage of the employed population, that is, civil servants and employees working in government agencies (table 3.2). Croatia has also been slow to reduce the size of its very complex state apparatus that resulted from the government's intrusive regulatory role in the economy, and the large number of administrative units at the central, county, and local levels. In 2009, it was estimated that Croatia's public-sector wages were about 11.1 percent of GDP (down from 12.4 in 2005) compared with 10 percent in Serbia.[10] But it is Montenegro along with Macedonia and Kosovo that have the largest overall proportion of those employed in the state and public sectors combined, averaging about one-fifth of those in the labor force. Most other Western Balkan states have from roughly 11 to 13 percent of their employed population in the public sec-

---

9. Bosnia-Herzegovina Federation TV, May 24, 2010. A recent report found that "the Federation accounts for the large majority of Bosnia's proverbial administrative bloat." International Crisis Group, *Federation of Bosnia and Herzegovina: A Parallel Crisis* (Brussels: International Crisis Group, 2010), 3.

10. These data are from Simon Gray, a World Bank manager in Serbia.

Table 3.2. *State Administration and Public Service, 2008 and 2009*

Country	Governmental, 2008–9				Legislative, 2008–9		
	State Civil Servants / Employees[a]	State Civil Servants / Employees as % of Employed Population	Total Public Service Employment[b]	Public Sector as % of Employed Population	Administrative Employees in Legislature	Number of Legislators	Staff per Legislator
Bosnia-Herzegovina	11,774	1.38[c]	105,298	12.4	79	57	1.38
Macedonia	13,203	2.24	110,000	18.6	196	120	1.63
Croatia	37,400	2.31	207,400[d]	12.8	283	152	1.86
Serbia	34,024[e]	1.28	357,318[f]	13.4	342	250	1.36
Montenegro	12,121	5.52	50,000	23.0[g]	96	81	1.18
Kosovo	8,206	2.20	73,221	13.3	157	120	1.30
Albania	13,790	1.15	105,134	11.4	145	140	1.03

[a]Without military and police.

[b]Includes those employed in education, health, culture, sport, judicial administration, and municipal/regional agencies (but excludes employees in public enterprises).

[c]Another 9,534 state employees work in the entity administrations (5,722 in the Federation, and 3,812 in Republika Srpska) or together with the 11,774 working in central "common" institutions a total of 21,308, or 2.5 percent of the employed population.

[d]Without Ministry of Interior or Ministry of Defense.

[e]In administrative bodies in the Republic of Serbia, including 3,400 part-time employees. A law at the end of 2009 limited the number employed at this level to 28,400.

[f]2009 Serbian Ministry of Finance Data without approximately 83,000 employees from the Ministry of Internal Affairs, Security-Information Agency, and Ministry of Defense.

[g]Estimated in reports near the end of 2009. In 2007, the equivalent figure was 44,015.

Sources: National Analytical Reports, EUROSTAT, and media reports.

tor. And although most EU countries on average have relatively higher public-sector wage bills than the Western Balkan states, they also have far more prosperous economies.[11] As may be seen in chapter 8, the costs of large administrative sectors in the Western Balkans place a heavy burden on their budgets and are a drag on economic development.

The high costs and low effectiveness of Montenegro's administration—linked to overlapping functions, weak coordination, blurred accountability among administrative units, and the inability of a small country to exploit economies of scale—have hampered decisionmaking and reduced the quality of service delivery.[12] Indeed, Montenegro's relative wage bill for "general government" in 2006 was higher than those of Croatia and Slovenia. Moreover, by 2008–9, Montenegro, like the other countries in the region, faced pressure for public-sector reduction just when there was a need to recruit new personnel to meet the requirements of EU integration and decentralization. Thus, unless such recruitment is compensated for by a corresponding decrease in staff, such pressures are likely to perpetuate large public-sector wage bills and to limit overall efforts to improve efficiency.

Macedonia's inflated bureaucracy has also been resistant to efforts at right-sizing. There are several reasons for this problem, not unlike those in neighboring countries: the use of highly politicized administrative posts as a mechanism for political party patronage, government perceptions that administrative jobs provide a way to reduce unemployment, and public perceptions that bureaucratic work is a "highly desirable opportunity" in difficult economic times.[13] The requirements of equitable ethnic representation and decentralization in the administrative sector mandated by the Ohrid Accord (see below) are also a factor in Macedonia. By 2009, some reports claimed that Macedonia's total public administrative sector had grown to 125,000 to 130,000 employees, although the country might not need not more than 70,000.[14]

11. International Monetary Fund, *Republic of Montenegro: 2008 Article IV Consultation,* Country Report 09/88 (Washington, D.C.: International Monetary Fund, 2009).

12. World Bank, *Montenegro beyond the Peak: Growth Policies and Fiscal Constraints—Public Expenditures and Institutional Review,* Report 46660-ME (Washington, D.C.: World Bank, 2008), 82.

13. Analytica, *Right-Sizing of the Public Administration in Macedonia* (Skopje: Analytica, 2009).

14. FOSIM, *First Quarterly Accession Watch Report* (Skopje: FOSIM, 2009), 54. In August 2010, Prime Minister Gruevski announced that 850 public admin-

Of course, the weaknesses of the Western Balkan states in administrative effectiveness and accountability do not derive solely from the fact that state structures are large in their spending levels and sizes (e.g., public employment levels). For example, the region's average size of government spending as a portion of GDP for most states in recent years was close to the average or lower than that for the current twenty-seven members of the European Union as a whole, roughly 47 percent—although in most cases, it was higher than in fast-growing economies such as Romania or Bulgaria (in 2008, 38.5 percent and 37.4 percent, respectively). General government expenditures across the Western Balkans in 2008 ranged from approximately 50 percent in Bosnia-Herzegovina to 33 percent in Albania (see table 3.1). Moreover, as already alluded to above, the fact that most of the Western Balkan states were in the very early stages of state formation considerably slowed and complicated their administrative development, as did setbacks caused by the direct and indirect consequences of recent regional conflict. Indeed, it is partly because of these aspects of path dependence, and also the political circumstances and sometimes political instability in individual states, that the considerable resources expended by the EU and international financial institutions to ameliorate problems in the region had only a limited impact during the post-2000 period.

But it was unrealistic for observers to assume that imported administrative models could quickly displace domestic habits of bureaucratic operation, or for them to entirely blame domestic elites for a failure of will. Thus, more often than not, the institution-building saga in the Western Balkans, as in most regions of the world, has resulted in an amalgam of old and new patterns of behavior in the administrative sphere. And although the *formal* legal restructuring of state administrations is not particularly difficult under EU conditionality pressures, the actual replacement of old administrative habits by new "European behavior" has proven very difficult.[15]

Indeed, the serious problem of improving the operation of the civil service has often continued during the postaccession phase for former

---

istrative employees had already been engaged to work on EU accession negations. *MIA,* August 6, 2010.

15. Arolda Elbasani, *EU Administrative Conditionality and Domestic Downloading: The Limits of Europeanization in Challenging Contexts,* Working Paper 2 (Berlin: Free University, 2009).

Communist states, particularly in highly polarized polities.[16] In the case of the Western Balkans, four particular and interrelated problems of administrative development have proven very intractable: (1) weak professionalization, (2) persistent politicization, (3) inequities in ethnic representation and power sharing, and (4) extensive and deeply entrenched patterns of corruption. These problems have historically plagued Southeastern European public administration, and they are also not unfamiliar to bureaucracies elsewhere. But as part of a broader context of difficulties, they have proven particularly detrimental to the effectiveness and democratic accountability of the public administrative sectors in the Western Balkans.[17] As a consequence, the notion of a merit-based public administration, which serves citizens and transcends the alternation of different governments and governing parties in a pluralistic system, has had considerable difficulty taking hold. It is useful to examine each of these four problems in more detail.

Weak Professionalization

Studies of Western Balkan bureaucratic structures frequently point to the shortages of skilled personnel in otherwise overly large public sectors, and also to the poor motivation of administrative employees compared with the private sector across the region.[18] Levels of administrative professionalization and politicization naturally vary from one country to another and from one ministry to another within countries. But the general reasons for problems in the region can usually be traced to low salaries, bad working conditions, poor qualifications and training, and the typically low prestige of civil servants in society. Thus, the qualifications of administrative employees, although improving slowly in the Western Balkans, remain unsatisfactory. A substantial number of civil servants have lacked any tertiary education—for example, roughly half of them in Serbia and Croatia during the period 2002–4.[19] Moreover, in the new states such as Montenegro and Kosovo,

16. Sigma, *Can Civil Service Reforms Last?* Working Paper (Paris: Sigma, 2010).
17. Dimce Nikolov, "Innovations in the Public Administration in the Balkan Regions," *Southeastern Europe* 31–32 (2005): 103–28.
18. Sigma, *Public Administration in the Balkans: Overview,* Assessment Report (Paris: Sigma, 2004).
19. Marijana Badun, "Governance and Public Administration in the Context of

even many young, highly educated individuals recruited to the public service in the post-2000 period have lacked experience or managerial and leadership skills.

Meanwhile, the older generation of officials, as in most other regimes in the Western Balkans, were often "equipped with outdated notions of management."[20] Throughout the region, it is also very difficult for the civil service to compete for highly qualified talent. For example, an October 2008 survey of nearly two hundred senior officials, managers, and other civil servants across the Western Balkans found that an overwhelming majority (91 percent) viewed international organizations as more attractive employers, and 60 percent considered private firms to be more attractive.[21]

Moreover, although new educational institutions specializing in public administration studies are a positive development, these institutions still do not have a strong reputation, and their limited number of graduates who enter public bureaucracies still constitute a minority struggling against well-entrenched negative practices. Indeed, in the 2008 survey, 40 percent of respondents across the region believed that traditional personnel practices in the civil service had not changed much by 2008, and 51 percent believed that another model is necessary for a "modern public service." Perhaps a hopeful finding of the survey was that 80.3 percent of the respondents claimed that the interests of citizens and business should be paramount in their work.

Unfortunately, the officials in the overstaffed and inefficient Balkan states too often compensate for their organizational weaknesses by a

---

Croatian Accession to the European Union," in *Croatian Accession to the European Union: Institutional Challenges,* vol. 2, edited by Katarina Ott (Zagreb and Skopje: Institute of Public Finance and Friedrich Ebert Stiftung, 2006), 152; and World Bank, *Serbia and Montenegro: Public Administration Development—Creating the Conditions for Effective Economic and Social Reform Policy Note* (Washington, D.C.: World Bank, 2004), 13.

20. This is from a Kosovo Capacity-Building Seminar, sponsored by United Nations Development Program, November 21–23, 2005. Vanja Ćalović, the executive director of a Montenegro nongovernmental organization lobbying for government and administrative overhaul, observed that his was a "really small country, so we have few government employees, and on the other side, our system of education does not prepare our people to do their job sufficiently well." *International Herald Tribune,* September 8, 2006.

21. Damir Ahmetović, "Attracting and Retaining Civil Servants in the Western Balkans," *Development and Transition,* April 2009, 11–13.

style of personal presentation—when doing business with foreigners, at domestic tax collection, border checking and traffic control, and so on—that projects strength, or an image of an ostensibly "strong state."[22] But below this veneer are found sizable or "big" states that are, however, "weak" or inadequate at delivering state-related services and are usually very unaccountable to their citizens. Indeed, fewer than 3 percent of those interviewed in the 2008 survey said that their own pursuit of a civil service career was motivated by a desire to perform public service. Job security and a regular salary were the main factors attracting people.

However, deficient educational and professional qualifications are only partially responsible for the poor performance and image of administrative sectors in the region, and their often undemocratic mode of operation. An equally important issue is the overall political mentality and motivational climate within the region's administrative structures. As a 2001 Croatian study put it: "Citizens consider the administration distant, formal and corrupted. . . . It is not perceived as professional and unbiased, but riddled with connections and the exchange of friendly services. . . . The people in the administration do not get there because of professional criteria, and they are not promoted according to expertise and performance."[23] A 2004 study by another Croatian analyst observed that "it is very difficult to break up the inheritance of clientelism and paternalism in which the administration has been focused too much only on itself. A culture of secrecy has been cultivated, favoring nepotism and arbitrariness, and citizens have always been made to feel subordinate in their encounters with the administration."[24]

Likewise, even after considerable EU assistance and pressure as part of Croatia's engagement in the preaccession process, a 2006 study concluded that "the capabilities of institutions to adapt to the requirements of modern and open societies" is still Croatia's "weakest spot;

22. Andras Inotai, *The European Union and Southeast Europe: Troubled Waters Ahead* (Brussels: Peter Lang, 2006), 249.

23. Ured za strategiju razvitka RH 2001, 7, cited by Marijana Badun, "Government and Public Administration in the Context of Croatian Accession to the European Union," in *Croatian Accession to the European Union,* vol. 2, ed. Ott, 150.

24. Marijana Badun, "Government and Public Administration in the Context of Croatian Accession to the European Union," in *Croatian Accession to the European Union,* vol. 2, ed. Ott, 152.

... changes in the public administration in the last couple of years show limited progress in the application of reforms that continue to be made partially. ... The goals necessary for public administration reform and various new incentives are proposed, but it is difficult to expect the necessary political will for their implementation."[25] A 2008 study of governance culture in Croatia found a strong "don't rock the boat administrative credo" among the country's political officials.[26]

Similar problems are apparent in the other Western Balkan polities and have been seriously exacerbated by the frequent change of ruling parties and party coalitions, and also by the climate of interparty polarization within government cabinets. Below the top tier of political ministers, among nonelected officials in the public administration, such changes, divisions, and uncertainty tend to feed bureaucratic inertia and nonaccountability. At the lower levels of public administration, such division and uncertainty have only solidified bureaucratic inertia. For example, one Serbian minister told visiting foreign experts in 2002 that "you can still find the old customs everywhere. The biggest problem is people's mental attitude. Our civil servants are used to seeing politicians [under the Slobodan Milošević regime] come and go. All initiatives are considered as transitory. Civil servants see no point in exerting themselves in support of the politicians. They will be gone tomorrow, and new people arrive with new ideas."[27] And a Serbian deputy minister remarked "that some ministries do not even function at all. The employees are neither interested nor involved in their work. They were employed because they once had the right connection, not because they might have been professionally qualified."[28] Still yet another deputy minister observed that "90 percent of the employees in his ministry are 'totally passive.' They don't actually do anything at all—not even damage. I don't even consider them part of the ministry."[29]

25. Katarina Ott, *Croatian Accession to the European Union: The Challenge of Participation* (Zagreb: Institute of Public Finance, 2006), 4, 8–9.

26. Saša Poljanec-Borić and Jadranka Švarc, "Transfer of Governance Culture: A Case Study of Socio-Cultural Barriers for Institutional Adaptation in Croatia," *Revija za sociologija* 39, no. 3 (2008): 123–44.

27. Agency for Public Administration Development, *The Serbian Central Government Administration: Organizational Challenges* (Belgrade: Government of Serbia, 2002), 83.

28. Ibid.

29. Ibid., 85.

Laying the groundwork for an improvement in the professionalization of Serbia's administrative structure proved difficult in the politically turbulent first six years that followed the downfall of the Milošević regime. Despite studies of the public administration and a host of recommendations for reform, recruitment to the ministries continued to be based more on party loyalty than on merit.[30] When more reform-oriented political forces finally assumed power in 2008, momentum for reform picked up. As one former Serbian official put it rather hopefully in 2009, "The people working within public administration fully understand their capacity, but they also perceive their shortcomings, and more importantly how to address them."[31] Unfortunately, the economic recession beginning in 2009 did not prove to be an auspicious period for administrative reform in Serbia or elsewhere. Efforts continued to educate and retrain civil servants to meet the current challenges in each country, but under conditions of austerity and wage freezes, it proved more difficult for the public sector to recruit top-level candidates and to instill a reform mentality.

Persistent Politicization

The difficulties of improving civil service professionalization in the region have been closely linked to the politicized character of public administration. Indeed, throughout the Western Balkans, efforts to depoliticize the civil service sector have gone very slowly. And despite a flurry of reform initiatives in the period 2002–5, politicization in most states actually increased.[32]

30. Jadranka Jelinčić, *Europeanization of Serbia: Capacities of Public Authorities and Local Self-Government Authorities* (Belgrade: Fund for an Open Society, 2006).

31. Tanja Miščević, "Serbia's Administrative Capacity: Driving European Integration," in *Serbia Matters: Domestic Reform and European Integration,* edited by Wolfgang Petritsch, Goran Svilanović, and Christophe Solioz (Baden-Baden: NOMOS, 2009), 93–98. See also Ministry of Public Administration and Local Self-Government, *Public Administration Reform Strategy in the Republic of Serbia: Action Plan for Serbian Public Administration Reform Implementation 2009–2012* (Belgrade: Government of Serbia, 2009).

32. Aleksandra Rabrenović and Tony Verheijen, "Politicians and Top Civil Servants in Former Yugoslav States: Back to Discarded Traditions?" September 28, 2005. The authors accurately point to the pattern of politicization that occurred in the successor states following the disintegration of socialist Yugoslavia. But they underestimate the degree of one-party political control from 1946 to the late 1980s,

The most important reasons for this problem are the region's deeply embedded tradition of political interference in administrative decisions, and the lack of a clear division between the public and private spheres. This legacy led to a situation where progress in reforming the state apparatus, including both the public administration and the justice sector, lagged behind developments in other areas such as trade, energy, and infrastructure. Members of the political elite often underestimated the importance of public administrative reform for economic development and, in most cases, incumbent decisionmakers simply wanted to maintain control of the bureaucracy in order to distribute positions and perks to their supporters. At the same time, the existing civil servants were often hostile to changes that disturbed their traditional modes of operation and personal networks (which could be summed up as characterized by inertia, which often frustrated younger professionals).[33] Indeed, administrative structures in the Western Balkans did not prove very willing or successful at allocating external assistance, or benefiting from such support for "good governance." Thus it is estimated that in Serbia and Croatia, only half of the EU assistance earmarked in 2001 for projects in public administration was actually dispersed by 2004.[34]

Studies of Serbia's administrative staffing in senior positions indicate that although Milošević was responsible for exacerbating the politicization of the Serbian civil service, the post-October 2000 experience under a multiparty system has been "even more politically colored."[35] As a high-ranking government official told one researcher in 2001, "We get a number of young people sent by political parties and with an order from the minister to employ them. They're usually arrogant, lack knowledge as to what a Civil Service career entails, and cannot fit in at all. You do not conflict with them if you want to survive. . . . New

---

and they exaggerate the "traditions of a professional strong and impartial civil service system" that the Western Balkan polities have been able to draw upon as a basis for recent administrative development.

33. Anke Freibert, "Problems and Challenges on the Path of Making the Civil Service in the Western Balkans Professional and Non-Political," *Hrvatska Javna Uprava* 8, no. 1 (2008): 31–45.

34. Svein Eriksen, "Promoting Good Governance in Eastern Europe: Domestic Responses to External Influences," unpublished paper, May 2006, 6–8.

35. Željko Sević, "Measuring Performance on a Local Government Level in a Transitional Country: The Case of Serbia," *International Journal of Public Service Management* 18, no.7 (2005): 597.

'political commissars,' that is what they are, and call themselves 'democrats' with a capital 'D.'"[36]

Part of the problem in post-Milošević Serbia was that the new reform-oriented prime minister in 2001, Zoran Djindjić, had little experience in governing and little idea of how to go about restructuring public services, other than to place them under his political control. As Djindjić told one interviewer just after assuming authority, he and his colleagues "were trained in opposing, not in exercising political power."[37] Serbia's very fragmented and polarized political party system also made it difficult to adopt reforms that might dampen administrative politicization.[38] A study by Croatian specialists in 2003 also revealed how the mentality of ruling parties made it extremely difficult to depoliticize public administration in the post–Franjo Tudjman period: "The relations between the government and administration are still treated as those of a *master* vis-à-vis an *apparatus* where the spoils system dominates in the political arena. This lessens or completely removes the need for the educated, professional, and ethical civil servants."[39] "Today," as one of the analysts put it in 2003, "the administrative profession is thought to be a mere servant of politics."[40]

The "spoils system" mentality throughout the Western Balkans has generally meant that each victorious incoming political party, or more typically a coalition of parties, not only changes the head of each ministry but also treats its entire administrative staff as its patrimony and as an opportunity for rewarding its supporters with patronage appointments. When the political process is driven by a new governing coalition, and ministries are allocated along party lines, it raises the problem

36. Ibid.
37. Svein Eriksen, "Unfinished Transition: Public Administration Reform in Serbia 2001–2004," unpublished paper, May 2005.)
38. Aleksandra Rabrenović and Zorica Vukasinović Radojićić, "Civil Service Reform in Serbia: Overcoming Implementation Challenges," in *Serbian Law and Transition: Changes and Challenges,* edited by Institute of Comparative Law (Belgrade: Institute of Comparative Law, 2009), 29–44.
39. Ivan Koprić, "Education of Administrative Personnel: Experiences and Challenges," in *Modernization of the Croatian Public Administration,* edited by Ivan Koprić (Zagreb: Faculty of Law, University of Zagreb, 2003), 210.
40. Ivan Koprić, "Modernization of the Croatian Public Administration: Issues, Proposals and Prospects," in *Modernization of the Croatian Public Administration,* ed. Koprić, 484.

of policy coherence among ministries—and sometimes even within ministries.

Thus, in Serbia, after a coalition of political parties won the legislative elections at the end of 2003, each ministry was managed by a miniature multiparty coalition of officials, with the result that individual ministries could hardly function at all.[41] After changes were made, and the ministries were allocated among winning parties on a party-by-party basis, the related problem of interministerial tensions and fragmentation arose, further undermining policy coordination. Indeed, cabinets in Serbian coalition governments often appear as a "confederation of fiefdoms" that have little capacity or will to function as a unified government. At worst, the government almost ceases to function, as it did during early 2007, when the formation of a new coalition was greatly delayed over the question of awarding ministerial posts.

The core of the problem resided within the polarized "democratic bloc," particularly between the Democratic Party (Demokratska stranka, DS) headed by President Boris Tadić on the one side, and the Democratic Party of Serbia (Demokratska stranka Srbije, DSS) headed by the caretaker prime minister, Vojislav Koštunica, on the other. For example, two different offers made by the DS to the rival DSS to constitute a new government proved unworkable: "Koštunica as prime minister, but without the award of strong ministerial positions to his parties, or DSS control of several ministerial positions, but without [Koštunica as] prime minister."[42] While deadlock continued through the spring of 2007, government and legislative policymaking was suspended and administrative effectiveness was impaired. The "feudalization" of the state administration by party machines continued after a democratic coali-

41. *Danas,* December 30, 2004.

42. One close observer of the Serbian bureaucracy notes that the politicization of ministries "has an impact on the quality and knowledge of office holders; on the one hand it prevents effective inter-ministerial and intra-ministerial cooperation. Not to mention the potential for violating the principle of equality before the law. It can even provoke competition among ministries, as well as different interpretations of the same law—regulation leading to uneven practices and application." Branislaw Malegurski, "How Can Administrative Procedures Either Foster or Hamper Economic Development? Experiences of an Outsider Dealing with Public Bureaucracies," paper presented at Sigma Regional Workshop on Public Administrative Reform and EU Integration, Budva, December 4–6, 2005. See also Slaviša Orlović, *Politički Život Srbije: Izmedju parkotratije i demokratije* (Belgrade: Službeni glasnik, 2008).

tion government (without Koštunica) was elected in 2008. And because each political party organization can decide on the placement of its loyalists in different ministries, it has almost been impossible for ministers to remove incompetent or redundant personnel. As one minister put it in 2009, "If you want to recall somebody, you have to ask approval from a coalition partner. If that partner has a strong position within the ruling coalition, it is not very likely that the recall shall occur."[43]

In some cases, where two strong parties have alternated in government, politicization has weakened the capacity for reform efforts in the Western Balkans by undermining, rather than entrenching, the continuity of the administrative sector. For example, one study of the Albanian civil service found that 30 to 35 percent of civil servants were changed for political reasons during the period from July 2005 to May 2006.[44] The Albanian political elite has, however, proven politically adept at paying lip service to EU demands for depoliticization and administrative reform. For example, on the eve of the 2009 election, the government hired 1,700 temporary staff, "mainly political militants," who could guarantee control over state agencies. As one analyst put it, EU mechanisms were unable to "break 'the informal rule' of reshuffling the state and starting anew after each political turnover. . . . The governing actors have not posed resistance to adoption of new rules, but showed great resistance to implement the laws."[45]

Similarly, in October 2006, Macedonia's government sacked more than five hundred public-sector managerial personnel in a three-day period after elections, despite EU criticism that civil servants must be shielded from political interference. As an EU official remarked in Skopje, "We have reacted to changing those people in whose training we invested."[46] Prime Minister Nikola Gruevski responded to such crit-

43. *BLIC,* May 25, 2009. See also Boško Mijatović, *Reforms in Serbia: Achievements and Challenges* (Belgrade: Center for Liberal Democratic Studies, 2008), 95–97.

44. Sigma Balkan Report, Albania Public Service, June 2006.

45. Arolda Elbasani, *EU Administrative Conditionality and Domestic Downloading: The Limits of Europeanization in Challenging Contexts,* Working Paper 2 (Berlin: Free University, 2009), 17–18. See also John O'Brennan and Esmeralda Gassie, "From Stabilization to Consolidation: Albanian State Capacity and Adaptation to European Union Rules," *Journal of Balkan and Near Eastern Studies* 11, no. 1 (2009): 61–82.

46. Sabina Fakić, *Macedonia Axes Public Servants on "Political Grounds,"* Institute for War and Peace Reporting, October 12, 2006.

icism by pointing out that "it is normal that a political team coming to power and with its own program wants to work with people it trusts." And a government spokesman observed that all the newly appointed officials were "professionals."[47]

Such responses, not inaccurately, underline the fact that all alternating governments in democratic systems have some level of politicization. However, the problem in Macedonia, and elsewhere in the region, is less the existence of political interference in routine administrative affairs and more the extent of politicization in appointments, both at the top of ministries and often more broadly. As one 2004 study in Croatia noted, "Croatia, in an institutional-managerial sense, . . . really doesn't have (a politically independent) administrative elite. The fundamental reason [seen in practice] is the perception of the political elite that the management of 'public affairs' isn't really a matter of well-educated professionals but primarily a question of 'the general affairs of politicians and employees.' Functionally, administrative individuals are considered part of a 'subordinate structure' and not an important developmental resource in the country."[48] The practice of considering assistant ministers as political appointees, which continued up to mid-2008, was a particular problem impeding administrative continuity and professionalization in Croatia.[49]

In Bosnia, the formation of a new civil service agency established professional criteria for public administration and eliminated the formal basis for overt political interference found in other states in the region. For example, a civil servant in Bosnia cannot be a member of a governing board of a political party and cannot follow the instructions of political parties. But research indicates that, in practice, below the level of the minister, politicization is still quite extensive with respect to personnel appointments. Although those who aspire to become civil servants are obliged to declare that they are politically independent, the Civil Service Agency of Bosnia does not monitor such declarations. Both agency officials and the public generally believe that most civil

47. Ibid.

48. Drago Čengić, Sanjin Dragojević, and Igor Vidačak, "Hrvatska administrativna elita i problemi upravljanja u procesu evropskih integracija," *Društvena istraživnaje* 13, nos. 1–2 (2004): 20.

49. Antonija Petričušić, "Reforming the Public Service as the Precondition for Public Administration Reform in Croatia," *Review of Central and East European Law* 32 (2007): 303–31.

servants belong to political parties or are closely connected to politics through family and personal ties.[50] And ministers began using the legal possibility of appointing "advisers" in their ministries in order to recruit loyal political personnel. This de facto practice soon acquired "epidemic proportions," and it has reportedly created a kind of "parallel administrative service."[51]

Moreover, Bosnia's legislative structure has not proven very effective at monitoring its civil servants.[52] In the past, the small size and lack of expertise in Bosnia's central legislature have contributed to weak legislative oversight over the administration. Indeed, except for Croatia (see table 3.2), Western Balkan legislatures have quite small administrative staffs to assist them in the monitoring of laws by very large public administrative sectors. Insufficient staff and resources have combined with the low levels of professionalization among legislators to weaken governmental accountability throughout the region.[53]

Meanwhile, in Kosovo, as governmental powers began to be transferred from UN interim administration to local authorities from 2005 to 2008, the major political parties engaged in a struggle to insert their loyalists into ministries—a pattern that appeared to intensify as the international community reduced its footprint. Kosovo's minister of public services in 2007 observed that, following a "formal recognition of the independence of Kosova," he expected a dismissal of civil service employees because the existing administration was already built on "political bias and has a difficult socioeconomic and political heritage and weak capacity."[54] Politically motivated personnel turnover became quickly apparent after independence was declared and Kosovo's new ruling party, the Party of Democratic Progress (Partija demokratskog

50. Reconstruction National Integrity Survey, *Reconstruction National Integrity Survey: Bosnia and Herzegovina* (Sarajevo: Reconstruction National Integrity Survey, 2007).

51. Esref Kenan Rasidagić, "Government Effectiveness and Accountability," in *Democratic Assessment in Bosnia and Herzegovina* (Sarajevo: Open Society Fund, Bosnia and Herzegovina, 2006), 204.

52. Nikhil Dutta, Christina Hajdu, et al., *Strengthening Legislatures for Conflict Management* (Princeton, N.J.: Woodrow Wilson School, 2006), 48–60.

53. See, e.g., *Transparency and Accountability in the Montenegrin Governance System* (Podgorica: National Democratic Institute, 2009).

54. Artan Mustafa, "Kosovars Concerned New Ministries May be Politicized," Institute for War and Peace Reporting, July 2005, nos. 5–7; Kosovo Live News Agency, February 27, 2007.

progresa, PDP), began axing civil servants and placing their supporters into public administration posts, whether or not the new appointees were qualified. "We can't afford to have people from other political parties operating key sectors of the economy and government," one PDP official observed.[55]

Inequities in Ethnic Representation and Power Sharing

In some Western Balkan states, the development of a public administration that is supportive of an inclusive and democratic society is linked to issues of ethnic representation. This ethnic dimension of administrative development in Bosnia and Kosovo, for example, is reinforced by internationally designed regime norms that institutionalize ethnic power-sharing practices and various policies for personnel selection on the basis of equitable representation. As elsewhere, views differ regarding the value of ethnic quotas. Do such methods and practices enhance overall stability by accommodating different groups? Or does ethnically based recruitment to state institutions compromise considerations of merit and professionalism in the public service? Answering these questions requires careful empirical research in multiethnic settings. In any event, accommodating the desire of ethnic constituencies and minorities to get their perceived fair share of administrative posts and resources is a major component in the political life and democratic consolidation of the Western Balkan states.

In Bosnia, Kosovo, and Macedonia, we see that where ethnic divisions have been particularly deep, domestic political authorities and international actors have paid considerable attention to the issue of balanced representation in the public sector. For example, in Macedonia, a good deal of progress has been made in achieving more equitable ethnic representation in the state administration, as stipulated by the Ohrid Accord of 2001. The 2009 EU Commission Progress Report for Macedonia observed that civil servants from non–majority ethnic communities (who made up 35.8 percent of the population in 2001) increased to 26 percent at the central level by September 2009.[56] The EU data suggest that ethnic Macedonians, who make up 64.2 percent of the

55. *Prishtina Insight,* June 14, 2008, 5.
56. EU Commission, *The Former Yugoslav Republic of Macedonia, 2009 Progress Report,* Commission Staff Working Document (Brussels: EU Commission, 2009).

country, constitute 74 percent of the central-level employees. Although this is an improvement from the situation that existed eight years earlier, recruitment targets under the accords are being made very slowly. Albanians, as the principal minority ethnic community, have made the most progress, but the ethnic Turkish and Roma communities remain considerably underrepresented.

Indeed, fuller and more detailed information provided by Macedonian agencies provides a more complete picture of the representation problem than the EU report. Thus Albanians, who made up approximately 25 percent of the population in 2001, increased their position in the state administration from roughly 12 percent in 2002 to 15 percent in 2005–6. And in some ministries—such as for the economy (19.8 percent), health (19.9 percent), and foreign affairs—the proportion of Albanians is even higher. However, in other sectors, such as the Ministry of Culture, there were only 90 Albanians out of 2,313 employees in August 2006, or 3.9 percent of those employed. In the judiciary, Albanians constituted only 8 percent of those employed, and only 3 percent of the public defense office, and there were no Albanians at all in the Republic Judiciary Council.[57] Moreover, 2008 data for designated civil servants in Macedonia's overall public sector indicate that although more Albanians have been appointed recently to a number of top jobs, ethnic Macedonians are still overrepresented in the core positions within the civil bureaucracy (see table 3.3). Meanwhile, members of non-Albanian ethnic communities are strikingly underrepresented below the very top positions.

In fact, Albanians are mostly represented at the top and bottom levels of administration. Still, the total Albanian representation among civil servants has grown impressively, from 5.6 percent in 2004 to 12.2 percent in 2006, and to 15.5 percent in 2008. This has been achieved, however, in large part by increasing the overall size of the civil service—from 10,352 individuals in 2004 to 13,203 in 2008. Indeed, 37 percent of the new employees hired from 2004 to 2007 were Albanians.[58] Efforts at

57. Data from Secretariat for Implementation of Ohrid Framework Agreement, August 31, 2006, in *Analysis of the Inter-ethnic Relations in Republic of Macedonia* (Skopje: Zaednichki vrednosti, 2009), 153.

58. Secretariat for Implementation of the Ohrid Framework Agreement, *Analiza i politikata i budzetskite implikacii za Soodvetna i previchna zastapenost na zaednicite* (Skopje: Secretariat for Implementation of the Ohrid Framework Agreement, 2008).

Table 3.3. The State Administration of the Republic of Macedonia, by Ethnicity, 2008 (percent)

Ethnic Affiliation	Total Population, 2001	General and State Secretaries	State Secretaries / Municipal	State Advisers	Directors and Assistant Directors of Departments	Directors of Divisions	Counselors	Higher Associates	Associates	Higher and Other Officers	Total
Macedonian	64.2	66.6	61.9	85.0	82.0	85.5	83.8	79.7	57.3	81.0	79.0
Albanian	25.2	19.0	28.5	10.4	13.3	10.2	11.1	14.2	37.8	12.9	15.5
Others	10.6	14.4	9.5	4.6	4.7	4.3	5.1	6.1	4.9	6.1	5.5
Total	100.0	100.00	100.0	100.0	100.0	100.0	100.0	100.0	100.0	100.0	100.0
Number		21	21	173	592	1,190	2,749	553	1,677	6,227	13,203

Source: Godišen izveštaj za podatocite od rigistarot na državnite službenici za 2008 godina (Skopje: Agencija za državni službenici, 2009).

more equitable representation have clearly begun to reverse an earlier pattern of the near exclusion of minorities, but only by expanding the bureaucracy, and with considerable resistance from the majority. But low-intensity interethnic resentments and a constant focus on the question of who is "winning" and "losing" are at least a partial improvement over the intergroup violence that occurred in 2001.[59]

The imperative of ethnic balance in administrative appointments and ethnic bargaining in decisionmaking has also been a major political issue in Bosnia that has sometimes subverted the promotion of professional standards and placed additional "stress" on governance building.[60] For example, the Dayton Peace Accords and the post-Dayton constitutional amendments in Bosnia have called for ethnic proportionality in the public services, in line with the prewar 1991 census.[61] But in practice, ethnic proportionality has meant little more than a consensus among the major ruling monoethnic parties to divide up central administrative posts in a more or less proportional manner, leaving minority groups underrepresented, particularly in the entity public services (the provisions of the Bosnian Constitution, which provide that only members of constituent peoples are eligible for top political positions, have had the same effect).

Moreover, because no census has been held in Bosnia since 1991, it is almost impossible to accurately determine the current ethnic representativeness of the state's public administration. This has recently resulted in increased interethnic squabbling regarding the issue of group representation. For example, in August 2009, Nikola Špirić, the incumbent chair of the Council of Ministers, claimed that a "certain imbalance" existed in the ethnic representation of top civil servants based on a report that the council had requested. According to Špirić, out of 383 top officials and government institutions, there were 163 Bosniaks

59. See Florian Bieber, ed., *Power-Sharing and the Implementation of the Ohrid Framework Agreement* (Skopje: Friedrich Ebert Stiftung, 2008), 7.

60. Sigma, *Balkans Public Administration Reform Assessment: Bosnia Herzegovina* (Paris: Sigma, 2004), 1. See also Sigma, *Balkans Public Administration Reform Assessment: Former Yugoslav Republic of Macedonia* (Paris: Sigma, 2004); and United Nations Development Program, *Macedonia, Blue Ribbon Report* (New York: United Nations Development Program, 2006), 64–66.

61. Dragan Ivanović, *An Ethnic Veto and Protection of Minorities on Sub-National Level in BiH,* Policy Brief (Sarajevo: Open Society Fund, Bosnia and Herzegovina, 2008).

(42.56 percent), 113 Serbs (29.5 percent), 93 Croats (24.8 percent), and 12 "others" from minority communities (3.1 percent).[62] Given that some calculations of Bosnia's 2009 population estimate Serbs as constituting approximately 34 to 37 percent of the population, Špirić's claim would have some, albeit very little, validity (although hardly any, when compared with the 1991 census, when Serbs made up 31 percent of Bosnia's population).

Meanwhile, Bosniak leaders have also complained of underrepresentation based on other evidence. Thus, Sulejman Tihić, the president of the Party of Democratic Action (Stranka Demokratske Akcije), claimed that during the period when Špirić presided over the Council of Ministers, 13 Serbs, 7 Croats, and 4 Bosniaks were appointed to leading administrative positions. This allegedly altered the balance in 60 state institutions to 25 Serbs, 19 Bosniaks, 15 Croats, and 1 majority person.[63] Tihić claimed that "there is an agreement between the Serbs and Croats at the expense of Bosniaks."[64]

Somewhat clearer evidence on ethnic representation in the two entities indicates the results of the ethnic reconfiguration ("ethnic cleansing") of the country that occurred during the 1992–95 conflict. Thus, in the Republika Srpska, more than 90 percent of civil servants are Serbs, while in the Federation of Bosnia and Herzegovina, the same proportion of posts are held by Bosniaks (66.5 percent) and Croats (26.19 percent) together.[65] The skewed ethnic composition of political and administrative posts in each of Bosnia's entities has reinforced an entity-centric outlook and entity-versus-center jurisdictional tensions, particularly between the Republika Srpska and the weak central state institutions. The Republika Srpska's prime minister, Milorad Dodik, went so far in December 2008 as to question whether "Muslim judges" in the central-level Court of Bosnia Herzegovina could be depended upon to fairly adjudicate an issue regarding the Republika Srpska.[66] And as has already shown in chapter 2, it is the predominantly Serb Republika Srpska that has been most culpable in blocking the initiatives of the central authori-

62. Quoted by Bosnian Serb Public Television, August 24, 2009, in *BBC Monitoring Europe,* August 27, 2009.

63. *Europa Magazine,* September 2009, 17. Croats have had the same complaints; see *Dnevni list,* August 10, 2008.

64. *Dnevni avaz,* August 25, 2009.

65. *Blic,* July 27, 2009; Erduan Katana, report from Banja Luka, June 24, 2009.

66. *ONASA,* December 10, 2008.

ties and institutions. In fact, the existence of administrative segmentation into two entities, a weak central government, the Brčko District, and ten cantons in the Federation have made it impossible to readily identify a unified administrative structure in the country.

Overall in Bosnia, disproportions in ethnic representativeness have been less responsible for political tensions and the lack of reform than have elite-driven jurisdictional rivalries, particularly between the entities on the one side (especially the Republika Srpska), and the central state institutions on the other. Decisionmaking paralysis increased in Bosnia during 2008 and 2009, as ethnic polarization in the political class intensified over the persistent issue of entity rights versus central government prerogatives. The new round of constitutional discussions that began in October 2009 (see chapter 2) was intended to strengthen the central institutions and the cohesion of the country. But that effort failed, and throughout 2010 the goal of constitutional change remained elusive. The major stumbling block was reaching a consensus on how to diminish the role of ethnic politics as channeled through the entities, and on how to moderate the use of the entity veto in the central legislature.

In Kosovo before 2008, affirmative action policies for the employment of minorities had been a centerpiece of the UN Mission in Kosovo's policy, as well as the Provisional Institutions of Self-Governance. By mid-2005, about 10.2 percent of the staff in Kosovo's central institutions were minorities, and about 7 percent were Serbs. But even such proportions of minority representation came under considerable criticism from members of Kosovo's Albanian majority, who argued that minorities were being "pampered" and that they did not perform their jobs adequately.[67] Following Kosovo's declaration of independence in 2008, the public administration not only became increasingly politicized, but many Kosovo Serbs also withdrew from the administration.[68]

67. "Serbs, Scroungers of Government," *Kosova Sot* (Priština), May 17, 2005, 3.

68. Organization for Security and Cooperation in Europe, *Human Rights, Ethnic Relations and Democracy in Kosovo (Summer 2007–Summer 2008)*, OSCE Background Report (Priština: OSCE Mission in Kosovo, 2008), 22. In Kosovo's central civil service, the representation of nonmajority communities decreased from 12 percent in 2006 to 9 percent in 2009, although such representation is higher in the judiciary. Organization for Security and Cooperation in Europe, *Communities Rights Assessment Report* (Priština: OSCE Mission in Kosovo, 2009).

Between 2008 and 2011, no significant progress was made in improving minority representation in political life.

Extensive and Deeply Entrenched Patterns of Corruption

In the Western Balkans throughout the post-2000 period, deeply entrenched practices of corruption have been especially corrosive to administrative development, and indeed to general economic growth and democratic consolidation. For example, comparative studies of the problem in 2001–2 indicated that citizen attitudes regarding the degree and tolerance of corruption differed little among the Western Balkan countries. Respondents in Macedonia, Bosnia, and Kosovo perceived corruption as particularly extensive.[69] Unfortunately, internationally assisted efforts by the regimes in the region to reverse the spread of corruption—an endemic problem in Southeastern Europe that was exacerbated by the pattern of conflict and state debilitation in the 1990s (that increased smuggling, human trafficking, war profiteering, and an illegal nexus between criminals and political officials)—have had only limited success. The comprehensive 2008 United Nations report on patterns of crime in the Balkans found that conventional criminality had decreased in the region but that a serious problem still existed as a result of the widespread collusion between politicians and criminals.[70]

Beyond the temptation of those active in the established political party organizations, and particularly those holding elected and appointed posts, to enrich themselves illegally (see chapter 5 for a discussion of political party financing), a number of additional factors have been responsible for the spread of corruption in the region. They range from the low salaries of officials to imperfect legislation and internal administrative controls, the legacy of problems from the precommunist and Communist periods (e.g., the blurred lines between the public and private sectors), the decline in public morality during the late Communist period, and the continued weakness of judicial and legal systems within individual polities. Recent research indicates (see below)

69. Vitosha Research, *Corruption Indexes: Regional Corruption Monitoring in Albania, Bosnia and Herzegovina, Bulgaria, Croatia, Macedonia, Romania and Yugoslavia* (Sofia: Vitosha Research, 2002).

70. United Nations Office on Drugs and Crime, *Crime and Its Impact on the Balkans* (New York: United Nations, 2008).

that most of the same problems apparent at the onset and end of the 1990s continued to manifest themselves throughout the next decade despite considerable regional efforts to control corruption. Generally in postcommunist states, a surfeit of anticorruption institutional innovation has not been able to improve integrity in public life in the absence of political forces that are committed to the task.[71]

During the post-2000 period, the emphasis of anticorruption efforts shifted from strategies of "awareness raising" to those of "capacity building," but numerous obstacles would impede the newer initiatives.[72] Each country had its own special difficulties. But three general problems afflicted the region: (1) mobilizing and sustaining sufficient civil society support for a long-term anticorruption agenda; (2) weak government commitment to such projects, which prevented follow-through on announced goals; and (3) the misuse or abuse of anticorruption mechanisms (specialized agencies, prosecutorial powers) as tools to attack political opponents. The result was typically to perpetuate low levels of popular trust in state institutions.

Anticorruption efforts throughout the Western Balkans have suffered from the polarized pattern of political party competition and elite dynamics (see chapter 5), along with the still-embryonic stage of civil society (see chapter 4). Support for anticorruption policies was also undermined by a mismatch between the desire of foreign donors for in-depth institutional reforms to eliminate corruption on one side and the general public's desire for quick results on the other side. Moreover, external donors frequently neglected the fact that policies stand little chance of success without the sincere and sustained commitment of the authorities at all levels within the region. As a study of corruption in Bosnia in 2005 remarked, "The mere existence of anticorruption efforts is not an indicator of how seriously the government is committed, . . . [and] the fact that a number of objectives set out in a strategy

71. Daniel Smilov, "Designing Anticorruption Institutions in Central and Eastern Europe," *Development and Transitions,* no. 12 (2009).

72. Martin Tisne and Daniel Smilov, *From the Ground Up: Assessing the Record of Anticorruption Assistance in Southeastern Europe* (Budapest: Central European University Press, 2004); Bryane Michael, "The Rise and Fall of the Anti-Corruption Industry: Towards Second Generation Anti-Corruption Reform in Central and Eastern Europe?" Stockholm School of Economics, n.d.; Alina Mungiu-Pippidi, "Corruption: Diagnoses and Treatment," *Journal of Democracy* 17, no. 3 (July 2006): 86–99.

have been achieved already is not a real indicator of commitment either, since ongoing reform efforts are largely driven by the international community."[73]

Bosnia is often deemed to be the most corrupt country in Southeastern Europe. For example, in 2010, Srdjan Blagovčanin, the executive director of Transparency International in Bosnia, claimed that Bosnia is a "captured state," with a ruling oligarchy in each ethnic group making laws to protect its respective interests. A former finance minister claims that public contracts are awarded to those willing to pay the highest bribes, and that anticorruption drives are designed to get even with political opponents. Blagovčanin feels that Bosnia's weak institutions, which were built from scratch after the war in the 1990s, are mainly to blame, along with the existence of either too little or too much state regulation, depending on the area. Such perceptions run from the elite to ordinary citizens. For example, a shop owner in Sarajevo recently said that she paid €7,000 to public officials to secure a cleaning job for her daughter: "I know that this is not right, but everyone does it and there is no other way. You have to pay to be properly treated by a doctor. You have to pay to enroll your children in school, and you have to pay to get them employed. This is normal."[74]

And in the case of Kosovo, longtime uncertainty about the status of the polity itself, plus confusing lines of responsibility and enforcement within the government structure, fed corruption.[75] The persistence of corruption and organized crime networks in Kosovo was a key factor behind the European Union's decision to place the European Union Rule-of-Law Mission (EULEX) at the forefront of plans to assist international supervision in the area once it achieved "supervised" independence in 2008. The difficulty of eliminating corrupt practices in Kosovo was particularly complicated by the role of traditional kinship connections and their role in clientism and nepotism. For example, a 2005 article in a Priština newspaper claimed that Albanian employees working in the public-service sector at the airport "did not call each

73. Vera Devine and Harald Mathisen, *Corruption in Bosnia and Herzegovina* (Bergen: Chr. Michelsen Institute, 2005), 56.

74. Quoted in "Lack of Political Will Thwarts Anti-Corruption Efforts," Center for Contemporary Relations, June 5, 2010.

75. Fron Nazhi, "Combating Corruption in Kosovo," in *The Anti-Corruption Action Plan: Social and Economic Necessity for Kosovo,* edited by Organization for Security and Cooperation in Europe (Priština: OSCE Mission in Kosovo, 2006.

other colleague or 'chief' but rather 'uncle,' 'nephew,' and 'cousin.'" According to the article, the head of airport security employed about seventeen cousins in the public company.[76] Anticorruption efforts by international officials to alter such patterns have had limited success. For example, a 2008 survey in Kosovo indicated that 91 percent of respondents believe that to get a job, it is better to have political connections than to be qualified.[77] A recent Gallup poll indicates that familial connections may actually be even more extensive in Montenegro—where clan-based connections remain very important—and in Bosnia.[78]

World Bank opinion surveys in the Western Balkans conducted during 2006 revealed quite "mixed" findings on the consequences of anticorruption efforts. For example, Croatia appeared to have made progress in reducing facets of "state capture," that is, corruption in the lawmaking process (particularly bribes to parliamentarians and government officials). But high levels of state capture were still perceived as a problem by respondents surveyed in Albania, Bosnia, Macedonia, Serbia, and Montenegro during the post-2000 period. Indeed, the problem of state capture seemed to be worsening in both Serbia and Montenegro, along with petty or administrative corruption.[79] A study of citizens' attitudes on corruption in Serbia carried out in 2006 was very similar to earlier World Bank surveys, as well as evidence from Transparency International studies.[80]

More recent Serbia-based research shows no fundamental reversal of corruption levels. The area of public procurement is a particularly corrupt sector. One official from the Association of Small and Medium-

76. *Express,* June 17, 2005, cited by Reconstruction National Integrity Survey, *Reconstruction National Integrity Survey: Kosova 2007* (Priština: Reconstruction National Integrity Survey, 2007), 46.

77. Leonard Ibrahimi and Faton Pocolli, *The Principle of Equal Opportunity in Kosovo's Employment System: A Survey of Citizen Perceptions* (Priština: KIMP, 2008).

78. Gallup Balkan Monitor, *2008 Analytical Report* (Brussels: Gallup Balkan Monitor, 2008), 31–33.

79. James H. Anderson and Cheryl W. Gray, *Anti-Corruption Transition 3: Who Is Succeeding and Why?* (Washington, D.C.: World Bank, 2006).

80. Vesna Pešić, *State Capture and Widespread Corruption in Serbia,* CEPS Working Document 262 (Brussels: Center for European and Policy Studies, 2007); and Transparency International, *Serbia Global Corruption Report 2006: Part 2* (New York: Macmillan, 2006), 235–36. In 2006, Serbia ranked 90th out of 146 countries in the Transparency International Corruption Index, 2006.

Sized Businesses observed: "We have passive and huge self-interests where the tacit rule is 'Don't touch me and I won't touch you.'"[81] A 2009 study of Kosovo, funded by the European Commission, found that a "culture of corruption" was "heavily embedded in institutions, and as a result citizens are encountering difficulties with the functions of the state and other institutions."[82] In 2010, high-profile anticorruption efforts against about twenty important officials were launched for the first time in Kosovo, but it remained to be seen if they would lead to convictions. And in Montenegro, the political elite's reputed involvement in the organized smuggling of cigarettes and also reported corruption in the public service gave the small state one of the worst reputations in the Western Balkans.[83]

Although Croatia was generally touted as a leader among the Western Balkan polities with respect to its efforts and successes at combating corruption, survey research continued to reveal corruption as a widespread problem in public institutions, particularly the judiciary, the health sector, and local government. For example, in February 2006, Croatian prime minister Ivo Sanader sent a negative signal to the international community by sacking his justice minister, Vesna Škare-Ožbolt, who had been an advocate of a bold anticorruption strategy and an independent judiciary. Though the move was connected to inter-party politics—the ex-minister belonged to a small party in Sanader's ruling coalition—the government subsequently watered down its anticorruption policy, and continued problems in the court system (millions of backlogged cases, a weak state prosecutor's office, and officials facing corruption allegations) represented serious deficiencies in the rule of law. Meanwhile, Škare-Ožbolt suggested that the condition of the Croatian court system was "weak," and that "the Croatian path to Europe will have further difficulties."[84] After Sanader abruptly left office in mid-2009, there were widespread rumors about his own involvement in or toleration of corruption.

81. RTSTV, May 13, 2010.

82. EU-AC, *Study of Corruption in Kosovo* (Priština: EU-AC, 2009).

83. Marijana Trivunović, Vera Devine, and Harald Mathisen, *Corruption in Montenegro 2007* (Bergen: Chr. Michelsen Institute, 2007); and UPCG, *Korupcija iz perspective poslodavaca* (Podgorica: UPCG, 2008).

84. Bojan Klima, "'Croatian Justice'—Članak Vesne Škaric Ožbolt u Wall Street Journalu," VOA News.com, February 2, 2006.

During 2008 and 2009, after a spate of further corruption scandals, the issues of honesty and integrity in the governmental system became a controversial domestic issue complicating Croatia's entry into the European Union. Indeed, it became a major issue in the presidential election of 2009–10. One of Croatia's top journalists, Davor Genero, put his finger on an issue that has plagued the political class in Croatia and the entire region. He pleaded with his readers to concentrate their attention on the matter of corruption when casting their votes: "Every relevant presidential candidate could be expected to have a clear anti-corruption strategy. But a strategy is not enough. What is needed most of all is a personal background that is free of even a whiff of corruption, which also means a clearly defined origin of personal and family assets, as well as a career devoid of suspicion of corrupt activities, especially suspicions of having created a network of associates and supporters by way of illicit activities and the spending of public money."[85] Following the election of Ivo Josipović in early 2010—who had an unblemished record and was strongly committed to fighting corruption—it appeared that he would be working closely on the issue with Sanader's successor as prime minister, Jadranka Kosor.

The Challenge of Judicial Reform

Problems associated with the establishment of an uncorrupted and independent judicial sector have also been a persistent obstacle to Western Balkan administrative and rule-of-law development. A comprehensive 2004 comparative study of judicial institutions in the region revealed that a "lack of the political preconditions for [judicial] independence is visible in many countries; . . . an insufficient culture of independence and separation of powers and functions still emerges in the whole region due to the presence of legacies of the political culture." The same study found that corruption was still a serious problem in the region, and this was in part due to the fact that the salaries of judges were "below the level of decency."[86] And although the system

85. Davor Genero, writing in *Vjesnik,* October 13, 2009.
86. Europe AID Cooperation Office, *Reinforcement to the Rule of Law, Division of Competencies and Inter-Relations between Courts, Prosecutors, the Police, the Executive and Legislative Powers in the Western Balkan Countries Final Report* (Brussels: European Commission, 2004), 25–26, 30–31. See also Directorate-

of financing courts had improved in Albania and Macedonia, the judiciary remained dependent on the executive and legislative branches of government in Croatia, and in Serbia and Montenegro. Mechanisms to ensure the accountability of judicial officials in the region were also seen to be "underdeveloped."

EU standards for combating judicial corruption have nonetheless made gradual progress in the post-2000 period. Structural changes and innovations have been slowly improving the administration of justice in some countries. Advances in the professionalization of the judiciary, encouraged by professional associations, have also improved the autonomy and role of the judicial sector.[87] For example, in Serbia, assertive members of the judiciary, particularly in the Serbian Society of Judges, sound deeply committed and outspoken about developing their profession as a sector that is an independent "branch of power." As Vida Petrović-Škero, the president of the Supreme Court of Serbia, put it in 2007,

> We do not agree to the dependence of a judiciary which involves itself with the dirty laundry of routine politics, instead of being a symbol of a law-governed state. We don't agree to conform to routine politics and judicial interpretations which are constructed by the political will of one or another [political] party, or the election of judges who are loyal, but are not competent. We don't agree to defend society from democracy, because democracy needs to be defended from the state. . . . We don't agree to silence about the embarrassments of the judiciary, if I'm already turning red from shame because of less than honorable decisions of the judiciary.[88]

Despite such a commitment, problems of judicial development in Serbia and throughout the region have been slow to change, especially where confronting a deeply embedded extralegal culture. As one of Serbia's leading human rights activists observed,

General for External Policies of the Union Directorate B, Policy Department, *Judicial Reform in Countries of South East Europe* (Brussels: European Commission, 2006).

87. See Milica Golubović, "Judicial Professional Associations: Fostering Judicial Reform through Civil Society Development," *Southeastern Europe* 33 (2009): 48–62.

88. Quoted in *Danas,* June 25, 2007.

Experience shows that people don't believe they can achieve much in the courts, that it is better to have good "connections." At least that's what our research shows. In Tito's time there was an office of the President of the Republic, and because Tito was a Marshal, it was called the Marshalat. Many people ignored the deadlines for appealing to courts because they directly appealed to the Marshal. That kind of desire by a subject to achieve rights, but not from the courts is a bad tradition in this country. Submissiveness to executive authority, to the top leader has lasted a long time and deformed the basic instinct [in Serbian society] regarding the equality of people.[89]

After a considerable period of political division and drift in Serbia from 2006 to 2008, the election of a more vigorous democratic coalition set the stage for judicial reform legislation in December 2008, and the establishment of a depoliticized High Judicial Council and State Prosecutorial Council in April 2009. There was optimism that "for the first time," according to the justice minister, "judicial selections between July 30 and December 2009 will be transparent and devoid of political influence."[90] However, in early 2010, the first indicators from the appointment of new judges and prosecutors suggested that the process remained nontransparent and had done little to remove doubts regarding nepotism and political influence in the judicial sector.[91] Several leading Serbian judges called the process "a slap in the face of the judiciary and democracy," and European officials put Belgrade on notice that the judicial reappointment process needed to be repeated in accordance with "European standards."[92] The problem of judicial independence was also problematic in neighboring Montenegro, where, by 2009, management rules for the judiciary had been put in place, but the judicial and prosecutorial services were still "visibly vulnerable to politicisation."[93]

Even for front-runner EU candidate states such as Croatia and Macedonia, persistent problems with corruption and judicial devel-

89. Vojin Dimitrijević, quoted in *Danas,* June 16–17, 2007.

90. *Tanjug,* July 30, 2009.

91. Vesna Pešić, "On the Appointment of Justices and Prosecutors," *Peščanik,* December 30, 2009.

92. Radio Serbia, December 23, 2009, in *BBC Monitoring Europe,* December 24, 2009. The High Judicial Council appointed 1,531 judges to permanent judicial positions and 876 candidates for first appointment to judicial posts. But 837 judges were not reappointed, without detailed explanation or legal recourse.

93. Sigma Assessment, Montenegro, Public Integrity System, May 2009.

opment have continued to slow these states' momentum in moving through the EU accession process. For instance, when visiting Croatia in April 2007, EU justice minister Franco Frattina asked that the fight against corruption be made a top priority and emphasized that politicians and judges are not above the law: "Legislative reforms are not enough. They need to be fully implemented."[94]

Recognizing such deficiencies and EU frustration on such matters, Croatia launched a major project in June 2007 to improve judicial efficiency, increase transparency, and reduce corruption.[95] At the same time, Croatia was hit by a national scandal regarding corruption by high officials of the country's troubled Privatization Fund, leading to calls for the resignation of the prime minister. Croatia's justice minister commented in 2009 that "the European Commission's grade on Croatia's progress in the judiciary could be described as C–. However, Croatia is preparing a package of laws on the independence of the judiciary, so one can expect the grade to improve to B– by the end of the year."[96]

Alan Uzelac, a Croatian legal development specialist, has usefully pointed out that members of the current judicial elite in Croatia—many of whom were educated in or adopted the "socialist legal tradition," which views law as instrumental to the ruling political order—have embraced the notion of "judicial independence," but only as a means of preserving and perpetuating the exclusive role of judges and magistrates in the judicial sector. This is not necessarily a desirable trend for developing judicial impartiality and democratic change. Indeed, the conservative values of Croatia's judiciary have been an obstacle to reform. Thus, by controlling all spheres of the judiciary (e.g., the High Judicial Council, professional associations, drafting of new legislation, the socialization of new judges), many unreformed members of the "judicial oligarchies" exercise considerable political leverage and "play a part in the political games." Professional legal elites can thus use the notion of "judicial independence" to entrench traditional values and ways of conducting the judicial process.[97]

In 2010, Croatia's new president, Ivo Josipović, emphasized the creation of an "independent and responsible" judiciary that was efficient

94. Quoted in *South East European Times,* April 18, 2007.
95. Eastbusiness.org, June 4, 2007.
96. *Hina,* October 15, 2009.
97. "Survival of the Third Legal Tradition?" paper delivered at International Association of Procedural Law meeting, Toronto, 2009.

and corruption free as a major priority of government policy. Until recently, he observed, "we were joking that there are issues [facing the courts] that are older than the judges. I hope this will come to an end." He also praised the indictment for corruption of "big fish," such as a former deputy prime minister. "There is always a bigger fish," he noted, "but a deputy prime minister is a very big fish. But it's up to the judiciary to determine his guilt."[98]

A 2009 study of Macedonia by the Organization for Security and Cooperation in Europe found that almost half (43 percent) of 421 surveyed judges felt that they were regularly subject to external pressure by executive, administrative, judicial, and political officers (37 percent said they were not, and 20 percent did not answer the question). Seventy percent of those surveyed believed that the members of the country's Judicial Council (composed of members of the legislature, the executive, and the judiciary), had been selected on the basis of "biased criteria." A retired Supreme Court judge who took part in the analysis inquired "how citizens trust such a judicial system, when significant numbers of judges do not believe in the system."[99]

In Albania, which trails among Western Balkan EU aspirants, corruption runs throughout the public administration, including the judicial sector, at a very high level, despite years of discussion and numerous policy statements regarding the issue. "Albania is in urgent need of reform of the judicial sector," remarked the country's justice minister in early 2007, as he announced a new €5 million EU project to improve the quality of trials and increase the number of judges.[100] The urgency of judicial reform in Albania was underlined by 2008 Gallup Poll results, which found that only 22 percent of Albanian respondents had confidence in their judicial sector and courts. This was the lowest level in the region, and close to the same low level was found in Macedonia. The regional median of 30 percent expressing confidence in the judi-

98. Legalis Hrvatski pravni portal, September 11, 2010.
99. Saše Dimovski, "Survey Shows Macedonian Judges Still Fear 'Pressures,'" BalkanInsight.com, January 6, 2010.
100. "Rilindja Demokratija," World News Connection, April 24, 2007, 54; "Citizen Trust in the Albanian Judicial System Is Low and Showed No Change from 2005–2006," in *Corruption in Albania: Perception and Experience Survey, 2006,* edited by Institute for Development Research and Alternatives (Tirana: Institute for Development Research and Alternatives, 2007). See also Organization for Security and Cooperation in Europe, *Analyses of the Criminal Justice System of Albania* (Tirana: OSCE Mission in Albania, 2006), 167–78.

ciary was approximated by the findings for Croatia and Serbia, and was considerably below the EU median of 47 percent.[101]

Meanwhile, in Kosovo, judicial institutions reflected the situation of a very "unfinished state," with overlapping and conflicting lines of authority. During 2009 and 2010, EULEX had not been able to eliminate a highly politicized judicial system, nor to establish a merit-based appointment process for judges.[102] The challenge for EULEX was complicated by the existence of a Belgrade-funded "parallel" justice system in Serb-controlled northern Mitrovica. At the end of 2009, Serbia's appointment of judges for the parallel system provoked a protest from EULEX and international actors.

The deep distrust and low evaluation of Western Balkan judicial systems not only reflected the malfunctioning of existing institutions and of judicial and administrative actors but also clearly had a transgenerational impact that impeded the development of a legal culture supportive of democracies. For example, a 2009 study of students and teachers in Bosnia found the "worrying fact" that they usually do not have a "trust in justice. . . . Three-fifths of students believe that the society in which they live is unjust, while even a third do not believe that justice wins over injustice."[103] A December 2009 study by the Organization for Security and Cooperation in Europe found that in the preceding twelve months, instances of undue political pressure on the Court of Bosnia and Herzegovina and the central prosecutor's office had reached an "unprecedented level."[104]

From 2007 to 2010, the Western Balkan countries all accelerated their efforts to fight corruption and deficiencies in the rule of law, but they were making up for the earlier loss of valuable time, and in many respects they were still in the take-off stage of meaningful state building, that is, implementation of legislation on these matters. For example, the 2009

101. Cynthia English, "Many in the Balkans Lack Confidence in Judicial Systems," March 10, 2008.

102. Vedran Džihić and Helmut Kramer, "Kosovo after Independence: Is the EU's EULEX Mission Delivering on Its Promises?" (Skopje: Friedrich Ebert Stiftung, 2009); and EULEX deputy head Roy Reeve, on Radio-Television Kosovo, June 4, 2010.

103. Regional Office for Southeast Europe, *Discrimination of Children in Schools in Bosnia and Herzegovina* (Oslo: Save the Children, 2009), 8.

104. Organization for Security and Cooperation in Europe, *Independence of the Judiciary: Undue Pressure on BiH Judicial Institutions* (Sarajevo: OSCE Mission in Bosnia and Herzegovina, 2009).

Progress Reports on the individual Balkan countries—important guide-posts for the region's political elites—suggested that corruption was still "widespread" (in Macedonia), "still prevalent in many areas" (Croatia, Serbia, Kosovo, Montenegro, and Albania), or that "little progress had been made in fighting corruption" (Bosnia). The judicial systems of the region were also identified as an area where reforms were taking place (with notable momentum in Macedonia) but still "remained to be tested in practice" (Croatia), were only "moderately advanced" (Serbia), or remained at "an early stage" (Kosovo, Bosnia, Albania).

Both EU and domestic officials have increasingly acknowledged that during the last two decades in the region's postcommunist countries, "the importance of the rule of law was sometimes underestimated." As the EU commissioner for enlargement put it in October 2009, "While in the early '90s [the] first, and often the only commandment was: 'Privatize,' they now underline that the most important thing was actually to put in place a modern Constitution, to reform the judicial system, including the courts, and to build credible law enforcement authorities."[105] Indeed, a report of the European Court of Auditors toward the end of 2009 questioned the sustainability of the European Commission's institution-building projects that had been conducted in the area of justice: "The reason for this was continued political weakness and lack of commitment (ownership) by the beneficiaries, as most projects did not come from within the region but from the Commission and other external stakeholders."[106]

Decentralized Governance and Democratization

Western Balkan elites have often resorted to various forms of decentralization as a way to combat corruption and address widespread citizen distrust toward public administration and judicial institutions. Each state in the region has pursed its own varied strategy of decentralization. But in all cases, they are aimed at promoting improved public

105. Olli Rehn, "Lessons from EU Enlargement for Its Future Foreign Policy," Speech 09/492, Brussels, October 22, 2009.

106. Maaten B. Engwirda, press conference, "Special Report 12/2009 on the Effectiveness of the Commission projects in the Area Justice and Home Affairs in the Western Balkans," ECA/09/57, European Court of Auditors, Brussels, October 13, 2009.

administration by enhancing the effective delivery of services and improving the accountability of government to citizens (through the local oversight of officials). Decentralization strategies are also sometimes touted as a way to nurture a new and more democratically oriented type of politician. And, in multiethnic settings, various modes of devolved authority are viewed as a way to satisfy demands for ethnocultural autonomy and/or to ensure the representativeness of local government to minority groups.

Because various schemes of decentralization and regionalization are so varied and complex—involving fiscal, administrative, and political decentralization—it is difficult to make sweeping generalizations about their success in the region. In some countries with deep ethnic divisions—such as Macedonia, Bosnia, and Kosovo, as discussed above—the centralization-versus-decentralization debate has often been extremely contentious and sometimes destabilizing. Other countries—such as Serbia, Croatia, Albania, and Montenegro—have experimented with modes of regionalization and the devolution of authority to municipalities, not primarily to accommodate ethnoregional or subcultural demands but rather to implement measures called for by both domestic and international actors for more effective democratic and accountable governance. Such initiatives have, in most cases, contributed to the formal *deconcentration* of governmental responsibilities and also stimulated considerable discussion of noncentralized models of organizing regimes. In comparative terms, considered in 2008 together with the experience of European nations and countries that belong to the Commonwealth of Independent States, most Western Balkan states could be ranked as "advanced intermediate decentralizers" (Macedonia, Albania, Croatia, Montenegro, Serbia, and Kosovo), because they have established "full systems of local government" and have made progress in "building the policy and legislative setting for decentralization." But legislative reform is only a first step. In Albania, for example, the establishment of a regional council is regarded as an "empty box," because regional and local officials often lack the capacity to deliver public services and promote economic development. The systematic turnover of local staff members after each municipal election has also weakened capacity in Albania.[107]

107. United Nations Development Program, *Decentralization in the European and CIS Region,* Discussion Paper (Bratislava: United Nations Development Program, 2008), 16.

Overall, efforts in the Western Balkans to combat local corruption, satisfy the demands of ethnic cultural groups, and foster political participation or create democratic linkages between citizens and the state through schemes of decentralization and regionalization have met with only limited success. Indeed, when the overall public administration sector is already riven by systematic problems such as organizational fragmentation, politicization, a lack of professionalism, and corruption, models of decentralization and regionalization can actually compound problems, at least temporarily. In Bosnia, for example, with three ethnopolitical elites and a host of ethnically oriented political parties dominating the scene, a weak central government and a multiplicity of regional and subregional administrative-political units has only accentuated fragmentation and a dysfunctional governmental system in which decisionmaking is impaired and corruption is rife. Strategies and "action plans" for fighting corruption have not been seriously implemented by central and local authorities that are sometimes closely associated with criminal elements. Corruption is also most widespread and apparent to observers at the local government level—especially in the legal, health, and education sectors—because of the direct personal contact between officials and citizens.[108] Of course, it is difficult to classify Bosnia as either decentralized or centralized, because its entities and cantons—that is, the middle level of governance—have considerable powers and resources vis-à-vis local governments. Thus, viewed from the local level, Bosnia is a case of extreme centralization, but not because of central institutions.[109] The renewed constitutional reform discussion, which began in Bosnia in 2009, is not likely to address decentralization on the local level, at least in the short run.

When intergroup tensions are at a fever pitch in a country, over-concentration on power distribution through decentralization can also deepen ethnocultural divisions. For example, in Kosovo, beginning in 2008, the radical Kosovo Self-Determination Movement had some success in convincing Kosovo Albanian citizens that internationally inspired decentralization plans to assist minority rights placed them

108. Srdjan Blagovčanin, *Korupcija u Bosni i Herzegovini* (Sarajevo: Friedrich Ebert Stiftung, 2009), 9.

109. Zdravko Miovčić, "Bosnia and Hercegovina between Centralisation and Decentralisation," paper for the conference "Decentralization between Regionalism and Federalism in the Stability Pact Countries of the Western Balkans," Tirana, June 9–10, 2006.

at a disadvantage compared with minority Serbs. And some Kosovo Albanians also perceive disadvantages from the transfer of power from the central government to local governments because the latter jurisdictions are financially weaker. Many Kosovo Albanians were already predisposed against decentralization because Serb communities in northern Kosovo and elsewhere had established what some in the country's ethnic majority considered a "state within a state."

By and large, however, most Kosovo Albanians regard the decentralization of powers to the Serbian community as a foregone conclusion because it is a core feature of the Ahtisaari Proposal—that is, the plan that paved the way to independence in 2008 (see chapter 2)—and would theoretically accommodate 80 percent of Serbs in local units of self-government. Most Serbs, meanwhile, have remained suspicious that any decentralization plan that is organized by the Kosovo state authorities and international actors will erode existing Serb structures of parallel authority (including control of schools and hospitals).[110] The participation of a small number of Serbs in the 2009 Kosovo local elections encouraged Kosovo officials to believe that their decentralization could move forward. But EULEX officials created a storm in early 2010 when they suggested that Belgrade's agreement to the dissolution of Serb control structures in northern Mitrovica might be linked to Serbia's chances to enter the European Union. Despite different views of decentralization between Kosovo's Albanians and Serbs, the actual administrative-organizational operations in the Albanian and Serb areas of the country have considerable similarity. Thus, in both cases local affairs are heavily influenced by central government party politics (in Priština for Albanians, and in Belgrade for Kosovo Serbs), and the direct accountability of officials to citizens is negligible.[111]

Macedonia has also been trying to implement a decentralization strategy since the Ohrid Agreement of 2001 provided for the devolution of greater power to municipal units. From its onset, the Ohrid decentralization strategy has been regarded by most ethnic Macedonians as a way for the predominantly ethnic Albanian municipalities to link up in some way to form a kind of "'enclavization' of municipalities" that

---

110. Kosovo Local Government Initiative, *Implementing Decentralization in Kosovo: One Year On* (Priština: Kosovo Local Government Initiative, 2009).

111. Gyorgy Hajnal and Gabor Peteri, *Local Reform in Kosovo: Final Report* (Priština: Forum 2015, 2010).

would eventually combine and lead to the federalization or collapse of the state.[112] Most citizens of Macedonia, however, grudgingly accepted that the decentralization mandated by the Ohrid Accord was necessary to prevent violence in the country. More enthusiasm for decentralized governance was shown on the Albanian side. In view of the strong political divide, the implementation of decentralization progressed slowly and nontransparently, with a kind of "centralized approach to decentralization."[113] For example, a 2004 referendum to overturn an early decentralization plan was defeated because turnout fell well below 50 percent. But because the referendum did not lead to further violence or instability, the vote was generally seen as a state-building success.

A new phase of decentralization began in July 2005. In 2006, out of eighty-four municipalities in Macedonia, thirty-two had a highly mixed ethnic composition and made up 41 percent of the state's total population. Another nineteen municipalities are dominated by minorities in the relative ethnic composition of their population, and sixteen have Albanians as the largest group. These municipalities made up about 28.6 percent of the population.[114] The ethnically mixed communities have provided at least an element of demographic political integration in the country. But because of Macedonia's political and party polarization on an ethnic basis (see chapter 5), such a mixed population does not provide for an improvement in interethnic relations. Thus, up until 2010, the decentralization model in Macedonia did little to de-ethnicize political loyalties or transcend intergroup conflicts, not to mention improve political participation, administrative accountability, or efforts to combat corruption at the local level. In fact, in 2009 four-fifths of surveyed respondents in Macedonia claimed that they had no influence over decisions made by local municipal governments, although a slightly greater number of Albanians felt that they now had some influence.[115]

112. Institute for Regional and International Studies, *The Process of Decentralization in Macedonia* (Skopje: Institute for Regional and International Studies, 2008).

113. Joseph Marko, "The Referendum on Decentralization in Macedonia in 2004: A Litmus Test for Macedonia's Interethnic Relations," *European Yearbook for Minority Issues* 4 (2004–5): 24.

114. Rizvan Sulejmani, "Decentralisation or Centralisation," paper for the Conference "Decentralization between Regionalism and Federalism in the Stability Pact Countries of the Western Balkans," Tirana, June 9–10, 2006.

115. United Nations Development Program, *People-Centered Analysis Report* (Skopje: United Nations Development Program, 2009), 82.

Albanian local politicians did have more influence in minority and mixed municipalities after 2005, and the danger of violence and territorial secessionism also diminished (due in part to greater minority rights with respect to education and language). And most citizens (78 percent) surveyed reported that interethnic relations in their municipality was "positive."[116] But decentralization in Macedonia has mostly benefited ethnic Macedonian and Albanian local party elites, who have been more concerned with their "petty interests" and "ethnic power sharing" as a means to control local institutions rather than in responding to the needs and views of citizens.[117] Significant progress has been made, however, in the area of strengthening the financial independence of municipalities (although it is still low in comparison with other countries in the region),[118] and by mid-2009, sixty-eight out of eighty-five municipalities had entered the second stage of fiscal decentralization.

Meanwhile, Serbia and Croatia have moved very slowly forward with initiatives to decentralize governance in the post-Milošević and post-Tudjman period. In part, both countries have faced difficulties in steering a course between pressure from the EU requiring more decentralization and the political realities of trying to avoid minority nationalism and state disintegration. This concern has been less serious in Croatia, where regional demands for autonomy in Istria have been moderate and well incorporated into the party system. However, Croatia lacks the dynamics of a generally decentralized system. Thus, there have been persistent delays in implementing decentralization plans in Croatia, and a Decentralization Commission has not proved able to act as a driving force in the process.[119] Moreover, enthusiasm for rapid decentralization to local government in Croatia has diminished somewhat in recent years,

116. Organization for Security and Cooperation in Europe, *OSCE Decentralization Survey 2009* (Skopje: OSCE, 2009).

117. King Baudouin Foundation, *A Guide to Minorities and Political Participation in South-East Europe* (Brussels: King Baudouin Foundation, 2009), 70; and United Nations Development Program, *Results of a Participatory Assessment, National and Local Capacities for Strengthening Inter-ethnic Dialogue and Collaboration* (Skopje: United Nations Development Program, 2010).

118. Tony Levitas, *Local Government Finances in Macedonia Today: Possible Reforms for Tomorrow,* IDG Working Paper 2009-08 (Washington, D.C.: Urban Institute Center on International Development and Governance, 2009).

119. United Nations Development Program, *Capacity Development for Quality Public Service Delivery at the Local Level in the Western Balkans* (Skopje: United Nations Development Program, 2009), 33.

owing to revelations of flagrant corruption by some municipal authorities.[120] Imbalance in the staff size of Croatia's local government units—the country has one of the largest numbers of territorial and local units in the Balkans, with 20 counties, 430 municipalities, and 126 cities—has also been an obstacle to administrative capacity and efficiency.[121]

In Serbia, there have been even greater difficulties with decentralization. Having recently experienced the breaking off of Kosovo and the cession of Montenegro, Serbia's elites are highly allergic to any further centrifugal initiatives. The 2006 Constitution actually increased the formal powers of the central government. However, there has been strong pressure for regionalization and autonomy, especially on the part of Serbia's minority communities, such as the Bosniaks in Sandžak, Albanians in South Serbia's Preševo Valley, and Hungarians in Vojvodina.[122] Indeed, demands in Vojvodina for more decisionmaking power go simply beyond minorities and include a portion of the majority (65 percent) Serbian community. In late 2009, the ruling coalition in Belgrade enacted a "Vojvodina statute" that granted some additional powers to the province (to be gradually implemented from 2010 to 2012).

However, nine years after the fall of the Milošević regime, Serbia was only beginning to initiate a broader countrywide process of decentralization, and this was largely conceived as a way to advance the country's case for candidate status in the EU preaccession process. A recent survey indicated that the majority of citizens (54 percent) expressed general support for the ideas of both regionalization and decentralization. But there existed considerable confusion about what such notions meant. Moreover, when asked whether they personally enjoyed any influence in local government, 57 percent of respondents said they had none, 19 percent said they had very little, 13 percent said they had only a little, and 9 percent said they had only moderate or considerable influence.[123] Local government influence in Serbian politics derives primar-

120. Marijana Badun, "Decentralisation, Corruption and Supervision of Local Budgets in Croatia," *Newsletter, Institute of Public Finance,* January 2009.

121. Ante Bajo, "The Structure of Employment in Local Government Units," *Newsletter, Institute of Public Finance,* July 2009, 1–9.

122. Beata Huszka, "Decentralization of Serbia: The Minority Dimension," Center for Policy Studies, July 2007.

123. Srećko Mihajlović, *Mnenje gradjana central Srbije o decentralizacija i regionalizaciji* (Belgrade: Center for Civil Society Development, 2008).

ily from the considerable power of local leaders and elites in various municipalities. Thus, popular local leaders who are able to garner significant voting support have increasingly become key partners of the major political parties operating at the central level of the state. Thus, a kind of traditional center-periphery form of clientalistic cooperation has been more important in Serbia than genuine decentralization.

Weak States in "Low-Capacity" Democracies

Despite the continued difficulties with fighting corruption, as well as in the areas of both judicial reform and decentralization, the Western Balkans did reveal improved governance capacity and democratic state building during its first postconflict decade. Thus, the useful data provided by the World Bank Governance Project offer cross-national evidence of a common pattern of both success and continued weakness in the region—some notable differences among states notwithstanding.

According to the World Bank Governance Project, three aggregate indicators focusing on the quality of governance are most illustrative with respect to the institutional focus of this chapter: (1) *government effectiveness,* including the quality of public services and the civil service, its degree of independence from political pressure, the quality of policy formulation and implementation, and the credibility of the government's commitment to such policies; (2) *the rule of law,* including compliance with societal rules, particularly the quality of contract enforcement, the police, and the courts, and also the likelihood of violence; and (3) *control of corruption,* including the extent to which public power is prevented from being exercised for private gain, which focuses on both petty corruption, such as "state capture" by the elite, and private interests. These governance indicators used by the World Bank draw on an aggregation of responses to a large number of surveys carried out by institutes, think tanks, nongovernmental organizations, and international organizations.

As table 3.4 indicates, most of the Western Balkan polities made progress with respect to their governmental effectiveness during the period from 1996 to 2008, with Croatia in the lead and Kosovo trailing behind. Control of corruption is a more problematic area of governance, even for Croatia. Kosovo and Albania are at the back of the regional pack, with the former suffering from an earlier pattern of deficient

Table 3.4. Selected Governance Indicators for the Western Balkan Region (percentile rank 0–100, worst to best)

Country	Government Effectiveness			Control of Corruption			Rule of Law		
	1996	2002	2008	1996	2002	2008	1996	2002	2008
Albania	55.0	32.2	44.5	59.2	23.3	39.1	53.3	19.5	32.5
Croatia	55.9	66.8	69.7	31.1	62.6	61.8	33.3	54.8	55.0
Bosnia-Herzegovina	5.2	12.8	35.1	46.1	42.2	45.9	54.3	29.0	43.5
Macedonia	47.4	37.0	50.7	11.7	30.1	54.6	52.4	33.3	43.5
Kosovo	N.A.	N.A.	18.5	N.A.	19.9[a]	30.0	N.A.	13.3	30.1
Serbia	36.5	31.3	47.9	18.0	29.1	53.1	16.7	20.5	41.1
Montenegro	N.A.	N.A.	56.9	N.A.	N.A.	47.8	N.A.	N.A.	53.1

Note: N.A. = not available.
[a]Kosovo, 2003.
Source: World Bank, *Worldwide Governance Indicators, 1996–2008* (Washington, D.C.: World Bank, 2009).

international management and new challenges of fledgling statehood, and the latter making a slow recovery in the decade that followed its 1997 state meltdown. Albania's scores in 2008 in all three areas selected were actually lower than in 1996. But even Albania, as shown from other evidence, made limited progress with administrative reform, and research indicated that support for a well-paid, merit-based civil service has been slowly developing within the ranks of senior administrative officials.[124] In view of the political difficulties faced by Serbia after Milošević, and the close links between criminal elements and politicians in Montenegro, corruption control in both countries has been slow. The rule of law as a general governance category shows steady forward momentum, but at levels that vary from country to country. International assistance has helped to advance Bosnia-Herzegovina in all areas, albeit not up to Croatia's level, and not yet exhibiting levels that will ensure sustainable progress once the present framework of foreign involvement and assistance is terminated.

Meanwhile, Kosovo, Albania, and Serbia also have deeply rooted rule-of-law problems. In the case of Serbia, this particular difficulty is closely linked to the broader issue of coming to terms with the recent past, not to mention the problem of dealing with entrenched criminal networks,[125] and two remaining high-profile war crimes cases. Macedonia's progress in the rule-of-law area dropped precipitously after the 2001 conflict, but later showed improvement. Overall, a comparison between Western Balkan trends in the rule of law, corruption, and government effectiveness with similar average aggregate data for the Eastern Balkans and Central and Eastern Europe reveals the relatively more favorable position of the latter two regions, which were fortunate in having faced the difficulties of postcommunist transition and democratic consolidation without postconflict burdens.

Although these selected World Bank indicators are subject to considerable margins of error, and cannot express the complex diversity of transformation within individual regimes and societies, the data usefully suggest relative standings and rates of progress. Most significantly, the

124. World Bank, *Global Monitoring Report 2006* (Washington, D.C.: World Bank, 2006), 152.

125. United Nations Development Program, *Serbia Corruption Benchmarking Survey Analytical Report* (Belgrade: United Nations Development Program, 2010).

aggregate measures indicate that from the vantage point of institutional strengthening or capacity building, the Western Balkan states still have a considerable way to go before they reach "European standards," although they have been making important progress since 1996. Aspects of the "intrusive state / weak state" syndrome nonetheless remain an outstanding issue for governance in region. The problem of state weakness has been a feature throughout the post-2000 period. A 2004 review of the region emphasized that the warfare in the 1990s had "fostered a culture of opacity, politicization, and corruption," leaving the countries and entities "generally weak in their capacities—the rule of law is respected neither by the executives nor the population, and judicial systems are incapable of enforcing it systematically."[126]

Referring to the performance of public administrations in the Western Balkan states as weak is simply a way of comparing their administrative structures to the longer-established and more professionalized administrative sectors in other European democracies. Typically, the so-called weak state lacks the "infrastructural strength," or the capacity to coordinate and carry out certain critical tasks, such as delivering selected services, protecting the rule of law and human rights, and avoiding corruption and the capture of governing institutions by various extrastate predatory forces and "opaque groups" in society. Indeed, even with the assistance of foreign state builders, the weak state usually lacks the capacity to obtain broad societal compliance for its policies.

Characterizing the Western Balkan states as weak does not suggest that they all suffer from the full range of problems generally associated with weak states in other regions, or that the same facets of weakness affect each country in the region. One feature, however, of the "weak society / weak state syndrome" that is perhaps most common to all the Western Balkan states—and one that they share with many other states especially following the impact of the recession (2008–10)—is the chronic lack of routine communication and trust between citizens and states (see also chapters 5 and 9).[127] The "implementation deficit" in actually getting laws translated into practice is another persistent

126. Sigma, *Public Administration in the Balkans: Overview* (Paris: Sigma, 2004), 7. On Balkan state weakness, also see Ivan Krastev, "The Balkans: Democracy without Choices," *Journal of Democracy* 13, no. 3 (July 2002): 39–53.

127. See Marko Grdešić, "Problem slabih država i slabih društva u istočnoj Evropi," *Anali Hrvatskog Politoloskog društva 2008,* 241–62.

regional problem. Indeed, the weakness of state institutions in the Western Balkans has been significantly affected by what has recently been referred to as a "culture of disrespect for state-sponsored rules," which is reflected in a deep "distrust of the state and its alienation from society." In most postcommunist states and throughout most of the Western Balkans during the past decade, such chronic disrespect for rules and their implementation has undermined the overall legitimacy and performance of the state, which is a prerequisite for progress in democratic consolidation.[128]

The selected features of state weakness displayed in the Western Balkans have negatively influenced the region's overall pattern of democratic consolidation. Thus, although the countries of the region have made considerable progress at state building and democracy building in the post-2000 period, most regimes have continued to manifest characteristics that Charles Tilly has referred to as "low-capacity democratic"; that is, they are regimes that have become more pluralistic and have expanded available civil liberties, but they are weak in the area of implementing policies and enforcing laws. "Capacity and democracy interact," as Tilly correctly points out, and though "governmental capacity does not define democracy, it looks like a really necessary condition for democracy on a large scale."[129]

The interaction between capacity and democracy is a vicious cycle. Thus, in the early stages of postcommunist transition, the nonconsolidated character of new democracies in the Western Balkans, and elsewhere in Eastern Europe, impeded capacity building in such regimes, and to some extent this problem persists. But more recently, the deficits in institutional capacity of the postcommunist regimes have become serious impediments to further democratic consolidation in the Western

128. Denisa Kostovicova and Vesna Bojičić-Dželilović, "State Weakening and Globalization," in *Persistent State Weakness in a Global Age,* edited by Denisa Kostovicova and Vesna Bojičić-Dželilović (Burlington, Vt.: Ashgate, 2009), 2–6. Susan Woodward, pointing to the progress that the Western Balkan states have made in reducing "conventional" crime levels, and downplaying the problem of corruption and organized crime, has questioned the utility of describing the region's governance achievements as weak in terms of capacity. Susan Woodward, "Measuring State Failure/Weakness: Do the Balkan Cases Fit?" in *Persistent State Weakness in a Global Age,* ed. Kostovicova and Bojičić-Dželilović, 151–64.

129. Charles Tilly, *Regimes and Repertoires* (Chicago: University of Chicago Press, 2006), 21–29.

Balkans. Such capacity deficiencies (especially in eradicating organized criminality, widespread corruption, and depoliticizing their judiciaries), and their links to other nonconsolidated features of democracy. (see chapters 4 and 5), have generated anxieties among elites and analysts both within and outside the region about future development. They wonder whether the Western Balkans have or can successfully develop the panoply of requisite institutional and political characteristics that will qualify them for fuller entry into the "European family," or whether the region will retain its familiar status as an area located "in between" on the East/West fault line. The fact that the most recent EU entrants from Southeastern Europe, Romania and Bulgaria, have remained severely challenged by postaccession problems related to fighting corruption and judicial development has been an added source of concern to EU elites as they ponder future enlargements in the region (see chapter 9).

Thus, as the first decade of the twenty-first century ended, most regimes in the Western Balkans were still trapped in an indeterminate and unstable intermediate zone—clearly no longer repressive authoritarian political systems, but not yet fully consolidated or strong democracies that demonstrate the capacity to effectively constrain egregious forms of corruption and the routine abuse of governmental power. And yet many of the obstacles to democratization that arose in the Western Balkans as part of the complex and prolonged consolidation phase following the transition out of Communist rule have been significantly reduced or, with the assistance of the EU, have begun to receive close attention (e.g., €3.5 billion in preaccession financial aid for the Western Balkans and Turkey covering the period 2007–11 was approved by the EU in mid-2007).

Clearly, the state structures in the region have not entirely recovered from the sharp downward slide they experienced during the late Communist period, and in the 1990s, with respect to their institutional capacity to carry out public functions. And many long-standing problems of state development—such as corruption and weaknesses with respect to the rule of law, and politicized administration and adjudication—remain troubling and difficult to dislodge. The relatively low or moderate levels of post-2000 institutional capacity in the Western Balkans have slowed progress in state building and democratic consolidation, if less in economic development until 2009, as we shall see in chapter 8. More rapid progress is, however, anxiously sought by the region's elites as a means to qualify for integration into the European Union. Still, as detailed in this and the preceding chapter, by 2010 improvements in constitutional design and in constructing the institutions of state authority and governance had undoubtedly made the Balkans a far different place than it was in 2000. Yet along with such gradual institutional advances, other dimensions of political life should be considered in making an overall evaluation of trends in democratic consolidation. Thus the next two chapters explore the emerging pluralist potential for the transformation of political culture, not only in the important areas of civil society development, gender equality, and media pluralism (chapter 4) but also with respect to political party development (chapter 5).

Chapter 4

Civic Engagement, Gender Politics, and Media Pluralism: Political Cultures in Flux

A vigorous and sustainable democracy requires not only effective state institutions but also a society with a dynamic civic ethos. Thus, the growth of civil society—largely composed of nongovernmental organizations (NGOs) and nonprofit organizations that function in the political space outside the state sector and other spheres such as the family and the market—constitutes a major dimension of democracy building. Indeed, many theorists of democracy believe that the development of civil society is the most critical dimension of democratic consolidation, although views differ about the level and nature of the associational activism that is essential to a sustainable democracy.[1]

In any event, the expansion of an authentic and free civil society can promote the type of associational life that facilitates linkages between the society and state, limits and monitors state power, and generally stimulates the participatory attitudes that constitute a democratic political culture. An enriched associational life composed of democratically oriented organizations generally contributes to both the civic engagement of citizens and the societal "embeddedness" of pluralist norms. A robust civil society sector can also engender the "critical distance" of society from the state, while still encouraging political institutions to be

1. See the discussion by Nikolay Valkov, "Membership in Voluntary Organizations and Democratic Performance: European Post-Communist Countries in Comparative Perspective," *Communist and Post-Communist Studies,* no. 42 (2009): 1–21. For a good overview of civil society's contribution to democratic change, see Stephen P. Osborne, ed., *The Third Sector in Europe: Prospects and Challenges* (London: Routledge, 2008).

responsive and accountable to societal interests and nonstate political actors.

Alternatively, or simultaneously of course, the growth of associational life may prove to be an impediment to democratization. Thus, NGOs can encourage the emergence or perpetuation of illiberal or "uncivil" perspectives, along with various traditional group bonds that serve to undermine democratic change. In some cases, the proliferation of "multiple civil societies" sharply divided along religious, ethnic, or linguistic lines will fragment a society and promote the kind of intergroup conflicts that detract from democratic development.[2]

The Development of Civil Society in the Western Balkans

Despite a pattern of intraregional variation and significant country to country, or subregion to subregion, specificities, it still is possible to discern three rather distinct, albeit overlapping, phases of civil society development throughout the Western Balkans: (1) the period of civil society takeoff following the emergence of pluralist political activity in the years just before, during, and immediately after armed conflicts in the region (1990–98/99); (2) a rapid stage of the post-1999 expansion of NGOs following the 1999 war in Kosovo, and the major post-1999–2000 leaderships changes in Croatia and Serbia; and (3) more recent (2005–11) and ongoing efforts of civil society organizations, on the one hand, and state policymaking bodies, on the other, to establish mutually acceptable, closer, and more "normalized" relationships with one another.

Civil Society Takeoff and "Colonization"

During the second half of the 1990s, as the Western Balkans began to slowly recover from the direct and indirect impact of Yugoslavia's violent disintegration, there was a noticeable surge in civil society development. The Communist legacy and the warfare of the early 1990s, as reviewed in chapter 1, had limited the region's experience with democratic political life. Still, the role of non–state-controlled associational

2. Geoffrey Pridham, *The Dynamics of Democratization: A Comparative Approach* (London: Continuum, 2000), 220–34.

activity was not totally absent. During the twilight decade of Yugoslav Communist development (1980–90), the erosion and disintegration of the authoritarian state structure provided substantial space for the growth of independent organizational activity.

But civil society development remained limited during this period, owing to the one-party regime's suspicion and fear of unofficially sponsored political participation—partially a legacy of the early Communist period, which led citizens to distrust associations outside traditional networks and familial circles (especially in Albania, but even in the former Yugoslavia, with its considerable basis for autonomous civic engagement)—and also the historically weak participatory political culture throughout the region. Moreover, in post-Tito Yugoslavia, illiberal elite entrepreneurs involved in the nationalist mobilization of the 1980s and 1990s also became major obstacles to democratic civil society development. But even in this period, there remained "oases" of an emergent civil society centered on alternative grassroots and critical intellectual civic groups that had first flourished in the 1960s and 1970s (especially in Zagreb and Belgrade, but also later in Sarajevo).[3]

As radical nationalism and the "ethnicization" of political life acquired more intensity in the 1990s, particularly in Serbia and Croatia, the differences in civil society development among the various republics would grow (and indeed would contribute to the process of Yugoslavia's dissolution), as well as create a fresh context for the next stage of organizational growth outside, and autonomous from, the state structure. In some of socialist Yugoslavia's republics—such as Croatia, Serbia, Montenegro, and Macedonia—national or ethnic concepts of emerging statehood would become more dominant, while in Slovenia a more civic or multiethnic, albeit sovereigntist concept, prevailed. Bosnia was more complicated, with the two conceptions strongly in conflict within and among the republics' constituent ethnoreligious communities. As Vukašin Pavlović has pointed out, the contrast was starkest and most significant between Slovenia and Serbia: "In Slovenia, the winning for-

3. Christophe Solioz, "Strengths and Weaknesses of Civil Society in the Balkans: Continuities from Conflict to Peace," paper prepared for Fourth Assembly of World Movement for Democracy, Istanbul, April 5, 2006. On the significance of legacy factors for civil society development, see Laszlo Bruszt et al., *Civil Society, Institutional Change and the Politics of Reform,* Working Paper 2010/38 (New York: United Nations University Press, 2010).

mula was 'nationalism plus civil society'; in Serbia, it was 'nationalism without civil society.'"[4]

Paradoxically, despite the antipluralist environment during Yugoslavia's violent dissolution from 1992 to 1995, various local antiwar, women's, and humanitarian organizations also began to function. Indeed, a wide range of different groups were formed in the 1990s throughout the region, including groups for peace, the environment, anticorruption, human rights, refugee return, social welfare, economic development, the disabled, minorities, and students. It is also noteworthy that although autonomous group activity was curtailed during the Communist phase—far more restrictively in Albania than in Titoist Yugoslavia—and organizational life was configured in a top-down manner, the societies in the region still had some experience with group or associational structures, albeit many of a downward "transmission belt" variety (e.g., for culture or sports). Thus, external evaluations of the region that characterize it as entirely devoid of associational activity before the 1990s are inaccurate and exaggerated. Indeed, as the tight corset of one-party control lifted during the first part of the 1990s, there was considerable spontaneous pressure, especially by opposition activists and younger urban elites, to organize societal forces and exploit the emergent, if still not completely unrestricted or entirely group-friendly, postcommunist pluralist framework.[5]

However, if the initial postconflict or takeoff stage of civil society development in the Western Balkans rested upon some positive "traditions" and recent experience, the setting was far from entirely benign for overall NGO development. Some polities, of course, had the benefit of externally assisted civil society promotion. Bosnia's position as

4. Vukašin Pavlović, "A Suppressed Civil Society," in *Democratic Reconstruction in the Balkans,* edited by Margaret Blunden and Patrick Burke (London: Centre for the Study of Democracy, 2001). Of course, nationalist mobilization in Serbia had an important grassroots base. See Jasna Dragović-Soso, "Why Did Yugoslavia Disintegrate? An Overview of Contending Explanations," in *State Collapse in Southeastern Europe: New Perspectives on Yugoslavia's Disintegration,* edited by Lenard J. Cohen and Jasna Dragović-Soso (West Lafayette, Ind.: Purdue University Press, 2008), 22–23.

5. Paul Stubbs, "Civil Society or Ubleha?" in *20 Pieces of Encouragement for Awakening and Change: Peace-building in the Region of the Former Yugoslavia,* edited by Helena Rill, Tamara Smidling, and Ana Bitoljanu (Belgrade: Center for Non-Violent Action, 2007).

an international quasi-protectorate after 1995 was quite exceptional in this regard, as, to a lesser extent, was the case of Albania after the 1997 intervention by a "coalition of the willing." In these two cases, a kind of "benevolent colonialism" allowed external states and organizations to nurture a donor-led and controlled pattern of civil society growth.[6] But throughout Serbia/Montenegro, Croatia, and Kosovo (until mid-1999), civil society groups functioned within the context of quasi-authoritarian or soft dictatorships in which associational life was constricted, and autonomous organizations were obliged to conduct an uphill battle against fundamentally illiberal regimes. Interestingly, however, because both the Slobodan Milošević and Franjo Tudjman regimes worried about their foreign image, both the Belgrade and Zagreb authorities often alternated between the restriction of the local NGO sector, on the one hand, and a limited tolerance for, and even official touting of, NGOs as an indicator of democratization, on the other hand.[7]

In the case of Kosovo, the Albanian population was able to develop a successful "parallel society" during the 1990s, which proved to be an important basis for later civil society development. But real independent and legal NGO activity only would flourish in Kosovo after it became a UN protectorate in 1999. Meanwhile, in Macedonia, which was neither authoritarian nor a protectorate, civil society expanded quickly, although the growing ethnic tensions that would eventually erupt in 2001 undermined and fragmented the impact of associational development.

Throughout this period, most decisionmakers and citizens of the region's new democracies still regarded NGOs with some suspicion. Thus the term "nongovernmental" was often perceived as meaning antigov-

6. See Steven Sampson, "Weak States, Uncivil Societies and Thousands of NGOs: Western Democracy Export as Benevolent Colonialism in the Balkans," in *Cultural Boundaries in the Balkans,* edited by Sanimir Rećić (Lund: Lund University Press, 2002); and Steven Sampson, "From Forms to Norms: Global Projects and Local Practices in the Balkan NGO Scene," *Journal of Human Rights* 2, no. 3 (September 2003): 329–37.

7. On the struggle of NGOs in Croatia and Serbia to achieve a "democratic breakthrough" against the Tudjman and Milošević regimes, see Sharon Fisher and Biljana Bijelić, "Glas 99: Civil Society Preparing the Ground for a Post-Tudjman Croatia," and Jelica Minić and Miljenko Dereta, "Izlaz 2000: An Exit to Democracy in Serbia," both in *Reclaiming Democracy,* edited by Joerg Forbig and Pavel Demes (Washington, D.C.: German Marshall Fund, 2007), 53–78, 79–100.

ernmental, antistatist, or disloyal to the existing states. And indeed, such an antiregime posture was the typical orientation of those liberal forces that struggled to replace illiberal regimes with democratic pluralism. The weak position of NGOs in this period was compounded by their limited experience and the fact that they initially depended heavily on resources from foreign states and organizations for both support and advice. The dominating role of external actors in local civil society development generated widespread domestic skepticism about NGO activity throughout the region—a perception often exacerbated by problems of corruption and the role of informal and personal factors within local organizations, along with the nontransparency of the new associational structures. There was also a blurring of the boundaries between civil society groups and the states, as many NGO activists migrated from one sector to the other, and indeed often served in both sectors simultaneously, while also in state-controlled bodies that posed as autonomous organizations as a means to obtain foreign funding.

The "NGO Boom": Empowerment and "Projectmania"

The departure from power of Croatia's Tudjman and Serbia's Milošević during 1999 and 2000, and the establishment of the Stability Pact for Southeastern Europe directly after the war in Kosovo, opened a new phase of civil society development. Throughout most of the Western Balkans a rapid proliferation in the number of NGOs (table 4.1), and a striking increase in the intensity of their activity, can be identified. For example, in mid-1999, according to the UN administration in Kosovo, the protectorate had 45 international and local NGOs. During 2001, approximately 626 new local NGOs were registered there. Clearly, the number of NGOs per se is a weak indicator of a civil society's vitality or its significance for democratic change. Indeed, the measurement of civil society's strength strictly by the quantity of NGOs officially registered ignores the quality and actual influence of NGO activity. The hyperproliferation of NGOs means very little if most such organizations are only intermittently active and ineffective owing to weak resources and management.

Thus, the sheer proliferation of NGOs can actually lead to the fragmentation of important societal interests in associational life, creating problems of coordination and the kind of networking necessary to accomplish important tasks. Practically speaking, inter-NGO competition

Table 4.1. Registered Nongovernmental Organizations in the Western Balkans

Country	1995–96	1999–2000	2006–7
Albania	300–350	400–800	1,000 (150 active)
Bosnia-Herzegovina	223	1,300 (300–500 active)	9,095[a] (4,629 active)
Montenegro	39	800	3,800 (400 active)
Serbia	519	2,000 (500 active)	10,500
Kosovo	10	400[b] (100 active)	2,394 (200–300 active)
Croatia	790	16,305[c] (1,000 active)	28,358 (2,000–3,000 active)
Macedonia	60	3,977 (400 active)	6,000 (300 active)

[a]This includes 6,658 in the Federation and 2,437 in the Republika Srpska (including 101 in Brčko District). For this period, unofficial information suggests 7,000 NGOs in Bosnia-Herzegovina with an estimated 1,200 active organizations.
[b]It is estimated that locally registered organizations rose from 45 to 400 in the period from June 1999 to June 2000.
[c]The total number of organizations rose to approximately 20,000 by the end of 2000.
Source: Compiled by the authors on the basis of local and foreign analyses.

for local and foreign funds may also supersede and detract from the attainment of NGO goals, undermine the public image of the civil society sector, and obstruct the institutionalization of a sustainable competitive pluralism. Moreover, under conditions of weak state development, the inflation of civil society groups can sometimes tend to overwhelm or supplant the state, creating a kind of hypersocietal activism or "NGO-centrism" that occurs without any corresponding state responsiveness or effectiveness in policy implementation.

Many of these problems have continued to plague Western Balkan civil society's development during the first decade of the twenty-first century. At the same time, the pronounced NGO proliferation after 1999 provides an interesting indicator of the Western Balkans' growing associational vitality, and also the comparative position of one country vis-à-vis another in fostering civil society development. For example, the lagging growth in the number of NGOs in Serbia, relative to its population, in comparison with the much larger organizational sector in demographically smaller Croatia, provides a useful measure of the comparative democratic progress in the two states (a broader topic that goes beyond civil society). Similarly, the relatively greater number of organizations in Macedonia in comparison with the much smaller NGO sector in Kosovo, a society with a similar-size population, is also illustrative and closely linked to the latter polities' special problems in achieving full sovereignty.

One negative feature that accompanied the initial NGO boom in the Western Balkans, including the dearth of domestic resources available to local organizations, was an overconcentration of NGOs on process rather than substance. This problem has been the source of considerable criticism because it resulted in a striking emphasis on project development specifically for the purpose of obtaining funds and sustaining organizational continuity. This phenomenon, which has been referred to as a "project culture" or "projectmania," resulted in "project elites" who were often distracted from carefully implementing or assessing the benefits of the myriad programs that they hurriedly developed. For example, Fran Nahzi, a Kosovo civil society activist, has thus described the initial situation of NGO growth in Kosovo after the 1999 war: "We had groups doing whatever there was money to do—whether or not it was in their mission statement. There was so much money available in 1999 and 2000 that people were literally getting money to plant grass in the front of restaurants. . . . Years later, along came people asking for accountability. . . . For the majority of NGOs, that appeared as a totally new concept."[8]

Thus, the situation of donor-generated civil society groups after 1999–2000 encouraged the development of projects that corresponded to the interests of NGO activists, rather than responding to the needs of those for whom the projects were designed. One chronicler of civil society development in the "post-Yugoslav space" points out that an obsession with seeking project funds often led to a paradoxical Janus-faced posture by some NGO activists toward state authorities: "You are authoritarian and against us; but you should have funded us."[9] Other analysts have complained that in the late 1990s, "with its focus on fuzzily-defined democratization initiatives, short-termism, and the disconnect with the grassroots perspective, the external efforts at civil society building was a process in which the donors' briefs shaped the creation and development of NGOs rather than the other way around. Consequently, civil society found it difficult in this period to profile itself as an effective counterbalance to the state."[10]

8. Quoted by Maggie I. Jaruzel, "Kosovo Today: Strengthening the Nonprofit Sector," *Charles Stewart Mott Foundation: News,* June 16, 2008.

9. Stubbs, "Civil Society or Ubleha?" 224.

10. Vesna Bojičić-Dželilović, Denisa Kostovicova, and Mary Martin, "Civil Society's Role in Advancing Human Security: European Union Policies in

Despite the problems of civil society development in the early post-2000 period, there is no doubt that much of civil society's activity proved beneficial to the citizens of the Western Balkans. For example, such activity was an important training ground for a new generation of activists committed to pluralism and socioeconomic modernization, the kind of "small steps" over a protracted period that gradually can assist the development of a democratic state-society nexus, and also long-term peace building. In many respects, the proliferating foreign-funded, small NGOs in this period were "actors without society." But they had begun to get their "'foot in the door,' a door that they could not pry open [and] they just managed to prevent it from closing completely."[11]

The NGO Sustainability Index developed by the US Agency for International Development (USAID) for the period between 1997 and 2009 provides interesting and useful empirical trend data concerning activities that have influenced Western Balkan civil society, and also civil society in several other regions. The index, which assesses NGO activity along several complementary dimensions—legal environment, organizational capacity, financial viability, advocacy, public image, service provision, and NGO infrastructure—reveals that NGOs in the Western Balkans lagged in relative terms compared with the countries of Central and Eastern Europe, although the gap between the two sub-regions has been gradually narrowing. The position of the Western Balkans is more favorable, however, when compared with other data for the post-Soviet states in Eurasia. Intraregional differences in the civil society of the Western Balkans are also very striking in the post-2000 period, with all the countries and entities in the area slowly beginning to move into a new phase of civil society development. These changes are taking the region beyond the "early transition" stage, although a phase of sustained "democratic consolidation" is still not evident.

Considering the entire decade from 2000 to 2010, NGO activity throughout the region has made notable progress on all the dimensions considered by the NGO Sustainability Index. However, specific areas,

the Western Balkans," *SudostEuropa Mitteilungen,* I, no. 47: 20–33. See also W. Benedek, ed., *Civil Society and Good Governance in Transition* (Belgrade and Vienna: Belgrade Center for Human Rights and Neuer Wissenschaftlicher Verlag, 2006).

11. Srdjan Dvornik, *Actors without Society: The Role of Civil Actors in the Post-Communist Transformations* (Berlin: Heinrich Boll Stiftung, 2009), 143.

such as financial viability, have proven extremely vexing to NGO sustainability for all the states in the Western Balkans, even before the economic downturn that began in the fall of 2008. In comparative terms (table 4.2), the composite index scores indicate that by 2008, Croatia—the country best positioned as the next likely candidate for EU integration—had the highest score in the region, with Macedonia and Bosnia doing reasonably well in their overall NGO development. Montenegro, Kosovo, and Albania have made less progress in civil society development. Meanwhile, Serbia, during the 2006–8 period, after making some notable improvements in the 2001–4 period, still had not advanced much beyond 2000 levels, that is, immediately following the end of the Milošević era. And although Serbia scored slightly better in 2008, its performance was still somewhat lower than those of other countries in the region, and on par with several of the Eurasian states analyzed by the NGO Sustainability Index.[12] Until 2008 at least, Croatia appeared to have a civil society whose development was advanced, while Serbia continued to be stalled in the early consolidation process.

Serbia's NGOs had, of course, played a decisive role in both laying the groundwork for, and then serving as a critical catalytic agent in, the events surrounding the collapse of the Milošević regime. And Serbia's civil society organizations after October 2000 had shifted from a "fight against" the regime, to a "fight for" democracy. But NGO progress was limited by a legacy of historical and political impediments to independent organizational activity, the dire economic situation of the country, and the renewed political instability and polarization that afflicted democratic forces during the post-Milošević period. As one 2005 study pointed out, "Current local governments claim that they are open and ready for any type of cooperation with NGOs, but so far they have been paying only lip service to the idea." Indeed, "according to the majority of activists, . . . actual cooperation is rare and anticipated cooperation is rarer. Activists feel that the cooperation with local government bodies must depend on partisan affiliation or the current disposition of the party in power at the local level, which is often the case."[13]

12. USAID, *The 2008 NGO Sustainability Index for Central and Eastern Europe* (Washington, D.C.: USAID, 2009).

13. Zdenka Milivojević, "NVO u Srbiji," in *NVO, moć, pregovaraja na lokalnom nivou u Jugoistočnoj Evropi,* edited by Zdenka Milivojević, Dino Djipa, and Klima Babunski (Belgrade: Argument, 2005), 37.

Table 4.2. NGO Sustainability Index Scores for the Western Balkans (potential scores range from a low of 7 to a high of 1)

Country	1997	1998	1999	2000	2001	2002	2003	2004	2005	2006	2007	2008	2009
Albania	4.4	4.2	4.8	4.6	4.6	4.3	4.1	3.9	3.9	3.9	3.8	3.8	3.9
Bosnia	N.A.	5.6	5.2	4.0	4.5	4.2	4.1	4.0	3.9	3.8	3.8	3.7	3.7
Croatia	4.6	4.4	4.7	4.3	3.8	3.7	3.5	3.5	3.4	3.3	3.2	3.2	3.1
Kosovo	N.A.	N.A.	4.4	4.6	4.6	4.3	4.2	3.8	3.8	3.8	3.9	3.9	3.9
Macedonia	4.4	4.4	4.6	4.6	4.2	4.0	3.7	3.6	3.6	3.6	3.6	3.6	3.6
Montenegro	N.A.	N.A.	4.6	4.6	4.7	4.6	4.5	4.3	4.2	4.2	4.1	4.1	4.1
Serbia	4.8	5.4	5.4	4.5	4.1	4.1	4.0	4.4	4.4	4.5	4.5	4.4	4.3
Average for Western Balkans[a]	4.5	4.8	4.8	4.4	4.3	4.1	4.0	3.9	3.8	3.8	3.8	3.8	3.8
Average for Central and Eastern Europe[b]	2.9	2.7	2.3	2.4	2.4	2.5	2.5	2.7	2.7	2.7	2.7	2.7	2.7

Note: NGO = nongovernmental organization; N.A. = not available.
[a]Calculated by the authors on the basis of data from the US Agency for International Development.
[b]Calculated by the US Agency for International Development for the Czech Republic, Estonia, Hungary, Latvia, Lithuania, Poland, Slovakia, and Slovenia.

Source: US Agency for International Development.

The exclusion of Serbia's NGOs from the country's constitutional reform process during 2006 illustrated the limitations on civil society development. Still, as one close observer who was active in promoting NGO activity during the post-2000 period noted, civil society in Serbia did have some influence on the overall democratic process, "whether through social support programs, cooperating as much as possible to the extent that government opens spaces, on the poverty reduction programs, on advocacy to implement legislation such as the Freedom of Information Act, or simply and importantly raising its voice when injustice, intolerance, hate speech, violence rear their ugly head. . . . In dealing with the past, civil society has been and is playing an important role, often working together with certain media outlets."[14]

Within each polity of the Western Balkans, there was also considerable variability throughout the post-2000 period along each specific dimension of NGO activity ranked by the NGO Sustainability Index. For example, in the 2001–8 period, improvement in the legal environment with respect to new legislation for NGOs contributed to progress in Kosovo, Macedonia, and Montenegro. Enabling framework legislation also accounted for legal progress in Albania, Bosnia, and Croatia. Serbia was the only country not to enact new framework legislation from 1997 to 2008. In countries such as Albania and Croatia, there was also a steady improvement in NGO advocacy capacity, including success at coalition building, the promotion of civic education, and the mobilization of voters. Montenegro (in the area of minority rights) and Kosovo (with respect to electoral reform) also made some incremental progress. By 2005 and 2006, NGOs in Macedonia were also having successes, and even Serbia moved forward (on electoral activity and in the coalition-building area as well as in advocacy), although in 2007–8, both the state elite and the NGO sector in Serbia were distracted by the Kosovo issue.

Overall, NGOs in the Western Balkans were gradually developing a closer partnership and participatory relationship with governmental agencies and in the policymaking process. NGOs in each polity in this period, with the exceptions of Serbia and Kosovo, also were assessed by USAID as making significant improvement in the delivery of services,

14. Testimony of Ivan Vejvoda, "Serbia: Current Issues and Future Direction," hearings before the Sub-Committee on Europe and Energy Threats, Committee on International Relations, US Senate, September 20, 2006.

although financial problems impeded more rapid improvement. The evidence indicates that regional NGOs faced their most critical challenges with regard to financial viability. Thus, while NGOs were recording achievements in several areas, including their infrastructures and support services, they were still, as in most areas of Eastern Europe and Eurasia, hampered by insufficient resources and a chronic overdependence on foreign donors.

This problem of limited resources and an overdependence on external support became even more critical with the onset of the global economic downturn at the end of 2008. Chronic dependency on external financing and control has contributed to the persistent high level of popular distrust or indifference to NGOs in the Western Balkans, despite the significant progress made during the past decade.[15] In 2009, the NGO Sustainability Index recorded a slight decline for Albania, where the economic crisis caused a financial squeeze on donor funds for NGO activity. Most states in the region made no progress with respect to NGO development. Only Croatia and Serbia achieved a slight forward momentum as a result of improved NGO cooperation with the government and some new legislation. But as a rule, NGOs in the region have been caught in a vicious circle: They cannot improve their public image and become more self-directed until they free themselves from foreign dependence, while at the same time their pressing financial needs dictate their ongoing dependence on external funding and guidance. However, as the next subsection suggests, the character of NGO activity was slowly changing, as was the response of government to civil society groups.

The Emerging State–Civil Society Nexus: Professionalization and EU-ization since 2005

During the second part of the decade after 2000, the NGOs in the Western Balkan region became far more experienced with regard to the dynamic of civil society activity in a democratic polity, as well as meeting the challenges of overcoming their many problems. The generation of NGO activists who had been most dominant in the initial takeoff

15. See, e.g., Gorica Atanasova and Simonida Kačarska, "The Role of External Actors in Civil Society Building: The Case of the Republic of Macedonia," *CEU Political Science Journal* 1 (2009): 48–75.

stage of postcommunist development during the 1990s was joined by a younger cohort of new activists who had been socialized in an environment that was far more tolerant of associational activities outside state control, and which was characterized by an organizationally denser and more robust civil society sector. The training and experience—as well as foreign tutoring for better or worse—of the newer generation of activists have made its members more sophisticated and professionalized than their early postcommunist predecessors. Indeed, enhanced NGO activity in the post-2000 decade has to some extent served as a "school of democracy" that has gradually, albeit imperfectly, contributed to a more sustainable and embedded pattern of pluralist development.[16]

Granted, by 2010, an independent civil society sector in the Western Balkans was still beset by traces of the same problems that had characterized its formative stage during the 1990s, particularly with respect to the matter of financial viability and other dimensions of NGO sustainability. However, general changes both within and outside the region, and in the experience of the local NGO sectors, created new challenges and opportunities. A systematic examination of individual countries reveals the detailed areas of progress and difficulties on a case-by-case basis. But before turning to country-case details, it should be noted that two broad patterns of difficulty preoccupied NGO activists and their organizations at the end of the twenty-first century's first decade: (1) fine-tuning and improving the relationship between civil society and the state; and (2) developing new and closer relationships with the European Union. Each Western Balkan polity has been challenged by many of the same domestic structural and societal impediments to civil society growth and functioning that they have chronically faced since the onset of postcommunist transition.

However, although the larger problems of relative weak-stateness and weak civil society development have not yet been overcome (i.e., compared with Central and Eastern Europe and certainly Western Europe),

16. Paul Stubbs aptly warned against "treating local actors as mere 'puppets' or 'cultural dopes' under the domination of all powerful external international actors. In reality, of course, whilst room for maneuver was limited and some inevitable compromises were made, the trajectories of diverse activists can not be reduced to notions of *selling out* or being rendered *ineffective.* Indeed the templates, processes and skills learnt or developed in NGOs may well have longer term relevance both in terms of individual career paths but also in terms of overall social development." Stubbs, "Civil Society or Ubleha?" 222.

at least the frequently noted imbalance between state power on the one side and civil society strength on the other is far less asymmetrical in favor of the state than at the outset of either the postcommunist or later postconflict periods. Thus, closer linkages and mutual modes of accommodation between the state structures and civil societies are now quite apparent.

For example, most states in the region are now more responsive to the involvement of civil society organizations (CSOs) in the policymaking process, as well as in consultation with state agencies, and in the formulation of national strategies to address key issue areas. The contentious discourse and initial antagonism between postauthoritarian state bodies and emergent civil societies have gradually been replaced with more "normalized" forms of interaction, and with a kind of natural tension or "contentious coexistence" between two sectors that need to cooperatively interact within emerging democratic polities.[17] Such dialogue has not guaranteed that civil society enjoys a decisive impact on state decisionmaking or on public policy—and the cooperation can sometimes serve as a legitimating façade for manipulative state officials—but there has definitely been an improvement in the basis for policy influence by Western Balkan civic organizations. Thus, in recent years, the problem for civil societies' qualitative improvement has had less to do with the intransigent attitude of the state and more often has been a matter of inadequate resources and the underdevelopment of research capacity within the civil society sector.[18]

Of course, the record of Western Balkan CSOs in influencing the state is quite mixed and varies from case to case. For example, the

17. George Schopflin has identified the need for a reciprocal relationship between the state and civil society in a democracy: "The state plays an important role in providing the integrative framework in which civil society operates and the latter cannot function properly without that. This would clearly include the rule of law as the ability of the state to create a degree of coherence without which civil society would rapidly become uncivil and potentially decline into chaos or anomie. But equally civil society must be free to challenge the state in order to preclude the bureaucratic rationality of state action from attaining the kind of paramountcy that would generate rigidity." George Schopflin, "Civil Society, Ethnicity, and the State: A Three-fold Relationship," paper delivered at the conference "Civil Society in Austria," Vienna, June 20–21, 1997.

18. Lorenzo Fioramonti, *How Civil Society Influences Policy: A Comparative Analysis of the CIVICUS Civil Society Index in Post-Communist Europe* (Tirana: CIVICUS, 2007).

CIVICUS Project's detailed investigations of NGO activity in selected Western Balkan states reveal that improvement in the impact of civil society on the state remains a gradual process. Thus, a CIVICUS study of Croatia in 2005 demonstrated that civil society was well positioned to influence the development of social policy, and that the "health of Croatia's civil society appeared to be improving."[19] Indeed, CSOs in the country had proved quite successful in providing social welfare services, assisting the needs of marginalized communities, and assisting victims of family violence. But as far as the ability of civil society to influence or monitor the state in Croatia, there were only some initial signs that these associational groups could hold the state accountable. In these circumstances, CIVICUS concluded that there was a "widespread reluctance among CSOs to 'bite the hand that fed them,'" and that "since 2004 the new government had limited its engagement with CSOs and civil societies' potential contribution to policymaking. In addition, CSOs lack capacity and experience to articulate their interests to government."[20]

However, a more recent civil society trend measurement in Croatia, which was critical of CIVICUS's methodology, claimed that by 2007 matters had improved considerably in Croatia and that most of the credit in this regard should go to "reform-minded leadership at the political helm. Certainly, "political will"—that old development nemesis blamed for so many policy failures in other countries—proved ready and willing to stand up and be counted in Croatia. But the political leadership could no longer act in a vacuum. Civil society was ready to seize the opportunity offered by devising, debating, drafting, and promoting new legislation.[21] Research indicated a growth in Croatia of the kind of social capital—that is, networks of trust and interaction among citizens—that is an important building block for enhanced civic

19. V. Finn Heinrich, *CIVICUS Global Survey of the State of Civil Society, Vol. 1, Country Profiles* (Bloomfield, Conn.: Kumarian Press, 2007), 71–72.

20. Ibid. See also Gojko Bežovan, Siniša Zrinščak, and Marina Vugec, *Civil Society in Croatia: Gaining Trust and Establishing Partnership with the State and other Stake-holders* (Zagreb: Ceraneo, 2005).

21. Harry Blair, *Final Evaluation of USAID Project for Support for Croatia's Non-Governmental Organizations (CRO NGO) 2001–2007* (Washington, D.C.: USAID, 2007), 40. On the problems of state–civil society interaction in Croatia, see Ariana Vela, *Sudjelovanje organizacija civilnog društva u zakonodavnom procesu u Republici Hrvatskoj* (Zagreb: Ured za udruge Vlada Republike Hrvatske, 2008).

engagement and democracy. As Croatia continued its modernization, this was particularly the case in the ranks of the younger generation and better-educated members of the middle class.[22]

In Macedonia, the potential for further civil society development was enhanced in January 2006, when the Macedonian government adopted a "Strategy for the Cooperation of the Government with the Civil Sector." But a CIVICUS report for Macedonia during 2007 concluded that civil society received only limited state support and had only a circumscribed role in public policy and "governance processes." Although deficient in influencing national budgets, or serving as a "watchdog of the state," Macedonian CSOs did have, however, an important impact on some policies affecting women, the disabled, and retirees.[23] A 2009 survey of the social responsibility of citizens in Macedonia revealed increased participation by citizens in nonpartisan political activities (protests, rallies, petitions, boycotts, etc.), which may be linked to dissatisfaction with the economic crisis. However, the extent of involvement of citizens and CSOs in the country remained low (10.2 percent indicated that they were actual members) and had not substantially changed from earlier years. Participation was highest among the younger age cohort, those having higher education, and those with an upper-middle or high-class standing.[24]

Indeed, as the impact of the global economic crisis hit Croatia and other Western Balkan states, civic activity seemed to acquire a new and more populist momentum. For example, beginning in the spring of 2009, student protests in Croatia began calling for free higher education. The student initiative continued into 2010 and was paralleled by even broader examples of civic engagement, such as trade union activity to collect more than 800,000 signatures demanding a referendum on a government proposal to modify the Labor Act, and then a massive expression of the popular will in Zagreb when civic activists led by an environmental group organized street protests to prevent the construction of a garage ramp that was to be a part of a planned business and residential complex in the city center's Varsavska Street. For some, these

22. Gojko Bežovan, "The Path Dependency of Civil Society and Social Capital: The Case of Croatia," in *Social Capital in Governance: Old and New Members of the EU in Comparison,* edited by Frane Adam (Munster: Lit Verlag, 2007), 267–85.

23. Heinrich, *CIVICUS Global Survey of the State of Civil Society,* 235–37.

24. Sašo Klekovski, Aleksander Kržalovski, et al., *Social Responsibility of Citizens: 2009* (Skopje: Macedonia Center for International Cooperation, 2009).

May and June 2010 street protests signaled the end of "authoritarian and submissive behavior" in Croatian society on matters of public interest. As the Zagreb sociologist Srdjan Dvornik put it: "Resistance usually appears in the form of resentment, grumbling, cursing politicians and mistrust of all institutions except the church and army. . . . This is people's right of course, but it doesn't help to change apathy. People have started realizing how untrustworthy the state and political institutions are—but also the kind of political power they have in their hands if only they act in an organized manner."[25]

In Montenegro, a CIVICUS assessment determined that civil society groups played a small but active role in service delivery, particularly in areas such as day care for disabled children, combating sex trafficking, and assisting marginalized groups neglected by the state. But CSOs in Montenegro had only very limited capacity, skills, and public support—factors that, along with an uncooperative government, impeded a strong role for civil society in influencing public policy.[26] The conclusions of the CIVICUS study for Montenegro were confirmed by another more recent 2009 analysis, suggesting that state officials tend to regard NGOs as more of a problem than as part of the solution, and only ask for NGO views on "relatively rare" occasions. Only about 44 percent of Montenegrins surveyed considered NGOs to be successful in solving major societal problems; and only about 4 percent exhibited a high level of trust in NGOs (32.4 percent expressed average trust, 20 percent had a low level of trust, and 15 percent did not trust NGOs at all).[27]

Research on Albania reveals a low level of civic activism with a financially weak civil society sector oriented heavily toward donor-driven goals. There is widespread citizen skepticism regarding the value of civic engagement, along with a widespread belief that "change comes from the top" and that policy processes and actors are not trustworthy. A 2010 CIVICUS report observed that "generally Albanian citizens display high levels of 'indifference' towards involvement in various social

25. Quoted by Barbara Matejčić, "Croat Activists Learn Active Street Democracy," *Balkan Insight,* July 1, 2010. See also Srećko Horvat and I. Stiks, *Pravo na pobunu: Uvod u anatomija gradjanskog otpora* (Zagreb: Fraktura, 2010).

26. Heinrich, *CIVICUS Global Survey of the State of Civil Society,* 255–57. See also Steve Muk, Daliborka Uljarević, and Srdjan Brajović, *An Assessment of Montenegrin Civil Society: Weak Tradition Uncertain Future* (Podgorica: Center for Development of Non-Governmental Organizations, 2006).

27. Maša Lekić, *Montenegrin Civil Society* (Brussels: Trialog, 2009).

actions, which is a common feature of societies in transition or early stages of post-transition with a relatively unsettled middle class and high levels of inequities."[28] There has been greater willingness for state actors to cooperate with CSOs, but such linkages are still not very extensive. Civil society in Albania appears to be only at the takeoff stage of capacity building, and civic activity is also hampered by the absence of coordination among state institutions and the polarization of the two major political parties.

Meanwhile, in Serbia, CIVICUS research revealed an active civil society sector playing an important role in the welfare system and social sphere, but also that CSOs were underutilized by the Serbian government. Owing to the CSOs' lack of advocacy skills and a "government that does not see civil society's impact in policymaking as important, . . . civil society is a rather marginalized sector in Serbia."[29] In 2006, Žarko Paunović, in a detailed analysis of Serbia's CSOs, concluded that "although relatively numerous and in some fields significantly developed, NGOs cannot achieve a substantial influence on overall social changes due to the poor status they have in the legal and political system of Serbia. Further development of civil society and strengthening of the nongovernmental sector will largely continue to depend on international support, harmonization of the legal system with European law, and adoption of new cultural and value patterns."[30]

Analysts have attributed Serbia's weak civil society sector to a number of factors. For example, Vukašin Pavlović observed that "the dilemma of whether the state or society should be given priority seems not to have existed in Serbia's political culture and tradition. A political culture that seeks solutions to all problems exclusively in the actions of a strong state has traditionally been dominant in Serbia."[31] Irena Ristić has attributed Serbia's problems in this area to the role of traditional collectivist cultural and religious values that have been in opposition to civic engagement on the part of individuals, along with "the underdevelopment of liberal elements in Serbia," and also the Communist regime's elimination of "all roots of civil political culture, and prop-

28. Gjergji Vurmo, *CIVICUS Civil Society Index Analytical Country Report for Albania* (Tirana: CIVICUS, 2010), 12, 29-30.

29. Heinrich, *CIVICUS Global Survey of the State of Civil Society,* 343–44.

30. *Nevladine organizacije-Pravni i politički status quo u Srbiji* (Belgrade: Službina Glasnik, 2006), 198.

31. Pavlović, "Suppressed Civil Society," 47.

erty rights awareness and sense of responsibility which existed prior to World War II."[32]

Such historical difficulties are important, but other factors are also at work. For example, following Milošević's departure, a large number of high-profile activists from the nongovernmental sector assumed positions in state institutions. Now ensconced in power, many former activists had little interest, or generally little opportunity, to alter the existing relationship between the state and civil society. However, following the assassination of Zoran Djindjić, many of these individuals migrated out of government and back to civil society groups, universities, and institutes, where they assumed the posture of a strident liberal, proreform, pro-European opposition that was highly critical of other democratic but conservative politicians who were still in power.[33]

Indeed, Serbian NGOs have been criticized for being less interested in encouraging young people to take part in political life or to productively cooperate with political authorities and more interested in simply criticizing political institutions and politicians.[34] At the same time, other analysts of Serbia's civil society have also been critical of the EU's tendency to support well-established or elite NGOs that focus on a "partnership" with political authorities, rather than more "radical" human rights advocacy groups that are critical of those in power.[35] In any event, even after the end of the Djindjić era, some opposition NGOs in Serbia continued to participate effectively in the country's policymaking using a variety of informal channels.

32. Irena Ristić, "Civil Society in Serbia: Theoretical Obstacles in Practice," unpublished paper presented at conference "Civil Society in Southeast Europe," Vienna, March 30–31, 2006. Olga Popović-Obradović downplays the impact of the Communist period and puts primary emphasis on the precommunist basis of Serbia's resistance to modernization. Olga Popović-Obradović, "The Roots of Anti-Modern Political Culture in Serbia," *Helsinki Bulletin,* no. 12 (April 2007): 1–7.

33. Vladimir Todorović, "State and Non-governmental Organizations in Process of Association to EU and Serbia: Through Partnership to Success," in *The State and NGOs in the EU Accession process in Croatia, Serbia and Bosnia-Herzegovina, Through Partnership to Success,* edited by Vedran Horvat, Vladimir Todorović, and Irham Ceco (Sarajevo: Open Society Fund, 2006), 155–80.

34. Mladen Joksić, "Democracy in Serbia after the Revolution: Bringing Youth Back In," Center for International Private Enterprise, October 15, 2007.

35. Adam Fagan, cited by Mladen Ostojić, "The EU and Civil Society in Serbia: Governance Rather Than Politics," *Balkanologie* 11, nos. 1–2 (December 2008).

Overall, the pronounced political polarization in the upper reaches of Serbia's "democratic bloc" during the first post-Milošević decade, and also the high level of political uncertainty in the country, severely impeded state–civil society relations.[36] Thus, on the eve of the May 2008 elections, one survey described Serbian civil society as "exhausted, confused, introverted, divided, and labeled a traitor to the nation. . . . NGOs [need to] fight not only to survive as organizations but also to stir positive changes in society."[37] The victory of democratic political forces in May 2008 opened a new phase for Serbian civil society, but one that was soon to be made quite difficult by the global financial crisis and a deteriorating economic climate.

However, for Milenko Dereta, one of Serbia's major civil society activists, the major problem lies not with the economy but in the attitudes held by the entrenched leadership of the principal political parties, including those in the 2008–9 ruling democratic coalition. As Dereta remarked in mid-2009: "After a full nine years of democratic changes, . . . Serbia is the only country in the region in which government has not established the institutional framework that would have, before anything else, created the underlying environment for the development of civil society. . . . Everything is present somewhere on paper and in sweet words, only that isn't enough to make anything happen. . . . Free citizens are a nuisance for every state, . . . especially a small partyocracy such as Serbia today."[38] In July 2009, Serbia finally enacted a Law on Associations. Despite its considerable difficulties and divisions, the NGO sector in Serbia had gradually begun making a contribution to enlarging the "landscape of political life."[39]

36. Zdenka Milivojević, *CIVICUS: Civil Society in Serbia: Suppressed during the 1990s—Gaining Legitimacy and Recognition after 2000* (Belgrade: CIVICUS, 2006).

37. Pontis Foundation, "Serbian Civil Society Brief: Déjà vu: Civil Society within a Five Year Perspective," March 14, 2008.

38. *Politika,* May 27, 2009.

39. On the complexity of state-society relations in Serbia, see Theodora Vetta, "'Democracy Building' in Serbia: The NGO Effect," *Southeastern Europe* 33 (2009): 26–47. Jelica Minić argued in 2007 that Serbia was a "deeply distorted society" but that NGOs "are very influential and extensively take part in introducing new values and standards into Serbian society." Jelica Minić, "Europe's Plan D and Serbia's Civil Dialogue," in *The Balkan Prism: A Retrospective by Policymakers and Analysts,* edited by Johanna Deimel and Wim van Meurs (Munich: Otto Sagner, 2007), 361–62.

In Kosovo, the impact of CSOs on policymaking has been retarded by the fact that up until early 2008, NGOs had to deal with a bifurcated "state" structure: on one side, the predominantly Albanian domestic actors in the Provisional Institutions of Self-Government, or "PISG 'State,'" which was really a pre-state or quasi-state arrangement; and on the other side, the international officials in the UN Mission in Kosovo (UNMIK), the United Nations Interim Administration for Kosovo. CSOs consulted with and made proposals to PISG on strategic direction (e.g., the drafting of the National Action Plan for Gender Equality formulated by a multiethnic group of women's NGOs and political leaders in 2003).[40] But an analysis of the local NGOs suggests that with UNMIK still in control, PISG was not regarded as the main arena in which to develop a potential state–civil society linkage in Kosovo.[41] Indeed, local observers noted evidence that, even as PISG gradually acquired more power during 2006 and 2007, it actually became less open to NGO influence.[42] Continued uncertainty about status and political power in Kosovo during this period, along with serious socioeconomic difficulties in the protectorate, probably accounted for the results of a poll taken by the United Nations Development Program, which found that more than 90 percent of the young Albanians and Serbs surveyed had no desire to participate in politics and NGOs.[43]

The unilateral declaration of independence of PISG authorities in February 2008 presented NGOs with an entirely new political situation. But the multiple sources of authority in the new state—Kosova government decisionmakers, a smaller but continued UNMIK presence, an EU International Civilian Office, the European Union Rule-of-Law Mission (EULEX), and parallel Serb authorities in the north—generated ambiguity regarding the locus of authority in the new state.

40. Bill Sterland, "Civil Society Capacity Building in Post-Conflict Societies: The Experience of Bosnia-Herzegovina and Kosovo," *Intract,* June 2006, 27.

41. Julia Nietsch, "Civil Society in Kosovo: The Interaction between Local NGOs and the Provisional Institutions of Self-Government," Arbeitspapier Nr. 54, Österreichisches Institut für internationale Politik, November 2006.

42. "Enabling Organizational Development: NGO Legal Reform in Post-Conflict Settings," *International Journal for Not-for-Profit Law* 9, no. 4 (August 2007).

43. Human Development Project, United Nations Development Program, "A New Generation for a New Kosovo," 2006. The record low electoral turnout of 45 percent in the November 17 Kosovo parliamentary elections—the lowest recorded since the 1998–99 war (compared with 53 percent in 2004)—is a reflection of the apathy, political disenchantment, and poor economic situation in Kosovo.

For example, during 2008 and 2009, EULEX Mission personnel were just beginning to fashion a relationship with the civil society sector in areas such as human rights, gender issues, and accountability. And although 46,000 NGOs were technically registered in Kosovo by 2008, the civil society sector remained on the whole very weak because of the small size of individual organizations, their sporadic activity, and a heavy dependence on short-term external funding. Thus, Kosovo was correctly described, as one study noted just before independence, as a polity "exhibiting features of a civil society that is heavily infected with democratic rhetoric, but empty of substance."[44]

Bosnia's record of state–civil society linkage reflects the considerable difficulties in the protectorate, but it has also undergone substantial improvement in recent years. For example, in May 2007, after several years of effort to establish a mechanism of cooperation between civil society and the government, a coalition of NGOs and the Council of Ministers signed an agreement "To Work and Succeed Together." An EU official optimistically described the agreement as a "historic moment," and promised that the EU would "continue to provide every kind of assistance, especially financial, for further development of the civil society sector in [Bosnia]." The agreement, which accorded formal recognition to the NGO sector, anticipated the active involvement of NGOs in the creation and adoption of laws, strategies, and initiatives.

How the agreement would work in practice remained unclear, however. Up until that point, Bosnia's NGOs had often criticized government officials for their unwillingness to cooperate or provide support. State authorities had also been accused of perceiving NGOs as "associations 'against' rather than 'for.'" The government sector also allegedly regarded CSOs as an "extended arm of the international community" and as guilty of "interfering" in the government's work.[45] One particu-

44. Arta Ante, "Exploring Social Capital: A Missing Link in the State-Building and Development Process in Kosovo," *L'Europe en Formation,* Autumn–Winter 2008, 349–50. See also United Nations Development Program, *Civil Society and Development: Human Development Report, Kosovo 2008* (Priština: United Nations Development Program, 2008).

45. Reima Ana Maglajlić and Edin Hodžić, "Political Participation," in *Democracy Assessment in Bosnia and Herzegovina* (Sarajevo: Open Society Fund, 2006), 322–23. See also Žarko Papić, "The Role of the Non-governmental Sector," paper presented at the Ninth International Conference of the Balkan Political Club, "Bosnia and Herzegovina: Crossing from Dayton's to Brussels' Phase and Role of the International Community," Sarajevo, May 6–7, 2006. Martina Fischer, "Preface

lar difficulty characterizing civil society–state relations in Bosnia was that multiethnic projects and proposals formulated by civil society actors were often undermined or rejected because of the ethnopolitical orientation of state actors, or, as Gajo Sekulić has observed, the "'ethnopolicy' of government elites as incompatible with civic concepts of society." Thus, the "ethnopoliticization of social structures" in Bosnia tends to fragment civil society efforts and undermine the cohesion of state structures.[46] Indeed, the fact that Bosnia has had both a governmentally fragmented structure (with central, entity, canton, municipal, and district centers of authority), and a de facto executive-centered political regime in which dominant power has been vested in the Office of the High Representative and international officials rather than in the weak domestic central state institutions, has also complicated efforts by NGOs to establish modes of cooperation with the government sector. Although the outcome of the 2006 elections was hardly an encouraging step forward in terms of the breaking down of the "ethnic pillarization" in Bosnia—hard-line nationalists were replaced with more "fashionable nationalists"—some civil society groups opposed to an ethnopolitical division of the country did emerge, such as Dosta! (Enough!) and GROZD (Civic Organizations for Democracy).[47]

Unfortunately, electoral rates of participation in Bosnia have been on the decline in recent years (see chapter 5), and disinterest in politics among young people has been on the rise.[48] Moreover, the level of interethnic polarization continued to intensify from 2007 to 2010, as political leaders sparred over how to reform the Constitution and restructure the state (see chapter 2). A September 2009 report, for example, concluded that Bosnia's civic groups "are significantly underdeveloped from the standpoint of entering the political fray and exercising power as issue advocates, government watchdogs and generally helping to set the agenda for political debate."[49] Bosnia's civic groups also often have

---

for the 2nd Edition," in *Peace-Building and Civil Society in Bosnia-Herzegovina Ten Years after Dayton* (Munster: Lit-Verlag, 2007).

46. Quoted by Ismet Sejfija, "From the 'Civil Sector' to Civil Society: Progress and Prospects," in *Peace-Building and Civil Society,* ed. Fischer, 125–40.

47. Fischer, "Preface."

48. United Nations Development Program, "Social Inclusion in Bosnia and Herzegovina," in *National Human Development Report* (Sarajevo: United Nations Development Program, 2007).

49. National Democratic Institute, *Bosnia-Herzegovina Democracy Assessment Report* (Sarajevo: National Democratic Institute, 2009).

an uncooperative relationship with the established political party organizations that are generally suspicious of any competition to their post–Dayton Accords control of the political landscape.

Gender Politics and Democratic Consolidation

During the post-2000 period, women's groups and networks throughout the Western Balkans have played a significant role in civil society and democratic development. But the struggle for the advancement of gender equality and gender representation in political life in the region has been extremely difficult, given that it is constrained by a legacy of traditional and recent obstacles. Thus, during the 1990s two pressures actually led to a striking regression in the position of women throughout the region: First, the breakdown of Communist rule eliminated the achievements that had been put in place (albeit often as tokens) by the Communist regime to promote gender equality; and second, the successor regimes were typically dominated by conservative elites and nationalist parties that upheld traditional and patriarchal patterns of authority, and also focused upon the retraditionalization of society at the expense of women's rights.

Democratic political structures were created in the Western Balkan states during the 1990s, but any suggestions of establishing genuinely "inclusionary" democracies were overshadowed by the warfare in the region, and also by the parochial state-building and survival strategies of the new "national elites." For example, during the wartime and early postwar period, female representation in the region's legislatures dropped from the high levels that had been symbolically orchestrated by the Communist regimes. For example, in the mid-1990s (see table 4.3), women's representation in every Western Balkan legislature was below 10 percent. At the same time, the new surfeit of postcommunist parties in each ostensibly "democratic state" paid little attention to either the socioeconomic or political empowerment of women. Issues related to women were part of the national discourse, but not in a manner that served the course of gender equality or empowerment. In Serbia, for example, as Wendy Bracewell has pointed out, the policy of the nationalist regime touted the ideals of motherhood and an increased birthrate, which were "not so different from those that operated under Yugoslav socialism. Both state socialism and authoritarian national-

Table 4.3. *Women in Western Balkan Legislatures and Government, Selected Years*

Country	Mid-1990s			Mid- to Post-2000s			2008		2009–10		Women Ministers, 2007–8	
	Year	Number/ Total	%	Year	Number/ Total	%	Number/ Total	%	Number/ Total	%	Number/ Total	%
Macedonia	1995	4/120	3.3	2005	23/120	19.2	35/120	29.2			3/22	13.6
Bosnia	1995	7/156	4.5	2006	10/57	17.5	6/57	10.5			0/9	0
Serbia[a]	1993	6/250	2.4	2004	27/250	10.8	51/250	20.4			4/24	16.7
Croatia	1995	8/138	5.8	2005	31/152	20.4	33/153	21.6	38/153	24.8[b]	4/17	23.5[c]
Albania	1995	8/140	5.7	2005	9/140	6.4	10/140	7.1	23/140	16.4	1/15	6.7[d]
Montenegro[e]	1996	6/71	8.5	2004	8/75	10.8	9/81	11.1	5/81	6.2	1/16	6.3
Kosovo	—	—	—	2001	34/120	28.3	36/120	30.0			2/9	10.5

[a]National Assembly of Serbia.
[b]As a result of changes, not an election.
[c]In July 2009, a woman was selected prime minister of Croatia.
[d]A woman is serving as president of the Assembly in Albania. In the 2009 election, there were 1,165 women candidates for the Assembly, or 30.2 percent.
[e]National Assembly of Montenegro.
Sources: Official Electoral Returns and National Statistical Reports.

ism approached reproduction and motherhood from a collectivist perspective; although in the former case the relevant collectivity was the
working class." In the 1990s, the official Serbian view and most public
discourse assumed that individual interests affecting women would "be
subordinated to the collective interests of the nation."[50]

The situation for women, of course, differed from state to state and
did not remain static during the 1990s. But women were the biggest
"transition losers" throughout the region, suffering from both a severely
deteriorating economic climate and a loss of the previously substantial
welfare measures provided by the various Communist regimes. A large
number of women were also the target of widespread abuses and depri-
vations during the warfare in the Western Balkans. Thus, Sonja Lokar
has pointed out that, during the 1990s throughout postcommunist
Central and Southeastern Europe, women generally chose to withdraw
from public life and to adopt "private strategies of survival."[51]

As the 1990s progressed, however, a new wave of feminism emerged
in the Western Balkans. Some women formed or joined new NGOs,
and they took advantage, with the help of foreign financial and organizational support, of the new environment of political liberalization
in order to organize and raise various issues such as violence against
women and freedom of sexual orientation—topics that had not even
been permitted on the political agenda during the former one-party
regimes. Moreover, as fighting engulfed the Balkans, many new wom-
en's groups sprang up in connection with the antiwar movement.[52] At
first, many of these NGOs sought to avoid any cooperation with the
male-dominated political parties, which were largely populated by conservative, nationalistic, and religiously oriented elites that generally
chose to either ignore or disdain gender-related issues. But the NGO
leaders from women's organizations soon realized they were unlikely
to be effective if they remained on the margins of the political system
or failed to network on a cross-gender and cross-ethnic basis in their
own countries (and with their counterparts in neighboring countries).

50. Wendy Bracewell, "Women, Motherhood, and Contemporary Serbian
Nationalism," *Women's Studies International Forum* 19 (January–April 1996): 31.
    51. Sonja Lokar, "Democracy in Eastern Europe: Women's Way?" *Development*
50 (2007): 110–16.
    52. See, e.g., Maria Lis Baiocchi, "Women in Black: Mobilization into Anti-
Nationalist, Anti-Militarist and Feminist Activism in Serbia, *CEU Political Science
Journal* 14, no. 4 (2009).

So increasingly during the 1990s, women's organizations made alliances with other non-gender-oriented NGOs, as well as with trade unions and political parties whose members believed that they might gradually be able to advance their respective causes.

The adoption of the Stability Pact for Southeast Europe following the 1999 war in Kosovo, and also the end of authoritarian rule in Croatia and Serbia (1999–2000), opened a new domestic phase—with a fresh commitment by extraregional actors for assistance—to address gender issues in the Balkans. The Stability Pact's Gender Task Force served as a key element for this forward momentum, and it was able to benefit from enhanced intergovernmental support and the utilization of experiences of women activists from the Central and Eastern European countries. A top-down strategy, which built on the experience of the European Commission and European "party families," was also combined with bottom-up grassroots pressure from local women's organizations. Male-dominated legislatures and governmental decision-making bodies were lobbied to expand the position of women in state institutions. Practices such as "awareness raising," and other training programs were employed, as well as coalition building that linked the fight for gender equality to other group causes in the political arena (constitutional, electoral, and judicial reform) or to the so-called free-ride strategy.

These new efforts paid off during the post-2000 period. In most countries of the Western Balkans, as may be seen in table 4.3, the percentage of women in legislatures increased noticeably, as did, to a somewhat lesser extent, the number of women ministers in governments. In some countries, such as Albania and Montenegro—which paradoxically have exhibited high levels of declared public support for "democracy" in surveys (see chapter 6)—female representation in legislative bodies lagged behind other countries in the region. Indeed, Albania until 2009 had the lowest level of female legislative representation in Europe, and in the February 2009 parliamentary elections in Montenegro, the number of women elected declined from 11.1 to 6.2 percent.[53] In such cases, the strength of patriarchal traditions and opposition by "old boys' networks" within the party system significantly slowed the advance of gender equality. Such resistance has proven to be a problem limiting the

53. Sometimes there was a postelection drop-off in female representation, as in Bosnia between 2006 and 2008.

extent of change throughout the region. But gradually, the use of legal quota regulations in most countries, both within individual parties and for entire electoral systems (e.g., in Macedonia, Kosovo, and Serbia), has significantly increased the number of women elected to public office. At the end of September 2008, even Albania's major political parties agreed to earmark 30 percent of their candidate lists for women, and as a result the number of women elected to the Parliament in June 2009 more than doubled.[54]

But female legislative representation still remained well below 50 percent throughout the region, and the influence of women in government cabinets—where the locus of decisionmaking power mainly resides—was much lower than in the parliamentary setting as a whole. In Croatia, a woman was selected as prime minister in 2009, but women constituted 20 percent of the Sabor (the Croatian legislature) in 2008, which still left the country 4 percent below the EU average. And quota systems, although helpful, do not easily overcome traditional attitudes.

Moreover, although quotas for women in legislatures have proven very useful, they are not the entire answer to securing influence for women in political decisionmaking. As a leading Kosovo female activist remarked in 2007, "Men in the Parliament still make decisions during their coffee breaks with their colleagues. . . . We are marginalized . . . not because we lack skills to face all the problems of Kosovar society, but because we are simply ignored by the male world. . . . Nothing would change even if we increased the number of women in Parliament to 50 percent.[55] A female deputy in Serbia observed in 2008 that in her country "the prevailing cultural and social model conceives of women as some kind of auxiliary intelligentsia, as second violins. Intelligent women are prized, but their intelligence needs to be supplementary, without being in the lead, and without prominence. . . . Women have learned to be on a secondary level, . . . and the majority will say: 'Why would I need to make a fuss in the Assembly when I can achieve my

54. Nicola Nixon has argued that women's problems in Albania can be attributed not only to past history, but also as a reaction to recent difficulties. Nicola Nixon, "'You Can't Eat Shame with Bread': Gender and Collective Shame in Albanian Society," *South East European and Black Sea Studies* 9, no. 1 (March 2009): 105–12.

55. Quoted by Kosova Women's Network, *Monitoring Implementation of United Nations Security Council Resolution 1325 in Kosova,* 2nd ed. (Priština: Kosova Women's Network, 2009).

goals through men?'"[56] A Serb female member of the Kosovo legislature was even more explicit:

> It is hard to be a woman in politics because you work only with
> men and they are not open to women. . . . Men do not have trust
> in women, they think we cannot do the work as well as them, but
> in fact we can do better. Male politicians are male chauvinists, they
> won't take our good ideas, even if they know it is a good idea. They
> only put us there where there is a lot of work to do, and they never
> put us in positions where we have a chance to get into a high deci-
> sion-making position. In order to be successful, we need to be pre-
> paring 'an army' of young, confident, educated women in the next
> 10 to 20 years.[57]

One area where female underrepresentation in politics remains quite
striking is in local legislatures and local executive posts. Indeed, generally speaking, the cause of gender equality has been less dramatic
in power positions above, below, and outside the highly visible central
legislative arena (where the attention of foreign officials and observers is most heavily focused). For example, in Serbia in 2007–8, women
made up roughly 17 percent of members of the central government
Cabinet, but only 6 out of 165 (4 percent) presidents of municipalities
(mayors) were women. In the 2009 local elections in Croatia, only 28
women were elected to 577 positions as mayors or heads of counties.
In 2007, Montenegro had only 1 female mayor out of 21 municipalities. And in Macedonia, only 13, or 3.4 percent, of the 378 candidates
for mayor in 2009 local elections were women, and not a single woman
was elected mayor in any of the 85 municipalities. All 65 mayors in
Albania in 2006 were men, as were 98 percent of 308 heads of com-
munes. In Kosovo, only 2 women in 2007–8 were serving as mayors in
30 municipalities. In Bosnia at the end of 2008, women were elected as
mayors in only 4 (2.8 percent) of 140 municipalities. According to one

56. "Gospodje poslanice," *Politika,* June 13, 2008. See also Ana Vuković,
"Stavovi Srpske političke elite o ženama u politici," *Sociološki Pregled* 42, no. 3
(2008): 343–63.
57. Quoted in "A Secure Future for Our Region: What Does It Take? Women
Leaders Speak Out," paper presented at conference sponsored by Regional
Women's Lobby for Peace, Security, and Justice in Southeast Europe with support
from UNIFEM, Priština, October 27–29, 2008.

women's NGO in Bosnia: "Women continue to be invisible in political negotiations regarding all the important questions in the life of citizens in Bosnia and Herzegovina, as, for example, the question of constitutional reforms. . . . Discussion about all important themes occur in narrow circles, and the international community supports this model. . . . The male elite is still not prepared to create more space for women in political decisionmaking."[58]

Increasing the number of female entrepreneurs and managers in the economy has also proven more difficult than improving attitudes in legislation on gender equality. Faced with this problem, domestic and internationally assisted efforts to improve the position of women in Western Balkan labor markets and in the business world have significantly increased. But throughout the region, women on average earn much less than their male colleagues in identical positions, are underrepresented in better paid positions, and also make up a disproportionately high percentage of the unemployed. In some Western Balkan societies—where efforts to improve the position of women in the economy began in conditions of severe economic backwardness—progress has been exceedingly slow. For example, a 2004 study of Kosovo revealed that only half the women from twenty-five to sixty-four years of age had received elementary education. In some rural areas, this figure was as low as 10 percent.[59] And in Montenegro, a study prepared in the early post-2000 period indicated (on the basis of data from the 1990s) that only 8 percent of women owned houses, 6 percent owned cars, and 10 percent owned a business or business premises. And in twelve companies of national importance, there was not a single female manager (seven of the twelve did not have even one woman on the executive board). In 1991, to put the challenges in further perspective, 41 percent

58. Republički Zavod za Statistiku, *Žene i muškarci u Srbiji* (Belgrade: Republički Zavod za Statistiku, 2008); Center za edukaciju, savjetovanje i istraživanje, *Žena u lokalnim izborima 2009 godine* (Zagreb: Center za edukaciju, savjetovanje i istraživanje, 2009); Zavod za statistiku, *Women and Men in Montenegro* (Podgorica: Zavod za statistiku, 2007); State Statistical Office, *Local Elections in the Republic of Macedonia, 2009* (Skopje: State Statistical Office, 2009); Statistical Office of Kosovo, *Men and Women in Kosovo* (Priština: Statistical Office of Kosovo, n.d.), 56; Instat, *Women and Men in Albania* (Tirana: Instat, 2006); Udružene žene, *Godišnji izveštaj za 2008 godinu: Udružene žene Banja Luka, Bosna i Hercegovina* (Banja Luka: Udružene žene, 2009), 8.

59. Freedom House, *Freedom in the World: Kosovo (Serbia-Montenegro)* (Washington, D.C.: Freedom House, 2006).

of the Montenegrin population was illiterate, of whom 82 percent were women.

Overall, however, gender equality and inclusion have slowly assumed a higher level of priority in the "pyramid of values" found in the Western Balkan countries. And in recent years, "patriarchal determinism" has had a less significant impact on Balkan politics than during the last decade of the twentieth century. By 2005, the countries of the region had either adopted gender equality laws, antidiscrimination legislation, or national action plans that included the improvement of gender-related issues. Unfortunately, the implementation of such laws and goals has remained extremely spotty. A 2006 study of "gender mainstreaming" in Bosnia observed, for example, that "there is a wide gap between de jure and de facto situations. Although legislation throughout the region has incorporated the principles of economic opportunities for women and men, in practice women still find it extremely difficult to realize these opportunities in either the public or private sectors."[60]

The employment of a large number of women in the informal (gray) economy, where official enforcement of laws is generally absent, has also limited the overall effectiveness of gender-related legislation. A 2008 study in Montenegro revealed that more than half the respondents believed the greatest discrimination against women was in the gray economy, while 37 percent felt the same way about small and medium-sized enterprises.[61] In Albania, the situation was even worse: "Albanian women now [2006] have the right to equal treatment under the law. However, the lack of effective enforcement of these laws has drastically exacerbated gender inequality with consequences to economic development, democratization and political stability."[62] In 2009, the Global Gender Gap Report found that out of 134 countries analyzed, Albania ranked 92nd, or just below Azerbaijan and Armenia.[63] Even in Croatia, where, during the post-2000 period, women had acquired considerable

60. Nada Ler Sofronić et al., "On the Road to the EU: Monitoring Equal Opportunities for Men and Women in Bosnia and Hercegovina," Open Society Institute, 2006, 9–10.

61. "Žene u Crnoj Gori Neravnoprave," *Tanjug,* 2008.

62. Artur Metnai and Somila Omari, "On the Road to the EU: Monitoring Equal Opportunities for Men and Women in Albania," Open Society Institute, 2006, 17.

63. Ricardo Hausmann and Laura Tyson, *The Global Gender Gap Report 2009* (Geneva: World Economic Forum, 2009).

visibility in the upper tier of the public and political spheres—and where in mid-2009 a woman assumed the post of prime minister for the first time (the journalist-turned-politician Jadranka Kosor)—there were numerous obstacles to the enforcement of gender discrimination rules: "The patriarchical status quo, the cultural pattern and attitudes toward the role of women in social practices that reflect it, remains stubbornly persistent, albeit going in cycles. The dominant attitude that a woman's natural place is in the home and with the family is often mirrored in the media and school textbooks."[64]

Despite the considerable difficulties facing women, especially at the local levels of politics and the economy, special governmental bodies have now been established in each state to promote gender-related issues. Important efforts to combat serious problems such as human trafficking and domestic violence are also in progress throughout the region. Perhaps most positively, gender issues in the post-2000 Western Balkan states have acquired a prominent place on the agenda of the European Union's strategy for the transformation and integration of the region. This is particularly significant with respect to the gender-mainstreaming program originally established by the Stability Pact's Gender Task Force. Thus, slowly, the "gender power imbalance" within the Western Balkan political parties has been reduced. By the years 2006–7, a study of the region's political parties indicated that the share of women members was roughly a third in most countries (with Albania and Montenegro still considerably below that level).[65] Levels of female membership vary from one party to another, as does the influence of gender issues, and are contingent on many factors, including party ideology. But the share of women in national executive party bodies has been rising—albeit still small in left-wing, centrist, and conservative party organizations—and has carried over to improvement in the number of women chosen to serve in governments.

In recent years, the increased activity of special women's organizations within political parties has also been significant. However, in 2010

64. Jagoda Milidrag Šmid, "On the Road to the EU: Monitoring Equal Opportunities for Men and Women in Croatia," Open Society Institute, 2006, 10.

65. E.g., of parties responding, 31 percent in Croatia, 30 percent in Kosovo, 37 percent in Bosnia, 31 percent in Serbia, and 36 percent in Macedonia, but less than a fifth in Albania, or 17 percent. Only one party responded in Montenegro. Stability Pact for South East Europe, "Gender Mainstreaming in South East European Political Parties, 2006–2007," March 2007.

the struggle to improve gender equality and empowerment, along with the entrenchment of the values that legitimate such efforts, remained a critical component of the challenges facing full democratic development throughout the Western Balkans. At a minimum, it was apparent that the effort to make progress in the area of gender equality was well under way and was receiving considerable attention from Western governments and the EU. As one of the most comprehensive research studies of this issue concluded in 2007, "The problems of inadequate levels of representation of women in politics have been rendered visible. This has sparked off a debate on the issue which has resulted in several attempts to come up with instruments for the elimination of disproportions indicated by the research."[66] Gradually, even in states where the cultural context was most unfavorable, the quality and quantity of female representation was improving and was contributing to overall democratic consolidation.[67]

The Media and Democratic Consolidation

The media play a critical role in shaping a country's civil society development, and in determining whether or not civic engagement strengthens a democratic political culture. Thus, in a postauthoritarian political environment such as the Western Balkans, the emergence of a free media sector that is substantially independent of state control, is professional, and is also capable of facilitating the expression of diverse viewpoints in society reinforces the ability of NGOs to link society to the state. Conversely, when the media sector is tightly controlled or influenced by state authorities, civil society organizations are impeded in effectuating such linkages and in carrying out their activities.

Whether the portion of the media sector that is not directly controlled by the state is considered part of civil society and included in the so-called third sector—or, as in the case of private media, described

66. See Elona Dhembo, "Women and Politics and Decision-Making in Albania: A Qualitative Analysis," *Journal of International Social Research* 13, no. 13 (2010): 73–85. It is also important to keep in mind that as of 2007, there were still seven EU member states—the Czech Republic, Cyprus, Ireland, Slovenia, Hungary, Romania, and Malta—where women still accounted for less than 15 percent of membership in the national legislature.

67. Ibid.

as the "fourth estate"—there is little doubt that the character of the media sector is closely linked to the extent of democratic change in a society. Such influence is not always positive. Thus, the reciprocal influence between elite-mobilized political nationalism during the 1990s in the Western Balkans and a media sector that was enlisted in the process of "forging war" was a prime tragic example of the kind of negative interaction that can erode democratic development. On the whole, however, media pluralism or "media democracy" not only broadens the marketplace of ideas but also promotes transparency by subjecting state institutions and ruling elites to the scrutiny that is necessary for accountable government.

A comparative analysis of media development in the Western Balkans reveals considerable, albeit uneven, progress in the post-2000 period, with many remaining impediments to media pluralism. Almost all states in the region share certain common problems. For example, throughout the Balkans, the ability of political and business elites to politically influence the media has been facilitated by the precarious economic and professional security of journalists and other media workers. Thus, a comprehensive 2008 study of labor relations in the region's media revealed that although journalists' salaries are above average for jobs held in the various countries, most journalists do not feel adequately rewarded for their work, and there is a considerable gap between those journalists employed in the capital cities and those working in smaller cities and towns. Frequent delays in salary payments, inadequate protections for journalists from dismissals, imprecise labor contracts, weak trade unions, low levels of professional solidarity among journalists, a very low awareness of the legitimate rights a journalist should enjoy, and insufficient court enforcement of such rights are all important factors contributing to the vulnerability of the media to outside pressure.[68] And most of these regionwide problems facing Western Balkan journalists have been exacerbated by the global economic recession that began in 2008.

Broad patterns of change, and the relative position of states in the region, are usefully illustrated by the annual Media Sustainability Index (MSI) issued by USAID (see table 4.4). The MSI evaluates media de-

68. Southeastern European Network for Professionalization of Media, "Labor Relations and Media: Analyzing Patterns of Labor Relations in the Media of SEENPM Member Countries," Chisanau, Moldova, February 2008.

Table 4.4. Media Sustainability Index for the Western Balkans

Country	2001	2002	2003	2004	2005	2006/07	2008	2009
Albania	1.76	1.97	2.01	2.02	2.27	2.41	2.21	2.20
Bosnia	1.66	1.66	2.09	2.52	2.41	2.90	2.64	2.81
Croatia	2.44	2.68	2.83	2.82	3.04	2.76	2.61	2.46
Kosovo	1.90	2.32	2.32	2.36	2.46	2.56	2.26	2.38
Macedonia	1.73	2.02	2.32	2.53	2.58	2.44	2.28	1.71
Montenegro	1.58	2.12	2.31	2.42	2.47	2.52	2.35	2.15
Serbia	1.86	2.42	2.52	2.46	2.50	2.47	2.36	2.35

Note: The Media Sustainability Index include these categories: unsustainable, anti–free press (0–1); unsustainable mixed system (1–2); near sustainability (2–3); sustainable (3–4).
Sources: US Agency for International Development, International Research and Exchanges Board.

velopment along a number of dimensions in a country's media sector, including an assessment of the existence of legal and social norms to promote free speech, the extent of free speech, the professionalization of journalism, the plurality of new available sources, the presence of business management practices and editorial independence, and the role of supporting institutions. Thus, each state is accorded an average sustainability score, but the subscore for individual dimensions of the overall index varies in each country considered.

In the eight years of MSI analysis (2001–9), the Western Balkan states have generally stood out among European and Eurasian post-communist countries in the average progress recorded. Thus, already in 2005, most of the region's media sector had acquired what has been termed by the MSI as "near sustainability" with regard to the various dimensions assessed. But beginning in 2006, the earlier positive trend in media development throughout the region ground to a halt, and in some polities there were discernible setbacks with regard to media progress in a democratic direction.[69] For example, in Kosovo, the backsliding reflects the politically and economically charged atmosphere connected with the 2007 and early 2008 drive toward independence that undermined media autonomy from political interference and also impaired the safety of journalists.

A study by the Organization for Security and Cooperation in Europe covering this period emphasized three main shortcomings regarding the Kosovo media: (1) The incumbents in leading political institutions such

69. The same negative trends were recorded by Freedom House's evaluation of the regime's media.

as the central government and legislature exhibit "little understanding" of the role played by free media and "the importance of media independence" from political interference for the development of a sustainable democracy; (2) independent media institutions (e.g., the broadcast regulator and the public broadcaster, Radio Television of Kosovo) lack the respect from politicians and the financial resources necessary to ward off political interference; and (3) media outlets of minority communities in southern Kosovo are underfunded and thus nonsustainable (the media in predominantly Serb northern Kosovo receive limited external assistance from the Belgrade authorities). The study acknowledged that Kosovo did exhibit "a very advanced legislative framework" to support freedom of expression and media freedom, and also has a large number of media outlets. But the absence of experienced journalistic personnel, and the very weak financial position of the print and broadcast outlets, allowed for extensive political manipulation of the media sector.[70]

MSI scores covering 2009 improved slightly in both Kosovo and Bosnia—mainly as a result of better management and the increased number of new sources in both countries—despite continued interethnic tension in both polities and serious problems within the media. In October 2009, the head of Europe's main association of broadcasters, the European Broadcasting Union (EBU), warned Prime Minister Hashim Thaçi that Kosovo's ambition for broader international recognition was being endangered by political interference in the work of Kosovo Radio-TV (RTK). The statement by the EBU chief claimed that RTK was being transformed "from being a balanced supplier of news into a media arm of the ruling party and of yourself as prime minister. . . . Critical or alternative voices have been suppressed."[71]

In Bosnia, difficulties at achieving positive media change during 2008 and 2009 could be traced to the heightened ethnic polarization and tensions that followed in the wake of the 2006 election (see chapter 5). Thus, media vulnerability to political pressure remained considerable

70. Organization for Security and Cooperation in Europe, *Human Rights, Ethnic Relations and Democracy in Kosovo (Summer 2007–Summer 2008)*, OSCE Background Report (Priština: OSCE Mission in Kosovo, 2008). Intimidation and removal of critical journalists continued during 2009 and 2010, although such reports were dismissed by the new state's government as exaggerated. In October 2010, the organization Reporters Without Borders dropped Kosovo's media ranking from seventy-fifth place in 2009 to ninety-second place. *Radio-Television Kosovo,* October 20, 2010.

71. OFAP, North American Service, October 26, 2009.

in Bosnia, as did corruption and low standards in certain media outlets. There was also a noticeable increase in threats to media freedom in Bosnia. Between 2008 and the summer of 2009, for example, the Bosnia and Herzegovina Union of Journalists registered sixteen verbal assaults and direct physical attacks, death threats, and other violations of journalists' rights, or a 20 percent increase compared with 2008.[72] Drew Sullivan, the director of the Center for Investigative Reporting in Sarajevo, observed that those who feel offended by press reports usually do not use the Press Council in the country to express their dissatisfaction: "Aggrieved businessmen, crime figures, or politicians will first go to the media owner, editor, or advertisers to extract satisfaction. . . . Some will resort to violence. Bosnia is a bully culture where important people simply bully those beneath them with their power and money."[73]

In Bosnia, political interference in the media and other obstacles to media pluralism have been closely linked to the country's unique ethnopolitical dynamics. For example, there has been a pronounced ethnic segregation of the media sector and continued obstacles to efforts at the "de-ethnicizing" of the state television network (part of Bosnia-Herzegovina Radio Television operating since 2004). Thus television, the most influential branch of the media sector, has been defined, as one commentator in Bosnia put it, as "national and political from the start" of the postcommunist period, not as a professional communications medium serving the citizens of the nations and the state. The state radio station has always been more multiethnic in personnel and content.[74] Each of the three major ethnopolitical communities and political parties has endeavored to use the media as a mouthpiece for its own interests, and, in the case of the nationalistically oriented Serb and Croat politicians, has claimed that the central state-run television is Muslim oriented in "the interest of one political option in Sarajevo." For example, in mid-2008, Milorad Dodik, the principal Serbian leader in Bosnia, claimed that he regarded TVBH as "foreign television."[75] Meanwhile,

72. "Thirty-Fifth Report of the High Representative for Bosnia and Herzegovina," November 30, 2008–April 30, 2009.

73. Quoted by Bill Ristow, "Sword and Shield: Self-Regulation in International Media," Center for International Media Assistance, May 2009, 12.

74. *Nezavisne novine,* December 17, 2008, 11, quoted by BBC, December 22, 2008.

75. *Tanjug,* July 14, 2008.

Croat political parties in 2008 and 2009 continued to push for a special public broadcasting channel in the Croatian language to match existing separate channels in the Serbian and Bosnian languages.[76]

It seemed that only the few investigative reporters who had engaged in a sweeping criticism of politicians and corruption in all three ethnic groups were subjected to criticism and intimidation by all three ethnic communities. For example, in early 2009, Bakir Hadžiomerodić of the Sarajevo TV show *60 Minutes* joked that he was "a little bit proud of the fact that we are receiving threats not only from Bosniaks [Bosnian Muslims], only from Croats, or only from Serbs . . . from the political/ criminal milieu; . . . this proves we are doing a good job."[77] The endeavor to achieve an ethnically unbiased state media and still nurture distinct cultural identities proved almost impossible in Bosnia throughout the entire 2000–2010 period. Even outside the state sector, media outlets are often compelled to ethnically profile their content in order to attract an audience. Still, the pan-ethnic impulses of economic activity, and the linguistic similarity of language groups in Bosnia, suggest that a non-ethnicized media may eventually attract support in the country.[78]

The persistence of strong organized crime elements in post-1995 Bosnia, and the state's enormous economic problems, have also made it extremely difficult for independent media outlets and journalists to function. In June 2008, Mehmet Halilović, the deputy ombudsman for media in the Muslim Croat Federation, observed that journalists cannot be independent because they are exposed to harassment in their salaries and often are not paid regularly. The situation, Halilović added, had deteriorated over the past few years.[79] But whether it declined as a result of ethnic politics, economic pressures, or political meddling,

76. Kamel Kurspahić has attributed the ethnification of Bosnia's media sector largely to the Dayton constitutional arrangement. Kamel Kurspahić, *Prime Time Crime: Balkan Media in War and Peace* (Washington, D.C.: US Institute of Peace Press, 2003).

77. BHTV, January 23, 2009, quoted by *BBC Worldwide Monitoring,* January 26, 2009.

78. Anna Fritzsche, "Pandora's Box of Nationalism: The Challenge of Public Broadcasting in Multi-ethnic Bosnia," *deScripto,* February 2007, 13–15; Amer Džihna, "The Public Broadcasting System in Bosnia-Herzegovina: Between Ethnic Exclusivity and Long-Term Sustainability," Open Society Foundation Bosnia and Herzegovina, 2008; Davor Marko, "Media and Politics in Bosnia-Herzegovina: Patron and Instrument of Ethno-Based Journalism," *Politička misla,* June 11, 2009.

79. "Journalists Above All," *Transitions Online,* June 9, 2008.

it has been a persistent fact of life in post–Dayton Accords Bosnia. In mid-2009, the director of the country's Communication Regulatory Agency (CRA), Kamel Huseinović, observed, for example, that political pressures on his agency had been constant since he assumed the post in 2003: "They [have] never stopped but only gone through different phases: at times they were stronger, and at different times more moderate. They have been the strongest as of late. . . . Politicians would like to have a [CRA] director that they can press on like a button and order him to punish a certain media outlet, to take away or give a frequency or revoke licenses and this is not exclusive to any people or entity."[80]

During 2008 and 2009, some quite negative trends also continued to plague the overall interaction between media and democratic development in other Western Balkan states. The crime-related assassinations in October 2008 of Ivo Pukanić, the owner of the Croatian weekly newspaper *Nacional,* and also his marketing director, shocked a country that had already been troubled by the frequent intimidation and assaults against key journalists (an estimated sixty journalists were injured and threatened in Croatia between 1991 and 2008).[81] Pukanić was renowned for his investigative reporting and had earlier been the subject of threats and an assassination attempt. The murders sent a chill throughout Croatia's media sector and sparked a countrywide debate regarding media freedom. The Croatian journalists' association claimed that political pressures on media independence remained a serious concern in both the public and private subsectors.[82]

President Mesić attributed many of the problems experienced by the Croatian media sector to the post-2008 economic problems. He also claimed that the economic crisis was being used as a pretext by employers to threaten journalists with dismissal and to intimidate those working on short-term contracts. He added, however, that some in the media were seeking to sensationalize issues that were essentially unimportant. The link between the global economic downturn and media difficulties was also emphasized by many in Croatia's independent media: "The

80. Bosnia-Herzegovina Federation TV, July 6, 2009. See also Mediamanifest, *Under Pressure: Research Report on the State of Media Freedom in Bosnia and Herzegovina* (Sarajevo: Mediamanifest, 2010).

81. "Politics, Organized Crime, and the Media in Serbia and Croatia, 1989–2009," *Eurozine,* March 20, 2009.

82. *HINA,* January 6, 2009. In June 2009, a suspect in the Pukanić case was arrested in Belgrade.

economic crisis has come like a tailor-made smokescreen. In times of recession, journalists are more eager to save their jobs than their professional dignity, and owners have a good excuse to do what they always intended to do: blackmail journalists with their existence."[83]

Some commentators in Croatia suggested that the most important impact of the ominous media climate would be to weaken the fight against corruption, particularly in the private media, where the injection of money and influence from media magnates and criminal elements was least transparent.[84] One leading Croatian journalist, though admitting that by 2009 "the media probably influences politics more than politics influences the media," nonetheless has warned his colleagues against being "manipulated by clever politicians who leak trivial stories and create artificial sensations."[85] Still, if media gullibility and vulnerability to financial power are now more important in Croatia than widespread systematic media intimidation by the authorities, then the country's media sector is slowly making progress.

Aspects of political interference, along with a pattern of ethnic fragmentation, have characterized Macedonia's sharply deteriorating media sector (the most precipitous drop in the region, according to the Media Sustainability Index survey). Although the quantity of media outlets in Macedonia per capita was one of the highest in the region during recent years (in 2008, for a country with a population of approximately 2 million, there were five countrywide television broadcasters, more than fifty local television stations, sixty radio stations, and some twenty newspapers), media freedom has been subjected to increasing assault. Thus, some of the owners of the most powerful television stations are leaders of political parties in the ruling coalition. Meanwhile, Macedonia Radio-Television, which is a public service created by the Assembly, is under the government's complete control. The government and ruling parties utilize their considerable funds for advertising and electoral campaigns to bring pressure on the media and ensure that the media exercises self-censorship. Media outlets that are excessively critical of the government find themselves denied stable financing. The fact that Macedonian journalists received the lowest wages in the region also makes them extremely vulnerable to economic pressure.

83. BBC, May 5, 2009, May 9, 2009.
84. *HINA,* June 16, 2009.
85. Davor Gjenero, in *Vjesnik,* October 20, 2009.

Even more ominous in Macedonia has been the use of the court system to fine and harass critical journalists. In May 2009, for example, it was estimated that some 160 lawsuits against journalists for slander and insult had been allowed to go forward during the previous two years, with many such suits resulting in large fines and juridical pressure on members of the media.[86] Owing to its substantial foreign ownership, the press market is less subject to domestic political influence than are electronic broadcasters. However, Albanian newspaper outlets in Macedonia are particularly susceptible to political influence because they are mainly financed by local economic and political elites.

During 2008 and 2009, the media sector in Serbia also experienced heightened politicization and various challenges to media freedom and the security of journalists. Thus, although a large percentage of Serbia's public believed that they were receiving detailed and comprehensive information from the media, roughly 70 percent in 2008 felt that the media was under control and censorship owing to editorial policies and political pressures.[87] For example, in May 2009 Nadežda Gaće, the president of the Independent Association of Journalists, remarked that during the previous year there had been a large number of threats against and pressure on journalists from local power holders—that is, not just local and major tycoons but also representatives of local bureaucracies, assemblies, and political party leaders, "whose reactions are horrendous whenever an article is not to their liking."[88] Violent incidents against media workers rose during 2009, leading some observers to conclude that media freedom remained fragile and unconsolidated.[89]

The economic vulnerability of independently oriented journalists and broadcasters in Serbia has provided a major avenue for political and business interference in the media. A contrast between the situation of the media in Serbia during 2009 and during the Milošević era was recently offered by Veran Matić, the director, editor, and owner of Belgrade B92, one of the country's best-known and most independent media outlets, and one that played a key role in the transition to democratic rule in late 2000.

86. *MIA News Agency,* May 3, 2009; BBC, May 4, 2009.
87. RTS Radio Belgrade, September 2, 2008, in *BBC Monitoring Europe,* September 3, 2008.
88. *BETA,* May 4, 2009.
89. "Attacks on Balkan Journalists Rise in 2009," BalkanInsight.com, December 10, 2009.

You can buy media and their opinions for money easier than ever. It is sad but true. . . . Today it is harder because it is more complicated and more complex. There are a lot more ways to apply pressure, to restrict freedom, and the more sophisticated they become, it is impossible to notice them at once. Often those who dictate the position of certain media come from the very times and places we would like to forget. . . . They are not your usual Eastern European tycoons and small fish who got rich overnight, these are people who are deeply involved in crime committed by the regime that was in power for over ten years. . . . In the past, we had only one strong center of power which had a monopoly on the force it used against the media; today, that power is decentralized, and the levers of power are varied.[90]

Unfortunately, many media practices in Serbia did not change substantially after the victory of a new coalition of democratically oriented parties in mid-2008. Indeed, once in power, the Democratic Party pragmatically decided to form an alliance with the Socialist Party, previously the instrument of Slobodan Milošević, and still in the hands of some of his former colleagues who claim to be modernizing and reorienting the party organization. Thus, the appointment of the new Socialist Party leader, Ivica Dačić, as interior minister in 2008 raised doubts about whether the Milošević-era crimes against journalists, including several prominent assassinations, would ever be prosecuted. And conscious of the political advantages of controlling the state media, the ruling Democrats and their allies have sought to consolidate tighter control over state media outlets.

Despite such difficulties, however, progress has occurred on Serbia's media landscape. In late 2006, the two largest journalists' associations managed to adopt a Journalist Code, which addresses the principles of reporting; and in February 2009, after considerable negotiation, a Press Council was established. Laws on broadcasting, telecommunications, and access to public information have also been adopted. But legal loopholes still permit media ownership to remain secret in Serbia, and antimonopoly provisions are frequently circumvented. Thus, a substantial portion of the media is still controlled by individuals who were formerly close to the Milošević regime, and also by foreign investors.

90. Veran Matić, "B92, Twenty Years Later," *Vreme,* May 22, 2009.

Continued media concentration and state pressure on the media have allowed Serbia's ruling political parties and party coalitions to continue having extensive influence on its media sector. For example, in 2007, some 80 percent of journalists in Serbia perceived their profession as highly politicized.[91] Journalists attributed such pressure mainly to politicians (70 percent), tycoons (59 percent), and the government (37 percent). Much of the political leverage on the Serbian media derives from the purchase of advertising by political parties.[92] The political influence on the Serbian media has been especially pronounced during election campaigns and has also escalated to a high pitch during sensitive periods, such as when Kosovo proclaimed independence and when Radovan Karadžić was apprehended. Political forces controlling the tabloid press have often deliberately fueled a struggle between so-called patriotic and "unpatriotic" media in these circumstances, and journalistic commentary tends to descend into mutual recriminations.[93]

A major clash of views erupted during the summer of 2009, when some members of Serbia's ruling coalition proposed amendments to the Public Information Law that would have the effect of prosecuting journalists and tabloids that flagrantly attack public authorities in a "nonprofessional" and "unethical" manner. Opponents of the initiative suggested that the law would reduce media freedom by imposing high fines on news media that violated it. Divided opinions on the bill split the ruling coalition and the opposition parties, along with the media sector itself. But the law was eventually enacted, after its most restrictive aspects were reduced by amendments. In the summer of 2010, there were also signs that Serbia's judicial and political bodies were beginning to take their obligations to protect journalists more seriously. The Constitutional Court upheld public information legislation, the perpetrators of an attack on a journalist were apprehended, and football extremists who had threatened the life of a journalist were sentenced and their convictions were upheld after an appellate process.

91. Helsinki Committee for Human Rights in Serbia, *Annual Report: Serbia 2007* (Helsinki: Helsinki Committee for Human Rights in Serbia, 2007).

92. Tamara Skrozza, "Serbian Media and Politics: Living in the Past," *Politička Misla,* June 11, 2009.

93. Balkan Investigating Network, *History Overshadowed by Trivia: Regional Media Coverage of Radovan Karadžić's Arrest* (Sarajevo: Balkan Investigating Network, 2009).

Montenegro also faced many of the same media difficulties experienced in Serbia and the other Western Balkan states. A substantial degree of media pluralism does exist in the quantity of media outlets and different points of view (with more than forty-five radio stations, twenty television stations, and a host of printed media outlets for some 670,000 inhabitants). The legal framework for free media is also in place. But overt and covert influence and pressure on the media from political and business elites remain considerable at both the national and local levels, and investigative reporting is underdeveloped and sometimes a high-risk enterprise. In 2004, the editor of an influential newspaper was killed, and in August 2009, a prominent Montenegrin journalist was attacked and seriously injured by the mayor of Podgorica, who was also a high official in the ruling party. The general scarcity of funds in the media sector and low incomes for journalists have also increased media vulnerability to financial interests and have weakened media professionalization.[94]

In sheer quantity, Albania's media sector is more pluralistic than most neighboring countries, with sixty-nine privately owned television stations, close to fifty privately owned radio outlets, and two hundred tabloid-style newspapers serving just over 3 million people. But such hyperpluralism of media reflects deeper difficulties that are detrimental to democratic development. Indeed, surveys indicate that Albanians generally believe that their media sector is free and that journalists can report on any topic they wish. But this high level of perceived media freedom is accompanied by considerable dissatisfaction regarding the actual information conveyed by the media.[95] Thus, according to one informed observer, the Albanian media scene in 2009 was "chaotic," "untransparent," and has "lamentably low" journalistic standards.[96] The Albanian media—in a manner even more pronounced than its Western Balkan neighbors—has a very "murky relationship to business and politics. In most cases, it's hard to determine who owns which media outlet. Media financing is also shrouded in mist. The presence of

94. Radojica Bulatović, "Montenegro: Politics and the Media," *Politička Misla,* June 11, 2009.
95. InterMedia Reseach, March 23, 2009.
96. Jonas Rolett at "Hearing on the Commission on Security and Cooperation in Europe: Albania's Election and the Challenge of Democratic Transition," Federal News Service, Washington, D.C., June 4, 2009.

so many stations in such a small market is a red flag. There simply isn't enough revenue to sustain them all."[97]

In recent years, there has also been flagrant politicization of Albanian state television and radio, with the ruling Democratic Party (reelected in June 2009) dominating appointments and the coverage of the ostensibly public media. This situation was particularly apparent during the months before the June 2009 election, when the government even threatened televisions stations with the loss of their licenses if they published opposition ads, and bulldozed billboards carrying opposition messages on the pretext that the structures were too close to the road. The TVKlan investigative program *Forbidden Area,* hosted by the very independent journalist Andi Bushati, was also prohibited by the station's owner— a well-known politically connected oligarch—from running a series of critical political portraits of major party leaders. As one Tirana newspaper put it, "The giant supermarket of the Albanian media," is characterized more by "manipulation instead of information; . . . politicians consider and treat the media and the journalists as mere instruments in their service, and whoever does not accept this role finds himself in a prohibited area."[98] Remzi Lani, the director of the Albanian Media Institute, has characterized the dangerous alliance between the media, politics, and business as "a brutal form of state capture."[99]

Unfortunately, the extensive "political instrumentalization" of the Western Balkan media by various self-interested legal and illegal actors, and also the "ethnification" of communications, especially in most multinational states, has considerably impeded the role of the media sector as a force for political reconciliation within the region's various states. Such a reconciliation between and among sharply polarized political forces and different ethnic groups is an important precondition for democratic consolidation that goes beyond simply the independent provision of information in society. Thus, when it comes to bridging sharp political antagonisms and dealing with sensitive and very controversial incidents from recent history, such as the prosecution of egregious war crimes

97. Ibid.
98. *Korreri,* June 11, 2009, in *BBC Monitoring Europe,* June 16, 2009.
99. Remzi Lani, "Media Clientalism: Between Politics and Business," notes from the conference "Ideology, Democracy and Social Change in the Western Balkans," Ohrid, Macedonia, June 26–27, 2009.

and alleged war criminals, the media can serve as either a moderating or polarizing influence. By and large, the media sector in the Western Balkans still has not proved very capable as a vehicle to transcend the sharp political and ethnic cleavages that have previously been the source of so much regional instability and violence. For one thing, reporting on war crimes can be exceedingly dangerous for individual journalists in the region, owing to an environment where bitter memories still prevail about relatively recent events and where politicians frequently take political advantage of such emotional issues.

Moreover, a declining but still not insignificant number of political and media personnel who engaged in war propaganda and hate speech during the 1990s remain on the scene and continue to influence the media's output and tone. And the deficits in the professionalization of journalists have often placed those working in the media in an uncertain and awkward position regarding their role in the process of reconciliation and "truth telling." The Serbian journalist Miroslav Filipović put the issue well in 2006: "Journalists who write about war crimes can be divided into two groups: a minority who report about war crimes committed by their compatriots; and a significantly larger majority who focus on crimes committed on their compatriots. I believe the duty of a journalist is to make his own society better and more humane. You should clean up your own mess before starting to point fingers at others."[100]

Not many journalists, for the reasons discussed here, including the issue of personal security, have adopted such a perspective toward war criminality and the experiences of their own countries. And many in the media sector cannot resist the appeal of writing tabloid stories—sometimes referred to as "media kitsch"—about war criminals who are on the run or evading the domestic and international authorities (as in the coverage of Radovan Karadžić's capture and of Ratko Mladić's fugitive status). Indeed, an early 2009 study of the mass media in Macedonia—a state where the two major ethnic communities remain "stubbornly locked into parallel worlds"—found that only about one-fifth of respondents surveyed believed that the media had a positive impact on interethnic relations in the country.[101]

100. Quoted by Marijas Šajkaš, "Transitional Justice and the Role of Media in the Balkans," International Center for Transnational Justice, August 2007.
101. United Nations Development Program, *People-Centered Analysis Report* (Skopje: United Nations Development Program, 2009).

Too often, the media play a divisive rather than a unifying role in the Western Balkans. Despite such problems, some members of the independent media, together with local civil society organizations, have endeavored to bridge intergroup divisions, and also to expand discussion of the past. For example, in Serbia, the most listened-to B92 radio show, *Hourglass,* which also appears in print and online, has promoted public debate over recent history. The program's motto is "If you believe that all is going well in the country, then this isn't the place for you" ("Ako vam je dobro, onda ništa").[102] However, the present ethnic divisions in the Western Balkan region, and the political value divide between and among groups in individual countries (see chapter 6), indicate that the media and NGO actors still face considerable challenges in the areas of objective historical analysis and attempted reconciliation.

One of the bright spots in the field of Western Balkans communications, which complements the media in information access and dissemination, and which also can potentially be a democratizing factor in the region, is the striking growth in the availability and use of the Internet. Comparative regional data with regard to the period from 2000 to 2008 indicate a spectacular increase in computer use and Internet penetration levels (table 4.5). In less than a decade, states like Albania, Bosnia, Kosovo, and Macedonia, which had only a very small number of Internet users in 2000, have recorded extremely rapid growth rates. And, as in many facets of regional political and socioeconomic development, Serbia's growth has lagged behind its neighbors (although the interesting role of personal computers in the mobilization against Milošević from 1996 to 2000 provided an early demonstration of the political potential of cybernetworking).[103] As in many other areas, Croatia was in 2008 a leader in the area of computer technology, while Kosovo and Albania have the farthest to go. Meanwhile, in recent years, Macedonia and Montenegro have made significant advances in Internet access. But leaving aside such regional inequities in cyberaccess and exclusion, the

102. See Verica Ripar, "Journalism and Political Culture in Serbia: A Case Study of *Hourglass* (Radio B92)," paper presented at the conference "Beyond East and West: Two Decades of Media Transformation after the Fall of Communism, Central European University, Budapest, June 2009.

103. Christopher R. Tunnard, "From State Controlled Media to the Anarchy of the Internet: The Changing Influence of Communications and Information in Serbia in the 1990s," *Journal of South East European and Black Sea Studies* 3, no. 2 (2003).

Western Balkan region has been gradually overcoming the "digital divide" between it and the rest of Europe. By 2008, almost two-thirds of the citizens of the EU's member states used the Internet. Usage was lower in the Western Balkans, but the region was rapidly catching up, and on the whole it was overcoming its earlier isolation from globalized information networks.[104]

A similar trend can also be seen with respect to the rapidly increasing use of Facebook, particularly among those in the age group between eighteen and thirty-five years of age. At the end of 2008, Croatia's prime minister, Ivo Sanader, created attention by ordering an inquiry into the activity of a young man—who reportedly was close to the leading opposition party, the Social Democratic Party (Socijaldemokratska partija, SDP)—who used Facebook to criticize the regime. Sanader's fans then launched a Facebook attack against the SDP leader. Not all political leadership sensitivity about Facebook is unwarranted. For example, in April 2010, the media reported that persons in Serbia used Facebook to threaten Serbian president Boris Tadić, whose office declined to comment. Data reported in 2009 indicated that Facebook users constituted roughly 15 percent of the entire population in Croatia, 11 percent in Serbia, 9 percent in Macedonia, and 8 percent in Bosnia.[105] By mid-2010, Serbia's Facebook users had grown 40 percent, and 56 percent of them were males.

Clearly, the Internet and its social networking media in the Western Balkans have begun to demonstrate their effectiveness in creating webs of interaction or "communities of interest" among users. Western Balkan politicians are also beginning to use social networking techniques during their electoral campaigns. Such interaction through social media can be an important aspect of social capital formation and potentially may help stimulate overall civic engagement in the region. Still, it remains to be seen whether Internet use and social networking in the Western Balkans will fulfill the kind of enhanced connectivity between citizens on the one side and the state on the other (including through channels such as the much-touted avenue of e-government),

104. By June 2010, Internet penetration was 55.9 percent in Serbia, 51 percent in Macedonia, 50 percent in Croatia, 44.1 percent in Montenegro, 43.5 percent in Albania, 31.2 percent in Bosnia, and 20.8 percent in Kosovo. *Internet World Stats,* October 6, 2010.

105. Adriatalk.com, May 6, 2009.

Table 4.5. Trends in Internet Usage: Western Balkan Countries and the European Union, Selected Years

Country or Group	2000		2006		2008		Use Growth, 2000–2008 (%)
	Internal Users (number)	Population Penetration (%)	Internal Users (number)	Population Penetration (%)	Internal Users (number)	Population Penetration (%)	
Albania	2,500	0.1	75,000	2.4	580,000	16.0	23,100.0
Bosnia	7,000	0.2	806,400	17.5	1,441,000	31.4	20,485.7
Croatia	200,000	2.6	1,472,400	32.9	1,984,800	44.2	892.4
Macedonia	30,000	1.5	392,671	19.1	906,978	44.0	2923.3
Montenegro[a]	N.A.		50,000	7.9	280,000	41.3	N.A.
Serbia[a]	N.A.		1,400,000	14.3	2,620,478	37.4	N.A.
Kosovo	N.A.	0.45[b]	N.A.	3.5	377,000	21.0	N.A.
European Union	86,796,800	22.9	252,818,939	51.3	300,233,365	61.4	218.1

Note: N.A. = not available.

[a]In 2001, it was estimated that Serbia and Montenegro had fewer than 200,000 Internet users, or less than 2 percent of the population.

[b]Estimated for 1999.

Sources: Authors' calculations based on selected national reports and *Internet World Stats.*

which may help promote democratization.[106] Thus, there is always the danger that politicians can use social networking media to manipulate voters in a plebicitarian manner, and that a serious gap or "civic divide" may open between a class of politicized citizens using these media to engage in political debate on the one side, and the nonpoliticized class, who use these media rarely or at most for recreational purposes. This would create a relatively new silent noncyber majority. Moreover, the "darker" side of social networking has also appeared in the Western Balkans, as ultranationalists and other extremists have begun to exploit it to spread hate propaganda—a practice one observer has termed "civic fascism."[107]

Forging a Participatory Political Culture

In only a relatively short period of time, the Western Balkans region has made very important progress in developing civil society, along with significantly improving the participation of women in political life and increasing the public's access to media choice and information. Of course, many traditional aspects of the region—captured by its frequent identification as an area having both weak states and weak civil societies—have persisted. And when compared with Central and Eastern Europe and Western Europe, civil society in the Western Balkans at the end of the twenty-first century's first decade still lags. But important progress has been made, albeit uneven and mixed, as a result of both internal efforts and outside assistance. Thus, there are far more democratically oriented and autonomous NGOs now present on the sociopolitical landscape, even if one takes account of the rather small number of legally registered organizations that are actively functioning on a full-time basis.

Granted, there has been considerable fluidity in associational life, with a large number of organizations dissolving or becoming inert, and many new organizations constantly forming. And most often, NGOs

106. Taylor Smith and Kathy Buckner, "Designing e-Participation with Balkan Journalists," *JeDEM* 1, no. 1 (2009). Political parties in Kosovo had even begun to utilize the Internet for election campaigns, as was demonstrated in the 2009 local elections; *Kijac News,* March 12, 2010.

107. Jelena Maksimović, "Serbian Extremism's Fresh New Face," *Transitions Online,* February 19, 2010.

are small in membership, have few resources, and enjoy only limited access to state policymaking bodies. The pervasive effects of significant dependency on foreign donors—even in quite successful cases of civil society development such as Croatia,[108] but especially in Bosnia and Kosovo—remain a problem limiting domestic democratic consolidation.[109] There are also marked disparities between urban and rural areas with respect to civil society development. Moreover, because NGO leadership is the preserve of the more educated and well-connected stratum of society, one encounters a kind of NGO elite in each polity that is generally quite separated from the bulk of the population in its lifestyles, attitudes, and behavior. This distance often detracts from the closer state-society nexus that civil society organizations are reputed to enhance.

Yet the Western Balkans is no longer the disrupted, dispirited, and politically immature region it generally was fifteen or sixteen years ago after the war in Bosnia, when it took its initial steps into the postconflict stage of postcommunist development. Moreover, the episodic opposition currents, grassroots movements, intellectual dissidents, and political protests that constituted nascent civil society development in the Communist period, and to a large extent laid the groundwork for the emergent spate of relatively weak NGOs that became part of the initial pluralist period, have been replaced by a far more organized, experienced, assertive, and internationally linked civil society sector. Moreover, in recent years, international donors and local NGOs have become more realistic about one another's respective strength and flaws. And as outside donors have increasingly departed from the

108. Srdjan Dvornik, "Politics from Below and 'Civil' De-Politicization," Center for European Integration Strategies, Working Paper, March 2007. For other issues in Croatia, see Paul Stubbs, "Aspects of Community Development in Contemporary Croatia: Globalization, Neo-Liberalization and NGO-isation," in *Revitalising Communities,* edited by Lena Dominelli (Burlington, Vt.: Ashgate, 2006).

109. Roland Paris and Timothy Sisk have argued that a large international presence in postconflict state building has built-in "participation dilemmas" on economic development and local politics, a kind of "distorting effect," "like a powerful magnet in an electric field." Thus, foreign influence can divert civil society activity away from local objectives, and also decrease local decisionmaking that is subject to popular control and accountability. Roland Paris and Timothy Sisk, *Managing Contradictions: The Inherent Dilemmas of Postwar Statebuilding* (New York: International Peace Academy, 2007), 6.

region, those local NGOs that have survived have tended to become more independent and sustainable.[110]

The NGO sector is also complemented, as shown above, by a more vigorous and active media sector that is able to express the views advanced by NGOs as they increasingly try to keep the state authorities accountable. Women's organizations have also begun to play a more active and accepted role in civic life, and female representation in decisionmaking bodies has been on the rise (except at the local level). If a "democratic political culture," as Alina Mungiu-Pippidi recently put it, is "democracy's oxygen," then the Western Balkan democracies are breathing better than ever before.[111]

This does not mean, however, that progress in the region has become irreversible, or as yet constitutes the fabric for substantially consolidated and sustainable democratic states. An April 2008 conference on civil society organizations functioning in the EU candidate and potential candidate countries pointed out a number of common problems facing all CSOs: (1) insufficient cooperation with public authority on all levels, (2) a need for improvement in CSO professionalization and expertise in lawmaking, (3) remaining weaknesses in the legal and financial framework pertaining to CSOs, (4) the low number of CSOs and the problem of communications with citizens, and (5) continued heavy dependence on external donors.[112]

Moreover, it is also important not to adopt an "NGO-centric" interpretation of democracy that neglects the significance of other components of democratic consolidation, such as political parties (see chapter 5) and the institutional structure of the state (see chapters 2 and 3). Democratic political culture is more than the culture of a democratic civil society, although certainly without the development of the latter it may be more difficult to sustain the former. As Serbia and other cases outside the Western Balkans markedly suggest, one needs to beware of the myth that NGO-assisted revolutions and regime change can them-

110. Ase Berit Grodeland, "'They Have Achieved a Lot Because We Have Paid Them to Do a Lot': NGOs and the International Community in the West Balkans— Perceptions of Each Other," *Global Society* 24, no. 2 (April 2010): 173–201.

111. Alina Mungiu-Pippidi, "Issue Paper: Working Session 3B," presented at the Council of Europe Forum for the Future of Democracy, Yerevan, October 19–21, 2010.

112. Draft conclusions, civil society conference sponsored by the European Union, Brussels, April 17–18, 2008.

selves ensure a linear or smooth path to the consolidation of sustainable democracies.[113]

Furthermore, the participation of some Kosovo Albanian NGOs in the anti-Serb protests of 2004, and some Bosnian Serb NGOs in resisting positive reforms in Bosnia, illustrates that the mere proliferation of organizations or improvement in their advocacy skills is not necessarily an indicator of progress and democratization. Value transformation in the development of civic and democratic attitudes has, for the most part, been slow and limited in the Western Balkans, and potentially dangerous islands of incivility and illiberalism still exist (see chapter 7). Well-entrenched enclaves of tradition continue alongside the clear and ever-more-dominant features of modernity. It is difficult, however, to generalize about the region as a whole, as this chapter's survey of intra-regional variation regarding state-society relations indicates. Indeed, in many respects the disparities in civil society development, and in overall democratization between and among the individual Western Balkan cases—particularly in those states that were former republics of socialist Yugoslavia—is greater today than it was during the 1990s. There is, of course, some virtue in looking at the region holistically, especially when evaluating its advancement in relation to other postconflict and postcommunist areas. But each polity still has a unique set of contextual difficulties that must be recognized and addressed.

As perhaps the most ambitious agent of state building on the global scene today, the European Union has naturally devoted considerable attention to ensuring that the states and political entities that are currently candidates or potential members for EU accession have relatively vibrant civil society sectors that are supportive of democratic change. Utilizing external funds, and particularly support from the EU's Instrument for Pre-Accession Assistance, will prove critical in the next period of Western Balkan civil society development. How this assistance is deployed will be an important part of the unfolding story of civil society development and democratic state building. Thanks to the impact of civil society growth, by 2010 the Western Balkans had a more participatory political culture. But the European Commission's hope of moving forward to a real "political culture of dialogue and tolerance"

---

113. Ivan Krastev, "Where Next or What Next?" in *Reclaiming Democracy: Civil Society and Electoral Change in Central and Eastern Europe,* edited by Joerg Forbig and Pavol Demeš (Washington, D.C.: German Marshall Fund, 2007).

will require sustained resources and political commitment from both within and outside the region. Such external support assumed even more urgency owing to the impact of the global economic crisis that spread to the Western Balkans by 2009–10. Thus, securing sources of external support became particularly challenging, just at the time when NGOs throughout the region were faced with domestic difficulties resulting from the economic slump. But before turning to the recent economic crisis and the promising advances that preceded it, the next three chapters address the political patterns and the social strains that surround civil society and frame the region's response to the critical challenge of European integration.

Chapter 5

The Transformation of Political Parties in the Western Balkans: From Embryonic Pluralism to Europeanization

As elaborated in the previous chapter, the development of civil society played an important role, both before and after 2000, in creating the foundation for more pluralistic political cultures in the Western Balkans. But progress toward fuller democratic consolidation also depends on other critical components of political development, such as the institutionalization of competitive party systems and the establishment of legitimated and uncorrupted electoral systems. The engagement and identification of citizens with political party organizations that are supportive of pluralism and the representation of citizen interests, and also the emergence of citizen trust and participation in the electoral system, are essential dimensions linking societies and state institutions in a democratic fashion.

In democratic polities, it is principally political parties that aggregate the voting choices of citizens and groups—and thereby through the formation of governments and oppositions (rather than simply by means of individual or prominent civil society dissidence during the late prepluralist period)—and thus serve to channel electoral outcomes to the formulation and monitoring of state policymaking. Political parties not only express the patterns of sociocultural and economic interests and cleavages in a society but also structure the alternative policies offered to citizens. And perhaps most significant for the focus of this chapter, parties in a democratic polity should provide the connective tissue between citizens and civil society actors on the one side, and state institutions on the other.

During the first two decades of postcommunist evolution in the Western Balkans, observers frequently noted specific features of political party development, which, albeit with variation from polity to polity, lagged significantly behind Central and Eastern European parties' transformation, and which contrasted even more sharply with Western European party systems. For example, in the late 1990s, when commenting on the formation of different parties along ideological lines in former Communist states, the Hungarian political scientist Attila Ágh observed that the Central and Eastern European parties had "come closer and closer to the West European party types," that is, can be considered as "'standard' parties," or "proper members of the ideological party families." But in his view, the "whole Balkan region should be considered as 'non-standard'"; "the parties have been less developed and important in the [region's] presidential systems, and yet have still played a central role in the lopsided development, that is, in both the paralysis and progress of democratization. The former [Communist] ruling parties have kept their places in the Balkans."[1]

Ágh, of course, was referring to the situation only a few years after the war ended in Bosnia, and before the departure of Slobodan Milošević and Franjo Tudjman from the political stage. But even in the early post-2000 period, observers generally described Balkan political party development as deficient. Explaining party divisions in the Western Balkans, one analyst claimed that the region could "be said to provide a more fractured political scene than the Western countries," and that this situation had led to "high volatility, . . . a very vague political environment and weak institutionalization. The important point to look for is whether the high number of parties will continue beyond the initial phase of democratization."[2]

In recent years, most commentators have characterized political parties in the Western Balkans in much the same way, noting the greater fluidity and instability in the party systems, in contrast with both older and newer EU member states. Indeed, the comprehensive Bertelsmann Transformation Index for 2008, which included important data on

1. Attila Ágh, *The Politics of Central Europe* (London: Sage, 1998), 123.

2. Murat Abus, "Democracy in the Balkans: 1990–2002," *Alternatives: Turkish Journal of International Relations* 12, nos. 3–4 (Fall–Winter 2003): 94.

democratic and economic change in 125 countries, utilized terms such as "fragmented," "shaky," "volatility," "polarization," and "instability" when referring to the deficiencies in most of the party systems throughout Southeastern Europe.[3] But while such characterizations were somewhat justified, depending on the particular polity under consideration, they often failed to explain important trends that have been under way in the countries of the region. The persistence of "traditional" or "Balkan" political and party features was sometimes exaggerated and often overlooked the complexity of recent regional party development. Indeed, stereotypical observations regarding political parties in the Western Balkans contributed to overgeneralizations about the region, and to the neglect of recent research findings.

This is not to downplay the important factors that have accounted for the retardation and distinctiveness of postcommunist party development in the Western Balkans. They include a limited tradition of democratic experience, the disruptive consequences of radical nationalism in several countries afflicted with deep subcultural cleavages, the direct and indirect impact of warfare and sectarian violence that occurred during the 1990s and beyond, and the persistent uncertainties and insecurities in the region with regard to the process of European Union enlargement. Such relatively well-known limitations certainly impeded or disrupted recent democratic party development in the Western Balkans, and deserve careful consideration. But it is important to evaluate the extent to which such issues constitute a significant obstacle to party development as the countries of the region have proceeded through the EU's preaccession process, and the likelihood of such factors persisting as obstacles to democratization. Indeed, there is substantial evidence that the ostensible fragmented, shaky, unstable, and volatile party systems of the Western Balkans have been gradually transformed as a result of both internal and external influences. This chapter examines the emerging party systems of the region and whether political parties are becoming more supportive components of democratic development. How have Western Balkan parties and party systems changed in recent years, and will negative legacies and continuities prove strong enough to significantly impede the process of democratic change?

3. Bertelsmann Stiftung, *Bertelsmann Transformation Index 2008 Political Management in International Comparison* (Berlin: Bertelsmann Stiftung, 2007).

Initial Political Party Pluralism: Trends and Traces

During the first part of the 1990s, each of the Western Balkan states legalized and elaborated the basic elements for multiparty competition and free elections. Citizens of nations in the region also acquired a familiarity with the basic mechanisms and dynamics of political party pluralism, although this rudimentary pluralism was troubled by the warfare and regional turbulence that accompanied the initial period of postcommunist transition. Turning from the legacy and conflict during the first elections, as treated in chapter 1, closer attention can now be paid to the fragmentation and instability that preceded the struggles for an institutionalized and Europeanized party pluralism during the past decade.

The oft-mentioned "neurotic" or "wild" pluralism that followed the end of one-party rule—both after Yugoslavia's self-managed socialism and Albania's state socialism—resulted in a plethora of political parties, most of which were small, without elaborate organizational infrastructures; were extremely shallow in terms of their loyal social support; and also typically lacked a coherent programmatic or ideological orientation. The socialist and social democratic parties that emerged from the ranks of the former Communist organizations were somewhat of an exception in this regard, although they had become pale shadows of the large prepluralist party organizations from which had they emanated. Most parties, both on the left and right ends of the political spectrum, were really leader-centered organizations, in which the attachments and loyalties of both voters and party elites were directed less to ideology or party programs and more to a charismatic or dominant personality.

The first stage of pluralist development was also one of considerable party fragmentation and party unification, as political party organizations were quickly formed, atrophied, or were reconfigured. The opportunity for citizens to express themselves politically after a long period of single-party constraints, during which the nascent and limited associational energies of citizens had been channeled mainly into the emergent civil society sector (chapter 4), resulted in a rapid proliferation of parties—a condition variously referred to as "hyperpluralism," "hyperpartyism," or "megapluralism." Legislation that typically allowed a relatively small number of citizens to form a party—50 individuals in Bosnia (and in Kosovo right after 1999), 100 in Serbia and Croatia, 200 in Montenegro, and 500 in Macedonia (changed to 1,000 in 2007)—contributed to a very rapid pattern of party formation in the initial years of pluralist development.

This extensive proliferation and fragmentation of political parties would continue well into the first decade of the twenty-first century, particularly in polities such as Bosnia, Kosovo, Montenegro, and Serbia, which, for one reason or another, were somewhat delayed in developing distinct home-grown party systems. For example, by the end of 1990, Serbia had 49 parties officially registered. In 1996, that number grew to 161 and continued to grow—to 184 in 1999, 274 in 2003, 287 in 2004, 301 in 2005, and 422 by the end of September 2007.[4] In mid-2009—when the number of officially registered parties had grown to nearly 600—Serbia finally adopted a law requiring the reregistration of parties on the basis of at least 10,000 signatures (and 1,000 for parties representing minorities). As a result of this law, 501 parties were decertified, and by May 2010, Serbia had registered 72 parties (including 24 who had members in the Assembly or government coalition). Forty-two of the parties represented minority groups.[5]

The overall number of parties was also striking in the other Western Balkan polities, although they fluctuated over time, and often increased just before elections. In Croatia, for example, 71 parties were registered in 2001, 93 in 2007, and 110 by 2010.[6] At the end of October 2006, 76 parties were registered in Bosnia, a slight drop from 83 organizations in 1999. For the October 2010 election, 47 parties were initially registered in Bosnia, although by September, only some 34 of the parties registered had nominated candidates. Seventy parties were registered in Montenegro during 2003, of which 15 were considered active; and this number dropped to 64 in May 2006, when a new law required the reregistration of parties and reduced their overall number to 24 (34 by August 2010).[7] Albania had some 47 parties registered with the Ministry of Justice in 2000, and 60 parties in 2004–5. Twenty parties were registered in Macedonia during 1990, but that number grew to 57 in 1998 and to 80 by 2006. But by 2010, formal party registration in Macedonia had declined to 26 organizations, and only about 12 were

4. *Tanjug,* September 27, 2007.
5. *Danas,* May 20, 2010.
6. *Političke stranke registrirane u Republici Hrvatskoj* (Hidra, 2009).
7. Vladimir Goati, *Političke partije i partijski sistemi* (Podgorica: Fakultet političkih nauka, Univerzitet Crne Gore, 2008).

active. Kosovo registered 49 parties and coalitions for the election in 2000, 35 in 2001, 68 in 2002, 33 in 2004, 27 in 2007, and 36 in 2009.

Clearly, if measured by the sheer formation and official registration of political organizations, the Western Balkan states were manifesting vigorous pluralist impulses. But most of these political parties—variously referred to as "telephone booth parties," or "ghost," "boutique," "ego," "couch," and "meteorite" parties—were very small, politically noninfluential, unknown to most of the general public, financially nonviable, and generally short-lived (although typically remaining on the registration books).

The fact that so many political parties were continuously founded and disbanded throughout the first two decades of Western Balkan pluralist development has accentuated the unstable appearance of the region's politics and party systems. In practice, however, only a small number of parties have actually been active and also electorally viable enough to win seats in legislative bodies. Thus, despite the striking proliferation of party organizations, generally only a dozen or fewer party organizations in each of the region's democracies enjoyed electoral success and gained parliamentary influence. In fact, as detailed later in this chapter, there was only a relatively small number of core or influential parties or party coalitions in each polity. Indeed, the limited number of parties organized on a countrywide basis, or were otherwise major players in the political game, often led to a kind of bipolarization or tripolarization in the party system. In most cases the group of core parties includes a former ruling Communist Party organization (that had undergone a makeover in its program and name), and a major anticommunist (nationalist, conservative, or center-right) party or coalition that emerged either before or during the first pluralist elections as a broad "national front," or counterforce to the former single party. This fundamental political duality tended to significantly constrain the pattern of overall hyperpluralism.

Of course, the actual number of parties winning a place in legislatures varies from case to case, depending on the specificities of the electoral system and the changing vicissitudes of routine political life. Moreover, a number of party organizations entered the new post-1989 pluralist scene with decided advantages in size, support, and resources (especially the former Communists, but also the major nationalist and anticommunist party or pre-party formations that developed in the late 1980s and early 1990s).

Usually, during the initial pluralist transition in each country, only one or at most two or three major political party organizations emerged as really strong contenders to challenge the former Communists, that is, the redesigned major left-wing party remaining on the scene. For example, in Croatia, the party formation that was able to effectively oppose the reconstituted League of Communists was the Croatian Democratic Union (Hrvatska demokratska zajednica, HDZ); in Albania, the Democratic Party (Partia Demokratike); in Bosnia, three nationalistic parties, the Party for Democratic Action (Stranka Demokratske Akcije), the Croatian Democratic Union in Bosnia-Herzegovina (HDZ-BiH), and the Serbian Democratic Party (Srpska Demokratska Stranka); and in Macedonia, the Internal Macedonian Revolutionary Organization–Democratic Party for Macedonian National Unity (Vnatrešna makedonska revolucionerna organizacija–Demokratska partija za makedonsko nacionalno edinstvo, VMRO-DPMNE).

In the case of Serbia, a hegemonic party organization emerged from the Communist Party and the auxiliary structures of the regime, namely, Milošević's Socialist Party of Serbia (Socijalistička Partija Srbije, SPS). However, the SPS was initially challenged by a politically divided and weak field of democratically oriented parties, owing largely to Milošević's ability to divide and infiltrate his opposition. It was only gradually that a more cohesive "democratic bloc" or opposition was able to coalesce into the alliance "Together" (Zajedno), and later into the Democratic Opposition of Serbia, and effectively challenge the regime (i.e., the former Communists now turned nationalists). A similar situation existed in Montenegro, where the then-Milošević-allied and hegemonic Democratic Party of Socialists (Demokratska Partija Socijalista) was only weakly challenged by rival opposition organizations such as the People's Party (Narodna Stranka, NS), and the Liberal Party of Montenegro during the 1990s.

The gradual adoption of electoral systems that provided for proportional representation (in full or in part) in most of the Western Balkan states also permitted several smaller political parties to obtain increased representation in each of the legislatures, and also typically to play a role in the postelection ruling coalitions that were formed. But because of the dynamics of party development directly after the end of one-party rule (and also the fact that majoritarian or mixed electoral systems were used initially in most countries), the parliamentary party landscape was not actually as fragmented or chaotic as it often seemed to outsiders, especially when considered against the plethora of small parties that were legally registered.

However, during the 1990s, the relative newness and unsettled character of political party systems, along with the still very weak identification of citizens with parties within and outside legislatures, coupled with the general turbulence in the region, acted to destabilize the Western Balkan political and party systems and to create problems that would complicate the next decade of pluralism (2000–2010). In Serbia, Milošević's antipluralist manipulation of an ostensibly competitive system created the one extreme case of party underdevelopment. Thus, in 1992, the then scholar–intellectual activist Vojislav Koštunica, who was the head of the small Democratic Party of Serbia (Demokratska stranka Srbije), which had broken away from the Democratic Party (Demokratska stranka) because of the latter organization's weaker nationalist posture), described the situation in Milošević's Serbia as follows: "Our party system is not even a true party system, . . . and with respect to the opposition parties, I think that parties do not exist here in the real meaning of the word; . . . elementary conditions for the work of political parties have not been ensured. We are not living in normal political circumstances, and we do not have a regular political life."[8]

Likewise, in January 1996, Shkëlzen Maliqi, the Kosovo sociologist and activist, described the character of political parties in Kosovo (then a province of Serbia under harsh political control from Belgrade): "Political organizations are not really political parties but merely pluralized elements of a national liberation movement whose overriding goal is the establishment of an independent Kosova."[9] And the situation in Albania was much the same. One Albanian analyst observed in 1998 that in his country, "the political parties have not found yet their human resources and social basis. They seem to be group[s] of interest but mainly in the sense that they collect individuals or groups, most by feelings or ideological convictions. . . . Due to the political elite's mentality, the political pluralism in Albania has been considered by the political parties mostly as a domination of government over the oppo-

8. *FBIS-EEU,* October 29, 1992, 50.
9. "The Albanian Movement in Kosova," in *Yugoslavia and After: A Study in Fragmentation, Despair and Rebirth,* edited by David Dyker and Ivan Vejvoda (New York: Longman, 1996).

sition rather than a cohabitation between political parties and sharing of power."[10]

Meanwhile, the intense polarization along ethnocultural lines of the fledgling political party systems in Bosnia and Macedonia—which obstructed state cohesion in both cases during the 1990s and beyond, and also led to violence and to sharp political-ideological differentiation between the major parties—undermined the basis for the emergence of moderate party pluralism functioning within broadly legitimated states. In some cases, such initial transition problems limited party development and have proved difficult to reverse. For example, a 2006 study by a analyst in Bosnia put it this way: "The multi-party system was characterized by segmented pluralism (highly fragmented, ideologically strongly polarized, and completely centrifugal), with a relatively large number of political parties. . . . In the party system of B-H [Bosnia-Herzegovina] there are no parties of the left, center, or right in the usual sense. . . . Parties in B-H do not have clear-cut programs, and certainly no credible political practice and vision of their own goals. Instead they mainly act on an ad hoc basis depending on their potential and their circumstances in B-H."[11]

The political parties in Croatia exhibited somewhat more structural stability than the other Western Balkan states during the 1990s, in terms of ideological differentiation and the beginnings of partisan identification. But the institutionalization of the party system in Croatia was obstructed by the authoritarian features of the Tudjman regime. As one Croatian political scientist argued in 2000, up until the post-Tudjman "second transition" began [at the end of 1999], the country's rulers had "made the overall political atmosphere impregnated with deep mutual distrust, uncertainty and public diversion on who is, and who is not, a democratic actor." Tudjman's ruling party, the HDZ, chose "to accuse other parties as being antisystem or state elements every time when the opposition has tried to criticize governmental policies."[12] The nine years

10. Kosta Barjaba, "Albania in Transition: Elite's Role and Perspective," June 1998.

11. Rebeka Kotlo, "Democratic Role of Political Parties," *Democracy Assessment in Bosnia and Herzegovina* (Sarajevo: Open Society Fund, 2006), 152–56.

12. Goran Čular, "Political Development in Croatia 1990–2000: Fast Transition Long-Postponed Consolidation," *Politička Misao* 37, no. 5 (2000): 39–41. See also Goran Čular, *Izbori i konsolidacija demokracije u Hrvatskoj* (Zagreb: FPN, 2005);

of soft authoritarianism in Croatia (1990–99), just as the personalization and concentration of power in Milošević's Serbia (1990–2000), seriously impeded the development of institutionalized party systems in both states. The problems of Western Balkan party development in the 1990s, and the resulting effects during the next decade, did not preclude the important changes throughout the region but rather imposed limitations that prevented a more rapid change in the institutionalization and development of democratic party systems.

Dilemmas of Institutionalization: Political Party Systems and Democratic Consolidation

In evaluating whether or not a particular political party system is institutionalized, analysts generally rely on a wide variety of criteria. To a large extent, these measures or indicators of party system institutionalization all are focused on the predictability, stability, or steadiness of a group of political parties to constitute the core organizations that play governance or opposition roles in a particular polity over time, and can regularly attract a substantial number of voters during elections. As one student of party institutionalization has put it: "The key element here is probably predictability, with strong party systems being highly predictable, and with weak or feebly structured party 'systems' being highly unpredictable. . . . The more predictable the party system is, the more it is a system as such, and hence the more institutionalized it has become."[13]

Various dimensions or indicators are typically examined by analysts to explore the degree of political party or party system institutionalization. For example, the institutionalization process depends upon the issue of the "volatility" or unpredictability of the electorate, in terms of voters moving from party to party; the frequency in the rise and fall of parties; the "rootedness" or "anchoring" of parties in the society;

---

and Ivan Šiber, "Structuring the Croatian Party Scene," *Croatian Political Science Review* 2, no. 2 (1993): 111–29.

13. Peter Mair, "The Freezing Hypothesis," in *Party Systems and Voter Alignments Revisited,* edited by Lauri Karvonen and Stein Kuhnle (London: Routledge: 2000). See also Fernando Casal Bertoa, "Party System Institutionalization in New Democracies: A Comparative Perspective," Leiden University, 2007.

the extent to which party systems are deemed by citizens and elites to be legitimate; and the degree of internal party democracy exhibited by the members of a party in relation to party elites and party policies. Needless to say, owing to the complexity and turbulence of the Western Balkan region, it has proven quite difficult for analysts to assess or operationalize such indicators of institutionalization. But sufficient evidence is available to explore some of these dimensions in order to determine the extent of the transformation, and attendant institutionalization, of Western Balkan party systems in the post-2000 period.

Party Legitimation: Evolving Public Attitudes to Party Pluralism

There is little doubt, as discussed above, that during the postcommunist period the political party systems of the Western Balkan states, to a much larger extent than those of the Central and Eastern European states, faced serious difficulties with respect to their development and institutionalization. Still, by the end of the 1990s, and certainly in the post-2000 period, few citizens of the nations in the region believed it would be wise to resurrect the old one-party system or doubted the intrinsic value of multipartyism.

Democratic rule was still by no means irreversible, or deeply valued and supported, by the region's population, but citizens had come to prefer a competitive process for choosing their decisionmakers. For example, a 2002 comparative study of the Yugoslav successor states revealed that most respondents believed that a democracy consisting of at least two strong parties was extremely important, or at least important.[14] Only 6 to 17 percent of respondents, depending on the polity in question, viewed such arrangements as unimportant. Those surveyed in Montenegro, Serbia, and Croatia viewed the value of a strong political party system the most positively, perhaps because their first decade of party pluralism had been plagued by a plethora of weak opposition parties, and also the personalized hegemony of authoritarian leaders fundamentally opposed to political competition. The most negative views regarding the value of party competition were expressed in Macedonia (16.5 percent less than a year after warfare in that state) and Bosnia (13.9 percent).

14. International Institute for Democracy and Electoral Assistance, "Southeastern Europe: New Means for Regional Analysis," 2002.

Although, after some ten years of pluralism, most citizens in the region may have come to believe in multipartyism as an ideal, this view is still a long way from any perception in the region that party pluralism is functioning properly. Indeed, there is considerable evidence from studies of individual Western Balkan states, and also from comparative research on the region, that public confidence or trust in political parties and party politicians has been extremely low, and in some cases has even declined during the first two decades of postcommunism.[15]

Some of this mistrust can be traced to a deeply entrenched cynicism regarding party politics and politicians that is a legacy of the prepluralist period. But the weak economic performance of political party elites during the postcommunist period, and also their role in fueling social and ethnic divisions in many cases, along with the continued presence of extensive corruption in political life, has reinforced negative perceptions about political parties. As the data in table 5.1 indicate, complete distrust of political parties in 2007 was the highest in Albania, Macedonia, and Serbia. There was a striking decrease of confidence in parties during the period between 1998 and 2002 in all cases, except in Serbia and Montenegro (where the level of distrust initially declined, probably because of the fall of Milošević). The data for 2007 reveal that the situation had improved somewhat in Macedonia and Bosnia but that the level of trust in parties had changed very little in Albania.[16] What is most striking and troubling, however, is that in 2007 more than two-thirds of the respondents in every Western Balkan state, except Montenegro, distrusted political parties. More recent surveys of public trust and confidence in political and governmental institutions within the region show the same low standing of political parties (see below).

Of course, some distrust—or a healthy level of skepticism on the part of citizens about their governing institutions, and about the activities of political authorities—may be normal and even a prerequisite

15. World Values Study Association and European Values Study Group, 1998, 2001, 2002; European Bank for Reconstruction and Development–World Bank Life in Transition Survey, "Trust in Political Institutions," 30.

16. A 2003 survey indicated that 66 percent of respondents in Albania believed that politicians felt they were above the law, and 70 percent thought that parties either only served the people to a limited extent or not at all. And in the case of urban youth, only 12 percent trusted political parties in 2004. Blendi Kajsiu, "Albanian Political Parties," in *Political Parties and the Consolidation of Democracy in South Eastern Europe,* edited by Georgi Karasimeonov (Sofia: Friedrich Ebert Stiftung and Institute for Political and Legal Studies, 2004), 9.

Table 5.1. Lack of Confidence or Distrust in Political Parties, Selected Years (percent)

Country	1998, from World Values Surveys			2001–2, from World Values Surveys			2007, from European Bank for Reconstruction and Development		
	Not Much	None at All	Total	Not Much	None at All	Total	Some Distrust	Complete Distrust	Total
Albania	56.1	18.7	74.8	37.5	31.3	68.8	16	57	73
Bosnia	38.1	14.0	52.1	57.1	27.6	84.7	21	46	67
Croatia	53.1	19.8	72.9	N.A.	N.A.	N.A.	27	44	71
Macedonia	42.6	39.7	82.3	42.0	47.0	89.0	13	56	69
Serbia	41.5	34.3	75.8	44.9	31.8	76.7	20	51	71
Montenegro	37.1	32.1	69.2	48.9	19.4	68.3	21	32	53

Note: N.A. = not available.
Sources: World Values Surveys; European Bank for Reconstruction and Development.

for democracy.[17] But the deep mistrust of political party organizations and party leaders throughout the Balkan region in recent years may have crossed the threshold of skepticism that is productive for democratic consolidation. In any event, when one examines the 2007 data on lack of confidence and distrust more closely, Montenegro has had the lowest percentage of respondents who express complete distrust in parties, whereas Albania and Macedonia have had the highest percentage among such respondents. Even in Montenegro, however, a majority (53 percent) remain distrustful of parties, and that state has the highest number of respondents indicating neutrality on the issue—that is, neither trust nor distrust—and only 6 percent express complete trust in political parties. But Montenegro does stand out with the highest proportion of respondents indicating some or complete trust in political parties (23 percent in total), whereas this figure is about 13 to 15 percent for all the other cases. The Montenegrin data might be accounted for by the fact that not long before the study, party leaders had successfully achieved independence from Serbia. Meanwhile, Croatia stood out with the lowest level (8 percent) of complete trust in political parties.

Party Corruption

The 2007 data for Croatia regarding trust in parties seem somewhat surprising in view of that country's front-runner regional position in several areas of political and economic development, and also the state's considerable progress in the EU preaccession process. But the Croatian situation might be explained by the higher levels of political corruption recorded in Croatia, and from the considerable public cynicism that has resulted from high-profile financial scandals involving party leaders (for the impact of the same factor on Euro-skepticism in Croatia, see chapter 8). Indeed, the low levels of confidence and trust in parties and party politicians throughout the region are undoubtedly linked to the broader and complex issue regarding the role played by money in politics. This aspect of Western Balkan political development includes the highly visible role of tycoons in political life, the corruption of parties by private and illegal interests, and also the low level of transparency in the funding of parties.

17. Charles Tilly, *Democracy* (Cambridge: Cambridge University Press, 2007), 94.

Almost all the Western Balkan states have established laws on the financing of political parties, and in most cases the legal regulation of political finance has improved considerably in recent years compared with the 1990s, as has state and public awareness of the issue's importance. At the same time, all the states in the region have experienced serious deficiencies in the implementation of such legislation, and recent surveys indicate that political parties are viewed by the public as the most corrupted of all political institutions. For example, in Croatia, only 21 percent of those surveyed in 2007 believed that legal provisions for financing campaigns were regularly adhered to by political parties. Supporters of the ruling HDZ were most positive (29.1 percent) in that regard. Roughly two-thirds of adherents in the major opposition parties responded negatively.[18] A detailed 2007 survey of party campaign financing in Croatia observed that "there has hardly been any party not involved in a scandal one way or another. Those involved in the scandals try to justify their behavior by making cynical statements about how such things existed all over the world." The same study concluded that "political party and electoral campaign financing legislation in the Republic of Croatia is deficient, and even when it exists it is often only dead letters."[19]

Serbia has had legislation regulating political finance since the mid-1990s, and it adopted new laws both before and after the Milošević regime ended in the fall of 2000. But a lack of actual transparency has protected the political parties from receiving close scrutiny. Things have improved in recent years compared with the Milošević period, when the practices of bribing leaders of the opposition parties and manipulating the system completely undermined the emergence of responsible and transparent pluralism. After 2000, a new law provided state financing for parties in a more generous and transparent manner.[20] However, party funding irregularities have persisted in Serbia, in large part owing to the politicization of the Central Election Commission by successive ruling

18. *Promocija Plus,* 2007.

19. Josip Kregar, Djordje Garadašević, and Viktor Gotovac, "Croatia," in *Political Finance and Corruption in Eastern Europe: The Transition Period,* edited by Daniel Smilov and Jurij Toplak (Burlington, Vt.: Ashgate, 2007), 62. See also Zdravko Petak, "Financing Political Parties in Croatia: Parliamentary Elections 2003," *Politička Misao* 40, no. 5 (2003): 68–74.

20. Vladimir Goati, "Political Finance in Serbia," in *Political Finance,* ed. Smilov and Toplak, 163–69. See also Miodrag Milosavljević, ed., *Finansiranje političkih partija: izmedzu norme i parkse* (Belgrade: Cesid, 2008).

party coalitions. Thus, the chairperson of Serbia's Anti-Corruption Council, Verica Barać, observed in 2007, that "the worst corruption is to be found in party funding, because if we knew who finances, we would know whose interests they champion. We would know why some laws are being passed or not passed. . . . We cannot find out how these parties are funded because the law has been conceived in such a way as to prevent this coming to light. And you cannot expect the parties to come out and admit who financed them."[21]

As a result of this situation, a small group of Serbian tycoons operating in the shadows have tended to exercise control over most political parties. In exchange for illegal cash transfers to parties, donors have been favored in public procurement deals and in competition for contracts. A 2009 study found that 69 percent of respondents in Serbia believed that political parties were the most corrupt sector of the political system.[22]

Meanwhile, in newly independent Montenegro, a 2007 study of corruption, which dealt in part with the financing of political parties and electoral campaigns, concluded that "there has been very little interest in the effective implementation of the law and numerous breaches of its provisions are committed by nearly all political parties to a certain extent, with little consequence."[23] A 2007 survey of campaign financing rules in Macedonia observed that they were "repeatedly violated, ironically by those who attempt to attract citizens' votes by promising to establish the rule of law. Even when there are initiatives to reform the electoral law, the issue of clear procedures for the control of campaign finance is readily overlooked."[24]

The most systematic analysis of Bosnia and Herzegovina with respect to laws regarding financing of political parties noted that "the area . . . is one of the most serious problems in the political life of

21. *BLIC,* May 21, 2007.

22. *Danas,* June 4, 2009. In May 2009, Vladimir Goati, the president of Transparency Serbia, observed that his country had experienced "20 years of complete financial irresponsibility and had arrived at a situation that required drastic measures. . . . Because we don't have a democracy without parties, but we must make them attractive and responsible." *Politika,* May 4, 2009.

23. Marijana Trivunović, Vera Devine, and Harald Mathisen, *Corruption in Montenegro 2007: Overview of Major Problems and Status of Reforms* (Bergen: Chr. Michelsen Institute, 2007), 9.

24. Renata Treneska, "Party Funding and Campaign Finance in Macedonia," in *Political Finance,* ed. Smilov and Toplak, 121.

BiH. . . . [State] budget financing of political parties is totally transparent, [but] financing of donations is partially transparent, if at all. Outside the official data, there is the insufficiently researched segment of the 'gray economy' directed by political parties, particularly the ruling ones."[25] Parties in Bosnia frequently failed to submit annual and postelection financial reports and information on property, and the media often accuse officials of money laundering by parties. One 2007 study by Transparency International in Bosnia concluded that the anticorruption campaigns promoted by international agencies have often "promoted political cynicism rather than a hope for political change." The same study observed that "the conclusion Bosnian voters have drawn from the institutionalization of anticorruption into every walk of life has been that no politician can be trusted." Moreover, anticorruption efforts may have actually assisted the nationalist parties: "The less trust people have in the broader political process, the more likely it is that parochial and local links will come to the forefront."[26] As in Bosnia, the legal regulation of political finance in Kosovo improved considerably after 1999. But political parties still received a good deal of funding from undisclosed sources, and organized crime groups have strong connections with political parties (a situation which both Kosovo's Albanians and Serbs agreed upon).[27] Meanwhile, in Albania, until 2010 there was still no specific law on party financing, and as a rule parties have not provided financial statements on their expenditures (as required by the electoral code). As the director of Albania's Central Election Commission observed in January 2008, "There is a consensus among the politicians to restrict the powers employed by the Audit Bureau of the State. . . . Political parties fill in a form to the Election Commission after the elections, but nobody verifies the authenticity of the statements. . . . We can do nothing more than take note of the statements of the various political parties."[28]

25. *Democracy Assessment in Bosnia and Herzegovina* (Sarajevo: Open Society Fund, 2006), 174–76.

26. Transparency International Bosnia and Herzegovina, *Bosnia and Herzegovina at the Crossroads: EU Accession or a Failed State?* (Sarajevo: Transparency International Bosnia and Herzegovina, 2007), 33.

27. Marcin Walecki, "Kosovo," in *Political Finance in Post-Conflict Societies,* edited by Jeff Fischer, Marcin Walecki, and Jeffrey Carlson (Washington, D.C.: US Agency for International Development, 2006).

28. "Albania: No Control over the Funding of Political Parties," Balkan Investigative Reporting Network, January 16, 2008.

Core Parties, Small Parties, and "Party Families":
Alignments and Cleavages

The extensive distrust of political parties in the Western Balkans, to-gether with considerable public cynicism regarding the role of party politicians in political corruption, undercuts the durability and predict-ability of support for existing party organizations, and has weakened overall party system institutionalization in particular countries. But despite the patterns of distrust described above and their accompany-ing causes, and also the previously noted plethora of parties that were constantly formed and disbanded in the region during the past decade, there has been considerable continuity with regard to the persistence of core parties within the legislatures of each polity. There has also been substantial popular or voter identification with the major parties that have been at the center of political life. As a result, one can observe important continuities with respect to distinct "party families," "ideo-logical families," or "party blocs" within each of the Western Balkan political systems, despite the fact that relations within, between, and among parties are often quite polarized, and also that rampant fac-tionalism has encouraged the frequent formation of breakaway party organizations.

Thus, in most countries, in almost all the elections held between 1990 and 2010, two or three successful parties, or coalitions of parties, which competed for seats in the lower houses of national legislative bodies have obtained the bulk of the votes cast. There are, naturally, fluctua-tions in the level of votes garnered by the major parties from election to election based on such factors as the changing political circumstances, the choices available, and the election rules. But as the data gathered in table 5.2 indicate, a few core parties in each country have been able to successfully dominate the multiparty landscape.

Indeed, when the major winners in terms of vote distribution are con-sidered, most of the political party systems in the Western Balkans have manifest essentially bipolar or tripolar patterns of party vote dispersion and alignment. Thus, generally in each of the Balkan polities, two or three of the same major parties—either on their own or typically allied with smaller parties in coalitions—constitute the poles around which the smaller parties pivot in a relatively structured manner. Most citizens perceive these core parties and party poles as the natural channels for participation in the political system. After elections, governments are

Table 5.2. Percentages of Votes Obtained by the Three Largest Parties or Contending Coalitions in Parliamentary Elections, Selected Years

Country	Years and Percentages of Votes Obtained							
Croatia	1990	1992	1995	2000	2003	2007		
	92.2	68.0	75.1	80.8	64.5	73.5		
Bosnia	1990		1996	2000	2002	2006		2010
	70.6		76.1	54.6	50.9	51.5		54.6
Serbia	1990	1992	1993	1997	2000	2003	2007	2008
	67.1	89.8	67.1	81.0	91.7	58.9	77.9	79.5
Montenegro	1990	1992	1996	1998	2001	2002	2006	2009
	90.7	73.9	82.6	91.6	90.5	91.0	65.9	89.4
Macedonia	1990		1994	1998		2002	2006	2008
	73.0		61.5	72.5		76.8	67.9	89.5
Albania	1991	1992		1996	1997	2001	2005	2009
	96.7	92.2		81.7	81.8	83.4	88.3	85.9
Kosovo		1992			2001	2004	2007	2010
		84.5			79.2	82.7	69.2	69.3

Sources: Authors' calculations from national reports.

usually composed of a ruling coalition made up of a core party that is allied with several smaller parties. Parties that fall outside the governing coalitions in opposition are generally small, single-interest parties, or party organizations focused on advocating the interests of regions and minority groups. But in most cases, even the principal minority parties are affiliated with the core parties or coalitions, thereby increasing the influence of such parties—a pattern that for the most part facilitates the incorporation of minority citizen interests into political life.

Toward Defragmentation

The continued presence of smaller political parties in each of the Western Balkan polities derives in part from the proliferation of party organizations during the first phase of postcommunist pluralism, and also from the political-cultural, socioeconomic, and historical cleavages in each society. But persistently high levels of party fragmentation have also been connected to the popularity of electoral systems with proportional representation (PR) throughout the region. As elsewhere, PR systems in the Western Balkans are generally perceived as a way to broaden participation and democracy, particularly after the political compression experienced during one-party rule. After the initial phase of experimentation with single-member district majority systems or mixtures of both types of electoral systems, PR systems have become the regional norm. However, in most cases, electoral laws include the use of threshold requirements that require parties and coalitions to have a sufficient number of votes to qualify for an allocation of seats in Parliament. Such threshold rules have somewhat reduced the fragmenting impact of PR electoral systems and, along with the political and financial imperatives of campaigning, have created incentives for smaller parties to join coalitions around the larger core parties. Moreover, electoral systems, such as the ones in Macedonia, Croatia, and Albania (after April 2008) that use so-called moderate PR systems that include several regional electoral districts, also tend to have a defragmenting impact on the distribution of seats. Thus, the pluralist landscape in the Western Balkans is far less extreme than the number of smaller party organizations officially registered in each country would suggest.

It was not surprising, therefore, that during 2008 and 2009, the smaller political parties in Albania strenuously objected to the country's mid-2008 adoption of a regionally backed PR system. One Albanian commentator observed that the law was really not against viable smaller parties but was simply a way of eliminating parties "which cannot fill a bus with supporters; . . . the ridiculous situation of having 60 to 70 political parties on the political scene will end very soon. It is hard to remember their names, let alone what they stand for."[29] Indeed, in the June 2009 election, the three major political parties in the country together won 86 percent of the vote. The leaders of Albania's smaller parties complained bitterly and blamed the situation on corruption in the vote count and on the new regional system for proportional representation.[30] The second-largest party organization, the Socialist Party (Partia Socialiste e Shqipërisë, PSSH), began a boycott of the country's legislature that remained in place throughout 2010.

The centripetal effects of threshold rules is offset to some extent by special rules aimed at facilitating the representation of smaller minority political parties in most Western Balkan legislatures. For example, in 2004, Serbia lifted the threshold requirement entirely for minority

29. *Shekulli,* April 26, 2008.
30. *Koha Johe,* July 9, 2009, in *BBC Monitoring Europe–Political,* July 10, 2009.

parties. Of course, difficulties can arise with regard to provisions designed to give an advantage to minority parliamentary representation. Thus, in April 2008, a month before the parliamentary election, the Serbian Constitutional Court ruled—on the basis of an initiative from the Serbian Radical Party (Srpska radikalna stranka, SRS)—that ethnic minority parties had to submit a list of 1,000 signatures and not the 3,000 signatures previously necessary for these parties to participate in elections. And in July 2006, Montenegro's Constitutional Court declared unconstitutional a plan that guaranteed minority party representation in the legislature. Minority party leaders in Montenegro, who had supported the government during the 2006 referendum on independence, felt betrayed. But some in the country believed, with the Court, that guaranteed seats for minority parties violated the idea of one person, one vote. The new Montenegrin Constitution of 2007 did not resolve the issue of direct minority representation, and majority/minority tension on the issue continued during 2008.

Overall, however, electoral provisions providing for a modified PR system to achieve minority representation have not contributed to instability in the Western Balkans. As the Croatian political commentator Davor Gjenero pointed out astutely, "absolutely proportionality" provokes hyperfragmentation. But PR systems that are modified by threshold requirements in several districts encourage four to five "serious" parties and stable political majorities that can govern through the executive branch, as well as stable coalitions. The "reduction of uncertainty" regarding the number of opposition parties in such party systems can facilitate democratic consolidation.[31]

Each polity's particular patterns of party alignment, of course, have been influenced by various country-specific factors, and these have evolved during the past two decades of pluralist developments. For example, Croatia has had an essentially bipolar pattern with—except for 1992—the HDZ and the Social Democratic Party (Socijaldemokratska partija, SDP) sharing the bulk of the votes and legislative seats throughout the postcommunist period. The smaller centrist/liberal Croatian People's Party (Hrvatska narodna stranka, HNS) has been allied closely with the SDP since the early 1990s, although after 2003 that alliance

---

31. *Vjesnik,* April 6, 2007. For the broader issue of minority political representation, see King Baudouin Foundation, *A Guide to Minorities and Political Participation in South-east Europe* (Brussels: King Baudouin Foundation, 2009).

came under strain, and HNS leaders appear determined to challenge the party system's bipolar orientation, and to eventually create a two-and-a-half- or three-party system.

In Bosnia, the three major nationalist parties, which emerged after the adoption of pluralism in 1990, remained dominant for a decade (including throughout the war). But in 2000, when these parties were weakened—in large part through the intervention of Bosnia's international high representative, but also through the public perception that the nationalists had been co-opted to the new reality of Bosnia under foreign direction—the civic-oriented (but predominantly Muslim) SDP formed the government. As the successor party to Bosnia's League of Communists, the SDP had been an important political force since 1990. But the ascendancy was short-lived, and in 2003 it was defeated at the polls when more "fashionable," "second-generation," or breakaway nationalist parties began to dominate the political scene (e.g., the predominantly Muslim Party of Bosnia and Herzegovina, Stranka za Bosnu i Hercegovinu, S-BiH, of Haris Silajdžić; the Serb Alliance of Independent Social Democrats, Savez nezavisnih socijaldemokrata, SNSD, of Milorad Dodik; and the new, albeit more conservative, Croatian Democratic Union 1990, Hrvatska demokratska zajednica 1990, HDZ-1990).

After 2006, two rival Muslim parties (the Party for Democratic Action, and the S-BiH), two Serbian parties (SNSD and the Party of Democratic Progress, Partija demokratskog progresa), and the two main Croat parties (HDZ and HDZ-1990) formed the main elements of a reconfigured but still essentially ethnically segmented tripolar arrangement. The weakened SDP, along with smaller civic-oriented parties, remained on the scene in Bosnia, but through the election of October 2010, ethnic cleavages still shaped the party system in large measure.[32] Part of Bosnia's problems, as the political analyst Zdravko Grebo aptly put it, is that there is a "tragic absence of a political spectrum in the traditional meaning of the word. Here [in Bosnia] both at the beginning and the end of the multiparty spectrum nobody can say with any certainty where the left stands, where the center is, and where

---

32. In the October 2010 election, the SDP considerably strengthened its position in Bosnia's central legislature and also in the Federation Parliament, but the ethnopolitical parties retained their hold on the country's executive and entity-level institutions.

the right is positioned; yet it is known with absolute certainty who is the Bosniak, who is the Croat, and who is the Serb."[33]

Montenegro has exhibited a more asymmetrical pattern of political party alignment than most Western Balkan states, owing to the hegemonic position of the Democratic Party of Socialists (Demokratska Partija Socijalista, DPS) and its smaller allies for the past two decades. Politics became more bipolarized in the country as the matter of independence arose in the post-2000 period—that is, between DPS support (with the help of the allied Social Democratic Party and smaller party organizations) for sovereignty on the one side and a number of divided opposition parties on the other. The Montenegrin political analyst Srdjan Darmanović observed in 2008 that the "ruling coalition in Montenegro is excessively powerful, and especially its core—the DPS. The system in which we live is theoretically called a multiparty system with a dominant party. Very different types of countries from Mexico to India, and also Italy, Japan, and Sweden have this kind of system."[34] No opposition party or coalition received more than 17 percent of the vote in 2009. The lack of unity among the opposition parties also facilitated DPS control. Thus, the divided opposition ran three separate candidates for president in April 2008 against the candidate selected by Milorad Djukanović, Filip Vujanović, who won the contest rather easily. Moreover, one portion of the opposition, the Socialist People's Party (Socijalistička narodna partija, SNP), which spearheaded the anti-independence bloc before 2006, has lost much of its popularity, except among voters of declared Serbian ethnic orientation.

In many respects, Macedonia has had essentially two separate and bipolarized party subsystems—an ethnic Macedonian system with two prominent parties, and another subsystem with two leading parties from the Albanian community. The two ethnic subsystems also include many smaller parties. But the weight of the two ethnic Macedonian parties, and the system of party alliances and coalitions, gives political life in the country a decidedly bipolar orientation. Thus, voter dispersion and governance have resulted in an essentially two-force competition, with the two ethnic Macedonian elements, VMRO-DPMNE and the Social

33. "Review," in *Ten Years of Democratic Chaos: Electoral Processes in Bosnia and Herzegovina from 1996 to 2006,* by Suad Arnautović (Sarajevo: Promocult, 2007), xv.

34. *Vijesti,* April 25, 2008.

Democratic Union (Socijaldemokratski sojuz na Makedonija, SDSM), alternating in power, typically in changing coalition partnership with one or another of the two major Albanian parties. In March 2008, the ruling VMRO-DPMNE appeared about to be left in the position of a minority government as its Albanian party ally, the Democratic Party of Albanians (Demokratska Partija na Albancite, DPA), suggested that it would pull out of the governing coalition in protest over the government's refusal to recognize Kosovo's unilateral declaration of independence and the government's failure to broaden the use of Albanian language and symbols. However, the scenario for minority government did not work out, and in the end all the major parties reached a temporary political consensus to bolster the unity of the country during its critical negotiations focused on NATO membership. And when the controversy over changing the country's name was used by Greece to veto Macedonia's membership in NATO at the Bucharest Summit in mid-2008, the government called a snap election for June 1.

As the country approached the election, one Macedonian commentator underlined the predictability of the process: "The election date and parties that are going to run are known. . . . [We] also know the plans and strategies of the political parties in relation to the electorate and their offers and projects are not secret either. In light of all this, there is no need for scanning every party individually because the objective of these elections is known beforehand. . . . We have two Macedonian political parties with dramatically opposed policies which from time to time make vain attempts to establish certain [ideological] principles."[35] Once again, the electoral contest centered around two major poles: one led by VMRO-DPMNE and supported by eighteen small parties; and the other by the SDSM, heading a coalition with five smaller parties. Macedonia was thought to have the largest number of registered parties per capita of any Western Balkan country. But its essentially bipolarized party system gave it an underlying structural continuity with regard to its core political actors.[36]

The June 2008 election—Macedonia's sixth as a pluralist polity—was marred by violence (one person killed and several injured), mainly between the principal Albanian parties, and fraught with electoral ir-

35. *Koha,* April 23, 2008.
36. See, e.g., Petar-Emil Mitev, Antonina Zhelyaz Kuva, and Goran Stoykuvski, *Macedonia at the Crossroads* (Skopje, 2008), 155–60.

regularities (intimidation, ballot stuffing, and fraud). About twenty people were arrested because of the violence, and the election had to be repeated in several districts. The final results indicated a major victory for the VMRO-DPMNE of Prime Minister Nikola Gruevski, which took roughly 48.3 percent of the vote (63 out of 120 seats). The opposition SDSM received only 23.4 percent of the vote (27 seats), and its leader, Radmila Šekerinska, announced her resignation. The bitterly divided two main Albanian parties, the Democratic Union for Integration (Demokratska unija za integracija, DUI) and DPA, received 18 and 11 seats, respectively. In early July, Gruevski formed a coalition government with the DUI, a move that intensified intra-Albanian political conflict. Thus, directly after the election, the DUI leader, Ali Ahmeti, claimed that the only way the country's politics could be "rehabilitated" was for the leader of the opposing DPA, Meduh Thaçi, to be "politically isolated." Thaçi in response claimed that Ahmeti had orchestrated the electoral violence, and that given Ahmeti's identification of "politics with shooting [in the 2001 fighting], it is hard for such a person to comprehend the power of democracy that can be accomplished with ballots not with weapons."[37] In the wake of the 2008 elections, the development of a fully democratic and consensual party political culture in Macedonia appeared to remain an elusive goal. Indeed, by the summer of 2010, Gruevski's alliance with the DUI was under severe stress.

Albania's party system has been strongly bipolarized between the PSSH and the Democratic Party (Partia Demokratike, PD), but with a good deal of factionalism and party splits, as is the case of most other parties throughout the region. But throughout the country's first two decades of pluralist experience, Albania has retained an essentially bifurcated or bipolarized party pattern, with a surfeit of smaller parties trying to overcome their weakness and marginal role by forming coalitions with the two major party organizations. When Prime Minister Sali Berisha was asked in April 2008 why he pushed through an important law on the judiciary with only the support of the country's two biggest parties, he answered: "Because the two of them together represent over 60 percent of Albanians. . . . It was impossible to convince all the smaller parties to back these amendments."[38] And though thirty-four

37. *Makfax News Agency,* June 5, 2008.
38. Shekulli, April 27, 2008. See also Fatos Lovanja, "The Introduction of Political Pluralsim in Albania: Contradictions and Paradoxes," in *Albanian*

parties and four coalitions competed in the election of June 2009, the right-wing coalition, Alliance for Change, headed by Berisha's DPA, took 49.92 percent of the vote, while the socialist's Union for Change coalition won 45.34 percent. The almost evenly divided polarization between the two principal parties and the reduction in support for the smaller parties was strengthened by the country's new regionally organized proportional representation system.

In Kosovo, three major political parties dominated the scene in all four elections from 1992 through 2007, and all the party organizations were focused on the quest for independence from Serbia. The largest party, the Democratic League of Kosovo (Lidhja Demokratike e Kosovës, LDK), saw itself as the legitimate heir to the existing regime in Belgrade, and it divided its energies between the quest for Kosovo's sovereignty and fighting off challenges from smaller parties in the Kosovo Albanian community.[39] After 1999, the major challenges to the LDK were the Democratic Party of Kosovo (Partia Demokratike e Kosovës, PDK) and the Alliance for the Future of Kosovo (Aleanca për Ardhmërinë e Kosovës, AAK), that is, the strongest parties to emerge from the forces of the Kosovo Liberation Army. The PDK and LDK took more than 70 percent of the vote until 2007, when party fortunes changed after the significant weakening of the LDK (in the wake of the death of its founder and longtime leader, Ibrahim Rugova), which led to the electoral victory of the PDK. However, in 2008, in the interests of mobilizing the Kosovo Albanian unity at a critical stage in the sovereignty-seeking process, the two major parties, the PDK and LDK, formed a coalition or unity government. But the PDK-LDK coalition was a marriage of convenience, and the weakened LDK was very much the junior partner (in October 2010, the LDK pulled out of the coalition in preparation for elections). Anxious to reverse traditional PDK and LDK control, Kosovo's right-wing parties, spearheaded by the AAK, actively engaged in discussions to form their own coalition.

Meanwhile, the small and fragmented Kosovo Serb party subsystem —which frequently boycotted the electoral process—has generally operated at the fringes of political life. Near the end of 2007, four of the six

---

Democratic Elections 1991–1997, edited by Kosta Barjaba (Berlin: WZB, 2004), 21–64.

39. Shkëlzen Maliqi, *Kosova: Separate Worlds, Reflections and Analysis* (Priština: MM Society, 1998), 28–32.

Kosovo Serb parties that took part in the November election formed a coalition, and they won a portion of the guaranteed minority seats in the legislature. Following Kosovo's declaration of independence, however, ethnic relations worsened in Kosovo, and on the eve of the November 2009 local election, many Serbs—urged on by the regime in Belgrade and the Serbian Orthodox Church—were still unwilling to participate in the new country's political system (although twenty-one small Serb parties registered to take part).

Dramatic Realignment in Serbia

Although Serbia has experienced more volatility in terms of people voting for one political party or another than most countries in the region, it has still exhibited a bifurcated political orientation with respect to the alignment of its parties.[40] Thus, during most of the 1990s, Serbia had an essentially two-bloc party system, with Milošević's SPS—together with the Yugoslav United Left (Jugoslovenska udruzena levica, JUL), the party dominated by his wife, and at times Vojislav Šešelj's SRS—politically dominating on one side—and a very divided "democratic bloc" of parties enjoying the main share of votes cast in opposition.

This asymmetrical dualism of forces was reversed after Milošević's defeat in October 2000, with the temporary marginalization of the SPS-JUL and SRS. From that "revolutionary" change in 2002 until March 2003, when Zoran Djindjić was assassinated, political dominance in Serbia was exercised by the eighteen-party coalition of democratic parties, the Democratic Opposition of Serbia (Demokratska opozicija Srbije, DOS). The first post-Djindjić election at the end of

40. Miša Djurković, "Problemi institucionalizacija partijskog sistema u Srbiji," *Srbija 2000–2006* (Belgrade: Institute for European Studies, 2007), 43. See also Slobodan Antonić, "Rascepi i stranke u Srbiji," in *Ideologija i političke stranke u Srbiji,* edited by Zoran Lutovac (Belgrade: Friedrich Ebert Stiftung, 2007), 51–66; Zoran Stojiljković, "Socijalni rascepi i linije političkih podela u Srbiji," Dragomir Pantić and Zoran Pavlović, "Stranačke pristalice i komponente političke kulture u Srbiji," and Srećko Mihailović, "Levica i desnica u Srbiji," all in *Političke stranke i birači u državama bivše Jugoslaviji,* edited by Zoran Lutovac (Belgrade: Friedrich Ebert Stiftung, 2007), 9–136; and Zoran Slavujević, "Ravzvrstavanje biračkog tela i relevantnih stranaka Srbije na osi levica-desnica," in *Osnovne linije partijskih podela i mogući parvci političkog pregrupisavanja u Srbiji,* edited by Jovan Komšić, Dragomir Pantić, and Zoran Slavujević (Belgrade: Friedrich Ebert Stiftung, 2003), 129–62.

2003 followed the breakup of the DOS coalition, which had swept to power in 2000.[41] But once again, a bifurcated pattern emerged between the resurgent nationalist-populist bloc of parties (with the SRS now at its core, instead of the SPS) on the one side, and the very divided but cooperating parties in the democratic bloc on the other. This duality was reflected in all parliamentary and presidential elections held between 2003 and the spring of 2008. For example, in February 2008, Boris Tadić narrowly won the presidency in a runoff against Tomislav Nikolić of the SRS (50.6 to 47.7 percent). The election once again mobilized the two sides (with a record turnout of 67 percent) of Serbia's divided body politic, but it left Tadić without the decisive legislative clout to push through reform and advance EU preaccession momentum. Serbia's party system was certainly more fragmented and volatile than those of most of its neighbors, but its essentially two-bloc division gave its politics a certain predictability, in the midst of considerable volatility of the voting public in lurching from one party to another on their respective sides of the basic political fault line.

For example, in the first months of 2008, the salience of the Kosovo issue in Serbian political life, and also the issue of Serbia's future association with Europe, led to a significant shift in Serbian party alignment. The center-right or conservative nationalist Democratic Party of Serbia (Demokratska stranka Srbije, DSS) of Vojislav Koštunica—a party that had previously been democratically oriented—but whose political fortunes had dropped precipitously during the preceding several years—engineered new parliamentary elections for May 11, 2008, and moved toward political cooperation with the traditionally extreme nationalist SRS of Šešelj. The public shift of Koštunica's DSS from a center-right position to a more nationalist posture in 2008 was based both on the weakened position of the DSS in the electorate and also on the strong impact of Kosovo's declaration of independence on Serbian party politics. However, the DSS had long had a rather schizophrenic orientation, carefully positioned as conservative nationalists close to the fault line—albeit on the democratic side—between the two prominent blocs in the Serbian party system. Surveys typically found that DSS supporters were less extreme in their nationalist views than were SRS adherents, and also more supportive of democracy than the SRS

41. For an overview of the divisions in DOS, which eventually led to its collapse, see Ognjen Pribićević, *Rise and Fall of DOS* (Belgrade: Stubovi Culture, 2010).

members.[42] The DSS's relations with the Democratic Party (Demokratska stranka, DS) had oscillated; the two parties came together to unseat Milošević, were then torn by rivalry between Djindjić and Koštunica, and later cooperated in the post-Djindjić period to form coalition governments. Meanwhile, there had been no love lost between the moderate-right DSS and the radical-right SRS, or between their leaders.

Still, the alliance of the DSS and SRS was hardly surprising in view of the decidedly strong feelings on the national question held by supporters in both parties since the early 1990s, when the two party organizations were founded. In the initial stage of Serbia's political development, the social base of the two parties was quite dissimilar, with the DSS having a more urban and educated makeup. But as it grew in size, the DSS underwent a process of "de-intellectualization," and it also acquired more members that had lower educational qualifications, as well as older voters, unemployed factory workers, and retirees and housewives. In brief, the DSS gradually became more like the SRS demographically (although the SRS voters have typically drawn even more heavily on voters who are male, older, uneducated, working class, unemployed, rural, and those who were "losers" in the transition process).

Therefore, to some extent, the alliance of Koštunica's DSS with the SRS reflected and reinforced a certain sociopolitical homogenizing of the nationalist bloc, and thereby the overall division of the two main orientations or clusters in Serbian political life.[43] The new bond be-

---

42. Regarding the place of the DSS on the center-right of the political spectrum, see Miša Djurković, *Konzervativizam i konzervativne stranke* (Belgrade: Službeni glasnik, 2007), 97–100. Some analysts had always situated the DSS, along with other conservative nationalists, as a separate pole between the "reformist" democrats to their left, and the far right.

43. Marko Blagojević has observed that the DSS appeals to a very heterogeneous group of voters. One portion of those voters is pro-European and democratically oriented, and also close to the Democratic Party. But one contingent in the DSS is more nationalistically inclined and closer to the Serbian Radical Party. When the DSS moved closer to the SRS in the May 2008 election campaign, the DSS lost about 200,000 voters; *Politika,* June 3, 2008. Jovo Bakić, one of Serbia's best sociologists studying the Radicals and populism, has observed that the high levels of unemployment, large numbers of peasants, workers, and lower-middle-class elements in Serbia's social structure, and the very low levels of vertical mobility in the country make it a "paradise for demagogues." And he adds that a kind of "egalitarian-nationalist syndrome which represents an interesting feature of popu-

252   The Transformation of Political Parties in the Western Balkans

tween the SRS and DSS was based both on a quest for power—that is, maintaining it for Koštunica, and acquiring it for Nikolić—and also the view that Serbia should only cooperate and seek entry into the European Union if Brussels recognized Serbia's claim to sovereignty over Kosovo. When Koštunica was asked in mid-April 2008 why, as in the past, he had not distanced himself from the SRS, he responded: "Parties should be allowed to change." And, he pragmatically added, the principles, which he had not abandoned, are "democratic and national," but they can be implemented "according to circumstances."[44] His alliance with the SRS left the DS of Boris Tadić (which advocated both assertive cooperation with the EU along with rhetorical defense of Serbia's claim to Kosovo), and its smaller allies (including the Group of Seventeen—or the G-17—Plus, which supported EU accession and the partition of Kosovo) to constitute the core elements of the democratic bloc in the May 2008 parliamentary election (in partnership with some minority and regional parties in Serbia). Meanwhile, the Liberal Democratic Party (Liberalno-demokratska partija, LDP), which eschewed any claim to Kosovo, and which originated as a factional break-off of the DS, positioned itself as a small antinationalist formation on the left side of the democratic forces.

The hopes of the allied SRS and DSS were dashed in the May 2008 parliamentary election, as the Euro-reformist, or pro-Europe, forces gathered in the coalition named "For a European Serbia" (Za evropsku Srbiju, ZES), which was led by the DS, surprised observers and achieved a major surge of electoral support. By taking 38.4 percent of the total vote, ZES essentially dethroned the SRS as the largest political group in the country. The SRS remained at about the same place it had been in 2003 and 2007 (increasing its popular vote very slightly but getting fewer parliamentary seats), and the DSS's share of the vote declined further. After 2003, the SRS had made some efforts at rebranding itself, endeavoring to mend its fences with the intelligentsia and trying

---

lism is pretty strong . . . in the Serbian political culture, . . . and Serbian radicals are prepared to exploit it." The SRS also exploits "a perceived ethnic threat, . . . whether the threat really exists or not," such as in areas where Serbs are interspersed with minority groups, especially in many border areas. Jovo Bakić, "Serbia: Populism. Populism? Populism! What It Looks Like and What Not to Do About It," paper presented at a conference sponsored by the Open Society Foundation, Bratislava, June 12–13, 2007.

44. *B92*, April 14, 2008.

to embody a procapitalist and populist response to the widespread corruption and confusion in Serbian political life.

However, even the emotional impact of the Kosovo independence issue during 2008 did not prove sufficient to overcome the widespread fear on the part of many Serbs that the SRS had not fundamentally changed its extremist stripes. And comments such as those by the SRS leader Šešelj at his Hague trial ten days after the election—in which he claimed that Zoran Djindjić's murderer deserves "the same glory as Gavrilo Princip in Serbian history"[45]—made it seem unlikely that the SRS's image and electoral prospects would quickly improve. The shift in fortunes in the election reflected and reinforced the realignment of political party organizations in Serbia, but the country's overall two-force division remained apparent in the voting outcome. As Srećko Mihailović, one of Serbia's leading students of electoral change, commented: "This kind of division of the 'national will' indicates a very strong value, ideological, party, political, and also social polarization. Serbia is really divided into two completely equal halves. Between them there is no agreement on any temporal aspect, neither in the viewpoint about the past, nor what to do in the present, nor in the future they wish to create for us. . . . One side is 'for Europe,' against Milošević's neosocialism, and for a soft approach to the Kosovo question. The other side is against Europe, more or less supports Milošević's neosocialism and represents a 'rigid approach' to the Kosovo question."[46]

The surge to power of the democratic bloc would initiate a fundamental reconfiguration of Serbia's party landscape. In a bold move following the May election, the leaders of the small and previously Milošević-dominated and only partially reformed SPS, together with its smaller allied parties that had typically been on the nationalist side of the Serbian fault line, decided to take pragmatic advantage of the opportunity afforded by the sharp polarization in the country. Thus, desperate to find the requisite number of seats to form a government, the DS and its pro-Europe coalition had decided to offer the SPS-led coalition—which possessed a small but politically critical number of seats (20 out of 250 seats, based on 8 percent of the vote)—a place in the new 27-person government (along with members of five other small

45. Radio B92, May 23, 2008.
46. *Danas,* May 15, 2008; Dragomir Pantić and Zoran Pavlović, *Political Culture of Voters in Serbia* (Belgrade: Institut društvenih nauka, 2009).

parties). Hungry for a seat at the governing table, the SPS accepted the entreaties of the DS and abandoned further talks with the SRS, Koštunica's DSS, and the other national-populist parties. By ostensibly tilting toward the moderate left, the SPS—emphasizing its "socially responsible" impulses, and muting the harder nationalist tendencies it had acquired in the Milošević era—ambitiously altered the political weight of the democratic side of Serbia's two-force cleavage structure, at least in the short run. This shift also demonstrated Serbia's less stable and less predictable party system in comparison with those of its neighbors in the Western Balkans. However, the possibility that the SPS might permanently jettison its earlier nationalist orientation and slowly become a modern left-center party—closer to, or possibly even integrated with, the DS—was regarded by some observers as a potentially hopeful sign of democratization in Serbia.

President Tadić suggested that the "strategic agreement" between his DS and the SPS might auger the beginning of a "national reconciliation," and he praised the SPS as having been the "authentic" representative of Serbian citizens during the 1990s, just as he said the DS had become after 2000. A DS-SPS working alliance, Tadić claimed, would help safeguard Serbia's territorial integrity and facilitate its membership in the EU. Indeed, pressured by the need to seal the new alliance, Tadić even went so far to assert that both the DS and the SPS were united by the fact that their former leaders—Djindjić and Milošević— are "not with them" and that both parties had already suffered their "pain." Tadić told his followers to "forget their former conflicts and to shake the hand of those who you were in conflict with in the 1990s, and together find a better future."[47] But many of Tadić's compatriots in his own party and smaller allied parties found the idea of equating Djindjić with Milošević completely unacceptable, and they worried that the SPS (which would control the Interior Ministry) might undermine Belgrade's potential cooperation with The Hague Tribunal. But they were well aware of Tadić's pragmatic need to prevent the SPS from joining together with its traditional nationalist-populist allies and forming a right-wing government.

The promising May 2008 electoral success of the DS and the Euroreformists, and their ability to form a government with the SPS, suggested that after a difficult and extended transitional period, Serbia

47. *Politika,* June 7, 2008.

might be entering a more hopeful period for democratic consolidation. The success of the DS was probably due in part to two critical factors: one, the fear of many voters in Serbia that the illiberal ultranationalist forces might actually come to power; and second, the fear that voting for political forces unenthusiastic or opposed to joining the European Union would seriously compound Serbia's already-difficult economic problems (unemployment, the low standard of living, etc.). Indeed, the EU's decision to sign a Stabilization and Association Agreement with Serbia on the eve of the election (which led to a decision by Fiat to once again invest in Serbia's automotive industry), played an important role in the outcome of the vote. Tadić's victory, and his alliance with the SPS, would soon precipitate further changes on the right wing of Serbia's party system (see below), which had the potential to move the country in a more moderate direction.

The Salience of Elite Behavior

By 2008, after about two decades of party pluralism, the major problem of democratic consolidation in most of the Western Balkans was no longer the excessive fragmentation or the volatility of voters and party organizations. Rather, the main problem was the fractured and stalemated nature of elite-level policymaking that had slowed reform throughout the region.

The issue of inter-elite disunity could be traced to the character of the elite political subcultures in each country, and the style and tone of their interparty dynamics. To a large extent, elite politics still put a premium on polarization, populist mobilization, and unbridled power seeking. Thus, in most of the region's polities there appeared to be a widespread, albeit sometimes challenged, consensus among the major parties and party elites regarding the values of democracy and market economics (see chapter 6), as well as the need to join the EU and NATO. But in most countries, a number of factors tended to disrupt continuity in policymaking—such as the zero-sum character of political interplay, boycotts of parliamentary life, the use of vetoes, persistent horse trading over patronage appointments in the public service, and frequent decisions to break up coalitions over noncritical matters.

The intensity and underlying reasons for sharp or polarized political cleavages at the societal and elite levels varied from one state to another—with ethnic distance and power-sharing issues being more important in Bosnia, Macedonia, and Kosovo; views on the state and national question, personality issues, winners and losers in the transition process, and urban/rural divisions mattering more in Serbia and Montenegro; and a left/right division regarding the state's role in the economy being most salient in Croatia and Albania. In each case, the particular socioeconomic cleavage underlying the party system was substantially different, but it primarily fell to party elites, for better or for worse, to translate and mobilize such societal materials into everyday political dynamics.

Therefore, the increasing predictability and defragmentation of Western Balkan political party systems did not necessarily translate into less polarization between and among party elites. And though relatively fair and free elections for the most part had become customary, the nature of elite competition in political campaigns often left lasting divisions in the interval between electoral contests. As a Serbian political scientist observed on the eve of Serbia's May 2008 election: "Negative campaigning has become the basis of political life; . . . the elections are transformed into a life and death struggle instead of a peaceful discussion of the future." Another analyst added: "Campaigns for the parliamentary election are very dangerous. The vocabulary and message sent to the voters are horrific. The deep differentiation which is the result of the campaign has consequences for our society. The average voter is confused, because everyone talks about Europe and has a wonderful view of European integration, but because they are not sincere about that, voters must separate the truth from the lies."[48]

Watching the May 2008 election campaign, the Belgrade psychologist Žarko Trebješanin observed: "We are witnessing a debacle of elementary political culture. . . . Both sides use excessive expression of false patriotism and the political elite create even more confusion in the people's heads because they refuse to tell the truth and accept the reality of Kosovo being lost in 1999."[49] The high representative in Bosnia also noted that the country was about to sign a Stabilization and Association Agreement with the EU in mid-June 2008, but that "the EU agenda has competition. Nationalism remains strong. In the forthcoming campaign for the municipal elections [October 2008], it

48. *BLIC,* May 9, 2008.
49. *BLIC,* April 14, 2008.

will lead to a rise in inflammatory rhetoric. Unfortunately, we must not be in any doubt that it is not just a short-term phenomenon. Nationalist politics is ever present, constantly exerting an undertow away from the positive dynamic of European integration. The simple arithmetic is: nationalism means votes and it has been a successful recipe for winning elections."[50] And even when ethnic division was not the primary political cleavage, as in the June 2009 election in Albania, the strong antipathy between the two major party organizations and their leaders helped to poison the election campaign and the postelection atmosphere. Thus, in the context of Albanian elite polarization, the advantages of party defragmentation did not necessarily contribute to democratic consolidation. Indeed, the second-place Socialists challenged the legitimacy of the elections and boycotted the fall session of the legislature. However, despite the polarized character of elite politics and party interaction, especially in cases such as Albania, and also in countries with a tradition of deep ethnic and ideological divisions, the character of party politics and party divisions within individual countries was slowly beginning to change.

Changing Cleavages and Patterns of Party Identification

The degree of rootedness or the anchoring of political party organizations in societal constituencies varies considerably across the polities of the region. Most parties are oriented more to personalities concerned with winning power rather than to ideologies and programs. But partisan identification, based upon a variety of factors, is still quite impressive with respect to the region's core parties.

For example, in Bosnia, the issues of ethnicity and power sharing trumps left/right ideological distinctions, and most voters are attached to parties representing their specific cultural or religious community. Much the same can be said about Macedonia. Citizens of the major ethnocultural communities in Bosnia and Macedonia have given steady support to either traditional or new nationalist organizations, and the civic parties with multiethnic programmatic orientations still have predominantly ethnic voting bases and have failed to develop their own solutions to the important national identity issues (e.g., the SPD in

---

50. Office of the High Representative, "Address of the High Representative to the UN Security Council," May 19, 2008.

Bosnia is roughly two-thirds Muslim in its membership and draws most of its adherents from the Muslim-Croat Federation).[51]

As mentioned above, the 2006 election in Bosnia saw an increase in support for predominantly nationally oriented parties having a more centrist orientation (the S-BiH and the Party of Democratic Progress) or a mixed "nationalistic–social democratic variety," the Alliance of Independent Social Democrats (Savez nezavisnih socijaldemokrata). And after 1995, the older and more traditional nationalist parties (the Party for Democratic Action, Stranka Demokratske Akcije, SDA; the Serbian Democratic Party, Srpska Demokratska Stranka; and HDZ-BiH) have been losing some of their strength. However, "real" social democratic parties advocating left-wing issues as well as civic values and multiethnicity also continued to lose ground. There was a bitter rivalry among several nationally oriented parties drawing their strength from one or another of the three major subcultural constituencies. For example, two major parties, the S-BiH and SDA, compete for the Bosniak vote; while three parties (and their small allies), Bosnia's HDZ, the HDZ-1990, and the Croatian Peasant Party–New Croatian Initiative (Hrvatska seljačka stranka–Nova hrvatska inicijativa), compete for the Croat vote. Thus, intraethnic competition has not lessened the fundamentally ethnically divided character of Bosnia's party system. As a rule, the various parties from the same ethnic group compete fiercely for votes, but they usually join together over matters critical to their subcultural community. New parties have joined the fray in Bosnia—such as the nonnationalist Naša Stranka, established in 2008 by several civil society actors, or the predominantly Bosniak-composed Union for a Better Future (Savez za bolju budućnost), led by the media magnate Fahruddin Radončić in the October 2010 election—but so far they have not altered the basically tripartite ethnic division.[52]

51. See Centar za humanu politiku, *Izbori u BiH 2006. godina: Analiza predizbornog i postizbornog procesa* (Sarajevo: Centar za humanu politiku, 2006); Srdjan Puhalo, "Socio-psihoški profil glasača i apstinenata u Bosni i Herzegovini," Banja Luka, 2007); and Puhalo, "Neke Socio-Demografske i Psihološke Karakteristike Glasača SNSD i SDP BiH-Dva Lica Socijaldemokratije u Bosni i Herzegovini," *Psihologija* 41, no. 2 (2008): 163–75.

52. On the problems faced by new civic-oriented parties in the region, see Paula Pickering, "Explaining Support for Non-Nationalist Parties in the Balkans," *Europe-Asia Studies* 61, no. 4 (2009): 565–91.

During the last two decades, Serbia has undergone more instability than neighboring countries regarding particular party fortunes: the meltdown of Milošević's SPS after 2000; the rapid strengthening of Koštunica's DSS in 2000, followed by its steady drop-off in support; the post-Djindjić breakup of the DOS coalition; deflation of voter support for the SRS of Šešelj and Nikolić following Milošević's departure, and then its striking comeback when the democratic bloc splintered in 2003–4; the near complete collapse of Vuk Drašković's Serbian Renewal Movement (Srpski Pokret Obnove) by 2007; and the emergence of smaller but important parties such as the G-17 Plus and the LDP.

Nonetheless, the two biggest political parties in Serbia up to 2008, the SRS and DS, maintained a large pool of "firm" adherents, and they also elaborated quite developed party machines. And between 2000 and 2008, voter identification with the two wings or party families within Serbia's broad bipolar division—the democratic bloc versus nationalist-populist bloc—was quite steady, albeit not deeply embedded or anchored in persistent support for the same parties belonging to the two major blocs. Most voter movement occurred on one side or the other of the fundamental divide, that is, among the nationalist-populist parties on one side or the democratic parties on the other. Thus, electoral volatility in terms of voters' changing from one party to another has been quite high, but has largely been limited to one or the other wing of the country's persistent two-bloc orientation. And in Serbia, considerably more voters, compared with those in neighboring countries, were typically focused on the issue of how different personalities and party elites approach the emotional national question. As Vladimir Goati, Serbia's most prominent student of party development, observed in 2008, the creation of an ideological perspective has not been the prime concern of any of the democratically oriented Serbian parties, but rather ad hoc "creative interpretation" of policies that "often change direction between democratic principles on the one side and the national principle on the other."[53]

No party in Serbia's democratic bloc, including the DS, which finally surged to victory at the head of a democratic coalition in 2008, proved completely "immune" to such "creative interpretation" or exploitation of nationalism (even Djindjić indulged in such instrumental use of

53. *Politika,* March 23, 2008.

nationalism during the war in Bosnia, and clerical nationalism after the war). Indeed, a study of Serbia's voters showed that half the respondents in 2004 thought that the DS was in the center of the political spectrum, while close to a fifth placed it on the left, and even a third believed it was on the right.[54]

Serbian survey data from 2006–7 indicated that only two-fifths of the electorate then had clearly defined party preferences (i.e., slightly more than 2 million out of 5.5 million voters). But the largest portion of the voters, about one-quarter, who identified with parties did so on the basis of support for the party leader or leadership. Leadership was the main motive for those identifying with all the major parties, except for the adherents of the DS, who indicated that "democracy" was their prime motive (27 percent), with leadership a close second (23 percent). Among members of both the extreme and moderate nationalist parties, the national issue emerged as the second most important motive for party membership next to leadership.[55] The continuity of such attitudes is not surprising in view of the important role of national issues in Serbia's political history, as well as during the emergence of the party system (1989–90), the subsequent ethnification of political life in the 1990s, and the more recent salience of national concerns surrounding the matter of Kosovo's independence.

The contending ambitions of rival leaders and the disputatious style of Serbian political culture have certainly been factors contributing to the polarization of party politics in Serbia. And, of course, the national question has been the principal polarizing cleavage that has influenced the Serbian political landscape. But as pointed out by Serbian scholars, Serbia's difficulty during the postcommunist and post-Milošević transition has not fundamentally been the deep polarization deriving from the primacy of symbolic and ideological divisions (e.g., "patriots"

54. This is based on Srećko Mihailović and Bora Kuzmanović, "Mesto stranačkih programa u identifakaciji gradjana sa političhkim stramkama," cited in *Politika,* March 23, 2008.

55. Srećko Mihailović, Zoran Stojiljković, et al., *Research of Public Opinion in Serbia, Early Autumn 2007* (Belgrade: CESID, 2007); Siniša Atlagić, *Partijska identifkacija kao determinanta izborna motivacija: Teorijske kontroverze i problemi empirijskog istrživanja* (Belgrade: Friedrich Ebert Stifung / FPN, 2007); Zoran Stojiljković, *Partijski sistem Srbije* (Belgrade: Službeni glasnik, 2006), 351–64; Vladimir Goati, *Partije i partijski sistem u Srbiji* (Niš: Odbor za gradjanskim incijativu, 2004), 191–236.

vs. "traitors," old regime forces vs. reformers), or even the socioeconomic cleavages in the country's political life. Rather, it is the particular *type* of exclusivist nationalism, which sought to exploit ethnicity
through the manipulation and deepening of symbolic or nondistributional cleavages. "This type of nationalism and its influence on the
type of cleavage," Dušan Pavlović and Slobodan Antonić emphasize,
"is what post-Milošević Serbia has inherited from the Milošević era."[56]
According to this view, it was the ability of the traditionalist, nationally oriented wing of the Serbian elite to mobilize and exacerbate exclusivist nationalism that resonated with a large sector of the Serbian
population, and prevented the elite from changing the direction of the
country. Indeed, as mentioned above, the significant electoral success
of the pro-European forces in the May 2008 election encouraged hopes
that the traditional nationalist character of Serbian politics might be
altered.

In 2008, two factors supported such speculation. First, as referred
to above, the transformation of the SPS away from Milošević-style nationalism, and its alliance with the DS, suggested that a new center-left
constellation focused more on social justice and the national interest
might be emerging in Serbia. Second, in mid-2008, as the global economic crisis loomed, a major development occurred on the right side
of Serbia's party spectrum when the SRS underwent a dramatic internal schism. Hard-line nationalists in the party remained loyal to the
jailed Šešelj, who had founded the SRS and who continued to direct a
rump SRS organization. But a new offshoot organization, the Serbian
Progressive Party (Srpska napredna stranka, SNS), led by former SRS
deputy leader Tomislav Nikolić, broke away and adopted a more moderate tone on domestic and international matters. The schism in the
SRS involved personality and internal programmatic differences. Many
former SRS members may simply have become tired of losing elections
and yearned for an organizational makeover.

It was initially unclear whether the new SNS would really jettison its
strident nationalism and live up to the more center-right perspectives
it had begun to espouse. In any event, the SNS quickly overshadowed
the SRS, and it emerged as a more popular party in local elections
during the years 2008–9. Thus, the SNS became the main competitor

56. Dušan Pavlović and Slobodan Antonić, *Konsolidacija demokratskih ustanova
u Srbiji posle 2000 godine* (Belgrade: Službeni glasnik, 2007), 290–93, 298.

facing the ruling DS. By late 2009, the DS and SNS had emerged as the core parties of the traditional two-bloc orientation in Serbia. This time, however, the strongest party on the nationalist-populist side of the divide was attempting to adopt a more moderate and European-oriented image, and although the two major parties differed in their core beliefs, their elites shared in a broad consensus that Serbia needed to join the European Union and that the struggle against Kosovo's wider recognition in the international community should be pursued in a peaceful manner.

Clearly, the programmatic gap between the DS and the newly formed SNS was not as big as the divide had been between the DS and the SRS (especially on the issue of joining the EU).[57] The challenge for both the SNS and the DS would be a competition to attract citizens who tended to gravitate between the right (more national) and left (more European-oriented) sides of the party system. Indeed, in a recessionary environment, the SNS seemed to have a real opportunity to attract voter support from the moderate part of the lower middle class, small businesspeople, retirees, and "losers in transition."[58] In any event, it appeared that Serbia had moved a considerable way toward a more deradicalized and less polarized two-bloc party system. Of course, substantial right-wing political forces and attitudes were still present in Serbia, and through 2010 at least emotional-symbolic and nondistributional issues still were very much part of political discourse in the country.[59]

Political party alignments in Croatia have generally exhibited lower levels of electoral volatility than those in its neighbor Serbia, and in recent years have demonstrated less concern with the kind of emotional national issues that have riven Serbia. Survey research in 2007 indicated that the average level of partisan identification in the Croatian electorate was roughly the same as in Serbia (approximately 40 percent), and that such commitments to a single party were strongest for HDZ members (68 percent), and those in the SDP (40 percent). But respondents in

57. Vladimir Goati, cited in *Politika,* August 12, 2009.
58. Dušan Pavlović, quoted in *Politika,* July 3, 2009.
59. See Vesna Pešić, "The Serbian Right," *Peščanik,* August 6, 2009. On the social basis of radical extremism before the party schism in the SRS, see Jovo Bakić, "Extreme-Right Ideology, Practice and Supporters: Case Study of the Serbian Radical Party," *Journal of Contemporary European Studies* 17, no. 2 (August 2009): 193–207.

Croatia indicated far less concern than voters in Serbia with leadership per se, or with a party's focus on the "national interest," as the primary motives for voting.[60] Most respondents in Croatia identified a party's perspectives on values and interests, and party concern with important socioeconomic problems, as the basis for their partisan identification.

Part of the reason for the decline of the national factor in Croatia as a dimension of partisan identification was certainly the more ethnically homogeneous character of the country in the aftermath of the events associated with Croatia's war for independence in the mid-1990s. Once the Krajina Serbs departed Croatia—both voluntarily and under duress—in the wake of advancing Croatian troops during 1995, Croatia no longer had a substantial minority territorial enclave to serve as the epicenter of nationalist agitation (unlike the Kosovo Serbs in relation to Serbian politics from 1999 to 2008). This contributed to an important shift in the basic cleavage structure of Croatia after the 1990s. Thus, the cleavages that divided parties and electorates along the territorial (regional)–cultural line (center vs. periphery, including border questions and ethnic relations between the Croat majority and Serbia minority), or along ideological-cultural lines (traditionalism/modernization, religion/secular, urban/rural, etc.) were overshadowed or lost their salience. In their place, socioeconomic cleavages (free economy / state distribution, management/labor, winners/losers in the process of transition and privatization) became critical factors in Croatian party politics.[61]

The change in Croatia's cleavage structure—and especially the waning of traditional cultural and internal territorial divisions—was the primary reason for a notable "defragmentation" in the country's party system and the consequent bipolarization of party political life. The victory of the left in 2000, with a two-thirds majority under the leadership of the SDP, revealed the centrality of economic and distributional questions in the country. But internal conflicts within the left-wing coalition soon led to the HDZ's return to power in 2003. Croatia was still substantially bipolarized, with the HDZ and SDP as the two key

60. Puls/International Republican Institute, "Analiza stavova gradjana republika Hrvatske," 2007.

61. Slaven Ravlić, "Transformacija predstavničke funkcije političkih stranaka," *Zbornik pravnog fakulteta u Zagrebu* 57, no. 6 (December 18, 2007): 1–27. See also Nenad Zakošek, *Politički sustav Hrvatske* (Zagreb: Fakultet političkih znanosti, 2002), 67–96.

collective actors along with a number of smaller left-wing, center-right, and right-wing parties. It was at this juncture that the new prime minister, Ivo Sanader—building upon and reinforcing Croatia's changed cleavage structure—pushed along the fundamental modernization of the HDZ, a process that he had initiated in the period 2000–2003. The HDZ underwent an "image conversion" or major rebranding, in which the party became, programmatically and in practice, a modern, conservative, center-right Christian Democratic organization (Tudjman had talked about doing this, but his illiberal rule had prevented the HDZ's real conversion).

Sanader was able to purge right-wing radical leaders from the party ranks, and also nudge the HDZ toward the center of the political spectrum. "I am usually not speaking about the past," Sanader commented in 2003, "because I am interested in Croatia's future."[62] He also reached out to the Serb minority, and by 2007 he even brought Serb party leaders into the government (he was reelected HDZ president in April 2008 but, as discussed above, he would resign suddenly in April 2009 and then vainly attempt to reenter political life). The deradicalization and shift to a right-center position by the formerly ultranationalistic Croatian Party of Rights (Hrvatska stranka prava) also contributed to the moderation of Croatian political life.[63] Such party transformations, along with Croatia's increasing post-1995 ethnic homogeneity, significantly diminished the basis for emotional national and territorial issues to continue to excite Serbian politics. It also permitted the core Croatian parties to clearly differentiate themselves on the basis of nonethnic policy issues and to focus more on the country's reform agenda in matters related to EU accession. But while Croatia came to enjoy the predictability of a substantially bipolarized party system, and certainly a more interest-based and unemotional style of politics than found in Serbia, the low levels of trust in the country's parties continued to detract from an overall increase in the party system's institutionalization. Still, Croatia's party dynamics increasingly mirrored political life in other European democracies—with the conservative (HDZ), socialist (SDP), and, to a lesser extent, liberal (HNS) party streams predominating.

62. Agence France-Presse, November 21, 2003.

63. See Zoran Malenica, "Neki problemi funkcioniranja političkih stranaka u Republici Hrvatskog," in *Kriza i transformacija političkih stranaka,* edited by Andjelko Milardović, Dražen Lalić, and Zoran Malenica (Zagreb: Centar za politološka istraživanja, 2007), 35.

Macedonia's major party subsystem, consisting of the country's two large and predominantly ethnic Macedonian parties, VMRO-DPMNE and SDSM, has reflected a political cleavage that can be traced to the Communist/anticommunist divide that was shaped at the time of independence in 1991. Questions of party ideology or socioeconomic cleavages between the two largest ethnic Macedonian parties have been less important. There has been considerable partisan identification by adherents within the two parties, and a low rate of voter movement between the two organizations. Meanwhile, the two predominant ethnic Albanian parties in Macedonia have been very sharply divided, primarily on the basis of support for personalities and their respective patron-client ties, rather than along ideological lines. But the low levels of confidence and trust that citizens of Macedonia have expressed for their parties indicates the imperfectly institutionalized character of the party system.

Neighboring Albania's party system, although characterized by two dominant parties, has some similarity to the situation in Macedonia (but without a minority party subsystem). Since the 1990s, the Communist/anticommunist divide in Albania has reflected the two-party face-off between the PD and the PSSH. Both parties have large and loyal party bases, although at election time they form coalitions with a pantheon of several smaller parties. The Democrats enjoy more support than the PSSH among the members of the younger generation and among the population of the northern and less developed parts of Albania.[64] Voters in the central region of the country have been affected by clientalism and tend to evaluate the government on the basis of its policies.[65] Shifts in voter choices in Albania have been often closely tied to voter perceptions of leaders, and also to the changing socioeconomic circumstances of the country. The Albanian electorate's perception of the endemic corruption in parties and elite circles has also contributed to changing party fortunes, and has accounted for the persistently high levels of distrust in the party system that has undermined overall party system institutionalization.

---

64. Altin Ilirjani, "Political Choice in Albania. The 2005 Parliamentary Election," *Albanian Journal of Politics* 1, no. 1 (2005): 75–86. See also Fatmir Zanaj, "The First Two Pluralist Elections and the Cleavage Structure in Post-Communist Albania," in *Albanian Democratic Elections 1991–1997,* ed. Barjaba, 101–30.

65. Klarita Gerxhani and Arthur Schram, "Clientalism and Polarized Voting: Empirical Evidence," *Public Choice* 1 (2009): 305–17.

Kosovo has had a sharply bifurcated and asymmetrical party system —a constellation of Albanian parties and a smaller group of Serbian parties—that has been divided along ethnic lines, with the parties on either side of the line not being clearly differentiated on a programmatic or socioeconomic basis. As Shkëlzen Maliqi put it in 2004, "The Kosova parties lack the aptitude, both financially to make clear what model of capitalism they stand for, or the type of social state they aspire to. . . . Almost all of our parties are in a big mishmash without a clear ideology as part of a movement."[66] Thus, before Kosovo's declaration of independence in early 2008, the Albanian parties all shared a strong commitment to acquiring sovereignty, although they had been deeply polarized over which party could best accomplish that task. After 1999, the LDK competed for that mantle, principally with the PDK and AAK, both offshoots of the Kosovo Liberation Army (in 2010, some 47 members of these parties in the 120-person legislature had previously been members of this army). But while the initial divisions among Kosovo's post-1999 Albanian parties can be traced back to their respective roles and views regarding NATO's war with Milošević's Yugoslavia, and also over how to deal with Serbia, such cleavages were becoming less and less critical for evolving party development in the new country. Meanwhile, the very small Serb parties in Kosovo, most closely tied to circles in Belgrade, were primarily divided over the best method of obstructing or coping with Kosovo independence. Thus, some Kosovo Serb parties are more militant and obstructionist, while others favor cautious cooperation with the Albanian and remaining foreign authorities.

On the Albanian side in Kosovo, a major shift in voter preference in the 2007–9 period badly weakened the LDK, whose troubles began with the death of Ibrahim Rugova in 2006 and worsened after its subsequent defeat at the polls in 2007. Moreover, with independence still outstanding before early 2008, some LDK members formed new parties or joined others (e.g., Nexhat Daci's Democratic League of Dardinia, which criticized the LDP but claimed a commitment to "Rugovism"; the New Kosovo Alliance, led by the Swiss-based millionaire Kosovar, Behxet Pacolli; and the Social Democratic Party of Kosovo, led by the former prime minister, Agim Çeku). Thus, voter volatility increased markedly, after some eighteen years with the LDK as the dominant Albanian

66. *BBC Monitoring Europe,* September 7, 2004.

party. The LDK has essentially become a significant party only in Kosovo's capital and some small pockets of the country.

Meanwhile, the PDK, which was previously dominant in the former war zones of central Kosovo, gradually grew in strength in places where the LDK lost support. Indeed, the PDK of Hashim Thaçi has slowly emerged as a national party. Beginning in 2008, the weakened LDK attempted to reconfigure itself within this fluid party situation. And in an interesting example of how pluralist dynamics begin to alter entrenched values and behavior, both the LDK and PDK sought to bolster their relative strength in the two-party government coalition by reaching out to small Kosovo Serb parties that were willing to cooperate. Embracing democratic norms was particularly difficult for the PDK's leader, Thaçi, who was undergoing a very slow political metamorphosis from guerrilla fighter to statesman. With the achievement of statehood in early 2008, and the arrival of the EU rule-of-law mission in Kosovo, Thaçi faced an even more challenging environment in which to demonstrate whether his conversion to democratic pluralism was genuine. Meanwhile, the opposition AAK has been primarily a party of western Kosovo, although The Hague Tribunal's 2008 acquittal of its popular leader, Ramush Haradinaj, gave the party added strength in the postindependence period.

A change in the overall cleavage structure of Kosovo politics appeared to be slowly under way in 2008–9, as the politics of the new and partially recognized state moved from sovereignty-related issues to matters of party building and state building within a confused structure of dual UN and EU supervision. Overall, however, Kosovo's party system in early 2010 was at quite a low level of institutionalization, lacked predictability, and was still not well anchored or highly legitimated. The new country remained at the takeoff stage of party system development in many ways, and the odd ruling coalition formed on the cusp of independence by its two largest and rival parties, the LDK and PDK, which lasted until October 2010, was really a temporary arrangement forced by the crisis of sovereignty and recognition.

As Kosovo underwent a new stage of state building in the years 2008–10—ostensibly sovereign, but within an altered pattern of international control—there was no clear ideological line dividing the polity's political parties. The PDK and LDK were mainly concerned with power and patronage, and during most of 2010 they still divided control of government ministries between themselves and a few minority parties (three minority ministers—two Serbs and a Turk—are also in the ruling coalition). Meanwhile, and still ominously for Kosovo's cohesion, an entirely new, albeit somewhat virtual, miniparty system has emerged among minority Serb party leaders elected to the legislature of the parallel Serb power structure created in the northern Mitrovica region as a protest against the constitutionalization of Kosovo independence.

From 2007 to 2011, the Montenegrin party system continued to exhibit many features of party development that were present before the country's achievement of independence in 2006. The disappearance of the cleavage between pro-union and pro-independence party blocs after 2006 changed the party dynamics and issues of party competition to some extent. Still, party divisions over the controversial issue of recognizing Kosovo's independence (recognition was finally attained in September 2008), overlapped closely with the earlier independence-versus-continued-union-with-Serbia cleavage that characterized pre-2006 party politics. Voter volatility among the core parties has been relatively low in recent years, and identification with parties is primarily on the basis of clientalistic ties and support of leaders.

The remarkable hegemony of the Democratic Party of Socialists in Montenegrin political life for nearly two decades derived mainly from Milo Djukanović's ability to transform his party from a pro-Milošević defender of old regime values (1990–96) into the paramount post-1997 advocate of democratic and market values, Montenegrin independence, and pro-EU sentiments. Djukanović used the DPS's strong party organization to assert leadership on the big issues in Montenegrin politics, thus overshadowing the smaller democratically oriented opposition parties, and leaving his former pro-Milošević allies in the Socialist People's Party (Socijalistička narodna partija) on their own as the representative of unpopular former regime beliefs. In recent years, the ability of the DPS, along with its close ally, the SDP, to dominate the political field (two smaller minority parties are also in the governing coalition), has derived mainly from Djukanović's charisma, agile political maneuvering, firm control over his party—even during his brief "retirement" from government in 2006–7—and the DPS's access to state resources. Djukanović claimed that his return to government service was prompted by his concern that "the anti-European lobby" enjoyed growing influence in Montenegro, and that EU accession, fostering investment, and anticorruption were his main goals. Despite the high level of political corruption often noted in Montenegro's political class—including in circles personally related to, and politically close to, Djukanović (who is one of the country's wealthiest men)—citizen distrust of the party system as a whole is not as high as in many other Western Balkan countries, albeit still very pronounced. Thus, the small state still lacked a party system that could be considered fully institutionalized,[67] and it probably will not be able to substantially develop in that direction until the conclusion of Djukanović's enormous imprint on the country's political life.

Party Democracy

The highly centralized pattern of control enjoyed by top leaders and party elites in the Western Balkans is another factor typically advanced to explain both the relatively low level of party institutionalization in the region and also weak democratic consolidation as a whole. As discussed above, the loyalty and identification of voters with political parties have been closely linked to the perception of party leadership. The surfeit of leader-dominated party machines also helps to account for the intense personalization found in the region's political party dynamics, including high levels of internal party factionalism, the frequent defections from existing parties, and the routine formation of so many new party organizations. Low levels of internal party democracy also contribute to the widespread voter distrust of political parties discussed above and undermine general public acceptance of democratic norms.

Recent research on internal party dynamics in the Western Balkan states reveals both aspects of cross-state convergence in the management of parties and also variation in the overall extent of party democracy.[68] Thus, on one level, during the last decade, there has been a significant degree of change and organizational adaptation by most parties throughout the region as they became more adept at internal party management and at the imperative of appealing to voters in a still relatively new pluralistic environment. Indeed, in practice, the pres-

67. Vladimir Goati, *Političke partije i partijski sistemi* (Gorica: CEMI, 2007). See also Zlatko Vujović and Olivera Komar, "Impact of the Europeanization Process on the Transformation of the Party System of Montenegro," *Journal of Balkan and Near Eastern Studies* 10, no. 2 (August 2008): 228–41.

68. Georgi Karasimeonov, ed., *Reshaping the Broken Image of Political Parties in South Europe: Internal Party Democracy in Southeastern Europe* (Sofia: GorexPress, 2007).

sures of competition and vote seeking have resulted in a high degree of organizational similarity among parties. The distinctive organizational legacies of most parties—such as a heritage of Communist mass mobilization techniques by most left-wing parties, the elitist nature of the liberal parties, or the anticommunist and nationalist features of many of the right-center parties—are becoming less significant as pluralist evolution proceeds. Most major parties in the region have acquired the features of "catch-all parties," striving to attract as many followers and votes as they possibly can to capture and maintain power. The comparative research on party democracy has considered factors such as the autonomy enjoyed by members of political parties (i.e., the formal rights of party members and local level influence on the party center) and the extent of inclusiveness practiced by party organizations (the actual participation of party members, particularly in choosing party executives, and the statutory power of party executives). By and large, despite many changes in structures and statutes, most parties in the region have remained highly centralized with strong party presidents, limited participation of party members, and recruitment processes still highly controlled by party elites.

For example, Goran Čular observed in 2005 that Croatia's parties "do not depart from the common postcommunist experience of party organizational life with a rather rigid structure, their organizational uniformity and little substantial change through time."[69] All Croatia's major parties followed what he called a "top-down model," with central party elites establishing and developing the party organizations. Čular emphasized that party leaders were politically socialized, even if originally anticommunist dissidents, "within the same socialist organizational culture and inherited the same organizational patterns. . . . These elites naturally tended to develop similar organizational styles and mutual copying." He found that top-down centralization was very pronounced in the most right-of-center party, the nationalist Croatian Party of Rights, but also was prevalent in the center-right Croatian Peasant Party (Hrvatska seljačka stranka) and in the core ruling party, the HDZ (following Prime Minister Sanader's resignation in 2009, factional disputes within the HDZ became more visible). The liberal HNS and the Social Liberal Party (Hrvatska socijalno liberalna stranka),

---

69. "Organizational Development of Parties and Internal Party Democracy in Croatia," in *Reshaping the Broken Image,* ed. Karasimeonov, 109–36.

and also the center-left SDP, had a less "radical way of imposing party discipline," but the central leadership of those parties "chose informal ways to put pressure on local leadership."

The intense internal discord over party leadership from 2007 to 2010 in the post-Račan SDP indicated the difficulties still faced by the SDP organization in achieving a more democratized internal operation. In September 2009, the SDP went so far as to postpone the implementation of its own party statute on the direct election of officials when matters did not seem to be turning out the way party leaders wished in the nomination of candidates for the December presidential election. The absence of provisions allowing party factions to operate within some Croatian parties has also led to the frequent expulsion of party dissidents, intraparty schisms, and the movement of strong personalities from one party to another.

In Bosnia-Herzegovina, Davor Vuletić found that all parties "arose as 'strong leader-driven' or 'elite-driven' parties and that in 2007 they were still in the process of becoming modern parties."[70] There are, of course, slight variations among the parties. Bosnia's two main Muslim parties, the post–Alija Izetbegović SDA and the S-BiH of Haris Silajdžić, are prototypical leader-driven parties. Indeed, Silajdžić even controlled party affairs tightly during the four-year period when he was officially absent from the leadership. In 2008, the SDA underwent a bitter internal struggle as the late Izetbegović's son, Bakir, sought unsuccessfully to unseat the politically weakened and ailing party chairman, Sulejman Tihić. (When, in October 2010, the younger Izetbegović was elected to the Muslim seat in the country's presidency, the stage was set for an internal struggle for party control. Although Izetbegović is a moderate, he is close to Reis Ceríc, the grand mufti of the Islamic community.)

The strong control of top elites has also been characteristic of Bosnia's main Croat parties (the HDZ-BiH and HDZ-1990), as well as in the Serbian Democratic Party (Srpska Demokratska Stranka). The leadership circles of those nationalist parties have been closely linked to ethnically based financial elites in the country. In Republika Srpska, Milorad Dodik's SNSD formally provides a somewhat larger role for local community organizations and the party membership, but

70. Davor Vuletić, "Internal Party Democracy in Bosnia and Hercegovina: The Interaction between Crises and Developments," in *Reshaping the Broken Image,* ed. Karasimeonov, 34–62.

the party is still highly centralized and leader-controlled (Dodik was reelected to the post of president of Serbia in 2010). The party statutes of the civic-oriented SDP in Bosnia have formally constrained the authority of party leaders and have placed a limit on the number of terms that can be served by party officials below the leader. But in practice, the dominant personality and style of the SDP leader, Zlatko Lagumdžija, has effectively limited the impressive formal provision for party democratization. The strong showing of the SDP in the October 2010 election strengthened Lagumdžija's party control and political prospects.

In Macedonia, Gordan Georgiev has argued that, procedurally, political parties exhibit a very weak basis for internal democracy and are prone to elect authoritarian leaders who typically impose their decisions on party members.[71] A nontolerance of party factions has resulted in the frequent establishment of breakaway parties. The SDSM has provided more formal mechanisms for internal party democracy than its main opponent, VMRO-DPMNE. But both core parties have had "renegade" groups split off and form new party organizations specifically with the goal of promoting internal party democratization. The two major Albanian minority parties that have alternated in forming government coalitions are also dominated by their leaders, and they are even more personality driven than the ethnic Macedonian organizations.

Besides rhetorical statements, Albania's two major parties have made little headway in democratizing internal party life under pressure from the EU. Thus, the right-center Democratic Party remains highly centralized and has been characterized for nearly two decades by the charismatic and domineering leadership of Sali Berisha. Reform momentum has been somewhat more successful in the PSSH following the departure of its long-term leader, Fatos Nano, in the wake of his party's defeat in the 2005 election. Beginning in 2006, the current socialist leader, Edi Rama, began to outline reforms that he ambitiously claimed were "intended to put the party members at the center of decisionmaking, . . . to make all party members equally important; to make the peasant in the remotest corner of the corner of the country equal to the party chairman, to make membership cards not mere documents and numbers, but expressions of the power of each PSSH member."[72]

71. Gordan Georgiev, "Political Parties in Macedonia: Democracy or Efficiency Dilemma," in *Reshaping the Broken Image,* ed. Karasimeonov, 136–52.
72. *Shekulli,* February 7, 2006.

Rama did succeed in bringing more women and young people into the socialist organization. But bottom-up party control has not been part of either Albanian political tradition or its still emerging embrace of democratic methods. Meanwhile, the PSSH has been plagued by an extreme factionalism that is competing in a fragmented field of smaller left-wing party organizations. Rama's inability to form an alliance between his own party and the smaller Socialist Movement for Integration (SMI, Lëvizja Socialiste për Integrim) allowed the PD of Berisha to narrowly win the 2009 parliamentary election (and form a coalition with the SMI).[73]

The case of Kosovo is very much in flux as noted above, but all the parties have been characterized by centralization and leadership domination. There is still some truth to the observation that Kosovo's recent political history (e.g., interethnic polarization, the 1999 war, and the struggle for independence), has bred "strong leaders and weak political parties."[74] Thus, most of Kosovo's citizens joined current party organizations during the emotional period surrounding the 1999 war. Moreover, in the context of high unemployment, those seeking jobs often depend on traditional political linkages that connect strong leaders to supporters, based on clan or patron-client networks. It is worth noting, however, that such linkages between patrons and clients, which have a premodern or predemocratic character, may be able to provide a degree of "clientalistic accountability" or responsiveness of those with political influence to ordinary citizens and voters in new democracies.[75] Until very recently, the empowerment of party leaders in Kosovo can also be traced to an election system based on closed-list proportional representation (the system was changed to an open-list method in 2008). The intraparty factionalism and party defections that have

73. For contending views on the impact of the 2009 election in Albania, see Ilir Kalemaj, "Authoritarianism in the Making? The Role of Political Culture and Institutions in the Albanian Context," *CEU Political Science Journal* 4, no. 2 (2009); and Tom Hashimoto, "Victory for European Albania: Democratic Elections as a Step towards 'Strong States,'" *European Perspectives—Journal on European Perspectives of the Western Balkans* 1, no. 1 (October 2009): 75–92.

74. United Nations Development Program, *Human Development Report: Kosovo 2004* (Priština: United Nations Development Program, 2004), 61.

75. Herbert Kitschelt and Steven I. Wilkinson, eds., *Patrons, Clients and Policies: Patterns of Democratic Accountability and Political Competition* (Cambridge: Cambridge University Press, 2007).

debilitated the post-Rugova LDK since 2006 also illustrate the difficulties that are generated when party cohesion is based on the near total control of a single personality. As a Kosovo Albanian political analyst put it in 2008, the LDK faced "the classic problem of movements and parties that depend on the will and authority of a single leader, as was Ibrahim Rugova. . . . He did not care to leave behind a successor with the authority and charisma close to his. . . . [In] the case of the LDK, the war for his legacy is destroying the party, . . . and some people still have not realized that not only has Ibrahim Rugova died but Rugova's LDK has died too, and that Kosovo has entered a new period which requires parties to create a profile and organize themselves on principles and practices that were not applied during Rugova's times."[76]

Political parties in Serbia have exhibited very little internal democracy since the advent of pluralist politics in 1990. Considerable research has indicated that most of Serbia's parties are leader driven in two senses: First, voters and party members tend to view parties very much in terms of the personality of the party president, who is the embodiment of the party program; and second, the various dominant party leaders identify themselves with the parties they closely control.[77] As a rule, party presidents have enormous influence on party personnel policy, and both extrastatutory practice and sometimes statutes allow top-down control over both the selection of candidates for internal party posts and those who are selected to be on the party list. There are, of course, as in other countries, variations among the parties with regard to their amount of internal democracy. As one might expect, the ultranationalist SRS was the party with the least devotion to democratic norms, and the one both formally and informally having the most powerful party president (Vojislav Šešelj). The schism in the SRS in 2008, which resulted in the party's acting leader in the country, Tomislav Nikolić, breaking with Šešelj and forming an entirely new party (SNS), was a vivid illustration of the difficulties of intraparty transformation in Serbia, especially on the right side of the political spectrum.[78]

76. Shkëlzen Maliqi, in *Express,* January 15, 2008, in *BBC Monitoring Europe,* January 19, 2008.

77. Dušan Pavlović, "Political Parties and the Party System in Serbia after 2000," in *Reshaping the Broken Image,* ed. Karasimeonov, 153-177.

78. The political marginalization and de facto expulsion of a top SRS local leader and party cofounder, the Novi Sad mayor, Maja Gojković, was another example of the intolerance toward internal dissent in the highly nationalistic SRS. "I

The Serbian political parties have also been characterized by a very low level of voluntary and democratically organized leadership succession. For example, in 1994, only a few years after it was founded, the DS had a major leadership change when Zoran Djindjić took control of the organization. But that leadership change was more like an internal coup rather than a procedurally democratic succession within the party elite. And the party's change of leadership in 2004 only came in the wake of Djindjić's tragic assassination. Meanwhile, leadership changed in Milošević's SPS only because of his incarceration at The Hague, and later his death. There has been no change at all at the summit of the DSS since it was founded by Koštunica's break with the DS in 1992 (he was reelected as party president in February 2010). Similarly, Šešelj has remained head of the SRS since the party was established in 1991, and in recent years he has managed the party organization from his jail cell at The Hague, while giving (up until late 2008) instructions to the party's deputy leader, Tomislav Nikolić (the SRS's failure to take power in May 2008 precipitated increasing tension between Šešelj and Nikolić and finally led to the previously mentioned SRS/SNS schism). Only the smaller G-17 Plus, which grew out of a nongovernmental organization specializing in economic analysis, underwent a leadership change through an intraparty election in 2006, when Mladjan Dinkić replaced Miroljub Labus. Labus was the Serbian deputy prime minister and resigned his state and party posts over the government's failure to arrest Ratko Mladić. The case of the G-17 Plus is rather an exception. As Srećko Mihailović has observed, in Serbia "it isn't considered abnormal that relations are undemocratic within a democratic party. . . . Nondemocracy is considered a necessary characteristic of political parties.[79] Leadership domination over Serbia's political parties may be related to the considerable tolerance in the membership of most parties for practices that are at variance with democracy as a system of governance. For example, survey data from 2005 revealed

---

spent a lot of time defining a different way of thinking," Gojković claimed. "And obviously they waited for me to go my own way and make things easier for themselves." Gojković and her followers ran on an independent ticket in the May 2008 elections, but they were only able to get 8 percent of the vote in Novi Sad. *Večernje Novosti,* March 19, 2008.

79. Srećko Mihailović, "Ima li tranzicje iz socijalnog haosa," in *Izmedju autoritarizma i demokratije III: Nacionalni i državni interes moderne Srbije,* edited by Dragica Vujadinović (Belgrade: Friedrich Ebert Stiftung, 2007), 99–143.

that 77 percent of respondents who identified themselves as members of the post-Milošević SPS, and 74 percent of SRS members, viewed the use of a "strong hand" in political life as being acceptable.[80] This compared with 61 percent of DS respondents and 54 percent of DSS members.

The unrivaled personal control exercised by Vojislav Koštunica over the DSS since its 1992 founding has not overcome the relatively low support expressed by DSS members for such a strong hand. Thus, Koštunica's domination over the DSS, both before and after he became the top elected actor in Serbian political life during 2000, was not paralleled by an effort on his part to build a strong countrywide party organization. This helped to weaken his party in the period from 2007 to 2010. Koštunica's diminished support, along with his deep nationalist convictions and antiglobalist and anti–United States perspectives, also help to explain his enthusiasm for a political alliance with the more extreme SRS during the run-up to the May 2008 parliamentary elections. Support for this coalition was reciprocated by the imprisoned SRS leader, Vojislav Šešelj. This so-called Voja-Voja alliance, or the cooperation between the DSS and SRS, personally negotiated by the two parties' nationally oriented leaders through intermediaries, illustrated the relatively inconsequential role played by party memberships in guiding the destiny of Serbia's political parties.

Interestingly, in 2003, the Serbian Constitutional Court ostensibly weakened party discipline by declaring that elected deputies rather than their parties (as had been the case earlier) were the "owners" of their mandates while serving in assemblies. This decision was rendered in response to the post-Milošević abuse of party control within the DOS parliamentary majority, when Zoran Djindjić engineered the ouster of DSS members from the Serbian Assembly. But when large numbers of deputies began to change their party affiliation and caucuses—some as a result of suspected bribery—the parties clamored to regain control over their elected deputies. Because the deputies were elected on party lists under the closed system of proportional representation and received party funds, the party organizations could make a reasonably

80. Zoran Stojiljković, "Demokratija (još) ne stananu ovde: Demokratski limiti 'partijskih naroda,' i karakter unutarpartijskih odnosa," in *Demokratija u političkim strankama Srbije,* edited by Zoran Lutovac et al. (Belgrade: Friedrich Ebert Stiftung and Institut Drustvenih Nauka, 2006), 137–38.

strong case for control over their elected members, including the right to discipline or expel them from assemblies if they departed from the policies of party caucuses. As a result, the new Serbian Constitution adopted at the end of 2006 included a provision (Article 102) allowing deputies to waive their mandates in favor of the parties that had listed them for the electoral campaign. Of course, deputies did not need to waive "ownership" of their mandates, but if they did not, they would forfeit being placed on a party's list.

For the reasons discussed above, the ruling party in independent Montenegro suffers from an even lower level of internal party democracy than most of the party organizations in Serbia. Thus, Milo Djukanović has enjoyed undisputed control over the DPS since the mid-1990s. But the DPS's hegemony in some measure derives from the similarly leader-driven character of opposition party organizations that have found it impossible to coalesce and effectively oppose the DPS. In April 2008, the high-profile anticorruption crusader, Nebojša Medojević, the presidential candidate of the opposition Movement for Change (Pokret za Promjene), went so far as to describe Djukanović's rule as the "last totalitarian regime in Europe"[81] (Medojević eventually placed third in the presidential contest.) Djukanović's long tenure, his links or perceived links to criminal circles, and his control over much of the governmental and judicial structure—who are more loyal to the DPS leader and his party than to the state administration—does not really qualify as "totalitarian rule." But his personalized domination of such a powerful party organization remains a problem for fuller democratic consolidation in Montenegro, and particularly party system development.[82]

In view of party diversity in each state, it is difficult to generalize about the internal democratization of political parties throughout the Western Balkan region, and even more challenging to measure the impact of internal party changes on overall democratic consolidation in any one country. But some organizational differences and trends can be identified. Thus, right-wing and center-right parties appear to have less internal party democracy than socialist and social democratic party or-

81. *MINA,* April 6, 2008.
82. At the end of 2009, Djukanović hinted that he was planning to step down soon. There was speculation, since justified, that Igor Lukšić, the deputy prime minister, might take Djukanović's place. *Dan,* January 23, 2010, 2 (see chapter 9).

ganizations that have undergone a transformation during the postcommunist period. Centrist, smaller democratic, and liberal parties exhibit a mixed pattern of internal democratization. Typically, the smaller liberal party organizations are often quite weak and highly elitist in terms of participation by their members. But such parties often stress local authority and decentralization when it comes to their formal party structures. In such parties, control is often in the hands of small groups of intellectual activists and officials, on both the local level and in top party bodies. But the larger democratically oriented parties are also often quite hierarchical and centralized, and indeed are leader dominated in their principles of operation and the extent of autonomy enjoyed by local party organizations. However, these parties often appear quite inclusive with regard to the number of members formally taking part in party meetings and voting on executive appointments.

It is quite difficult, however, to ascertain how differences among "party families," with respect to their internal levels of democracy, influence trends in overall patterns of democratization. Thus, democratically oriented parties that are centralized, hierarchical, and oligarchic in operation may still prove critical to the democratic development of a country, considered in terms of the party's overall impact.[83] Similarly, the deputies in democratically oriented parliamentary party caucuses can achieve considerable autonomy from the control of central party offices, but in doing so they actually become less accountable to their party memberships. In brief, the relationship between internal party democratization and democratic consolidation is not an entirely straightforward one, and it may be far less significant than other factors such as the values, style of behaviors, and achievements of elected party representatives and party officials. In the final analysis, it is the outlook and decisions of a party's leaders that are most important in determining what the party stands for, how it functions, and its overall significance for political change.

83. For example, at the end of 2009, Boris Tadić, the president of the DS, and president of Serbia, asked that the DS be reformed in a more "centralized direction. . . . I believe that only a centralized DS can implement the process of decentralization so that the integrity of Serbia will be preserved." A longtime Democratic Party stalwart, Dragoljub Mićunović, admitted that the term centralization "is now associated with something undemocratic, but this need not be the case . . . political parties should be united. . . . It is a matter of political discipline." *Danas,* February 3, 2010.

The "Participation Deficit" and the Europeanization of Western Balkan Parties

Clearly, party systems and political parties have made some quite important, albeit often still tentative, steps toward greater institutionalization throughout the Western Balkans during the second decade of the region's postcommunist development, from 2000 to 2010. Thus, substantially fair and regular elections took place during the two decades of pluralist politics, and citizens of the area became more accustomed to, and supportive of, competitive political life. But as discussed above, widespread distrust toward parties and party politicians remained, and there has been only limited accountability of most party leaders and party elites to the members of their own organizations. Most important, political parties in the region have not been very successful at facilitating the citizen-state linkage that is a core component of a representative democracy. Parties in the region have certainly performed the function of mobilizing and articulating some of the major cleavages in Western Balkan societies, including ethnic, socioeconomic, and various ideological divisions. Yet they are not popularly regarded as organizations that have effectively responded to pressing public concerns and the desire of citizens to move effectively ahead with such things as economic development, enhanced social inclusiveness, and the desire of most citizens to join the EU, or at least achieve an EU standard of living.

The Problem of Electoral Abstention

It has frequently been argued that the Western Balkan region suffers from a serious "crisis of representation," which has alienated citizens from elites and has undermined the region's overall stabilization and democratic consolidation. This is reflected not only in the low level of trust for parties discussed above but also in a serious participation deficit that has impeded the development of a democratic political culture. For example, an examination of patterns of voter turnout in the region reveals a major decline in the years following the emergence of competitive political dynamics (see table 5.3). Reasons underlying the high levels of voter abstention, of course, vary from country to country and from election to election, and thus they cannot be blamed solely on the political parties themselves.

Table 5.3. Voter Turnout in Western Balkan Parliamentary Elections, 1990–2009 (percent)

Country	Years and Voter Turnout							
Croatia	1990	1992	1995	2000	2003	2007		
	84.5	75.6	68.8	76.5	66.8	63.5		
Bosnia	1990		1996	2000	2002	2006		2010
	77.0		82.0	64.4	55.4	54.5		56.3[a]
Serbia	1990	1992	1993	1997	2000	2003	2007	2008
	71.5	69.7	61.6	57.4	57.7	59.3	60.4	61.4
Montenegro	1990	1992	1996	1998	2001	2002	2006	2009
	75.8	68.9	67.1	76.0	71.5	77.5	71.3	65.0
Macedonia	1990		1994	1998		2002	2006	2008
	84.8		77.3	72.8		74.6	56.0	57.2
Albania	1991	1992		1996	1997	2001	2005	2009
	97.0	91.0		81.1	72.6	54.0	49.2	50.8
Kosovo		1992			2001	2004	2007	2010
		87.8			64.3	49.5	40.1[b]	47.4

[a]Preliminary data for the October 3, 2009, election provided by the Central Election Commission.
[b]In the November 2009 local election—Kosovo's first postindependence contest that was regarded by domestic actors as equivalent to a national vote—the turnout was about 43.5 percent, and only a small number of Serbs took part.
Sources: Reports of state electoral commissions.

Comparative research on voter turnout suggests various explanations for high abstention. For example, the routinization of pluralist politics and the frequency of elections often leads to a general pattern of electoral fatigue in countries. Voter turnout often drops off sharply after a country's founding election, and it may continue to decline for some time.[84] Moreover, citizens of a region such as the Western Balkans, who experienced a painful transitional economic recession and war-related trauma during the 1990s, and who faced continuing difficulties with making a living and surviving in troubled economies, simply may not have had the time, inclination, patience, or energy for party politics and elections.

However, research on the particularly sharp and declining pattern of turnout in the Western Balkans—some 10 to 30 percent less than during the first stage of pluralism (and sometimes even steeper de-

84. See Tatiana Kostadinova and Timothy J. Power, "Does Democratization Depress Participation?" *Political Research Quarterly* 16, no. 3 (September 2007): 363–77.

clines in Kosovo and Albania)—reveals that disillusionment with the performance of parties and the activities of party politicians probably has played a key role in turnout levels. Low voter turnout may also be traced to the difficulties that civil society organizations have faced in all the postcommunist states since the initial transitional period (see chapter 4). In some cases, the rise of new parties has also overshadowed civil society groups, crowding them out from the available political space, and thereby weakening their role in bridging the elite/mass divide. Disenchantment with the slow pace of reform, the gap between the political promises of party leaders and their actual accomplishments, and the high level of political corruption in the region (see chapter 3), have been especially dispiriting to the younger generation in the Western Balkan polities, who consequently often disengage from the political process.

Low rates of turnout also derive from popular views regarding the fraudulent character of elections, along with the lack of trust in legislative institutions found throughout the region, factors that themselves contribute to the general crisis of representation.[85] Whatever the reasons, high levels of abstention in the region have undermined the entire process of democratic consolidation. Thus, party politicians who garner only small segments of the eligible voting publics are hardly likely to be very responsive to the broad general public will. The former high representative and EU special representative in Bosnia, Christian Schwarz-Schilling, put it very well in the fall of 2006: "We face a depressing and dangerous vicious circle. Politicians are scandalously indifferent to the interests and aspirations of voters. This makes more and more voters apathetic about participating in politics, and this in turn makes politicians indifferent to the voters' aspirations." And he added: "The figures are frightening—and in democratic terms, unsustainable. . . . Election turnout in Bosnia Herzegovina has decreased steadily from about 2.4 million votes in 1996 to 1.3 million in 2002. The country is saddled with a political establishment that appears unable or unwilling to develop

85. Gallup Survey data on the Western Balkans reveals a very low level of confidence in the honesty of elections: 24 percent in Albania, 34 percent in Macedonia (28 percent among Macedonia's Albanians), 36 percent in Bosnia, 37 percent in Croatia, 43 percent among Kosovo's Albanians, 45 percent in Montenegro, and, interestingly, at the highest level, 61.7 percent in Serbia (although minorities in Serbia show a 25 percent lower level of trust). *Gallup World Poll* (Princeton, N.J.: Gallup Europe, 2006–7).

and explain policy, and . . . appeals to and depends on a shrinking and unrepresentative base of popular support."[86]

This view regarding participation is not just a position taken by a detached foreign official. The Sarajevo analyst Zdravko Grebo put it this way: "The last [2006] and past elections showed the level of abstention was enormous. The abstainers were primarily the young and people from urban environments. Resigned, melancholic, and apathetic, they no doubt concluded that it wasn't of any value to participate because the results were known in advance. Their nonvoting helps consolidate the ethnonationalistic elites constituted in the political parties."[87] Turnout increased only slightly in the October 2010 general election, and without much consequence to the entrenched ethnopolitical elites (Bakir Izetbegović, the son of the late Alija Izetbegović, replaced Haris Silajdžić as the Bosniak member of the state presidency). The rate of invalid votes was also exceptionally high in the 2010 election.[88]

A good deal of research has been conducted recently in the Western Balkans on citizen disaffection with the role of political parties in governance, and also the role that such perspectives play in the region-wide participation deficit. For example, in a December 2007 survey in Macedonia, respondents expressed very little confidence that citizens could influence the political agenda of party organizations.[89] Only 28 percent of the respondents expressed a belief that citizens could have such an impact, down from 44 percent in March 2007. Interestingly, belief in the proposition that citizens can have an influence was greater among ethnic Macedonians (56.6 percent) than Albanians (44 percent), but almost 40 percent of Albanians surveyed refused to answer the question or claimed not to know the answer. Clearly in Macedonia, the general distrust of parties illustrated in these comparative trend data continues to be a serious problem. Thus, 53 percent of those surveyed had a total mistrust of parties, and only 1.7 percent expressed strong confidence in parties. Albanians in Macedonia exhibited less mistrust of political parties than ethnic Macedonians, a finding that may be

86. Office of the High Representative, Sarajevo, September 22, 2006.
87. *Izbori 2006,* September 2006, 28.
88. For factors relating to low participation in Bosnia, see *Uzroci apstinencije mladih i žena pri izlasku na izbore u Bosni i Hercegovini* (Sarajevo: Heinrich Böll Stiftung, 2010).
89. United Nations Development Program, *People-Centered Analysis: Report* (Priština: United Nations Development Program, 2008), 70–71, 71–77.

connected with the fact that ethnic Albanians have not played as large a part in legislative policymaking and have been more extraparliamentary in their general political activities.

Analysts of electoral behavior in Serbia point out that their country has only enjoyed the conditions for democratic consolidation since October 2000, and that because of the turbulent course of politics during the next several years, Serbia only achieved the minimum legal, political, and social conditions for "normal" elections beginning with the January 2007 parliamentary contest.[90] Recent research on Serbia also indicates that citizens have a more positive attitude about the efficacy of elections than they do about parties, and that those who identify or sympathize with particular parties are the most likely citizens to participate in elections. Among those citizens who said they would not be voting, almost all expressed a lack of belief in the preelection promises of political parties.

Thus, citizens' perceptions of parties and party elites and also identification with parties are closely linked to the development of a participatory political culture supportive of democratic institutions. One Serbian analyst commenting on the rare and relatively large voter turnout in the two rounds of the February 2008 presidential election—when Boris Tadić narrowly beat Tomislav Nikolić of the SRS—remarked that "a large electoral abstention over the previous years was an expression of open disappointment with the lack of party direction on policy, but also a protest against the abuse of the very institution of elections. At the parliamentary elections last year [2007], the citizens sent one message while parties distributed power within their coalition in a manner quite different from the voters' will. The politicians played a good game and established themselves solidly, clearly demonstrating that the essence of their politics was the fight for power and not concern for the welfare and prosperity of the people."[91] The turnout for the critical May 2008 legislative election in Serbia was only slightly higher (61 percent) than for the 2003 and 2007 contests, although it assisted in the victory of Tadić's democratic coalition. Serbian analysts attributed the low turnout to several factors: voter fatigue with elections, voter confusion, and

90. Djordje Vuković, "Izborno zakonodavstvo u Srbiji," in *Parlamentarni izbori 2007: Okolnosti i rezultat,* edited by Srećko Mihailović (Belgrade: Službeni List, 2007), 128.

91. Dragoš Ivanović, "Presidential Election in Serbia, 2008," *Republika,* February 2008.

the fact that people can no longer see that elections produce a result, although politicians keep characterizing them as "decisive." But once again, highly pragmatic interparty bargaining over the formation of a coalition to govern appeared to undermine the kind of nexus between voters and decisionmakers that could be perceived as democratically accountable.

The level of electoral abstention has been especially high in Kosovo, rising to 60 percent in 2007. Indeed, in recent years, more Kosovo voters chose to abstain than those voting for the major parties.[92] A report of a Kosovo think tank, Forum 2015, attributed low electoral turnout to political dissatisfaction, the (in)efficiency of political parties, a lack of restraint in campaigns, the perception that the individual has no influence, massive corruption in politics, division about Kosovo's status which make elections secondary, and technical problems.[93] Kosovo Serbs have generally boycotted elections since 1999 at the urging of their community leaders, the Belgrade authorities, and the Serbian Orthodox Church. There was only a slight change in the November 2009 local election, the first since independence. Thus, a small number of Serbs decided to participate in the election and were able to win a majority in three municipalities. But the total turnout in those localities was only 23.6 percent in Gračanica, 25.4 percent in Klokot, and 13.9 percent in Ranilug. In the Serb-controlled northern Kosovo districts, the usual boycott prevailed, with almost no turnout (0.75 percent in Zvečan, 6.64 percent in Zubin Potok, and 0.83 percent in Leposavić). Granted, all the Serbs did not boycott the election, but the nationwide abstention rate dropped only slightly to 56.5 percent. Prime Minister Thaçi's party, the PDK, won control in twenty out of thirty-six municipalities. But his claim that Kosovo and the PDK have passed the test of democracy" and have "risen above party and ethnic flags" seemed a tad premature.[94] In Belgrade, the official in charge of Kosovo put it differ-

92. Parties in Kosovo have also been rather smug about declining rates of electoral participation, in part because all parties have felt that they should focus primarily on their "core voters" rather than on "nonvoters" or the apathetic. Kosovar Institute for Policy Research and Development, *Voting Trends and Electoral Behavior in Kosovo: 2000–2004,* Policy Research Paper 6 (Priština: Kosovar Institute for Policy Research and Development, 2006).

93. *Koha Ditore,* November 16, 2009.

94. Central Election Commission, November 15, 2009; Agence France-Presse, November 16, 2009.

ently: "There is a crack between the Serbs (from central enclaves) and the Serbs in the north, but also between them and the government."[95]

Survey results in Kosovo and elsewhere in the Western Balkans have indicated that reluctance to participate in political life has been especially pronounced among young people. For example, 94 percent of Kosovo youth surveyed in 2006 claimed that they had no interest in getting voluntarily involved in politics. Little difference existed on this matter between young people from the two major ethnic communities. This situation makes it very difficult for parties to mobilize young people for either party activity or electoral campaigns, and in turn it leaves young people with very little influence on decisionmaking. Ostensibly, there is considerable interest in voting. Thus, 81 percent of Kosovo Albanian youth claimed to be looking forward to electoral participation once Kosovo became independent; and such a perspective was not insubstantial (63 percent) among Kosovo Serb respondents. But fewer than 30 percent of Albanian youth in Kosovo found the electoral system fair and democratic, and only 5 percent of Serb youth in Kosovo did so.

Such survey results did not bode well for a reduction of the participation deficit in an independent Kosovo.[96] As one foreign observer noted in 2008, "Kosova presently has experienced political leaders who know how to craft a message that resonates with the general population," and it is also host to numerous think tanks run by intellectuals for almost every facet of public policy. The problem, however, in his view, is that "the political leaders do not fully trust the intellectuals, and intellectuals disdain partisan politics. Political parties put all of their energies into jockeying for favor with the internationals, more foreign donor support and competition over the spoils. . . . Too many young people—almost all of them with real education and talent—stay away from politics."[97] Macedonia's young people also seem to be disinterested in politics (only 20 percent trust parties—the lowest support for any institution in the country, and only 7 percent express any political interest at all), and

95. Agence France-Presse, November 16, 2009.

96. United Nations Development Program, *Youth: A New Generation in Kosovo: Human Development Report 2006* (Priština: United Nations Development Program, 2006), 83–84. For turnout in the 2009 local election see the note in Table 5.3.

97. Henry H. Perritt, "Making Civil Society Meaningful in Independent Kosovo," *New Kosovo Report,* March 27, 2008.

they tend to blame the country's persistently troubled interethnic relations on parties more than any other institution.[98]

Comprehensive studies of young people in Croatia between 1999 and 2004 indicated that three-quarters of the country's youth believed that the younger generation is insufficiently represented in the country's political life. On the positive side, the number of young people completely disinterested in politics decreased somewhat in the first five years of the twenty-first century—a period when Croatia underwent its initial post-Tudjman "second transition"—and there was increasing acceptance by the younger generation of fundamental liberal democratic constitutional principles. But the level of interest in politics was still much lower among young people than in the older generation. And although most young people indicated a willingness to take part in politics, the number of young respondents participating in parties and other political organizations dropped substantially. Croatian youth who were surveyed attributed the political marginalization of their peers to beliefs about the unfairness of politics, the failure of politicians to deal with issues relevant to young people, and the preoccupation of the younger generation with their own existential problems, along with the discontent and self-marginalization of many young people. The paternalism of the older generation and a lack of acceptance toward giving young people a broader role in political decisionmaking were also viewed as important reasons for the political marginalization of the younger generation.

Thus, well over a decade after the introduction of a multiparty system, research indicated that most Croatian young people—about 21 percent of the overall eligible electorate—still chose to distance themselves from political activity. Research on Croatian youth in 2004 also indicated that two-fifths of young people expressed a desire to spend a long period of time working and studying abroad, and that a quarter of those surveyed wished to leave their country permanently.[99] And though

98. Dane Taleški et al., *Youth Aspiration Survey in the Republic of Macedonia* (Skopje: Friedrich Ebert Stiftung, 2006).

99. Vlasta Ilišin, "Youth and Politics," in *Youth and Transition in Croatia*, edited by Vlasta Ilišin and Furio Radin (Zagreb: Institute for Social Research, 2002), 157–204; Vlast Ilišin, "Political Attitudes and Participation of Youth: Continuity and Change," and Vlasta Ilišin and Ivona Mendes, "Youth and European Union: Perceptions of the Consequences of Integration," both in *Croatian Youth and European Integration* (Zagreb: Institut za društvena istraživanja, 2007), 69–149, 209–71.

Croatia was in the lead among Western Balkan countries queued up to enter the EU, Eurobarometer research indicated that in 2007 only 8 percent of Croats surveyed had confidence in their country's political parties, and this dropped to only 4 percent in 2009. This was the lowest support expressed by Croatian respondents for any of their country's national institutions; the equivalent figure in 2009 was 12 percent for the central legislature, 15 percent for the judiciary, and 46 percent for the military.[100]

The European Road to Political Participation and Party Transformation

One of the more interesting dimensions of the so-called crisis of representation that has afflicted most Western Balkan countries—and is an area of convergence with citizens in many of the EU member states—is the belief that the institutions of the European Union can be trusted *more* than their respective national governments and parliaments. For example, Eurobarometer data from Croatia and Macedonia, the two Western Balkan states that are already formally EU candidate countries, is highly illustrative in this sense. Thus, in the spring of 2008, 21 percent of Croatian citizens surveyed tended to trust their national government, and 40 percent of citizens in Macedonia expressed the same regard for their government. The equivalent trust levels for the EU as an institution were 37 and 64 percent, respectively.[101]

Interestingly, more politically troubled and less economically developed Macedonia reveals a level of trust in the EU that is considerably higher than such expressions of trust for the EU in Croatia. But even in the more Euro-skeptic Croatian public during 2008, significantly more Croats believed that things were going well in the EU compared with those who thought things were going badly, although the opposite was true with respect to perceptions about Croatia itself. Similar findings are also apparent when Croatian and Macedonian citizens' confidence in their legislatures is examined and compared with their views of the

---

100. Eurobarometer, *Eurobarometer 68: Javno mnijenje u Europskoj uniji, nacionalni izvještaj, Hrvatska* (Brussels: European Commission, 2007); Eurobarometer, *Eurobarometer 72: Javno mnijenje u Europskoj uniji, nacionalni izvještaj, Hrvatska* (Brussels: European Commission, 2009).

101. Eurobarometer, *Eurobarometer 69: European State of Mind* (Brussels: European Commission, 2008).

EU. The high levels of distrust in governments and parliaments are in large part linked to the extremely negative views held by citizens of both countries regarding the role played by political parties (which is also quite high in the EU's twenty-seven member states, albeit at a lower level than in the Western Balkans).

In any case, the paradox that both EU-candidate and most non–EU-candidate Western Balkan states share with the EU member states that were formerly Communist is that public opinion is generally more favorably disposed toward European political institutions than toward their respective domestic national structures. This is not to ignore the substantial anti-European and/or also Euro-skeptic parties and segments of public opinion in the Western Balkans (see chapter 8). Rather, it only suggests that a strong motivating factor behind the high levels of support for EU accession in the region is the hope of escaping from the problems of highly imperfect domestic political structures, and especially deficient political party performance.

Indeed, evidence from Central and Eastern Europe has shown that during the EU accession process, a majority of voters viewed the EU as "an ally in controlling corrupt local elites."[102] Thus, many citizens in the Western Balkans view EU accession as a way of circumventing their own problematic domestic political structures and of quickly improving their prospects of sharing in the European promise of democratic and economic development. Such evidence suggests that there may be more willingness to turn a blind eye to the EU's own democratic deficits—which are widely decried within the EU member states—when one's own state's democratic deficiencies are even more pronounced, and are sometimes even viewed as intractable.

One negative effect of such views in the Western Balkans is, of course, that the expectation of imminent inclusion in the higher-capacity and more democratically seasoned institutions of the EU as a panacea for domestic democratic deficits may actually detract from the commitment of Western Balkan citizens and elites to finding solutions to the

---

102. However, Ivan Krastev argues that once countries enter the EU, the bureaucratic elite in Brussels become an ally of national elites and a way for domestic elites to avoid democratic accountability. Unfortunately, this can lead to a popular backlash, as in Central Europe recently, where there is a "structural conflict between elites that are becoming increasingly suspicious of democracy and angry publics that are becoming increasingly anti-liberal." "The Populist Moment," *Eurozine,* September 18, 2007.

problems of their national institutions and electoral processes. Thus, elites from candidate countries, or potential candidate countries, engaged in the EU preaccession process may perceive little need to go beyond a superficial remodeling of their domestic institutions to meet EU requirements. Such limited structural renovations are not likely to create sustainable institutional capacity or a popular legitimation of local institutions.

The Europeanization of Political Party Organizations

The level of enthusiasm for the European Union exhibited in polls and surveys varies from one Western Balkan state to another. Moreover, the issue of EU accession is often manipulated or politically exploited by political party elites in each particular country. But the Europeanization of the Western Balkan party systems and parties is occurring in other and very practical ways. For example, the decision by a state to pursue membership in the EU, and the formal entry of a country into the EU preaccession process, unleash changes in the country's political environment that have an influence on its political parties. Indeed, a whole subfield of party development literature has emerged dealing with such Europeanization, conceptualized as political party adaptation to the opportunities and constraints of European integration, and how that adaptation relates to the democratization process. On a very general level, Europeanization can be conceived as a set of processes whereby the EU's "formal and informal rules, procedures, policy paradigms, styles, and 'ways of doing things,' and shared beliefs and norms" are gradually "incorporated into the logic of domestic discourse, identities, political structures and public policies."[103] Indeed, the entire debate regarding EU integration taking place in postcommunist countries, including the discussions and controversies in the Western Balkan states that have yet to make it through the entire process, make up part of the Europeanization process, broadly conceived.

Judging by the earlier experiences of the Central and Eastern European countries, a number of changes influence party development dur-

103. Claudio Radaelli, "Whither Europeanization? Concept Stretching and Substantive Change," *European Integration On Line Papers* 4, no. 8 (July 17, 2000): 4.

ing the lead-up to, and direct involvement in, the EU accession process, including the increased programmatic, value, and organizational convergence between Western European and Central and Eastern European political parties. This generally includes a gradual restructuring of party competition in a manner similar to Western European left-right beliefs and party orientations. Thus, pro-European right-wing parties often begin to move away from their extreme positions and mimic aspects of the programs developed by Western European socially conservative Christian and nationalist parties. Left-wing parties also move more toward the center. Parties in preaccession countries also begin to focus on the reform agenda of the EU *acquis communautaire,* and thus they form direct transnational party linkages with parties already in the EU member states. Such linkages and the process of Europeanization have been well under way in the Western Balkans during the last few years.

For example, some parties in the region have been undergoing an externally nurtured process of party socialization toward European democratic norms owing to their membership (at the full, associate, or observer level) in transnational European political parties, such as the center-right European People's Party and the European Liberal and Democratic Reform Party, as well as in regional and international organizations that bring together like-minded political parties. Thus, Western Balkan parties such as Croatia's HDZ (a full member in June 2008), Macedonia's VMRO-DPMNE, the Democratic Party of Albanians and Albania's Democratic Party, and Serbia's DSS and G-17 Plus are all affiliated with the European Democratic Union (a branch of the International Democratic Union), which brings together right-wing and right-center parties. And the Socialist International (SI) includes Albania's Social Democratic Party, Bosnia's SDP, Macedonia's Social Democratic Union, the Social Democratic Party of Montenegro, Montenegro's dominant DPS, Bosnia's Alliance of Independent Social Democrats, Serbia's DS (these last three parties became full members in July 2008), and the Social Democratic Party of Serbia. Croatia's Social Democratic Party is also a member of the SI, and one of its female deputies, Mirjana Ferić-Vac, was elected vice president of the SI in July 2008, as was Radmila Šekerinska, the outgoing head of Macedonia's SDSM. Meanwhile, the region's smaller liberal parties—such as the Liberal Party of Serbia, Montenegro's Liberal Alliance, the Liberal Democratic Party in Macedonia, the Social Liberal Party in Croatia, and the Liberal Party of Kosova (Partia Liberale e Kosoves)—are all in the Liberal International.

A number of Western Balkan parties are also members and observers in the Christian Democratic International (CDI), including the Democratic League of Kosova, the Albanian Democratic Party, the small Christian Democratic Party of Serbia, Bosnia's small New Democratic Initiative, and Croatia's HDZ. At a September 2007 CDI Summit in Rome, HDZ president (and Croatian prime minister) Sanader asked CDI members "to stand by those capable of explaining to the public that the insecurity it felt over the Western way of living could be overcome with basic values. It is values from the Christian heritage that can help combat world poverty. . . . I personally believe in successfully bringing Christian democratic values to Croatian politics."[104] Sanader frequently referred to HDZ membership in party internationals to justify or legitimate his own reformist and centrist orientation, and also to garner support for Croatia's EU accession goals. Indeed, the desire to receive international legitimation is an important motivation for the effort by Balkan elites to forge links with external party organizations.

To some extent, the experience of Western Balkan parties in such regional and international associations—even when countries are still not deeply engaged in the mechanics of the preaccession process—reduces differences among similar parties across the region (i.e., the diversity deriving from their national settings or country-specific factors) and increases similarities within party families across European borders. It creates a constellation of European (and internationally) linked party "families" whose members, including parties in the Western Balkans, become, in varying degrees, more "European," moderate, and cooperative in their orientations. These family associations also have a positive influence on interstate relations. Within specific countries of the region, the linkages of specific parties to their families on an international level can also increase the contrast between and among parties, offering voters a clearer choice (although the imperative of parties to cast a wide net and achieve catch-all type gains also tends to blur party contrasts to some extent).

In any event, the establishment of transnational party linkages can have an important modernizing and democratizing impact. Domestic

104. *HINA*, September 21, 2007.

parties seeking ties to democratically oriented European and international party organizations must have their party programs reviewed, have their activities vetted by the European and transnational party organizations, and respond to advice and assistance from external party offices in order to become eligible for financial assistance that can facilitate organizational development. The impact of party practices from the EU member states on the EU-candidate and -aspirant states can encourage specific facets of party and democratic development, such as the improved status and empowerment of women and ethnic minorities in a country's party system.

The real and symbolic value of a political party becoming a member of a democratically oriented regional or international organization was recently demonstrated when the SPS—seeking to jettison its past as Milošević's party and become a modern social democratic party—applied to join the SI at the organization's July 2008 Congress in Athens. Although initially unsuccessful, the SPS's application to the SI caused considerable controversy and led Bosnia's SDP to walk out of the meeting. Meanwhile, there was also a controversy in the European People's Party because one of its associated members, Vojislav Koštunica's DSS, had moved farther to the nationalist right and temporarily formed links with the SRS. Clearly, familial party status in Europe was increasingly becoming a factor in Western Balkan political life.

It is also worth noting that the influence of outside values and party experiences on the postcommunist states, or the top-down importation of foreign models of party development, can also occur at the expense of improved local party linkages with civil society groups and the public, and thereby can exacerbate the broader crisis of representation. Imitation of party centralization as practiced in the EU countries may encourage a tendency toward elite control in parties. When elitist proclivities occur in countries at the early stages of democratization, as in the Western Balkan states, which already have very hierarchical and personalized internal power structures, external influence can actually weaken organizational links between the state structure on the one side, and civil societies and the public on the other side. Occurring in this manner, the process of Europeanization has the danger of increasing the alienation of voters and intensifying the participation deficit. Moreover, in weakly institutionalized party systems where parties are already excessively connected to the state administration and are not very responsive to the grassroots, party linkages to broader European and international organizations may undermine the democratic accountability of party leaders to local voters in the short run.

And because the implementation of EU preaccession requirements is typically managed from the executive wing, not by parliaments where different party organizations and especially opposition forces have the most influence, European integration may also have a centralizing and elitist effect that can undermine the establishment of closer linkages between party organizations and citizens. Of course, even elite-centered party development may not always be helpful to EU accession in the absence of political will. As Tanja Miščević, the head of Serbia's EU Integration Office, observed just before the May 2008 election: "There is already a clear majority in the public in favour of [EU entry]. But it is the political elite that is responsible for EU integration, not the people."[105] In the longer run, once countries become members of the EU, elitist tendencies may lead to an alliance between elites in Brussels and in the new member states that may stimulate anti-elitist and populist sentiment in domestic settings. Thus, it would be incorrect to simply equate the Europeanization and modernization of political parties with easy progress in democratic consolidation. Still, on the whole, the fact that the Western Balkan states have been moving, albeit at very different rates, through the EU preaccession process has generally been a positive development (see chapter 9).

Summing Up: Party Development and Democratic Consolidation

By 2010, the transformation of the political party systems in the Western Balkan nations had become a significant part of the democratic consolidation process. The transformation of these party systems appeared to be midway between Western European development patterns, on one side, and the experiences farther east in Europe, in Eurasia, and in the nations belonging to the Commonwealth of Independent States, on the other. Generally, levels of party system change have reflected, and have also been responsible for, the positioning of the states in the queue to join the European Union. This is hardly surprising, because the activities of party organizations and party elites determine so much of

105. *Die Presse,* April 18, 2008.

294 The Transformation of Political Parties in the Western Balkans

what is going on as a whole in the transformation of states. For example, Croatia has undergone a marked metamorphosis in the social cleavage structure underlying party development, and in the rebranding and conversion of core parties. Serbia's party system, for a number of well-known reasons, lagged behind up to 2008, but it subsequently underwent important changes. In Bosnia and Macedonia, the salience of ethnic cleavage has impeded party transformation. Albania's party system, although less fragmented than earlier, is still a highly polarized case of pluralism. Meanwhile, the newest state in the region, Kosovo, remains very much in the takeoff stage of party development. But in the area of party development, as with economic change, there are certain advantages of backwardness and newness that can assist rapid transformation and continued democratic consolidation.

Granted, the political party systems in the region may only be partially and imperfectly institutionalized.[106] But as shown above, by 2010 predictability in the strength and role played by core parties in most states, and embeddedness with respect to the societal anchoring of those parties, had become quite substantial. Part of this situation can be traced to the length of time these parties have now been on the political landscape, and also to the survivability of certain larger parties—a kind of path dependence—that entered pluralist politics in the 1989–91 period with certain assets. Considerable party fragmentation remains—partially as a result of the proportional representation electoral systems used throughout the region, which also include low threshold rules for party entry into legislatures, and partially because of the evolving cleavage structure in the very diverse societies. However, the catch-all syndrome exhibited by parties that tried to obtain as many votes as possible, and also in some cases the reduction of the type of cleavages and emotional issues that strengthened interparty polarization in the 1990s, have pushed parties toward the center of the political spectrum. The same factors have weakened smaller and extreme parties, and have contributed to a defragmentation and emergence of a two-bloc pattern of alignment between the main parties and coalitions that obtain legislative representation. In some countries such as Croatia and Serbia, which underwent significant changes in the leadership and outlook of major parties during the post-2000 period and

106. See, e.g., Vera Stojareva and Peter Emerson, eds., *Party Politics in the Western Balkans* (London: Routledge, 2010).

came to resemble relatively stable bipolar systems, partisanship in the elite was becoming less of a divisive force and more of an integrating factor supportive of democratic consolidation.[107] Overall, Western Balkan party systems have become less unstructured than they were twenty years ago, when the democracies of the region were far more fragile and unconsolidated.

The legitimation of political parties and party systems by citizens of the region is still, of course, quite uneven. Few citizens currently would wish to return to single-party rule, but public opinion in the Western Balkans still exhibits high levels of distrust toward political parties and electoral systems, and the very high rates of electoral abstention are still a concern. Political corruption and the failure of ruling parties and coalitions to achieve faster reform and economic progress are key reasons for the lack of confidence in party organizations and their leaders. The ability of Western Balkan parties to make progress with respect to internal party democratization has not been very impressive, and in some cases the strong personalization and top-down control of party structures apparent in the 1990s has changed very little, even though new personalities are gradually advancing to positions of party leadership. However, internal party democracy may be a less important factor than the increasing commitment to democratic norms on the part of party elites and voters (see chapter 7 on value transformation). Thus, the linkage between the institutionalization of parties and party systems (as measured by such traditional factors as trust in parties, internal party democracy, and even the fragmentation and volatility of party systems), on the one side, and the democratic consolidation of political systems, on the other, is not an entirely straightforward matter. In fact, parties and party systems can be imperfectly institutionalized—as they appear to be in most of the Western Balkan cases—and still make a significant contribution to overall democratic consolidation.

107. On the relationship between partisanship and polarization, see Zsolt Enyedi and Bojan Todosijević, "Adversarial Politics, Civic Virtues and Partisanship in Eastern and Western Europe," in *Political Parties and Partisanship: Social Identity and Individual Attitudes,* edited by John Bartle and Paolo Bellucci (London: Routledge, 2009), 121–61. Croatia's post-2009 pattern of dual executive cohabitation between a moderate president from the SDP and a moderate prime minister from the HDZ opened an especially promising, but also challenging, stage in pluralist development. Davor Gjenero, "Nova stranačka arhitektura," *Vjesnik,* February 21, 2010.

Clearly, even the relatively cohesive and reasonably predictable core political parties of the Western Balkan nations are far from perfectly functioning or model organizations, and they are held in low esteem by a great many of these countries' own citizens. But during the past decade, the party organizations in the region have contributed more effectively to the basic operational requirements of democratic rule and to the quality of democracy than they did during the initial pluralist transition period. This suggests that the institutionalization of parties and party systems in new democracies may essentially be more of a by-product than a cause of democratic consolidation.[108]

The institutionalization of political parties in the region thus can still be one of the key factors reinforcing democracy, even if not the critical motor force in democratic change. In brief, party pluralism in the Western Balkans has become a substantially established component of the "only game in town," even if the style of this democratic game sometimes appears quite unusual and flawed to outsiders, the rules of the game are frequently breached, and citizens express their considerable suspicion of the players. Finally, party pluralism in the region has become more and more of a European game, encouraged through the socialization of Western Balkan political parties and elites by Western European and international party organizations. As the Western Balkan parties become even more deeply engaged in the EU preaccession process, various transformative and Europeanizing pressures will certainly increase. The process will be gradual, hardly unilinear, and probably— as recently suggested by the populist and disruptive facets of party life in the more politically advanced states of Central and Eastern Europe —not without some worrying setbacks.

---

108. Gábor Tóka, "Political Parties in East Central Europe," in *Consolidating the Third Wave Democracies,* edited by Larry Diamond, Marc F. Platter, et al. (Baltimore: Johns Hopkins University Press, 1997), 118–22.

Chapter 6

The Social Basis for Democratic Development: Elites, Middle Classes, and the Struggle against Poverty

This chapter proceeds on the premise that social transformation is one of the critical variables that influences the course of economic development as well as democratic change. Thus, the sustainability of economic growth and the consolidation of democratic regimes are conditioned by the evolution of societal features such as class structure, educational structure, and levels of urbanization, as well as the fundamental values and more routine attitudes of various social strata regarding sociopolitical issues.

A substantial body of social science literature goes farther, supporting the general proposition that the emergence of a middle class in society constitutes the critical instrument or social force through which modernization can positively influence the process of democratization. This research indicates that the existence of a relatively well-educated and urbanized middle class, which also subscribes to pluralist values and the rule of law, can dampen extremism in society, buffer the destabilizing impact of intergroup conflicts, and reduce the longevity and prospects of authoritarian rule. This is not to suggest, as the principal modernization theorists have cautioned, that class-driven democratization is an inevitable, linear, or irreversible cause and consequence of economic development. Indeed, the role of distressed and impoverished middle-class elements (especially the "petty bourgeoisie") in the rise and maintenance of authoritarian rule is well documented.

But it is fair to say that the social structure of more economically developed societies is more supportive of democracy than the social structure of nonindustrialized countries with a primarily rural economy.

297

Thus, nuanced versions of modernization theory identify the virtues of a large and prosperous middle class in the emergence and sustainability of democracy without any determinism regarding the impact of changes in social structure on specific political outcomes. Adam Przeworski put it well after extensively exploring the relationship between economic development and political change:

> There is no doubt that the probability that a democracy survives increases with per capita income; . . . that relationship will survive anything. It's monotonic, and it's strong, unbelievably strong. . . . Democracy becomes more stable in more developed societies because as people become wealthier, too much is at stake in attempting to subvert democracy. Intense political mobilization is risky in general, and in wealthy democracies it is even more risky because people have too much to lose.[1]

Because, historically, the Western Balkans have not benefited from "a social structure favoring democracy,"[2] at least not for any prolonged period, exploring the formation of middle classes and how they may influence democratization in the region is of particular interest to this study.

Elite Reconstruction and Middle Class Development in the Balkans

There is no question that economic growth in the Western Balkans during the past several decades (to be detailed in chapter 8) has resulted

1. Adam Przeworski, "Capitalism, Democracy and Science," in *Passion, Craft, and Method in Comparative Politics,* edited by Gerardo L. Munck and Richard Snyder (Baltimore: Johns Hopkins University Press, 2007), 470–71. See also Larry Diamond, "Economic Development and Democracy Reconsidered," in *Re-examining Democracy: Essays in Honor of Seymour Martin Lipset,* edited by Gary Marks and Larry Diamond (Beverly Hills, Calif.: Sage, 1992), 93–140; Larry Diamond, *The Spirit of Democracy* (New York: Times Books, 2008), 88–105; Ronald Inglehart and Christian Welzel, "How Development Leads to Democracy: What We Know about Modernization," *Foreign Affairs* 88, no. 2 (March–April 2009): 33–48; C. Boix, *Democracy and Redistribution* (Cambridge: Cambridge University Press, 2003); and Daron Acemoglu and James Robinson, *Economic Origins of Dictatorship and Democracy* (Cambridge: Cambridge University Press, 2006).
   2. Alina Mungiu-Pippidi, Whim van Meurs, and Vladimir Gligorov, *Plan B:*

in more prosperous societies with higher levels of national income and wealth. But the societies of the region are still troubled by the economic, social, and political legacies from their rapid and turbulent early transformation (see chapter 1). The consequences of these legacies created uncertainties about these states' further economic development even before the current international financial and economic crisis, and also uncertainties about the consolidation and maintenance of their new democratic institutions.

Important questions arise regarding the capacity of the new Western Balkan states to address these uncertainties. For example, how have the elite structures of these states been transformed during the past two decades of postcommunist development? To what extent have factors such as occupational change, entrepreneurial activity, and educational reform contributed to the formation of robust and self-conscious middle classes that can influence democratic change in coming years? Considering recent changes in the region's elites and middle-class formations, how has the less fortunate bottom tier of society fared, especially those who are classified as living in poverty? How successful have efforts to fight poverty been in the Western Balkans? This chapter explores these questions and other social features of the region, before we turn in the next chapter to examine the related issue of whether the changing values of Balkan elites and classes have become more supportive of a democratic political order.

Retarded Social Transition in the 1990s

The collapse of one-party regimes in the Western Balkan states at the outset of the 1990s, and the reconfiguration of political power and ownership in each society, led to changes in the region's elite structures and patterns of class stratification. For the most part, throughout the 1990s the region's political and economic elites were a composite of three segments: (1) a substantial number of personnel who had served in the old regime and had quickly adapted themselves to, or benefited from, the new postcommunist environment (e.g., through the "crony capitalism" discussed above); (2) a generally younger group of political

---

B for Balkans—State-Building and Democratic Institutions in Southeastern Europe (College Park: Center for Applied Policy Studies, University of Maryland, 2007), 35.

and economic actors who became involved in the new pluralist regimes and their mixed (or dual) public and privatized economic structures; and (3) the top members of various politically connected rent-seeking elites (including mafia-type or illegal networks, tycoons, media barons, and others) who had corruptly acquired substantial political and economic influence and wealth.

As discussed in chapter 1, the considerable opportunities afforded to this third elite sector during the 1990s were closely linked to the transitional economic recession of the initial postcommunist period, and also to the economic disruption and sanctions that accompanied, or were an indirect result of, the "wars of the Yugoslav succession." Of course, the specific size and influence of each postcommunist sub-elite varied from country to country. One notable feature of all the Western Balkan states, however, is that the collapse of one-party rule was characterized by the extensive "reproduction" or continuity of personnel within elite structures, in contrast to the pronounced "replacement" or "circulation" of elites, which was more typical in Central and Eastern Europe.[3]

For example, in Croatia, after the end of Communist rule in 1990, the most senior political members of the old regime lost their posts, but former members of the elite from the League of Communists still constituted a substantial proportion (approximately one-third) of the higher echelons of the various political parties in the new competitive political party system of each state. The "reproduction" of old regime elites was greater within the economic leadership—about 46 percent of postcommunist Croatian managers had held elite positions in 1989—than among politicians (24.1 percent) who had served in earlier elite posts.[4] Thus, while Croatia in the decade after 1990 was under the dominant control of Franjo Tudjman's Croatian Democratic Union (Hrvatska demokratska zajednica, HDZ), the introduction of parliamentary democracy meant that a substantial number of leading personnel from the former League of Communists remained top

3. Frane Adam and Matevž Tomšić, "Elite (Re)configuration and Politico-Economic Performance in Post-Socialist Countries," *Europe-Asia Studies* 54, no. 3 (2002): 435–54.

4. Duško Sekulić and Željka Sporer, "Political Transformation and Elite Formation in Croatia," *European Sociological Review* 18 (2002): 85–100; Alija Hodžić, "Development of the Political Elite in Croatia," unpublished paper, 2002, http://esr.oxfordjournals.org/misc/terms.shtml.

leaders of various political parties (especially the Social Democratic Party that had been reconfigured from the former Croatian League of Communists, but also leaders of other parties, including Tudjman himself). Moreover, elite circulation did not necessarily mean a fresh perspective. For example, although the managerial elite in Croatia revealed a high level of personnel circulation (54 percent), the new leaders were recruited by the dominant ruling party of Tudjman, which exercised a high level of control over the economy.

As a result, the "new entrants" into the postcommunist Croatian elite were recruited from the ranks of the large stratum of professionals or individuals with university degrees that had been trained during the Communist period. Interestingly, the overall educational level of the Croatian political and economic elites was lower during the first postcommunist period. Thus, holdover or recycled members of the Communist elite were less educated, as were the newly recruited members within the political and managerial elites. The overall lower educational level of the immediate postcommunist Croatian elite (76 percent of the politicians and 54 percent of the managers) derived in large part from the fact that the members of new ruling HDZ were recruited on the basis of populist-nationalist appeals and had only limited support from the upper-class intellectual circles in Croatia or from the important Croatian Diaspora. Moreover, the centrist parties, which drew more upon the support of middle-class elements and also of the humanistic and technical intelligentsia, were unable to achieve political influence until after the end of HDZ rule in early 2000. Indeed, for the first decade of postcommunist rule, members of the Croatian elite were not only dominated by a nationalist-populist party, which was less well educated than its Communist predecessors, but also was older and more homogeneous in its ethnic composition. Political regime "circulation" had occurred as a result of the political transition from a one-party to a multiparty system, but the level of reproduction or continuity in elite personnel was striking, along with other features of elite style, behavior, and orientation that would constitute impediments to democratization, and to the further modernization of society.

The blocked development of a prosperous and democratically oriented new middle class was an additional aspect that distorted modernization in Croatia. Initially, there was no social formation to replace the old socialist class of enterprise directors, managers, and officials, whose own position had both economically and politically deteriorated owing primarily to the economic downturn, the wartime environment of 1992–95, and the highly politicized pattern of the new regime's privatization programs, which favored friends of the top leader and his party machine. Croatia's "crony capitalism" spawned an elite of new owners and managers who were closely linked to the ruling party. Based on "tycoon privatization"—Tudjman actually called at one point for the creation of 200 wealthy families that would own the economy (eventually, there were only 117 families)—this insider elite undermined the development of a strong and independent business class devoted to the rule of law.[5]

The case of Serbia during the 1990s provides another example of "blocked modernization" that derived from an incomplete process of elite circulation, and which had an adverse impact on the development of a reformist and robust middle class. As in Croatia, both the political and economic elites consisted of mixtures of holdover personnel from the Communist period, and also new members—that is, "elite reconstruction," having aspects of both reproduction and circulation. Moreover, during the war both these elements often became closely linked to illegal and corrupt networks, thereby forming a kind of kleptocratic third elite pillar, which strongly influenced political decision-making. Evidence regarding Serbia's elite development indicates that the Slobodan Milošević regime was able to replicate the political and societal monopoly of the former Serbian League of Communists (Savez komunista Srbije, SKS), by its control of an interlocked elite composed of party-state and economic officials associated with the apparatus of the Socialist Party of Serbia (the SPS, or heir to the SKS). Mladen Lazić, for example, found that in 1993, 65 percent of the Serbian elite were from the "old nomenklatura," although the number had fallen to 56 percent by 1997.[6] Meanwhile, the top leaders of the recently formed opposition parties—most of whom had also been members of the League of Communists—also remained isolated from power,

5. D. Čengić, ed., *Menadzersko-poduzetnička elita i modernizacija: Razvojna ili rentijerska elita?* (Zagreb: Institut društvenih znanosti Ivo Pilar, 2005); Damir Grubiša, "Political Corruption in Transitional Croatia: The Peculiarities of a Model," *Politička Misao,* no. 5 (2005): 66–67.

6. Lazić cited by Adam and Tomšić, "Elite (Re)configuration," 452. See also Mladen Lazić, "The Adaptive Reconstruction of Elites," in *Elites after State Socialism,* edited by John Higley and Gyorgy Lengyel (Oxford: Rowman & Littlefield, 2000), 123–40.

manipulated by the governing elite, and deeply divided among themselves. Thus, the Serbian elite structure during the 1990s was sharply fragmented between those working with the ruling party and those who were outside this network—for example, some leaders of the "opposition" parties, independent members of the intelligentsia elites, and the few private entrepreneurs not controlled by the regime.

During the Milošević regime, Serbia's interlocked political and economic elites used the benefits of insider privatization, and the illegal opportunities afforded by warfare in the region, to greatly improve their material position and status. Thus, though the overall economy remained in crisis or stagnated, there was increasing social polarization between the governing elite on the one side (which included a small, emerging entrepreneurial elite or nouveau riche stratum closely linked to the regime), and a very large and impoverished agglomeration of strata on the other side (most from the old middle class, the agricultural population, and the industrial working class). The class structure of both Yugoslavia and Serbia during the socialist period had been less egalitarian than the other Communist societies (owing to the market aspects of the economy and considerable managerial autonomy). But after a period of diminishing inequalities during the first half of the 1990s (due to runaway inflation and general impoverishment), material inequalities and social tensions slowly began to rise again throughout the region. For a decade, however, using an admixture of socialist and nationalist appeals, Milošević was able to engineer a coalition of class elements—a kind of "class amalgam" in support of his regime. This internally contradictory interclass coalition consisted of parts of the former Communist nomenklatura and the depleted middle class—the members of which had turned away from socialist ideology in favor of private interests, privileges, and material interests—and the bulk of the lower strata who were mobilized behind the ideas of collectivist-populist nationalism and egalitarianism.[7]

The pattern of elite reproduction and blocked transformation of Croatia and Serbia during the first decade after one-party rule (1990–2000)—along with warfare, obstacles to reform, and other serious difficulties facing the states of the region during the same period—gave observers good reason to conclude that the link between economic

7. Mladen Lazić, "Postsocjalistička transformacija u Srbiji," *Danas,* October 14, 2010.

growth, elite change, and democratization had been derailed in the Western Balkans.[8] Moreover, excessive intervention by the state in the economy, and various distortions in the privatization process, had also considerably slowed the growth of independent middle classes through-out the regions. The continuity of a striking gap between elites and nonelites in the postcommunist Western Balkans, the material inequali-ties in society, and the fundamentally antimodernizing and illiberal features of important segments in the elite structures throughout the region made it very difficult for the countries of the Western Balkans to advance toward greater prosperity and democracy, not to mention catching up with the rest of Europe.

Yet despite such regionwide problems during the 1990s, it would be incorrect to conclude that the Communist-era middle classes—includ-ing the substantial subgroups of specialists and professional person-nel that had been produced during the period of one-party controlled modernization—had somehow been completely extinguished in the Western Balkan states. Clearly, the relative socioeconomic position of the middle classes had sharply deteriorated during the transition of the 1990s, and they had lost most of their former political influence. But middle-class elements, especially in the larger Western Balkan states, still retained a preferential niche in the social hierarchy and a good deal of potential strength. The region's emergent middle classes had been "impoverished" and reduced by the events of the 1990s, but they still remained on the social landscape. For example, in Serbia, Lazić has persuasively demonstrated that members of the middle strata retained "a significantly higher living standard in the 1990s in comparison to low social strata."[9] This was particularly a result, he argues, of their better living conditions, greater savings, and regular pay, but also a conse-quence of the fact that during the period of economic sanctions against the country the middle strata relied upon the gray economy, which rep-resented approximately 40 to 45 percent of the economic structures. Just as during the pre-1990 Communist period, the surviving middle class of the Milošević period after 1990 remained highly dependent on

8. Will Bartlett, "Economic Transformation and Democratization in the Balkans," in *Experimenting with Democracy: Regime Change in the Balkans,* edited by Geoffrey Pridham and Tom Gallagher (London: Routledge, 2000), 133.

9. Mladen Lazić, *Promene i otpori: Srbija u transformacijskim procesima* (Belgrade: Filip Višnjić, 2005), 136.

the state, and they thus lacked a firm basis for playing a substantial or independent role in political life.

But research indicates that during Milošević's illiberal rule, segments of the middle strata continued to embrace and express prodemocratic values and "openness toward the world." For Lazić, the most important illustrations of the persistent underlying potential of the middle class in Serbia during the 1990s was its "overt rebellion" against the Milošević regime during the winter of 1996 and 1997, and the later electoral and "street revolution" that brought down the regime in September and October 2000. In fact, Serbia's antiregime counter-elites, largely drawn from the urban educated middle sectors of the class system (particularly those involved in nongovernmental organizations), played a critical leadership role in both manifestations of antiregime popular mobilization.[10] For Croatia, perhaps the best analogies to the Serbian case are the fall 1996 street demonstrations in Zagreb, where protesters marched against the closure of the prodemocratic Radio 101, and the 2000 electoral results, where voters rejected the former ruling HDZ party following Tudjman's death at the end of 1999. The Croatian demonstrations and the subsequent vote against the ruling party occurred, of course, with far less drama and extra-institutional public protest than the case of Serbia. But as in Serbia, it was the more urban and educated activists from the middle strata that played the key role in ending quasi-authoritarian rule in Croatia. Middle-class weakness in both countries did not prevent a breakthrough toward democracy, although the changes that occurred could not be considered irreversible. Indeed, both democratic breakthroughs took place only a decade after severe economic setbacks and turbulence in the region seemed to have destroyed any prospect of steady middle-class advancement toward democratic rule.

In both Tudjman's Croatia and Milošević's Serbia at the end of the 1990s and early post-2000 period, the divide between the governing regime elites and the antiregime elites, and also the division between

10. Mladen Lazić, ed., *Protest in Belgrade: Winter of Discontent* (Budapest: Central European University Press, 1999). Lazić and Vladimir Vuletić recently observed that the Milošević regime was removed "by a combination of a middle class movement, the finally united opposition parties, and the new economic elite, with pressures from the USA and EU." Mladen Lazić and Vladimir Vuletić, "The Nation State and the EU in the Perceptions of Political and Economic Elites: The Case of Serbia in Comparative Perspective," *Europe-Asia Studies,* August 2009, 988.

the elite on one side and the lower social strata on the other, were the most salient cleavages in the social structure. Ethnically, elites in both these states were quite homogeneous, with representatives from the minority groups holding only a negligible portion of the top-level positions. The elite configuration in Montenegro was much the same, and also occurred in the context of a high level of ethnic homogeneity in the ruling apparatus, even after the break with Milošević near the end of the 1990s. Deep political elite and party divisions also fragmented Albania's substantially monoethnic elite throughout the 1990s (along with some aspects of regional and clan differentiation). Each of the two major party elites in Albania was also closely linked to public and private economic leaders in a kind of power-business/business-power symbiosis that dominated political and economic decisionmaking.[11] The schism within the divided Albanian elite only increased the obstacles to economic development and democracy already caused by the alienation and social differentiation of the population from the elite as a whole. As a local resident cynically told a visiting analyst to Albania in 2003, "The rich in Albania are now 10 percent—they speak over mobile phones, while the rest of the people talk to themselves."

Bosnia, Macedonia, and Kosovo (which was a province closely controlled by Serbia until 1999 and did not become a state until 2008) were riven not only by deep programmatic political divisions among contending political party elites, and by the elite mass cleavages typically found in the region, but also by very deep and persistent ethnocultural cleavages. For example, the postcommunist ethnopolitical polarization of communities in Bosnia, nurtured by domestic power-seeking elites who were encouraged by outside forces in Serbia and Croatia, eventually precipitated the state's collapse and descent into intense warfare. But even after hostilities ended in late 1995, the provisions of the peace accord did not facilitate an elite consensus among the three major ethnic communities.

Meanwhile in Kosovo, throughout the 1990s parallel Serbian and Albanian elites became ensconced and were unable to overcome their mutual hostility. When party and other elite-level cleavages on the Albanian side in Kosovo finally led to a fundamental change in strategy by segments of the province's independence-seeking Albanian activists, the stage was set for interethnic violence and the NATO war of 1999 (pronounced intra-Albanian elite cleavages would persist even after the establishment of a UN protectorate).

In the case of Macedonia, deep elite divisions between Slavic Macedonians and the state's Albanian party leaders also impeded progress in state building and eventually contributed to open violence in 2001. Both ethnic contingents in Macedonia's elite structure—each of which included the typical mixture of rival legal and illegal sub-elites—operated independently of any serious accountability to the rest of the population, and particularly to the very large lower class working in industry and agriculture. And, as elsewhere in the region, Macedonia experienced a contraction in the size and strength of its middle class. One Macedonian analyst observed in this regard that processes "completely different from the one [the American sociologist] Seymour Martin Lipset was talking about for a rich society occurred in the country. The social pyramid in Macedonia has not turned into a rhombus [i.e., diamond]. But rather the opposite has happened; the rhombus [has] turned into a pyramid with a big base."[12]

The deep ethnic divisions and eventual conflicts in Bosnia, Kosovo, and Macedonia during the period from 1992 to 2001 not only helped to weaken the influence of reformist leadership elements but also assisted corrupt rent-seeking elites (war profiteers, military commanders, and many politicians) in greatly profiting from the general breakdown of stability in the region. The successive conflicts in the three cases opened an economic niche for networks engaged in smuggling and money laundering (on all sides of the ethnic fault lines in these societies), which contributed to the criminalization of the emerging postcommunist elite structure of those states and those of their neighbors. For example, the astute Sarajevo-based analyst Zdravko Grebo has observed that while the process of elite formation took years to unfold in most postcommunist countries, the same development occurred almost overnight in Bosnia, thereby permitting relatively new elite actors to convert criminal capital amassed on a large scale in the war into political capital.[13]

12. Lidija Hristova, "Trade Unions as Political Actors," in *Reframing Social Policy: Actors, Dimensions, and Reforms,* edited by Gerovska Mitev (Skopje: Friedrich Ebert Stiftung, 2007), 230.

13. Peter Andreas, "The Clandestine Political Economy of War and Peace in Bosnia," *International Studies Quarterly,* 48, no. 1 (July 2004): 29–52.

The linkage that was forged during the war among prewar nationalist politicians (including many former Communists), military leaders, and newer criminal elites would exercise a strong grip on Bosnia's politics during the fifteen years following the 1995 Dayton Peace Accords.[14]

Postconflict Social Transformation

The transitional economic disruption and warfare of the 1990s, and the economic difficulties of its immediate aftermath, provided a welcoming environment for the corrupt and nationalistically oriented sub-elites who had helped to spawn the Western Balkan conflicts in the first place. But a discernible new stage of elite and class development in the region would emerge following the 1999 war in Kosovo (and in Macedonia after the 2001 interethnic fighting), a development facilitated by the more robust involvement of the international community in the region and the end of quasi-authoritarian regimes in Croatia and Serbia. The legacy of the 1990s, including the continued influence of rent-seeking elites and other old nomenklatura, would continue to burden Western Balkan societies for some time. But after the period 1999–2001, a more pacific and benign political climate, along with serious efforts to fight corruption and residual destabilizing influences, encouraged the acceleration of several important political, social, and economic factors, which together had a transformative impact on elite and class development.

Collectively, these trends would influence the course of modernization and democratization in the Western Balkan states. Two factors were particularly important in elite and class change during the post-2000 period: (1) the growing size of the entrepreneurial class that was associated with the expansion of both the private sector and small and medium-sized enterprises (the SMEs discussed in chapter 1), and (2) the enhanced profile of highly educated professionals and experts within both the technical and humanistic intelligentsia (including highly skilled individuals directly involved in political and governmental activity). The features and combination of these two factors varied among the Western Balkan polities, but they both became increasingly

14. Nerzuk Curak, Djordje Cekrlija, Eldar Sarajlić, and Sead Turcalo, *Politička elita u Bosni i Hercegovini i Evropska Unija: Odons Vrijednosti* (Sarajevo: Institut za Društvena istraživanja, 2009).

important as the region entered a new and more normalized phase of postcommunist development. The post-2000 period would therefore be significantly different from the preceding decade, but the differences unfolded gradually through externally assisted incremental change rather than a radical acceleration in elite and class transformation.

The destabilization of the Western Balkans during the mid-1990s had disrupted a process of private sector development and economic elite formation that had begun quite slowly and chaotically following the breakdown of the socialist economic structures and the transitional shocks in the early period after 1989. Thus, a "new" private entrepreneurial class had started to emerge throughout the region during the 1990s, but its ability to operate in a modernizing and reformist manner was limited by the presence of so many old nomenklatura and criminal elements in the elite structure, and also as a result of the only partially democratic context within which economic leadership operated. For example, as Mladen Lazić has remarked, regarding Serbia's private entrepreneurial elite at the time, that the circumstances in which it was forged "made it a conservative rather than transforming social force" or essentially a "new anti-modernizing elite."[15]

Still, during the 1990s the rudimentary entrepreneurial activities and sentiments of nonstate managers and owners had, at least to a limited extent, formed a nucleus of a private-oriented middle class, and had helped to alleviate the socially destabilizing effects of the economic deterioration found throughout most the region. But as the Western Balkans entered the second decade of postcommunist development after 1999, local observers, not without good reason, were rarely optimistic about future elite prospects and continued the long tradition of identifying elite actors as the primary culprits in the region's retarded modernization.[16]

However, after 2000, as gradually increasing privatization and SME development accelerated, the size of the private sector grew considerably, as did the influence of newer economic and managerial elites.

---

15. Mladen Lazić, "Old and New Elites in Serbia," in *Serbia between the Past and Future,* edited by Dušan Janjić (Belgrade: Forum for Ethnic Relations, Institute of Social Sciences, 1995), 49.

16. See, e.g., Drago Čengić and Ivan Rogić, eds., *Upravljačke elite i modernizacija* (Zagreb: Institut društevenih znanosti: Ivo Pilar, 2001); and Latinka Perović, *Srbija u modernizacijskim procesima 19 i 20 veka: Uloga elita* (Belgrade: Cigoja Stampa, 2003).

For example, after Serbia and Croatia initially became partially "de-blocked" with the opening of the post-Tudjman and post-Milošević periods, there was renewed momentum in both states' privatization processes, and in SME development. Those employed in the Serbian private sector, for example, had grown from 2.4 percent of the labor force in 1990 to 14.4 percent in 2000.[17] But after new privatization legislation was adopted in 2001, there was a spurt of private-sector activity in an economy that had been badly stalled. And although most of Serbia's labor force remained largely in state-owned or socially owned firms, the number of private entrepreneurs and persons independently employed, and those working for such employers, grew from 17 percent of the labor force outside agriculture in 2001 to 23 percent in 2004 and 28 percent by 2007 (i.e., from 349,000 to 569,000).[18]

Meanwhile, in Croatia the number of those employed in SMEs grew from nearly 404,000 in 2003 to more than 591,000 in 2007. Nearly 84,000 individuals were classified as entrepreneurs in 2007, of which roughly 82,000 were in SMEs employing fewer than 10 workers. And although the number and growth rate of active SMEs in relation to the size of the population were substantially lower than in most of the new EU member states, it is the overall trend and direction of SME development that is most important in comparison with the prior socialist and early postsocialist periods. For example, in Macedonia the number of SMEs increased from 9,703 in 1991 to more than 33,000 in 2001 and to approximately 44,000 by 2005.[19]

In Macedonia, as in Kosovo, nearly all active firms were small or microenterprises. Additionally, Macedonia had a total of only 340 large enterprises in 2005, while Kosovo's SME sector increased particularly quickly in the post-1999 period, from 27,000 at the end of 2003 to nearly 56,000 in 2006. Small business and entrepreneurial development had

17. Silvano Bolčić, *Blocked Transition and Post-Socialist Transformation: Serbia in the 90s,* William Davidson Working Paper 6 (Ann Arbor: William Davidson Institute, University of Michigan, 2003). See also Silvano Bolčić, "Preduzetnica i preduzetničke firme u Srbije 1992–1996 godina: Ima li značajnih promena?" in *Društvo rizika: promene, nejednakosti i socijalni problemi u današnjoj Srbiji,* edited by Sreten Vujović (Belgrade: Institut za sociološka istraživanja, 2008), 73–106.

18. *Privredna Komora Beograda,* 2007.

19. GFA Consulting Group, *Small Enterprise Development in the Former Yugoslav Republic of Macedonia: An Overview* (Hamburg: GFA Consulting Group, 2007).

been quite vibrant in Kosovo before 1999—that is, within the Kosovo Albanians' parallel reality under the Milošević regime—but the end of Serbian control created the potential for the protectorate's Albanian middle class to become more robust, notwithstanding that it was still badly traumatized by the 1999 war. But at the end of 2006, there were only 35 large enterprises in Kosovo—that is, those employing more than 250 workers—out of a total of 55,884 registered companies.[20]

Clearly, the Western Balkan private and SME sectors after 2000 remained quite weak compared with Central and Eastern Europe and with the EU member states. And the obstacles to faster business start-ups (for procedures and cost of business registration, etc., see chapter 8) were still considerable. Additionally, in some countries corruption, unfair competition (especially from the informal sectors of the economy), a lack of financial resources, and unstable legal systems have impeded more rapid SME development.[21] Such problems also limited the role of the private sector and SMEs in job creation, which was urgently needed to reduce high unemployment and the continuing struggle against poverty in every state.

But notwithstanding these serious problems, the steady expansion of the private and SME sectors assisted, to a limited extent, in creating a larger middle class throughout the Western Balkans, which at least potentially can serve as a strong underpinning for at least resumed economic growth, democratic politics, and EU reforms. It is no surprise in these circumstances that EU efforts to assist the Western Balkans in recent years have placed considerable emphasis on entrepreneurship and SME development.

Owing to problems of data collection and comparability, it is difficult to form an accurate picture of the similarity and differences in private-sector and entrepreneurial development from one society to another in the Western Balkans. But the available evidence regarding private employment indicates certain instructive patterns and trends. For example, the secondary analysis of data from the World Bank's impressive Life in Transition study has examined the employment history of the labor force in Western Balkan societies. The study shows the substantial flow of individuals from the state/social sector into the

20. Kosova Chamber of Commerce, 2006.

21. Biljana Ačevska, "Entrepreneurship under Difficult Circumstances: Factors Hindering SME Growth in the Republic of Macedonia," *SEER–South East Europe Review for Labor and Social Affairs,* no. 1 (2002): 109–21.

private and self-employed sectors between 1990 and 2006, a trend that was particularly marked for Croatia.[22]

Indeed, by 2001, private employment exceeded state employment in the whole region, although Bosnia, Macedonia, Montenegro, and, as already noted, Serbia have been latecomers in this movement from one sector to another. The study also indicates that there was a more pronounced shift to private-sector employment during the initial stage of the transition process, which was subsequently followed by a flow of many workers from the private sector to self-employment. Significantly, during the post-2000 period, the critical shift in the labor force is cross-sectoral—that is, from state employment to private and self-employment—rather than any massive upward mobility from one income level to another.

Comparative data on SME development also indicate some interesting differences among the states in the region. Thus, Kosovo, Macedonia, Croatia, and Albania are regional front-runners in the density of SMEs per thousand population during the post-2000 period.[23] But in Albania—an early leader in privatization and SME formation—the rapid growth of the population gradually overtook the speed of business development (although by 2005, 81 percent of those employed were already working in the private sector. Trend data are not available for Kosovo, which also has a very high birthrate). And though, in recent years, Serbia has steadily increased its SME sector in absolute numbers, with the most growth in SMEs, it ran considerably behind its neighbor in SMEs per capita (mainly because of a long period of stalled reform and interparty deadlocks). The development of SMEs has also lagged in Bosnia, which reveals the lowest rate of SMEs per capita in the early post-2000 period. Indeed in 2005, the participation of the SME sector in Bosnia's total gross national product was just 36 percent compared with 40 percent in Albania, 56 percent in Croatia, 47 percent for Serbia and Montenegro, and 42 percent for Macedonia.[24]

22. Irina Denisova, Markus Eller, and Ekaterina Zhurnavskaya, *Labor Market Flows in Transition* (Moscow: Center for Economic and Financial Research at New Economic School, 2007).

23. Organization for Economic Cooperation and Development, *SME Policy Index 2007: Report on the Implementation of the European Charter for Small Enterprises in the Western Balkans* (Paris: Organization for Economic Cooperation and Development, 2007), 37.

24. Ibid.

Bosnia's ethnopolitically divided politics continues to be an important cause of its slow reform. Overall, however, up until the 2008 economic downturn, the Western Balkan region exhibited considerable momentum in small business development.

One additional indicator of emerging entrepreneurial spirit associated with this trend can be found in data regarding occupational choice preferences by young people during 2002 and 2003.[25] Thus, the choice of becoming a businessman or businesswoman ranks first of several choices when young people are asked to rank their preferences for a career. The very high preferences expressed for a business career among young people in Kosovo, and the Republika Srpska in Bosnia, may result from the lack of opportunities in those regions compared with the preceding decade. A very large number of respondents surveyed in Kosovo in 2004 and 2005 also indicated a general interest in business as a preferred sector of activity. This was also the case among Macedonian young people. Meanwhile, adults as a group in Serbia appeared far less enamored with business as an endeavor than young people in that society.

Such data on career preferences may be of considerable importance to levels of economic development in the Western Balkans. But the findings do suggest that the earlier antibusiness mindset in the region—which can be traced to both a heritage of collectivism and egalitarianism, later reinforced by socialist ideology—is probably slowly eroding.[26] Possibilities for entrepreneurial activity and perceptions of that activity would be negatively affected by the global economic crisis that began in 2008, and the states that had trailed behind in better years, such as Bosnia, suffered the most.[27]

The increasing number and role of highly trained professionals, or what might be termed "intelligentsia elites," and technical experts, have

25. Dragan Popadić, Jovan Savić, and Strahinja Dimitrijević, *Regional Research on Young People* (Belgrade: KIZ and Altera, 2005); Vedrana Spajić-Vrkaš and Vlasta Ilišin, *Youth in Croatia* (Zagreb: University of Zagreb, 2005).

26. Dragomir Pantić, "Interesovanje gradjana Srbije i Crne Gore za Biznis," in *Biznis i Država* (Belgrade: Institute of Social Sciences, 2006), 263–73.

27. See, e.g., *GEM BiH 2009, Recesija reducirala poduzetničku aktivnost u BiH* (Tuzla: Entrepreneurship Development Center, 2009). At the same time, perceptions of the positive status of entrepreneurship and views about it being a desirable career remained quite high in Bosnia. See also *Preduzetnici u očima Srpske javnosti* (Belgrade: Vreme, 2010).

also been an important feature of Western Balkan social development. Indeed, a glance at the occupational structure of the region's workforce in recent years can provide insights into the underpinning of the emerging middle class. Because occupational status is so closely correlated with income, such information can help to assess the relative size of the middle class. In comparative terms, managerial personnel and intelligentsia elites, together with a less-well-educated stratum of technical employees, constitute roughly from one-fifth to one-quarter of those employed (table 6.1) in most countries.

Moreover, if intelligentsia elites and technicians are considered together with a thin top stratum of higher political and managerial personnel in these states (roughly from 3 to 7 percent of the employed population), one can identify an upper and middle tier of the social pyramid constituting approximately one-fifth to one-third of the employed population in each Western Balkan country. Those political/managerial personnel, intelligentsia elites, and technicians are situated above a relatively thin less-educated and well-paid stratum of service employees and also the working-class segments of the population (both the agricultural and nonagricultural sectors), which constitute the remaining components of the employed population (45 to 55 percent in most states). Apparent anomalies, such as the fact that Kosovo appears to have a relatively large specialized elite, derived from the new state's broad mode of classification regarding "experts" and the fact a very large segment of the population falls outside the employment structure. In addition, the data do not include persons who are unemployed, inactive, working in the gray economy, or engaged in criminal structures. Such categories of the population are not included in table 6.1 or in labor studies, but they can nevertheless have an important influence on the society (as in the case of criminal elements on corruption and political party life).

Overall cross-country variations in the occupational structure of the employed labor forces in individual Balkan states are not that extensive, and they are usually accounted for by the evolving size and peculiarities of various economic sectors from state to state, or differences in the statistical classification of the workforce. For example, in Montenegro the service sector makes a very large contribution to the country's gross domestic product (GDP) (about 69.4 percent in 2007, mainly in tourism) and to the number of all workers employed in activities related to

Table 6.1. Occupational Composition of the Employed Workforce, about 2008 (percent 15–64 years of age)

Occupations	Macedonia, 2008	Kosovo, 2007	Montenegro, 2009	Serbia, 2009	Croatia, 2008	Bosnia, 2008	Albania, 2008
Legislators, higher officials, managers	6.5	7.3	7.1	5.6	5.3	3.0	4.1
Professionals/experts	8.9	13.8	11.3	11.5	9.9	8.7	8.9
Technicians/associated professionals	10.0	9.7	16.2	14.1	15.0	9.2	5.7
Employees/clerks	6.8	6.3	11.0	6.0	11.8	6.9	1.9
Service workers/ shopkeepers	14.1	20.4	22.9	12.9	14.4	16.6	9.9
Agricultural workers, forestry, fisheries, basic occupations	26.4	22.2	13.2	29.5	19.5	28.0	53.2
Craftsmen and trade workers	12.1	14.4	9.9	12.8	13.5	17.6	10.6
Plant and machine operators	13.9	5.7	8.1	7.3	10.2	9.1	5.1
Military	1.2	—	—	0.3	0.5	0.8	0.6
Total	100.0	100.0	100.0	100.0	100.0	100.0	100.0
Number	609,015	371,490	213,600	2,590,188	1,605,300	890,239	1,122,989

Source: National Labor Force Surveys, reconfigured by authors.

this sector (about three-quarters of the labor force, which is even higher than in the current twenty-seven members of the European Union—hereafter, the EU-27—or 67.1 percent in 2007).

Indeed, it is also important to bear in mind, if viewed in longitudinal terms (which is not possible for occupational data), that there have also been considerable changes in the economic activities of the workforce in each Western Balkan country. For example, as the data in table 6.2 illustrate, during the last two decades there have been some important changes in the contribution of different economic sectors to total GDP in each country, although the region's sectoral profile still differs from the rest of the "European family." Almost all the states in the region have undergone an expansion of their service sectors and a contraction of agriculture, although at different rates. Leaving aside the cases of Albania and Kosovo, the economic sectors of the five other Western Balkan states are roughly the same size. Croatia's service sector was already quite sizable in the early 1990s and has remained about the same size. Economic transformation has been most striking in Albania and Kosovo. In 2007, for example, Albania's service sector contributed 59 percent of GDP as opposed to 16 percent in the early 1990s, while the agricultural sector in the same period had been halved from 40 to 21 percent, and industry from 44 to 20 percent. Thus, while some 59 percent of those employed in Albania worked in agricultural activities in 2006, that sector only contributed approximately one-fifth of the country's overall GDP. The sectoral changes in Kosovo were very similar to Albania, although when the postcommunist transition took off after mid-1999, the contribution of the service sector was quite a bit higher in Kosovo.

However, the Western Balkans remain significantly behind the EU in terms of an "optimal economic structure" for a modern European state. In 2007, Croatia's agricultural sector (at 7.2 percent of GDP) came closest to the EU-27 average levels of 2.1 percent, and Albania was at the other extreme (at 21.4 percent).[28] The shift from one sector to another in the Western Balkans has depended, of course, on changing conditions of political stability, evolving economic policies during

28. Zoran Arandjelović, Vladislav Marjanović, and Dejan Djordjević, "The Change of Economic Structure of Balkan Countries as a Condition for Integration in European Union," conference paper presented at the University of Niš, Faculty of Economics, May 18, 2007.

Table 6.2. Economic Structure of the Western Balkan States by Contribution to Gross Domestic Product, Early 1990s Transition and 2007

Country or Group	Agriculture		Industry		Services	
	Early 1990s	2007	Early 1990s	2007	Early 1990s	2007
Albania	40	21.4	44	20.0	16	58.6
Bosnia	14	9.8	25	21.6	59	68.6
Croatia	13	7.2	34	31.6	63	61.3
Macedonia	17	12.0	42	29.5	41	58.5
Serbia	17[a]	13.0	28[a]	28.4	55[a]	58.6
Montenegro		19.5		20.0		69.4
Kosovo[b]	31.3	20.0	35.3	20.0	32.4	60.0
EU-27, 2006	—	2.1	—	27.1	—	70.7

Note: EU-27 = EU with the current twenty-seven members.
[a]Early 1990s data are for Serbia/Montenegro.
[b]Kosovo data for 1990s are from 1995.
Sources: Encarta, US Central Intelligence Agency.

the last two decades, and the level of violence and disruption within each society. But all countries in the region have undergone significant decrease in the contribution of agriculture to GDP, and also, Croatia and Serbia aside, a reduced role for industry while gradually increasing the size of their service sectors.

Moreover, if such changes are considered over a longer historical period, they are even more striking. For example, the contribution of agriculture to GDP in Kosovo dropped from 83.8 percent in 1947 and 64 percent in 1961 to approximately 20 percent in 2007. Such sharp changes in the economic dynamics of the Western Balkan states during a relatively short time span—especially when taken together with other elements of political disruption—have had enormous socioeconomic consequences because of job destruction, unemployment, and the internal movements of affected populations. The formation of the region's emerging class divisions and elite development must be viewed against the background of such major forces affecting social readjustment and societal cohesion. What is most important for the discussion in this chapter, however, is that there has been a discernible, albeit quite gradual, development of economic activity and occupations, which can over time provide a basis for the kind of robust middle class that can potentially assist further economic and democratic development.

Brain Drain and the Challenges of Educational Development

In the post-2000 period, the Western Balkan states have clearly undergone a reconfiguration in the size of their private sectors, the contribution made by nonagricultural branches of economic activity, and the expansion of entrepreneurial and professional activities. In light of these changes, it seems fair to ask why sociopolitical change in these countries and others has not been more rapid. A number of factors must be considered, some of which have continued to retard the region during the most recent phase of economic transformation, elite formation, and democracy building. For example, two major problems throughout the region have been brain drain and deficiencies in educational development.

Out-Migration and Overcoming Isolation

Throughout the postcommunist period, all the Western Balkan states have suffered from a substantial loss of talent caused by the out-migration of professionals and skilled workers from the region. Successive migratory waves of highly skilled personnel leaving several Balkan states beginning in the early 1990s—particularly from Albania, Kosovo, Serbia, Bosnia, and Macedonia—have made it difficult for those states to muster the necessary human capital to meet the challenges of economic progress and democratization.

Of course, this problem was not entirely a new one. Emigration in search of better opportunities has certainly been a historical tradition in Southeastern Europe, and it has included an outflow of hundreds of thousands of "temporary workers" from the former Yugoslavia to Western Europe during the 1960s, 1970s, and 1980s (the majority leaving permanently). But the wars associated with Yugoslavia's breakup, and the chaos in Albania in the second part of the 1990s, precipitated a new wave of emigration. Moreover, the well-known brain drain phenomenon not only resulted in personal trauma for those forced or motivated to leave their societies in search of better prospects but also weakened the capacity of societies to nurture and stabilize the broader elite and class formation needed for economic development and an active civil society. In many cases, changing economic circumstances and job destruction have also led to "brain-waste," that is, when highly qualified specialists seek more profitable jobs in the private or informal sectors of the economy that are not directly connected with their area of expertise.

For example, during the period from 1990 to 2003, an estimated 25 percent of Albania's population, or 35 percent of the labor force, left the country.[29] In Albania, emigration or internal migration of elite-level personnel, especially intellectuals, professional, and businesspeople, deprived the country of thousands of qualified specialists who had been trained locally and abroad during the Communist period. It is estimated that more than 50 percent of Albania's university lecturers and research workers went abroad between 1991 and 2005.[30] And the internal migration of specialists from smaller towns to more developed urban areas also unbalanced the pattern of regional development. Moreover, during the 1990s, most graduates who left their country for additional training never returned to Albania. The massive out-migration and displacement of Bosnia's war-ravaged population between 1992 and 1995 as a result of the warfare had especially severe consequences. Thus, a large segment of Bosnia's university and research elite left the country, were no longer able to pursue their careers, and in some cases were killed in the fighting and ethnic cleansing. Brain drain continued in the postwar period. It is estimated that in the decade after 1995, 79 percent of research engineers, 81 percent of master's degree holders in science, and 75 percent of PhD graduates in science left Bosnia (in May 2010, Bosnia's minister of human rights and refugees reported in Sarajevo that 1.3 million persons of Bosnian descent currently live abroad).[31] A large share of the populations from all the Western Balkan countries live abroad.

In 2002, Serbia's minister for science estimated that 40 to 50 percent of the best scientists and up to 70 percent of new graduates had left

29. Mirela Bogdani and John Loughlin, *Albania and the European Union* (London: I. B. Tauris, 2007), 84.

30. United Nations Development Program, *From Brain Drain to Brain Gain: Mobilising Albania's Skilled Diaspora* (Tirana: United Nations Development Program, 2006), 6–7.

31. "Southeast Europe Turns 'Brain Drain' into 'Gain,'" *SETimes,* June 25, 2007; *Srna,* May 21, 2010. For Bosnia and Albania, the number of expatriates is estimated as equal to approximately one-third of the respective resident populations. The equivalent figures are between 9 and 15 percent for Croatia, Macedonia, Serbia, and Montenegro. Marcel Kopiszewski, ed., *Labor Migration Patterns, Policies and Migration Propensity in the Western Balkans* (Warsaw: Central European Forum for Migration and Population Research, 2009), 104.

the country.[32] The emigrants from Serbia with a university degree—both during and after the Milošević regime—account for the very large contingent of educated and qualified personnel in the Serbian Diaspora, especially in the United States and Europe. It has been estimated that during the 1990–2000 period, 73,000 people emigrated from Serbia and Montenegro, of whom 17,000 or 23 percent were highly educated.[33]

At the end of 2004, the Belgrade sociologist Srećko Mihajlović observed that the inability of young people to fulfill their "desires"—specialization, career advancement, a decent life, security, and so on—had created a second post-1990s generation of young people "waiting to graduate and emigrate."[34] In Serbia and Bosnia, difficulties in carrying out political reform, and also in relating more effectively to the EU accession process, have seriously compounded the state's ability to slow the younger generation's desire to seek a better life abroad. And in most countries of the Western Balkans, many of those hoping to get ahead are simply fed up with the slow pace of change and the continued politicization of institutions and the economy. For example, a recent study concluded that Albania's leaders had made little effort to prevent highly qualified young people from leaving, or to attract them back home: "The reality is that Albania's leaders seem more comfortable governing a country from which the smartest, most educated, civilized, and skilled citizens leave every day. . . . A country like Albania where advancement and progress depends on political affiliation rather than meritocracy will lose bright people to societies and countries where talent and 'brain' is appreciated."[35] In Macedonia, analysts estimate that in the decade before 2003, between 12,000 and 15,000 educated and highly skilled workers left the country, and that in 2003, 85 percent of the younger generation planned or wished to emigrate after the completion of their studies.[36]

If, as many analysts have observed, economic development and democratization are in large part an "elite-crafted" dimension of change

32. Yoanna Dumanova, *South-east Europe Review,* no. 4 (2003): 24–25.
33. Vladimir Grećić, "The Role of Migrant Professional in the Process of Transition in Yugoslavia," *International Problems,* 2002, 3.
34. *Večernje novosti,* December 29, 2004.
35. Bogdani and Loughlin, *Albania.*
36. Cited by Vedran Horvat, "Brain Drain: Threat to Successful Transition in Southeast Europe?" *Southeast European Politics* V, no. 1 (June 2004): 84.

of societies, then the Western Balkans have paid very heavily for the outflow of its intellectual capital on such a large scale. Advances, inertia, and setbacks in reform are inextricably linked to the availability or absence of competent and forward-looking political, economic, and professional elites. Expatriate elites and the diasporas can also play a key role in the reforms of their countries of origin. But the "brain circulation" of such talents and skills by those who have gone abroad requires the existence of a critical mass of reform-oriented elites back home who are also willing to recognize and use expatriate skills. For whatever reasons, the numbers returning to the Western Balkans have been too few to help significantly.

Surveys of economic executives interviewed in the Western Balkans during 2007 and 2008 indicated that the brain drain of talented people to pursue opportunities in other countries continues to be a serious problem affecting economic activity, particularly in Serbia, Macedonia, Bosnia, and Albania. Studies of Western Balkan brain drain have also observed that many students often enter their home universities with the specific intention of using local training as a stepping-stone to later employment abroad. Indeed, the adverse circumstances of economic life and political instability in the Western Balkan region have exacerbated a "culture of flight" that has often been reinforced by the weaknesses of local educational institutions. Thus, the issues of reversing brain drain, the quality of local higher educational institutions, and the broader issues of economic prosperity, political stability, and middle-class development are all closely linked.

Data from Gallup surveys concerning the attitudes of Western Balkan citizens toward travel and migration indicate that the majority of respondents perceive better prospects abroad than in their own countries.[37] Nearly three-quarters of those surveyed in Kosovo, for example, felt that way, as did roughly two-thirds of respondents in Albania and more than half of those polled in Bosnia and Macedonia. Only in Croatia (53 percent) and Montenegro (43 percent) did respondents view opportunities as better in their own countries than abroad. But, except for Albania, a majority of respondents in each state preferred to stay in their own country if they had a choice. Croats were the most inclined to avoid emigration, while in most countries about one-

37. Gallup Balkan Monitor, *Focus on the Impact of Migration* (Brussels: Gallup Balkan Monitor, 2009).

fifth preferred to go abroad. And except for Bosnia and Montenegro, a majority of those who said they would like to move abroad also claimed that they would like to return home one day.

The evidence suggests that the pretext for the continued out-migration from the Western Balkans still exists, mainly prompted by the perception that local conditions are unsatisfactory. Granted, levels of preference for going abroad appeared to drop from 2006 to 2008 for all the countries in the region, but in the same period there was increased dissatisfaction with the situation by citizens in every country except newly independent Montenegro and Kosovo. Such dissatisfaction appeared to increase as a result of the global economic recession that began in 2008. For example, a 2010 survey of students at the University of Belgrade conducted to "determine the outlook of the future social elite" revealed that more than two-thirds of students contemplated leaving Serbia after graduation.[38] Indeed, when asked what "single biggest assistance" the international community could provide to their country, roughly one-third of respondents in most countries chose travel and visa "liberalization." Albanian citizens (53 percent) and those in the Bosnian Federation (54 percent) expressed the most eagerness to travel freely, while least concern was expressed in Croatia (16 percent), a country that already enjoyed visa-free travel in 2009.

In the summer of 2009, the European Commission announced a plan for visa liberalization beginning in January 2010 for Serbia, Montenegro, and Macedonia. But citizens of Bosnia, Kosovo, and Albania were disappointed, particularly the Bosnian Muslim population, who felt that their country's Croat and Serbian citizens would benefit from their ability to travel by taking advantage of the better situation in neighboring Croatia and Serbia. Kosovo Albanians felt the same way about ethnic Serbs in Kosovo, who could potentially utilize Serbian passports. How the new provisions would affect the issue of brain drain would not be clear for some time. It may be significant that although young people in the region express the most desire to go abroad, those feelings drop somewhat for those having a higher education. But this feeling may reflect the fact that so many university professionals have already left the region.

---

38. *Nedeljni Telegraf,* May 20, 2010.

Human Capital and the Challenges of University Reform

In what has become a vicious circle, Western Balkan educational systems have not only been badly weakened by brain drain and brain waste from the region during the last decades, but the region's educational institutions have also failed to compensate for the outflow of human capital. As a consequence, Western Balkan countries have serious deficiencies when it comes to growing the resource base to facilitate faster economic development and democratization, that is, the creation of a substantial pool of well-educated professionals and specialists in the middle strata who can staff public and private institutions. Evidence of the problem can be seen in the region's low level of educational attainment compared with the EU states (table 6.3). Overall levels of tertiary educational completion naturally vary considerably within the region—with Kosovo, Albania, and Bosnia at the lowest end of the range. Only Serbia, Montenegro, Croatia, and Macedonia have proportional tertiary attainment rates that are close to the levels of the older states in the EU or to the newer member states.

Efforts to significantly improve higher educational development have been stymied owing both to the relatively low tertiary enrollment rates in the region and also to high dropout rates from higher educational institutions. Gross enrollment ratios in tertiary education—that is, the number of students enrolled at that educational level as a share of those theoretically eligible from that cohort in a country—are much lower in the Western Balkans than in the Central and Eastern European and EU member states. The figures are particularly low in Kosovo, Albania, Bosnia, and Macedonia, but still well below the EU states for Serbia and Croatia, the Western Balkan enrollment front-runners.[39] Low graduation rates and high dropout rates in the Western Balkan universities also contrast unfavorably with the countries that belong to the Organization for Economic Cooperation and Development and with

39. World Bank, *Kosovo Quarterly Economic Briefing (October–December 2007)* (Washington, D.C.: World Bank, 2007), 2. See also Toby Linden and Nina Arnold, *From Fragmentation to Cooperation: Tertiary Education Research and Development in South Eastern Europe* (Washington, D.C.: World Bank, June 2008); and Martina Vukasović, ed., *Financing Higher Education in South Eastern Europe: Albania, Croatia, Montenegro, Serbia, Slovenia* (Belgrade: Center for Education Policy, 2009), 73.

Table 6.3. Tertiary Educational Attainment Rate of the Population 25–64 Years of Age, Early 2000s (percent)

Country or Group	%
Albania, 2004	9
Bosnia-Herzegovina, 2004	10
Croatia, 2003	16
Kosovo, 2003	1
Macedonia, 2005	14
Serbia, 2005	17
Montenegro, 2005	17
EU-15 (old member states), 2002	22
EU-10 (new member states), 2002	15
Bulgaria, 2005	21
Romania, 2005	11

Source: Jean-Raymond Masson and Anastasia Fetsi, "Human Capital and Education Reforms in the Western Balkans," in *Labor Markets in the Western Balkans: Challenges for the Future,* edited by European Training Foundation (Turin: European Training Foundation, 2007), 73.

the Central and Eastern European countries, particularly in the cases of Bosnia, Albania, and Serbia. According to 2006–7 data from the Center for Educational Policy in Belgrade, only 16 percent of university students in Serbia pass each year of study with success, and roughly 40 percent of students in higher education never complete their studies.[40]

Such low levels of tertiary enrollment and university success have slowed the acquisition of skills for economic development, but they have also been an obstacle to the social inclusion of vulnerable groups in society, and the general social mobility of those strata that are denied the opportunity for higher education. Thus, though there is an absence of systematic empirical data, the evidence suggests that students who perform the best on university entrance examinations have enjoyed the opportunities to attend the best pre-tertiary schools. Moreover, there is also extensive anecdotal evidence regarding the widespread use of corrupt practices in entrance procedures for higher education in the Western Balkans, a situation that also favors more affluent families.[41]

40. Helsinki Committee for Human Rights in Serbia, *Helsinki Annual Report: Serbia 2007—Self Isolation: The Reality and Goal* (Belgrade: Helsinki Committee for Human Rights in Serbia, 2008), 339–42; and Biljana Čučković, "Serbian Students: Empowered or Disempowered?" *European Education* 38, no. 1 (Spring 2006).

41. Recent Serbian data have shown that university students are four times more likely to have parents with higher education than members of the general

Deficiencies in tertiary education enrolment and attainment have had a very detrimental impact on human capital accumulation in the Western Balkans. A comprehensive recent study of the problem concluded that the supply of a highly skilled labor force with tertiary qualifications to meet the region's need for higher educational skills is insufficient. Expenditures on tertiary institutions in the region are quite low compared with other countries in Europe, and the quality of higher education has not kept pace with recent European developments. The difficulties encountered in higher educational development in the Western Balkans derive both from policy failures and poor resources, and it is only in the last several years that the need for the Western Balkans to catch up with Europe has received systematic attention.

The participation of Western Balkan countries in the Bologna Process has at least created the potential for major improvement in the quality of teaching and learning. The Bologna Accords, first signed in 1999, endeavor to establish a European educational sphere that provides common degree standards and comparable quality assurance norms. The philosophy of the Bologna Process, though separate from the EU accession process, coincided with the aim of the EU's so-called Lisbon Agenda, which seeks to improve the competitiveness of Europe in innovation and with respect to the "knowledge economy." However, the important opportunities provided by the Bologna Process and other significant EU projects to assist educational development are still only in their early stages of development, and they have encountered many problems of implementation in the Western Balkan region. Unfortunately, more attention has been paid to the bureaucratic changes supporting the Bologna Process and not enough to curriculum redesign and actual teaching.

Each country in the Western Balkans has, of course, experienced its own unique problems in adopting and implementing Bologna Process goals. Inadequate expertise, weak preparedness, insufficient resources, and a lack of will have impeded implementation goals, along with bureaucratic resistance and the sheer politicization of the process. For example, in Serbia some of the resistance has resulted from excessive pride in established local institutions, and also from prejudice against foreign models of operation that are advocated by activists from non-

population. Martina Vukasović, "Visina školarina: Da li je naše visokoškolsko obrazovanje jednako dostupno mladima u Srbiji," July 7, 2008.

governmental organizations who seem to be bent on holding Milošević generation academics to account. The brain drain of younger university academics starting in the 1990s has also limited the number of persons who have embraced or understood modern university management.

But some reformists and forward-looking members of the university community view educational modernization as critical and adherence to Bologna guidelines as a "psychological boost" for a country that has become rather isolated from European trends. The Serbian educational specialist Srbijanka Turaljić put it well: "After 2000 surfacing from the nightmare of prolonged isolation we found ourselves in a deeply changed world. When we went into hibernation [in the 1990s] we left behind a world dominated by nation-states where education and culture were integral, with the coherent core of values. When we woke up the global economy, multiculturalism, consumerism, knowledge society, information and communication technologies, were the buzzwords."[42]

Innovative reforms have often, however, been accompanied by prolonged conflict over implementation. For example, in Serbia after the new 2005 Act on Higher Education gave university faculties more autonomy, the issue of avoiding a "disintegrated university" became a highly debated issue in the country's tertiary educational structure. The first years of Bologna implementation in Serbia (2003–8) therefore proceeded very slowly, unevenly, and contentiously. Thus, in 2008, a policy proposed by Belgrade University that would prohibit professors from working at private university faculties was rationalized as a way to improve the quality of teaching. Critics of the proposal argued, however, that the policy was misguided because quality could be maintained, if—as provided for by Bologna—students were asked to evaluate the work of professors. The problem, critics argued, that there was only lip service being paid to Bologna, but that the Bologna provisions were not actually being implemented. Thus, as Serbia continued to struggle to become "Bologna compliant," its educational system still confronted problems on many levels: underfunding, difficulties in the transfer and accumulation of course credits, resistance by professors to changing their teaching methods, and problems with standardizing the amount and nature of student work.[43]

42. "Institutional Approaches to Entrepreneurialism and the University of Belgrade," *Higher Education in Europe* 31, no. 2 (2006): 136.

43. Igor Jovanović, "Serbia, The Slow Pace of Change," *Transition On Line,* February 13, 2009.

Croatia has suffered no less from the internal difficulties that delayed educational reform in Serbia, but in recent years it has made considerable progress in the implementation of the Bologna procedures. The groundwork for the recent educational reforms in Croatia was, at least, laid in 2001–5 through legislative changes and a transformation of the curriculum. Thus, beginning in the 2005–6 academic year, a new phase of educational reform was able to focus on reforming university governance and management, teaching and learning, and internal quality assurance. Still, notwithstanding these advances, in May 2008 students across Croatia demonstrated against what they viewed as the government's poor track record of implementing the Bologna Accords. In particular, students were most concerned that new rules were being inconsistently applied and that the country's educational system continued to be a mixture of the new Bologna provisions and the "old system." Croatia still seemed to be suffering from what one student placard described as "Bologna à la Balkans."[44] Indeed, this description was quite apt for most Western Balkan states, which were either at the takeoff or transitional stages regarding the Europeanization of their higher educational institutions.

In Bosnia, for example, the challenges to the implementation of the Bologna goals and new practices have been especially daunting owing in large measure to the wrangling among different ethnic groups and territorial jurisdictions, a problem that blocked the adoption of higher education legislation until mid-2007. Bosnia's Serbs in particular objected to the creation of a national accreditation agency that would effectively link Bosnia's eight universities. Officials in the ten cantons of the Bosniak-Croat Federation, who have authority and financial control over education, were also resistant to any educational integration. As a result, quality assurance in the country's education system suffered badly (including in newer private universities), and citizens with foreign diplomas could not easily attain recognition of their degrees. This situation also made it very difficult for returning Bosnian refugees to obtain university positions, and for the country to utilize their badly needed research skills; at the end of 2007, the University of Sarajevo was still at 40 percent of its prewar staffing levels. Individual faculties in the country began adoption of Bologna-related reforms despite the

44. Croatian Public Radio, HRI, May 7, 2008, in *BBC Monitoring Europe-Political,* May 7, 2008.

absence of a national education law, but such unilateral practices often enhanced the country's general proclivity toward fragmentation. The adoption of new legislation in 2007 thus unfortunately failed to resolve the issues of student and teacher mobility, cross-border recognition of qualifications and degrees, and equity in educational funding that the country badly needed, and it perpetuated the type of local governance and control by ethnoregional party politicians that had previously existed in the country.

One result of Bosnia's failure in educational integration was an inability to increase spending on education. For example, it was estimated that in 2005, Bosnia spent €56.75 million on higher education, or about €550 per student. The same year Croatia, which had a student population of only 20,000 more than Bosnia, spent six times that amount on tertiary education. Postsecondary educational funding shortfalls, in turn, made it difficult to improve the quality of instruction as student enrollment rose. This situation, together with the inability to address cross-border accreditation within Bosnia's fragmented structure of university jurisdictions, and also between Bosnia and the rest of the world, seriously impeded the country's ability to fulfill its Bologna goals. In this regard, the head of the Organization for Security and Cooperation in Europe's Bosnia mission observed in April 2008 that, though universities in the country claim to have already implemented Bologna provisions, "in practice very little has changed, which is one of the reasons for the dissatisfaction of students. There are no visible concrete improvements."[45]

Kosovo's tertiary educational sector has also suffered from a lack of integration, both among predominantly Albanian institutions and between those institutions and the Serbian university in Kosovska Mitrovica. A 2008 study of education in the new state observed that although aspects of the Bologna process were being implemented, "higher education is still perceived [as] elitist and often an arena for political incidents rather than a field for education and research. Both public universities [Priština and Mitrovica] are striving with great difficulties for a minimum of European standards. . . . On the structural level, central institutions and mechanisms are still missing, or not yet fully in operation."[46]

45. OSCE Mission in Bosnia, "OSCE Concerned about Implementation of Bologna Process in Bosnia," April 15, 2008.

46. Klaus Schuch, *The Matić Report, Science and Technology in Kosovo/UNMIK*

Moreover, although young Kosovars might exhibit a preference for the perceived political advantages and modern lifestyle associated with a business career, the educational system does not yet operate as a vehicle to facilitate the achievement of such goals. Thus, "the higher [system] of education in Kosovo is still characterized by a scrupulous academic orientation and by the mentality of the 'stay away from business-type' which does not generate the required balance between the offerings of the educational programs and the demands of the market."[47] The weak linkage between university faculties and education, on the one side, and the needs of the economy, on the other side, is a general problem throughout the Western Balkans. As one observer noted: "We need the academic education of a *new democratic and cosmopolitan elite,* cosmopolitan meaning truly European. This elite will be able to attract exchange with other parts of Europe, and at the same time explain to the people at home why they must trust in a deferred gratification pattern, since there are no real returns to be expected from a growing market and a higher education without a sustainable labor market" (emphasis in the original).[48]

Middle Classes and Elites: A Decade of Renewal and Challenges

The expansion of private entrepreneurial activity in the Western Balkan states, together with the increased role of highly educated professionals and experts in the labor force, and the expansion of the service sector and postsecondary education, gradually altered the social structure of the region during the decade after 2000. Such changes began to slowly broaden the size and role of the middle class, although, owing to the many challenges faced by the region, to a lesser extent than in Central

(Vienna: Information Office of the Steering Platform on Research for the Western Balkan Countries, 2008).

47. Ministry of Education, Science, and Technology, *Strategy for Development of Higher Education in Kosova (2005–2015)* (Priština: Ministry of Education, Science, and Technology, 2004), 10.

48. Michael Daxner, "The Balkans on Their Way to Europe and to Themselves: An Agenda for Higher Education," paper presented at EUA Conference "Strengthening Higher Education and Research in South East Europe: Priority for Regional and European Cooperation," Vienna, March 2–3, 2006, 4.

and Eastern Europe. As the Western Balkan countries have moved forward in their quest for EU membership, the question of whether these recent social changes have helped to deepen democratic sentiments or "European value perspectives" on the part of the political, economic, and cultural elites and middle class also acquired more significance (see chapter 7).

For most analysts, elite groups are distinguished by the fact that their members exercise substantially more power and influence in a specific sector of societal activity than does the general public. The middle class occupies a place below the elite and the top tier of income and property ownership in society, but above the less-advantaged groups in the social structure, which are mainly composed of those working in industry and agriculture, and also the unemployed. The specific lower and upper boundaries of the middle class are usually based upon arbitrary assumptions, and depend on the particular analytical perspective adopted. Thus, in some analyses, the middle class might include the better-educated and prosperous segments of the industrial and agricultural workforce, while in other studies members of the professional or economic elites may also be included. Moreover, the top tier of the class structure may or may not be differentiated from the relatively small group of tycoons and magnates in each country that enjoy extensive wealth and influence or "super-elite" status.

Although each state in the region has manifest specific patterns of social change and class stratification, the general trends during the post-2000 period are quite similar. For example, the Croatian sociologist Zoran Malenica described the "higher stratum" or "elite" of Croatian society as consisting of about 10,000 people (0.29 percent of the society, including the political nomenklatura, tycoons, higher managers), a middle stratum of some 600,000 citizens (17.6 percent drawn from managers of small firms, craftsmen, higher and lower professional specialists, and a "lower middle class" employed in the service sector), and 2.8 million in the lower class (82.1 percent, made up of industrial and agricultural workers, retirees, the unemployed, and the homeless). By 2006, Malenica argues, Croatian society was already characterized by a "capitalist class" of the "second generation," or families that have secured elite educations for their children and have a "specific class consciousness." The higher professionals in the middle class include judges, lawyers, university professors, scientists, and doctors; the lower professional class is made up of teachers below the university rank, nurses, social workers, and most of the technical and humanistic intel-ligentsia.[49] According to Malenica, the socioeconomic position of the higher professional subgroup improved in the post-2000 period. More recent research has found that the post-2000 middle class in Croatia rebounded to its earlier mid-1990s levels. Moreover, a gradual "retreat" of the state's role reduced the previous overrepresentation of public sector employees within the overall middle class.[50]

Other research has revealed that, between 1990 and 2007, the highly qualified professionals with expert knowledge—that is, intelligentsia elites—have also become the core of Croatia's parliamentary elite. A closer analysis of the legislative elite also demonstrates that in recent years, the members of the social or "humanistic intelligentsia" are found more typically among left-wing parliamentary representatives, and also that "technocrats" are more often found in the right-center parties.[51] Meanwhile, Malenica has shown that even before the post-2008 global economic crisis, the bottom segment of the middle class (consisting of salaried employees, administrative personnel, and salesclerks in small shops, supermarkets, and department stores), had suffered a deteriora-tion of their socioeconomic standing, although their overall proportion in the population had grown. And the lowest substratum of society, constituting the largest portion of the class structure, saw its social and economic position substantially stagnate during the same period (al-though the segments of that substratum have experienced a consider-able restructuring in the nature of their work, i.e., the character of their agricultural and industrial jobs).

Another Croatian sociologist, Dražen Lalić, argues that the lower professional segment of the middle class is hardly differentiated in terms of its income from the working class. However, Croatia's middle class is smaller and sociopolitically weaker than the same social group in Western European countries such as Germany, and it often faces prob-lems similar to those that prevailed during the period of late socialism and the difficult transition of the 1990s (e.g., finding resources for the

49. *Ogled u hrvatskom društva* (Zagreb: Golden Marketing, 2007).

50. Iva Tomić and Joanna Tyowicz, "What Happened to the Middle Class in the New Market Economies? The Case of Croatia and Poland," *Croatian Economic Survey* 12, no. 1 (April 2010): 9–44.

51. Vlasta Ilišin, "The Social Structure of the Croatian Parliament in Five Mandates," *Politička misao* 44, no. 5 (2007): 45–70.

education of its children, business investment, travel, and other status symbols). Members of Croatia's middle class in recent years have also found it difficult to exercise influence over government circles and public policy. But commenting on the 1990s, Lalić concluded that not only did the Croatian middle class not wither away, it actually had been "pruned and strengthened by the difficult transition years."[52] An important 2006 survey on the "Quality of Life" in Croatia indicates that the gaps between rich and poor, and between management and workers, continue to be regarded as creating serious social tensions. Such subjective inequality far outweighs popular perceptions of divisions relating to gender, age, or ethnicity.[53] Because of the formation of a stronger middle class, however, Croatian society no longer faces the sharp bifurcation between rich and poor, the elite and mass pattern that had characterized the 1990s. Inequalities have grown in society, but so has the role of the middle class as a buffer between society's upper and lower tiers.

In Serbia, it took several years following the end of the Milošević regime for a sizable middle-class sector to reconstitute itself. But by 2005, the Belgrade sociologist Gordana Matković could already identify the dimensions and limitations of such reemergence:

> When you are in Belgrade one sees that the middle class has returned in some sense. It's a big question whether we will ever have as big a middle class as earlier that has money to go every year on summer holiday, on a winter holiday, to spend a little time abroad, for households to regularly spend money on new things, to drive a nice car, to wear good clothes. I think we see changes although mainly in Belgrade and Vojvodina. In the rest of the country things are difficult. . . . Subjective poverty the personal perception of one's own poverty is much greater in the Western Balkans [than Eastern Europe], simply because people in this region at one point lived considerably better than today.[54]

By 2007–8, the evidence from Serbia revealed considerable similarity to Croatia with regard to the relative size of social strata in the two

52. "Srednja klasa ipak ne odumire," *Poslovni dnevnik,* May 12, 2008.
53. United Nations Development Program, *Quality of Life and the Risk of Social Exclusion in the Republic of Croatia* (Zagreb: United Nations Development Program, 2006).
54. *Vreme,* July 7, 2005.

countries. Scholars at Belgrade's Institute for Sociological Research, for example, suggested that during the post-Milošević period, the country had slowly been able to form a middle/capitalist class. The study estimated the social stratification of Serbia's employed population as follows: 50,000 (1.4 percent) in the elite or highest tier; 800,000 (23.8 percent) in the middle sector; leaving the largest social group, or roughly 2.15 million people (74.4 percent), situated at the bottom of the social structure. Yet many members of the lower class perceive themselves to be part of the middle stratum, including skilled workers, technicians, and others who are well paid. But objectively, the study emphasized, they do not constitute part of the middle class because of their low educational qualifications, different habits, and behavior.[55]

The middle class, according to one of the study's authors, Slobodan Cvejić, is composed of highly educated people (professors, specialists, engineers, managers and directors of small enterprises, doctors, teachers, et al.). "Members of the middle class have an apartment or house, can send their children to school and afford a better education, take plane trips, mostly to Greece or Turkey."[56] The middle class is not unified, but can be differentiated into those who are in either the public or private sectors, or subgroups with different interests concerning economic and societal transformation. The entrepreneurs in the private sector, according to Cvejić, are more liberal, whereas those in the public sector are more supportive of "state capitalism" (see below). About 10 percent of the middle stratum can be considered a "higher middle class." A lower subgroup in the middle class has a postsecondary education, not because they are jobless, but they are losers in this transitional period and constitute the "sacrificed" (perhaps 100,000 people). As the post-2008 global economic crisis hit Serbia, the position of the lower portion of the middle class deteriorated. The test of who belongs to the middle layer, observed one Belgrade social scientist in mid-2010, "is a person who can afford a paid vacation, and not just go to a friend's weekend cottage. Or to loan a friend €2000. Today the so-called lower middle class is nailed to the poverty line, and is simply eradicated by the present crisis. Only the upper middle class can be called that name in the full sense of the word."[57]

55. *Politika,* September 10, 2008.
56. Ibid.; *Politika,* February 18, 2008.
57. *Politika,* June 14, 2010.

There is no doubt that the middle class or middle stratum in Serbia, despite political difficulties during the post-2000 period, has strengthened its position and potential role. Whether this development will serve to moderate social tensions and also contribute to democratic consolidation in the future remains an open question. The Serbian sociologist Vladimir Vuletić has pointed out that "the middle class is a guarantor of stability and represents a buffer zone between the working class and the elites. But the more blurred those boundaries are [between classes and elites], the greater the possibility of staving off protests, revolutions."[58] Thus, at least until the downturn near the end of 2008 in Serbia, economic differentiation and conspicuous consumption in all forms had been on the rise. Members of the Serbian government tasked with economic development hoped that prosperity could help diffuse social tensions. As the vice premier of the Serbian government, Božidar Djelić, put it in 2007: "We hope that more citizens in Serbia see themselves as potential entrepreneurs in order to form the backbone of a specifically European society with a middle class," so that Serbia "does not just have a division between the poor and the tycoons."[59] But an opposition leader was less charitable about the government's persistent recruitment of highly qualified administrative officials in recent years, which she referred to as the formation of a "false middle class, . . . not the growth of a middle class which germinates from the dynamic of a market economy, but rather from the dynamic of state power, on the backs of the people."[60] Miša Brkić, a leading economic journalist, shared the same general view in 2007:

Owing to defects in the Serbian tradition state officials are the biggest part of the middle stratum. . . . The government has a populist policy and constantly raises salaries in the state administration, regardless of their performance. Today service in the state administration is the only secure work in Serbia. . . . In stable societies, the middle class gives security to the social system. In Serbia, state officials give security to the political system; to the parties in power they

58. *Večernje novosti,* August 17, 2008.
59. Božidar Djelić, *BLIC,* December 20, 2007.
60. Vesna Pešić, "Lažna srednja klasa," speech in the National Assembly, December 12, 2007.

are the guardians of political oligarchy and believe that the middle stratum will rapidly expand and soon will be broader than Tito's.[61]

As the Serbian regime felt a pressure to reduce salaries and make personnel cuts in the public administration during the period 2008–10, it was unclear how middle-class officialdom would react and evolve in the postcrisis period. For example, Mladen Lazić and Slobodan Cvejić are rather skeptical of the prospects for Serbia's middle class—substantially made up of professionals, lower- and middle-class managers, and small entrepreneurs—to evince a sufficient level of autonomy from the state and also the kind of liberal values to push ahead with the socioeconomic development of Serbia in the direction of democratic capitalism. Serbia's traditional pattern of state intervention may, in their view, be reinforced by persistent statist anticrisis strategies that can stifle a market economy and democratic reform.[62]

Another issue potentially complicating social stability and democratization in Serbia is that even before the current economic crisis, social mobility had become more difficult, there had been a trend toward the "closing of the elite strata," and greater difficulty moving into the middle class and moving upward into its various subtiers. Thus, there are fewer and fewer elite members in Serbia whose fathers were manual workers or peasants. By and large, the new Serbian business elites are the offspring of the middle strata and higher class. Should the middle class contract as a result of the global economic crisis, there is always a danger that elite circles will become even more self-perpetuating.

Aware of the very negative impact that the post-2008 economic climate was having on the poor and middle class in Serbia, and also the increasing social differentiation in the country, President Boris Tadić decided to launch a populist-style attack on those he described as the "indecently wealthy." The "middle class still exists in Serbia," he claimed, but they are people who have "no sense of responsibility and use the money only for personal pleasures."[63] He withheld specific names, however, claiming he did not want to be the tycoons' "judge and jury." But some tycoons publicly reacted. For example, Milan Beko, a

61. *Politika,* July 13, 2007.
62. "Post-Socialist Transformation and Value Change in the Middle Class in Serbia," *European Sociological Review,* August 4, 2010, 1–16.
63. *BETA,* June 6 and 7, 2010.

co-owner of the Port of Belgrade, spoke to a meeting of entrepreneurs: "I don't think I'm indecent, and wealth is a relative term." In any case, he added, this "indecent wealth" was not created during Milošević's rule but after October 5, 2000. "If we are anyone's tycoons, we are the ones of Djindjić, Koštunica, and Tadić, rather than Milošević."[64]

Montenegro began the post-2000 period with a largely undifferentiated and hardly prosperous majority sector of the population—perhaps 75 percent of the country—who were mainly state employees and workers of various kinds. That "middle sector" was situated below a relatively well-off political-economic stratum and above those who were living in extreme poverty. As Montenegrin growth rates and living standards improved, the position of the middle sector gradually expanded to include a new subgroup of experts and entrepreneurs, not to mention a very rich class of domestic and foreign businessmen. Class stratification and inequality also increased, and the gap between the new middle class and the working class gradually expanded. Thus, a 2007 survey of Montenegrin attitudes regarding social status and the quality of life indicated that approximately 55 percent of respondents viewed themselves as belonging to the "middle stratum," and about 5 percent as belonging to the elites.[65] But from the perspective of influence on decisionmaking in the country, the middle class still remained largely on the margin of events.[66]

As for Albania, middle-class development there has been very slow, and some observers have cast doubt on the real existence of the middle class as a social grouping in the country. A recent study concluded, for example, that "in Albania there is a middle class in terms of its education and professional qualifications, but not of its income (in this respect the middle class is poorer than the other less educated strata of society). It is sometimes remarked that 'Albania built socialism without workers, and today is building capitalism without the bourgeoisie.'"[67] Meanwhile, the brain drain problem continues to impede the formation of a "knowledge elite" that could contribute talent to the emergence

64. *Ekonom-East,* June 23, 2010.

65. Marina Blagojević, *Rodni barometer u Crnoj Gori: Društveni položaj i kvalitet života žena i muškaraca–2007 godina* (Podgorica: Vlada Crne Gore, 2007), 86.

66. This point was made by the sociologist Srdjan Vukadinović in *Slobodna Evropa,* June 21, 2009.

67. Bogdani and Loughlin, *Albania,* 75.

of a broader educated middle-class sector. Still, in recent years, the number of think tanks and research institutes in Albania has grown. Moreover, the substantial urbanization of the country, both before and after 1990, has gradually increased pressure for better housing, and also whetted the appetite of city dwellers for a middle-class lifestyle and standard of living.

The evidence (table 6.4) indicates that Albania trails most of its neighbors in urbanization (only Kosovo has a larger rural sector), but the rapid migration from the countryside to cities is impressive compared with past decades (from about 20 percent urban in 1950 to 48 percent in 2010), and will substantially increase, according to forecasts. The speed and enormous social consequences of Albania's urbanization can be traced to the earlier stringent Communist controls against urban growth and freedom of movement—restrictions not lifted until 1990. It is estimated that the population of Tirana alone grew from about 200,000 in the early 1990s to nearly 800,000 by 2005 (or a five times greater migration flow than the average for developing countries).[68] Unofficial estimates put the capital's population at about 1 million by 2010. Perhaps most important, Albania's economic growth in the post-2000 period (at least until late 2008), raised the country out of extreme poverty.

Together with urbanization, the availability of mortgage financing, remittances from the large diaspora community, and the growth of the SME sector, Albanian economic growth has strengthened the basis for urban middle-class formation. In recent years, many more Albanians have been able to spend money on real estate and also the education of their children abroad (especially in Italy). But the position of the country's small middle class (businessmen, politicians, academics, professionals, journalists, highly qualified workers, et al.) remained quite fragile; indeed, it constituted a relatively thin social layer between a handful of rich beneficiaries of the recent trends on the one side, and a large very poor population on the other. Compared with the neighboring Western Balkan countries, Albania's social structure also remained in an unfavorable position. A World Bank unit estimated, for example, that in 2007 Albanian professionals earned an average of $8,100 and a skilled worker about $3,500, compared with about $14,000 and

68. Genard Hajdina et al., *Health in Albania. National Background Report* (Tirana: Republic of Albania Ministry of Health, 2009), 17.

Table 6.4. Urbanization in the Western Balkans (percentage of urban population)

Country	1950	1980	1990	2000	2005	2010
Albania	20.5	33.8	36.4	41.7	44.8	48.0
Bosnia	13.7	35.3	39.2	43.2	45.7	48.6
Croatia	22.3	50.1	54.0	55.6	56.5	57.8
Macedonia	23.4	53.5	57.8	62.9	65.4	67.9
Serbia	20.3	46.1	50.4	51.1	51.5	52.4
Montenegro	12.7	38.8	48.0	58.5	61.2	59.4
Kosovo	14.6	32.5	37.3	34.9	—	42.0[a]
	(1953)	(1981)	(1991)	(2001)		(2009)

[a]Some experts suggest a 50/50 breakdown between the urban and rural sectors.
Sources: United Nations, *World Urbanization Prospects, The 2007 Revision—Highlights* (New York: United Nations, 2008); UN Mission in Kosovo, *Kosovo State of the Environment Report* (Priština: UN Mission in Kosovo, 2003), 9.

$5,700, respectively, in Macedonia.[69] Moreover, the Albanian middle class is mainly concentrated in and around Tirana and still struggles for a social identity, given the chaotic pace of urbanization, and also the country's highly uneven and lagging development. As one observer described Tirana in mid-2006:

> Ruined peasants (subsidies vanished) rushed from mountain to city, making Tirana into a Brazilian-style agglomeration of slums and temporary housing. Few know where the many live. Utilities are measured by inspectors who overtax the wealthy to offset costs the poor can't pay. Electricity is stolen absurdly (thieves tap into snarled lines), and local and national taxes make sense only in the abstract. Standards, whether for fresh meat or anti-seismic building material, are often in the eyes and pocket of the beholder. The city is a cult of shifting alliances, most informal and deeply personal. Big projects take priority over local business development because there is more money involved, and few in the city can yet speak in terms of a common interest.[70]

Kosovo has faced some of the same challenges as Albania. A private sector favoring development and entrepreneurial activity has created

69. Altin Raxhimi, "Europe Keeps Door to Albanians Closely Guarded." *BIRN,* November 15, 2007.
70. Christopher Winner, "A Backwater Capital Makes Its Own Brave New World," in *Articles on Tirana* (Tirana: Municipality of Tirana, 2008).

the foundation for middle-class development, especially among own-ers of small family-run businesses. But serious employment problems, demographic issues, and chronic, albeit reduced, poverty, together with political problems, have limited the pace of progress. Some Kosovo so-ciologists have observed, for example, that there effectively is no middle class in the new country, or what is sometimes described as a middle stratum is actually a very weak social formation struggling to survive. "In Kosovo there is no class that stands between the capitalists and the proletariat," one sociologist remarked in 2007. "Here we have a few capitalists and others who belong to the class of wage earners."[71] Still, the roughly one-third of Kosovo's employed labor force who are in managerial, professional, and technical positions—not that different from the situation in most other Western Balkan societies—provide a basis for a future middle-class formation. Moreover, Kosovo's propor-tional urban population has grown from approximately 15 percent in 1953 to about 42 percent in 2009.

Social change has brought about increased inequality. A 2005 survey of Kosovo citizens indicated that 67 percent of respondents believed that over the previous decade differences between the rich and poor had increased (the view of 75 percent among those surveyed in Priština, and 83 percent of Serbs interviewed). As a consequence, "social envy" is quite high, especially among those with lower levels of education and income.[72] But the new class of teachers, managers, and professionals expresses less social envy. Such envy was admitted to by an above-average number of respondents from smaller ethnic minorities in Kosovo, but was lower among Serbs. Interestingly, the overwhelming number of respondents chose to self-classify themselves as being in the middle of the class structure: 10 percent as "upper middle class," 60 percent as "middle level," and 17 percent as "lower middle level." Only 4 percent of those surveyed self-classified as "upper level," and 9 percent as "lower level." The self-classification process in Kosovo was strongly related to education and occupation, with university graduates, managers, and professionals most likely to place themselves in the upper-middle strata.

71. The sociologist Xhavit Shala, quoted by Muhamet Ibrahimi, Alfred Marleku, and Astrit Gazhi, "Disappearance of the Middle Class," *Prezja,* November 11, 2007.

72. Theodor Hanf, *Attitudes and Opinion on Society, Religion and Politics in Kosovo: An Empirical Survey* (Eschborn: German Society for Technical Cooperation, 2005), 10–17.

A clear majority (62.3 percent) also felt that the majority of people "are in the middle class with a few people who are rich or poor." At least in Kosovo, the research suggests, middle-class convictions may serve as a kind of social buffer, a rather hopeful sign that may somewhat offset the deep ethnic fault line in the country.

In Bosnia, the warfare of the mid-1990s (which killed about 100,000 people), and attendant physical and emotional injuries, population displacement, emigration, and economic breakdown substantially eradicated the country's former middle class. Before the disintegration of Yugoslavia, most citizens of Bosnia at least subjectively saw themselves as part of a relatively well-off and growing middle stratum. Following the war, most of Bosnia's population regarded themselves as divided largely into "haves" (including a thin layer who would prosper from the wartime parallel economy) and "have-nots."[73] It was only the difficult postwar reconstruction during the next fifteen years (1996–2010), and the return of refugees in large numbers, that would very gradually result in a resurgence of Bosnia's middle class. But as a social formation, it is smaller, weaker, and more divided than those in its neighboring Western Balkan states.

Meanwhile, Bosnia's ethnopolitical cleavages remain deep, particularly among both the political and economic elite. In this regard, the veteran Sarajevo journalist Senad Pećanin observed that "Bosnia and Herzegovina has the misfortune to have a political elite which combined war criminals, nationalists, unscrupulous criminals and incompetent dilettantes who are principally involved in pursuing their own interests and the [ethno] national rights of the nations they represent. It is really about one cast of people completely insensitive to social problems, and the social disaster in which the majority of citizens live."[74]

73. Dino Djipa, Mirsalia Muzor, and Paula Franklin Lytle, *Consultations with the Poor: National Synthesis Report, Bosnia-Herzegovina* (Washington, D.C.: World Bank, 1999).
74. Quoted by Amir Suzanj, "Ima li B-H politička elite?" *Infoservis za promociju suradnje razumijvanja regionalne paralele,* February 23, 2006. Some observers do not really think that decisionmakers in Bosnia constitute a real elite. E.g., the Banja Luka political analyst Tanja Topić remarked in 2006: "You have one stratum of people who spin around on the political stage, who don't have a minimum of responsibility to the citizens, but who control all spheres principally in the economy and finances, and simply wish to decide everything. We don't have a political elite, nor do we have an intellectual elite, nor a critical mass. The special role accorded

The Banja Luka analyst Miloš Solaj places a good deal of the blame for the situation in Bosnia on the formative period of the country's current elite: "At the end of the 1980s and the beginning of the 1990s the old Communist elite effected a merger with the economic elite. The members of the Communist elite wish to enrich themselves, but they were not as economically literate nor experienced in making money and they rubbed shoulders with a new commercial and smuggling elite who did not shrink from criminal methods of acquiring money. The result was general corruption. In the final analysis the profile of Bosnian tycoons in a value and educational sense is far below the average in Eastern Europe."[75]

In recent years, a newer and younger generation of leaders and professionals who were not directly involved in the wars of the 1990s has gradually acquired influential positions in Bosnia's parties and various legislative bodies. But as yet, they have not been able to supplant the nationalistically oriented party elites or to become the vanguard of a strong and relatively united pan-ethnic middle-class grouping. Moreover, as elsewhere in the region, many of those in the middle class remain highly dependent on the state for their employment and are still not prepared or inclined to influence political life.[76]

Trends in Poverty and Inequality, 2000–2010: The "New Poor"

The slow expansion and renewal of the middle-class sector throughout the Western Balkans during the decade after 2000 has facilitated and fed on the region's economic growth (see chapter 8) and has been a hopeful, if not yet robust, trend for the region's democratic consolidation. But significant sectors of social vulnerability and social exclusion also remain in the region. Thus, the transitional economic hardships and conflicts during the 1990s not only seriously weakened the size and

---

to the international community and the High Representative also limit the political ambit of domestic leadership. Decisions in the country are often made by networks of the wealthy local actors outside of public view." Ibid.

75. "Nacionalizam dobitna karta," *Danas,* October 24, 2008.

76. Sabina Čabaravdić, "Gde je sada srednja klasa," Radio Slobodna Europa, September 20, 2009.

prosperity of middle classes as a whole but also impoverished a large segment of the population in each Western Balkan society. Most significant for the bottom tiers of the class structure, governmental efforts to overcome the problems of poverty proved quite modest during the first part of the post-2000 period.

National differences in calculating poverty limited the comparability of data collected in this period, but the evidence indicates a pattern of considerable intraregional variation.[77] Data on absolute poverty levels based on World Bank evaluations indicated that Croatia had the lowest level of poverty (4 percent in 2004), while Kosovo, with 50 percent of the population estimated to be living in poverty in 2002, and Albania, with 25 percent during the same year, were at the high end. Macedonia, with 21.7 percent under the poverty line in 2003, and Bosnia, at 17.8 percent in 2004, were also at the higher end. The equivalent figure for Serbia in 2002 was 10.6 percent, and for Montenegro, 9.4 percent.

Studies conducted during this period and subsequently revealed that poverty was especially prevalent among the unemployed, the less educated, households with several children, the elderly, those in rural or underdeveloped regions, persons with disabilities, refugees and displaced persons, and more disadvantaged minority groups such as the Roma. Certain geographical regions of each country also suffered from higher levels of poverty, such as northern Kosovo, the north and east of Albania, southeastern Serbia, and northern Montenegro. It is also important to recognize that during this period, a very large portion of the population in each society was concentrated just above the poverty line. Thus, changing the national thresholds of poverty could significantly alter the share of the population considered to be impoverished. And only a slight downward shift in economic circumstances by a portion of the population could change the landscape of poverty in a particular society. Thus, particularly when one considers the lowest segments of the middle stratum in Balkan societies, there is not much difference in the economic status of those classified as "poor" compared with many of those generally identified as "nonpoor" members of the middle class.

77. See, e.g., Gordana Matković, "Overview of Poverty and Social Exclusion in the Western Balkans," *Stanovništvo*, no. 1 (2006): 7–26; Sanjay Kathuria, "How Can the Small Countries in the Western Balkans Continue to Grow?" World Bank, July 2008; and European Commission, *Social Protection and Social Inclusion in the Western Balkans: A Synthesis Report* (Brussels: European Commission, 2009).

Large portions of the nonpoor lower middle class were highly vulnerable, or "at risk" of sudden downward mobility, when facing a period of economic deterioration.

The pattern of poverty in the Western Balkans also included quite a large segment of the population that was living in extreme poverty. This was particularly true, for example, in Kosovo (12 percent in 2005) and Albania (4.7 percent). Extreme poverty was especially apparent in the large Roma population in several countries. A 2004 analysis of Roma poverty rates across the Western Balkans indicated that Roma below the threshold of earning $4.30 per day constituted 78 percent of the group in Albania, 59 percent in Kosovo, 57 percent in Serbia, and 34 percent in Macedonia. In each of the countries, however, a substantial portion of the poverty-stricken Roma was living on less than $2.15 a day (39 percent in Albania and 26 percent in Serbia).[78]

During the second half of the decade after 2000, each of the Western Balkan polities accelerated measures to reduce poverty, with some progress—albeit quite uneven. Thus, despite the region's decade of impressive economic development, poverty rates have remained high. As a consequence, poverty in all the countries has persisted as an important social issue and a significant impediment to consolidating sociopolitical stability. As in other areas of development, Croatia has been in the best position. For example, poverty continued to be relatively low and shallow, albeit persistent, in Croatia from the late 1990s onward (in the years right after switching to Eurostat methodology in 2001, poverty was estimated at roughly 16–18 percent).[79] In 2006–7, about 11 percent of the population was regarded as poor, with approximately another 10 percent located near the borders of poverty, and roughly 1 percent viewed as being in serious poverty. In 2006, it was estimated that 80 percent of the impoverished came from households headed by persons with only primary education.[80] In February 2007, President Stejpan Mesić drew attention to such data, but he added that three-quarters of the households in Croatia still had problems meeting their monthly

78. United Nations Development Program, *Roma and Displaced in Southeast Europe at Risk* (Bratislava: United Nations Development Program, 2006), 13.

79. Zoran Milenica, "Extent of Poverty and the Struggle Against Poverty in the Republic of Croatia," *South-east Europe Review,* no. 4 (2001): 83–96.

80. World Bank, *Croatia Living Standards Assessment, Volume 1: Promoting Social Inclusion and Regional Equity* (Washington, D.C.: World Bank, 2006).

costs. Before 2008, at least, the level of income inequality in Croatia had been relatively low and on par with the average for advanced transition countries.[81]

However, extremely interesting research done in 2009 indicates that a large portion of Croats express a feeling of negative social mobility. For example, 39 percent of those surveyed felt that their position in 1989 was above average, but only 14 percent of those individuals surveyed in 2009 believed that their social position had not worsened. Objectively, the analysts point out, the middle class is larger today because of economic growth, but subjective feelings are another matter. Thus, feelings of "symbolic inequality" can override objective improvements, especially at a time of deteriorating economic conditions. For many, the "transitional optimism" so evident twenty years earlier had been supplanted in 2009 by a feeling of "insecurity, uncertainty, and fear regarding the future" or "transitional pessimism."[82]

Economic conditions in the post-2008 period have likely had a negative impact on social conditions. For example, a 2010 World Bank study indicated that the global economic crisis had eliminated welfare improvements during the preceding years, and that between 2008 and 2009 consumption-based poverty rose 3.5 percentage points. The share of households in Croatia living on less than a poverty line of $380 per adult per month went from 10 percent in 2008 to 13.5 in 2009. The lower middle class was hit hardest by such a decline, while the very poorest in society and the economically inactive were less affected because of social assistance benefits. By 2009, the surge in poverty had created a new situation in Croatian society, the "new poor," who were better educated and younger than the "old poor," who, having lost their jobs during the crisis, still were looking for new jobs.[83]

Relative poverty (70 percent of median equivalent expenditures) has changed very little in Macedonia—from 30.2 percent in 2003 to 28.7 percent in 2008, rising to 31.1 percent in 2009 as the results of the global

81. World Bank, "Country Partnership Strategy for the Republic of Croatia," August 13, 2008. See also Predrag Bejaković, "Jaz izmedju bogatih i siromašnih gradjana u Hrvatskoj manji je nego u Izraelu," *Poslovni dnevnik,* December 9, 2009.

82. Ivan Burić and Dragan Bagić, "Tranzicijski pesimizam izmedju objektivnog i subjektivnog," unpublished paper, Zagreb, 2009.

83. World Bank, *Croatia, Social Impact of the Crisis and Building Resilience, Main Report* (Washington, D.C., World Bank, 2010).

economic crisis were felt in the country.[84] Northeast Macedonia has an extremely high "at risk of poverty rates." The largest family groups are the most vulnerable economically, with 58 percent of the poor living in households with five or more members. A 2009 study indicated that Macedonia has a "very sharp level of income inequality for the country as a whole, and among ethnic groups. The richest 20 percent of the population in Macedonia, for example, received 42 percent of the disposable income, while the poorest 20 percent received just 5 percent of the total income.[85]

The poverty index in Bosnia was 19.5 percent in 2001 and only dropped to 18.6 percent by 2007 (20.2 percent in the Republika Srpska and 17.4 percent in the Federation of Bosnia and Herzegovina). Another 22.9 percent constituted the "near poor" in 2007, and they were extremely vulnerable to economic shocks. A comprehensive 2007 study of poverty in Bosnia and Herzegovina concluded that poverty over the previous six years had remained "substantially unchanged" and that "for a country that in the last ten years had a 'robust economic growth,'" this was a "reason for concern." A similar "concern" is also expressed regarding data on consumption inequality, indicating that Bosnia's richest 20 percent utilized about 41.5 percent of total consumption in the country, whereas the poorest 20 percent used only 7.2 percent of consumption.[86] In 2009, approximately 17.8 percent of Bosnia's population still lived below the poverty line.[87]

Research conducted by the United Nations Development Program in Bosnia, Macedonia, Croatia, and Montenegro during 2009 indicated that Bosnia had the largest number of those surveyed (88 percent) who indicated that there is considerable tension between rich and poor groups. Social tensions even exceeded the percentage indicating the existence of an ethnic cleavage (79 percent). The next highest figures

84. The 2009 figures for Macedonia are from *MIA,* September 14, 2010.
85. United Nations Development Program, *People-Centered Analysis* (Skopje: United Nations Development Program, 2009), 30–33.
86. Bosnia and Herzegovina Agency for Statistics, *The BiH Household Budget Survey 2007, Poverty and Living Conditions* (Sarajevo: Bosnia and Herzegovina Agency for Statistics, 2009).
87. *SEEbiz,* December 19, 2009. For the expectation that the economic crisis would reverse antipoverty gains in Bosnia, see World Bank, *Protecting the Poor during the Global Crisis: 2009 Bosnia and Herzegovina Poverty Update,* Report 51847 (Washington, D.C.: World Bank, 2009).

were for Macedonia, where 57 percent indicated tensions between rich and poor, but only 36 percent identified ethnic tensions as substantial. What is striking about the results for Bosnia—particularly in research conducted near the start of the global and regional economic crisis— is the combination of serious perceived intergroup tensions of both a socioeconomic and ethnic character, a finding that separates Bosnia from all the other states in which research was conducted.[88] Indeed, as the impact of the financial and economic crisis spread to Bosnia during 2009 and 2010, although not as severely as to other areas, additional research indicated an increase in unemployment among youth, reduced remittances, significant levels of social discontent (begging, theft, and rising levels of domestic violence), and deteriorating ethnic relations.[89]

In Montenegro, a comprehensive study of poverty completed in June 2008, and using 2005–6 data, concluded that 11.3 percent of the population, or 71,000 persons, were living in poverty. More than twice that number, approximately 150,000 people, were on the brink of poverty. The study also pointed to a deep gap between the rich and poor, although consumption and income inequality seemed to be slowly declining. Earlier data on consumption inequality, gathered in 2002, had shown Montenegro at the upper range for the region (second only to Serbia).[90] However, a 2009 study found that 10.8 percent of the population lived below the poverty line, 28 percent of citizens were economically endangered, and consumption inequality was on the rise.[91] Strong regional differences also existed. For example, the poverty rate was 19.2 percent in the northern region, which was highly vulnerable to economic fluctuations (62 percent of all the poor resided in the north), but 8.5 percent in Podgorica (although there is severity of poverty owing to greater inequality in the capital).[92]

88. Lidija Gaper, "Measuring Quality of Life and Social Exclusion in the Western Balkans," *Development and Transition* 15 (June 2010): 17–19.

89. Nicola Nixon, "Assessing Social Exclusion in Bosnia and Herzegovina," *Development and Transition,* June 2010, 1–5; United Nations Development Program, "Key Findings of the Early Warning System Report," 2009.

90. See *Analiza Siromaštva u Crnoj Gori,* cited in Monitor, October 24, 2009; and ISSP, *Household Survey Report No. 7* (Podgorica: ISSP, 2003).

91. *Nacionalni izvještaj o razvoju po meri čovjek, 2009–društvena isključenost* (Podgorica, 2009).

92. United Nations Development Program, *National Human Development Report 2009: Montenegro—Society for All* (Podgorica: United Nations Development Program, 2009).

The poverty rate in Kosovo has not changed substantially in recent years; it was 43.5 percent in 2003–4 and 45.1 percent 2005–6. But the "extreme poor" increased from 13.6 percent of the population in 2003 to 16.7 percent in 2005. This was mainly due to the pronounced increase in poverty among Serb-headed households. Generally, however, poverty is quite shallow in Kosovo, with a large portion of the population just under the poverty line. This shallowness suggested, at least until the global economic downturn of 2008, that employment-generating growth in Kosovo might push many people out of poverty.[93] Consumption inequality is also low (although income inequality was rising slowly in rural areas up to 2008 owing to lower remittances from abroad). Overall, however, poverty in Kosovo remains widespread and the highest in the region. And vulnerability to poverty is also very high.

Until 2008 at least, poverty reduction strategies fared better in Albania and Serbia. In Albania, the portion of the population deemed as living in poverty was halved, falling from 25.4 percent in 2002 to 18.5 percent in 2005 and to 12.4 percent in 2008. Approximately 200,000 of 575,000 poor people in 2005 were "lifted out of poverty." Those defined as extremely poor dropped from 5 percent in 2002 to 1.2 percent in 2008. With the exception of Albania's mountainous areas in the north and east of the country, differences across regions also narrowed. Albania, with an estimated 7.1 percent growth rate between 1998 and 2008, appeared to exemplify how high and sustained sectoral growth could assist in poverty reduction. The evidence also indicated that Albania had a modest level of inequality compared with other states in the region.

In Serbia, according to research from 2007, poverty declined by roughly 50 percent, from 14 percent in 2002 to 6.6 percent in 2007. Subjective poverty also fell from 23.5 percent to 15.4 percent in the same period. But about 490,000 people still lived under the poverty line in 2007. The poverty level of refugees and internally displaced persons was considerably higher—although declining in the same period. The most vulnerable segments of Serbian society were the unemployed, those with low educational levels, the elderly, and those living in rural

93. Statistical Office of Kosovo, *Kosovo Quarterly Economic Briefing,* April–June 2007; and Statistical Office of Kosovo, *Kosovo Poverty Assessment, Volume 1: Accelerating Inclusive Growth to Reduce Widespread Poverty* (Priština: Statistical Office of Kosovo, 2007).

areas, and poverty was most serious within the Roma minority.[94] And although the government claimed that its antipoverty efforts had halved the number of poor people in the country between 2003 and 2008, the economic downturn during the following year drove up the poverty level to an estimated 9.2 percent (approximately 697,000 people) by the end of 2009 (perhaps rising to 720,000 by May 2010).[95] Research also indicated a relatively high inequality of income in Serbia (with the Gini Index perhaps rising from 0.28 in 2003 to 0.35 in 2007[96]), outstripped in the region only by Macedonia and Bosnia. Indeed, in 2007 the richest 10 percent of the population spent six and a half times more than the poorest.[97]

The significance and sustainability of middle-class reemergence and expansion in the Western Balkans that occurred from 2000 to 2010 appear more tenuous when considered against the still large and persistent sectors of those living in poverty and those at risk of poverty in most countries of the region. A substantial portion of those in the middle class enjoyed income only marginally higher than those considered poor (but who were not living in extreme poverty).

Thus, the economic downturn of 2009–10 both undermined progress in the struggle against poverty and put the position of the middle class, and particularly its lower tier, in jeopardy. It also reopened the issue of whether the Western Balkan middle classes would prove sufficiently stable, cohesive, and attitudinally inclined to contribute to building consolidated democratic states. This issue was especially pertinent as measures were taken in each state to find new tax sources and savings in government expenditures at a time of declining growth rates, rising unemployment, and lower remittances from abroad.

However, in some cases, such as Serbia, the upper and middle classes fared the best during the first years of economic contraction. Thus

94. Gorana Krstić, "Poverty Profile in Serbia in the Period from 2000–2007," in *Living Standard Measurement Study* (Belgrade: Statistical Office of Serbia, 2008), 9–28.

95. *Novosti,* November 25, 2009. See also *Newsletter on Social Inclusion and Poverty Reduction,* November 2009; *Analiza Karakteristika Siromaštva u Srbiji* (Belgrade: Vlada Republike Srbije, 2009); and *B92,* May 4, 2010.

96. The Gini Index measures income inequality, with 0 signifying perfect equality and 100 perfect inequality.

97. Cited by Goran Nikolić, "Pad ekonomske nejednaknosti u Srbiji," *B92,* June 20, 2008.

those fully employed in the public sector (legislators, officials and managers, civil servants, those covered by social insurance, those in the military, those in the education sector, and skilled workers in agriculture) remained social "winners" during the global economic crisis. The majority of the "losers" were the uneducated, those with only a primary education, and the older portion of the population—those same groups that had experienced the greatest decrease in poverty in the precrisis period.[98] Before returning to the issue of the ongoing economic crisis in the last chapter, it is important to examine the values and attitudes espoused by the Western Balkan populations, and particularly those in the middle class and elite, before the crisis. For example, does the pattern of value transformation in the region appear to promote intergroup tolerance and the stable management of social, ethnic, and gender divisions that is necessary for further democratic consolidation?

98. Gordana Matković, Bosko Mijatović, and Marina Petrović, *Impact of the Financial Crisis on the Labor Market and Living Condition Outcomes* (Belgrade: Center for Liberal-Democratic Studies, 2010).

Chapter 7

The Transformation of Values: Coexisting Democratic and Illiberal Beliefs

As detailed in the previous chapter, the gradual appearance of new middle class and elite actors in the Western Balkans during the first decade of the twenty-first century has been a potentially promising feature for the region's further economic growth and democratic development. But whether such potential will be realized depends in substantial measure on the beliefs and behavior of the new actors and social formations that have recently emerged, and on their relationship to other societal forces. For example, do elites and other citizens of the Western Balkans subscribe to the type of democratic beliefs and market institutions that—to varying extents and with different nuances—are found in the EU member states? To what extent have civic values acquired importance in the Western Balkans? And how much do ethnic identities remain a basis for political mobilization? Additionally, if certain values have changed in the region, do those changes constitute a democratic political culture that is sustainable?

Indeed, whether an improved climate for economic and democratic development can be sustained in the region is closely linked to the strength of those societal and political constellations that are resistant to reforms, and especially to the vitality of extremist actors who are deeply disposed to antidemocratic or illiberal value perspectives. As with many other parts of the world, the Western Balkan region exhibits the interplay of forces connected with both modernity and tradition. Although particular *values* or subsets of values (e.g., civic and ethnic

350

values) may appear to change, entire *cultures* or the broader configuration of attitudes and norms change very slowly.[1]

Examining the Empirical Evidence

Fortunately, there is some empirical evidence that can provide insights into the changing value perspectives of classes and elites in the Western Balkans, and the extent to which there is broad societal support for "European values," which are presently so widely endorsed by governments, officials, and opinion makers in the region. For example, the "Life in Transition Study," a comparative investigation undertaken by the European Bank for Reconstruction and Development and the World Bank in 2006, sketched the landscape of general values found across the region's societies at a point roughly sixteen or seventeen years into their postcommunist evolution (table 7.1).[2] On the basis of interviews with 1,000 persons in each polity (except for Kosovo), the findings indicate that, declaratively at least, support for democracy and market economic systems was moderately strong throughout the region. There was substantial variation from country to country, with respondents in Montenegro and Albania indicating very strong support for democracy, and those surveyed in Serbia indicating less enthusiasm. Meanwhile, Bosnia and Macedonia stood out as having the highest levels of respondents who were supportive of authoritarianism. Croatian respondents exhibited a middle-level position as far as support for democracy, and also with respect to the minority who supported authoritarianism.

Enthusiasm for market economics was generally not as strong as the preference for democracy in the region, with Albania and Montenegro again exhibiting the highest levels of support. Quite substantial support for a planned economy existed in Bosnia. More detailed analyses of the same data that linked attitudinal preferences for various types of political systems with views on economic systems revealed that in the Western Balkans, as in many other postcommunist states, a considerable portion

1. Thorleif Pettersson and Esmer Yilmaz, eds., *Changing Values, Persisting Cultures. Case Studies in Value Change* (Leiden: Brill, 2008).

2. World Bank, *Salient Findings of the Life in Transition Survey: Europe and Central Asia Region* (Washington, D.C.: World Bank, 2007).

Table 7.1. Attitudes in the Western Balkans, 2006: Support for Democracy and the Market versus Authoritarianism and Planned Economy (percent)

Country or Group	Political System			Economic System		
	Support Democracy	Support Authoritarianism	Does Not Matter	Support Market	Support Planned Economy	Does Not Matter
Albania	66	9	25	65	13	22
Bosnia	61	19	19	34	39	27
Croatia	55	14	31	36	27	37
Macedonia	47	18	35	34	29	37
Montenegro	73	8	18	47	26	27
Serbia	51	14	35	45	21	34
EU member states	55	18	27	42	25	33

Source: World Bank, *Salient Findings of the Life in Transition Survey: Europe and Central Asia Region* (Washington, D.C.: World Bank, 2007), 22–23.

of the population was unconvinced about the virtues of regimes that combine democracy and market economies. Indeed, slightly more than 10 percent of those surveyed in Bosnia (13 percent) and Macedonia (11 percent) indicated a preference for a regime that is both politically authoritarian and has a planned economy. That preference was only 4 percent in Montenegro, 5 percent in Albania, and 6 percent in Serbia. Support for authoritarianism and a planned economy was more typically found among the elderly and lower-income groups. Similar data from a 2005 study of Kosovo also indicated that positive attitudes toward democracy tended to increase with education and income level. Thus, more than three-fifths of the respondents in Kosovo thought that democracy was the best solution. But between 21 and 38 percent did not object, at least in theory, to a type of political system in which "one group (majority or not) rules over the others, and people that refuse to accept this have to keep quiet or leave."[3]

One of the most interesting facets of the 2006 "Life in Transition" data is that the regional averages for the Western Balkans as a whole revealed higher levels of general rhetorical support for democracy in most countries than the same data indicated for the postcommunist states that were already in the EU. Moreover, support for an authoritarian political system was also lower in the Western Balkans than in the EU. And average attitudes on the economy were almost identical in the Eastern European EU member states and in the Western Balkans (except for the very high support for democracy and the market in Albania). These expressions of enthusiasm of course could have reflected the eagerness of many Balkan residents to portray themselves and their countries in the best possible light—especially to fellow Europeans in the EU. The citizens of the postcommunist Central European states already in the EU may also have grown somewhat disenchanted with the fruits of democracy. Moreover, the nature of the survey avoided any details regarding what is meant by the term "democracy."

The actual meaning and significance of poll results is, of course, difficult to ascertain. For example, a 2008 survey conducted in the Western Balkans by the Gallup Organization found that a "disturbingly large minority"—approximately 27 percent—of respondents in Montenegro

---

3. Theodor Hanf, *Attitudes and Opinion on Society, Religion and Politics in Kosovo: An Empirical Survey* (Eschborn: German Society for Technical Cooperation, 2005), 33.

believed that "most people in their country were afraid to express their political views." Roughly another 20 percent in Montenegro felt that many are afraid to voice their political opinion. Less than a majority of Montenegrins (47 percent) were confident that their compatriots were unafraid of exercising their freedom of expression.[4] But another question in the 2008 Gallup data indicated that Montenegro had the largest number of citizens in the region who thought that the government's performance was excellent. Thus, paradoxically, a strong endorsement of the government coexisted in Montenegro with a high level of stated belief that widespread fear existed regarding the open expression of one's views.

When compared with the 2006 "Life in Transition" survey data on Montenegro, such strong reservations about the extent of freedom in the country suggest that the practice or "quality of democracy" may have been lower than at first glimpse. And although the 2008 Gallup data for Kosovo revealed that the protectorate had the highest proportion of respondents who felt that "nobody was afraid" to speak out in public, or only some were afraid, those results must take into account the sharp difference between Kosovo Albanians and Kosovo Serbs. Thus, Serbs in Kosovo expressed considerable fear. The belief in the extent of freedom was also quite high in Croatia. According to the 2008 data, only 12 percent of the respondents in Croatia believed there was widespread fear of free expression. But such a strong endorsement of the idea that Croatia was an "open society" was at odds with what one might conclude from the very moderate level of support for democracy in Croatia indicated in the "Life in Transition" study. It also seemed doubtful that democracy actually enjoyed less support in Croatia than in Albania, Bosnia, and Montenegro.

Such inconsistencies remind one that it is impossible to accurately gauge the intensity or sustainability of commitment to democratic values from such snapshot and contradictory surveys on public opinion. It is even more difficult to interpret the implications of the findings for the longer-term consolidation of democratic systems. At most, such data can provide useful insights into the general value profile or makeup of different political cultures at a particular moment, and thus assist in making broad comparisons among states.

4. Gallup Europe, Gallup Balkan Monitor, *2008 Analytical Report* (Brussels: Gallup Europe, 2008), 24.

Whatever the contradictions of public opinion in the Western Balkans and the limitations of survey research regarding the region taken as a whole, the evidence does indicate that in the last several years, there has been substantial expressed support for democratic practice and market institutions. And though good time-series data are not available, the 2006 data suggested that support for democracy has grown in recent years, relative to the situation found at the end of the 1990s or during the early post-2000 period. Moreover, although the persistence of anti-democratic values in some quarters poses a continuing problem for the countries of the region, as have threats to democratic expression, such illiberal views appeared to enjoy only minimal support, or at least have become politically incorrect.

Still, when evidence on values for some countries is probed more deeply over time, one finds continued cause for concern regarding the prospects of democratic consolidation. For example, survey data for Albania in the 2000–2002 period indicated that 16 percent of the respondents preferred "a strong leader who can decide things quickly," rather than a parliament; 33 percent perceived dictatorship as the best form of government under certain circumstances; and 63 percent felt that important decisions "should be made by experts and not the government and parliament."[5] Further details on the attitudes of Albanian citizens suggest that observers must be very cautious when interpreting the intensity and implications of general support expressed in surveys for broad notions such as "democracy" or "free expression," concepts that are prone to various interpretations and also glib or politically correct responses, not to mention considerable confusion on the part of individual respondents.

Thus, a 2006 cross-country survey among ethnic Albanians in Albania, Macedonia, and Kosovo reveals a deep "conflict of conduct norms" among respondents. Roughly 51 percent (394 out of 726 respondents) agreed that their country needed a strong dictator and harsher prison sentences to respond to criminality. As a rule, the more dissatisfied people were with the political and economic situation, the more they supported dictatorial rule and harsh sentences. The study

5. European Commission, *Value Systems of the Citizens and Socioeconomic Conditions: Challenges From Democratisation for the EU—Enlargement* (Brussels: European Commission, 2007); Jana Arsovska, "Social Confusion on the Road to Modernity: The Meaning of Violence and Crime in Ethnic Albanian Contexts," CERGEEI GDM Project, June 2007.

also found that Macedonia's Albanians were mostly in favor of dictatorship (144 of 193 surveyed), as were people from villages and from the Gheg tribal grouping. Approximately one-third of respondents felt that a democratic legal system cannot be a model for their country because it would be incompatible with domestic cultural traditions. The authors concluded that Albanian society, within the countries surveyed, was still in a state of flux, and that "while traditional values have been severely weakened, new ones have not yet taken their place."[6]

A July 2009 study of attitudes related to political culture in Albania found that its citizens are generally concerned about political life and are familiar with democratic values but are also very disillusioned about how democracy actually works in their country. Those Albanians surveyed believed that the irresponsible behavior of the political class in their country, and the lack of influence citizens have on decisionmaking, absolve citizens from a responsibility to participate more in the political process. Some 40 percent of those surveyed were not surprised to be treated unfairly by public officials, and 44 percent thought that the best remedy for bad treatment was to seek the help of "a powerful person."[7]

Ambivalence regarding support for democracy was also found in a 2005 study of attitudes in Kosovo: "The overall perception of democracy except for a minority of respondents remains inconsistent, and makes for a very diffuse picture of support for democracy."[8] More recent research on Kosovo found that "traditional national values" are still very strongly entrenched, and political actors who advance "more cosmopolitan, urban, and civic" ideas are widely seen as a threat. As the two researchers put it,

6. European Commission, *Value Systems of the Citizens and Socioeconomic Conditions;* Jana Arsovska and Philippe Veruyn, "Globalization, Conduct Norms and 'Culture Conflict': Perceptions of Violence and Crime in an Ethnic Albanian Context," *British Journal of Criminology* 48, no. 2 (2008): 226–46.

7. Belina Bedini, "Albanian Political Culture in Transition: Helping or Stumbling the Democracy's Consolidation, *International Journal of Arts and Sciences* 3, no. 8 (2010): 20–28. For the argument that the authoritarian political culture of political elites in Albania has distorted the country's democratic institutions, and that therefore Albania cannot be considered a consolidated liberal democracy, see Ilir Kalemaj and Dorian Jano, "Authoritarianism in the Making? The Role of Political Culture and Institutions in the Albanian Context," *CEU Political Science Journal,* no. 2 (2009): 232–51.

8. Hanf, *Attitudes and Opinion,* 31–37.

Kosovo has a very liberal and contemporary constitution and legislative framework with regard to individual rights. Nevertheless there is quite a lot of mismatch between the liberal constitution and the conservative values dominating society. This is mostly a result of the international presence and the top-down nature of the way in which laws were written and approved during recent years. . . . Take for example the issue of homosexuality, which is seen by the vast majority of the citizens of Kosovo as something completely unacceptable.[9]

The Kosovo-based authors of the study also concluded that there was a hesitation by political parties to take a stand or embrace a clear set of values for fear of upsetting the predominantly conservative society. "Lack of discussion on these issues increased the gap between Kosovo society and societies that aspire to join in the future (read the EU) and strengthens the backward mentality that prevails in a fair portion of the newest country in Europe."[10]

Thus, although surveys may indicate that express levels of support in the Western Balkans for democracy and for a market economy may be higher than, or at very similar levels to, those of the member states in the EU, the perception of what constitutes a "democracy" may be quite different and fraught with contradictory beliefs. An important issue regarding the question of democratic support in the Western Balkans—particularly for elites and publics within the EU who are pondering the region's admission (see chapter 9)—remains how deeply notions such as elite accountability to citizens, intergroup tolerance, and the rule of law have actually become entrenched and how those notions are understood compared to the countries of the EU. There is, of course, certainly considerable variation within and among the EU states themselves concerning perspectives on democracy. But the entry of the Western Balkan states into the EU is premised upon the minimal acceptance and practice of certain kinds of democratic principles.

Determining whether or not citizens from majority groups in a society, as well as governing elites, promote intergroup tolerance in the political process, protect minority rights, and encourage the incorporation of minorities into the political process can also help to indicate

9. Kuschtrim Shaipi and Agon Maliqi, *Party Attitudes toward the Society: Values, Religion, State and Individuality* (Priština: Friedrich Ebert Stiftung, 2009), 16, 38.
10. Ibid.

the extent to which a democratic political culture has emerged and has significantly contributed to the overall process of democratic consolidation. Political regimes in which minority groups feel excluded from, or are outside of, the state structure are likely to be unstable and also vulnerable to extreme and extra-institutional forms of political mobilization. A closely linked issue is whether the members of the elite and general population primarily view themselves and other cultural groups in civic terms—that is, as being equal citizens of a society or, in contrast, identify themselves solely with the interests of one particular ethnic community.

For example, the same 2005 survey referred to above, conducted when Kosovo was a protectorate of the United Nations, found that 68 percent of the Kosovo Albanians interviewed described themselves as ethnic Albanians first, while 20 percent identified themselves as "citizens of Kosovo." Another 11 percent viewed themselves as "Muslim," and 1 percent as "European." Meanwhile, the Serb respondents in Kosovo identified themselves mainly as Orthodox (37 percent), Serbian (36 percent), or "citizens of Serbia." Only 8 percent of the Serbs surveyed regarded themselves as "citizens of Kosovo." And a December 2007 study of views in Kosovo—conducted shortly before the declaration of independence—found that two-thirds of the Serbs blamed tense interethnic relations within the society on the attitude of Kosovar Albanian leaders. Kosovar Albanians viewed the regime in Belgrade as the main culprit contributing to poor ethnic relations.[11] And, though Albanian government leaders in Kosovo frequently declared their support for minority rights, a May 2008 poll in Kosovo, following the declaration of independence, found that only 3 percent of Serbs felt ethnic relations were improving, or a drop from 17 percent in December 2007 (and from 87 percent in June 2007).[12] The smaller non-Serb minorities in Kosovo continued to believe that interethnic relations were improving in the new country. During most of 2008, the predominantly Albanian-run government of Kosovo was focused on obtaining international representation for its new polity. For example, the president of the new state,

11. United Nations Development Program, *Fast Facts* (Priština: United Nations Development Program, 2007), 6.
12. *Early Warning Report* (United Nations Development Program and US Agency for International Development), no. 20/21, special edition, January–June 2008.

Fatmir Sejdu, claimed that "the Republic of Kosova is a democratic country, which belongs to all citizens, without ethnic distinction."[13]

But the problem of integrating the Serb minority remained a major impediment to the cohesion and democratization of Kosovo throughout 2009 and 2010, and also to the desire of its political elites to join the EU and NATO. An April 2010 study by the United Nations Development Program found that the portion of Kosovar Serbs willing to work with Kosovo Albanians had dramatically fallen to an all-time low of only 3 percent. And only 37 percent of Albanians were willing to work with Serbs.[14] "Kosovo: The Young Europeans" was the catchy brand developed by public relations experts for the new state. But a considerable maturation of democratic norms will be necessary to support Kosovo's substantial democratic consolidation.

Sharply divided attitudes regarding democracy and identity are also starkly present in Bosnia. Survey research indicates that there is a large discrepancy between the expectations and efforts of the EU and the international community to build a multiethnic democracy in Bosnia on the one side, and the reality that exists in the country on the other. A good deal of the difficulty in Bosnia stems from the wartime period of the 1990s, which destroyed interpersonal trust and interethnic relations in the country. Such divisions were subsequently reinforced when, as part of an effort to obtain peace, the Dayton Accords contributed to a substantial extent to the institutionalization of ethnoterritorial cleavages. Moreover, the impotence of a governance model imposed from outside the country, and also the replacement of a "minimum-social differentiation society" by a more deregulated liberal economic system,[15] presented Bosnia's citizens and leaders with a new, cumbersome, and fragmented set of institutions that were premised upon unfamiliar internationally sanctioned norms. Subsequent foreign tinkering with the Dayton model during the decade and a half following the war, and also domestic circumstances, did little to improve the situation.

For example, a 2007 study indicated that a majority of respondents in Bosnia-Herzegovina wanted to change the Dayton political structure,

13. *Kosova Live,* October 21, 2008.

14. *Early Warning Report: Kosovo* (United Nations Development Program), April–June 2010.

15. "Bosnia-Herzcegovina: Navigating a Turbulent Business Environment," *Thunderbird International Business Review,* July–August 2007, 437.

but 8 in 10 of the respondents interviewed were not even aware of the internationally led efforts to rewrite the Constitution.[16] Bosnia stands out across the Western Balkans with respect to the very large number of people who claim that they are totally uninterested in politics and who are also very mistrustful of political structures. Bosnia also has an exceptionally large number of citizens—especially young people—who wish to leave the country in pursuit of a better life. Expressions of support for "democracy," such as those indicated in the "Life in Transition" study, must therefore be viewed in context. Even more critical, in the case of Bosnia-Herzegovina, is the large number of citizens who consider their ethnoreligious identity as being their primary identity, and who only secondarily feel themselves to be "B-H citizens."[17] Granted, most people in Bosnia ascribe to multiple identities. But approximately 57 percent of respondent feel "above all" that they are Bosniak, Croat, or Serb. Meanwhile, only 43 percent declare they are first and foremost citizens of Bosnia and Herzegovina (57.8 percent of respondents in the Muslim-Croat Federation, and only 18 percent in the Republika Srpska). Three-quarters of those interviewed who express an ethnoreligious identity also claim that they have a second or dual entity ascription as Bosnia and Herzegovina citizens (including 56.9 percent in the Federation). A smaller group appears to completely reject the idea of Bosnia-Herzegovina citizenship—one in seven respondents (14.2 percent in Bosnia)—as part of their identity makeup. These "non-Bosnia identifiers," or rejectionists, are mainly Orthodox believers by religion (i.e., ethnic Serbs who live in the Republika Srpska), are low income earners, have a low to middle level of education, and in many cases were displaced from their homes during the war (and did not return home).

Those who identify themselves most as citizens of Bosnia tend to be more educated, have higher incomes, and live in the Federation of Bosnia and Herzegovina. The rejectionists also are more willing (13.6 percent) to use violence, or to say that they might do so (22.9 percent) under certain circumstances. Those who have an exclusivist or non-Bosnia-Herzegovina identity also favor preservation of the status quo in the country. Those who primarily identify with Bosnia citizens are

16. Oxford Research International, *The Silent Majority Speaks* (Oxford: Oxford Research International, 2007).

17. Ibid.

less supportive of the Dayton model (13.6 percent) and its ethnically and territorially segmenting features. Thus, overall, most respondents in Bosnia have a dual identity, but ethnoreligious identification has the greatest salience. Optimistically, the substantial multi-identity, or "middle-Bosnia cluster," would seem to provide a basis for the country's cohesion in the future. But whether the middle cluster proves to be more oriented toward their ethnoreligious beliefs, or favor a countrywide identity, will depend on evolving political and socioeconomic circumstances in the country, and particularly the type of guidance and encouragement they receive from political leaders. Moreover, those with an exclusivist ethnoreligious identity, and who completely reject Bosnia and Herzegovina citizenship as an overarching basis for allegiance, still represent a substantial political risk for the country. Generalizing from the sample survey, this latter group may constitute several hundred thousand members of the population.

Regrettably, judging by the recent rhetoric of political leaders and party elites in Bosnia, and also the results of both the 2008 local elections and the 2010 general election, it would appear that stimuli favoring ethnoreligious identity currently trump any pan-Bosnia notion of citizenship. For example, the United Nations Development Program's early warning survey data from March 2008 revealed that some 83 percent of Bosniaks in Bosnian-majority areas were proud of being citizens of the country, but only 31 percent of Croats in Croat-majority areas felt such pride, as did only one-fifth of Serbs in Serb-majority areas.[18] Nearly fifteen years after the Dayton Accords, the extent of legitimacy enjoyed by Bosnia as a state was highly lopsided among its three principal ethnic communities. Indeed, 30 percent of the Serbian respondents and 20 percent of the Croats claimed that they lacked pride in the country or thought the matter of pride to be of any importance.

Bosnia's degree of state cohesion appeared to be so brittle by the fall of 2008 that some external observers were suggesting that the country might unravel unless the international community continued playing a robust role through, for example, continuation of the Office of the High Representative. In yet another warning to the stalemated political class of Bosnia—the kind of threat that had become a staple of post-Dayton

18. United Nations Development Program, *Early Warning System: First Quarterly Report—March 2008* (Sarajevo: United Nations Development Program, 2008), 42, 53.

political life—EU enlargement commissioner Olli Rehn warned that "the lack of a common vision among the country's leaders about its future in the absence of consensus on EU reforms harm its European prospects."[19] As the country experienced the impact of the global economic crisis after 2008, and approached its October 2010 election, the low level of attachment to the Bosnian state among Serbs and Croats remained substantially unchanged.[20] Among the elites representing the three major ethnic groups in the country, and a substantial number of their constituents, there was no shared notion of how the state should be configured or, in many cases, if the state should even exist.

As pointed out in chapter 5, considerable blame for the polarized political situation in Bosnia from 2006 to 2010 can be placed on the policies and political saber-rattling between the Bosniak leader, Haris Silajdžić, and the prime minister of the Republika Srpska, Milorad Dodik. Some analysts speculated that these two politicians not only contributed to the deteriorating interethnic conflict in the country but have worked together to prevent an improvement in the country's overall situation in order to consolidate their own power. Doubtful as this is, both Dodik and Silajdžić became accomplished at blending or alternating between civic and ethnic appeals when the leaders address voters and international officials.

Indeed, Dodik openly advocated a federalized state that would replace the constitutional arrangements established in 1995 and the establishment of three territorial units more or less along ethnic lines. As he put it in 2006: "Some people here suddenly want to become citizens only, and nothing beyond that. I am not that type of an idealist. I think that nations and ethnic feeling are still far more important and stronger than civic and universal principles, but I do prefer civic values within the concept of national and civic equality in Bosnia-Herzegovina. . . . Bosnia is a Christian majority country. Croats as Roman Catholics and Serbs as Christian Orthodox people have the majority here over Bosniaks who are of Islamic faith."[21] Near the end of September 2010, Dodik went so far as to suggest that Bosnia and Herzegovina existed

19. Olli Rehn, quoted from Europa Press Release, October 22, 2008.

20. United Nations Development Program, *Annual Report 2008* (Sarajevo: United Nations Development Program, 2008), 60. See also *Nema suglasja medju bosanskohercegovačkim narodima o budućnosti BiH* (Zagreb, Ipsos Puls, 2010).

21. Sarajevo TV, September 15, 2006, as translated in *BBC Monitoring Europe–Political,* September 18, 2006.

only in the minds of certain foreigners who believe that universal principles of organization apply to all situations in the world."[22]

Meanwhile, Silajdžić had a consistent record of favoring "citizen representation" over ethnic representation. But his strident insistence that the prerogatives of the Republika Srpska should be extensively downgraded, that the role of the central government should be greatly strengthened, and also his incessant public attacks on the wartime crimes of the Serb side tended to ethnicize political discourse and fuel interethnic antagonism. In October 2010, Bakir Izetbegović defeated Silajdžić in his bid to be reelected to the presidency. After the victory, Izetbegović claimed that Silajdžić had badly "assessed the effects of the policies he had adopted, negotiated in the style of all or nothing, and he received nothing, or almost nothing. The reactions of the Americans, Europeans, and Serbs living in Bosnia was not what he expected. . . . And it cost us."[23]

Members of Bosnia's political class persistently evince their commitment to democracy, but throughout 2010 the actual dynamics of political life in the country continued to encourage intergroup mistrust and noncivic or ethnonationalist values. And though, rhetorically, democracy may be "the only game in town," the tone and content of elite politics encouraged cynicism regarding established "democratic" political institutions. Moreover, the highly decentralized Dayton system, which also allowed elite stakeholders to function informally in a very nontransparent and nonaccountable manner, led to the "deinstitutionalization" of the official state structures and the "blockage of reformist modernization processes." As one observer noted in 2008, "The joint practice of 'exchanging favors,' and of 'connections and contacts' among the elites and people dates back to the real socialism era, and continued in [the] ethnicized [Bosnia-Herzegovina] society. . . . The Dayton political system (competitive elections, a parliamentary and a multiparty system, ethnically defined state institutions, and an authoritarian arbitrator of an international semiprotectorate, existing at the same time) enabled the reproduction of an authoritarian, antidemocratic, approach to politics by the society."[24]

22. *Politika,* September 24, 2010.
23. *Politika,* October 18, 2010.
24. Bodo Weber, "Političke elite i politička kultura u bih i izazovi evropskih integracija," in *Zbronik radova: Bosna i Herzegovina i proturječnosti procesa integracija* (Sarajevo: Heinrich Boll Stiftung, 2008), 89.

Together with other indicators of ethnic distance—such as the continued ethnic segregation of the school system[25]—the pattern of polarization in Bosnia and Herzegovina demonstrated the failures and outstanding challenges to democratically oriented value transformation at both the mass and elite levels. Further value transformation that is supportive of democracy would be necessary before pluralist political arrangements could become irreversibly entrenched in the country. The high representative in Bosnia put it well just before the 2010 election campaign began:

> Democracies don't work on automatic pilot. They need to be protected and upheld through the determined and active support of citizens. The common thread in the experience of countries that have made the transition from authoritarian to democratic rule is that the process involves change that goes beyond writing constitutions and enacting laws. It requires a shift in popular perception and it requires a shift in the way people understand the right to acquire and exercise power. . . . The problem is that many in Bosnia's political establishment have failed to make the psychological shift to living and operating in a democracy.[26]

In Macedonia, the development of a modern civic and democratically oriented value structure among leaders and citizens has also faced significant challenges. Thus, during the last few years—owing to the implementation of the 2001 Ohrid Framework Agreement—there has been substantial improvement in interethnic cooperation and in protections for the Albanian minority. Slow and very costly progress, for example, has nonetheless been made in achieving fair minority representation in various state institutions and also in providing facilities for minority education. But considerable mistrust continues to exist between ethnic Macedonians and ethnic Albanians, and domestic politics still revolves primarily around an "ethnic axis" rather than civic notions of shared values. A 2009 survey also indicated that twice as many Macedonians as Albanians believed that their society was tolerant.[27]

25. UNICEF Bosnia-Herzegovina, *Divided Schools in Bosnia and Herzegovina* (Sarajevo: UNICEF Bosnia-Herzegovina, 2009).

26. Speech by Valentin Inzko, Sarajevo, February 4, 2010.

27. Open Society Institute, *How Inclusive Is the Macedonian Society?* (Skopje: Open Society Institute, 2009), 11.

Thus the substantial ethnocentrism apparent in both political and educational life had tended to generate a pattern of ethnic segregation in both spheres.

Overall, ethnic Albanians and other minorities have appeared to express more openness to interethnic social contact than ethnic Macedonians. Ethnic Macedonians also perceive a higher risk of ethnic conflict in the state than Albanians (who feel that there is almost no danger). But high numbers of Macedonian respondents (60 percent) and Albanians (50 percent) feel that "central level politicians" are the principal drivers of ethnic tensions in the country, and respondents in both ethnic groups express considerable mistrust toward politicians from the other ethnicity. The media is also viewed by members of both groups as another significant contributing factor to interethnic difficulties.[28]

However, in contrast to Bosnia—where state cohesion is often regarded as tenuous and the leaders of large ethnically dominated territorial entities accord the state and central government very little legitimacy—value conflict between elites in Macedonia does not appear to seriously threaten the routine operation or existence of the country. As one analyst remarked in 2008, "Hot spots in particular regions in the country exist [but] tensions over ethnic issues have been subdued since 2001. Neither are there important segments of Macedonia's Albanian community ready to take up arms to fight over these issues. Most party leaders among the local Albanians have all been in power at one point or another, and have accepted the democratic rules of the game. In fact all the political elites accept the workings of the political system despite occasional dissatisfactions with electoral results or functioning of particular governments."[29] One former minister from the Albanian community described the situation as "a lack of supportiveness towards the specific constitution, but not towards the Macedonian state."[30]

28. United Nations Development Program, *The People-Centred Analyses Report* (Skopje: United Nations Development Program, 2008), 64.
29. Zhidas Daskalovski, "The Independence of Kosovo and the Consolidation of Macedonia: A Reason to Worry?" *Journal of Contemporary European Studies* 16, no. 2 (August 2008): 267–80. See also Florian Bieber and Soren Keil, "Power-Sharing Revisited: Lessons Learned in the Balkans?" *Review of Central and East European Law* 34 (2009): 337–60.
30. Simonida Kačarska, "Political Parties and the State in the Republic of Macedonia: Implications for Democratic Consolidation," *CEU Political Science Journal* 1 (2008): 49–71.

Thus, most elite members from the major ethnic communities exhibit support for the spirit of the Ohrid Framework Agreement, although in practice their supportive behavior has been rather shallow and inconsistent. Moreover, most major party leaders typically seek advantages from the "ethnicizing" of routine political discourse. Still, Macedonia has made some real progress in ethnic relations and in reaching an elite consensus on democratic values within and across ethnic lines. Thus, in "achieving instrumental unity" political leaders—even when engaging in corrupt activity—appear to have crossed a critical hurdle in regime transition by practicing "politics as bargaining" rather than "politics as war."[31] That said, the violence which occurred during the 2008 elections, and an increase in interethnic tension in 2009, suggested that political stability remained fragile, and that if unfavorable circumstances arose, the country was still susceptible to violence and instability.[32]

In the decade following the Franjo Tudjman era, Croatia made impressive strides in the realm of democratic development. This advance was acknowledged by the EU's early awarding of candidate status for the country (2001), and it was subsequently reflected in Croatia's steady progress through the EU accession process. But there have also been serious impediments to Croatia's consolidation of democracy—obstacles in part traceable to the country's imperfect embrace of modern values. Thus, islands of opposition to the "Europeanization of Croatia" still

31. Roberts Hislope, "When Being Bad Is Good: Corrupt Exchange in Divided Societies," paper prepared for the Conference "Postcommunist States and Societies, Transnational and National Politics," Maxwell School of Syracuse University, September 30, 2005.

32. The EU Commission's 2008–9 "Draft Report on Macedonia's Progress" put it more gently: "The lack of constructive political dialogue between major political parties and actors adversely affected the functioning of the political institutions." A recent survey indicated that 80 percent of Macedonians claimed to have friends or acquaintances who are of a different ethnic origin. But the country also faces serious challenges with respect to intolerance toward non-ethnic minorities, particularly people of different sexual orientations. European Commission, *Discrimination in the EU 2009: Eurobarometer 71.2 Results for FYROM* (Brussels: European Commission, 2009). A recent study by the Organization for Security and Cooperation in Europe found that students in Macedonia are keenly aware of the existence of ethnic prejudice within the school system; MAXFAX, February 4, 2010. See also "Report on the Former Yugoslav Republic of Macedonia, 4th Monitoring Cycle," European Commission Against Racism and Intolerance, Brussels, June 15, 2010.

persist, including marginal elements that are even prepared to use violence in the pursuit of their political goals.

For example, survey research conducted by the Zagreb political sociologist Vlasta Illišin and her associates indicated that at the end of the 1990s and the early post-2000 period, there was already a high degree of acceptance by both Croatian youth and adults regarding "basic liberal democratic values." But such "proclaimed values," Illišin emphasized, "is a necessary but not sufficient base for adequate (democratic political behavior)."[33] Thus, the liberal values necessary for "constituting a democratic order (a multiparty system, rule of law and national equality) were lower than generally stated liberal values concerning freedom, human rights and equality."

Illišin concluded that this gap constitutes a "deficit in democratic traditions." And her findings indicated that a substantial majority of citizens are ready to subordinate specific interests to the interests of the nation and agree with the idea that respect for individual interests can harm the general interest of the state. In Illišin's opinion, this demonstrated a "misunderstanding of political competition" among Croats. But they also represent views that are likely to slowly erode with more democratic experience. "These attitudes can be recognized as a reflex of the fetishization of the nation and state as collectives during the 1990s which left a conspicuous trace in citizens awareness."[34] Illišin worries that "the failings in democratic awareness" is linked to high levels of distrust for various institutions (parties, government, the Parliament, the judiciary, large companies, and public services). Together, they create "a base for the rise of authoritarian political opinions. . . . Croatia has had much experience with that type of political behavior and recent experience demonstrates that political protagonists are too often prepared for undemocratic behavior." But overall, the prospects for democratic breakdown are seen as "minimal" by Illišin, and democratic consolidation in Croatia is viewed as having clearly achieved considerable momentum.

In recent years, Croatian political leaders, such as Prime Minister Ivo Sanader and President Stipe Mesić, expressed pride in having developed

33. Vlasta Illišin, "Political Values and Attitudes," in *Democratic Transition in Croatia: Value Transformation, Education, and Media,* edited by S. P. Ramet and Davorka Matić (College Station: Texas A&M University Press, 2007), 113.
34. Ibid.

a "new paradigm of patriotism" in Croatia that includes intergroup tolerance and the encouragement of minority rights. And although findings from the 2006–7 "Quality of Life in Croatia" survey indicated that the country had a much higher level of intergroup tension than existed in the EU member states, tension between rich and poor (perceived by almost two-thirds of Croatian citizens) was much higher than perceptions of interethnic tension in the country (34.9 percent). To some extent, the reduced size of Croatia's minority groups as a result of the war during the 1990s may account for improved views on interethnic relations (in the 2001 census, only 7.5 percent of Croatia's population was made up of minorities, with Serbs constituting the largest proportion, 4.5 percent).[35] Interestingly, however, it is the youngest subgroup of respondents (eighteen to thirty-four years of age) that expressed a higher than average perception of ethnic tensions in society.[36]

Indeed, arguments that Croatia has firmly established liberal nationalism as a predominant value configuration[37] tended to neglect or ignore the country's remaining problems with minority representation, strong ethnic distance in ethnically mixed areas that have a record of intergroup violence, remaining facets of religious nationalism, and also residual nationalism in education, culture, and the media.[38]

35. For decreasing intolerance toward Serbs in Zagreb, see Martina Topić, "Nacionalističke predrasude i socijalna distanca-od vanjske prema unatarnjoj prijetnji," *Godišnjak za sociologiju* 15, no. 5 (2009): 63–83.

36. Croatia continues to be one of the most religious countries in Europe, and this has increased among younger people. Gordon Crpić and Siniša Zrinšćak, "Dynamism in Stability: Religiosity in Croatia 1999 and 2008," *Društevna Istraživanja* 19 (2010): 3–27.

37. E.g., Davorka Matić rather optimistically argues that the illiberal side of nationalism in Croatia was eliminated once the "high stress and general uncertainty arising from the war and occupation" of the 1990s came to an end. "Is Nationalism Really that Bad? The Case of Croatia," in *Democratic Transition,* ed. Ramet and Matić, 347–48.

38. See, e.g., Siniša Tatlović, "National Minorities and Croatian Democracy," *Politička Misao* 43, no. 5 (2006): 45–59; Boris Banovac and Željko Boneta, "Etnička distance socijalna (dez)integracija lokalnih zajednica," *Revija za sociologiju* 37, no. 1 (2006): 21–46; Vjekoslav Perica, "Religion and Ethnic Nationalism: The Making of the 'Church of the Croats,'" unpublished paper, October 10, 2009; Dejan Ajduković and Dinka Čorkalo Biruški, "Caught between the Ethnic Sides: Children Growing Up in a Divided Post-War Community," *International Journal of Behavioural Development* 32, no. 4 (2008): 337–47; and Zan Strabec and Kristan Ringdal, "Individual and Contextual Influences of War on Ethnic Prejudice in Croatia," *Sociological Quarterly* 49, no. 4 (2008): 769–79.

Croatia's leadership has been sensitive to the need to entrench a civic form of nationalism and guard against intolerance. Thus, in August 2009, President Mesić felt obliged to suggest that "religious symbols should not be placed in state institutions in the police and the military as people of various denominations are employed there. . . . Therefore let us learn to be tolerant."[39] Later in the year, Mesić chastised Croatian diplomats for formally objecting when Switzerland denied entry to a right-wing Croatian pop singer whose songs glorified genocide.[40]

The use of traditional religious symbolism, and support for racist singers in certain quarters, does not, of course, define a political culture as illiberal. But in a country with Croatia's historical record during World War II, and again in the 1990s, there is always a danger—greater than in longer-established democracies—that internal pressures and a changed international climate might quickly combine to provoke an outbreak of nationalist sentiments against internal minorities or putative external foes. In September 2009, after a local politician in Split made deprecatory comments against Serbs in a national TV show, one Croatian journalist observed that this was done with the knowledge that it would appeal to a wider audience: "Extreme nationalism has retreated and withdrawn into the private sphere, into conversations, commentaries and actions among confidants. And so now we have a secret club of those who hate Serbs, who represent a substantial part of the voting public and are found in the state and among those on the local level."[41]

Recognizing that, by 2010, far-right parties were highly fragmented and marginalized in Croatia, some Croatian commentators are nevertheless concerned that extremist views might arise after the country would enter the EU. "Once Croatia has entered the EU," observes Andjelko Milardović, "large numbers of foreigners will come and settle here. From the European north to the south, the far right is characterized by an anti-immigrant attitude, xenophobia of every sort in reaction

39. *HINA,* August 12, 14, and 17, 2009.
40. *HINA,* October 11, 2009.
41. *Nacional,* October 27, 2009. Nenad Zakošek pointed out in 2007 that after 2000, Croatian politics experienced gradual moderation and democratic consolidation, but that "societal discourse didn't follow the democratic turn of the political discourse and remained strongly polarized." Nenad Zakošek, "The Heavy Burden of History: Political Uses of the Past in the Yugoslav Successor States," *Politička Misao,* no. 5 (2007): 29–43.

to globalization and a multicultural society. Croatia is not going to be spared." And Žarko Puhovski also argues that there is a potential in Croatia "for the creation and growth of the far right, namely, groups like skinheads, war veterans, and other victims of war, along with those who come from families where radical right-wing attitudes are handed down from one generation to another."[42] Fortunately, the democratic perspectives and "constitutional patriotism" endorsed by recent Croatian leaders, and the centrist attitudes expressed by most members of the elite and public irrespective of political affiliations (particularly Ivo Josipovič, who was elected president in early 2010), along with the prospects that Croatia will soon enjoy the positive side of EU membership, are all good omens for the country's future.

Stalled modernization and various democratic deficits linked to the deeply entrenched forces of radical nationalism and authoritarianism that persisted after the demise of the one-party regime account for Serbia's pronounced lag in transforming values. Indeed, strong resistance to the abandonment of traditional beliefs and methods and to the adoption of "European values" by sizable segments of the political elite and intellectual circles is a frequently noted feature of Serbia's modern history that has continued to have strong echoes, both during and in the aftermath of the Milošević regime. The continuity of antiliberal, anti-European, and strongly conservative attitudes in Serbia—sometimes reduced to a conflict between tradition (particularly patriarchal, collectivist, and egalitarian views) and modernity—is often explained by the political defects or violent fate of reformist leaders, the polarization of political divisions historically entrenched in the elite culture, the country's rather abbreviated democratic experience, and the Serbian inability to transcend traumatic episodes in the country's turbulent history (e.g., historical nostalgia and a sense of victimization).[43]

42. *Vjesnik,* October 11, 2010.

43. Dragomir Pantić, "Value Systems, Civil Society and Tolerance as Prerequisites for Democratic Development in Serbia," in *The Balkans: Searching for Solutions,* Conference Proceedings, edited by Stein Kuhnle and Dzenal Sokolovic (Bergen: Stein Rokkan Centre for Social Studies, 2003), 89–117. See also Mladen Lazić and Slobodan Cvejić, *Promene društvene structure u Srbiji: Slučaj blokiranje post-socijalističke transformacije,* in *Transformacija i trategije društvenih grupa,* edited by Andjelka Milić (Belgrade: Institut za sociološka istraživanja, 2004), 59–76; Jelena Pešić, "Persistence of Traditional Value Orientations in Serbia," *Sociologija* 8, no. 1 (2006): 208–305; Mladen Lazić, "Serbia a Part of Both the East and the West?" *Sociologija* 45, no. 3 (2003): 194–215; Vladimir Vuletić, *Izmedju nacio-*

At the same time, many intellectuals and portions of Serbia's middle class, as well as certain renowned political leaders, should be credited with promoting and preserving modern European democratic ideas within the political culture. But following the collapse of one-party politics in 1990, and again throughout the decade after Milošević's fall from power, demagogic or populist leaders and party elites proved very adept at obstructing the implementation and momentum of democratic reforms. Reflecting on the problem over a longer duration, the Belgrade historian Dubravka Stojanović recently compared Serbia's difficulty in consolidating democracy to "oil on water." In her view, the country's problem is not an absence of democratic impulses and leaders over the past two hundred years but rather that democratic norms and institutions fail to become the dominant motif in the political culture, "the democratic forces always remained isolated, as oil remains isolated from water."[44]

Many Serbian analysts believe that the syndrome of elite division and disunity regarding democracy is a problem that has continued undiminished throughout the first decade of the twenty-first century. "Research shows," writes the prominent educational sociologist Srbijanka Turajlić in early 2008, "that the greatest resistance to the modernization of Serbia and the acceptance of European values is not located as one might expect—among the impoverished parts of society, but among the elite including [at the] university. That is another very important difference between us and other countries in transition."[45] The political sociologist Mladen Lazić is more inclined to separate elite responsibility for Serbia's delayed modernization and weak record of democratic development, on the one hand, from the positive role played by the new urban middle class, on the other. In Serbia, only 10 to 15 percent of the population lives a rather well-off style of life as a "solidly established middle class." Still, according to Lazić, this "newly consolidated middle class alongside of the economic and political elites is the principal defender of forward-looking changes that have recently

---

nalne prošlosti i Evropske budućnosti (Belgrade: Službeni glasnik, 2008); Bojan Todosijevic, "Politics in Serbia 1990–2002: A Cleavage of World Views," *Psihologija* 39, no. 2 (2006): 121–46; and Veljko Vujačić, "The Serbian Political Tradition: How Exceptional?" *Nova Srpska Politička Misao*, nos. 3–4 (2008): 135–56.

44. Dubravka Stojanović, "Ulje na vodi," *Pesčanik,* June 11, 2010.

45. Nedim Sejdinović, "Srbijanka Turajlić, Profesorka univerziteta: Elita je najslabiji deo našeg društva," March 16, 2008.

occurred in this society: They are completely conscious of their interests because they have something to defend, quite different from the poor who neither recognize their interests nor can advance some political alternatives. They [the poor] are abstainers or are disoriented, who can't differentiate demagoguery from real promises; only when they will know what they are electing, or when they will have alternatives will we be able to say we have democracy. Thus we have the illusion of democracy which unfolds as an elite game—an elite which leads us astray."[46]

Until 2008, routine political discourse within both Serbia's elite structure and the middle class was typically not characterized by differences over the means to a common end but rather reflected a deeper value divide with respect to modern democratic principles. Indeed, what appeared most distinctive about Serbia was not just the coexistence of old and new values but the fundamental division between those who advocated various shades of conservatism and nationalism, on the one side, and those supporting liberal notions and more tolerance in society, on the other. Each side of this sharp value fault line was also fragmented into contending sub-elites, depending on their particular and frequently changing choice of party affiliation (see chapter 5). Still, research by Serbian analysts, and also recent political developments in Serbia, indicate that a general transformation in beliefs away from traditional and authoritarian notions was gradually occurring in Serbia's middle class and elite circles.

According to Lazić and others, a good deal of the problem accounting for elite polarization has been the admixture of several antagonistic value patterns in the country—premodern, presocialist, traditional, socialist, postsocialist, postmodern—all of which in whole or in part have continued to compete for dominance, or have fused in a counter-

46. *Politika,* August 14, 2008. Slobodan Antonić has recently suggested that Serbia's middle class expected that the removal of Milošević would provide them with the opportunity to overcome the deteriorated situation they had suffered in the 1990s, and to resume their former position in society. When this restoration of status did not occur, a portion of the middle class tended to identify with a new "transnational capitalist class" (TNKK) and to endorse beliefs that are highly elitist and antipopulist. Antonić argues that one part of Serbia's ostensibly democratic elite and middle class urban strata regards the lower strata in Serbian society as their "chief enemy," and typically describes them as retrograde, traditional, nationalist, conservative, and rural. "Postoji li u Srbiji Transnacionalna Kapitalistička Klasa," in *Društvo rizika: Promene, nejednakosti i socijalni problemi u današnjoj Srbiji,* edited by Sreten Vujović (Belgrade: Institut za sociološka istraživanja, 2008), 51–72.

productive and somewhat confused manner.[47] But Lazić also joins other analysts in giving the middle class the bulk of the credit for putting pressure on the Milošević regime during the late 1990s, and eventually unseating it. He admits, however, that Serbia's middle class has not been blameless for the country's problems and the continued strength of former regime values. Thus, one can point to the relative political apathy of Serbia's middle class, compared with its counterparts elsewhere in Eastern Europe, as well as its acquiescence to nonreformist programs in the years following Milošević's fall. "Liberal values are most represented among representatives of the elite and the specialists," Lazić commented in 2005. "However, they are hardly the majority. In Serbia no social consensus exists concerning liberal values, nor is the societal elite dominantly oriented to such values. Part of the elite is, but it is has a relatively weak base in the population in order to firmly insist on reforms."[48]

The assassination in 2003 of the reformist prime minister Zoran Djindjić was a major setback to the cause of reform in Serbia, and it also encouraged tendencies toward radical forms of nationalism. Thus, during the five-year period from 2003 to 2008, there was relatively little progress in developing a consensus on liberal political values (see chapter 5). In fact, the "blocked transition" that aptly described Serbia in the 1990s turned into a "postponed" or "prolonged" transitional period. Still angered by the NATO attack on Serbia in 1999, and faced with foreign pressure for the extradition of war criminals, Serbia's ruling elite, dominated by the conservative democratic nationalist Vojislav Koštunica, followed a policy that has sometimes been described as kind of a "European anti-Europeanism," or more even more critically as an anticommunist variety of "renewed Miloševism." "Stateness" issues connected to the drive for independence in Montenegro and in Kosovo, and they also fomented antiliberal sentiments within those segments of the elite, middle class, and general population most attracted to aggressive nationalism.[49]

    47. Mladen Lazić and Slobodan Cvejić, "Class and Values in Post-Socialist Transformation in Serbia," *International Journal of Sociology* 27, no. 3 (Fall 2007): 59–60.
    48. *Politika,* October 9, 2005.
    49. Vesna Pešić, of the Liberal Democratic Party, has recently argued that when democratic opposition forces overthrew Milošević in October 2000, they chose to temporarily rally behind Vojislav Koštunica because he was "Milošević's double," that is, "continuing with the national [project] and adding democracy." And by

Such factors—which included the introduction of religious classes in the schools, the legitimation of the World War II Chetnik movement, and ethnopopulist appeals to voters by political parties on the right—fueled a new period of "retraditionalization" and "desecularization" that strongly resembled aspects of earlier elite-driven nationalism during the 1990s. Continued aspects of ethnocentrism and xenophobic tendencies also made it difficult for the elites and citizens of that country to come to terms with the negative facets of Serbia's roles in the wars of the 1990s or to fully cooperate with international bodies in apprehending war criminals—that is, measures that could have proved crucial in reducing radical nationalism, as well as in achieving some semblance of interethnic reconciliation, both domestically and regionally.[50]

Research studies in Serbia during the post-2000 period, however, did indicate that nationalist and authoritarian views were becoming less prevalent among the more educated and younger segments of the population. Support for the more postmaterialist values of self-expression and nonconformism had begun to reflect a generational change in values that potentially could become more supportive of interpersonal trust in society, as well as for the democratic development and further modernization. But there were also still indicators of pronounced ethnic distance and materialist values in certain segments of the younger population who are disillusioned about the possibility of change.[51] More than anything else, Serbia throughout most of the decade after 2000 seemed to manifest a "confusion of values," or the persistence of elite and mass perspectives both strongly opposed to, and supportive of, the development of civic and European values in the country.[52]

---

also cooperating with paramilitary units and organized criminal elements to push Milošević out, the democratic forces introduced "a terrible kind of instability . . . into the [political] system. . . . Mafia and organized crime started blackmailing and saying: Well we were the ones who put you in power. . . . The two leaders [Koštunica and Djindjić] became hostages" of those who carried out the coup. *Pesčanik,* October 6, 2010.

50. On the role of Serbia's elite in trying to rewrite history or rework the past in a manner that led to a return of "anti-antifascism," see Todor Kuljić, "The New (Changed) Past as a Value Factor of Development," *Sociologija* 48, no. 3 (2006): 219–29.

51. Zagorka Golubović and Isidora Jarić, *Kultura i preobrazaj Srbije: Vrednosna usmerenja gradjana u promenama posle 2000.godine* (Belgrade: Res publica i Sluzbeni glasnik, 2010).

52. On the intergenerational continuity and discontinuity of values in Serbia re-

The coexistence or confrontation of contradictory values is not, of course, atypical for a pluralist society. But in Serbia, the division and collision of values ran very deep, making it extremely difficult for forces committed to a civic value perspective to achieve a decisive breakthrough or to acquire the substantial legitimation characteristic of a consolidated democracy. In 2007, reviewing and elaborating his extensive research on Serbia completed during the 1989–2004 period, Lazić concluded with the rather "melancholic prognosis" that "political and economic elites in Serbia did not form a consistent value system either at the beginning of post-socialist transformation [1989], nor fifteen years later [2004]; and consequently members of both groups did not unequivocally internalize liberal economic and political values. . . . Bearing in mind that these two strata decisively influence the formation of dominant value horizons of the whole society it is obvious that the stabilization of dominant value patterns inside the wider social strata could be even less probable. This will certainly extend the process of building a political pluralism and market economy in Serbia and make it more uncertain."[53]

Lazić's research indicated that liberal values had strengthened among members of both the political and economic elites in Serbia, but "the change is ambiguous and less than expected." Thus, the survival of elite views supportive of "an authoritarian orientation" and also "statist-redistributive" values, which offer a positive evaluation of state intervention, persist in Serbia together with positive evaluations of "capitalist forms of private ownership and of [a] free public sphere." Moreover, managers and professional elites in Serbia appeared only marginally more liberal than unskilled workers. Some Serbian analysts, however, were more confident that the country was gradually establishing the basis for a sustainable "democratic orientation." For example, Srećko Mihalović argued that by 2007, a "syndrome of modern value orientation and corresponding behavior" had become "socially rooted in the middle class and the better part of the entrepreneurial class."[54]

---

garding the recent past, see Todor Kuljić, *Sociologija Generacije* (Belgrade: Cigoja, 2009), 186–90.

53. Mladen Lazić, "Spread of Value Orientations amongst Political and Social Elites in Serbia," *Romanian Journal of Political Science,* no. 2 (2007).

54. Srećko Mihalović, "Can There Be a Transition from Social Chaos?" in *Between Authoritarianism and Democracy, Volume 3 of Serbia at the Crossroads,* edited by Dragica Vujadinović and Vladimir Goati (Belgrade: Friedrich Ebert

As discussed in chapter 5, the electoral victory in May 2008 of the Democratic Party–led coalition "For a European Serbia" provided an impetus for the kind of broader coherent and more sustained elite and mass consensus on liberal values and reform that could help overcome Serbia's longtime value divisions. Indeed, during 2008 and 2009, Serbia's party structure underwent the kind of reconfiguration that had the potential to weaken nationalist attitudes and strengthen the country's genuinely prodemocratic centrist forces.[55] But traditional forces on the illiberal right—although undergoing some structural and image reconfiguration—retained considerable strength. And a substantial segment of the Serbian "democratic elite" has remained unwilling to risk opposing intolerant values. As one Belgrade public opinion analyst observed, research reveals a paradox with a majority supporting EU integration, but "when asked about the EU's fundamental values, they are crudely against their implementation in our society."[56]

For example, extremist elements that express both radical nationalist and homophobic beliefs have managed to retain their disruptive potential throughout the post-Milošević period. After extremist groups violently disrupted a gay rights parade in 2001, Serbia's lesbian, gay, bisexual, and transgender population was too frightened to attempt another march for seven years. In September 2009, the government canceled a gay rights parade in Belgrade, suggesting the potential for serious violence in the capital. Indeed, there was evidence of continuing problems in Serbia regarding tolerance for minorities.[57] The October

---

Stiftung, 2009), 139. Looking at the period from 2000 to 2007, Zoran Vidojević takes the view that no social class, including the middle sector of the social structure, constituted a force for democracy in Serbia, and that Serbia's political culture reflects a dominant "subject" or conformist orientation. Zoran Vidojević, *Demokratija na zalasku* (Belgrade: Službeni glasnik, Institute društvenih nauka, 2010).

55. Dušan Pavlović, "Symbolic and Distributional Cleavages in Serbia after 2000," in *Serbia Matters: Domestic Reforms and European Integration,* edited by Wolfgang Petritsch, Goran Svilanović, and Christophe Solioz (Baden-Baden: Nomos, 2009), 165–81.

56. *Danas,* September 19, 2009. Srdja Popović has argued that although most parties in Serbia abandoned any proposals regarding the use of force by their country, aspects of nationalistic ideology remained present even in the democratic bloc of parties. Srdja Popović, "Gene of Nationalism in the Democratic Party," *Peščanik,* February 14, 2010.

57. Strategic Marketing Service, *Javno mnjenje o diskriminaciji i nejednakosti u Srbiji* (Belgrade: Strategic Marketing Service, 2009).

10, 2010, "gay pride" parade held in Belgrade again brought Serbia's value divide and democratic fragility into sharp focus. Determined to protect the parade, and realizing that its success was a litmus test of the state's commitment to human rights that would be watched closely in Brussels, the government put more than 5,000 police officers on the streets of Belgrade in order to contain more than 6,000 anti-march rioters. But violence organized by far-right groups led to major clashes and widespread destruction of property throughout the city (including to the headquarters of the ruling Democratic Party). A brief parade of approximately 1,000 persons (including some liberal party leaders) was held, but fighting between hooligans and police engulfed Belgrade. Nearly 150 police officers were injured, and more than 250 persons were arrested. Serbia's defense minister called it a "sad day" for his country, and "an attack on Serbia's European path and democratic values."[58] The synchronized character of the hooliganism was the result of planning by ultranationalist organizations such as "Obraz," which had been responsible for earlier episodes of violence in the country.[59]

The October 2010 "battle of Belgrade" demonstrated Serbia's capacity to restore order—albeit with great difficulty using armored vehicles and tear gas—and no deaths occurred. But the events exposed a deep undercurrent of extremism, social dissatisfaction, and persistent organized and violent antidemocratic sentiment in the society. Thus, while hooligans carried out the violence in Belgrade, the strong expressions of antigay sentiment by various ultraright groups and parts of the Orthodox Church establishment—under the guise of protecting family values and the territorial integrity of Serbia—indicated the continuing threat to democratic consolidation and the destabilizing potential from illiberal forces in the country.[60]

58. Reuters, October 10, 2010.

59. Ultranationalist groups and violent football fans have been involved in riots when Kosovo declared its independence from Serbia in February 2008, after the arrest of Radovan Karadžić in July 2008, and in September 2009 when a French football fan was beaten to death by supporters of the Belgrade team "Partizan." On the features of extremism in Serbia, see Barbara N. Wiesinger, "The Continuing Presence of the Extreme Right in Post-Milošević Serbia," *Balkanologie* 11, nos. 1–2 (December 2008).

60. A riot in Geneva by Serbian fans at an Italy-Serbia European soccer game on October 12 was believed to be coordinated by the same organized elements. Serbia's minister of sport emphasized that not all young people in her country should be linked with hooliganism, and that the reasons why young people between

The attack on the gay pride parade was simply a pretext for the extreme right to launch an attack on the democratic parties and the state. But those behind the organized hooliganism counted on the context of dissatisfaction and traditional intolerance for selected minorities. For example, a September 2010 Gallup Monitor Poll reported that 70 percent of respondents in Serbia believed that homosexual relations were always wrong, and three-quarters believed that gays should not exhibit their sexual preferences. Serbia had the highest score on such issues for the entire Balkan region; the next highest figures were 64 and 66 percent, respectively, in Bosnia. Approximately 82 percent of Serbs also expressed the view that homosexual acts are immoral, a view widely shared in the region (by 91 percent in Kosovo, 89 percent in Bosnia, and 65 percent in Croatia).[61] Another survey of Serbian public opinion found that among those who have negative attitudes toward homosexuality, there is a very large portion that question democracy as a system, and distrust it. Some 70 percent of those opposing democracy were "fully" or "mostly" homophobic, while supporters of democracy were more tolerant toward homosexuality (21 percent was the average level of tolerance, 36 percent for democracy supporters).[62]

Serbia's overall value transformation has also been complicated by the difficulty of getting "past the past," and particularly dealing with war

---

fifteen and thirty years of age engage in violent activity, especially at sports events, should be sought in the influences to which they have been exposed: "They were about 3 years old when the conflict started in the former Yugoslavia. They were 5–7 years old when sanctions were introduced. They were 15–16 years of age when the Prime Minister was assassinated. . . . These young men were constantly exposed to images of violence and its part of their inherited situation. It's what they were exposed to in their youth." "Koji su uzroci navijačkog nasilja?" Radio Slobodna Evropa, October 11, 2009. The Belgrade psychotherapist Zoran Milivojević has suggested that "the average hooligan" comes from the periphery of Belgrade or from the interior of Serbia: "They are members of a sub-cultural that cherishes as its core values courage, strength, honesty, justice. Many of them are sports fans so they have no fear of the police. They have been regularly fighting them as well as fans of opposing teams. . . . Their parents are struggling to survive, although there are those who come from well-off families, but they are spoiled kids. Their main characteristic is black-and-white thinking, they believe they know what is right and what they should not accept. There is no compromise with them, or it is very difficult for them to accept a compromise." *B92*, October 13, 2010.

61. Gallup Monitor Poll, October 11, 2010.

62. Gay Straight Alliance, *Prejudice Exposed: Homophobia in Serbia, 2010* (Belgrade: Gay Straight Alliance, 2010), 28.

crimes in terms of self-criticism and accommodating international pressure for the extradition of major war criminals. For example, a 2009 survey supported by the Dutch government (which has pressed extremely hard for Serbia to arrest the indicted Ratko Mladić and Goran Hadžić) indicated that a large portion of the Serbian population still held a very negative view (72 percent of the respondents) of the International Criminal Tribunal for the Former Yugoslavia. The most negative views were held by those more than forty-five years of age who belonged to the nationalist-populist grouping of parties. But even 89 percent of both "modernized" and ostensibly "deradicalized" members of the Socialist Party of Serbia (Socijalistička Partija Srbije, SPS), and the breakaway former Radicals in the Serbian Progressive Party (Srpska napredna stranka, SNS) felt the same way.[63] By 2010, ethnic distance by Serbs toward traditional foes had declined, although still high especially toward Albanians.[64] Serbia's most liberal opposition figures remained skeptical that modernization has become the dominant trend in their society. For example, Vesna Pešić, of the Liberal Democratic Party (Liberalno-demokratska partija), suggested that continued "anti-European feeling in Serbia is another word for a poisonous Serbian nationalism which still exists in excessive doses and sometimes overdoses us. . . . Serbian nationalism remains some kind of temporary state waiting for some kind of unification of 'Serbian lands.' This is the main obstacle for Serbia to construct a decent society for its citizens. They must reject the nationalist vagaries."[65] Yet by early 2010, signs of moderation were also increasingly apparent in Serbia both on the elite level and in the voting public. Thus, a new generation of political leaders on the democratic side of the party divide, as well as some seasoned but more moderate clerics—such as the eighty-year-old newly elected patriarch of the Serbian Orthodox Church (Irinej Gavrilović, who was formerly bishop of Niš)—who are more accepting of Serbia's need to join the EU and for Belgrade to carry

63. *Public Perceptions in Serbia of the ICTY and the National Courts dealing with War Crimes* (Belgrade: Organization for Security and Cooperation in Europe, 2009).

64. Srbobran Branković, *Bliskosti i distance u Srpskom društvu na kraju prve dećenje XXI veka: Strahovi gradjana Srbije* (Belgrade: Megatrend Univerzitet, 2010).

65. *Danas,* September 15, 2010. On the continuing importance of nonmodern beliefs in Serbia, see also Nikola Bozilović, "Tradicija i modernizacija (Evropska perspective kulture na Balkanu)," *Sociologija* 52, no. 2 (2010): 113–26.

out its international obligations, may help steer the country away from
strident and dysfunctional nationalism.[66] President Boris Tadić's efforts
to achieve regional state-to-state reconciliation with other Balkan leaders were also very encouraging.

The decision by Montenegro's political establishment to break with the
Milošević regime during the last part of the 1990s, and subsequently to
chart its own course toward state independence, considerably improved
the climate for the growth of civic and liberal values in the country.[67] But
although breaking with the Belgrade regime, Montenegro's small elite
and middle class began their separate state-building journey; they were
still operating within a society steeped predominantly in traditional, collectivist, statist, and egalitarian notions. As relations soured between the
Montenegrin regime and Milošević's successors after October 2000—
and particularly after the murder of Zoran Djindjić in 2003—those supporting the "civic option" combined forces, temporarily at least, with
those ethnically oriented state-seeking Montenegrin nationalists who favored sovereignty. Members of the Montenegrin elite tried very hard to
garner international support by strongly endorsing democratic norms in
theory, and disassociating themselves from the very conservative brand
of nationalism that had become stronger in post-Djindjić Serbia. Civic
consciousness was also stimulated by Montenegro's increasing integration into the global world economy, which impelled elites in the country
to focus on European and international integration and to place less
emphasis on an exclusive "national" program.

Montenegro's modern history and structure of ethnic identity also
encouraged the regime to promote a more civic form of identification.[68]

66. In early 2010, the SPS decided to vote for a resolution that would condemn
the crime committed at Srebrenica. And the vice president of the SNS, Aleksandar
Vučić, a leader of the former Radical Party, even admitted that "in Srebrenica a
horrible crime was committed, a horrible crime and it is with shame that I must
say that the people who committed that crime belong to the same nation to which
I belong." *Politika,* January 21, 2010. The views of religious leaders have also been
slowly changing. "Historically, we belong to Europe," the new centrist Patriarch observed in February 2010. "Every form of togetherness is constructive, and we hope
that Europe will respect our religion." Inter Press Service News Agency, February 1,
2010.
67. Florian Bieber, *Montenegro in Transition: Problems in Statehood and
Identity* (Baden-Baden: SEER and Nomos, 2003).
68. Miloš Bešić, "Nationalities versus Civic Option in Montenegro," in *Between
Authoritarianism and Democracy,* ed. Vujadinović et al., 217–32.

For example, the Communist regime from 1946 to 1990 had attempted to circumvent deep historical cleavages between north and south, Whites and Greens, traditionalists and modernizers, by balancing and keeping ambiguous categories such as Montenegrin identity and Serbian identity, and also by pushing for the integration of both identities under the broader concept of "Yugoslavism." As a result, by the post-2000 period, Montenegro was essentially an aspirant nation-state "without a nation."[69] This allowed the regime to place an emphasis on a distinct Montenegrin identity as a way to provide the cohesion necessary for a complete break with the Belgrade regime, and eventually for state sovereignty. Such factors helped to explain the high level of support expressed for democracy by Montenegrins in survey research, and also the weak endorsement of authoritarianism and nonmarket notions.

However, there is reason to believe that the depth of support for civic notions in Montenegro has remained quite shallow. In 2005, for example, Veselin Pavićević, a political analyst in Podgorica, pointed out that Montenegrin society has no tradition of democracy or a political "enlightenment" to draw upon. At the time, he estimated that only 7 percent of the population actually subscribed to civic-oriented democratic values.[70] Following independence in 2006, there is also evidence of considerable ethnic distance between Montenegrins and Serbs on the one side (who are politically polarized), and smaller minority groups such as Albanians, Bosniaks, and Roma. However, those respondents in surveys who indicate a civic value orientation exhibit the lowest level of ethnic distance from other groups.[71]

Strong Potential for a Democratic Middle Class?

The trends examined above that were identified in the Western Balkan countries during the post-2000 period indicate a noticeable shift in the direction of more democratic tolerance and postmaterialist values, and a growing acceptance of civic norms. But the transformation toward

69. Siniša Malešević and Gordana Uzelac, "A Nation-State without the Nation? The Trajectories of Nation-Formation in Montenegro," *Nations and Nationalism* 13, no. 4 (October 2007): 695–716.

70. Radio Free Europe / Radio Liberty, South Slavic, April 28, 2005.

71. Miloš Bešić and Veselin Pavićević, *Ethnic Distance in Montenegro* (Podgorica: Nansen Dialogue Centre, 2007).

liberal democratic values has been uneven. And the extent of commitment to democratic values on the part of elites and ordinary citizens remains quite shallow and ambivalent. Moreover, and not surprisingly, elite and citizen conceptions of democracy in the Western Balkans are often quite distinct from the way democratic norms are conventionally understood in the more established European democracies.

In some countries, for example, beliefs about participation and accountability are often linked primarily to involvement in traditional clientalistic networks based upon ethnicity, clan, or locality, rather than civic notions of equal representation through broadly legitimated institutions. Citizens are voting in elections and participating in political parties and nongovernmental bodies as detailed in earlier chapters, but such "civic engagement" is paralleled by an extensive use of personal connections and patron-client networks to a larger extent than typically seen elsewhere in the democracies of the Euro-Atlantic community. Uneven value change in the Western Balkans is a good demonstration as to why analysts and observers (and particularly policymakers) need to take account of both modernization theory and culturalist interpretations when they endeavor to explain value transformation and the potential for democracy. Those who completely reject culture in explaining the value component of democratic consolidation are likely to be badly disappointed by their sometimes glib expectation that economic development will ensure pluralist politics.

Thus, as societies develop economically, they are pushed in a common direction toward a higher level of cultural convergence by modernization, while at the same time the speed and extent of such convergence is contingent on the particular cultural and historical contexts of the societies in question.[72] There is no single "Balkan political culture"

72. As Ivan Rimac and Siniša Zrinščak observed in a recent analysis of values: "The impact of a Communist past has to be considered a crucial factor in shaping the cultural values of communist countries irrespective of the considerable socioeconomic development experienced after the fall of communism." Ivan Rimac and Siniša Zrinščak, "Social Legacy and Social Values: A Post-Communist Experience," in *Mapping Value Orientations in Central and Eastern Europe,* edited by Loek Halman and Malina Voicu (Leiden: Brill, 2010), 110. See also R. E. Inglehart and W. E. Baker, "Modernization, Cultural Change and the Persistence of Traditional Values," *American Sociological Review* 65 (2000): 19–51; Sjoerd Beugelstijk, Ton Van Schail, and Wil Arts, "Towards a Unified Europe? Explaining Regional Differences in Value Patterns by Economic Development, Cultural Heritage and Historical Shocks," *Regional Studies* 4, no. 3 (May 2006): 317–27; and Frane

that determines the character of political life throughout the region. Reversing the impact of a difficult history is not impossible, and no nation is "doomed to perpetual poor governance."[73] But in each state in the Western Balkans, there are historically shaped patterns of behavior and beliefs, which both combine and coexist with newer values and which continue to significantly—in some settings and institutions more than others—influence the nature and speed of democratic consolidation.

An important issue is whether the emerging Western Balkan middle classes support democracy and have embraced a democratic political culture. As demonstrated in the last chapter, the middle strata within the Western Balkan states now occupy a significantly larger part of the social structure than immediately after the crises of the 1990s, which eroded, and then nearly destroyed, their relative position in society. But the region's middle classes remain very much in the first postconflict or early posttransition stage of development. By and large, they still lack a sense of confidence regarding their position in society, or their autonomy from the state. And if they lack solidarity and depth, they also lack breadth.

Thus, in the Western Balkans, the middle class is predominantly found in urban areas, mainly in the capitals and larger cities. No wonder, therefore, that in the less developed rural sectors, and among the lower middle class and working class at the edge of urban areas, the right of center and extreme political parties have been able to attract many voters (see chapter 5). Moreover, the outlook of the middle class in each society is not uniformly supportive of European or liberal values. The region's continued economic difficulties, even before the global downturn that began in 2008, and its outstanding problems with cor-

---

Adam, Matej Makarović, Borut Rončević, and Matevz Tomšić, *The Challenges of Sustained Development: The Role of Socio-Cultural Factors in East-Central Europe* (Budapest: Central European University Press, 2005). For the combined influence on Balkan politics from both cultural-historical factors and situational factors related to transition, see Wolfgang Hopken, "Gibt es eine 'balkanische' politische Kultur?" *Sudosteuropa Mitteilungen,* no. 6 (2009): 30–47.

73. Alina Mungiu-Pippida, "Fatalistic Political Cultures Revisited," in *Democracy and Political Culture in Eastern Europe,* edited by Hans-Dieter Klingemann, Dieter Fuchs, and Jan Zielonka (London: Routledge, 2006), 308–35. See also Susanne Pickel, "Political Culture(s) in Eastern Europe: An East European Map of Political Support," in *Mapping Value Orientations,* ed. Halman and Voicu, 193–232.

ruption, have also led to a certain general skepticism regarding the reality and benefits of democratic institutions, even among urban educated citizens. A substantial portion of the middle class in each state is also made up of public-sector employees, a kind of bureaucratic bourgeoisie that is often quite conformist and more loyal to the ruling coalition of the moment than to general democratic principles.

Moreover, substantial illiberal constituencies remain on the political landscape and continue to undermine the process of consolidation in the region. And particularly in multiethnic settings, the elite political manipulation of subcultural and religious cleavages, along with continued intergroup resentments, can help sustain the persistence of sentiments vulnerable to demagogic and populist appeals. By 2011, we see a growth of middle-class values supportive of democracy, but still not to the level of a discernible tipping point that would suggest a strong social basis for democratic consolidation has been achieved.

Overall, the evidence would seem to support the views of some modernization theorists that the termination of authoritarian regimes and the mere installation of democratic institutions per se "does not quickly or automatically produce a democratic political culture." But as Ronald Inglehart optimistically notes, incremental, intergenerational shifts usually occur in the direction of "more democratic notions and self-expression values." And he adds, "It seems that economic development gradually leads to social and cultural changes that make democratic institutions more likely to survive and flourish."[74]

Such directional "shifts" provide the hope that former Communist countries that have undergone traumatic conditions and economic difficulties—as in the case of the Western Balkans—can acquire the developmental momentum and modernization that, over time, underpin sustainable democratic political cultures. Taking part in the EU pre-accession process has certainly been an enormous help to the region, and will be in the future (see chapter 9), but the obstacles to advancing democratic consolidation still remain daunting.

Nonetheless, the evidence suggests that the elites and emergent class formations of the Western Balkans are gradually embracing democracy. And significantly, throughout 2010–11, the region's governing elites

74. Ronald Inglehart, "East European Value Systems and Global Perspective," in *Democracy and Political Culture in Eastern Europe,* Deiter, 83.

and emergent middle classes demonstrated an ability to weather the economic turbulence caused by the global financial crisis. But can the economics of the region draw on the recent social changes, as well as the newer political and administrative dynamics and advances in civic engagement explored in previous chapters, to meet the critical economic challenges of the postcrisis period, and also the steep qualifications required for EU membership? To address these questions, the following chapters review the recent record and persisting or current problems.

Chapter 8

Belated Economic Transitions:
Promise and Problems

Bearing in mind the daunting political and social challenges of democracy building just reviewed, we turn finally to the postconflict economic transition in the Western Balkans. It was too much delayed, deferred, or corrupted to speak of its consolidation during the course of the 1990s. The full systematic transition to a legal economy of independent private enterprise remained for the most recent decade to address. Only in 1999 did the European Union acknowledge the region's credentials for potential membership, as part of the wider international commitment that followed NATO's intervention in Kosovo. Only from that time forward could the EU expand trade preferences for the region. These concessions combined with the arrival of European banks several years later to provide a substantive connection between the Western Balkans and the EU membership's economies. Rising rates of economic growth and a range of domestic reforms have also distinguished the region's economic record from the faltering fits and starts of the 1990s. The subsequent decade has seen the signing of Stability and Association Agreements (SAAs) with the EU across the Western Balkans.

The more promising record of this "second transition" nonetheless left problems in place even before the international downturn of 2009. Impressive annual increases in gross domestic product (GDP) and foreign direct investment (FDI) for the period 2004–8 accompanied declining deficits in state budgets, significant tax reforms, low inflation, with the exception of Serbia, and declining unemployment, with the exception of Macedonia. At the same time, the region's trade deficits remained high. Exports were barely one-half of imports, and incomes per capita were one-third of the EU average, Croatia excepted at one-half. Some initial success in the market-based mobilization of capital also left labor forces, Croatia included, still lacking the needed size and set of skills.

Both capital and labor are needed to promote the growth of income and opportunity independent of political favor. But for private competition to replace party or state control to the advantage of society as a whole, a market economy must draw on more than access to capital and labor. For the self-sustaining growth that is economic development, those basic factors of production must rest on a framework—political and civic, social and educational—that supports innovation and improves efficiency. In an economist's terms, this is the nonquantitative "residual" that increases "total factor productivity" and turns extensive into intensive growth. The preceding chapters have addressed the region's struggle to build political and social capacity. Its struggle has been the central concern of this volume, the fate of liberal aspirations for responsible governance, the rule of law, and a free society popularly perceived as democratically representative. Such a combination of private and public capacity provided the economic foundation on which the liberal democracies of Western Europe were able to recover and prosper following World War II. This residual combination stands behind the technology, entrepreneurship, and organization that accounted for nearly half their sustained economic growth, leaving the other half to increased supplies of capital and labor drawn to the most productive sectors.[1]

Such a combination continues to face difficulties across the Western Balkans, as specifically suggested by the political resistance to reforming public administration detailed in chapter 3. Let it also be noted that the EU's own "conditionality" has grown while still allowing prospective member governments no bargaining rights for special conditions.

1. On the Golden Age of increasing labor productivity for Western Europe, spanning the years 1950–73, see Barry Eichengreen, *The European Economy since 1945: Coordinated Capitalism and Beyond* (Princeton, N.J.: Princeton University Press, 2007), 15–51. On the recent concentration on "total factor productivity," including the residual left after capital and labor are quantified, and applied in particular to postwar Western Europe, see Stephen N. Broadberry, "Total Factor Productivity," in *The Oxford Encyclopedia of Economic History,* vol. 5 (London: Oxford University Press, 2004), 128–32; and Nicholas Crafts, "Long-Term Growth," in *The Cambridge Economic History of Modern Britain,* edited by Roderick Floud and Paul Johnson (Cambridge: Cambridge University Press, 2004), table 1.4, 11.

The provisions of the swollen *acquis communautaire* also challenge the absorptive capacity of public sectors that are both overstaffed and un-derqualified. In short, embracing democracy and embracing the EU at the same time, although they share the same standards, is not a single, seamless process.

This chapter begins, hopefully, with what have seemed promising financial transitions since 1999. Leading the way across the Western Balkans have been the privatized banking sectors. They have opened the way to a competitive mix of EU-member banks and the arrival, primarily through access to enterprise privatization, of FDI. Fiscal re-form has played an important supporting role. Lower rates of income and corporate taxation were successfully combined with the introduc-tion of transparent value-added taxes to increase the revenue collected. The post-1999 pursuit of balanced budgets attracted the same interna-tional support as had the creation of stable currencies, which were al-ready in place by then (as noted in chapter 1). Guarding against budget deficits and inflation were, after all, the two main policy legs on which the Washington Consensus, the original neoliberal prescription for an essentially financial transition to a market economy of privatized en-terprises, sought to stand. At the same time, the pegged or managed exchange rates prescribed by the Consensus have left the region's gov-ernments with no monetary leverage to stimulate lagging exports and thus reduce the huge trade deficits that they all face.

Together, these changes did nonetheless facilitate the advance of legal, private sectors. They have also fueled a promising five-year rise in real annual growth of GDP, despite the persisting distance from EU levels of income and outsized trade deficits, as shown in table 8.1. Inflation remained low across the region until a short-lived upturn in 2008, when rates moved toward Serbia's persisting rate of 10 percent. Without the financial transition, this combination of income and export deficiencies, even with the Western Balkans' improved if still imperfect political standards, would not have permitted the signing of SAAs with the European Union. With offers to Serbia and Bosnia-Herzegovina in 2008, these prospective arrangements now blanket the region. Only the newly independent Kosovo is yet to be included.

At the same time, the entire region faced the interrelated challenge of raising incomes to reduce the striking disparity with EU averages while also increasing exports to trim trade and current account deficits. The largest part of the region's foreign trade has already shifted to EU

Table 8.1. Growth of Gross Domestic Product (GDP), Low Income Levels, and Trade Deficits, 2001–8

Country	GDP Real Growth, 2001–8 (%)		GDP per Capita PPP (as % of EU-27), 2008	Export as % of Imports (as % of GDP), 2008
	Annual Average, 2001–5	Annual Average, 2006–8		
Albania	5.8	5.7	6,400 (25)	27.6 (8)
Bosnia-Herzegovina	4.9	6.3	6,800 (27)	42.5 (40)
Croatia	4.7	5.1	15,600 (62)	47.1 (30)
Macedonia	2.9	4.3	8,200 (33)	60.1 (58)
Serbia	5.5	6.3	9,400 (37)	49.3 (32)
Montenegro	2.3	6.5	11,500 (46)	30.0 (29)
Kosovo	—	3.3	—	9.5 (12)

Note: PPP = purchasing power parity.
Sources: Vienna Institute for International Studies, *WIIW Handbook of Statistics 2009* (Vienna: Vienna Institute for International Studies, 2009), 8-11; ICEG European Center, *Quarterly Forecast on the Western Balkans and Turkey, Spring 2009*; Economist Intelligence Unit, *Country Report, Eastern Europe and the Former Soviet Union* (London: Economist Intelligence Unit, 2009), 7, 8; Mimosa Kusari-Lila, "Sustainable Development in Kosovo? Challenges and Opportunities," EES Noon Discussion, Woodrow Wilson Center, April 22, 2009.

members, linking the future prospects of the Western Balkans to further integration. What obstacles stand in the way? Simply said, there are two main ones: capital was becoming an obstacle even before the 2009 downturn, and labor continues to be the other. Their availability threatens the longer-term capacity of the region's economies, in the words of the Copenhagen Criteria, "to cope with competitive pressure and market forces within the EU." With domestic privatization largely concluded and international credit markets contracting, we leave the question of reviving FDI and revisiting the question of privatization to a concluding chapter. For now, it is enough to say that governments and state budgets must be denied the political leverage over the private sector that they abused during the 1990s.

Yet the conflicts of the 1990s still left public expenditures and administration with a longer-term problem beyond the political burdens discussed in chapter 3. A public sector under pressure to contract also faced the socioeconomic costs of a smaller, less skilled labor force than the one presumably in place in 1989. The costs come from an aging population and losses of educated young people to emigration, as detailed in chapter 6. An untaxed gray economy persists across the region, adding to fiscal constraints—hence the dilemma in meeting domestic imperatives (and EU standards) for educating the young and protecting the old. Both international financial institutions and the EU are belatedly acknowledging these challenges. World Bank reports now speak of the need to provide social services that will give "flexicurity" to an existing labor force that is still too immobile. Bank projects and the EU have joined local voices in calling for educational reform that will offer professional training and promote research.

These initiatives, along with broader efforts to make public administration more responsive and transparent as well as more efficient, were already moving beyond the narrow, neoliberal confines of the original "Washington Consensus" well before the current downturn. As early as 1999, John Williamson of the World Bank, who originated the term, was suggesting that this new turn, away from simply restraining inflation and state budget deficits to give private investment and enterprise free rein, should already be called "the Post–Washington Consensus."[2] The global financial crisis has now expanded the search for a new post-

2. John Williamson, "What Should the World Bank Think about the Washington Consensus?" *World Bank Research Observer* 15, no. 2 (August 2000): 251–64.

monetarist consensus that features regulatory and social responsibility. It remains to be seen whether this broader, arguably more democratic, and surely more public agenda will empower an expanded managerial and professional elite to support a political culture grounded in civic rather than ethnic identity.

Competitive Credit Markets and the Rise of Foreign Banks

Transparent access to affordable credit has long been regarded as one foundation stone of a successful market economy. Lending from a competitive banking system reduces risk, mobilizes savings, and monitors enterprise management. Freeing management from political appointees or party ties also promised to keep their leverage from undermining the democratic political framework to which the Western Balkans region has committed itself. A strong and independent financial sector has already helped the region to adjust to the sharp decline in bilateral assistance since the 1990s, a decline that cut overall development grants from $3.2 billion in 2002 to $2 billion by 2007. Shares of international aid in GDP dropped from 6 to 4 percent everywhere but in Bosnia and Herzegovina, where they also fell from 7.4 to 5.7 percent. For Croatia, the figure stayed under 0.5 percent. The region has been left to rely primarily on aid tied to the EU's accession process, itself first scaling back from the €1 billion provided in 2000 to an annual average of less than €700 million for the period 2003–7 under the Community Assistance for Reconciliation, Development, and Stabilization (CARDS) program but now back more than €1 billion under the Instruments for Pre-Accession Assistance program for 2007–13.[3]

Reacting against the reckless political lending of Yugoslavia's banks during the 1980s and the pyramid schemes in Albania, Macedonia, and

3. A useful summary of international assistance through 2005 is provided by William Bartlett, *Europe's Troubled Region, Economic Development, Institutional Reform and Social Welfare in the Western Balkans* (London: Routledge, 2008), 170–92. EU assistance, in particular for 2000–2006 and as projected as Instruments for Pre-Accession Assistance (IPA), is given by Franjo Štiblar, *The Balkan Conflict and Its Solutions, Creating Conditions for Peace, Stability and Development in the Western Balkans* (Ljubljana: Manet, 2007), 209. For the IPA aid projections for 2007–13, see Milica Uvalić, *Serbia's Transition: Toward a Better Future* (London: Palgrave, 2010), tables 8.1 and 8.4.

Serbia during the mid-1990s, their still state-controlled survivors were offering only minimal credits as the decade drew to a close. Interest rates regularly exceeded 20 percent. The cost to the state budget of cleaning up the several bank failures of 1997–98 in Croatia has been estimated at 8 percent of GDP, and the cost of the pyramids' 1997 collapse in Albania has been estimated at 12 percent of GDP. By 1998, while some 55 percent of Albania's bank loans were nonperforming, the figure for Macedonia reached 85 percent. Yet by 2008, the flood of new properly vetted lending from Western banks in both Albania and Macedonia had combined with negotiated write-offs of bad debts to reduce the share of nonperforming loans to less than 10 percent. Not coincidentally, the state's share of commercial bank assets had fallen to 10 percent everywhere in the Western Balkans except Serbia and Montenegro, where it had declined to 21 percent. Interest rates in what had now become a competitive, largely private banking system also fell by 2007, to less than half the earlier level for Croatia and much less for the others. Lending rates were 10 percent or less everywhere except Albania and Serbia, with real rates several points lower because of inflation. At the same time, total bank assets as a fraction of GDP had risen significantly. Already in 2005, as noted in table 8.2, these fractions ranged across the region from one-half up to three-quarters of GDP for Bosnia-Herzegovina and past 100 percent for Croatia. By 2008, Montenegro's fraction had jumped to 72 percent and Croatia's to 127 percent.

The 2007 European Commission–World Bank report and more recent International Monetary Fund and World Bank reports from which these data are taken makes clear the primary source of the striking upturn: It was the entry of foreign banks into a now accelerated process of privatization, a process that eliminated the major loss makers and reduced the total number of banks by half in Serbia/Montenegro, Croatia, and Bosnia-Herzegovina.[4] Major Italian and Austrian banks

---

4. Daniel Müller-Jentsch, "Financial Sector Restructuring and Regional Integration in the Western Balkans," Office for South-East Europe, European Commission–World Bank, Brussels, February 2007; International Monetary Fund, *Republic of Montenegro,* IMF Country Report 08/50 (Washington, D.C.: International Monetary Fund, 2008); International Monetary Fund, *Former Yugoslav Republic of Macedonia,* IMF Country Report 09/60 Washington, D.C.: International Monetary Fund, 2009); World Bank, *World Development Indicators 2009* (Washington, D.C.: World Bank, 2009), 252–54.

Table 8.2. Private Finance and Foreign Banks, 2005

Country, Number of Banks	Bank Assets as % of GDP	Major EU Banks % of Assets	Private Loans as % of GDP	Deposits as % of GDP
Albania, 17	60	90	10	47
Bosnia-Herzegovina, 33	75	66	45	35
Croatia, 34	110	94	65	60[a]
Macedonia, 20	50	50	25	34
Serbia, 40	52	72	22	23
Montenegro, 10	42	75	11	24
Kosovo, 6	55	61[b]	20.3[a]	37.5[a]

[a]2004.
[b]2003.

Sources: EC-WB Office for Southeastern Europe, *Financial Sector Restructuring and Regional Integration in the Western Balkans* (February 2007), 6–10,18–29; Bank Austria Creditanstalt, *Banking in South-Eastern Europe* (September 2005), 6, 63.

led the way in restructuring the survivors, starting in Croatia. Greek, Slovenian, and then Hungarian banks followed suit across the region. Their combined shares of bank assets by 2005, as may be seen in table 8.2, ranged from 94 percent in Croatia down to 50 percent in Macedonia. It was there, not incidentally, that regulations for the transfer of bank ownership remain limited by procedures started in the late 1980s by the Marković reforms (see chapter 1). But by 2008, with the passage of a commercial bank law in 2007, the foreign, largely Slovenian and Greek, share of Macedonian assets had jumped to 85 percent. Elsewhere, earlier bank legislation opened the way to Central European and French arrivals. Croatia also topped the list in private loans and bank deposits as a share of GDP at 70 percent, with total bank assets nearly four times the size of those in Serbia's otherwise comparable economy.[5] The surprisingly high Bosnian figures across the range of these indicators reflect the fact the EU banks have provided the largest part of FDI in an otherwise struggling economy. This helps to account for the absence in Sarajevo, at least until sparked by the recent financial crisis, of the public resentment and political criticism of such dependence on foreign banks seen in Zagreb or Belgrade. There have been enough of these EU-member banks, five or more, in all the economies of the Western Balkans save Kosovo's, to establish competitive credit markets, so far preventing the monopolistic leverage threatened by individual banks that are subsidiaries in much larger entities.[6] Avoiding the withdrawal of credit lines from these European banks in the current financial crisis has, however, become a new challenge posed by this leverage. Only in Sarajevo has Italy's Unicredit actually withdrawn some of its capital.[7]

Another reason for the initially broader public acceptance of the EU banks in Bosnia and also in Albania has been the rising demand

5. For survey data suggesting a generally positive impact from the predominance of foreign banks in Croatia, see Evan Kraft, *How Competitive Is Croatia's Banking System?* Croatian National Bank Working Paper W-14 (Zagreb: Croatian National Bank, 2006).

6. This is the threat raised by Ingrid Ulst, *Linkages of Financial Groups in the European Union, Financial Conglomeration in the Old and New Member States* (Budapest: Central European University Press, 2005). Answering with evidence of competitive results so far for our region are George Stubos and Ionnis Tskripis, "Regional Integration Challenges in South East Europe: Banking Sector Trends," *Southeast European and Black Sea Studies* 7, no. 1 (March 2007): 57–82.

7. Franjo Štiblar, *The Impact of the Global Financial Crisis on Montenegro and the Western Balkans* (Podgorica: Central Bank of Montenegro, 2009), 210.

for access to credit as the remittances and foreign aid on which they relied more heavily throughout the 1990s than any other economy in the Western Balkans began to decline. Remittances are still high, at 12 percent of GDP for Kosovo, 14 percent for Albania, and 18 percent for Bosnia-Herzegovina in 2008. Still, they have come down by one-quarter since the late 1990s. International assistance peaked and began falling even earlier, declining to half of the 1996–99 high point by 2001–4 for Bosnia and by one-third for Albania.[8]

Further aiding the rise of Albania's foreign banks, fourteen of only seventeen in all, was the virtual absence of commercial banking before they arrived. After the long isolation under Enver Hoxha's Communist regime, the few new, fledgling banks had seen their reputations destroyed by the pyramid crisis of 1997. Their collapse had only encouraged the reliance on the cash-based economy in which the large informal and illegal sectors were already operating. The turn to reliance on bank deposits and credits began, after initial resistance, with the payment of public employees' salaries into bank accounts. Overall, Albania's financial sector remains the smallest in the region, with a limited range of banking services and little access to insurance. Indeed, a lack of credit ratings and collateral, and even of land titles until a full cadastral survey is completed, has limited bank loans and deposits as a fraction of GDP to 10 percent.

At the other end of the spectrum, with the aforementioned 70 percent of GDP, is the loan and deposit base of Croatia's financial sector. Its thirty-four banks operated through 1,100 branch offices by 2005 with a full range of services, from credit cards to mortgage, corporate, and consumer loans. The initial boom in household lending prompted the central bank, the Croatian National Bank, to introduce a series of restrictions starting in 2003. Some two-thirds of consumer loans have contained a "currency clause," requiring a payment equivalent to the kuna's value in euros at the time of the loan. This stipulation helped to discourage devaluing the otherwise slightly overvalued kuna in order to promote exports and restrain imports. It did not stop the growth of real

8. John R. Lampe, *Balkans into Southeastern Europe, A Century of War and Transition* (London: Palgrave, 2006), table 8.2, 291. On remittances, see World Bank, *European Development Indicators, 2008* (Washington, D.C.: World Bank, 2008); and Jens Bastien, "External Anchors to the Rescue: Economic and Financial Crises in Southeastern Europe," *Eliamep,* October 2009, 32.

credit from averaging 14 percent a year from 2003 to 2008. By 2008, the domestic credit boom and looming international financial crisis pushed the central bank to review reserve requirements for commercial banks and guarantee depositors' accounts up to €56,000.[9] By 2009, domestic pressures on the kuna had finally forced a depreciation approaching 5 percent, enough to make the loans repayable at the higher borrowed rate a further burden. But the European banks, largely Austrian and Italian, appeared to be staying the course, even increasing the capital base of their Croatian subsidiaries.

Filling out a full financial sector are insurance firms, which provide for 6 percent of all assets and the largest stock market in the Western Balkans. The 182 companies listed on the Zagreb Stock Exchange accounted for half the region's formal capitalization. Representing 21 percent of Croatia's financial assets by 2006, this was by far the largest fraction in the region, although still well short of the percentages for Poland, the Czech Republic, or Bulgaria.

Serbia could only start on financial reform in late 2000, following the demise of the Slobodan Milošević regime, but it has made up for lost time since then.[10] To support that widely corrupt regime, an unsupervised banking system had provided politically tied credits, laundered money, and overseen covert transfers abroad. It remained burdened domestically with nonperforming loans and frozen foreign accounts. The regulatory overhaul that followed from 2001 simply closed twenty-five insolvent banks. Even with debt/equity swaps to recapitalize some others, the reduction from eighty-seven to thirty-six banks has been the sharpest in the region—hence, a banking sector by 2006 that was one-quarter the size of Croatia's with twice the population. Yet with the arrival of Austrian, Italian, French, and more recently Greek banks, credit

---

9. World Bank, "Global Financial Crisis Is Affecting EU 10, Croatia Coped So Far," http://www.worldbank.org/website/external countries/ecaext/0,contentMDK... 2/22/2009; Ivana Prica and Milica Uvalić, "The Impact of the Global Economic Crisis on Central and Southeastern Europe," Conference on Economic Policy and Global Recession, Faculty of Economics, University of Belgrade, Belgrade, September 25–27, 2009, 11.

10. For a progress report through 2005, see World Bank, *Serbia, Economic Memorandum* (December 2005), 63–90; and Gerhard Fink, Peter Haise, and Mina von Varendorff, "Serbia's Banking Sector Reform, Implications for Economic Growth and Financial Development," *Southeast European and Black Sea Studies* 7, no. 4 (December 2007): 609–36.

totals grew by nearly twice the high Croatian average for 2003–8. The sum of bank deposits and private loans climbed from 15 to 22 percent of GDP. The privatization of Serbia's two leading insurance firms has only recently begun. Listings as well as capitalization on the expanding stock exchange are still about one-fifth of the Croatian figures.

Montenegro's ten banks are the smallest in number across the region, but their combined assets jumped up from 42 to 72 percent of GDP between 2005 and 2008. They had remained in operation after hundreds of offshore banks, operating to launder profits from the extensive smuggling of cigarettes and other goods during the 1990s, were closed down by order of the Constitutional Court in 2002.[11] The Central Bank of Montenegro's initial switch to the German deutsche mark as the official currency in 1999, followed by the euro in 2002, helped to establish the new regulatory framework. Its establishment and the continued advantage of straight euro transactions brought in first the Slovenian and then French and Hungarian banks that already accounted for three-quarters of bank assets by 2005. But by 2008, an International Monetary Fund "stress test" of bank accounts found "surging deposits," up fourfold since 2005, and "soaring credit growth" to be responsible for pushing up nonperforming loans, often in real estate. Now restraints from the credit crisis on parent banks, Hungary's OTP in particular, are expected to join new, domestically imposed reserve requirements, credit ceilings, and a centralized credit registry in contracting the previously explosive growth in domestic lending.[12] The struggle of the small stock exchange to get started has prompted discussion with others in the Western Balkans about forming a regional exchange, perhaps linking up with the Austro-Hungarian consortium recently formed by the Vienna Stock Exchange.[13]

The fit with international assistance has worked as a common advantage in the region's financial transition, both in the boom times through 2007 and in the present downturn. Transition aid that started with the IMF and the World Bank, soon joined by US Agency for International

11. Dragan Djurić, "The Economy of Montenegro," in *Montenegro in Transition, Problems of Identity and Statehood,* edited by Florian Bieber (Baden-Baden: Nomos, 2003), 154.

12. International Monetary Fund, *Republic of Montenegro.*

13. Müller-Jentsch, "Financial Sector Restructuring," 12; interview with Nikola Fabris, chief economist, Central Bank of Montenegro, October 3, 2005.

Development (USAID) and US Treasury projects, served to provide expertise and experience in bank reform, if not in privatization and other sweeping structural changes. Initial projects in Croatia from 1995–96, and by 2000 elsewhere, were already dealing with restructuring balance sheets, establishing auditing procedures, and eliminating bad debts in the existing individual banks. Joint IMF–World Bank regulatory reviews under the Financial Sector Assessment Program were soon incorporated into the EU's monitoring of its Copenhagen Criteria, set forth in 1993 as economic and political standards to be met for membership. In the actual privatization of state-owned banks starting in 1996, the European Bank for Reconstruction and Development (EBRD) joined with the World Bank's International Finance Corporation to aid in the restructuring needed to meet standards of accountability that easily included the new regulatory emphasis. Even in the 1990s, USAID, the EBRD, and the World Bank provided seed money for the region's own economic authorities to launch a series of successful programs, as detailed below, for microcredit lending to small and medium-sized enterprises. More recently, these same international agencies have joined the European Commission in projects to promote compliance with the financial chapters of the EU's massive *acquis communautaire*.

The assistance has also been tailored to address some of the specific problems facing the various economies. In Albania, credits and loans have gone to procedures for declaring bankruptcy and providing collateral, a cadastral survey of rural property included. The support for previously unknown financial instruments like mortgages has fortunately included no connection to the international "securitization" that spread disastrously from the United States. In Bosnia-Herzegovina, the focus has been on establishing a common regulatory framework and integrated financial market between the two otherwise divided entities. These efforts have allowed one Austrian bank to conduct statewide lending. In Macedonia, the EBRD was obliged to take on some initial holdings in prying several of the major banks loose from the aforementioned insider privatization of the early 1990s. The recent rise in foreign bank investment, led by the National Bank of Greece and by Slovenia's Ljubljanska Banka, did succeed in largely eliminating nonperforming loans.

But by 2009, following new central bank standards for reserve requirements and household credit in particular, commercial banks were pushing interest rates up from 8 to 12 percent and requiring property or multiple incomes to secure consumer loans. At least bank customers were also receiving deposit guarantees, as in Croatia and Montenegro.[14] For Croatia first and later for Serbia plus Montenegro, the EBRD has also eased privatization with equity participation. Excepting Croatia, Financial Sector Assessment Program reviews from the IMF and World Bank were linked to restructuring and regulatory loans. Credits to expand access to insurance have proceeded successfully, but the pension reforms—typically requiring higher contributions, lower benefits, or both—have proved controversial.

For all these economies, it remains to be seen whether the ongoing financial monitoring from both the international organizations like the IMF or the World Bank and the home bases of the now-predominant EU-member banks can sustain the public approval that they received initially in return for replacing a broken system of domestic banks. Significant increases in amounts of consumer credit, exceeding the increases in enterprise credit, helped initially and then accelerated with little restraint. By 2008, as already noted, efforts to rein in such household credit were already proceeding under constraints imposed first by domestic central banks and then by foreign commercial banks. At least in Croatia, credit to corporations had in fact caught up with surging consumer credit by 2005.[15] And across the region, it should be emphasized, this largely imported set of banks had up to that point served to provide the financial stability that was sorely lacking in the 1990s.

But while this financial framework promoted high macroeconomic rates of growth and maintained competitive market standards through the boom times, it did not achieve the widespread rise in living standards that would be the surest defense against a political backlash.[16] And obviously compounding this political risk, there would be reduced access to the previously ample lending resources of these parent European banks. Their own overextensions and subsequent struggles with the general contraction in international credit markets that began late in 2007 raised alarms that they would retreat from the Western Balkans.

14. International Monetary Fund, *Former Yugoslav Republic of Macedonia;* authors' interview with the Council of Foreign Economic Relations, Skopje, June 1, 2009.

15. Author's interview with Evan Kraft, Croatian National Bank, Zagreb, June 5, 2008.

16. For a detailed critique of the risks from bank concentration, see Ulst, *Linkages of Financial Groups.*

But no such retreat had appeared by 2009, even in a Croatian economy that is the most heavily involved with such credit. Its lending rates have risen slightly and terms stiffened as elsewhere, but the regional range of interest rates remains at 8 to 12 percent. Damping down fears of a retreat has been an explicit commitment by ten leading European banks, as announced in Vienna in March 2009, to stay in Serbia and elsewhere in the region. The Greek banks, despite their troubled parent banks, hold large bases of local deposits, and several banks from Central Europe have provided infusions of new capital assets. The domestic central banks have also worked to keep capital shares of commercial bank assets high, up to 20 percent in Serbia.[17]

Trade Routes and the Trade Deficit, the EU and CEFTA

The clear imperative across the small economies of the Western Balkans during the past decade has been the need to increase exports. To connect an improved financial framework with domestic growth and rising incomes, the same export sector that led the way for the Western European economies on the 1960s needs to step forward here. The domestic economies of the Western Balkans are even smaller in population and income than, say, the original Benelux members of the Common Market. The 24 million people in these six economies, now seven with Kosovo, amount to only 5 percent of the total for the existing EU membership. With a combined GDP that is less than 0.5 percent of the EU's, the purchasing power of their individual domestic economies is even more limited. The region's export markets and the pattern of persisting trade deficits nonetheless offer some potential for domestic initiative and FDI to generate export-led growth. Without such growth, the region's political and public support for European integration will be hard to sustain.

17. This initial optimism for Croatia was the unanimous view at a symposium organized for John Lampe at the Economics Faculty, Zagreb University, by Ivo Bićanić, June 2, 2008. For the more recent and less optimistic forecasts of regional credit contraction led by the European banks, see Laza Kekić, "East European Economy: The Outlook Continues to Worsen," Economist Intelligence Unit, *Viewswire,* November 18, 2008; and Steven Wagstyl, "Variable Vulnerability," *Financial Times,* February 26, 2009. For a more hopeful view based on the growing cooperation of the EBRD and the IMF with European banks, see Bastien, "External Anchors to the Rescue," 18–31.

Table 8.3. Trade Growth, 1996–2008

Country and Measures of Growth	1996	2000–2004 Average	2005	2006	2007	2008
Albania						
Export annual % growth	15.4	16.4	7.2	5.2	7.5	6.8
Imports annual % growth	34.5	19.2	10.1	7.8	28.2	12.3
Exports as % of GDP	12.3	20.4	22.3	25.1	27.8	28.5
Imports as % of GDP	35.2	42.4	46.3	49.2	54.3	55.0
Bosnia-Herzegovina						
Export annual % growth	118.5	5.6	16.2	13.7	12.6	8.2
Imports annual % growth	121.6	0.3	4.6	–6.9	14.2	9.0
Exports as % of GDP	23.6	27.4	33.0	36.6	39.1	34.6
Imports as % of GDP	83.9	72.9	74.7	66.4	73.7	64.4
Croatia						
Export annual % growth	14.3	7.8	3.7	6.5	4.3	1.7
Imports annual % growth	9.1	8.8	3.9	7.4	6.5	3.6
Exports as % of GDP	35.8	42.6	42.6	43.4	42.8	41.9
Imports as % of GDP	42.4	48.5	49.1	50.4	50.4	50.3
Macedonia						
Export annual % growth	–12.9	1.0	13.6	9.2	11.8	9.6
Imports annual % growth	–8.6	4.9	8.7	10.9	15.2	4.7
Exports as % of GDP	28.2	41.5	44.7	48.1	53.2	56.0
Imports as % of GDP	38.5	58.7	62.0	66.8	72.2	77.3
Serbia						
Export annual % growth	N.A.	11.1	14.4	4.9	16.3	12.1
Imports annual % growth	N.A.	20.3	–4.9	2.8	23.9	12.0
Exports as % of GDP	N.A.	21.3	25.2	28.7	29.4	31.4
Imports as % of GDP	N.A.	40.4	47.3	49.4	51.5	55.5
Montenegro						
Export annual % growth	N.A.	2.5	4.2	8.6	10.3	7.7
Imports annual % growth	N.A.	2.5	4.2	8.6	10.3	7.7
Exports as % of GDP	N.A.	36.6	43.5	49.4	46.3	41.1
Imports as % of GDP	N.A.	55.6	61.1	77.7	84.9	74.0

Notes: GDP adjusted for purchasing power parity; N.A. = not available.
Source: World Bank, *World Development Indicators 2009,* Online Database.

All these economies have recorded significant increases in exports but have seen imports grow as fast or faster, maintaining export totals generally half the value of imports (see tables 8.3 and 8.1). Reducing if not closing these trade deficits is a goal that is particularly relevant to successful European integration because so many of the region's exports and imports already go to or come from EU members. Autonomous Trade Preferences already launched by the European Commission in 1998 virtually eliminated EU tariffs on exports from the Western Balkans. Hence the jump in the EU's share of the region's exports from

48 percent in 1996 to 68 percent by 2005. Import shares have lagged slightly behind these percentages because regional tariffs have been reduced but not eliminated. The reductions for industrial imports were indeed significant, falling for 2001–5 from 8.8 to 5.2 percent ad valorem overall and from 7.6 to just 2.4 percent for Croatia. But the rates for agricultural imports actually increased from 11 to 11.2 percent, led by Serbia/Montenegro's boost from 13.7 to 16.8 percent.[18]

In part because of these tariff changes, the direction of regional exports had already shifted toward the EU by the period 2000–4, as noted in table 8.4, as had the composition of exports. Food, feed, and agricultural raw materials have seen their share drop from 21.1 to 15.8 percent. But all manufactures are up only slightly to 66 percent, as a drop in textile and chemical exports has canceled out the rise in metals, machinery, and miscellaneous manufactures from 31.7 to 39.8 percent.[19] By 2009, of course, the drop in steel and other metal prices and European demand was also cutting into these exports.

Even before the present downturn, total export values struggled against the aforementioned high exchange rates maintained for the domestic currencies in the interest of financial stability and attraction to FDI. Those same high rates have instead made imports cheaper and discouraged the domestic production that has attempted to compete with them. Exports as a share of GDP adjusted for purchasing power parity have nonetheless risen since 2000, as may be seen in table 8.3. Unadjusted, they were still low by EU standards in 2005, at 11 to 17 percent for all but Croatia. There its share had risen to 32 percent, within sight of the EU average of 37 percent, on the strength of services. For merchandise exports, the share was lower still, averaging 4 to 8 percent, with Croatia again higher at 13 percent.[20] And in the meantime, the significantly larger import shares than average grew still larger for Albania, Croatia, and Serbia/Montenegro while holding steady elsewhere.[21]

Both from within the Western Balkans and from the EU, the major efforts for increasing export potential have focused on intra-regional

18. World Bank, *Western Balkan Integration and the EU: An Agenda for Trade and Growth,* available at web.worldbank.org., June 2008, tables 2.1 and 2.4, 28 and 35.
    19. Ibid., table 2.6, 40.
    20. Ibid., table 2.3, 31.
    21. World Bank, *The Little Data Book 2007* (Washington, D.C.: World Bank, 2007), passim.

Table 8.4. Trade Distribution, 1996–2008

Country and Measures of Growth	1996	2000–2004 Average	2005	2006	2007	2008
Albania						
EU share of exports	86.0	92.4	89.5	87.7	82.5	68.1
EU share of imports	76.3	76.9	67.3	65.3	59.6	61.5
Western Balkans share of exports	3.8	4.6	2.6	3.7	4.5	4.4
Western Balkans share of imports	3.6	3.5	3.2	4.2	5.3	4.9
Bosnia-Herzegovina						
EU share of exports	44.4	75.7	69.3	71.2	72.0	72.4
EU share of imports	36.8	69.8	68.1	65.8	61.5	62.0
Western Balkans share of exports	33.5	17.5	19.9	20.7	22.4	22.1
Western Balkans share of imports	32.1	23.3	25.0	25.0	26.7	25.7
Croatia						
EU share of exports	51.0	66.1	63.3	64.0	60.3	60.4
EU share of imports	59.4	71.1	67.4	67.3	64.8	64.1
Western Balkans share of exports	13.7	14.7	15.5	13.4	22.3	23.4
Western Balkans share of imports	1.3	2.2	3.2	3.6	5.0	5.0
Macedonia						
EU share of exports	42.8	53.6	57.0	61.3	70.1	60.6
EU share of imports	38.7	52.8	54.7	53.1	60.8	60.2
Western Balkans share of exports	7.4	28.8	30.3	32.8	31.7	31.1
Western Balkans share of imports	3.5	12.3	11.5	10.7	10.4	9.2
Serbia and Montenegro						
EU share of exports	76.2	86.4	79.6			
EU share of imports	66.4	79.6	75.1			
Western Balkans share of exports	N.A.	0.6	0.9			
Western Balkans share of imports	N.A.	0.3	0.1			
Serbia						
EU share of exports				56.3	57.7	57.4
EU share of imports				45.9	11.2	20.7
Western Balkans share of exports				30.3	29.9	29.2
Western Balkans share of imports				7.8	8.4	8.2
Montenegro						
EU share of exports				92.7	98.3	98.6
EU share of imports				80.4	76.4	77.2
Western Balkans share of exports				N.A.	N.A.	N.A.
Western Balkans share of imports				N.A.	N.A.	N.A.

Note: N.A. = not available.
Sources: International Monetary Fund, *Direction of Trade Statistics Yearbook, 2003, 2007, 2008, 2009* (Washington, D.C.: : International Monetary Fund, various years); International Monetary Fund, *Direction of Trade Statistics Quarterly, December 2009.*

trade. The more the region becomes a single economic space, as economic theory teaches us, the larger the domestic market and the greater the chance for comparative advantage in combining resources and facilities to produce more competitive exports. The effort began in 2002 with a series of bilateral free trade agreements soon spreading across the region. By 2004, they numbered thirty-two in all. By 2005, this network of agreements had indeed increased this broader intra-regional trade, but only by recapturing the 2.5 percent lost to Asian and Russian imports between 1996 and 2005. As noted in table 8.4, Bosnia-Herzegovina, Serbia, and Macedonia sent 35 to 40 percent of their exports to elsewhere in the region, and Montenegro sent 45 percent, but Croatia only sent 21 percent (with 15 percent for Bosnia-Herzegovina) and Italy-bound Albania sent 2 percent. Import shares were much lower across the board, averaging 12.1 percent of total value versus 27.1 percent for exports. Though Serbia and Macedonia approximated the import average, Montenegro with 47 percent and Bosnia-Herzegovina with 30 percent, mainly because of the aforementioned flow from Croatia, were exceptions at one end, and Croatia and Albania were exceptions at the other, with 4 and 2 percent.[22] Thus the chances for intraregional exports to reduce overall trade deficits seemed to rest with raising the Croatian share.

Then, in 2006, the Western Balkans took another step toward creating a single economic space by agreeing to multilateral free trade under the newly revived Central European Free Trade Association (CEFTA). This framework has raised expectations for increased intraregional trade. There were also complaints that it should have been in place before the tariff-free openings to the EU, and its capacity to improve the overall competitiveness of those exports has been called into question. One detailed regional analysis of its prospects finds that the chances for increasing interregional trade and also overall trade by as much as half do exist, but only if supported by internal institutional reforms and some protection against import substitution.[23] Conversely, a "gravity model" prepared by the World Bank suggests that the region and indeed all of Southeastern Europe are already "overtrading with each other." It therefore concludes that CEFTA may indeed help the region,

---

22. Štiblar, *Balkan Conflict,* table 8.1, 241.
23. Ibid., 254–65.

but only as a greater attraction to FDI rather than a direct stimulus to increased intraregional trade.[24]

Problems with Privatization and Prospects for Foreign Direct Investment

Expectations for the economic and export growth needed to raise living standards rest with private enterprise and FDI across the Western Balkans. Government plans for Serbia's economic development for 2006–12, and now under a new government for 2009–12, were, like other medium-term plans in the region, counting on new investment in the private sector to lead the way in increasing incomes, employment, and productivity.[25] Not yet included in these plans is a turn to the targeted state investments advocated by some critics of the Post–Washington Consensus and its still-market-based institutions. Advocates point to the East Asian success stories as providing the pattern to follow.[26] But their approach faces two obstacles to relying on industrial policy in the Western Balkans. One is the legacy of political clientism left behind by the monopolistic abuses of the Communist regimes and the corruption of their successors during the 1990s. The other is the continuing limit on state capacity, even with ongoing efforts to strengthen its institutions. Still, in the absence of any overall plan, several targets of opportunity have come forward. They connect private foreign investors into large, hard-to-privatize enterprises, with a minority share staying in state hands.

Overall, privatizing large industrial enterprises and utilities has not preserved residual public ownership. Starting in the late 1990s, the region's newly democratic regimes have all expended considerable political capital to reprivatize industrial enterprises left to insiders or taken back from them directly by the state. They have proceeded primarily by sale tenders or auctions at market prices, recently moving the utilities

24. World Bank, *Western Balkan Integration,* 39.

25. "Država ima plan, nacionalna strategija privrednog razvoja Republike Srbije, 2006–2012," *NIN,* January 18, 2007; International Monetary Fund, "Serbia—Fall 2008 Staff Visit, Aide Memoire," September 24, 2008, 3.

26. For a review of the arguments over neoliberalism versus industrial policy, see Daniel Yergin and Joseph Stanislaw, *The Commanding Heights: The Battle for the World Economy* (New York: Free Press, 2002).

serving national networks. Public utility sales in particular have commanded the higher prices that only foreign investors can pay, although their status as natural monopolies has made the political defense of potential foreign ownership more difficult. At the same time, the rise in direct FDI from 2004 to 2008 coincided with the sort of annual increases in GDP that will be needed to attract further investment and raise living standards. The question thus looms large of how quickly FDI and regional growth can return to or just approach these promising levels following the 2009 downturn.

Consider first the cases of the region's two largest economies, Croatia and Serbia. As shown in table 8.1, both saw sizable 5 to 6 percent increases in real GDP annually for the period 2006–8 and received the largest GDP shares of FDI. Their "gray economies" of informal or illegal activities were reduced to under 15 percent of GDP for Croatia and under 30 percent for Serbia, versus the higher, less certain figures still applying in Albania, Bosnia-Herzegovina, and Kosovo. Serbia belatedly joined Croatia in increasing access to entry and credit for small and medium-sized enterprises. Both states have shared the same problems in moving away from the political privatizations and state takeovers of the major "socially owned" enterprises under the Franjo Tudjman and Milošević regimes. The continuing gap between Croatia's EBRD ratings for privatizing and restructuring large versus small enterprises, as noted in table 8.5, is particularly striking. So is the disparity between Croatia's ranking as having the region's least "perceived corruption" and one of the poorest scores for the "ease of doing business," also shown in table 8.5. This disparity suggests the greater importance of official obstacles than unofficial ones.

For the Croatian Privatization Fund, its efforts to restart the process under new legislation following the end of hostilities in 1995 resulted only in an extension of the state's share of ownership vouchers. Half the assets in the 900 enterprises that had already been partly privatized were in fact held by the state. But this was a modest collection of mainly medium-sized enterprises, now joined by larger firms whose vouchers led the state's portfolio to jump from €500,000 in 1996 to €4.2 billion by 2000. By the next year, the belated start of sales by tender and auction had trimmed the state's holdings down to €1 billion. Subsequent sales pushed the number of enterprises still waiting for transfer from the Privatization Fund and its state holdings down from 2,500 to 1,100 by 2004, now including fewer than 100 with significant state shares.

Table 8.5. Privatization, Restructuring, and Business Indicators, 2007–8

| Country | Privatization[a] | | Large Enterprise Restructuring[a] | Perceived Corruption[c] | Ease of Doing Business[c] |
	SMEs[b]	Large Enterprises			
Albania	92	69	54	105	135
Bosnia-Herzegovina	69	69	46	84	117
Croatia	100	77	69	69	107
Macedonia	92	77	62	84	79
Serbia	85	62	54	84	91
Montenegro	85	77	46	79	84

[a]According to the "transitions indicators methodology" in www.ebrd.com/country/sector/econo/stats/timeth.htm, a rating of 4.33 equals 100 for large enterprises, representing 75 percent of assets privately owed and under effective corporate governance, and for SMEs, no state ownership and land effectively tradable, both types operating with standards and performance typical of advanced industrial economies. The same scale applied to the restructuring of large-enterprise management and organization yields lower ratings all around.
[b]Small and medium-sized enterprises.
[c]Rank in 2008 of 180 economies for perceived corruption and 178 economies for ease of doing business by ten criteria ranging from start-up days, licenses, and registration to credit, taxes, trade, and enforcing contracts.
Sources: European Bank for Reconstruction and Development, Online Database, 2007; Transparency International, *Corruption Perceptions Index 2008* (Berlin: Transparency International, 2008); World Bank and International Finance Corporation, *Doing Business 2008* (Washington, D.C.: World Bank, 2007), 103–62.

These still included the largest firms and the major utilities until those sales began in 2003 with Deutsche Telekom's purchase of the majority holding in Croatia Telekom. FDI has gone ahead since 2003, led by Austrian capital. The share devoted to manufacturing has not kept pace. Still, the large, profitable investments in Pliva's pharmaceutical complex, at least under its new US owner since 2006, and Podravka's food-processing enterprise showed what could be done. The bulk of FDI has flowed instead to the banking sector, joined recently by housing, first on the Dalmatian Coast and then into Zagreb, and by retail outlets, some along the new superhighway from Zagreb to Zadar on the coast.

Goods have contributed far less than services to the share of exports coming from FDI. The struggles of large firms to extricate themselves from the loss-making operations and politically appointed managements of the 1990s have been responsible in part for limited merchandise exports. The six shipyards distributed between Pula, Rijeka, and

Split are the outstanding examples, which still have not been privatized at this writing, despite ongoing EU pressure, and only a couple of which have undertaken enough restructuring to produce competitive car carriers or military vessels. By 2009, the most profitable shipyard in Pula was soliciting FDI, with minority shares for the state and existing employees. Another barrier to restructuring for exports has come from the many medium-sized enterprises that were privatized into the hands of insiders or political favorites. They often used the scarcity of investment capital as an excuse to strip the assets and dismiss employees. A belated 2003 audit of some 1,300 privatized firms, mainly medium-sized, found that 20 percent had been left to bankruptcy proceedings.[27]

Although less likely than large firms to boost exports, new private small and medium-sized enterprises (SMEs) have, conversely, come forward to advance Croatia's annual share of entering firms in the existing total from 1 to 5 percent between 2000 and 2005. They bring the SMEs' share in enterprise employment up to 67 percent. As pointed out in chapter 6, their 50 percent share of GDP was the region's highest, except for Albania with its dearth of large enterprises. Already in the late 1990s, such new firms in Croatia had access to microcredits offered locally through a program launched by a new Division for SME Development in the Ministry of Economics and supported by USAID grants.[28] They have gone on to record better results in profits and labor productivity than any other category of enterprise, leading Croatia's privatization and enterprise restructuring indicators for SMEs to the region's highest World Bank rating, as noted in table 8.5. Obstacles persist from the daunting delays in the registration process, which still takes forty-nine days in Croatia, and the judicial framework. The courts are still caught between uncertain property rights and the earlier political appointees, some from the Communist period, as noted below.[29]

27. Domogoj Račić and Vladimir Cvijanović, "Privatization, Institution-Building and Market Development: The Case of Croatia," in *Path-Dependent Development in the Balkans, The Path of Privatization,* edited by Siniša Kušić (Frankfurt: Peter Lang, 2005), 53–67. On the Pula shipyards and other Croatian prospects for joint FDI-state projects, see EBRD, *Transition Report, 2009,* 132.

28. Bartlett, *Europe's Troubled Region,* 88–89, 96–101.

29. For a study drawing on interviews of Croatian entrepreneurs as well as published data, see Nevenka Čučković and Will Bartlett, "Entrepreneurship and Competitiveness: The Europeanisation of Small- and Medium-Sized Enterprise Policy in Croatia," *Southeast European and Black Sea Studies* 7, no. 1 (March 2007): 37–56.

One part of Serbia's post-Milošević effort to make up for lost time in encouraging new SMEs was a new Agency for SME Development and Entrepreneurship. It took a regional lead in cutting down the time and funding needed to establish a new business, reducing the number of days from fifty-one to ten and the required founding capital from €5,000 to €500 by 2005. These measures and several modest improvements in the regulatory framework were responsible for Serbia's ranking, as noted in table 8.5, putting it ahead of Croatia in the World Bank's indicators for *Doing Business 2008* and *Doing Business 2009,* and thus reversing the two nations' previous positions.

We find the same superior performance for these new private firms, typically more medium-sized in Serbia than in Croatia. By 2004–5, their sales were exceeding those of comparable old firms by upward of 20 percent. Labor productivity and profits on investment were higher as well. Without the same head start in microfinancing as in Croatia, these firms also faced comparable problems in contract enforcement and judicial recourse.[30] As now in Montenegro, however, the number of new firms has advanced at the faster Croatian pace thanks to the streamlining of the regulatory framework. Still, for both Serbia and Montenegro, SMEs still accounted for only half of all enterprise employees and 40 percent of GDP by 2007.

The belated pace of privatization for the largest firms is another, less fortunate Serbian distinction shared with Montenegro. Starting in 2001 in Serbia and 2002 in Montenegro, new privatization laws did at least turn away from insider or political management in favor of market sales by tender, auction, or stock purchases. By 2004, three-quarters of the Serbian firms offered had been sold, with most bought at auction. The mass distribution of investment vouchers to 400,000 original employees, plus new procedures for declaring bankruptcy and compensating redundant workers, have allowed Montenegro to restructure its insider-privatized enterprises at a similar, apparently rapid pace. But missing in both Serbia and Montenegro have been a majority of the largest industrial firms and, until recently, also the utilities. The privatization of seventy-six such firms in Serbia and seventeen in Montenegro was delayed into 2005. In addition to losses that made their purchase unattractive, public opinion opposed their sale to anyone except their original, precommunist owners and also kept some attachment to the

30. World Bank, "Serbia, Economic Memorandum," December 2005.

pre-1989 notion of "social ownership." Elements of its ill-defined social property rights were reportedly surviving in some five hundred Serbian enterprises in 2009.[31] But since 2005, sales primarily to foreign investors from Russia in Montenegro and to EU or Russian firms in Serbia have gone ahead.

These large sales were primarily responsible for boosting the share of FDI in GDP past 7 percent for Serbia and 30 percent for Montenegro's much smaller economy in 2006. They have only generated more criticism in the media and the political opposition. Admittedly, they do not constitute so-called greenfield investments in new enterprises. Their long-term plans acknowledge that they must rely on such new investment once these sales of existing firms have been completed. But the examples of US Steel's Smederevo plant purchase in Serbia and now the Russian multinational Rusal's acquisition of the KAP aluminum complex in Montenegro have increased their respective shares of exports. Smederevo became Serbia's largest exporter, while KAP has added to its already-dominant position in Montenegro. More promisingly, US Steel's restructuring of enterprise management has combined with tough but transparent union negotiations and an unavoidable reduction in the labor force, first from 8,000 to 3,000 but then back to 6,000. Profitability and productivity rose in the process to levels needed to encourage other types of investments, greenfield projects included, to follow suit. For its part, US Steel agreed in 2008 to make a further investment of $100 million. But for its part, the Serbian government had already assumed the enterprise's past debt of more than $1 billion. For Montenegro, the planned construction of two new American hotels on the Adriatic Coast, which already attracted one large Russian luxury hotel along with a flood of private Russian house purchases, have been the major greenfield prospects, though they are now threatened by the downturn starting in 2009. Aluminum exports from KAP and steel exports from Smederevo fell by half in 2009, it should be added, from their 2008 levels.

31. Milica Uvalić, "Serbia's Transition to Market Economy," Wilson Center Noon Discussion, Woodrow Wilson International Center for Scholars, Washington, D.C., May 13, 2009; and Božidar Cerović, ed., *Privatization in Serbia, Evidence and Analysis* (Belgrade: Faculty of Economics, Belgrade University, 2006). Also see European Commission, *Serbia and Montenegro, Progress Report,* SEC 1428 (Brussels: European Commission, 2005); and World Bank's first separate "Republic of Montenegro, Economic Memorandum," October 27, 2005.

For Serbia, new Western investment was already holding back, awaiting an end to the political uncertainty following Kosovo's declaration of independence (as Kosova) in February 2008 and the parliamentary elections in May. In the meantime, only the Russian purchase of the oil and gas utility had gone ahead, with the prospect of further Russian investment only adding to Western uncertainty. Although the victory of the pro-EU Democratic Party and its subsequent coalition with the now similarly inclined Socialist Party did not end the impasse over Kosovo, the new government did succeed in winning long-delayed parliamentary approval for an SAA with the EU. This was enough for Italy's Fiat to step in by September 2008, promising sizable funding of €600 million to take more than 70 percent of the struggling Zastava auto enterprise in Kragujevac. The Serbian state retains the other 30 percent. The deal, delayed but signed in 2009, does not come cheaply for the Serbian side. It is to provide land at no cost and is obliged to cover two years of back wages for the labor force. Serbia's easier access than its neighbors to the big Russian market also played a part. This is a market targeted for a new model to be produced in larger numbers than the domestic market could accommodate.[32]

Aside from the exceptional case of Montenegro, favored by heavily demanded nonferrous resources and an accessible tourist seacoast, the other small economies of the Western Balkans have faced the problems of privatization without the transfusions promised by major FDI. Their informal or illegal sectors still account for roughly 30 percent of economic activity. By 2006, neither Albania and Macedonia nor the two long-standing protectorates, Bosnia-Herzegovina and Kosovo, approached the size of Croatia's economy, at least four times their GDPs in 2006. Nor did any of them match the per capita income of Serbia. Its population of 7.5 million is twice the likely Bosnian total and higher still when compared with Albania's 3.1 million and the 2 million each in Macedonia and Kosovo. Together, these four small economies barely number 10 million people. Hence they share the still greater reliance on a regional market as well as on European integration, a subject to which we shall return in chapter 9.

The significant rise in FDI across the region since 2000 had nonetheless surpassed external assistance across the region by 2004 and was five

32. "Fiat Srbija u Kragujevcu," *Vreme,* October 2, 2008, 10–12; interview with *Vreme*'s Miša Brkić, October 6, 2008.

times the total for 2007. For FDI, their economies averaged $10.3 billion a year, versus just $1.7 billion for the period 2000–2002. As may be seen in table 8.6, increased shares of FDI in GDP have covered at least some of the region's unusually large deficits on current account and made up for low rates of domestic investment, further restrained by much lower rates of domestic saving. The only exception is Croatia. By 2007, its FDI alone covered the current account deficit, while domestic savings rates were approaching 25 percent of GDP to match those of the so-called EU-8, the eight new EU members admitted from Eastern Europe in 2004.[33]

Albania and until 2005 Macedonia still ranked at the bottom of the region's recipients of FDI, even calculated in table 8.6 as a percentage of their lower GDPs. In both cases, disincentives to foreign investors have derived not from the absence of privatization but from the way it was conducted and largely completed in the 1990s. Insiders' ownership and their unaccountable managements stayed in place even after the disruptions and conflicts spilling over from the Kosovo crisis of 1999 had subsided. Meanwhile, for the entire region, as may also be seen in table 8.6, the external assistance from international and bilateral donors has continued to decline from the peak levels of 2000–2 to one-fifth of FDI.

In Albania, fully 75 percent of enterprises, mainly SMEs and most of them taken from agricultural land held by state and collective farms, had been transferred to private owners by 1996. For agriculture, the new or restored old owners were rural families receiving more than 450,000 small, subdivided shares of land. They have continued to resist any recombination into any larger, export-oriented holdings. Manufacturing enterprises still account for only one-quarter of GDP, the smallest sector in the region. Their managers are typically those in place since 1991. They took over controlling shares after the initial mass voucher distribution foundered on the pyramid schemes of the mid-1990s. Past managers were the auction bidders politically favored by local "privatization boards" to take control after the pyramids' collapse in 1997.

At the state level, the only major change was an initiative during the period 1998–2001 to open up the previously unprivatized nonferrous

33. World Bank, *Western Balkan Integration and the EU: An Agenda for Trade and Growth* (Washington, D.C.: World Bank, 2008), 7–20; World Bank, *World Development Indicators 2009* (Washington, D.C.: World Bank, 2009), 376–823.

*Table 8.6. Foreign Direct Investment and Aid versus Current Account
Deficit, and Domestic Savings and Investment versus Savings Deficits,
2000–8 (as percentage of gross domestic product)*

Country and Period	Foreign Direct Investment	Aid	Current Account Deficit	Domestic Savings	Domestic Investment	Savings Deficits
Albania						
2000–2002	4.0	7.4	−7.5	20.0	27.4	−7.4
2003–5	3.6	4.5	−7.1	17.9	25.0	−7.1
2006–8	3.6	3.4	−8.8	19.1	28.6	−9.5
Bosnia-Herzegovina						
2000–2002	2.6	13.5	−14.0	2.5	16.5	−14.3
2003–5	4.0	7.0	−17.3	−1.2	16.1	−17.3
2006–8	11.0	4.2	−11.9	−14.6[a]	18.2	−32.8
Croatia						
2000–2002	4.9	0.9	−4.7	17.1	22.0	−4.9
2003–5	2.4	0.4	−6.4	23.4	29.8	−7.2
2006–8	7.5/10	0.5	−8.3	19.0	29.0	−10.0
Macedonia						
2000–2002	6.6	6.9	−6.2	14.5	20.6	−6.1
2003–5	2.3	4.8	−4.1	16.4	20.5	−4.1
2006–8	4.5	3.2	−6.0	16.6	25.1[b]	−8.6
Serbia and Montenegro						
2000–2002	1.4	10.4	−4.4	6.8	11.0	−4.2
2003–5	4.8	5.1	−8.1	7.2	14.3	−7.1
Serbia						
2006–8	8.0	5.0	−13.9	10.0	24.5	−14.5
Montenegro						
2006–8	24.4	4.1	−34.3	−0.75[c]	26.8	−27.5

[a]Foreign savings.
[b]2007–8.
[c]2006–7.

Sources: UNCTAD, Online Database, 2008; UNCTAD, *Handbook of Statistics, 2009*
(Geneva: UNCTAD, 2009); World Bank, *World Development Indicators,* 2009; Vienna
Institute for International Studies, *WIIW Handbook of Statistics 2009* (Vienna: Vienna
Institute for International Studies, 2009); International Monetary Fund, *Serbia Country
Report,* Country Report 10125 (Washington, D.C.: International Monetary Fund, 2010);
International Monetary Fund, *Macedonia Country Report,* Country Report 09160
(Washington, D.C.: International Monetary Fund, 2009); International Monetary Fund,
Montenegro Country Report, Country Report 09188 (Washington, D.C.: International
Monetary Fund, 2009); Croatian National Bank, *Financiska stabilnost* 2 (2009), 16;
Economist Intelligence Unit, *Country Forecast: Economies in Transition: Eastern Europe
and the Former Soviet Union* (London: Economist Intelligence Unit, 2009); World Bank,
Country Assistance Strategy Progress Report for Albania, FY 06–FY 08, No. 43346-AL
(May 9, 2009), annex 6.

mines and the network utilities to wider auctions that welcomed foreign investors. And indeed, it has been in these "strategic sectors," as the initiative called them, that Italian investment in chrome mines and the electricity network, Turkish investment in copper, Greek investment in telecommunications, and even US investment in air traffic control have come forward.[34] But in the seventy-two large enterprises dominating the export capacity of the manufacturing sector, only the textile and shoe firms providing raw material to Italian firms as subcontractors have proved to be profitable. It is instead the urban construction boom for residential and commercial housing, now including Greek and Italian contractors, that has made this rapidly growing sector the one primarily responsible for rates of growth in real per capita GDP that have been the highest in the Western Balkans since 2001.

The problems facing Albania's manufacturing enterprises may of course be traced in part to aging and inferior Russian and Chinese equipment, the last of which arrived in the early 1970s. But with the arrival of foreign banks since 2000 and the potential access to affordable credit they have brought with them, the notion that there is simply no way to replace this equipment is hard to support. Still barring the way, however, as described by one Albanian economist, is "an uncontrolled free market including some wild, dynamic entrepreneurs" but still missing "the nails needed everywhere" to promote the accountability and the transparency required for access to credit from the expanded banking sector.[35] Less than 30 percent of GDP is estimated to pass through the budgetary accounts of tax authorities. This figure poses a particular problem for legally registered SMEs competing with informal enterprises paying no taxes. A stock market has existed formally since 1996, but it remains inactive because only one private industrial enterprise has been prepared to make its assets public.

The wider constructive role that even a limited amount of new FDI could play may be judged from the immunity even from requests for normal, informal payments reported by Lockheed Martin's air traffic

34. Economist Intelligence Unit, *Albania Country Profile 2004* (London: Economist Intelligence Unit, 2004), 31–41. For the details, see Fatmir Mema and Inez Dika, "Privatization and Post-Privatization in Albania: A Long and Difficult Path," in *Path-Dependent Development in the Western Balkans: The Impact of Privatization,* edited by Siniša Kušić (Bern: P. Lang, 2005), 193–220.

35. Interview with Dhori Kule, dean of the Economics Faculty, Tirana University, April 21, 2005.

control project. USAID's Albanian-American Enterprise Fund and the private Albanian American Bank have pursued large new investors with just this "demonstration effect" in mind, at least attracting a Kuwaiti contract to build the new Sheraton Hotel in Tirana. But hopes for agricultural processing remain frustrated by the aforementioned unwillingness of rural smallholders to participate. Missing provisions for access to water, energy, and waste disposal plus uncertain property rights also leave the topographically stunning potential of the Adriatic coast for tourism untapped.

Macedonia lacks any comparable potential for tourism, but its economy was already doing better by 2005 with an agricultural sector that has better memories of cooperative enterprise from the Communist period. Here, just the sort of encouragement to foreign investors sought by both the World Bank and US representatives in Albania came forward in the form of a USAID project implemented by the US dairy company Land O'Lakes. Working through the Macedonian Agricultural Marketing Association, established in 1999, the project's Seal of Quality program has brought meat, dairy, and poultry production up to EU-compatible standards. But beyond that agricultural enterprise, the industrial sector was still struggling by 2005. All but one of its dozen largest firms were managed by the insiders or political favorites who took them over early in the 1990s (as noted in chapter 1). Strikes by employees threatened with layoffs and the threat of Albanian/ethnic Macedonian warfare derailed the reprivatization under discussion at the end of the decade. Political payoffs have discouraged any real changes. Their managers typically had no knowledge of foreign languages, the Internet, or modern marketing practices. In fairness, they were also obliged to deal with a shifting set of legal requirements and a court system notorious for delayed decisions. But encouraged by a start on the SAA-related reforms and less certainly by a controversial government campaign to attract foreign investment, FDI had averaged 5 percent of GDP for the period 2006–8 (see table 8.6), more if company loans are included, before declining in 2009.[36]

36. Economist Intelligence Unit, *Macedonia Country Report 2008* (London: Economist Intelligence Unit, 2008), 15; International Monetary Fund, *Economies in Transition, Eastern Europe and the Former Soviet Union* (Washington, D.C.: International Monetary Fund, 2009), 38; International Monetary Fund, *Former Yugoslav Republic of Macedonia;* interview with Verica Hadživasileva-Markovska, Analysis and Advisory Group, Skopje, June 3, 2009.

Already by 2005, the voucherless privatization of some 1,700 SMEs had been completed, with nearly half in management-employee buy-outs and the rest in auction sales.[37] Private firms still faced the fifty-one days and numerous steps needed to establish a new enterprise that the Skopje weekly *Kapital* contrasted enviously in October 2005 with the sharp Serbian reduction noted above. A still greater reduction to fifteen days has however followed since then, reflecting in part constructive exchanges on business reform between Serbia and Macedonia that began with the implementation of the value-added tax (VAT). Led initially by a large number of new SMEs established by Albanian Macedonians and now freed from the sanctions-busting of the 1990s, their share in enterprise employment passed 75 percent in 2005.[38] In addition, as the next section suggests, the fiscal framework if not the public administration required for a legal, market economy had moved ahead in Macedonia—although with more determination than actual accomplishment, it was still enough for the EU to agree, surprisingly, in December 2005 to offer an SAA.

Neither Bosnia nor Kosovo, the two territories that continued as international protectorates through 2007, succeeded in securing such recognition, primarily for the way that their economies operate, until Bosnia-Herzegovina signed a tentative agreement with the EU in June 2008. In Kosovo, a near decade of supervision under the UN Mission in Kosovo (UNMIK) saw its economy make less progress toward a legal market framework based on a private sector attractive to FDI than any of the others in the Western Balkans. Part of the problem came from unresolved issues of indebtedness, accountability, and compensation from Serbia's takeover of all socially owned enterprises under the Milošević regime. As may be recalled from chapter 1, their initial transfer to or merger with firms in Serbia followed in 1997 after they had first been declared state property. Their subsequent damage in the NATO bombing and asset stripping during the Serbian departure of 1999 admittedly left UNMIK with a difficult task. The initial influx of

37. Interview with Borko Handžiski, Economics Faculty, Skopje University, October 4, 2005; Sašo Arsov, "Post-Privatization Perspectives of Macedonia: Could We Have Done It Better?" in *Path-Dependent Development,* ed. Kušić, 165–91; Economist Intelligence Unit, *Macedonia, Country Profile 2005* (London: Economist Intelligence Unit, 2005), 30–42.

38. Bartlett, *Europe's Troubled Region,* 88, 101–4.

aid funds did allow the repair of damaged facilities and some replacing of outdated equipment.

But how, even after independence was declared in 2008, to detach the management of the small industrial sector and the several large utilities from the political management of the leading Kosovar Albanian parties that now replaced Milošević's appointees? This problem remains, made worse by the failure to return of many of the trained Kosovar staff fired in 1989 and forced to emigrate. By 2002, UNMIK had put forward three successive proposals for privatization. After the first failed because of objections from the UN's Head Office for Legal Affairs, the second foundered over the diffused ownership that would have resulted from simply distributing 60 percent of stock shares to existing employees. The third initiative finally set up an independent Kosova Trust Agency, comparable to other privatization agencies in the region, but its efforts to auction or sell enterprises were delayed or postponed until the years 2006–7. The few actually transferred, twenty-fours before the postponement in 2004, employed fewer than 4,000 workers between them.[39] Those numbers approached 15,000 after the successful privatization of some construction firms and wineries and helped to double the total number of privatizations in 2007.

Until then, a majority of enterprises remained managed instead under the leasing arrangements, or "commercialization contracts," that US and German advisers suggested as at least a temporary way of keeping them operating while the process of privatization unfolded. The leading political parties divided these positions among themselves, and the managers appointed were under no obligation to make their assets or operations transparent in the privatization ongoing since then, so the same political interests and payments remain the rule.[40] They are now free of the uncertainty in which previous Serbian obligations left them. Yet they still struggle under the serious deficiencies in public administration and the judicial system (to be detailed in the next section). The

39. Isa Muhaj, "Delayed Privatization in Kosovo; Causes, Complications and Consequences of the Ongoing Process," in *Path-Dependent Development,* ed. Kušić, 123–63.

40. Iain King and Whit Mason, *Peace at Any Price: How the World Failed Kosovo* (Ithaca, N.Y.: Cornell University Press, 2006), 184–87; Mimosa Kusari-Lila, "Kosova's Economic Transition," Wilson Center Noon Discussion, Woodrow Wilson International Center for Scholars, Washington, D.C., April 22, 2009.

political assumption in Priština and also in Washington was that independence would push up FDI beyond the minuscule amounts recorded through 2005 or match the privatization-based high points of $400 million for 2006 and $600 million for 2007. But FDI had already declined to $500 million in 2008, before the international credit contraction took hold. At least the 2006 creation of the Central Banking Authority for Kosovo had begun putting a regulatory framework in place for a fledgling financial structure of six banks and nine insurance companies. By 2009, there were now eight commercial banks, which were 80 percent foreign owned, and their large deposit base and low rate of bad loans secured their continued presence. And despite a recent financial scandal involving its director, a proper central bank had emerged in Priština.[41] As elsewhere in the Western Balkans, such a central bank was providing not only independent policy but also the most reliable source of economic statistics. Unlike the rest of the region, however, international aid will continue to provide a larger share of foreign funding than FDI, although the previous disproportion has been greatly reduced.[42]

The case of Bosnia-Herzegovina has been both more promising and more complicated. The Dayton Agreement left its two entities, the Serbs' Republika Srpska and the Federation of Bosnia and Herzegovina, subdivided into ten cantons—Bosnian Muslim, Croat, or mixed—with more local authority than UNMIK has given to Kosovo. Nor was this authority compromised by the need for a final settlement with Serbia. The promise of a single integrated Bosnian market economy was there from the start of the postwar recovery. Under an initiative from USAID rather than the international authority of the Office of the High Representative, privatization plans were first developed at the two entity levels and then harmonized by 1998. Given the initial lack of domestic capital or much prospect of FDI, the joint plan fell back on the mass distribution of vouchers to employees, most according to years of em-

41. Kusari-Lila, "Kosova's Economic Transition"; ICEG Information Center, Budapest, *Quarterly Forecast on the Western Balkans and Turkey, Spring 2008,* 35–36.

42. At the Donors Conference of July 2008, the EU, its member states, and the United States pledged another €1.2 billion of assistance to Kosovo for 2009–11, slightly exceeding the projections for FDI. For 1999–2007, essentially the same set of donors contributed €2.7 billion, versus a total for FDI of less than €800 million. EU–World Bank Web site, http//:www.seerecon.org; Central Bank of the Republic of Kosovo. See Steven Whalen, "Kosovo: Current Issues and US Policy," Congressional Research Service, 7-5700, August 19, 2009.

ployment but with some share for veterans and all adults. This effort to preserve the presumed social ownership of the Yugoslav system had already proved unsatisfactory in the Marković reforms of the late 1980s. The same concentration of ownership in managers and political favorites followed from the same secondary market for overvalued shares as elsewhere in the region, but with an additional handicap. The entities and cantons resisted losing direct control over their large "strategic enterprises," despite the fact that links for production and supplies with the other entity or other cantons were essential to their profitable operation. The turn in both entities to tender sales for these large enterprises in 2000 did not help the process as it had for their neighbors.

The troubled process of voucher distribution went ahead more rapidly for SMEs than for large firms. Even there, privatization was not close to complete. By 2003, 73 percent of SMEs had been privatized in the Federation of Bosnia and Herzegovina and 55 percent in the Serb entity. Only sixteen of fifty-six large Federation enterprises and four of sixteen in the Republika Srpska had been privatized by that time. Assisted by a new international proposal for more transparent tender offers, sales followed in 2004 for half the remaining strategic enterprises in the Federation. They included the first large FDI, the $131 million purchase of a 51 percent share in the Zenica steelworks by the huge multinational Mittal.[43] Several others have followed, now in the Serb entity as well. They pushed the Bosnian total for FDI in the years 2006–7 at least past the figure for Albania given in table 8.6. But the process of privatization has gone little further, stalled by repeated changes in the legislation from both entities and then the struggle to reharmonize them yet again. The private share of GDP is still only one half, minus a nonobserved sector for informal and illegal activity that continues to add at least another one-third.[44] For foreign investors, navigating across the Federation among each canton's own set of separate regimes for registration, regulation, and the judicial process across the Federation remains daunting. Simply registering successfully in one

43. T. Donais, "The Politics of Privatization in Post-Dayton Bosnia," *Southeast European Politics* 3, no. 1 (2002): 3–19; Economist Intelligence Unit, *Bosnia-Herzegovina Country Profile 2005* (London: Economist Intelligence Unit, 2005), 32–33.

44. World Bank, *Bosnia and Herzegovina, Addressing Fiscal Challenges and Enhancing Growth Prospects,* Report 36156-BA (Washington, D.C.: World Bank, 2006), 10–13.

canton does not automatically qualify a firm to do business in the others. As a result, some investors have turned to the Serb entity with its single centralized regime.[45] Still, the major attraction for foreign investors remains a single Bosnian economic space with the obstacles to integrating its resources removed.

For the Western Balkans as a whole, however, the private sector has now attracted significant FDI and been supported by a more comprehensive financial transition. These features have helped to hold the European Union to its 1999 offer of a genuine pathway to membership for all the region's states. The predominance of EU-member banks in all financial sectors has surely helped to provide the framework under which SAAs were concluded by 2007 with Croatia, Macedonia, Albania, and Montenegro, in that order. Signings with Serbia and Bosnia-Herzegovina, both with conditions attached, followed in 2008, with inquiries about an SAA already emanating from newly independent Kosova. The new dilemma is how to proceed if the banking sector that was the leading recipient of FDI suffers the same downturn that new bank investment now faces globally.

Two earlier and also contradictory dilemmas remain within the region's economies, both of them troubling for the fulfillment of those promising agreements and final EU membership. One is to match the advances in fiscal reform with the restructuring of swollen public sectors and politicized commercial courts—that is, how to make them more efficient at less expense. The other dilemma is how to marshal these scarce budgetary resources to educate or train the human capital needed to advance the public and private sectors. For the labor force, only increased productivity can provide such an advance, given that populations will barely grow any more in the years ahead than their minimal advances since 1989. We consider these two challenges in order.

The Transition from Fiscal to Administrative Reform

Since 2001, the "structural reforms" requested in return for International Monetary Fund or World Bank funding have generally succeeded in

---

45. Economist Intelligence Unit, *Bosnia-Herzegovina Country Profile 2007* (London: Economist Intelligence Unit, 2007), 19–21; interview with Ivailo Izvolski, senior country economist, World Bank, Sarajevo, June 5, 2007.

freeing private enterprise from inflation threatened by budget deficits and depreciating currencies. This was the primary concern of the original Washington Consensus. The exchange rates pegged to or managed around the euro across the region have held the line against depreciation, at the cost of higher export prices and any independent monetary polices. This has confined their governments' economic leverage to fiscal policy. The resulting focus on fiscal reform has extended to the introduction of lower but more enforceable rates of income tax. At the same time, a variety of sales taxes were replaced with the VAT that is common practice across the EU. The region's own governments deserve the bulk of the credit for carrying through these reforms and seeing their ratings in the international bond markets rise accordingly.

Less progress has been made until now in reforming public administration, despite its prominence in the "conditionality" attached to EU membership. Simply improving the collection of tax revenues is not enough. Most public employees are paid too little and a few are paid too much, their overall numbers are too large, and their training or expertise is too limited. The judicial process struggles with corruption and a lack of transparency. As detailed in chapter 3, all this continues to trouble the consolidation of legal market economies as well as the public perception of executive authority and its capacity for democratic governance. Here, our focus falls on the resulting inefficiency or corruption as a series of economic obstacles—in particular to expanding the private sector for legal business and to attracting FDI.

The large size and still-limited capacity of the public sector itself remains a major economic problem. For Serbia and Montenegro, as we already saw in table 3.1, the value of public expenditures has approached 45 percent of GDP and surpassed it for Croatia. In addition to these still-top-heavy state budgets for Croatia and Serbia, table 8.7 indicates that their public and external debt has become a much higher fraction of GDP. Promising reductions in those fractions await the decentralization that is supposed to come with the EU's emphasis on regional and local government. For Bosnia-Herzegovina, public expenditures fall short of 40 percent of GDP but primarily because of divisive decentralization, not only to the two entities, the Bosnian Muslim–Croat federation and the Serb republic but also to the federation's ten cantons. For Macedonia, Albania, and now Kosovo, the biggest problem is weak central government. As noted for all three over a longer period in table 3.1, their public expenditures

Table 8.7. State Budget Balances, Gross Domestic Product (GDP) Share, and Public External Debt, 2005–7

Country	Budget Balance as % of GDP	Expenditure as % of GDP	Public Debt as % of GDP	External Debt as % of GDP
Albania	−1.1	23.6	54.9	22.0
Bosnia-Herzegovina	2.3	39.1	20.5	57.5
Croatia	3.3	43.2	41.0	85.7
Macedonia	0.5	31.7	33.5	37.4
Serbia	−2.2	45.8	50.4	59.3
Montenegro	4.3	23.6	43.7	29.5

Sources: World Bank, *The Little Data Book* (Washington, D.C.: World Bank, 2008); ICEG European Center, *Quarterly Forecast on the Western Balkans and Turkey, Spring 2008;* World Bank, *World Development Indicators 2009.*

amount to the lowest fractions of GDP. Recall that their indicators for "perceived corruption" given in table 8.5 are among the worst in the region. Yet once again, we find that a combination of local and international initiatives has recently paid promising attention to a legal market economy's need for transparent state authority.

Croatia comes first in paying such attention. With the largest economy in the Western Balkans, half again the size of second-place Serbia's with barely half its population, it has also advanced furthest in its candidacy for EU membership. Its legal market economy, up from 60 to 70 percent private, increasingly dominates the smallest gray economy in the region, down under 15 percent of GDP, as already noted. The rate for personal income taxes has come down to a range from 15 to 35 percent, and the corporate rate is 20 percent, combining to win Croatia a high 80 percent for fiscal freedom in the Heritage Foundation's 2008 Index of Economic Freedom.

Yet the Croatian economy also struggles with a large public sector and the region's largest foreign debt as a fraction of GDP. Total debt has moved well past its neighbors' to 98 percent of GDP in 2007, approaching the record high of the former Yugoslavia in 1982. Annual debt service now amounts to one-third the value of exports and remittances combined.[46] Warning signals sent by a budget deficit that already had climbed past the IMF target to 4.8 percent of GDP by 2004 have, however, prompted restraint. By 2007, with the assistance of a

46. World Bank, *World Development Indicators 2009,* 360.

questionable decision to exclude pension debts, the budget deficit was cut back to 2.7 percent. It thereby dipped under the EU's own benchmark of 3 percent. At least the public share of the burgeoning foreign debt declined from 50 percent to less than 20 percent, doubtless helped by the completion of the expensive new road from Zagreb to Zadar and Split. The economic boom encouraged along this divided highway and on the Dalmatian Coast thereby connected with Central Europe helped to push the annual growth of GDP past 5 percent for the period 2006–8.

Better training and standards for public employees and better pay for judges and judicial staff remain important, as noted in chapter 3. A replacement for the Institute of Public Administration abandoned in the 1990s has been proposed but remains on the drawing board. Meanwhile, law faculties teaching graduates much as they were trained before 1989 hardly helped to reduce the welter of Communist-era stipulations required for a private business to start or succeed. Real estate regulations have been a particular problem. At least the swollen numbers in police and military positions—often war veterans, as in the staffing of comparable positions in Tito's Yugoslavia by former Partisans—have been bought down since 2002. By 2007, the overall number of state employees had been reduced to less than 5 percent of the population and the wages bill approached 5 percent of GDP, both representative figures for new EU members from Eastern Europe.[47] But the new agencies needed for EU membership may push the numbers back up.

As private incomes have risen, judges in the lower courts typically earn less than notary publics. Such low salaries tempt them to neglect the backlog of unresolved cases or to accept payment for favorable rulings. Many judges in the higher courts, though well paid like the bulk of civil servants, remain unchanged from Tudjman's Croatian Democratic Union (Hrvatska demokratska zajednica, HDZ) regime of the 1990s, with too many of them originally appointed in the Communist era, as noted in chapter 3. The initial Social Democratic government that replaced Tudjman's regime hesitated to make changes

47. World Bank, *Croatia Country Economic Memorandum,* W25434-HR (Washington, D.C.: World Bank, 2003), 60–65; Vienna Institute for International Economic Studies, *WIIW Handbook of Statistics 2009* (Vienna: Vienna Institute for International Economic Studies, 2009).

in the judiciary, and changes have now been further delayed by the return of the HDZ to power since 2003. The commercial courts' backlog
has stretched into several years in enough business disputes, typically
involving property rights, to prompt some foreign investors to demand
access to contract arbitration outside Croatia.[48] These conditions continued sufficiently into 2009 to keep Croatia near the bottom of the
table for the Western Balkans in the World Bank's annual Index for the
Ease of Doing Business, ahead only of Bosnia and Albania, as already
noted for 2008 in table 8.5.

Although the judiciary still struggles, domestic initiatives to meet
EU economic standards in other chapters of the *acquis communautaire* have made progress. By 2009, Croatia had opened negotiations
on twenty-two of thirty-five chapters, although provisionally closing
only seven of them. These efforts earned Croatia second place in the
World Bank's index of leading reform economies for 2006–7.[49] The average time required to register property was cut from three years to six
months. The procedures for starting a business have at least been consolidated into the sort of one-stop shop encouraged by projects from
USAID in particular. A new credit bureau and a registry for movable
property helped the total for domestic business loans to rise to 58 percent of GDP by 2007. This is by far the largest in the region, although
well below the world average of 138 percent. Finally, amendments to
the insolvency law have set professional if hard-to-enforce requirements for bankruptcy proceedings and shortened time lines.

Serbia still struggles with a somewhat larger gray economy, accounting for 27 percent of all wage earners in 2005, and a smaller private share
of the legal market, under 60 percent, than Croatia. It has correspond-
ingly poorer marks for corruption to show for it. But for its ease of doing business, as recorded in table 8.5, Serbia does better than Croatia,
ranked 94th versus 105th of 175 countries in the World Bank rankings for *Doing Business 2009*. Tax policy is the most tangible difference.
Taxes on profit and personal income have come down repeatedly since
2002, now simplified since 2005 to flat rates at 20 percent for dividends

48. Heritage Foundation, *Index of Economic Freedom 2007, Croatia* (Washington, D.C.: Heritage Foundation, 2007).

49. World Bank and the International Finance Corporation, *Doing Business
2008* (Washington, D.C.: World Bank, 2007), 2–8; World Bank and the International
Finance Corporation, *Doing Business 2009* (Washington, D.C.: World Bank, 2008),
2–8.

and capital gains and 12 percent for salaries. With revenues boosted by broader collection and also a VAT of 18 percent since 2005, their total climbed to 45 percent of GDP by 2005, while expenditures were reduced to 43 percent. In the process, the combined burden of "contributions"—that is, the *doprinosi* familiar from the former Yugoslavia, which also include health and social payments in deductions from the wage bill—have come down to 35 percent from 40 percent or more, as they have across the rest of the region, with the exception of Bosnia and Montenegro.[50] But by 2006–8, the small surplus in the state budget had given way to annual deficits of 2 percent of GDP, which was small but worrisome at a time when private-sector spending in Serbia was nearly 20 percent in excess of income and the current account deficit rose to 20 percent of GDP by 2008.[51]

Momentum to make changes after the demise of the Milošević regime in 2000 provides another reason for the relatively greater ease of doing business in Serbia. Already in 2001, a movement came forward to purge the state capture set in place under the Milošević-era economy. At an international conference, "Corruption in Serbia," organized in Belgrade, the new minister of finance, Božidar Đjelić, called for anticorruption councils within the government and from the various nongovernmental organizations (NGOs) to aid in preparing new legislation. Facing a larger initial problem than Croatia, the effort nonetheless made enough changes to improve investor protection, access to legal credit, tax payments, and procedures for starting a business. According to the aforementioned World Bank rankings, all these benchmarks topped Croatia's. By 2006, the reduction and simplification of start-up procedures available in Serbia were providing a model for similar measures in Macedonia.[52]

50. Unpublished table of tax rates and contributions for Southeastern and Central Europe prepared by Jean Tesche from European Tax Handbook 2005, Regional Ministries of Finance, 2007, available at www.worldwide-tax.com; International Social Security Association, *Social Security Programs throughout the World: Europe 2006* (Geneva: International Social Security Association, 2006).

51. International Monetary Fund, "Serbia—Fall 2008 Staff Visit"; FREN, "Kvartalni monitor ekonomiskih trendova i politika u Srbiji, Okt.-Dec., 2007," http://www.fren.org.yu/sr/vesti/htm.

52. For an extensive treatment of post-Milošević progress in this area, see Milica Bisić, "Public Finance Policies," in *Four Years of Transition in Serbia,* edited by Boris Begović and Boško Mijatović (Belgrade: Center for Liberal Democratic Studies, 2005), 117–86.

The judicial system in Serbia has nonetheless remained the same weak point as in Croatia and elsewhere across the region, not only for democratic practice (see chapter 3) but also for the economy. Low marks for license approval and contract enforcement in the *Doing Business* ratings typically trace back to delays in court proceedings or judges still seeking political approval (or reimbursement) for favorable decisions. Data compiled by the Organization for Security and Cooperation in Europe and the UN International Crime and Justice Research Institute indicate that only 14 indictments and one conviction had been recorded through 2005 against more than 500 suspicious financial transactions since 2000.[53] The Serbian Parliament has continually failed to pass legislation clarifying property rights against claims for restitution or social ownership. Here is another handicap for the courts, adding to the above-mentioned delay in privatizing the remaining large social enterprises, typically operating at a loss and with unpaid debts unresolved.

The far smaller economy of Montenegro, politically separate from Serbia since 2006, had already started down the same path to tax cuts and other business reforms, again leaving the judicial system too little changed. Tax reduction and standardization started in 2002. Profit taxes were cut to 15 percent for smaller enterprises and income taxes to 25 percent. A single VAT rate of 17 percent was introduced in 2003. Since then, Montenegro has moved closer than the rest of the region in single rates. It joined new EU members Estonia and Slovakia in trimming the corporate income tax to a flat 9 percent as well. Unfortunately for private companies, the share of "contributions" in the wage bill is still the highest in the region, at 52 percent. The contributions account for 19 percent of GDP, versus 13 percent in Serbia.

Reducing corruption in an economy with the same gray legal proportions as Serbia's has benefited from the blow to cigarette smuggling and money laundering that came with end of sanctions on neighboring Serbia and the above-noted closing of numerous offshore banks by 2002. Still, with a police force of 6,000 that is inordinately large, the share of state expenditures in GDP noted in table 8.6 matches the high level for Serbia, if it is slightly lower than Croatia's. The match with Serbia continues in the itemized breakdown of the index for *Doing Business*. Again, the procedures requiring judicial approval or defining

53. "OSCE Crime Report Warns Belgrade to Clean Up Money Laundering," *Belgrade Times,* October 12, 2006, 7.

legislation receive low marks. License approval and property rights pose the same difficulties. Lengthy delays in court decisions burden contract disputes in particular. Commercial courts take up to one year to settle the hard cases involving bankruptcy or liquidation.[54] Responding to the incentive to complete the EU *acquis communautaire*'s chapter on the judiciary, a major initiative from its Finance Ministry in 2007 faced less opposition from the Interior and Justice ministries than such efforts were still facing in Serbia. In general, Montenegro has been able to accelerate its candidacy on the basis of wider public support for EU membership than in Serbia.

Standing against the same sort of progress in the larger economy of Bosnia-Herzegovina are the divisions of the Dayton Agreement. In addition to the largely separate administration of the Republika Srpska, the ten cantons of the Federation of Bosnia and Herzegovina each operates its own separate set of agencies, judicial, and educational systems, as outlined out in chapter 3. The cantons alone accounted for 45 percent of total public employment and 39 percent of the wages bill in 2005, with the Republika Srpska adding another 33 and 23 percent. The shares left to the joint Bosnian state government are minuscule, 7 percent of employees and 11 percent of wages. The proportion of civil servants appointed under nonethnic standards is even smaller, across the board.[55]

Thus it is little wonder that considered as a single country, as its candidacy for EU membership is irrevocably framed, Bosnia-Herzegovina receives a significantly lower ranking for ease of doing business than all its neighbors. Most responsible are the separate cantonal sets of agencies and courts wherein both foreign and domestic enterprises must register to work. Inconsistencies and extra charges, which are often corrupt, abound. A single central administration has come to give the Republika Srpska an advantage in attracting FDI, as noted above. In both entities, a month or more has been needed to start a new business and also for completing annual financial, market, and labor inspections. Only in 2007 did new court facilities aim to reduce registrations to five days and trim inspection procedures down to ten days or less.[56]

54. World Bank, *Republic of Montenegro: Economic Memorandum,* W32623-YU (Washington, D.C.: World Bank, 2005), iii–vi.

55. World Bank, *Bosnia and Herzegovina, Addressing Fiscal Challenges and Enhancing Growth Prospects,* Report W36156-BA (Washington, D.C.: World Bank, 2006), 56–63.

56. Ibid.

The Federation of Bosnia and Herzegovina has at least taken the lead in reducing the overall size of the gray economy toward 30 percent of GDP and pushing the legal private share toward 50 percent, still short of Serbia's, let alone Croatia's, shares. Overall, despite state budget expenses holding to 40 percent of GDP, the territory's wage bill for public employees remains high thanks to cantonal salaries that account for 61 percent. But by 2004, military demobilization had gone far enough to trim the share of population so employed to 4 percent, under the regional average and well under the average for the EU when it had fifteen members (hereafter, "the EU-15").[57] Also, the avoidance of the significant budget deficits common to the region helps to explain the absence of the growing foreign debt, troubling Croatia in particular.

This restraint has unfortunately not been accompanied by sufficient tax reform. The pace elsewhere in the Western Balkans has made the conduct of private business more predictable and attractive. The need for an inter-entity agreement delayed a VAT until 2006, when it was finally introduced at 17 percent. The delay kept the Federation of Bosnia and Herzegovina from undertaking the global reform needed to reduce the tax rate on other individual incomes from 30 to 50 percent to the 10 percent set for wages or to cut the rate on corporate profits from 30 percent. In addition, the cantons still retain some limited tax authority. These impositions combine to keep "contributions" at 45 percent of an enterprise's wage bill, down from 80 percent in the late 1990s but still the highest in the region. The Republika Srpska took advantage of its separate authority to cut both profit and income taxes to 10 percent in 2002. But its high health and public order charges have kept contributions at virtually the same discouraging rate as the Federation's.[58]

Tax reform has gone ahead in Macedonia, with state expenditures that generated virtually no budget deficits until 2008. Even then, the deficit of 2 percent came from expenses that were still only 38 percent of GDP. But while public foreign debt had fallen to 20 percent of GDP by 2008, the private share had nearly doubled since 2004 to 38 percent.[59] The limits of fiscal reform help us to understand the paradox of the Macedonian economy's international rankings. They are at the forefront of the region in the ease of doing business and near the bottom

57. Ibid.
58. Tesche, "Tax Reform."
59. International Monetary Fund, *Former Yugoslav Republic of Macedonia*.

for corruption, just the reverse of Croatia's position. Low inflation and tax rates with maximums for incomes at 18 percent and corporations at 15 percent, then cut to a 10 percent flat tax, earned 90 percent rankings for monetary and fiscal policy from the Heritage Foundation's aforementioned Index of Economic Freedom 2007. By then, the number of days required to start a new business had been brought down from forty-eight, with thirteen procedures, to four or five days and the same number of procedures. From 2003, a VAT of 18 percent has accounted for the largest part of state revenues.

So far, so good, within a framework that allowed the EU to designate Macedonia in 2005 as "a functioning market economy," as required by the Copenhagen Criteria for the SAA that it was duly offered. But two deficiencies have deterred the FDI that might otherwise have been expected to follow. They were the privatization problems for large enterprises noted above and the burden of widespread corruption. The smuggling and tax avoidance that had started with the sanctions against Serbia, then including Kosovo, during the 1990s kept the gray economy's share of GDP well above 30 percent, and closer to 45 percent by some estimates. Although police salaries were raised in the mid-1990s to reduce temptation, the pay levels for public employees at the lower grades have kept the incidence of bribery high. Increases of 10 percent in public salaries for both 2007 and 2006 have helped, but further increases would require cutting tens of thousands of employees from a public labor force of 130,000, as noted earlier in chapter 3, which thus stands as having the region's largest share of the total population, at 6.5 percent. There has been no serious proposal for such a reduction. Encouraged by the region's highest level of unemployment, the major parties continue think of themselves as employment bureaus for loyal members or large donors. Indeed, since the sweeping victory of the coalition led by the Democratic Party for Macedonian National Unity (Vnatrešna makedonska revolucionerna organizacija–Demokratska partija za makedonsko nacionalno edinstvo) in the 2008 elections, the public rolls may have actually increased by another 10,000 or more. At the same time, the "absorptive capacity" for reform or the use of external funds remains low, sometimes compounded by EU requirements for new agencies or auditing.[60]

60. Interviews with Borko Handžiski, economics officer for the EU Commission Delegation, Skopje, and Abdylmenaf Bexheti, rector of Business School, Southeast

The distribution of these jobs as a political right extends, not surprisingly, into the judicial system. The delays and the difficulty of favorable judgments against politically connected defendants are nicely illustrated by the longest listing on the American Embassy Web site for the top ten judgments outstanding. A USAID loan through its Media Development Fund for new transmitters went to pay for its local director's imports of meat, from the United States no less, for his own retail shop. The 1998 judgment of a New York court remained unenforced into 2005.[61]

For Macedonia's public administration, the economic burden of corruption is joined by the political challenge of proportional representation for the large Albanian minority, which makes up 25 percent of the population according to the official census of 2002. As detailed in chapter 3, the Albanians' share of employment in the various ministries has risen but remains well below their share of the population.[62] This discrepancy adds to the difficulty of drawing the Albanian minority into the payment of taxes and away from the illegal interaction with Kosovo that is a major part of the gray economy. The interrelated problems of economic corruption and minority representation have not, however, gone unchallenged. With NGO sponsorship, an initial "corruption conference" in 2002 saw the creation of a state Anti-Corruption Commission, while a second in 2004 renewed the effort after a major money-laundering scandal. By the end of 2007, Prime Minister Nikola Gruevski launched a "Macedonia without Corruption" campaign, again with NGO support, but also on the basis of his own party's manifesto in the recent elections.[63] This time, meeting EU standards

European University, Tetovo, October 4, 2005; with Elizabeta Georgieva, Office of the EU Special Representative, Skopje, June 1, 2009, and with Sašo Ordanoski, ALSAT National Television, Skopje, June 1, 2009. Also see Economist Intelligence Unit, *Macedonia Country Profile 2005* (London: Economist Intelligence Unit, 2005), 31–36; and International Monetary Fund, *Former Yugoslav Republic of Macedonia.*

61. Interview with Michael Latham, economic officer, US Embassy, Skopje, October 5, 2005.

62. Interviews with Naim Memeti, legal adviser to the vice prime minister, Skopje, September 5, 2005, and Agim Selani, *Analytica,* Skopje, June 3, 2009.

63. On the first two conferences, see Foundation Open Society Institute–Macedonia, *Macedonia and the Corruption, Situation and Challenges* (Skopje: Foundation Open Society Institute–Macedonia, 2005); and on the 2007 initia-

for membership have added a new incentive. Another stimulus came from greater Albanian participation in the new government (as noted in chapter 5), and from the promising economic start to the reduced set of local districts that put Albanian and ethnic Macedonian populations together. At least in districts such as Gostivar, the new local authorities were able to draw on tax and utility payments previously ignored by the Albanian population and begin the much-needed improvement of municipal facilities.[64]

In Albania itself, and even more in the former UN protectorate that is now independent Kosova, the size of state expenditures and foreign debt compared with GDP have not posed the problems seen across the rest of the region. Kosovo's expenditures and external debt like Albania's, as noted in table 8.7, remain under 30 percent. VATs again provide the bulk of revenues. Income and enterprise rates are set higher than the regional average, at 20 percent, but end up collecting less revenue because of tax evasion. The larger share of revenues collected in the Kosovo protectorate, reaching 37 percent of GDP in 2004, were also a testimony to the effectiveness of the Central Fiscal Authority, a Kosovar Albanian institution created in 2001 to coordinate excise and customs collections as well as the VAT. The resulting surplus was simply allowed to accumulate in the absence of the standing needed as an independent entity to borrow on the international market. Nor did the number of public employees in either Albania or Kosovo move past the 4 percent of total population share that ranks at the lower end of a regional standard that is itself under EU member norms.[65]

The principal problems as widely perceived for Albania and Kosovo have instead been the public corruption and organized crime that feed off gray economies nearly as large as or larger than the legal market

tive, see International Republican Institute, "IRI Helps Macedonia Combat Corruption," January 8, 2008.

64. Islam Usufi, Wilson Center Conference on European Integration of the Western Balkans, Woodrow Wilson International Center for Scholars, Washington, May 6, 2009.

65. World Bank, *Albania: Public Expenditure and Institutional Review,* Alia Mouhayed, principal author (Washington, D.C.: World Bank, 2006), 90–94; Rakia Moalla-Fetini, Huikki Hatanpaa, Shehadan Hussein, and Natlia Koliadina, *Kosovo, Gearing Policies toward Growth and Development* (Washington, D.C.: International Monetary Fund, 2005), 20–25; Government of Kosovo, *Kosovo: Public Expenditure and Financial Accountability (PEFA) Assessment Report,* April 2007, 9–12.

economy. Albania's rankings for corruption and property rights are by far the region's least favorable in the Heritage Foundation's Index of Economic Freedom 2007, as are its overall ranking as the worst in the World Bank's *Doing Business 2008* and Transparency International's "perceived corruption" index. (In 2009, sweeping reforms in business registration and construction permits in Albania jumped from 135 to 86 in the World Bank rankings). The three indexes do not appraise Kosovo, but all other indicators suggest even lower rankings. One regional specialist makes a persuasive case for the core of the problem as being "a disorganized state, not organized crime."[66] And indeed, the weakness of state institutions has done much to exacerbate corruption, which has not only discouraged the growth of a legal market economy and FDI but also facilitated the regional networks for smuggling goods and trafficking in drugs and humans that continue to be centered in Albania and Kosova. At least the arms trade has subsided since 1999.

Starting from a lower level of development than Kosovo, Albania has begun to acknowledge the economic disadvantages that the weakness of public administration poses for business enterprises. Evidence that no more than 30 percent of GDP passes through state budgetary accounting has generated efforts, now spurred on by the signing of an SAA for the EU, to push up that percentage upward. The rise of a modern banking sector noted earlier in this chapter has helped to reduce the tendency to do business in cash and hence to cut down the chances for money laundering. The flood of unauthorized settlement surrounding Tirana, perhaps doubling its total population to 900,000, has called attention to the need to regularize title registration and the procedures for property rights. Customs collection, hospital visits, and the judicial process have been identified as the major public services routinely requiring private payments.[67] Politically appointed judges, open to intimidation along with bribery, and to secretive, often delayed decisions, tarnish the reputation of a court system that enterprises try to avoid by seeking private agreements to settle disputes. As noted above, at least the few Western firms operating directly in Albania seem to have been

66. Interview with Remzi Lani, director of Albanian Media Institute, Tirana, April 15, 2006.
67. For a survey of corruption and crime, see Mirela Bogdani and John Loughlin, *Albania and the European Union, The Tumultuous Journey towards Integration and Accession* (London: I. B. Tauris, 2007), 148–62.

spared these pressures, perhaps because of their access to their own legal systems.

With World Bank assistance, a half-dozen new "transparent courts" are now operating in Albania. Three-quarters of all court decisions are being enforced, and a general effort is under way to staff more positions throughout the public administration with competitive appointments to a civil service that was barely 5 percent of the public-sector total in 2000.[68] The addition of a Department of Strategic Planning to the Ministry of Economics in 2005 reflects an Albanian readiness, further encouraged by the SAA, to join with a full set of international donors in pursuing a single coordinated strategy for administrative reform. As in neighboring Montenegro and Macedonia, public support for EU membership exceeded 80 percent. This helps a crowded field of international donors that includes the World Bank, the IMF, and the UN as well as USAID and Western embassy programs to work on the same page with the EU in reforming governance.[69] Yet the ongoing political division between President Sali Berisha's Democratic Party and the opposition Social Democrats (noted in chapter 3) continues to trouble the judicial system at the highest level. Witness the prolonged struggle during the years 2006–7 to control the anticorruption Office of the Special Prosecutor.

In newly independent Kosovo, the Central Fiscal Authority joins the aforementioned Central Banking Authority as a positive legacy bequeathed from Kosovo's near decade as a UN protectorate. Its success in tax collection had already reduced its dependence on external assistance in total public expenditures from 69 percent in 2001 to 12 percent by 2005. Otherwise, however, the last review under the UNMIK protectorate gave public financial management the lowest possible grades for comprehensiveness, transparency, disbursement procedures, and multiyear planning.[70] This is hardly surprising, given a gray economy accounting for some half of economic activity. Its size also limits the capacity to resist abuse or corruption in the territory's fledgling public administration, the Ministry of Finance included. Political ap-

68. World Bank, *Country Assistance Strategy for Albania, FY06–FY09,* Report W34329-AL (Washington, D.C.: World Bank, 2006), 51–55.

69. Interview with Greta Minxhoxi, deputy country manager, World Bank, Tirana, April 16, 2006.

70. Government of Kosovo, *Kosovo: Public Expenditure Financial Accountability, 2007.*

pointments to high positions and family members to their staffs have predominated even under the so-called EU pillar authorizing their provisional creation.[71] Whether independence will advance the more accountable public finance and more independent public administration functions needed to encourage international lending, let alone attract FDI in a newly discouraging international climate, remains to be seen.

Jobless Growth and Population Problems

Lying ahead for all the independent states of the Western Balkans, now numbering seven with Kosovo, are longer-term limitations on their labor forces. These limits will challenge their successful accession to the EU, even if attracting private investment and reforming public administration would proceed, as they had begun to do by 2006. The largest state is Serbia, but its population of 7.5 million is small by EU standards. The other states are smaller still, down to 640,000 for Montenegro. Their small economies are additionally burdened with low rates of birth and employment, compounded by too little flexibility in their labor markets. Their various economic ministries at least recognize the need (as detailed in chapter 6) to upgrade education and training to replenish a professional class that has been depleted by the skilled young people who have emigrated since the early 1990s. Already, these combined limitations have kept the promising 2004–8 upturn in GDP growth across the region from generating any significant increase in employment. Hence the specter of "jobless growth" and poverty for the unemployed raised in recent reporting on all these economies. In the process, the focus of international assistance and also domestic debate within the region shifted from financial management to job training and educational reform, at least before the international credit crisis of 2009.

The dilemma of negative growth rates in the overall population is a familiar one across Europe in the past two decades, particularly in the formerly Communist Eastern Europe. The number of retirees increases as the younger cohort declines. The EU's answer has been to push for higher rates of participation from the existing labor force. In 2005, the European Commission refocused its Lisbon Agenda on job

---

71. King and Mason, *Peace at Any Price,* 224–31.

growth, first put forward in 2000 with the general aim of making EU economies globally competitive. The specific target is an employment rate of 70 percent. As may be seen in table 8.8, all the economies of the Western Balkans fall well short of this benchmark. One reason is surely that the EU has based its benchmark on the same qualitative standard for "flexicurity" as originally advanced by the International Labor Organization. This standard is based on the Dutch model of a more flexible market for formal part-time and contractual employment that is still undergirded by the same social support for health, pensions, and other benefits familiar across the EU-15.[72] For the Western Balkans, such flexibility has appeared mainly in the informal, often illegal sector of the aforementioned gray economy. Its employees make no payments to the already-strapped system of social support left over from the failing Communist economies. The social system's burden on state budgets remains at more than 20 percent of GDP everywhere except Albania and Macedonia, prompting political struggles yet to be resolved over some sort of socially acceptable but fiscally affordable reforms.[73] Unemployment rates, even including work in the gray economy, are still well above the EU standard—or, for that matter, the Bulgarian and Romanian reductions to 7 percent recorded before rising again in 2009.

The cases of Serbia and Croatia are again the most comparable. The Serbian economy's struggle with its labor market has, however, unfolded against the less promising political background detailed in previous chapters. Its EU candidacy has suffered accordingly but did proceed, as noted above, to a tentative SAA in 2008. Responding to its economic challenge has been made more difficult, politics aside, by a declining population. Death rates passed birthrates per 1,000 in 2005. Fully half a million younger, better-educated people had emigrated during the 1990s (as noted in chapter 6), and few have returned. They have been replaced by a half million aging, less-educated Serb refugees from Croatia, Bosnia, and finally Kosovo. Thus the projection for 2005 to 2020 foresees a drop of more than 200,000 in the labor age cohort

72. On the origins of "flexicurity" and a comparison of relevant employment rates and labor flexibility across the post-2004 EU members plus Croatia, see Sandrine Cazes and Alena Nesporova, *Flexicurity: A Relevant Approach in Central and Eastern Europe* (Geneva: International Labor Office, 2007), 3–55.

73. For a detailed discussion of social policies and welfare costs across the region, see Bartlett, *Europe's Troubled Region,* 140–68.

Table 8.8. Population Growth, Labor Force, and Employment, 2008

Country or Group	Population, 2008 (in thousands)	Natural Increase by 2010 (%)	Participation Employment % of Labor	Unemployment
Albania	3,177	0.70	53.8	13.1
Bosnia-Herzegovina	3,842	−0.20	33.6	23.4
Croatia	4,435	−0.42	44.4	8.4
Macedonia	2,048	0.30	37.3	33.8
Serbia	7,350	0	44.4	13.6
Montenegro	628	0	42.3	17.2
Kosovo	ca. 2,000			45.0
EU 15	395,294	−0.10	67.3	7.1

Sources: Vienna Institute for International Studies, *WIIW Handbook of Statistics 2009* (Vienna: Vienna Institute for International Studies, 2009); European Commission, Eurostat Statistics Database, 2010; Mimosa Kusari-Lila, "Sustainable Development in Kosovo? Challenges and Opportunities," EES Noon Discussion, Woodrow Wilson Center, April 22, 2009.

of fifteen to sixty-four years. The employment rate already declined to a low point of 51 percent in 2005 after reaching 58 percent in 2001, while unemployment moved back to more than 20 percent before falling briefly in the boom years of 2007–8. As in the Croatian case, the employment rate for women was well below that for men, 41 versus 60 percent. The unemployment rate also included the same huge fraction, four-fifths, who had been out of work but looking for a job for more than a year. Like Croatia, the greatest number of jobs was in services, but with fewer of them in the private sector, which accounted for only 52 percent of all legal employment in Serbia.[74] As noted above, "informal employment" still accounted for 27 percent of all wage earners.

Limited mobility has further restricted the capacity of Serbia's labor force to support the growth need to narrow the income gap with EU members. New labor laws in 2001 and 2003 sought to advance the ease of hiring and firing, according to the guidelines for a competitive European economy set forth in the EU's original Lisbon Agenda of 2000. With encouragement from World Bank consultants and the prospect of financial assistance, the legislation allowed some progress in loosening the restrictions set in place by the Milošević regime in 1996. But political pressure from the Vojislav Koštunica government to mar-

74. World Bank, *Serbia, Labor Market Assessment* (Washington, D.C.: World Bank, 2006), 7–14.

ginalize the World Bank guidelines and accommodate trade union demands rolled back these looser regulations in 2005.[75]

Croatia's case is somewhat more encouraging. Its economy is not only closest to qualifying for EU membership, but its numbers of legally employed also began to inch upward. In contrast to the declines continuing elsewhere in the region, its unemployment rate fell from a peak of 20 percent in 2002 to 10 percent by 2007. In addition (as noted in chapter 6), fewer than 5 percent of its population had incomes falling below the World Bank's poverty benchmark of $4.30 a day at purchasing power parity, versus levels ranging from 25 percent in Macedonia up to 40 percent for Serbia and 70 percent for Albania. Croatia's substandard incomes are largely confined to pockets of rural Croats in Eastern Slavonia and the Dalmatian hinterland, plus the rural majority of the 90,000 Serbs who have returned since the warfare of the 1990s. Only in these pockets does unemployment remain above 20 percent.[76]

Accompanying these encouraging trends, however, has been the same negative rate of natural increase seen in the region's populations, Albanians excepted. According to table 8.8, Croatia's employment rate is still below 55 percent. Moving toward the Lisbon target of 70 percent would indeed facilitate the continued 5 to 6 percent rate of annual GDP growth needed even to increase per capita income from one-half to two-thirds of the EU-15 average. Narrowing this income gap would also require increased labor mobility and productivity, beyond the employment rate per se. Major incentives to remain registered as unemployed were removed in 2004 with a new labor law that reduced benefit periods after entitlement for health insurance had already been decoupled.[77] Movement away from the eastern and coastal areas of rural underemployment has at least been encouraged by the example of the new job opportunities in the towns along the new highway from Zagreb to the coast, although most of the labor for constructing the highway itself had to be imported. The scarcity of low-cost rental housing in the towns has finally been recognized. The lower employment rates for

75. Boško Mijatović, "Reform of the Labor Market and Labor Relations," in *Four Years of Transition,* ed. Begović and Mijatović, 302–24.

76. Sanja Crnković-Pozinć, "Croatia," in *Flexicurity,* ed. Cazes and Nesporova, 93–99; World Bank, *Croatia, Living Standards Assessment,* Slaman Zaidi, lead author (Washington, D.C.: World Bank, 2007), vii–xv.

77. Economist Intelligence Unit, *Croatia Country Profile 2004* (London: Economist Intelligence Unit, 2004), 35–36.

women, 47 percent versus 61 percent for men, suggest that increasing their participation would also help the advance toward the Lisbon target. Some increase in the low level of benefits for child care would encourage this advance.

Upgrading Productivity through Higher Education: Back to the Bologna Process

For increased participation in a labor force already employing more people in the service sector than in industry or agriculture, levels of education and training will also need to rise. Only with these higher levels can labor productivity expect to increase. Only with these higher levels can the region's lagging research and development generate the innovation on which intensive growth always depends. Only Croatia and Serbia spend even 1 percent of their GDP on research and development. As table 8.9 indicates, the low overall rankings for global competitiveness across the Western Balkans follow from deficiencies in higher education and even more from the lack of innovation.

This brings us back to the Bologna Process, the post-1999 program discussed in chapter 6. European-wide but not connected to the EU, the purpose of this process was to create standard programs and transferable credits for undergraduate and graduate degrees. But beyond connecting the swelling number of university students across the Western Balkans with a single set of European standards, the Bologna Process was presumed to be of particular importance for the region's economies. Its reforms were, after all, intended to advance education for employment and innovation. They assumed that better training would promote the rise in the productivity especially needed in limited labor markets. Wages could then increase with more competitive exports.

Croatia was the first regional state to sign on formally to the Bologna Process, and by 2003, a new minister of education was championing the changes, including the introduction of new textbooks on a regular basis. Although its introduction has proved troublesome, Croatia's economic interest in educational reform seems clear. Following the emigration of the 1990s, only 11 percent of the reduced population have university degrees, and another 11 percent have the *gimnazija* degree, which adds at least a year to an American high school's curriculum. State funding for education did rise, from 4.2 to 4.7 percent of GDP by

Table 8.9. Global Competitiveness, Higher Education, and Innovation, 2007–8

Country	Overall Ranking	Higher Education and Training Ranking	Higher Education Enrollments[a]	Innovation Ranking
Albania	109	103	21.7	131
Bosnia-Herzegovina	106	98	25.2	121
Croatia	57	46	36.3	50
Macedonia	94	75	21.2	92
Serbia	91	82	N.A.	78
Montenegro	82	79	N.A.	104
Bulgaria	79	66	40.1	88
Romania	74	54	43.7	76
Slovenia	39	24	83.2	30

Note: N.A. = not available.
[a] Percentage of population in 2005, age 19–24 years.
Source: Toby Linden and Nina Arnhold with Kirill Vasiliev, *From Fragmentation to Cooperation: Tertiary Education, Research and Development in Southeastern Europe,* World Bank Education Research Working Paper 44748 (Washington, D.C.: World Bank, 2008), 2, 9.

2005, the region's highest fraction and close to the EU-15's average of 5 percent. Of those funds, however, only 0.8 percent of GDP was spent on higher education, two-thirds of the EU average. Meanwhile, the Croatian share of its cohort of nineteen to twenty-four years enrolled in higher (or tertiary, in European terminology) education jumped ahead to 30 percent in 2000 and 36 percent in 2005. It is the region's highest proportion, although still short of the EU-15 average of 62 percent. There followed a disparity that has grown between student numbers and state support. This gap is as much at issue in recent student strikes as have been problems with the Bologna Process.[78]

The large number of students now crowding into Zagreb University, up by one-third from 2000 to 2007 to 67,000, find that the technical and business training most relevant to the economy (and to the EU's Bologna Process for reforming higher education), are relatively neglected. The Economics Faculty added a small program in business

78. Toby Linden and Nina Arnhold with Kirill Vasiliev, *From Fragmentation to Cooperation: Tertiary Education, Research and Development in Southeastern Europe,* Education Working Paper 4748 (Washington, D.C.: World Bank, 2008), 7–20; Council of Europe Development Bank, *Social Challenges in South Eastern Europe* (Strasbourg: Council of Europe, 2005), 25–27; World Bank, *Little Data Book for 2009* (Washington, D.C.: World Bank, 2009), 15, 65.

administration only in 2005. A few small private business schools have now opened, but as noted above, plans for a new Institute of Public Administration and International Affairs have not gone forward.

Overall, the Bologna framework has encouraged student discipline and introduced faculty evaluations. Still, it has otherwise failed to raise the quality of university education. A large number of students, perhaps one-third, enrolled beyond the state-funded quota or needed extra years for graduation. They took the lead in resuming student strikes in 2009. Their principal demand is an end to the annual fees of roughly €1,000 and a return to the free enrollments of the Communist era.[79]

For their part, Zagreb's faculty members continue to resist the single, coordinated university administration also mandated under Bologna that would save some of the costs of making fees essential, as it has at Tuzla University in Bosnia. Rijeka and the four new smaller universities at Pula, Split, Zadar, and Dubrovnik have adopted such unified administrations and faced shorter-lived strikes. A new curriculum for tourist management has started with USAID encouragement at Dubrovnik, while Rijeka is moving to comply with the faster completion of the more employment-oriented degrees mandated by the Bologna Process.[80]

Serbia's Ministry of Education had also signed on to the process later in 2003 with similar hopes of upgrading the labor force. Both the government's "National Strategy for Economic Development, 2006–2012" and its successor's plan for 2009–12 openly acknowledged the challenge of increasing productivity or simply falling further behind the EU level. Only a significant increase in productivity would allow the 45 to 50 percent rise in GDP and in exports by 2012 that would start to close that gap, a post-2009 recovery permitting. And it is the very increase in technical and business education promised by the Bologna Process that the Serbian plan is counting on to boost productivity accordingly.[81]

It remains to be seen how rapidly this reform can proceed with the lowest state share of GDP spent on education in the region, 3.8 percent, and with same swelling student numbers as in Croatia, up to 200,000 overall and 90,000 in Belgrade University alone. The funding short-

79. Linden and Arnhold, *From Fragmentation to Cooperation.*

80. Interviews with Vesna Pusić, member of Parliament, June 4-5, 2006, and with Ivan Grdešić, professor of political science, Zagreb University, Zagreb, June 2, 2008.

81. "Država ima plan" (The State has a Plan), *NIN* (Belgrade), January 18, 2007, 39–51.

fall has prompted the charging (and protesting) of fees for the further two years of training needed for the much-desired master's degree. The economy needs more undergraduates who have completed even the three-year course of study introduced by the Bologna plan. It also needs a publicly supported business school, although the financial course offered by the Economics Faculty of Belgrade University offers a business-related economics degree, and Singidunum University, the largest of a growing number of small private schools, provides a similar degree or a master's in business administration. Such training is particularly important for a service sector whose employment share already exceeds one-half, as elsewhere in the region.[82] As for wider European connections, at least the lifting of the long-standing Schengen visa restrictions on Serbia in December 2009 should begin to increase the number of university students who have visited an EU country. According to the Belgrade faculty, it stood at a minimal 3 percent in 2005.

The three small states of what some have called the Southern Balkans—Montenegro, Macedonia, and Albania—face the same challenge of using educational reform to raise the productivity of a limited labor force. Their combined population is less than 6 million. Their three sets of ministries and universities have nonetheless gone ahead with comparable national plans. Bosnia could not pass a plan until 2007. Frustrating agreement and limiting any integrated funding or economies of scale were its above-mentioned division of budgetary authority between the two entities and the Federation of Bosnia and Herzegovina's cantons. Nor was there any planning to link education and the economy in UNMIK-administered Kosovo, even on the Kosovar Albanian side of the budgetary and political divide.

The national plans in the three states of the Southern Balkans confront population problems that are more daunting than those already outlined for Croatia and Serbia. Smaller populations, ranging from 3.1 million for Albania and 2 million for Macedonia down to 640,000 for Montenegro, have also ceased to grow, if not beginning to decline as in their two larger neighbors. Even the more sizable rate of Albania's population growth declined to 0.7 percent a year for 2004–8, versus 0.2 to 0.3 percent for Montenegro and Macedonia. In addition, the employment rates for all three do not even reach the 50 percent marks exceeded by Croatia and Serbia. Albania appears to be an exception,

82. World Bank, *World Development Indicators 2009*, 48–50.

with an overall rate of 57 percent, well ahead of Montenegro, at 41 percent, and Macedonia, at only 36 percent in 2005. But for its urban economy, where the prospects of productivity and even employment gains surely lie, the Albanian rate is only 47 percent. It is instead an employment rate of 65 percent in the region's largest and least-productive rural economy, still accounting for 56 percent of total population, which brings up the overall rate.[83]

The apparently striking differences in rates of unemployment between the three states appear less significant when the sizes of their respective urban sectors, where almost all the registered unemployment occurs, are taken into account. Thus, Albania's lower level of unemployment, until joined by Montenegro's fall to 12 percent in 2007, has come from a relatively smaller urban population. Its urban share of 44 percent and unemployment rate of 14 percent for 2005 compare instructively to 62 percent and 37 percent, respectively, for Macedonia. Reducing unemployment, as elsewhere across the region, are the chances for informal work in the aforementioned gray economies. Discouraging formal employment in every case are the aforementioned "contributions" (*doprinosi*) for social services and local charges that discourage legal employers. For the unemployed in all three economies, as in Croatia and Serbia, those seeking jobs for more than one year remain some four-fifths of the total. Their skills, whatever they might have been, erode with this passage of time.

The declining pools of employed labor in all three countries have therefore been able to take advantage of the rising growth rates since 2002 and thus have seen their wages increase, most strikingly in Montenegro. There, the 7 percent drop in legal employment from 1998 to 2004 was accompanied by a literal doubling of net monthly wages. In 2004 alone, this advance amounted to a 9 percent increase in real wages. Macedonia, with the group's lowest annual increase in GDP for 2004, short of 4 percent, still managed to boost real wages for the legally employed by 7 percent. Both boosts far exceeded the increase in labor productivity achieved in the industrial and services sectors where these wages were paid.[84] Only the training provided for younger work-

83. World Bank, *Albania: Trends in Poverty and Inequality, 2002–2005* (Washington, D.C.: World Bank, 2006), 3–5.
84. See the detailed presentation of this productivity gap for Montenegro given by World Bank, *Republic of Montenegro, Economic Memorandum,* Report 32623-

ers coming out of an improved system of education can promise expanded employment and higher productivity.

Despite the disparity in overall educational expenditures as a percentage of GDP, the systems of higher education in all three nations have made efforts to start dealing with generally comparable problems. It is true, as noted in chapter 6, that Montenegro spent 5.4 percent of GDP on education in 2005, Macedonia 4 percent, and Albania only 3.4 percent. One further Albanian challenge is to establish the faculties for engineering and related technical subjects that were left to Russian oversight and training in the Soviet Union when the first Albanian university was founded in Tirana in 1957. The regime's split with the Soviets a few years later ended these links. Its attraction to Mao Zedong's Cultural Revolution saw no need to replace them during the subsequent Chinese connection (1962–78). The emphasis on these subjects in the former Yugoslavia has meant that the universities in Podgorica and Skopje did not enter the postcommunist period with this disadvantage.

Otherwise, the three systems have experienced the same surge in university applications and enrollment since the 1990s, while trying to adjust to the Bologna Process. They have begun to promote training in business and public administration. Such an emphasis has replaced primary education as the focus of international assistance, particularly from the World Bank. The placement of computers in a large number of these schools has been one accomplishment, sponsored privately by Intel in Montenegro and by USAID in Macedonia and Albania. The training of secondary school teachers has, however, languished as salaries have remained low. In Montenegro and Albania in particular, there is a growing shortage of teachers, given the discouraging prospect of an assignment to isolated rural areas where declining enrollments threaten closure.

The increase in university enrollment has been most striking in Macedonia. In Skopje and Bitola, both state universities, the student/faculty ratio has climbed to 27/1. And as their combined enrollment rose from 25,000 in 1994 to 45,000 in 2002 and then to 65,000 (Skopje alone to 50,000) by 2007, faculty salaries failed to keep pace even with

---

YU (Washington, D.C.: World Bank, 2005), 20–38. For Macedonia, employment data are from the Economist Intelligence Unit, *Macedonia Country Profile 2005*, 22–25, 57.

the average wage. Since 2006, the Gruevski administration has addressed at least the overcrowding in Skopje by opening new faculties at Bitola and a new university in Stip, but to uncertain effect.[85] Bitola's specialization in tourism and catering has specifically targeted one existing gap.

A broader gap is business education, but a major initiative has come from the Southeast European University in Tetovo. Connected to Indiana University, it enrolls the largest part of the 10,000 students in the half-dozen private universities. Its business school graduated its first class in 2005, and ethnic Macedonians primarily from Skopje accounted for one-quarter of a student body that was originally all Albanian Macedonians. For the university as a whole, this non-Albanian fraction still held in 2009.[86] All university classes are taught in English, Albanian, and Macedonian. This practice sets it apart from the exclusive use of Macedonian in the two state universities noted above and of Albanian in the other one, the long-resisted, now-accredited Tetovo University.

The University of Montenegro, as it has been called since 1992, has yet to establish a business school or separate business major in its Economics Department in Podgorica. Among the eight of its fifteen faculties located there, the four devoted to engineering have the strongest reputation. Some 11,000 students are enrolled across these fifteen faculties. Of the seven not located in Podgorica, only the Faculty of Tourism and Hotel Management in Kotor provides training directly for the economy. In Podgorica, the Department of Political Science has, however, taken the lead in establishing a separate program for EU studies and public administration. There is also the new Mediterranean University, established in 2006 as Montenegro's first private university, to develop six faculties, among them Tourism and Hotel Management, Information Technologies, and Business Studies per se.

Despite a population of 3.1 million that is five times Montenegro's, the authorized full-time enrollment of 18,000 in Albania's eight state universities amounts to less than twice Montenegro's 11,000. Here is

---

85. Interviews with Ordanoski and Selani, 2009; Anthony Morgan, "Higher Education Reform in the Balkans," *Academe,* September–October 2004, http://www.aaup.org/publications/Academe/2004/04so/04somorg.htm.
86. Interview with Bexheti; US ambassador's roundtable discussion, Skopje, June 2, 2009.

one indicator of an educational system that is starting from a lower position than any of the others in the Western Balkans. Another is a national average number of only 8.5 years in school, also the lowest in the region and six years under the Europe-wide average for members of the Organization for Economic Cooperation and Development.[87] Among the existing university graduates in the 1990s, some 40 percent are said to have emigrated. Among the current cohort, fewer than 10 percent are training for or pursuing teaching careers. This aggravates the aforementioned shortage of primary and secondary school teachers in the upland areas of declining population. As for higher education, only half the limited full-time enrollments graduate, versus fewer than 10 percent of the large number of part-time students crowding into the two large state universities of Tirana and Shkodra for no fees charged. Applications for full-time admission and scholarship support rose to twice the number the available places, encouraging false documentation in a sizable fraction of applications.

At the same time, a strong desire not to fall further behind European standards and the EU economies in particular prompted university officials and the Ministry of Education to support Albania's signing of the Bologna Declaration in 2003. Efforts to adopt the new three-tier system of degrees more oriented toward employment have encountered less faculty opposition than elsewhere in the region. Already in 2002, the Economics Faculty at Tirana and Shkodra universities entered an agreement with the University of Nebraska that featured four-month exchanges of faculty. Their purpose was not only to benefit the younger and less experienced Albanian faculty but also to introduce class participation and more frequent exams into their courses, precisely the direction desired by the Bologna Process.

By 2006, Tirana's Economics Faculty could count 7,000 full-time students, with many of the further 1,200 already employed students attracted to the new master's in business administration (MBA) program.[88] In response to the sizable number of Albanian students seeking to study abroad, the late Gramoz Pashko established the New York University of Tirana in 2002 as Albania's first private university, modeled on the comparable State University of New York affiliates in

87. World Bank, *World Development Indicators 2009,* 80–96.
88. Interview with Dhori Kule, dean of the Economics Faculty, University of Tirana, Tirana, April 21, 2006.

Prague, Athens, and other locations. Still small, with 500 undergradu-ates, the new institution launched its own MBA program with Swiss and British collaboration in 2004. The fees needed for operation are a barrier to rapid expansion. So are the fees charged in the other new private university opened in 2006 or the fifty private high schools now functioning. The models provided by these two MBA programs, one public and one private, nonetheless suggest that Albania, despite start-ing from further back than its neighbors in the Western Balkans, can make economic use of the Bologna Process if the state budget and pri-vate enterprise can mobilize sufficient support.

Balance Sheets for Postconflict Economies from the Post-1999 Decade

Where then do the similar, although hardly identical, balance sheets for the transition economies of the Western Balkans stand a full decade after the violent conflict and open warfare of the 1990s? Before turning to the international financial crisis and the road ahead in a conclud-ing chapter, some recognition is due the progress of the past decade. The fiscal discipline of governments and the financial discipline of a banking sector restructured around private and foreign competition are major accomplishments. The competitive privatization of industrial and service enterprises has been pulled along in the process. Small and medium-sized enterprises are entirely privatized and have become the most profitable and productive sector of legally registered businesses. They have also drawn constructively on international assistance.

The privatization of large firms—particularly the network enter-prises for fuel, utilities, and communications—has faced a variety of obstacles. Most common has been domestic political resistance to ac-cepting foreign control of the monopoly powers inherent in such en-terprises, however abused domestically in the past and however much the shortage of domestic capital calls out for foreign funds. One conse-quence for Croatia in particular has been the reemergence of the same state borrowing that created foreign debt in the former Yugoslavia and whose servicing encouraged further borrowing. In general, however, the region's governments and central banks have favored FDI over state recourse to foreign borrowing, typically overcoming the popular oppo-sition to FDI. The only new state initiatives have been linked, as with

Serbia's automobile production, to majority ownership and control by a private foreign partner.

Meanwhile, low birthrates on top of the emigration that peaked in the late 1990s have created shortages of trained labor and educated professionals. These shortages have in turn threatened the capacities of the domestic economies to grow. And they need to grow enough to begin closing the striking differences in income from the EU average, and to increase exports enough to narrow the equally striking trade deficits that divert domestic savings to imports. Across the Western Balkans, the imperatives of improving the training of management and increasing the productivity of labor have at least been widely recognized during the past decade. Also emerging well before the Greek crisis of 2010 has been the need for more effective public administration, smaller in size but with the greater absorptive capacity that EU membership will demand (see chapter 3). In sum, the region has already come to see a public-private nexus, rather than any lingering neoliberal reliance on privatization per se, as the only way to make the scarce domestic resources of capital and labor more productive.

The growing awareness of these imperatives across the region has been a major achievement of the past decade. The narrower economic imperatives treated in this chapter will surely need the wider social consolidation of a new middle class, already posed as a major challenge for embracing democracy in chapter 6. Together with a vibrant and open pluralism (with competitive parties and an engaged civil society), the rule of law, and a regulated market economy, they provide the four cornerstones on which a democratic political culture stands, the same foundation on which the original members of the European Union began building more than a half century ago. How the nations of the Western Balkans might now proceed into the next decade, advancing toward EU membership as functioning democracies as well as "functioning market economies," concerns the concluding chapter.

Chapter 9

Democracy Building and EU Accession during a Global Recession

The preceding chapters have systematically explored the complex dimensions of political and socioeconomic transition in the Western Balkan states, particularly in the post-2000 period. Overall, the evidence indicates that by 2010, the seven states in the region had overcome the instability and malaise of the early postcommunist and postconflict stages of development, and most had made impressive strides forward in both political democratization and economic growth. But substantial developmental deficiencies also jeopardized the effort of all states in the region to become more prosperous, stable, and democratic, and also hampered their individual efforts to be smoothly integrated into the European Union. Thus, in 2010, and relative to the Western European and Central and Eastern European member states of the EU, the countries of the Western Balkans remained low-capacity or weak democracies, with lower-income economies and weaker legal markets.[1] More specifically, the region still struggled with its own "democratic deficits"—particularly in the routine implementation of the formal rules that have already been put in place—as it faces an EU seeking to overcome many similar difficulties. And now, as noted in the previous chapter, the income gaps and trade deficits supporting the economies of the Western Balkans faced the further burden of the international financial and economic crisis that began at the end of 2008.

---

1. See also Will Bartlett, "Economic Development in the European Super-Periphery: Evidence from the Western Balkans," *Economic Annals* 54, no. 181 (April–June 2009): 21–44.

The Region's Uneven Record since 1999

On the positive side, as detailed in earlier chapters, the first decade of the twentieth century was a period of substantial economic and sociopolitical progress for the Western Balkans. The pattern of striking economic growth during the years 2004–8 had laid the groundwork for the region's potential prosperity, reversing the impact of the transitional recession and the economic consequences of warfare during the 1990s. At the same time, democracy building and state building made significant progress. On the eve of the global financial crisis that began in the fall of 2008, most states in the region had already established substantially privatized economies, modern and largely civic-oriented constitutional frameworks, and increasingly professionalized public administrations. Growing and more engaged civil societies, less fragmented and more stable party systems, and larger and more urbanized middle classes had gradually evolved, which included activists and political actors who were adapting to the institutions of pluralist politics, and also beginning to embrace tolerant and more moderate political values. New interactive communication technologies also made information more accessible to citizens, which potentially could assist democratic participation.

However, although in the decade after 2000 a discernible democratic consolidation phase had clearly supplanted the initial period of postauthoritarian transition, very serious obstacles to further democracy building remained. For example, throughout the region the continued politicization of administrative and judicial agencies, and widespread corruption both in the public and private sectors, seriously impeded efforts to achieve a breakthrough to more advanced and sustainable levels of institutional effectiveness and democratic accountability. The shallow membership of nongovernmental bodies and their heavy dependency on foreign financing, along with the problematic independence and security of the media sector and continued obstacles to more extensive female participation, particularly in political and economic life at the local level, also impeded the creation of more robust democratic political cultures. The highly polarized character of political party life and elite politics, in which many actors were only "contingent democrats," who were more obsessed with seeking and preserving power than with effective policymaking and accountability to voters, also weakened governmental performance and derailed the implementation of reform-oriented legislation. Aspects of social exclusion, social inequalities, and pockets of poverty also marred the class structure of the states in the region, and complicated efforts to broaden opportunities and establish more socially open societies. A tier of superrich tycoons at the apex of each social structure often corrupted political life, and they had little accountability to established national institutions. Advances in the size and security of the middle classes were clearly slowed by the economic recession and stimulated the persistent brain drain of human capital from the region. The incomplete reform of tertiary education also complicated efforts to achieve the progress in "brain gain" that is required for the region's future development. And although radical nationalism diminished appreciably across the region in the post-2000 period, the continuing ethnic stratification and ethnic distancing in some states perpetuated enclaves of interethnic strife, exclusion, and intolerance, threatening both firmer state cohesion ("stateness") and regional stability.

The EU and Western Balkan State Building

Starting with the conflict-laden 1990s, a plethora of internal and external actors—international, regional, and state agencies, and private organizations—have been engaged in promoting, assisting, and monitoring the political and economic transformation of the Western Balkan states. But particularly in the decade that followed the adoption of the Stability Pact for Southeastern Europe in 1999, the European Union served as the major external actor shaping the region's advances and ambitions. The EU has provided the preferred template of reform in Southeastern Europe, and it has also been the primary organization evaluating how well or poorly the states in the region were achieving reform. Thus, progress is gauged by both EU and domestic Balkan elites as being fundamentally a question of advances in the process of "Europeanization," understood as "EU-ization." Indeed, the entire enterprise of regional transformation since 1999 has been directed at the eventual accession of the region's states to the European Union.

The EU's procedures and requirements for the accession of new members have sought to reduce the democratic deficits or illiberal practices that have troubled acceding "candidate" and "potential candidate" states. Indeed, the EU preaccession process has been one of the most ambitious democracy-promotion efforts ever attempted. The endeavor has relied upon a toolbox of mechanisms that are used to condition or leverage acceptance of the Europeanization process. In brief, the EU has utilized a reward-based approach in which Western Balkan governments—just like the Central European states before 2004, and Bulgaria and Romania before 2007—have been required to comply with certain conditions and to introduce various prointegration reforms in order to obtain assistance and be deemed ready to progress through the stages of the preaccession process.

The rewards for adhering to the EU's preaccession program have been considerable. Starting with only €1.4 billion for 1991–94, and €3.1 billion for 1995–99, financial assistance to the Western Balkan states in 2000–2006, coming under the Community Assistance for Reconciliation, Development, and Stabilization (CARDS) program as part of the Stabilization and Association Process, exceeded €5 billion. And starting in 2007, a new framework, the Instrument for Pre-Accession (IPA), replaced earlier assistance instruments. For 2007–13, IPA allocated €10 billion in financial support for Western Balkan EU candidate and potential candidate countries (and another €1.5 billion for Turkey). IPA includes five components: transition assistance and institution building, cross-border cooperation, regional development, human resources development, and rural development (the potential candidate states have access only to the first two components).[2]

Milada Vachudova has usefully outlined four mechanisms through which the EU has typically endeavored to exercise leverage on domestic political change in countries that have been engaged in the preaccession process.[3] Two of these mechanisms were most apparent immediately following the end of the one-party Communist order, when illiberal elites or predemocratic constellations of political forces were still in partial control of the postcommunist political process: first, the role played by European institutions as a "focal point for cooperation" among opposition forces to the illiberal elites; and second, the creation of incentives for opposition politicians to "adapt" their agendas to the EU and other international organizations. Two other mechanisms usually became more significant after so-called watershed elections that

2. Tamás Szemlér, "EU Financial Support for the Western Balkans: Well Suited to Real Needs?" paper for workshop: "Roadmap for the Western Balkans," Brussels, October 11, 2007. See also Milica Uvalić, *Serbia's Transition: The Thorny Road to a Better Future* (London: Palgrave, 2010).

3. Milada Vachudova, "Promoting Political Change and Economic Revitalization in the Western Balkans: The Role of the European Union," *Slovak Foreign Policy Affairs,* Fall 2005, 67–73.

were deemed to result in the political ascendancy of reform democrats committed to a more fundamental break with the Communist past: "straightforward conditionality" that is reward based, and the process of "credible commitment to reform" itself. For example, elections such as those in Romania (1996), Bulgaria (1997), Slovakia (1998), Croatia (2000), Bosnia-Herzegovina (2000), Serbia/Montenegro (2000), and Macedonia (2002) were viewed by the EU as turning points, although in some cases subsequent setbacks occurred. In such elections, reformist forces achieved electoral success and begin to evince a "credible commitment to reform" that seem to make democracy more irreversible, and the regimes themselves more susceptible to the kind of EU conditionality that could have positive consequences.

The EU's conditionality-based assistance in the Western Balkans has played a very important part—along with domestic efforts and the work of other organizations and agencies—in the region's partial progress during the decade after 2000. Moreover, it has been the frequently mentioned "gravitational pull" of EU prosperity that has kept the troubled Western Balkan regimes focused on moving in a democratic direction. But a systematic assessment of the region's democratic consolidation reveals a mixed picture of successes and continued difficulties. All too often, political life in the region has exhibited a coexistence of democratic rules and democratic rhetoric with nondemocratic practices. In any event, the imperfectly consolidated character of Western Balkan democracy has combined with the region's checkered history and reputation in Western and Central Europe to prompt considerable skepticism within EU public opinion about a rapid pattern of EU enlargement.

Generally speaking, however, the EU enlargement process, especially until the latter half of the post-2000 period, was an elite-driven enterprise, and therefore accession moved forward at a rather steady pace. But in 2005, after the French and Dutch votes against constitutional change chilled the atmosphere for rapid enlargement, considerable skepticism arose in EU public and elite opinion about the urgency of accession for the Western Balkan states. And after Bulgaria and Romania entered the EU in 2007—subject to new oversight in order to deal with perceived deficiencies in their performance—it became clear that entry into the EU for the remaining states of the Balkans would not come quickly or easily.[4] The EU subjected Bulgaria and Romania to a for-

---

4. On the mixed record of accomplishment by states that have recently entered the EU, see Graham Avery, Anne Faber, and Anne Schmidt, eds., *Enlarging the*

mal, post-entry process, the Cooperation and Verification Mechanism (CVM). Its annual reviews denied funding to Sofia and criticized Bucharest over judicial compliance. Their qualifications for entry now questioned, the Western Balkans will now face more pre-entry scrutiny than did their two Balkan neighbors. The terms for Croatia's pending entry in 2013 provide for EU monitoring of compliance with several *acquis* chapters both before accession and extending afterwards, without a formal CVM, for two years. The Romanian and Bulgarian cases also illustrate that it is a political decision by EU elites, rather than ideal performance vis-à-vis a set of criteria or benchmarks, that plays the crucial role in shaping the EU accession calendar.

Already in 2006, Eurobarometer data indicated that the majority of the population in the twenty-five EU member states supported the eventual accession of most Western Balkan states, *providing* that the countries of the region would comply with all the conditions stipulated by the EU as mandatory for membership.[5] But even if the Western Balkan states could demonstrate compliance with EU norms and requirements, the extent of support for accession of those candidate and potential candidate states was quite shallow (for Macedonia, 49 percent; Bosnia, 48 percent; and the former Serbia and Montenegro—including Kosovo—47 percent). EU citizen support was greatest for Croatia (56 percent), while a majority of EU citizens were opposed to the entry of Albania (with 47 percent against and only 41 percent in favor). According to the EU respondents surveyed, the major challenges facing all the Balkan countries were respect for human and minority rights (43 percent), reconciliation and cooperation with neighboring countries (31 percent), and democracy (30 percent). Skepticism in the EU regarding the advantages of admitting the Western Balkan states in particular derived from a variety of factors, including the kinds of economic issues and anti-immigrant stereotyping that arose during the referendums in France and the Netherlands. But along with such domestic influences, there was also a persistent public perception in the EU that the Western Balkan states—as discussed in earlier chapters—

European Union: Effects on the New Member States and the EU (Brussels: Trans European Policy Studies Association, 2009). See also Daniel Korski and Richard Gowan, *Can the EU Rebuild Failing States? A Review of Europe's Civilian Capacities* (London: European Council on Foreign Relations, 2009).

5. Eurobarometer, *Special Eurobarometer 255: Attitudes toward European Union Enlargement* (Brussels: European Commission, 2006).

continued to lag in the Europeanization of their political cultures and to suffer from a profound democratic deficit in comparison with the old EU member states, and also the newer ones that had entered the EU in mid-2004.

Such negative perceptions, along with the EU's own constitutional problems in adopting the Lisbon Treaty up to late 2009, and also the interstate differences and rivalries among EU member countries regarding whether and how best to proceed with European integration, weakened interest in rapidly moving forward with the accession of new members. Much to the chagrin of Western Balkan elites, Europe seemed to be deeply afflicted by the well-known "enlargement fatigue" that many observers believed might place the region in a "ghetto" or "dark hole" surrounded by EU member states. At the summit of EU leaders in June 2006, a declaration suggested that constitutional momentum—derailed by the 2005 French and Dutch "no" votes—remained a high priority, and set the end of 2008 as an endpoint for the organization's debate on further European integration. But support for further expansion of the EU remained problematic. For example, large segments of the public in France (54 percent), Germany (52 percent), Luxembourg (50 percent), Finland (47 percent), Austria (45 percent), the Netherlands (44 percent), and Belgium (41 percent) indicated that they felt frustrations, annoyance, or fear when they heard discussions about EU enlargement.[6] And on a general level, a systematic qualitative analysis of attitudes within the EU member states, conducted in February–March 2006, revealed a climate of uncertainty and anxiety about the future.[7]

The basis for such concern lay in fears about job security, the impact of globalization, and a weakening of the social protection systems. There were also widespread concerns about the existence of threats to the integrity of the "social fabric," including worries about traditions being lost. In some EU member states—such as Germany, the United Kingdom, Cyprus, and Estonia—there appeared to be a strong sense of "defensive anxiety," whereas in some new member states, large segments of the population still expressed a "rejection of the "Westernization" of

6. Eurobarometer, *The Future of Europe* (Brussels: European Commission, 2006).
7. Eurobarometer, *The European Citizens and the Future of Europe, Qualitative Study in the 25 Member States* (Brussels: European Commission, 2006).

society" or a feared "'dispossession' of the natural economic heritage." Throughout the EU, a great many respondents expressed concern about a number of EU failures, including "the lack of a collective spirit," concern that enlargement has been "too great and too rapid" (and often a special worry about the potential entry of Turkey), and "the absence of a 'European identity' able to attract people's support." When asked to explain the remaining gap between the EU's own ideals and reality, a number of different reasons were noted by the Europeans surveyed, including the different interests among the member states, the significant economic and cultural difficulties among countries, inefficient EU governance, and hostile feelings and national resistance in the course of Europe's complex history. Thus, well before the economic recession of 2008–10, and even before the challenges of digesting Bulgaria and Romania as new members in 2007, European public opinion expressed significant anxiety about EU enlargement and the accession of more Balkan states.

Another Eurobarometer survey conducted in the spring of 2008 suggested that such anxiety and skepticism was persistent over the future enlargement of most of the Western Balkan region (see figure 9.1). Thus citizens in the current twenty-seven member states of the European Union favored accession for Norway (78 percent), Switzerland (77 percent), and Iceland (72 percent). But Europeans favored entry for Croatia by only a slim majority (52 percent). Majority support for the other Western Balkan states was lacking: Montenegro received 41 percent; Macedonia, 40 percent; Bosnia, 40 percent; Serbia, 38 percent; Albania, 34 percent; and newly independent, albeit not widely recognized, Kosovo, 34 percent. Turkey lagged behind as a possible future member state (31 percent).[8] A relative majority polled in the EU considered that the accession of the Western Balkans states would help to stabilize the region (48 percent), but a substantial number disagreed (39 percent). As might be expected, the two Western Balkan states that had already been officially deemed by the EU as "candidate members" (and whose public opinion was therefore polled) felt strongly—Macedonia (84 percent) and Croatia (62 percent)—that accession would constitute a stabilizing factor. But as the global economic recession began to bite more severely in Southeastern Europe during 2009 (see below), European majority opinion favoring enlargement gradually diminished,

---

8. Eurobarometer, *The European Union Today and Tomorrow* (Brussels: European Commission, 2008), 28–35.

Figure 9.1. Support for the Accession to the EU of Western Balkan States by Citizens of EU Member Countries, 2008 (percent)

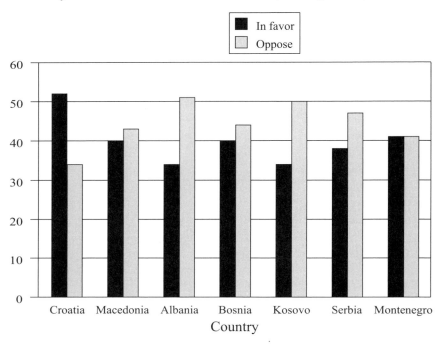

Source: Eurobarometer, *Public Opinion in the European Union Based on Field Work in June–July 2009* (Brussels: European Commission, 2009).

and the future of the accession process became less certain. However, in the new member states that entered the EU in 2004 and 2007, a large majority still favored further enlargement (64 percent for, 21 percent against), whereas in the fifteen older member states, the situation was reversed (38 percent in favor, 52 percent opposed).[9]

Patterns of Euro-Enthusiasm in the Balkans

Within the Western Balkans, just as in the EU itself, the impetus for enlargement was mainly led by elites. However, in contrast to the EU's

9. Eurobarometer, *Public Opinion in the European Union Based on Field Work in June–July 2009* (Brussels: European Commission, 2009).

public skepticism over the accession of the Western Balkans states, citizen attitudes within the region itself have been relatively positive. Still, the views of Western Balkan citizens and political party leaders were hardly uniform regarding to what extent and how quickly various EU conditionality provisions should be fulfilled. Generally in the Western Balkans, as elsewhere, Euro-skeptic views and party pronouncements on programs concerning the pace or manner of European accession have been political posturing or a part of the rhetorical discourse found in interparty competition. Most skepticism has lacked any deep principled or ideological opposition to Europe or to European integration (e.g., based on rejection of or hostility to transferring national sovereignty or to integrating economies, or opposition to the acceptance of democratic norms).

Thus, just as in Central and Eastern Europe during the postcommunist period, and up to that region's EU accession in 2004, the major political parties in most Western Balkan countries exhibited a large measure of ideological convergence in support of European integration. Where this convergence was weakest, as in Serbia (owing to the heightened significance of nationalist sentiments and specific factors such as the NATO bombing of 1999 and the widespread, albeit incomplete, EU support for Kosovo's February 2008 declaration of independence), higher levels of Euro-skepticism prevailed for quite some time. The pro-European position of party elites in the Western Balkans was not, of course, unresponsive to public opinion in the region. So as democratization proceeded, elites needed to be sensitive to popular views, including the perspectives of nonparty actors and pressure from the media. Because each party elite in the region was eager to mobilize voter support in order to remain in power, it tended to calibrate its outlook in accordance with current issues and events, and this determined the temporary extent of a party's Euro-enthusiasm, or its "softer" and "harder" levels of skepticism.

Thus, political party and popular attitudes toward membership in the EU continuously fluctuated in each country. For both most major parties and elites in the region, a fear of their country's isolation has trumped Euro-skepticism or a preoccupation with the past. Even in Serbia, after the Serbian Radical Party (Srpska radikalna stranka, SRS) fractured in late 2008, the more powerful breaking-off segment, the Serbian Progressive Party (Srpska napredna stranka, SNS), chose to endorse a pro-European position. Most political leaders in the

Western Balkan states shared a desire not to be left behind their regional neighbors in the EU accession process. Indeed, in some cases, where the party system was divided along ethnic lines, there was a concern by some party elites that their own ethnic community might be disadvantaged if their country remained outside the EU. For example, in Bosnia, many Muslims felt that Bosnian Serbs and Croats might benefit from the advance to the EU of nearby Croatia and Serbia, and thereby leave the majority Muslim community isolated.

Typically, specific levels of support for association with the EU, within either general public opinion or political elite ranks, tend to rise and fall with changing circumstances and routine political events. Thus, although levels of enthusiasm for joining the EU generally held steady across the region, perceptions about accommodating EU conditionality requirements have proved more volatile. Segments of public and elite opinion often bristled at EU obligations for "regional cooperation" that raised territorial issues, and "compliance with international obligations," which implied full cooperation with The Hague Tribunal. For example, in late 2006 and early 2007, a Gallup survey of Serbian voters found 62 percent expressing the view that their country's membership in Europe was "a good thing," and just 9 percent saying it was "a bad thing."[10] Indeed, levels of support for Serbia's entry into the EU were approximately 60 to 70 percent for several years before 2008. Thus in February 2008, 59 percent of respondents surveyed still indicated that they supported Serbia's entry into Euro-Atlantic institutions and approximately a quarter opposed such a development. But half those surveyed felt that the protection of Serbia's territorial integrity and sovereignty needed to be safeguarded as part of Serbia's participation in the process of Euro-Atlantic integration, and only 36.4 percent were willing to be included in that process if it meant accepting special conditions.[11] A poll in February 2008, conducted the day before Kosovo's declaration of independence, indicated that three-quarters of the Serbian respondents would not trade European membership in exchange for acknowledging Kosovo's independence.[12] And many Serbian voters seemed to be quite ambivalent about EU accession, ow-

10. Julie Ray, "Serbians' Views on EU Membership Key to Vote: Presidential Election is Seen as a Referendum on Future Path with Europe," Gallup Poll, January 18, 2008.

11. *BETA*, March 22, 2008.

12. *Balkan Insight*, March 1, 2008.

ing to the contradictory rhetoric of the political elite. A survey reported on April 25, 2008, indicated that about a quarter of the public held "anti-European" views, up from 15 percent about three years earlier. About 16 percent of those surveyed were explicitly for entry into the EU—that is, hard Euro-enthusiasts—whereas earlier that figure was 29 percent.[13] Essentially, Serbian voters appeared to be conflicted and frequently shifting between moods of Europhobia and Europhilia that were linked to outside pressures and the changing circumstances in the country.

Also, until mid-2008 Serbia's political elite, attuned to such views, and in some measure responsible for their existence, was itself divided with respect to its "EU orientation." Although one survey indicated that 64 percent of elite members interviewed in Serbia had an EU orientation, only 35 percent were regarded as having a "strong orientation." The survey also revealed that the business elite was substantially more EU oriented, and indeed had no strong orientation regarding the primacy and interests of the nation-state (in comparison with nearly a fifth of party politicians).[14] The victory of a pro-European democratic coalition in Serbia in May 2008 reduced the degree of Euro-skepticism in the country, and at the end of 2008 the SRS split also helped the pro-European cause in the country. Thus, by 2009 there was substantial elite consensus in Serbia on European accession, further aided by the lifting of the EU's visa requirements in December. Of course, what the notion "European orientation" meant for one elite actor or another, or one party or another, varied significantly.

In recent years, the prevalence of Euro-skeptical public attitudes in Croatia has been quite striking. In part, such views were motivated by a reaction against EU pressures regarding the extradition of Croatian indictees to The Hague Tribunal. But such Euro-skepticism was also related to Croatia's economic difficulties, and to considerable anxiety regarding the uncertainties of what European economic integration would require. Ironically, Croatian concerns regarding EU integration were also connected to Croatia's relative success at internal reforms and its front-runner status for EU entry among the Western Balkans. As earlier in Central and Eastern Europe, the closer a country had moved

13. *Politika,* April 25, 2008.

14. Mladen Lazić and Vladimir Vuletić, "Intune Elite Survey in Serbia," Central European University, Budapest, November 27, 2007.

toward EU accession, the greater the popular anxiety and resistance to prospects of becoming an EU member. For example, in the summer of 2008, 60 percent of Croatians interviewed felt that membership in the EU would lead to a severe or general deterioration in their personal or financial position, compared with a quarter or less who had a similar feeling in other states. In any event, a February 2008 poll indicated that 60 percent of the respondents in Croatia supported joining the European Union (up about 10 percent from November 2007). But Zagreb's conflict with Slovenia over its Adriatic Sea border made Croatians very allergic to any outside interference. Thus, 56 percent of Croats surveyed in 2008 favored remaining outside the EU rather than give up their right to control half the disputed bay. Indeed, throughout the Western Balkans, such country-specific issues play a prominent role in determining the rise and fall of both public and elite attitudes toward European integration.[15]

For example, Macedonian support for EU accession was quite high, especially after the EU granted it candidate status in 2005. But the spring 2008 rejection of Macedonia's bid to join NATO at the Bucharest Summit (because of Greece's objection to the name "Macedonia") temporarily diminished overall support for Euro-Atlanticism in the country. Shortly before the negative decision on NATO, 83 percent of respondents in Macedonia rejected changing their country's name in order to become a NATO member, and by implication an EU member.[16] During the same period in Albania, popular support for EU and NATO membership was about 90 or 95 percent, and after the country's Euro-Atlantic incorporation into NATO at the Bucharest Summit, positive feelings were reinforced (as was also the case in Croatia as a result of its entry into NATO).[17]

Meanwhile, in Montenegro, a July 2008 survey found that three-quarters of respondents supported EU accession for their country. Indeed, only 5 percent were partially or fully against EU entry (but 31 percent were fully or partially against joining NATO).[18] Different atti-

15. *Balkan Insight,* March 3, 2008.

16. *Angus Reid Global Monitor,* March 13, 2008.

17. Inter Press Service News Agency, March 20, 2008. NATO has played a significant role in Balkan state building through its efforts at the democratic transformation of the region's armed forces.

18. Agence France-Presse, July 2, 2008.

tudes toward EU integration also reflected internal ethnic divisions. In Kosovo, a February 2007 survey indicated that 63 percent of Albanians in the state-seeking polity viewed the role of the EU very positively, as opposed to 3 percent of Kosovo Serbs. In Bosnia, despite high levels of general support for EU membership (70–80 percent in 2008), there remained striking differences between the two entities regarding the necessity to meet the conditions required by the EU.[19] For example, 61 percent of respondents in the Republika Srpska felt that the existence of separate entity police forces—opposed by Brussels—was more important for their entity than membership in the EU. Only 32 percent held the same view in the Muslim-Croat Federation of Bosnia and Herzegovina. Still, agreement on the partial reorganization of the police forces in Bosnia was finally reached in mid-April 2008, and the country moved on to sign a Stability and Association Agreement with Brussels in June 2008.

Gallup Balkan Monitor survey data collected in 2009, after the advent of the global economic recession, indicated that in most countries of the Western Balkans, support for EU accession did not diminish a great deal, probably because both elites and citizens throughout the entire region recognized the critical role that the EU would need to play in the immediate and long-term recovery of the region from the ongoing crisis (figure 9.2). Thus an absolute or relative majority of those in all the Western Balkan countries continue to support EU membership, although the extent of support has continued to vary considerably. In some countries—such as in Croatia, Macedonia, Serbia, and Kosovo—support dropped somewhat. But in Kosovo, the ethnic division remained. Albanian support was 93 percent, while only 22 percent of the Serb minority felt similarly. Meanwhile, in Montenegro and Albania, support for EU accession actually increased. And in Bosnia there was a striking increase in support. But the 2009 data for Bosnia also indicated that sharp differences between ethnic groups and regions persisted. Some 76 percent of citizens in the Federation of Bosnia and Herzegovina thought that EU membership was a good thing, whereas only 48 percent approved in the Republika Srpska. During 2009, the regional attraction of EU membership did not seem to be much affected by the international financial crisis. However, the wider threat of

19. *SETimes,* February 12, 2008.

Figure 9.2. Support for the Accession to the EU of Western Balkan States by Citizens of Western Balkan States, 2006–9 (percent stating that accession is a good thing)

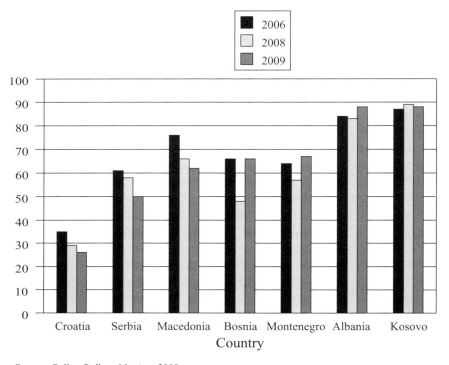

Source: *Gallup Balkan Monitor*, 2009.

a slow European recovery to the EU accession prospects of the Western Balkans still needed to be addressed.

The Economic Dimension: Crisis, Recovery, and EU Prospects

The financial consequences of the international financial crisis descended on the Western Balkans starting in late 2008 but seemed less threatening than for the leading Western economies. Central bankers around the region could point hopefully to their large reserves of capital supporting stable rates of currency exchange and to the absence of any involvement by their predominantly foreign banks in the hedge funds or debt equity swaps threatening the dangerously complex Western financial superstructure. Consumer loans taken for lower interest rates in euros or Swiss francs would not face the repayment problems descending on neighboring Hungary by mid-2008 as long as their currencies did not sharply depreciate, as the forint had. The predominantly pegged rates have stayed in place, and the managed floats for Croatia's kuna, if not increasingly for Serbia's dinar, have held depreciation against the euro to 5 or 6 percent.[20] In early 2009, as we saw in chapter 8, the variety of Austrian, Italian, German, French, Greek, and Slovenian banks that account for 80 to 90 percent of the private financial sector acted to calm fears that they might be leaving because of problems with the parent banks. The price of their staying has, as also noted, included tighter terms and higher interest rates for domestic borrowers.

However, the contractions that confronted the region's economies in 2009 came from more than newly restricted access to credit. The high 5 to 6 percent rates of annual growth that had held up through 2008, slipping only to a gain of 2.4 percent in Croatia, now turned negative everywhere except Albania. More significant for these striking reverses were the delayed effects on the region from the wider European contraction that was already under way in 2008. These repercussions hit hardest at exports from and foreign direct investment (FDI) to the Western Balkans. Both fell off sharply and in turn reduced the region's capacity for imports. The negative rates for gross domestic product (GDP) and the rising budget deficits as a fraction of GDP in 2009, as noted in table 9.1, match up instructively with the dramatic declines in exports, imports, and FDI shown in table 9.2. Here were the largest declines in the major economic indicators from 2008. Note that the minimal increases in GDP forecast at this writing for 2010–11 are significantly below the promising advances of 2004–8.

Even if growth rates revive to a more realistic 3 to 4 percent a year, it should be pointed out that this rate adds another five to ten years to the region's advance toward the 1989 levels in Western Europe, promised for 2020 by the 5 to 6 percent rates. We join a recent study of the region's future prospects in judging the resumption of such rates as

20. See Nikola Bokan et al., "The Impact of the Financial Crisis and Policy Responses in Croatia," Croatian National Bank, January 5, 2010; and Rodovan Jelašić, "Current Monetary and Economic Developments," National Bank of Serbia, Belgrade, November 29, 2009.

Table 9.1. Main Economic Indicators in the Financial Crisis, 2007–11

Country or Group and Indicators	2007	2008	2009	2010[a]	2011[a]
Albania					
GDP (real change % against preceding year)	6.0	8.0	1	3.5	3.4
Unemployment (rate in % annual average)	13.5	13.1	15	16	14
Current account (in % of GDP)	−10.6	−14.7	−14.5	−13.7	−13.2
Budget deficit (in % of GDP)	−3.5	−5.7	−6.3	7.4	−5.8
Bosnia-Herzegovina					
GDP (real change % against preceding year)	6.1	5.7	−3.1	−0.8	2.2
Unemployment (rate in % annual average)	29.0	23.4	24.1	27	27
Current account (in % of GDP)	−10.4	−14.9	−6.8	−5.5	−5.3
Budget deficit (in % of GDP)	−0.1	−3.0	−5.7	−4.5	−3
Croatia					
GDP (real change % against preceding year)	5.5	2.4	−5.8	−1.4	1.3
Unemployment (rate in % annual average)	9.6	8.4	10.5	11	10
Current account (in % of GDP)	−7.6	−9.4	−5.2	−2.6	−2.1
Budget deficit (in % of GDP)	−2.5	−1.4	−3.3	−3.6	−3.5
Macedonia					
GDP (real change % against preceding year)	5.9	4.9	−2	1.7	3
Unemployment (rate in % annual average)	34.9	33.8	34	33	33
Current account (in % of GDP)	−7.2	−13.1	−10	−8	−8
Budget deficit (in % of GDP)	0.6	−1.0	−2.8	−2.5	−2.5
Serbia					
GDP (real change % against preceding year)	6.9	5.4	−4	1.3	3
Unemployment (rate in % annual average)	18.1	13.6	18	20	20
Current account (in % of GDP)	−15.7	−13.9	−6.9	−9.3	−8.6
Budget deficit (in % of GDP)	−1.9	−2.4	−4.5	−5.1	−4.0
Montenegro					
GDP (real change % against preceding year)	10.7	8.1	−3	1.1	2
Unemployment (rate in % annual average)	19.3	17.2	19	20	20
Current account (in % of GDP)	−22.9	−30.1	−15	−10	−10
Budget deficit (in % of GDP)	6.4	−1.5	−6.2	−7.9	−4
EU-27					
GDP (real change % against preceding year)	3.0	.5	−4.3	1.5	1.5
Unemployment (rate in % annual average)	7.1	7.0	9.4	10.9	N.A.
Current account (in % of GDP)	−0.4	−0.1	−1.9	−2.0	N.A.
Budget deficit (in % of GDP)	−0.8	−2.3	−5.8	N.A.	N.A.

Note: GDP = gross domestic product; N.A. = not available; EU-27 = EU with the current 27 members.
[a]Projections.
Sources: Vienna Institute for International Studies, *WIIW Handbook of Statistics 2009* (Vienna: Vienna Institute for International Studies, 2009), table 1; EBRD, Online Database, 2010; IMF, Country reports for Albania, Bosnia-Herzegovina, Croatia, Macedonia, Montenegro, and Serbia, and *World Economic Outlook, 2010–11.*

Table 9.2. Foreign Trade and Foreign Direct Investment, 2008–9 (millions of dollars)

Country and Years	Merchandise Exports	Merchandise Imports	Foreign Direct Investment
Albania			
2008	11,356	4,907	844
2009	1,125	4,662	640
Bosnia-Herzegovina			
2008	5,194	12,286	1,003
2009	4,600	10,500	800
Croatia			
2008	14,356	30,419	4,576
2009	10,580	24,575	2,731
Macedonia			
2008	3,971	6,522	612
2009	2,300	4,300	300
Serbia			
2008	960	3,192	805
2009	723	2,501	638
Montenegro			
2008	10,956	22,213	2,717
2009	8,000	15,400	1,400
Total			
2008	36,773	79,539	10,557
2009	27,328	61,938	6,519
2008/2009 %	74.3%	77.9%	62%

Sources: European Bank for Reconstruction and Development, Online Database, 2010; European Bank for Reconstruction and Development, *Transition Report 2009: Transition in Crisis* (London: European Bank for Reconstruction and Development, 2009); Vienna Institute for International Studies, *WIIW Handbook of Statistics 2009* (Vienna: Vienna Institute for International Studies, 2009), 41, 246–81.

unlikely.[21] The overheated expansion of credit also seems to make the boom years an exceptional period. Even the more financially feasible and historically consistent revival of growth to 3 to 4 percent a year will require a revival in recently sagging FDI.

Such a revival, if not the easy credit to go with it, will nonetheless be needed to address the two major structural problems detailed

21. Ivo Bićanić, Jasena Kukavčić, and Vjerana Spajić, "The Post Recession Growth Prospects of South East European Economies," *Southeastern Europe* 34 (2010): 193–221. The study identifies the recent high rates as an historical anomaly in a region that could not even record them in the 1950–73 period of maximum postwar growth, East and West.

in chapter 8. First are the deficits on current account, primarily trade deficits, covered at least in part before 2009 by rising FDI totals. If the debt-creating trade deficits are themselves to be reduced, an FDI turn from financial institutions and services to export-promoting investment would be required. Second are the labor issues. The "jobless growth" of 2004–8 saw only Croatia cut its unemployment to under 10 percent. The longer-term challenge is to compensate for populations that have ceased to grow and are aging by improving the education and training of the smaller younger generation, keeping them in the country, and thereby increasing productivity per capita.

In the short term, both structural problems seem to be less threatening. A sharp decline in imported services has cut into the current and projected deficits on current account for 2009–11. As may also be seen in table 9.1, unemployment has moved back to the high levels of 2007 and slightly beyond. But for the inflow of badly needed European services to resume and any significant reduction in high levels of unemployment to occur, the slow pace of recovery in overall growth rates must accelerate. Given the central role of foreign trade and investment in these small economies, any acceleration will depend in turn on the revival of the European economy in general and their major trading partners in particular, namely, Germany, Italy, Austria, France, and Greece. At this writing, the Western European revival is off to a slow start, with the possible exception of Germany. Greece faces severe fiscal restraints to reduce its high budget deficits if it is to service its equally high foreign debt. Neither its modest trade totals with the Western Balkans nor parent bank support for its regional affiliates can be expected to bounce back.[22] This leaves the region's own chances more dependent on a full Western European recovery that may now stretch into the next decade, not the next couple of years.

For the Western Balkans, this time line presents the daunting prospect of a third decade of transition, moving past not only the armed conflicts of the first decade but also the second decade's credit- and debt-heavy growth. More such growth would leave serious structural

---

22. On the exposure and role of Greek banks in the region, with market shares of one quarter in Albania and Macedonia and 16 percent in Serbia, see Jens Bastien, "External Anchors to the Rescue: Reaching Out in a Time of Economic and Financial Sector Crisis in South Eastern Europe," *Eliamep,* October 2009, 24–27.

problems unattended in the region's substantive approaches to EU membership, and also rankling its own public's opinion. As the international financial crisis cut growth short, voices from the region joined a chorus of Western complaint. It is indeed tempting to generalize from the Anglo-American case about overconfident neoliberal reliance on an unregulated, self-correcting market mechanism. For the Western Balkans, critics range from Croatia's president, Stjepan Mesić, who has asserted that "neo-liberalism has exhausted itself. The dogma about the omnipotent market . . . has definitely failed," to the Serbian leader of the SPS, Ivica Dačić, who has claimed that "the defeat of neoliberal capitalism has shown that the future lies in Socialism."[23] Such sentiments typically include calls for a larger but unspecified state role at the expense of the prolonged and generally unpopular process of privatization. Yet these calls do not spell out how public ownership might be financed nor speak of a return to the political management of "socially owned enterprises," as in the former Yugoslavia.

More important for the present analysis, the politically popular notion that the Western Balkans proceeded through the past decade by relying only on the neoliberal principles of the original Washington Consensus from the 1990s is simply not true. As pointed out in chapter 8, the search for a "Post–Washington Consensus" began almost at once in 1999. The very international organizations presumed to be the guardians of neoliberal orthodoxy lent their support to strengthening the public sector. The World Bank has addressed the need for affordable state support of social services and improved education, seeking a floor to allow greater labor mobility through what it has called "flexicurity." Both the International Monetary Fund and the European Bank for Reconstruction and Development (EBRD) have tied their lending not only to the reduction of overly large state sectors but also to the reform of public administration and more effective state regulation. How to resolve the apparent contradiction between reducing the size and expanding the reach of the state framework at the same time remained a dilemma, even in the years of rapid economic growth (see chapter 3). Yet the priority of a "functioning market economy," in which the state plays only a supporting role, still informs the international organizations in the current downturn. In the words of the EBRD's chief economist, Erik Berglöf, this current crisis has

---

23. Quoted in *HINA,* May 16, 2009; and in *Večernje novosti,* May 12, 2009.

confirmed a view which has been gaining traction over the last decade, namely that transition to a market economy is about much more than building markets and shifting economic responsibilities from the state to the private sector. It also involves developing certain state functions, and improving how the state interacts with the private sector. The crisis has brought home the importance of market-supporting policy institutions and policies, particularly in the financial sector. This does not necessarily mean more regulation, but it certainly means better regulation, focused on improving incentives.[24]

Across the Western Balkans, both the elected governments and their central banks have already focused their efforts on creating an effective public framework for a market economy. The idea of reinstating price controls or trade restrictions has attracted no support. None of the respective finance ministries have resisted the fiscal reforms that have introduced a value-added tax, cut income taxes, increased revenues, and limited expenses so as to keep state budgets closer to balance than a number of EU members (see chapter 8). But the struggle for a legal market economy operating with an independent judicial system and under a system of transparent regulation has not been yet been won. Corruption and clientism still obstruct competitive standards. The efforts of the several international institutions and the aid programs of Western governments have indeed contributed to overcoming these problems, which would be far more serious if open markets were to be replaced by politically staffed agencies. But now the principal responsibility for balancing the public and private sectors rests with the Western Balkans region itself, with its multiparty politics and with its public institutions (see chapters 2, 3, and 5).

To strike that public/private balance and also to reconnect to rapid growth while addressing the persisting problems with exports and employment, the economies of the Western Balkans must nonetheless depend on the rest of Europe in two respects. One is beyond their control, the aforementioned recovery of the wider European economy. The other, full integration with that economy as EU members, is hopefully not. The European recovery's protracted duration, as projected above, does have the advantage of coinciding with what is now the likely length of the EU accession process for the region. Only Croatia may be

24. EBRD, *Transition Report 2009* (London: EBRD, 2009), vii.

on track for acceptance before 2018, with prospects for 2012–13 at this writing. As in recent years, an even longer period of EU incentives and conditions is nonetheless the best chance that these economies will have to advance their private sectors and improve their public sectors. This best economic chance also includes counterproductive challenges and a major policy question. Together, they leave some sharp corners ahead, even on an open road toward EU accession. This mixed prospect will also confront the political prospect for "functioning democracies," as argued below, to deal with a prolonged accession process.

The advantages of the process leading to EU membership have been widely recognized since Spain and Portugal used it to eliminate the last vestiges of their authoritarian regimes and corporatist economies, before both joined the EU in 1986. The same result has been presumed to follow for the former Communist regimes, although with a longer delay in accession for Central European members than may have been needed and a shorter one for the Baltic and now Balkan members. For the Western Balkan states, the economic advantages of undergoing the process seem to still be in place, but the process itself has grown more complicated and its conditionality has become heavier.

As already mentioned, the financial support for EU accession is considerable. More than €1 billion a year for the period 2007–13 amounts to several times the combined amount that projected aid or loans from the EBRD and the World Bank might provide. The only other source of such support is the IMF, but borrowers complying with its terms do not advance to membership privileges and further support, as with the EU. Instead, as for Serbia's new standby loan of €2.6 billion over a twenty-seven-month period and Bosnia's €1 billion over three years, the subdivision into tranches allows payment of the subsequent installments only if the terms of compliance have been met in the preceding tranche.[25] The terms do fit EU stipulations demanding reforms in public administration along with a reduction in state employees. But the rigor of IMF oversight has prompted Montenegro to delay agreement on much smaller loans (€200–300 million), and Croatia and Macedonia to defer in favor of their own bond issues. For the EU's less onerous

---

25. International Monetary Fund, *Country Report for Serbia,* Country Report 10/25 (Washington, D.C.: International Monetary Fund, 2010); International Monetary Fund, *Country Report for Bosnia and Herzegovina,* Country Report 09/225 (Washington, D.C.: International Monetary Fund, 2009).

new Instrument for Pre-Accession program, it should be noted that the majority of these funds are being directed toward technical assistance. This leaves the major infrastructure investments in energy or transportation to the limited resources of the state budgets.

Such technical assistance has nonetheless promoted a more efficient and transparent public sector, helping to strengthen the weak states that still characterize the region (see chapter 3). So have the institutional guidelines laid down in the *acquis communautaire*'s thirty-five chapters and the regular reports required before and under the current set of Stability and Association Agreements, which have now been signed and approved by the EU everywhere except in Bosnia and Kosovo, as noted in table 9.3, to chart the way to a more efficient and transparent public sector (see chapter 3). At the same time, the need to establish and staff new agencies required by the *acquis* have burdened governments seeking to reduce the number of public employees and keep the most able ones in place. The Macedonian experience cited in chapter 8 is hardly unique. Still, such new agencies are typically charged with oversight and auditing the economy, thereby internalizing regulation.

Clearer advantages of the accession process have come from the impetus toward trade integration with its existing membership and the new stipulation for regional cooperation. During the course of the past decade, duty-free access to EU markets has led the way in making these members the main trading partners for the region, with shares ranging from 60 to 80 percent of their exports and imports. The same partners have also been the major source of FDI, the most promising way to reduce current account deficits in the short run and increase exports in the long run. In addition, the EU demand to demonstrate regional cooperation has played a decisive part in the entire region's signing off on the multilateral Central European Free Trade Agreement (CEFTA) in 2006. CEFTA replaced the myriad bilateral agreements that had been reached since 1999. Still, as noted in chapter 8, the chances for CEFTA to increase overall trade significantly will depend on a revival of FDI and the same set of institutional reforms required for EU membership. For the coordination of integrative reforms, some help may be coming from the new Regional Cooperation Council, which was set up in Sarajevo in 2008 to finally supersede the 1999 European Commission–World Bank Stability Pact for Southeastern Europe with a local body.

Table 9.3. EU Relations with the Western Balkan Countries, 1999–2010

State	Year of Feasibility Study	Stabilization and Association Agreement			Application for EU Membership	Status in 2011	Special Missions
		Signed	In Force				
Albania	2002	June 12, 2006	April 1, 2009		April 28, 2009	Potential candidate	
Bosnia-Herzegovina	2003	June 16, 2008	Pending		—	Potential candidate	EUFOR/Althea Mission: 1,975 troops as of January 19, 2010; EUPM: 166 international police, 35 civilian staff, 220 Bosnian staff
Croatia	2000	October 29, 2001	February 1, 2005		February 21, 2003	Candidate country as of June 18, 2004	
Macedonia	1999	April 9, 2001	April 1, 2004		March 22, 2004	Candidate country as of December 16, 2005	
Montenegro	2005	October 15, 2007	Pending		December 15, 2008	Candidate as of December 17, 2010	
Serbia	2005	April 29, 2008	Pending		December 22, 2009	Potential candidate	
Kosovo[a]	Proposed in November 2008, but pending	Stabilization and Tracking Mechanism (STM)	STM: November 6, 2002		—	"Clear European Perspective"	EULEX Mission: 1,650 international and 1,050 local staff

[a]Five EU member states have not recognized Kosovo's independence: Greece, Spain, Cyprus, Slovakia, and Romania.

There remains a dilemma of short-run policy for both some EU members and the Western Balkan states: How to expand state emergency spending for investment and job creation in a context of retrenchment to reduce budget deficits? The case of Greece again comes quickly to mind. An outsize budget deficit of 12.7 percent, plus a foreign debt exceeding GDP, has prompted draconian EU demands to reduce the number of state employees, along with the same reforms in public administration being asked of the Western Balkans.[26] Here the region benefits from its existing involvement in reforming the public sector, and budget deficits fell far short of the Greek level, even after rising in 2009. They typically included the sort of small "stimulus packages" familiar from Western Europe and the United States, amounting to less than 1 percent of GDP. Room for more such state initiatives may come from the IMF's Stand-By Agreement with Serbia. Citing the need for "fiscal stabilizers to work," it accepts a budget deficit of 4.5 percent in 2009 and 4 percent in 2010, as opposed to the 3 percent borrowed from the conditions of the European Monetary Union.[27] As noted in table 9.1, deficits for Albania, Bosnia, and Montenegro exceeded this benchmark for 2009.

In the long as well as the short terms, FDI still offers domestic market economies the best prospect for job-creating investment. Papers from a recent Belgrade conference of economists from around the region supported this conclusion while also presenting well-argued criticisms of the international financial system.[28] Several recent deals in Serbia and prospects in Croatia, whereby the private foreign investor agreed to partial state ownership or interest, have stirred new attention to the Southeast Asian model for industrial policy. The Fiat agreement to retool and expand the Zastava automobile works in Serbia, leaving a one-third share in state hands, is exhibit A. As also noted in chapter 8, there are two similar deals in place in Serbia, one in Montenegro, and two pending in Croatia. Only the Fiat venture, Montenegro's alu-

26. "Briefing: Greece's Sovereign Debt Crunch," *The Economist,* February 6, 2010, 75–77. See also Jens Bastien, "Greece in Southeastern Europe, Political Opportunities and Economic Challenges," *International Policy Analysis,* February 2010.

27. International Monetary Fund, *Country Report for Serbia,* 7–9.

28. Aleksandar Praščević, Božidar Cerović, and Momir Jakšić, eds., *Economic Policy and the Global Recession,* 2 vols. (Belgrade: Faculty of Economics, Belgrade University, 2009).

minum complex, and the Pula shipyard project will produce manufactured goods for export. Otherwise, these projects have been confined to energy or utility investments in what had been state monopolies, joined in 2009 by a Chinese credit of €1.25 billion for power plants in Serbia.[29] These few cases are best described as targets of opportunity rather than the basis for a new program requiring targeted investments from constrained state budgets. Calls for such a program would need to rely on a huge infusion of EU capital and a regionally coordinated development plan, both of which are unlikely at this writing.[30] Still, the individual projects deserve a chance to prove themselves. An alternate approach, less likely to generate large FDI but more likely to attract greenfield and small business projects, involves industrial parks that offer infrastructure and communication facilities already in place.[31]

Some combination of the two approaches may help to address a major challenge facing the economies of the Western Balkans in the decade ahead: how to raise the competitive level of exports from their already-functioning market economies so that they will not only increase exports and reduce the large trade deficits but also attract foreign investors to their enterprises. In the process, the higher quality of exports would allow their economies' long-overvalued exchange rates to be reduced with higher sales following from lower prices, as they would probably not now. The other major challenge is to increase productivity, not only from a better trained labor force but also from public administration and economic regulation. Together, the legal market and a stronger state can squeeze out the gray economy and the wider corruption that still discourage both the region's own young professionals from staying and foreign investors from coming in. Meeting both challenges would also constitute compliance with the economic chapters of the EU *acquis communautaire,* which is a crucial requirement for membership.

29. EBRD, *Transition Report, 2009,* 156, 216; *Balkan Watch,* February 15, 2010.

30. For an argument in favor of such a funded development plan as the region's only alternative for advancing into the EU, see Vassilis Monastiriotis and George Patrakis, "Twenty Years of Economic Transition in the Balkans: Transition Failures and Development Challenges," *Southeastern Europe* 34 (2010): 149–69.

31. Two industrial parks are already operating in Serbia, with another dozen on the drawing board. Interview with Mihailo Crnobrnja, dean, Singidunum University, Belgrade, January 18, 2010.

The Political Dimension: Democracy Building
in Crisis and Postrecession

The initial impact of the global financial and economic crisis during 2008 and 2009 also seemed to present a serious threat both to democracy-building progress in the Western Balkans and to the region's hope of joining the EU. Thus, as the crisis unfolded, most observers naturally worried that it might unravel the reform accomplishments that had been made in the region during the previous decade, compound remaining difficulties in both the economic and political spheres, and delay the EU accession calendar for individual countries. When a slow recovery from the crisis seemed evident at the end of 2009, some of those commentators were deemed to be doomsayers by pundits who feigned 20/20 insight regarding past and future economic events. However, in the initial phases of the crisis, it was extremely difficult for observers to gauge how events would eventually unfold.

For example, there were legitimate concerns that economic problems might strengthen populist and extremist parties, and presage a resurgence of radical nationalism. Moreover, if there was a deep and prolonged crisis throughout the region, the potential of the emergent middle classes—including the large contingent of state employees—to serve as a politically stabilizing force in each country would likely also be jeopardized. Western Balkan elites openly worried about the danger of social unrest, and also that increased regional disenchantment within the EU might endanger the further prospects for enlargement. Against this background, two closely related questions became increasingly pertinent: What would be the short-term and long-term domestic political consequences of the global recession for the states in the region? And how would these consequences affect the region's "European perspective" and future democratic consolidation?

As shown above, enthusiasm for EU accession was very substantial within Western Balkan public opinion. But would the global and general European economic difficulties make Western Balkan elites and publics turn away from a closer EU embrace? Or would faltering economic conditions in the Euro-Atlantic region simply reinforce the views of those already predisposed to Euro-skepticism while buttressing the pro-European perspectives of those who had always regarded the EU as an answer to Western Balkan problems? And how would EU elites and citizens—themselves deeply affected by the economic downturn—

feel about moving forward with enlargement once the short-term and long-term repercussions of the crisis unfolded?

Fortunately, the democratic progress already achieved in the region between 2000 and 2008, albeit accompanied by serious problems, proved sufficient to withstand the limited sociopolitical impact of the recessionary climate that began at the end of 2008. In terms of their capacity to manage state functions, and the accountability of elites to citizens, the democracies of the region remained "weak" or "low intensity" in character (see chapter 3). Still, the region's state institutions exhibited enough infrastructural strength and political legitimacy to maintain their pluralist character and to survive the turbulence generated by the economic crisis, albeit assisted by external actors. Thus, most political discourse in the Western Balkans during the crisis focused upon its causes, consequences, and the necessary response strategies, rather than stimulating sharp internal conflict regarding the fundamental legitimacy of the democratic system itself or the basic integrity of the state. In most states, the conflict associated with the highly emotional issues of borders and territorial questions had diminished considerably, at least compared with the decade before 2000. Episodic interterritorial and local ethnic flare-ups occurred, but not the earlier pattern of mass violence.

By the time of the global financial and economic crisis, a substantial elite consensus had also emerged in the individual Western Balkan states that supported the value of adhering to EU norms of democratic behavior and economic practice (see chapter 7). This allowed most regimes in the region to maintain a relatively moderate—if, in some states, still quite polarized—form of elite politics throughout the crisis. In Serbia, as already noted (chapter 5), formerly disruptive or authoritarian-oriented political parties such as the Milošević-founded Socialist Party of Serbia (Socijalisticka Partija Srbije, SPS), and the dominant fraction of the former SRS that broke off and formed the SNS, had begun to engage in a more pluralist and pro-European brand of politics even before the crisis began. Genuine commitment to democratic and European principles in Serbia's political party system, and in many parties in other Western Balkan countries, continued to be arguably somewhat superficial or shallow, but the general deradicalization of political life in the region helped its regimes face the economic crisis with considerable political maturity. Democracy in the Western Balkans, although still under considerable pressure during the crisis, had consolidated sufficiently to become "the only game in town" (see the Introduction). Major political changes took place during the recessionary environment of 2008–10, but they occurred within each state's relatively new democratic frameworks (e.g., the sudden resignation of Croatia's prime minister Ivo Sanader in mid-2009, and the dramatic political party developments already referred to in Serbia). Of course, such stability does not ensure that the region's political outlook would not again darken if its hesitant economic recovery from the global crisis were to badly falter. But the positive facets of democratic consolidation detected in the preceding analysis (see chapters 2–5) present an important barrier and counterweight to any authoritarian revival.[32]

Moreover, although levels of social capital, interpersonal trust, and trust in institutions were quite low when the crisis began, regime stability in each state benefited from the fact that *diffuse* support for democracy as a value—if not *specific* support for particular institutions (especially parties)—had improved considerably (see chapter 7). And significantly, citizens in the region were able to fall back upon the familial and traditional social networks that are often critical for surviving sharp economic downturns of limited duration. Of course, the impact of the crisis on patterns of mistrust in the region remained worrisome. Thus trust in political institutions and in the political class has certainly not improved during the crisis, and has undoubtedly decreased in some quarters, even as political stability has prevailed and limited signs of economic recovery have been observed.

This trust deficit was illustrated by the presidential campaign in Croatia that took place during late December 2009 and early 2010. The presidential election of Ivo Josipović, a moderate and democratically oriented law professor who favors tolerance and the rule of law and is dedicated to fighting corruption, appeared likely to prove helpful in Croatia's quest to make an unruffled entry into the European Union. But turnout in the election—44 percent of eligible voters in the first round, and roughly 50 percent in the second round (lower than in 2005)—reflected the poor standing that politicians, parties, and the electoral process have in public opinion. Such apathy demonstrated distrust in the

---

32. In January 2010, Freedom House also noted, but did not explain, the "encouraging resilience" in the Western Balkans during a period of "freedom recession" globally. See Arch Puddington, "Freedom in the World 2010: Erosion of Freedom Intensifies," Washington, D.C., January 12, 2010.

electoral process and is characteristic of most of the Western Balkan states (see chapter 5). Together with the impact of the crisis on all institutions (a decline in "systemic trust"), such views can hardly be considered positive for democratic consolidation. Indeed, compared with survey responses in the Scandinavian countries, where positive levels of interpersonal trust range from approximately two-thirds to three-quarters of respondents, similar responses in the Western Balkans range from a tenth to a fifth of those surveyed.[33]

Thus, although traditional social bonds such as family and friends have proved initially helpful to societies undergoing crisis in the region—as pointed out in recent studies of Serbia, Bosnia, and Croatia—a decline in both institutional and interpersonal trust can generate a kind of "negative social capital" that is detrimental to longer-term democracy building and economic development.[34] Therefore, just as the record of democratic consolidation over the past decade is a mixed one, the political recovery from the current crisis remains uneven and uncertain. And while even a low level reservoir of social capital in the Western Balkans proved useful for coping with the crisis, this reserve has been depleted by the recent experience, making future stability and democracy building more precarious. As Paul Stubbs wrote in November 2009, "In societies where there is little trust in institutions, strong memories of hyper-inflation and banking collapses which wiped out savings, and continued concerns of parallel power structures, 'crony capitalism' and unfair privatization, the region's untested 'crisis management capacity' is under threat."[35]

33. Robert Manchin, "The State of Balkan Integration 2009 October," Gallup Balkan Monitor, 2009.

34. See Felix Roth, "Effect of the Financial Crisis on Systemic Trust," CEPS Working Document 316, July 2009. See also Siniša Zarić, "The Level of Social Capital in Serbia: Problems and Prospects in a Recession," paper presented at the conference "Economic Policy and Global Recession," Belgrade, September 25–27, 2009; *The Ties That Bind: Social Capital in Bosnia and Herzegovina* (Sarajevo: United Nations Development Program, 2009); *Corruption in Albania: Perception and Experience: Survey 2009* (Tirana: Institute for Development Research and Alternatives, 2009), and Predrag Bejaković, "Tax Evasion, State Capacity, and Trust in Transitional Countries: The Case of Croatia," *Društvena istraživanja*, no. 45 (2009): 787–805. For Croatia and Macedonia in comparative perspective, see *Second European Quality of Life Survey: Overview* (Dublin: European Foundation for the Improvement of Living and Working Conditions, 2009).

35. "Building Capacity to Promote Social Integration and Social Inclusion in the Western Balkans," paper presented at the Expert Group Meeting on Practical

Fortunately, the low levels of citizen trust in the Western Balkans do not appear to be a precursor of warfare in the region, or even of significant episodic violence (although such eventualities cannot be entirely ruled out if tenuous confidence in governments combines with other difficulties).[36] Indeed, the experience of the Western Balkans appeared to confirm arguments suggesting that recessions generally do not generate regime change or revolutions.[37] The concern, rather, is that the persistent weakness of the region's democracies might collectively leave the Western Balkan states—whether outside or inside the EU—as a permanently weak or marginalized area still separate from the European mainstream. Such a fringe condition or reputation has long bedeviled the Balkan region, and an effort to overcome the situation is precisely the reason why its elites have sought membership in the EU.

The future European and democratic prospects of the Western Balkan states will depend heavily on the influence, attitudes, and behavior of the middle classes that have been slowly reemerging in the region during the post-2000 period (see chapters 6 and 7). The social standing and strength of these classes appeared to be in serious jeopardy during the recent economic recession, and it remains unclear whether and how quickly their position will rebound during a likely protracted period of recovery. The fact that during 2008–9 each Balkan state experienced a striking reduction in the number of small and medium-sized businesses (7,000 in Croatia alone during 2009, and approximately 10,000

Strategies to Promote Social Integration, "Lessons Learned from Existing Policies and Practices," Accra, November 17–19, 2009.

36. As a recent analysis put it, the "uneasy inter-ethnic condominium" in Bosnia and the problem of the Serb minority in Kosovo represent "principal challenges to stability in Europe in 2010." Dennis C. Blair, *Annual Threat Assessment of the U.S. Intelligence Community for the Senate Select Committee on Intelligence* (Washington, D.C.: Office of the Director of National Intelligence, 2010). The weakness and politicization of security forces also create the potential for local incidents to escalate into ethnic clashes, such as those that have occurred at soccer games in Bosnia. Bodo Weber, "West's Last Chance to Get Serious in Bosnia," *Balkan Insight,* December 1, 2009. For a very pessimistic view of the region's stability and democratization by a Russian-funded think tank, see *Kosovo 2009: Ten Years of International Administration, One Year of Independence* (Paris: Institute of Democracy and Cooperation, 2009).

37. Minxin Pei and David Adesnik, "Why Recessions Don't Start Revolutions," *Foreign Policy* (Spring 2000): 138–51; and Julia Brower and Thomas Carothers, "Will the International Economic Crisis Undermine Struggling Democracies?" Carnegie Endowment for International Peace, Washington, D.C., April 2009.

in Serbia during the first six months of 2009), had an especially negative impact on middle-class development.[38] Thus, as pointed out in chapter 6, small and medium-sized business development broadens the base of stakeholders in a country and facilitates the emergence of a middle class of property owners and taxpayers that can support stability and democracy.

Equally worrisome is the fact that poverty levels began to slowly climb in the region during the economic recession. The ability of the region's poverty reduction programs to effectively resume their efforts is therefore critical to preventing potential social unease and its typical negative repercussions for political life. Thus, an estimated 30 percent of the population in the Balkans lives on less than $5 a day and is only slightly worse off than the highly vulnerable portion of the lower-middle-class stratum found throughout the region.[39] During the post-crisis period, Balkan political elites will undoubtedly face the challenge of how to protect those with low incomes and the middle class from the impact of crisis-generated austerity measures. How to blend fiscal responsibility with social sensitivity is therefore a critical problem throughout the region. The case of Greece undoubtedly offers a cautionary tale, although in the Western Balkan region, unlike Greece, the weakness and atomized character of trade unions lessens the prospects of widespread or destabilizing labor unrest.[40]

Accession Prospects and the Dilemmas of the Decade Ahead

Early in the recent global financial and economic crisis, it seemed that the EU might significantly backpedal on its prior commitments to EU accession for the Western Balkans by continuing to use "soft power" to

38. *HINA,* December 27, 2009; *Tanjug,* July 17, 2009.

39. Paul Stubbs and Moises Venancio, "Compounding the Crisis? International Assistance in the Western Balkans," *European Perspectives–Journal on European Perspectives on the Western Balkans* 1, no. 1 (October 2009): 27–52. See also *The Impact of the Global Financial Crisis on the Macedonian Economy and the Economic Situation in the Macedonian Households* (Skopje: Friedrich Ebert Stiftung, 2009); and *Protecting the Poor during the Global Crisis: 2009 Bosnia and Herzegovina Poverty Update* (Washington, D.C.: World Bank, 2009).

40. Heribert Kohl, *Freedom of Association, Employees' Rights and Social Dialogue in Central and Eastern Europe and the Western Balkans* (Berlin: Friedrich Ebert Stiftung, 2009). Greece does bear a close resemblance to the Western Balkans

nurture democracy but scaling back financial assistance in the region and postponing enlargement plans. For example, Germany's Angela Merkel did call for a "time-out" on EU enlargement following the expected Croatian accession in the near future. But EU officials and most elites in member states continued, to their credit, to advocate the integration of the Western Balkans. And the EU commissioner for enlargement, Olli Rehn, admitted in 2009 that all Euro-Atlantic institutions, including "both the EU and NATO, suffer from enlargement fatigue." But, he added, "It's always harder to enlarge in a recession; . . . while combating the economic recession, we must not make EU enlargement a scapegoat for a problem it did not create. . . . Europe's economic troubles are not created by Czech auto workers or Serbian civil servants. They stem from errors of financial capitalism—and originate from Wall Street, not the Main Streets of Prague or Belgrade."[41]

For most EU officials, it seemed that the very existence of the deep public skepticism within the EU states that now endangered the integration of Europe was precisely the reason the Western Balkans region should move forward as rapidly as possible with domestic transformation and accession. According to this view, these countries slated for eventual accession should be fully assisted in their preparations for EU entry, and earlier promises by Brussels to the region still needed to be fully honored. The unpalatable alternative had already been demonstrated by the Western Balkan warfare and deep recession during the 1990s, and subsequent frustration and problems in the region.

The EU made a particularly important contribution to progress in the Western Balkans in mid-2009 when it committed itself to a partial visa liberalization plan for the region. Keeping the promise that visa restrictions would be lifted in late December for citizens of Serbia, Montenegro, and Macedonia (Croatia had already been free of such requirements) wishing to travel to the EU buoyed spirits there as well. The visas had first been introduced when the former Yugoslav Socialist

---

in terms of its high poverty and unemployment rates, low level of social capital, popular mistrust of politicians and civil servants, frequent incidents of corruption, and the inefficiency of the state bureaucracy. Nikoleta Jones, Chrisovaladis Malesios, Theodoros Iosifides, and Costas M. Sophoulis, "Social Capital in Greece: Measurement and Comparative Perspectives," *South European Society and Politics* 13, no. 2 (2008): 175–93.

41. "EU Enlargement Five Years On: A Balance Sheet and What Next," EU Commission Speech/09/292, Brussels, June 10, 2009.

Federation was dissolving in 1991. And although these restrictions remained in place for Bosnia, Albania, and Kosovo, the EU had sent an important signal during a difficult period that access to Europe was possible for the citizens of the Western Balkans and that such a change was linked to internal reforms. (By October 2010, EU lawmakers had voted to lift visa requirements for Bosnia and Albania, and if the EU ministers approved this decision, the new provisions could be in place by 2011. But Kosovo was not yet part of this expanded liberalization.) The fact that EU financial assistance continued to flow into the Western Balkans during 2009 and 2010 as previously promised also reflected Brussels' continuing commitment to the region's fragile democracies. And the entry of Croatia and Albania into NATO during 2009 and closer relations between NATO and the other countries in the region was an additional factor boosting the region's Euro-Atlantic orientation.

Before leaving office in July 2009, Javier Solana, the European Union's high representative, observed that EU foreign policy had been "born" in the Balkans, and that the EU had "invested too much to allow the countries of the region to slip away from the EU power of attraction. And it will be harder and costlier in five years' time."[42] In early 2010, as the global crisis and economic downturn gave way to some signs of hesitant recovery, it seemed that EU leaders had realized they needed to forge ahead, albeit cautiously, with the accession of the Western Balkan states. Thus, a new foreign policy team in Brussels, working under the terms of a very recently ratified Lisbon Treaty, struck an upbeat mood regarding the accession prospects of the Western Balkan states. For example, as he prepared to assume his post as the new enlargement commissioner, Štefan Füle observed that the EU was committed to overcoming the Western Balkans' "huge historical and political baggage," and he hoped that new member states would be able to enter the European "family" during the next five years.[43] But he also underlined the need to be clearer about enlargement in order to counter the "fatigue" still expressed in European public opinion. And he emphasized that there were to be no "shortcuts to membership" in the EU, and that countries would need to demonstrate their "positive contribution to Europe."

42. Ditchley Foundation Lecture, July 11, 2009.
43. Hearings at the European Parliament, January 12, 2010.

The signal was becoming clear: Enlargement momentum would continue, but at a slow pace and with considerable scrutiny over the process. By mid-2010, Angela Merkel was able to formally persuade her colleagues (at a meeting of the Committee of Permanent Representatives in the European Union, or the Comité des représentants permanents, COREPER) of her earlier view that EU eastern enlargement would need to pause temporarily after Croatia acceded to the EU. As Germany's foreign minister, Guido Westerwelle, explained during a Balkan tour in August, the Greek budget crisis meant that the EU needed to maintain strict requirements for membership. "That is why," he said, "there will be no rebate on the accession criteria. If we loosen the rules, we would only sow concerns [in the EU] about taking on new members."[44]

The comments by Füle and Westerwelle reflected an attempt to straddle the long-standing divide within EU elites about just how quickly to move forward with enlargement. On the one side are the advocates of what has been termed "shock integration." They maintain that EU candidate and potential candidate countries should be rapidly advanced toward membership. The underlying assumption of the so-called fast-track perspective is that efforts at further stabilization and democratization of the Western Balkans, and hopes of diminishing threats to stability in the region, can better be fulfilled if the states of the region are "under the tent" of the EU. In this view, the same special arrangements for postaccession monitoring of progress, along with aid restrictions until Brussels is satisfied—already introduced for Bulgaria and Romania—may be needed. Such a framework is more desirable, it is argued, than further exclusion of states from EU membership, and the possibility of their potential frustration with regard to a "European perspective." Speaking to the European Parliament in November 2009, Adrian Severin, a Romanian member and foreign policy specialist, summed up the importance of a future-oriented perspective: "We should . . . avoid any conditionality which is not linked directly to the capacity to be interoperable with us from the legal, institutional, political and cultural point of view. . . . We should not impose conditionality which is not linked with these criteria. We should remember that enlargement is about a better future, not about a better past. We think too much about the past."[45]

44. Agence France-Presse, August 25, 2010.
45. Speech to the European Parliament, Strasbourg, November 25, 2009.

The opposing view calls for a more stringent and deliberate approach to EU accession, or what has alternatively been called the "tough love" or the "no discounts" perspective. In this approach, countries applying for membership to the EU should be required to meet a high threshold for entry. Any watering down of conditionality would be highly detrimental to the EU in the long run. For example, Chris Patten, a former EU commissioner for external affairs, worried in November 2009 that EU policy in the Western Balkans was "starting to show (for example in Bosnia-Herzegovina) a dangerous disinclination to apply tough conditionality."[46]

Ultimately, the speed of further EU enlargement will not be determined by any ideal set of criteria that provides for either fast-track or high-threshold measures of entry. The reality of the EU accession calendar is shaped largely by the evolving political and economic climate, and by the national interests of EU member states and their ability to reach a policy consensus. Whether or not a particular state is deemed ready for EU entry—is digestible or indigestible—is largely a political question that is decided after a state has already been subject to transformative EU soft power for a protracted period.

The debate about how vigorously the EU should apply conditionality requirements to a particular state or region, of course, begs the question of whether such considerations actually make much difference to the speed and sustainability of changes in values and behavior that are requested by Brussels. The mixed record of success in democratic consolidation underscored in this book is in part the result of uneven compliance by Western Balkan elites with EU demands. The factors that motivate Balkan elites to implement or reject the conditionalities stipulated by the EU for progress in the preaccession process are not always readily apparent. But certainly the basis for compliance includes both the domestic power imperatives of Balkan leaders and their perception of the legitimacy of the requests made by the EU. Moreover, recent research indicates that the incentives and penalties proffered by the EU are only part of the compliance story. Thus even the advent to power of reform-minded political elites and political parties "embracing the EU's philosophy" do not guarantee high levels of receptivity to EU conditionalities. When EU demands are deemed by Western Balkan elites—whether reformist or antireformist—to be inappropriate

46. *Irish Times,* November 24, 2009.

or lacking in legitimacy (because they conflict with local identity, state-hood, or moral concerns), the incentives ("carrots") for compliance with the EU do not have much impact, or only elicit superficial imple-mentation.[47] As a rule, the ultimate success of EU leverage depends on numerous factors. As Heather Grabbe, a former senior adviser to the EU enlargement commissioner from 2004 to 2009, has recently observed:

> On the demand side, conditionality transforms countries most ef-fectively when would-be members have strong states, a cross-party consensus giving priority to accession and substantial inflows of foreign direct investment. The Central European countries that had the most capable national administrations made the fastest progress towards EU membership. But in the Balkans, states are weak.[48]

By the end of 2010, the transformation and Europeanization of each country in the Western Balkans had clearly evolved, and their acces-sion prospects had improved. Indeed, there was a reasonable basis for speculation that by the end of another decade (2020), all the region's states, except for Kosovo, would be members of the EU.[49] However, for

47. Gergana Noutcheva, "Fake, Partial and Imposed Compliance: The Limits of the EU's Normative Power in the Western Balkans," *Journal of European Public Policy* 16, no. 7 (2009): 1065–84. See also Tanja A. Borzel, *The Transformative Power of Europe Reloaded: The Limits of External Europeanization* (Berlin: Freie Universität, 2010). On the limitations of EU conditionality for state building in "awkward states" where elites in substate units are skeptical of the central au-thority, see Florian Bieber, "Building Impossible States? State-Building and EU Membership in Kosovo, Bosnia and Herzegovina and Serbia and Montenegro," *Europe-Asia Studies,* forthcoming.

48. Quoted in *Prague Post,* February 24, 2010.

49. The EU does not announce dates of future accessions until negotiations are nearly completed. For example, Croatia began its negotiations in 2005, and in 2010 was acknowledged as being in the last stages of that process. One recent analysis of Serbia put the issue into perspective: "In the best case scenario, without interven-tion of political elements that could slow the process Serbia could not receive the status of candidate country before 2011. In fact the earliest date for the beginning of accession talks would be 2012 with the conclusion in 2016 which leads to the fact that Serbia could not become a member before 2018. Indeed, having in mind easily anticipated complications Serbia could encounter, the year 2020 is the most realistic estimate." Željko Pantelić, "Through Blood, Sweat and Tears Serbia Could, at the Earliest Enter the EU in 2018," *ISAC Policy Perspective,* December 2009.

Table 9.4. Salient Problems of Democratic Consolidation in the Western Balkans, November 2010

Country	EU Evaluations of Governance in 2010 Progress Reports
Albania	Parliamentary institutions and procedures do not function properly. Substantial shortcomings regarding the independence, transparency, and accountability of the judicial system. Proper implementation of the legal framework remains a concern, as do the lack of transparency and accountability in appointments and the politicization of the public administration.
Bosnia-Herzegovina	The Constitution established a complex institutional structure which remains inefficient and misused. State-level executive and legislative bodies are negatively affected by the prevalence of ethnically oriented considerations; little progress has been made in the area of public administration. Corruption is widespread throughout the public and private sectors; anticorruption policies and measures are not adequately implemented. Development of an independent and effective judiciary in line with European standards remains at an early stage.
Montenegro	Corruption remains prevalent in many areas and constitutes a particularly serious problem. Political interference and nepotism exist in appointments and promotions and undermine the quality and efficiency of public administration. The judiciary still has to demonstrate its independence, accountability, and efficiency.
Serbia	Additional efforts are needed to improve the compatibility of some constitutional provisions with European standards, particularly in the judiciary; the reappointment procedure for judges and prosecutors was carried out in a nontransparent way, putting at risk the principle of the independence of the judiciary. Corruption remains prevalent in many areas and continues to be a serious problem; the number of final convictions, especially in high-level cases, remains low.
Kosovo	Public administration reform remains a serious challenge. Kosovo is at an early stage of addressing priorities in the area of justice. Political and other interference is an issue of serious concern. Corruption remains prevalent in many areas and still constitutes a very serious concern.
Croatia	The legal basis for building a modern and professional civil service is still incomplete. The new judicial system has yet to be tested in practice. There has been limited progress in the prevention of corruption.
Macedonia	Limited progress was made in implementing the reform of the judiciary. Significant further efforts are needed to ensure the transparency, professionalism, and independence of public administration.

Source: Compiled by the authors on the basis of European Commission 2010 progress reports.

the moment, most countries continued to face accession issues associated with their mixed records at democratic consolidation. Persisting deficiencies related to governance issues—such as corruption, the rule of law, judicial administration, and the performance of public administrations (as detailed in chapters 2 and 3)—continued to be the most vexing problems (table 9.4).[50]

Of course, as noted throughout the study, the reasons for incapacities and malfunctions of democratic development differed from one country to another in the Western Balkans. Even after years of democracy promotion and state building in the region, the EU regarded such governance deficiencies as major obstacles to the full "Europeanization" of the Western Balkans. What worried some observers about the states in the region—both among political elites and academic analysts—was that a failure to overcome the root causes of governance problems might persist into the postaccession dynamics of these states, as local actors continued to operate according to informal rules and culturally based practices, while paying lip service to formal EU-inspired conditionality provisions. Such difficulties, particularly in developing modern-based standards of professionalism and depoliticized behavior in the public administration, continued to be a problematic area for many postcommunist countries even after EU accession. The cases of Romania and Bulgaria were very instructive in this regard.[51] The possibility that a similar pattern might emerge in the Western Balkan states strengthened the argument for a "tough love" approach to enforcing requirements for future accession to the EU. A lack of agreement regarding how candidate and potential candidate members would fare once they had entered the EU also made it imperative that policymakers fully understand the background, character, and strength of domestic reform difficulties facing each Western Balkan state.

50. Communication from the Commission to the European Parliament and the Council, *Enlargement Challenges and Main Challenges, 2009–2010* (Brussels: European Commission, 2009).

51. Antoaneta L. Dimitrova, "The New Member States of the EU in the Aftermath of Enlargement: Do New European Rules Remain Empty Shells?" *Journal of European Public Policy* 7, no. 1 (January 2010): 137–48; and Dimitris Papadimitriou and Eli Gateva, "Between Enlargement-Led Europeanisation and Balkan Exceptionalism: An Appraisal of Bulgaria's and Romania's Entry into the European Union," *Perspectives on European Politics and Society* 10, no. 2 (June 2009): 152–66.

By the end of 2010, Croatia, which had first applied for EU membership in 2003 and started accession talks in 2005, was clearly on the verge of EU entry. Moreover, the outcome of the presidential election in January 2010, as mentioned above, had certainly elevated the country's prospects. Indeed, EU officials had already signaled that Croatia was about to conclude the preaccession process. Only the need to reform its judicial sector and intensify the fight against corruption and organized crime seemed to stand in Zagreb's way of entering the EU. Euro-skeptic sentiment was still substantial, but the ruling political elite appeared determined to avoid derailing their country's chances for EU entry, now projected for 2013. As one observer put it during the Croatian election, anticorruption had become "the new nationalism," with every presidential candidate endeavoring to demonstrate that he or she was the most uncorrupted choice.[52]

At his inauguration, the newly elected president, Ivo Josipović, clearly stated the country's challenge: "We have established a state, but justice and equity are values which we have yet to discover in their fullness."[53] Josipović also quickly undertook reconciliatory initiatives with fellow leaders in Serbia and Bosnia to underline that he intended to turn a new page in Croatia's foreign policy. He benefited from the fact that he could find a partner in another major regional leader, Serbia's president, Boris Tadić, who was of a similar age, had opposed the wars in the 1990s, and was modern and nonnationalistic in orientation.[54] Relations between Serbia and Croatia, as the two most populous and influential polities in the region, have long been the centerpiece of regional amity or discord in the Balkans, and thus the rapport between Josipović and Tadić was highly significant. Meanwhile, Croatia's territorial dispute with Slovenia had been set aside for international arbitration, and would—unless the Slovenes renege—not block Zagreb's path to the EU. Euro-skeptic anxiety remained strong in Croatia, but that sentiment may be the premonition of a feeling of what one Romanian scholar called "the unbearable lightness of Europeanization," that is, "once the intensely sought-after accession takes place, the anesthetic

52. Ines Sabalić, cited in *The Economist,* December 28, 2009.

53. *HINA,* February 19, 2010.

54. This view is emphasized in remarks by Dejan Jović, one of Josipović's advisers. "Croatia and Serbia: New Initiatives for Regional Cooperation," unpublished paper, 2010.

effect of the effort disappears, and the ache [of a state's unfinished transformation] resurfaces."[55]

Serbia's government, full of optimism at the invitation, formally applied for EU membership at the end of 2009, after the EU ministers had unblocked a suspended trade agreement and Belgrade had received a positive appraisal regarding its effort to deal with the issue of war criminals. The Serbian government continued to maintain that it would never recognize Kosovo's independence—as had been done by twenty-two of the twenty-seven EU member countries. But at both the popular and elite levels in Serbia, there was also a grudging recognition that Kosovo's independence was unlikely to be reversed. Kosovo ranked seventh on a list of citizen priorities in a recent Serbian public opinion poll, and only 10 percent of citizens perceived Kosovo as the most significant problem facing the country. Half of those polled wanted Kosovo reunited with Serbia, but only 15 percent believed that to really be possible.[56] More moderate segments of the Belgrade elite were focused on the future, not on Kosovo and the past. "Our program is simple," claimed President Tadić. "We want Serbia in the European Union with our own identity."[57]

Increasingly, it appeared that Serbia's leaders had overcome the earlier and sometimes self-destructive interpretation of its identity and interests—a problem that had badly delayed the pace of Serbia's European integration. For example, in September 2010, without recognizing Kosovo, Belgrade "took note" of the International Court of Justice's ruling that Kosovo's declaration of independence was legal, and Serbia's leaders agreed to a dialogue with Kosovo on other matters (although momentum toward the start of talks was slowed by the prospects of an early 2011 election in Kosovo). Serbia's new approach seemed to temporarily again put Serbia on track in the EU accession process. It was too early to tell, however, whether the new spirit of EU-Belgrade accommodation would prove to be a turning point or only a brief window that would eventually close. It seemed that Brussels would move ahead with Belgrade's application to become a candidate member of the EU, thereby increasing the amount of aid given to the country. However, Serbia still had many technical and reform challenges

55. Alina Mungiu-Pippidi, *The Bridge* 1, no. 4 (2007): 55.
56. *BETA,* September 16, 2010.
57. BBC, December 20, 2009.

ahead if it hoped to satisfy EU benchmarks and requirements. Indeed, democratic consolidation, the most crucial issue of the entire post-2000 period, still remained a fundamental challenge. "Serbia," as President Tadić observed in January 2010, "has not yet crossed the critical boundary, which it must cross as soon as possible in order to strengthen the process of democratization, institutionalization, and modernization. Until that critical boundary is reached, there is always the danger of Serbia falling back politically, economically, and socially."[58]

Macedonia, which received EU candidate status in 2005, and Montenegro and Albania, which applied for EU membership in 2008 and 2009, respectively, all had country-specific governance difficulties that impeded their accession hopes. As noted above, Macedonia faced the special burden of a Greek veto over its progress because of the persistent "name dispute." The fact that by the summer of 2010 Albania's opposition parties had boycotted the central legislature for more than a year hardly helped to advance its course of reform. In Montenegro, chronic problems with corruption and organized crime, and also the longtime political dominance of the same leader and political elite, were sources of particular concern.[59] Meanwhile, Bosnia's EU hopes remained on hold because of the impasse between its two entities over constitutional reform. Bosnia's frequently noted pattern of interethnic and interelite polarization prevented any breakthrough on a number of reforms. The country's hopes of joining NATO were blocked by the same problems. Nearly fifteen years after the Dayton Accords,

---

58. "Demokratizacija nije gotova," B92, January 27, 2010. Serbia's progress in the EU preaccession process was also complicated by the fact that during 2010 Ratko Mladić and Goran Hadžić continued to evade the jurisdiction of the International Criminal Tribunal of the Former Yugoslavia (ICTY). The ICTY is expected to finish its work with the completion of the Radovan Karadžić trial and likely appeal in 2014. But its chief prosecutor, Serge Brammertz, suggested that a kind of "sleeping tribunal" might be left in place at The Hague that could be activated if fugitives are arrested at a later stage. In a February 2010 conference assessing the ICTY legacy, Brammertz also suggested that national judiciaries in the Western Balkans had begun to take an effective role in continuing the work of the ICTY. *Beta,* February 24, 2010.

59. Kenneth Morrison observes that although Djukanović "possesses qualities that are held in high regard in Montenegrin society (bravery, strength, ruthlessness, charm, physical presence), . . . it is—in the final analysis—inherently unhealthy for one individual (or even a small group of individuals) to dominate a country's political process for almost two decades." Morrison, "The Political Life of Milo Djukanović," *Sudosteuropa* 57, no. 1 (2009): 25–54.

observers were nonetheless hoping that the election in October 2010 would usher in a "fresh start." On the eve of the contest, the high representative, Valentin Inzko, pleaded that "if people would only have a little bit of goodwill, it would be easier [to have a better-functioning state], even without the Constitution." And, he added, "If criminals can work together regardless of religion, language, and ethnic affiliation, why would not fine people be able to cooperate?"[60] But the electoral results were not very encouraging.[61]

Kosovo, the newest state in the region, which enjoyed only supervised independence and still faced serious internal problems—particularly the challenge of territorial integration of the Serb-populated north and improving interethnic relations—remained at the end of the EU accession queue. And like Bosnia, Kosovo was still functioning under foreign oversight, including the presence of foreign troops—a condition that continued to bring the sustainability of its state-building efforts into question.[62] On the bright side, the new state was receiving "more efforts and money" per capita from the EU than any other place in the world from anyone.[63]

Overall, the intraregional hierarchy of state-building progress among the seven Western Balkan states had not changed very much during the previous decade—Croatia at the vanguard, and Kosovo farthest behind—although both the domestic and international landscapes had undergone dramatic changes and the future looked more promising. When visiting the region in February 2010 for the first time as EU foreign policy chief, Catherine Ashton asserted to a Belgrade audience that the EU member states "want the peoples of the Western Balkans

60. *ONASA,* October 1, 2010.

61. The results of the 2010 election did not appreciably change the overall situation in Bosnia, although the outspoken and uncompromising Bosniak member of the presidency, Haris Silajdžić, was replaced by the more pragmatic and moderate Bakir Izetbegović. Because it would be several months before a new government would be formed (Bosnia's Election Commission also ordered a recount of void ballots cast for the Serb seat in the tripartite presidency), whether a new period of "constructive dialogue" could begin in the country, as the EU urged, remained an open question.

62. Kosovo remained essentially bifurcated along ethnic lines, with North Mitrovica still outside the control of the authorities in Priština. Belgrade had even taken the step of appointing judges to serve in courts in Kosovo.

63. EU high representative Catherine Ashton, quoted in *Koha Ditore,* February 21, 2010.

to feel—and be—part of Europe." But, she added, "we will have to recognize that the integration of the whole region into the EU will take time."[64]

Clearly, at the end of 2010, major obstacles remained for democracy building and the EU accession hopes of the Western Balkan states. Moreover, the crisis-generated economic and political uncertainty in the region, and also in Europe and internationally, could alter the precise timetable of reform in a particular state or its chances of entering the EU. But "Euro-optimism" throughout the region was in the air as never before. And in contrast to the serious difficulties that each polity had experienced during the 1990s, the more recent decade has given the Western Balkan states the realistic prospect of becoming sustainable and prosperous democracies. If the European economic slowdown ends soon enough, the voices resisting the virtues of the democratic embrace will grow still fainter.

64. Catherine Ashton, "The EU and the Western Balkans in a Changing World," Speech 10/32, February 18, 2010. Ashton emphasized that "the EU will never accept the breakup of Bosnia and Herzegovina."

Epilogue: The Western Balkans and Postauthoritarian Lessons

In early 2011, as a dramatic wave of civil activism and regime change swept the Middle East, the Western Balkan region moved purposefully but unevenly ahead along the past decade's well-trodden path of reform and democracy building. Each state in the Western Balkans exhibited genuine intentions and some of them made significant progress toward meeting the democratic standards—both political and economic—that are explicitly set for their accession to the European Union. Yet other troubling limitations still plagued this region burdened by legacies of the pre-1989 political culture, patterns of deficient governance, and the warfare of the 1990s. The financial crisis that began in 2008 also buffeted the region, and its hesitant recovery from the postcrisis recession generated politically unsettling constraints. Thus, badly needed access to international credit has been available only in return for the domestic fiscal austerity demanded by the European Union and the International Monetary Fund. This is a hard bargain to strike in the short run, however essential pension and public-sector reform are in the long run.

The Western Balkan experience with democratic change has also had an impact beyond the region, particularly as a model for collective protest and social media in political mobilization. For example, the substantially nonviolent mass protests that ushered in the post-2000 democratization of Serbia were directly emulated by the young cyberactivists leading Egypt's anti-Mubarak April 6th youth movement, who consulted the Belgrade activists who had led the anti-Milošević Otpor resistance movement.[1] Lessons from the Western Balkans should be of

1. Before the 2011 anti-Mubarak street demonstrations, Egyptian activists

492

similar comparative utility during the difficult postauthoritarian transition period faced by new democracies. Thus, the warfare of the 1990s in the Western Balkans provides a tragic example of the dire consequences that can befall democratizing states. The more recent postconflict evolution of the region's countries, and especially the post-2000 period detailed in this volume, reveals how the complex and illiberal legacies of early postauthoritarian failures in democratization may retard and complicate subsequent stages of political and economic development. So unless certain institutional reforms and changes in political culture become embedded and legitimized "after the revolution," new pluralist states face the danger of breakdown or may gradually regress into forms of liberalized authoritarian rule.[2] Indeed, this is precisely what happened in a number of the Western Balkan states during the first decade of postcommunist development, a legacy that still troubled the region's next and more positive phase of political change. The Western Balkan states, just like the recent cases generated by the "Arab spring" of 2011, have all wrestled with the dangerous potential for an "aborted transition" and the equally unfortunate possibility of becoming "lost in transition."

The Western Balkan case particularly illustrates the importance of distinguishing between the role of *social media* and *social capital* in democratic consolidation. Thus, the Internet's social networking media constitute an enormously valuable tool for creating the initial solidarity

---

had met with former Otpor personnel now working in Belgrade's Center for Non-Violent Action and Strategies, known as CANVAS. The Egyptian activists in the April 6th youth movement also adopted Otpor's clenched fist logo, and borrowed ideas from an Otpor published book on nonviolent resistance. The Serbian experience was also used by activists in several other antidictatorial collective protests, such as in Georgia, Ukraine, Burma, Belarus, and elsewhere.

2. In mid-2011, regime transition generated by the Arab Spring was obstructed owing to old regime resistance in Libya, Yemen, Syria, and Bahrain. At the same time, the momentum of democratic consolidation encountered significant difficulties in Egypt and Tunisia. Larry Diamond astutely observed: "Even if the Arab Spring comes in fits and starts, it will eventually bring fundamental change. But whether democracy is the end result depends in part on how events unfold and how regimes and actors engage the opposition forces. . . . Real prospects for democratic development exist alongside the very real risks of Islamist accession, political chaos and humanitarian disaster." "A Fourth Wave or False Start?" *Foreign Affairs,* May 22, 2011. See also Fred Lawson and Abdelwahab Shaker, "Breakdowns of Democracy Revisited: Transitions from Liberal-Democratic to Authoritarian Regimes around the Mediterranean Littoral," paper presented at Twelfth Mediterranean Research Meeting, Florence, April 6–9, 2011.

and fearlessness necessary to mobilize citizens against an authoritarian regime. But during the transition away from such a regime, it is also essential to accumulate the social capital—that is, the interpersonal and intergroup trust—that can facilitate the capacity for compromise and other political skills that are supportive of a liberal democracy. Building a well-organized civil society and democratic culture requires not only modern technology for communication among citizens but also the kind of trust that permits pluralist politics to proceed in a routine and face-to-face manner within widely valued and accountable institutions. Indeed, excessive postrevolutionary use of online social networks by young activists can even reduce the number of people voting and directly participating in political life.[3]

One of the most important lessons of the Western Balkan case is that the pace of democratic consolidation is mainly attributable to the willingness of postconflict elites to work together in tackling the entrenched sources of authoritarian resilience. Thus, Western Balkan democratization during the last decade has moved ahead in fits and starts in large part because many of the region's top leaders have only been "contingent democrats" who are inadequately socialized in the practices and values of pluralist politics and are often little equipped or interested in creating genuinely accountable, uncorrupted, and effective modes of governance.[4] But in the post-2000 period, a generation more deeply committed to democratic habits and goals has slowly been emerging in the region. This has been most evident in the 2010–11 working alliance for advancing intergroup reconciliation and democratic methods established by the presidents of Serbia and Croatia. The joint efforts by Boris Tadić and Ivo Josipović to transcend the past antagonisms between their two countries, and move beyond old patterns of mutual recrimination, have not of course received unanimous support

---

3. Ivan Krastev, "Authoritarianism 2.0," *IWMpost*, September–December 2010.

4. A recent UN study observed that "leadership and institutional development are symbiotic. Leaders create institutions, but they must then be willing to accept to submit themselves to those institutions. . . . Leadership is not an isolated activity done by one greatly endowed person. It is an endeavor of collective community action dependent on followers who trust the leaders enough to jointly work toward mutual goals. Confusion about who will succeed the top leaders causes mistrust to cascade through all levels of government." United Nations, *Reconstructing Public Administration after Conflict: Challenges, Practices, and Lessons Learned* (New York: United Nations, 2010), x, 35.

from their compatriots.[5] Nor will these initiatives in and of themselves ensure future stability and democratic consolidation for the two states. But the new and encouraging approach of the top leaders in Belgrade and Zagreb regarding both past events and the current imperatives of democracy building have nurtured a positive and hopefully contagious climate that will help overcome previous patterns of intolerance and arbitrary rule.

In Serbia, for example, Tadić has not only endeavored to improve relationships between countries but has also practiced a domestically inclusive and catch-all style of party pluralism that has involved the co-operation of his ruling Democratic Party (Demokratska stranka, DS) with a variety of forces on both the left and right of the party spectrum. Moreover, by 2011, the salience of nationalistic politics in Serbia—around such rallying points as the Kosovo issue and the "Serbian question" in Bosnia—had considerably diminished. Aspects of militant nationalism and extremism can, of course, still be found on the political landscape, especially among the most radical and fringe intellectuals, and also within the most anti-intellectual and hooligan-type circles. But pluralist and interest-based politics has increasingly overshadowed radical ideological and emotional symbolic politics in the country. An interesting example of such change and style is illustrated by the case of Ivica Dačić, the politically agile successor to Slobodan Milošević as head of the Socialist Party of Serbia (Socijalistička Partija Srbije, SPS). Dačić, who currently holds the post of minister of the interior in the DS-led government, recently remarked: "We are no longer Communists, we are no longer nationalists. Today we are socialists. . . . Today we are drawing a line on all the stories about our past. . . . We will not find strength in going back into museums and measuring who likes the current leader more and who prefers the former leader [Milošević]."[6]

Despite the SPS's express commitment to European rather than Russian ties, questions remain about the ability of Dačić to push aside the several remaining hard-liners in the SPS leadership and also se-

---

5. Old mentalities often die hard in political cultures and are reinforced by different sectors not easily replaced by reformist forces. E.g., on the use of the educational curriculum and textbooks to perpetuate negative interethnic and interstate images, see Dubravka Stojanović, "An Explosive Device with a Delayed Effect: Image of the Wars of the Nineties in Serbian History Textbooks (1993–2005)," *Peščanik,* April 18, 2011.

6. *Večernje novosti,* December 14, 2010.

cure the support of the wider membership for the competitive standards of a market economy. So do concerns about the balance between Europeanism and homegrown populism in the new Serbian Progressive Party (Srpska napredna stranka, SNS), which was founded in 2008 to break with the irredentist nationalism of the Serbian Radical Party (Srpska radikalna stranka) and is now the much larger party. The SNS's public statements favoring EU accommodation point to a general retreat from extremism in Serbia's party system, an important step toward democratic consolidation. In its mass demonstration staged in Belgrade in February to demand immediate elections, the SNS leaders voiced their appeal in populist terms, but only to charge corruption and to challenge the economic rather than the foreign policy of the coalition government led by the DS and President Boris Tadić. Rather than seeking to reclaim Kosovo, the SNS endorsed the objections of retirees and public-sector employees to the government's austerity budget. Meanwhile, as inflation mounts, the coalition faces resentment for dividing up access not only to public sector employment (see chapter 3) but also to jobs in the remaining unprivatized enterprises (e.g., the JAT airline). Growing income disparities, shrinking pensions, and persistent unemployment have also helped to fuel public discontent. If its current lead in opinion polls were to bring the SNS to power in 2012, this recently formed party would still face the same hard political bargain as does the present government. It would have to reconcile the conditions for EU accession with measures to ensure social peace. But in the continuing absence of any specific SNS program to strike this bargain, the Tadić coalition may still survive the elections, particularly if Brussels approves the start of Serbia's accession talks (see below) before the end of 2011.[7]

In Croatia, the top leadership of the country—both Josipović and the moderate elements in the ruling Croatian Democratic Union—have finally begun to wage a vigorous campaign against corruption. For example, in December 2010, the former defense minister received a four-year sentence for corruption. This new policy also precipitated the flight from Croatia of former prime minister Ivo Sanader, and the February 2011 demand of Croatia's leaders for his extradition from Austria to

7. The SNS's electoral prospects appeared to weaken in mid-April, when SNS chief Tomislav Nikolić staged a week-long hunger strike as a means to force early elections. In Serbia, Nikolić's strike was widely viewed as a stunt that would backfire.

stand trial in Zagreb on corruption charges. President Josipović has asserted that in the fight against corruption, "there will never be untouchables" and that 2010 was "the key moment in the development of democratic society. Nothing will be the same in Croatia after this, especially the politicians' perception of their work."[8]

It has taken Croatia two decades of postcommunist development, and a full decade of postauthoritarian development (from 1999 to 2010), for its political institutions and leadership to become fully engaged in an anticorruption struggle. Indeed, the ongoing battle with corruption in the country remains far from over, and may yet delay Croatia's accession to the EU and indeed its future after becoming a member state.[9] The antigovernment protests held in several towns throughout Croatia during early March 2011 also indicated, just as did the SNS-organized February demonstration in Serbia, the substantial support for populism that still exists during a period of socioeconomic malaise. In the Croatian case, protestors came from a broad cross-section of society, including dissatisfied war veterans, workers, farmers, fishermen, small business owners, retirees, Facebook users, students, and middle-class professionals.

Assuaging popular discontent and the task of reform leadership in Croatia was made more difficult in mid-April, when two Croatian generals on trial in The Hague were given long sentences by the International Criminal Tribunal for the Former Yugoslavia (ICTY) for crimes committed against civilians during the country's 1995 military action against Serb secessionists in the Krajina border areas. Many Croats were particularly angered over the ICTY's finding that the wartime policies of state founder Franjo Tudjman and others amounted to a "joint criminal enterprise." Eager not to disturb their imminent prospect of EU accession, Croatia's ruling circles could do little except express their strong dissatisfaction with the verdicts and also promise to appeal the convictions. But there was deep popular discontent that Croatia was being equated with Serbia as a perpetrator of war crimes. Support for international justice and the EU temporarily waned in the country. However, other voices urged Croatia to avoid the obstructionist stand taken by the shrinking nationalist circles in Serbia then still

8. Interviewed in *Koha Ditore,* December 30, 2010.
9. See *Interim Report from the Commission to the Council and the European Parliament on Reform in Croatia in the Field of Judiciary and Fundamental Rights (Negotiation Chapter 23),* COM (2011) (Brussels: European Commission, 2011), 110.

shielding the accused Bosnian Serb general Ratko Mladić (prior to May 2011) from the ICTY, and to work in full accord with international legal institutions—even when expressing disagreement with specific judicial decisions.[10]

The recent spate of mass protests in Croatia and Serbia, and elsewhere in the Western Balkans (see below), also reflects the "demonstration effect" of popular unrest in North Africa and the Middle East. But the protests in the Western Balkans have grown out of antigovernment sentiments that were already considerable in the region, owing to the impact of the economic crisis and persistent political corruption. For example, when addressing the Belgrade demonstration held by his party in February, the SNS leader told protesters that "elsewhere in the world, people are telling government they should listen to the people. I know you are disenchanted and bitter over this dishonest government which is tormenting you. Let us torment government instead." But unlike many earlier street protests in Serbia, the most recent demonstration was nonviolent (as were demonstrations in May to protest the Mladić arrest). Croatia's antigovernment demonstrations in February and March that condemned corruption and economic difficulties were also substantially peaceful. Moreover, the Croatian government treated the protests as a normal part of democratic politics, and police behavior was highly professional.[11]

Although the populist protests in Serbia and Croatia have hardly been free of some illiberal elements, both states have made important strides in democratic consolidation, particularly with regard to the deradicalization of political party leadership. Unlike mass protests in North Africa and the Middle East, where those participating in demonstrations have been taking their first critical steps in overcoming fear of repression, most citizens attending the antigovernment rallies in Croatia and Serbia were expressing their frustration and disappointment with already established but imperfectly democratized regimes that were finding it difficult to fulfill popular expectations. Thus, the institutional and political development of Croatia and Serbia has already reached a more advanced stage. As their respective governments struggle to implement further economic reforms, consolidate the rule

10. Davor Gjenero in *Vjesnik,* April 18, 2011.
11. Dražen Lalić, "A Sociological Analysis of Protests in Croatia," *PSRC Monthly Report,* March 11, 2011.

of law, and eliminate rampant corruption, their ruling parties and elites find themselves in a politically vulnerable position. Faced with such challenges, the regimes in Zagreb and Belgrade have been fortunate to be led by more democratically oriented and European-focused political leaders than most neighboring states, although this is hardly a guarantee of smooth progress.

Elsewhere in the region, potentially hopeful patterns of leadership succession could also be identified at the end of 2010 and the first months of 2011, albeit with more limitations and less impact on political life. For example, in Bosnia, the October 2010 election of the politically moderate Bakir Izetbegović to the Muslim/Bosniak seat in the country's three-person presidency (replacing the more uncompromising Haris Silajdžić) appeared to bode well for efforts to overcome the state's ethnically polarized style of politics. At a February 2011 conference in New York, Izetbegović congratulated Prime Minister Josipović for his readiness to "confess and not accuse" regarding Croatia's intervention in Bosnia during the 1990s. But Izetbegović also suggested that Bosnia would not be able to overcome its current internal divisions until Bosnian Serbs "accept one country," an allusion to the exclusivist and polarizing views of the Bosnian Serb leader Milorad Dodik.[12] Izetbegović brings a less strident tone to politics in Bosnia, but his lack of experience in political leadership, and alleged earlier association with corrupt actors, may diminish his ability to break the pattern of elite paralysis within the country. The leadership deficit in Bosnia was also reflected in the inability of political parties to form a central government during the six months following the October 2010 elections.[13] Interethnic relations on a popular level exhibited the same uneven pattern of development in Bosnia. Thus, there are some recent indicators in Bosnia of increasing interethnic trust among ordinary citizens over

12. Remarks at the conference "America at the Crossroads: The Dayton Accords at the Beginning of 21st-Century Diplomacy," New York University, February 9, 2011.

13. Some European officials, frustrated by elite stalemate in Bosnia and caught up in the climate of Middle Eastern street demonstrations, called for the country's young people to begin mass protests. This suggestion did not prove popular among the entrenched ethnic leaders in Bosnia. For example, one local Croatian politician in Bosnia observed: "Problems can't be solved on the streets. . . . If people come into the streets, especially young people, that is no longer democracy and we don't need elections." *Nezavisne Novine,* February 23, 2011.

the past five years. But there is also polling evidence that such views do not translate into a "pervasive belief in the future of peaceful cohabitation in [a] multi-ethnic state."[14] As yet there is little evidence of a consensus in Bosnia regarding its past, present, or future. And without such a consensus, especially within the divided elite, Bosnia probably cannot become an EU member state, and its governance will continue to resemble that of an international protectorate.

In Montenegro, political succession and generational change have made some progress, owing to the late December 2010 resignation of the long-serving and politically dominant Milo Djukanović, who was replaced by his thirty-four-year-old protégé, Igor Lukšić.[15] The scandal-driven replacement of some of Djukanović's longtime associates added to the impression of elite renewal in the country. But Djukanović remained at the head of his ruling party, did not rule out running for president in 2013, and has by no means abdicated political influence or severed his reputedly close links to Montenegro's murky world of wealth and illegality. It should also be noted, conversely, that Lukšić is a London-trained economist who has served as finance minister for the past five years.[16] "We are waging a fierce struggle against [corruption]," Lukšić claimed at the end of March 2011. "We have been quite successful. It may be that it is the younger people who no longer want this old political style."[17] A recent survey indicating high levels of corruption

14. Gallup Balkan Monitor, "Focus on Bosnia and Herzegovina," *GBM Focus On,* November 2010, 4. Research by nongovernmental organizations indicates that Bosnia's citizens have the lowest level of trust in their institutions since 2005; see *Izvještaj u stanju učešća gradjana u odlučivanju u BiH* (Banja Luka: Centri Civilnih Inicijativa, 2010). See also Gerard Toal and Carl T. Dahlman, *Bosnia Remade: Ethnic Cleansing and Its Reversal* (New York: Oxford University Press, 2011), and *Thirty-ninth Report of the High Representative for Implementation of the Peace Agreements on Bosnia Herzegovina to the Secretary-General of the United Nations, 16 October 2010–20 April 2011* (New York: United Nations, 2011).

15. Lukšić quickly opened a page on Facebook and sent greetings to his first "500 friends." One of his friends appreciatively noted that "the prime minister has found a way to approach citizens; he did not choose to be an 'untouchable god' as some postcommunist leaders." *Tanjug,* January 24, 2011.

16. For an excellent discussion of succession contingencies in Montenegro, see Kenneth Morrison, *Change, Continuity and Consolidation: Assessing Five Years of Montenegro's Independence,* LSEE Papers on Southeastern Europe 2 (London: London School of Economics and Political Science, 2011). In May 2011, Djukanović was reelected head of the ruling DPS for a fifth successive mandate.

17. *Der Spiegel,* March 28, 2011.

and ruling party influence in Montenegro's state administration suggests that Lukšić will have an uphill battle.[18]

Other states in the Western Balkans have manifested fewer signs of intergroup rapprochement or the moderating tendencies of significant elite-level change. Thus, in Albania and Kosovo, elite dynamics and political life suggest a continuation of the zero-sum politics and turbulent style that have convulsed the recent histories of those societies. For example, in early 2011, Albania experienced an escalation of the already highly polarized standoff between government and opposition forces that had begun with the contested results of the 2009 election. In January 2011, opposition protests in Tirana turned violent, resulting in four deaths and injury to dozens of citizens. An EU-appointed negotiator was quickly sent to the country to calm the situation and encourage peaceful political dialogue. For his part, Prime Minister Sali Berisha accused the opposition leader, Edi Rama, of trying to take power through a coup, and claimed that the demonstrations would not force new elections before 2013.

As a consequence of the protests, the distrust between political forces in Albania deepened, and its prospects for further democratic consolidation and advancement in the EU accession process remain tenuous. The highly polarized pattern of politics in the country since the beginning of its postcommunist transition has allowed political activity to spill over from weak institutions onto the streets, and also to a dependence on third-party foreign mediation to restore political calm. The country presents a case study in what can happen when a postauthoritarian evolution fails to move forward and instead slips backward. Thus, although the largest part of Albania's political and professional elite express genuine support for democratic principles, the leaders of the two largest political parties exhibit a fundamental conceptual misunderstanding of what is entailed in a pluralist electoral system, including the necessity for the graceful alternation and competition of parties in a genuine democracy. In the process, Albania's candidacy for EU membership has, at least for now, been derailed.

Meanwhile, Kosovo's democratic development turned more problematic in late 2010 and early 2011. Thus, a Council of Europe report

18. Directorate for Anti-Corruption Initiative and United Nations Development Program, *Survey of the Capacity and Integrity of the State Administration Sector in Montenegro* (Podgorica: Directorate for Anti-Corruption Initiative and United Nations Development Program, 2010).

prepared by the Swiss member of Parliament, Dick Marty, indicated that the new state's prime minister, Hashim Thaçi, and some of his close associates were probably aware of trafficking in human body parts during and after the 1999 war.[19] Thaçi denied the allegations, threatened to sue its authors, and orchestrated a campaign against the report by Albanians throughout the region. But there were also calls in some quarters for Thaçi's resignation and for launching an internationally organized investigation. The Marty report appeared directly after the victory of Thaçi's party in the December 2010 Kosovo election, a contest fraught with accusations of fraud and many irregularities. A leading Kosovo commentator remarked that the "elections were a major test for Kosova. . . . We can say that Kosova failed the test. . . . We have followed the example of Albania, . . . which cannot provide the minimum of representative democracy, ensuring a free and fair election."[20] The political turbulence unleashed by the Marty report, other allegations in a leaked NATO document regarding Thaçi's role in organized crime,[21] and the widespread electoral fraud not only seriously tarnished Thaçi's legitimacy but also cast a shadow over the EU-managed dialogue between Kosovo and Serbia that began in March.[22]

In February 2011, questions regarding Thaçi's commitment to democratic practice were made worse by his use of pressure to secure—without a constitutionally proper quorum in the Kosovo Assembly—the election of the construction tycoon Bexhet Pacolli as the country's new president.[23] And only thirty-five days after Pacolli became president,

19. "Inhuman Treatment of People and Illicit Trafficking in Human Organs in Kosovo," Council of Europe, December 12, 2010.

20. *Koha Ditore,* January 23, 2011.

21. *Guardian,* January 24, 2011.

22. Serbia's chief negotiator in the talks claimed that Kosovo is "unquestionably part of Serbia," while Kosovo's negotiator emphasized that "the status issue [independence of Kosovo] is a closed chapter." Agence France-Presse, March 8, 2011. The initial talks did, however, make some progress on technical issues such as land registries and energy sharing.

23. Haki Abazi, the director of the Rockefeller Fund for the Western Balkans, claimed that the manner in which Pacolli was elected (on the third round of voting, with 62 votes out of 120 and only 67 present in the legislative chamber following an opposition walkout and a 45-minute break in the proceedings called by Thaçi in order to lobby the remaining deputies) "make the President an unrespected figure who does not reflect the unity of the state and its citizens." Division of Public Information, UN Mission in Kosovo, February 23, 2011. Immediately following Pacolli's election, the deputies from his very small New Alliance of Kosovo (Aleanca

Kosovo's Constitutional Court ruled that his election was constitution-ally invalid. After initial ambivalence about the prospect of resignation, Pacolli stepped down and was briefly replaced by an interim president. But in April, under strong US pressure and choreography, Thaçi and his allies quickly took steps to obtain a legislative majority for the election of a new and less controversial president—thirty-six-year-old Alifete Jahjaga, one of Kosovo's leading woman officials. After receiving some Western training, she made a professional career in the country's police force and has no previous party affiliation or experience in political life. Pacolli temporarily took the post of deputy prime minister under Thaçi, but soon indicated that after the next elections in the country, he would again seek the presidency.

Kosovo's "presidential crisis" of 2011 occurred fewer than six months after Pacolli's predecessor had been forced to resign on constitutional grounds (see chapter 2). Although some in Kosovo blamed the entire crisis on constitutional problems—such as a lack of specific provisions for the resignation of the head of state—others suggested that viola-tions of the Constitution and nondemocratic practices by members of the ruling parties were to blame. The crisis also threatened the con-tinuation of the coalition between Thaçi's Democratic Party of Kosovo (Partia Demokratike e Kosovës) and Pacolli's New Alliance of Kosovo (Aleanca Kosova e Re), thereby raising the prospect of early parlia-mentary elections. In some respects, Kosovo's political difficulties in selecting a president can be regarded as typical of a new democracy's normal institutional growing pains. But when considered along with the country's other troubling issues, and the continued deep internal division between Albanians and Serbs, Kosovo clearly faces more than its share of democracy's initial challenges.

The problematic post-Milošević democratization of Kosovo illus-trates the naïveté of international expectations regarding antidictatorial insurgencies led by self-proclaimed "democrats" who have very little or no genuine commitment to liberal principles and practices. Military backing for such insurgencies by established democratic states may help to reduce civilian suffering and also achieve political traction for those

---

Kosova e Re) voted with Thaçi's party to form a government with the support of 65 legislators. Thaçi's "vote trade" with Pacolli and their constitutionally questionable tactics were widely criticized in Kosovo. *Koha Ditore,* March 1, 2011.

opposing dictatorship, as recent events in Libya have shown. Indeed, the imperative of removing murderous dictatorial regimes may morally justify arming insurgents who have a very tenuous commitment to any inclusive agenda. But such external assistance does not necessarily ensure robust postconflict momentum in a democratic direction. Indeed, the Kosovo experience suggests that once ensconced in power, many former insurgents may condone or become involved in criminal activities, which can seriously impede reform and democratic consolidation. Making the transformation from "freedom fighter" to democratic state builder has proven extremely difficult for Kosovo's first postconflict generation of political leaders. In late March 2011, substantially more than a decade after Kosovo was removed from Serbia's control, the European Union Rule-of-Law Mission (EULEX) arrested several former insurgents suspected of war crimes. The EULEX chief, Pieter Feith, observed that "some in the KLA [Kosovo Liberation Army; also, Ushtria Çlirimtare e Kosovës] resistance who were heroes may have committed crimes or things which they have to answer themselves and to render account. . . . This is a process that may take a bit of time."[24] The EULEX action prompted street demonstrations led by the KLA veterans' organization, which requested that legal protection be given to KLA "war values," and that EULEX be stripped of its executive authority. In such a climate, whether or not the current generation of political leaders will be able to kick-start meaningful democratic consolidation remains open to question.[25]

Macedonia's internal political scene was somewhat less troubled than those of neighboring Albania and Kosovo, but hardly conducive to untrammeled democratic consolidation. The unresolved "name dispute" with Greece—and the Macedonian claim to the country's ancient origins—continues to drain time and energy away from the reform process. Intergroup relations between ethnic Macedonians and Albanians

24. International Civilian Office Transcript, Priština, March 24, 2011.
25. A recently published report finds that although the country's legislation regarding political participation "meets international standards," its slow implementation and poor monitoring have opened a significant credibility gap in public perception. . . . The hurry to bring Kosovo into technical alignment with EU standards has raised expectations far beyond actual performance, and also Kosovo's capacity to deliver results even where real and visible efforts are being made." United Nations Development Program, *Kosovo Human Development Report 2010* (Priština: United Nations Development Program, 2011), 80.

in the state also remain chilly, although nonviolent.[26] As the country celebrated ten years of interethnic coexistence under the Ohrid Accord, Macedonia still lacks the kind of political leadership that is able to represent ethnic group interests while moving beyond old agendas and the politics of mutual distrust. Despite the absolute majority won with its Albanian partner in the last elections, the ruling VMRO-DPMNE party has faced a parliamentary boycott from the rival Social Democrats as well as criticism for the closing of an independent television station. The crisis finally precipitated an early election in June 2011. VMRO-DPMNE's nationalist rhetoric and policies helped mobilize ethnic Macedonian support, and their coalition took nearly 40 percent of the vote with 56 seats in the 123-member assembly. Combined with the allied Albanian DUI that took 15 seats in parliament, VMRO will be able to form a government. But the VMRO-led coalition won fewer seats than in the last election, while the Social Democrats increased their parliamentary representation from 27 to 42 seats. The high turnout (63.5 percent) was a decided upturn from the last two elections (see chapter 5). Prior to the election, Prime Minister Gruevski's populist style and the concentration of power in his office sometimes gave Macedonia's governance the appearance of a *demokratura*—a mixture of democratic and authoritarian practices. Relations between ethnic Macedonians and Albanians remained tense in the country, but political disagreements are being effectively channeled through an open electoral process. Its observance embeds a prerequisite for further evolution towards liberal democracy.[27]

Aside from the important breakthroughs in elite succession and efforts at reconciliation in leading states such as Croatia and Serbia, it was the continued commitment of the European Union to the Western Balkans' eventual accession that provided the major hope for the region's further democratic evolution. In the spring of 2011, Croatia was in the last stage of its quest for EU membership, and its application was receiving close attention from Brussels. The EU decision to allow citizens of Bosnia and Albania to obtain visas in order to enter

26. Aleksandar Kržalovski, *Diskriminacijata vo Makedonija po osnova na etnička pripadnost* (Skopje: Macedonian Center for International Cooperation, 2011).
27. See Sašo Ordanoski, "The Story of Macedonian Populism: 'All We Want Is Everything!'" in Jacques Rupnik, ed., *The Western Balkans and the EU: 'The Hour of Europe'* (Brussels: European Union Institute for Security Studies, June 2011), Chaillot Papers, no. 126, 95–110

the border-free Schengen area beginning in mid-December 2010 was also a hopeful sign for those states. Montenegro's elevation to candidate member status in December was also likely to encourage domestic concentration on meeting EU standards, and also foreign investor confidence. Montenegro has made faster progress in the accession process than many of its neighbors, but the country also exhibits a pattern found throughout the region, namely, the adoption of formal democratic rules and norms that are typically ignored or very inconsistently applied. As a Montenegrin sociologist remarked in February 2011, "Standards differ from reality. . . . We should not be surprised when we hear the frequently used saying that our laws are European while the practice is Balkan."[28]

Still, Serbia stands a good chance of consolidating recent gains in democracy-building. The decision at the end of May by the Serbian government to extradite Serb General Ratko Mladić to The Hague (after he was finally arrested in northern Serbia) will undoubtedly improve Serbia's chance of obtaining the status of EU candidate membership before the end of 2011. Surmising that the bulk of Serbia's urban educated middle class would be supportive of Belgrade's cooperation with The Hague as a means to expedite EU accession, President Tadić took a calculated gamble that opposition to the arrest would be relatively small and of limited duration. And in fact protests by nationalist elements against Mladić's arrest and extradition were considerably smaller than after the 2008 arrest of Radovan Karadzić (see chapter 7). Over the long run, Serbia's now more promising advance toward EU membership is likely to assist its democratic consolidation and also aid regional reconciliation. But should the EU impose stiff new conditions on Belgrade to obtain candidate status—such as Belgrade's recognition of Kosovo's independence even after the July 2011 arrest of Goran Hadžić removed the last remaining high-profile fugitive indicted in war crimes—Tadić's own political prospects and support for the ruling democratic coalition may still suffer.

Most importantly, Serbia's significant social and economic difficulties could still be exploited by those who remain skeptical of an EU-managed model of Europeanization. Serbia has crossed the tipping point in its democratic intentions and deeds, but the sustainability of its

28. *Dan,* February 10, 2011.

democratic course remains fragile. Indeed, both Serbia's and Croatia's protracted problems in dealing with wartime criminality and its aftermath provide a reminder to other new democracies of the difficulties and episodic violence that can occur during the early postauthoritarian stage, and the even more lengthy and complex matter of meting out justice and consolidating the rule of law.

Should Belgrade complement the May arrest of the long-sought General Mladić with robust anticorruption efforts and other reforms, Serbia is likely to advance more quickly toward EU candidacy and eventual entry. Indeed, at the end of 2010 and early 2011, a team of specialists in Belgrade worked for forty-five days preparing a thirty-seven-volume set of answers to the EU questionnaire that is required before Belgrade can acquire candidate status. Following through to accession on a successful set of answers will require that the reforms and fiscal discipline being implemented by the present government survive despite growing economic hardship and public discontent. But Serbian opinion polls still favor EU accession by two to one, and a positive decision from Brussels in December to start EU accession talks will reinforce that majority and may vindicate President Tadić and the DS-led government. As elsewhere in the region, the previous gains of the middle class have been seriously eroded by the recent economic crisis and recession.[29] Democratic consolidation without renewed middle-class development throughout the Western Balkans will prove highly problematic.[30]

---

29. E.g., in Serbia, the number of people falling under the poverty line grew from 6.9 to 9.2 percent in the 2008–10 period. Rural poverty is at 13.6 percent, compared with 5.7 percent for urban areas. Focusing on the much larger proportion of the population at risk of poverty, the minister of labor and social policy claimed that "in Serbia everyone is poor who is not rich. The entire middle class is disappearing"; *Tanjug,* April 29, 2011. In Croatia, the sociologist Zoran Malenica warned that the lower tiers of the middle class—especially small entrepreneurs, craftspeople, administrative employees, workers in the retail sector, and lower-level professionals such as teachers—have been losing ground because of the sluggish economic recovery; *Novi list,* February 27, 2011. In Bosnia and Macedonia, similar trends of a shrinking middle class have been noted, with its members migrating into either the ranks of the poor or the wealthier sectors; *Vijesti.ba,* April 10, 2011, and *Vreme* (Skopje), May 10, 2010.

30. For example, near the end and directly after the Milosević regime, the middle class was instrumental in advancing democratic change (see chapter 7), although it gave only weak support to market-oriented reforms. Mladen Lazić,

A cautionary note needs to be sounded concerning the pace and conditions of recovery in Serbia and Croatia, the region's two largest economies. Fiscal imbalances remain, despite strong financial sectors. Serbia is making greater progress on its public debt and budget deficit but only at the expense of politically perilous pension cuts. The slow growth projected for both economies in 2011 is accompanied by even slower growth of employment, with little indication of closing the gap between exports and imports or, for Serbia, reversing the sharp decline in foreign direct investment since 2009.[31] For both economies, the continued rise in interest rates has particularly burdened the small and medium-sized enterprises that have given the middle class its greatest economic opportunities. In Serbia, these enterprises have been forced to borrow more not only because of the region's highest inflation rate but also because of delayed payments owed to them by large, monopolistic, but debt-ridden enterprises such as the Delta food sales complex. One alternative here may be a new publicly funded facility for low-interest, small-scale lending to supplement the further structural reforms required for both economies by the market-based standards of the EU's *acquis communautaire*.[32] Both Serbia and Croatia will need more competitive economies and exports if they are to take advantage of EU membership.

For the half-dozen Balkan states that still remain outside the European Union following Croatia's imminent membership, the ongoing political and socioeconomic challenges of accession will not be easy to overcome.[33] In this regard, it is noteworthy that Croatia became a candi-

---

Čekajući kapitalizam: Nastanak novih klasnih odnosa u Srbiji (Belgrade: Službeni Glasnik, 2011). "Without a strong domestic bourgeoisie," Lazić also claims, "the future of democracy is uncertain." *Vreme,* May 5, 2011.

31. On aggregate Serbian data, see FREN, *Quarterly Monitor: Economic Trends and Policies in Serbia,* no. 23, October–December 2010; and for Croatia, see National Bank of Croatia, *Bulletin,* no. 167, February 2011.

32. Interview with Božidar Cerović, chair, Ekonomski Fakultet, Belgrade University, March 21, 2011. The case for microeconomic structural reform is advanced by the World Bank, "Sustainable Economic Recovery for Croatia," Zagreb, November 30, 2010. On the case for a new state-sponsored facility for development lending in the EU framework, see Milica Uvalić, *Serbia's Transition toward a Better Future* (London: Palgrave, 2010), 264–67.

33. Public opinion in the twenty-seven EU member states at the end of 2010 indicated that 47 percent of those surveyed favored Croatia's membership, but only

date country in June 2004, a year after beginning negotiations with the EU for eventual entry. By the time the country enters the EU in July 2013, a full decade of active preparation will have elapsed.[34] But despite the remaining distance that most Western Balkan states must still traverse before reaching their democratic and EU accession goals, they have on the whole covered a good deal of ground. This is clear when they are compared with countries that still are struggling to develop the preconditions of pluralism—such as political party systems, civil societies, rule-of-law institutions, a free media sector, market-oriented economies, and a substantial middle class. Perhaps most important, the Western Balkan states have already in varying measure reached the takeoff stage in acquiring a democratic political culture that endorses, if not always exhibits, genuine support for consensus politics, compromise, tolerance, and minority rights. Illiberal remnants are not gone from the political landscape, but earlier notions of authoritarian governance have little support. Although the road to EU accession and democratic consolidation has been much longer and more difficult than most leaders and citizens within the Western Balkan states initially an-

---

36 percent supported entry for Montenegro, 35 percent for Macedonia, 35 percent for Bosnia, 34 percent for Serbia, and 29 percent for both Albania and Kosovo. European Commission, *Eurobarometer 74: Autumn 2010* (Brussels: European Commission, 2011).

34. "The accession process has taken ten years," remarked President Josipović in May 2011. "Our virtual membership during the coming year as well as during the first years of EU membership will continue to have a very strong impact on our transition." *Ured Predsjednika RH*, May 28, 2011. Josipović called the violence at a gay pride parade in Split on June 12, 2011, a "national disgrace," and a sign that Croatian society still contains "non-European components." HINA, June 12, 2011. For a caveat regarding Croatia's remaining democratic deficits, see Andrea Despot and Dusan Reljic, "Croatia's Rush to Join the EU," *SWP Comment* (June 2011), no. 14. Dejan Jović recently cautioned that a substantial body of Croatian elite and public opinion supports a narrative that celebrates the war and conflict of the 1990s, and is an obstacle to creating "a more liberal, open-minded and tolerant Croatia." EU membership not only can offer an opportunity for liberal antinationalists but also "nationalist anti-globalists." The latter group will try to "disassociate Croatia from the 'remaining Balkans'" and oppose further enlargement to other Western Balkan states. "Turning Nationalists into EU Supporters: The Case of Croatia," in Jacques Rupnik, ed., *The Western Balkans and the EU: 'The Hour of Europe'* (Brussels: European Union Institute for Security Studies, June 2011), Chaillot Papers, no. 126, 43–44.

ticipated, the end of that journey is now more clearly in sight. And in a world where a new wave of democracy building has only just begun to capture the imagination of millions of citizens—and when the danger of authoritarian nostalgia always lurks in the shadows, the experiences of the seven states discussed in this volume offer useful insights regarding both the opportunities and the obstacles of postauthoritarian change.[35]

35. In the wake of the Arab Spring the EU has announced a new initiative "in building deep democracy—the kind that lasts. . . ." *A New Response to a Changing Neighborhood, European Commission, High Representative of the European Union and Foreign Affairs and Security Policy* (Brussels, May 25, 2011). During the current period of slow economic recovery, all the transition countries were facing difficulties in maintaining earlier gains in democracy-building and democratic value change. Thus, the results of a new EBRD survey published at the end of June 2011 indicated that in many transition countries, including those in the Western Balkans, the economic downturn of 2008–10 had a discernibly negative impact on support for democracy and the establishment of a market economy in comparison with the situation in 2006 (see chapter 7). Few respondents supported a return to one-party rule. But in some countries, such as Albania, Serbia, Bosnia, Macedonia, and Montenegro (the study was not conducted in Kosovo), respondents felt that some important features of a stable democracy were clearly absent. *Life in Transition after the Crisis* (London: European Bank for Reconstruction and Development, 2011).

Abbreviations

AAK	Aleanca për Ardhmërinë e Kosovës (Alliance for the Future of Kosovo)
BSA	Bosnian Serb Army
CARDS	Community Assistance for Reconciliation, Development, and Stabilization (of the EU)
CDI	Christian Democratic International
CEFTA	Central European Free Trade Agreement
COREPER	Comité des représentants permanents (Committee of Permanent Representatives in the European Union)
CSO	civil society organization
DOS	Demokratska opozicija Srbije (Democratic Opposition of Serbia)
DPA	Demokratska Partija na Albancite (Democratic Party of Albanians)
DPS	Demokratska Partija Socijalista (Democratic Party of Socialists), Montenegro
DS	Demokratska stranka (Democratic Party), Serbia
DSS	Demokratska stranka Srbije (Democratic Party of Serbia)
DUI	Demokratska unija za integracija (Democratic Union for Integration), Albania
EBRD	European Bank for Reconstruction and Development

EU	European Union
EULEX	European Union Rule-of-Law Mission
FDI	foreign direct investment
FRY	Federal Republic of Yugoslavia
GDP	gross domestic product
HDZ	Hrvatska demokratska zajednica (Croatian Democratic Union)
HDZ-BiH	Croatian Democratic Union in Bosnia-Herzegovina
HDZ-1990	Hrvatska demokratska zajednica 1990 (Croatian Democratic Union 1990)
HNS	Hrvatska narodna stranka (Croatian People's Party)
ICJ	International Court of Justice
ICTY	International Criminal Tribunal for the Former Yugoslavia
IFOR	Implementation Force (of NATO)
IMF	International Monetary Fund
IPA	Instruments for Pre-Accession Assistance (of the EU)
JNA	Jugoslovenska Narodna Armija (Yugoslav National Army)
JUL	Jugoslovenska udruzena levica (Yugoslav United Left)
LDK	Lidhja Demokratike e Kosovës (League for Democratic Kosovo)
LDP	Liberalno-demokratska partija (Liberal Democratic Party), Serbia
MBA	Master's in Business Administration
MSI	Media Sustainability Index (of USAID)
NATO	North Atlantic Treaty Organization
NGO	nongovernmental organization
NS	Narodna Stranka (People's Party), Montenegro
OHR	Office of the High Representative (for Bosnia)

OSCE	Organization for Security and Cooperation in Europe
PD	Partia Demokratike (Democratic Party), Albania
PDK	Partia Demokratike e Kosovës (Democratic Party of Kosovo)
PDP	Partija demokratskog progresa (Party of Democratic Progress), Serbia
PIC	Peace Implementation Council (for Bosnia)
PISG	Provisional Institutions of Self-Government (in Kosovo)
PPSh	Partia e Punës e Shqipërisë (Albanian Party of Labor)
PR	proportional representation
PSSH	Partia Socialiste e Shqipërisë (Socialist Party), Albania
SAA	Stability and Association Agreements (with the EU)
SAP	Stabilization and Association Process (of the EU)
S-BiH	Stranka za Bosnu i Herzegovinu (Party for Bosnia and Herzegovina)
SDA	Stranka Demokratske Akcije (Party for Democratic Action), Bosnia
SDP	Socijaldemokratska partija (Social Democratic Party), Croatia
SDSM	Socijaldemokratski sojuz na Makedonija (Social Democratic Union of Macedonia)
SFOR	Stabilization Force (of NATO)
SI	Socialist International
SKS	Savez komunista Srbije (Serbian League of Communists)
SMEs	small and medium-sized enterprises
SMI	Socialist Movement for Integration (Lëvizja Socialiste për Integrim), Albania
SNP	Socijalistička narodna partija (Socialist People's Party), Montenegro

SNS	Srpska napredna stranka (Serbian Progressive Party)
SNSD	Savez nezavisnih socijaldemokrata (Serb Alliance of Independent Social Democrats)
SPS	Socijalistička Partija Srbije (Socialist Party of Serbia)
SPSEE	Stability Pact for Southeastern Europe
SRS	Srpska radikalna stranka (Serbian Radical Party)
UÇK	Ushtria Çlirimtare e Kosovës (Kosovo Liberation Army, also KLA)
UN	United Nations
UNICEF	United Nations Children's Fund
UNMIK	United Nations Mission in Kosovo
UNPREDEP	United Nations Preventive Deployment Force
UNPROFOR	United Nations Protection Force
US	United States
USAID	US Agency for International Development
VAT	value-added tax
VMRO-DPMNE	Vnatrešna makedonska revolucionerna organizacija–Demokratska partija za makedonsko nacionalno edinstvo (Internal Macedonian Revolutionary Organization–Democratic Party for Macedonian National Unity)

Index

Figures, notes, and tables are indicated by f, n, and t following the page number.

515

Sigurimi (Albanian secret police), 30, 34, 62
Silajdžić, Haris, 92, 271, 362, 363, 490*n*61
Singidunum University, 441
Sisk, Timothy, 219*n*109
60 Minutes (TV show), 206
Škare-Ožbolt, Vesna, 147
Slovakia, elections in, 453
Slovenia: civil society in, 170–71; economic development of, 28; elections in, 30, 31–32
small and medium-sized enterprises (SMEs): credit for, 406; development of, 309–11, 312, 337; and employment, 416; and entrepreneurial class, 308; and middle class, 479; and privatization, 309–10, 312, 408–9, 412, 419; women, discrimination against, 199
Smederevo steel plant (Serbia), 410
SME Development and Entrepreneurship Agency (Serbia), 409
SME Development Division (Croatia), 408
SMEs. *See* small and medium-sized enterprises
smuggling operations, 45–46, 55, 147, 426, 432
social capital, 48, 183–84, 216, 476–77, 493–94
Social Democratic Party (Socijaldemokratska partija, SDP): in elections, 57, 65, 96–97; and Facebook investigation, 216; and party defragmentation, 243–44; and party democracy, 271–72; and party identification, 262, 263–64, 268
Social Democratic Party of Kosovo, 266
Social Democratic Union (Socijaldemokratski sojuz na Makedonija, SDSM), 106, 245–46, 247, 265, 272, 290

"social envy," 339
Socialist International (SI), 290, 292
Socialist Movement for Integration (Lëvizja Socialiste për Integrim, SMI), 273
Socialist Party of Albania (Partia Socialiste e Shqipërisë, PSSh): in elections, 36, 60, 64; and executive powers, 108; and party defragmentation, 242; and party democracy, 272–73; and party identification, 265
Socialist Party of Serbia (Socijalisticka Partija Srbije, SPS): and Dacić, 495; in elections, 29, 32, 53–54, 56; and ICTY, 379; and media sector, 210; and party democracy, 275, 276; and party identification, 259, 261; and party pluralism, 229; and party realignment, 253–54, 255; renaming of, 52; and Socialist International, 292; and Yugoslav United Left, 249
Socialist People's Party (Socijalistička narodna partija, SNP), 245
Social Liberal Party (Hrvatska socijalno liberalna stranka). *See* Croatian Social Liberal Party
social media, 216, 218, 493–94
social structures, 19–20, 297–349; brain drain and educational development, 318–23; and elite class, 298–317, 329–41; human capital and university reform, 323–29; and middle class, 297–317, 329–41, 348; out-migration and isolation, 318–22; and poverty, 341–49; and social transformation, postconflict, 308–18; and social transition, 299–308
Socijaldemokratska partija (SDP). *See* Social Democratic Party
Socijaldemokratski sojuz na Makedonija (SDSM). *See* Social Democratic Union
Socijalistička narodna partija, SNP (Socialist People's Party), 245